Writing the Nation: National Historiographies and the Making of Nation States in 19th and 20th Century Europe

General Editors: **Stefan Berger, Christoph Conrad** and **Guy P. Murchal**

National histories form an important part of the collective memory of the peoples of Europe and national bonds have been, and continue to be, among the strongest bonds of loyalty. This new series is the main outcome of a five year research programme funded by the European Science Foundation between 2003 and 2008 entitled 'Representations of the Past: The Writing of National Histories in 19th and 20th Century Europe'.

As a transnational and comparative investigation, this series will explore the structures and workings of national histories; enhance our understanding of the diversity of national narratives in Europe; and open up a dialogue for understanding among European nation states. In particular, the books will bring together the histories of Western and Eastern Europe in an attempt to bridge the historiographical divide cemented by the long division of the continent by the Cold War.

The series will compare the role of social actors and institutions, as well as the importance of diverse narrative hierarchies in nationally constituted historiographies. It attempts to organize the comparison between historiographical and other representations of the past in order to draw conclusions about the effectiveness of diverse forms of representation within specific historical cultures. It promotes comparisons between different nationally-constituted historical cultures in order to take account of their various contexts, interactions, exchanges, misunderstandings and conflicts.

The series will focus on, first, the institutions, networks and communities that produced national histories and were themselves influenced by the idea of national history, secondly, the construction, erosion and reconstruction of national histories and their relationship with other master narratives structuring diverse forms of historical writing (e.g. class, race, religion and gender), thirdly, national histories and their relationship with regional, European and world histories, and, finally, territorial overlaps and contested borderlands and their impact on the writing of national histories.

Titles include:

Ilaria Porciani and Lutz Raphael (*editors*)
VOL I. ATLAS OF THE INSTITUTIONS OF EUROPEAN HISTORIOGRAPHIES, 1800–PRESENT

Ilaria Porciani and Jo Tollebeek (*editors*)
VOL II. SETTING THE STANDARDS
Institutions, Networks and Communities of National Historiography

Stefan Berger and Chris Lorenz (*editors*)
VOL III. THE CONTESTED NATION
Ethnicity, Class Religion and Gender in National Histories

Matthias Middell and Lluis Roura (*editors*)
VOL IV. TRANSNATIONAL CHALLENGES TO NATIONAL HISTORY WRITING

Tibor Frank and Frank Hadler (*editors*)
VOL V. DISPUTED TERRITORIES AND SHARED PASTS
Overlapping National Histories in Modern Europe

Stefan Berger and Christoph Conrad
VOL VI. THE NATION AS HISTORY
National Identities and Historical Cultures in Modern Eur

GW00761452

Stefan Berger and Chris Lorenz (*editors*)
VOL VII. NATIONALIZING THE PAST
Historians as Nation Builders in Modern Europe

R.J.W. Evans and Guy P. Marchal (*editors*)
VOL VIII. THE USES OF THE MIDDLE AGES IN MODERN EUROPEAN STATES
History, Nationhood and the Search for Origins

Writing the Nation series
Series Standing Order ISBN 978–0230–50002–0 hardback
(*outside North America only*)

You can receive future titles in this series as they are published by placing a standing order.
Please contact your bookseller or, in case of difficulty, write to us at the address below with
your name and address, the title of the series and the ISBN quoted above.

Customer Services Department, Macmillan
Distribution Ltd, Houndmills, Basingstoke, Hampshire RG21 6XS, England

The Contested Nation

Ethnicity, Class, Religion and Gender in National Histories

Edited by

Stefan Berger
Professor of Modern German and Comparative European History, University of Manchester

Chris Lorenz
Professor of Theory of History and of Historiography, VU University Amsterdam

EUROPEAN
SCIENCE
FOUNDATION
SETTING SCIENCE AGENDAS FOR EUROPE

palgrave
macmillan

© The European Science Foundation 2008, 2011

All rights reserved. No reproduction, copy or transmission of this publication may be made without written permission.

No portion of this publication may be reproduced, copied or transmitted save with written permission or in accordance with the provisions of the Copyright, Designs and Patents Act 1988, or under the terms of any licence permitting limited copying issued by the Copyright Licensing Agency, Saffron House, 6–10 Kirby Street, London EC1N 8TS.

Any person who does any unauthorized act in relation to this publication may be liable to criminal prosecution and civil claims for damages.

The authors have asserted their rights to be identified as the authors of this work in accordance with the Copyright, Designs and Patents Act 1988.

First published in hardback 2008 and in paperback 2011 by
PALGRAVE MACMILLAN

Palgrave Macmillan in the UK is an imprint of Macmillan Publishers Limited, registered in England, company number 785998, of Houndmills, Basingstoke, Hampshire RG21 6XS.

Palgrave Macmillan in the US is a division of St Martin's Press LLC, 175 Fifth Avenue, New York, NY 10010.

Palgrave Macmillan is the global academic imprint of the above companies and has companies and representatives throughout the world.

Palgrave® and Macmillan® are registered trademarks in the United States, the United Kingdom, Europe and other countries.

ISBN: 978-0-230-50006-8   hardback
ISBN: 978-0-230-30051-4   paperback

This book is printed on paper suitable for recycling and made from fully managed and sustained forest sources. Logging, pulping and manufacturing processes are expected to conform to the environmental regulations of the country of origin.

A catalogue record for this book is available from the British Library.

A catalogue record for this book is available from the Library of Congress.

10   9   8   7   6   5   4   3   2   1
20   19   18   17   16   15   14   13   12   11

Printed and bound in Great Britain by
CPI Antony Rowe, Chippenham and Eastbourne

Contents

List of Maps

Notes on the Contributors

David Mota Álvarez is writing a PhD thesis on 'Castilla y España en la Historiografía Portuguesa. Del Vintismo a la República (1820–1910)' at the University of Salamanca, Spain. He has previously collaborated with the research project 'Castilla y España en las historiografías española y portuguesa contemporáneas'. He has published extensively on the relationship between historiography and nationalism in Portugal and Spain.

Peter Aronsson is Professor of Cultural Heritage and the Uses of History at the multidisciplinary Culture Studies Department, Linköping University. His dissertation dealt with the historic conditions for creating a durable democratic culture. The role of historical narrative and consciousness to direct action has been the focus in recent research both as regards historiography proper and the uses of the past in historical culture at large. Currently Aronsson is coordinating several international projects exploring the uses of the past in national museums, see www.namu.se and *Historiebruk – att använda det förflutna* (2004).

Stefan Berger is Professor of Modern German and Comparative European History at the University of Manchester. He is the chair of the five-year European Science Foundation programme on 'Representations of the Past: Writing National Histories in Nineteenth and Twentieth Century Europe' (2003–8) and one of the series editors of the Palgrave Macmillan series accompanying the programme. He has published widely on the comparative history of national identity and nationalism, historical theory and labour history. His most recent monograph is *Inventing the Nation: Germany* (Hodder Arnold, 2004).

Marnix Beyen is an assistant professor at the University of Antwerp, Belgium, where he heads the Research Group on Political History. Among his main publications are: *Held voor alle werk. De vele gedaanten van Tijl Uilenspiegel* (1998) and *Oorlog en Verleden. Nationale Geschiedenis in België en Nederland, 1938–1947* (2002). His most recent work (with Philippe Destatte) is the last volume of *La Nouvelle Histoire de Belgique*, concentrating on the period 1970–2000 (2008).

Gita Deneckere is Associate Professor of Modern History at Ghent University, Belgium. She is author of, among others, *Sire, het volk mort. Sociaal protest in België 1831–1918)* (1997); *Het katoenoproer van Gent in 1839. Collectieve actie en sociale geschiedenis* (1999); *Les Turbulences de la Belle Époque (1878–1900)* (2005); *1900.*

België op het breukvlak van twee eeuwen (2006) and editor (with Jeroen Deploige), of *Mystifying the Monarch. Studies on Discourse, Power and History* (2006). She is currently writing a biography of Leopold I titled *The Melancholy of a Prince Who Became King of the Belgians.* With Bruno De Wever, she recently founded the Institute of Public History which aims at closer connections between academic and public history.

Hugo Frey is Principal Lecturer and Head of History at the University of Chichester, England. He is the author of *Louis Malle* (2004) and has co-edited (with Benjamin Noys) special issues of the journals *Rethinking History* 'History in the Graphic Novel' (6, 3, 2002) and *Journal of European Studies* 'Reactionary Times' (37, 3/4, 2007). In 2003, his work (with Christopher Flood) regarding the French extreme right was reprinted in the Routledge Reader series, James D. Le Sueur (ed.) *Decolonization: A Reader* (New York, 2003). Currently, Frey is writing *Filming France.*

Narve Fulsås is Professor of History at the University of Tromsø, Norway. His books include *Historie og nasjon: Ernst Sars og striden om norsk kultur* (1999) and *Havet, døden og vêret: kulturell modernisering i Kyst-Noreg 1850–1950* (2003). He is editor of the series *Henrik Ibsens skrifter* vols. 12–15 (2005–) Ibsen's letters with introductions and comment.

Pertti Haapala is Professor of Finnish History at the University of Tampere, Finland, a long-time head of the department, Director of the Finnish Doctoral School of History and director of many major research projects. He has published several monographs on the social history of Finland in the nineteenth and twentieth centuries. He also lectures and writes on historiography and history politics in Finland. Currently he is running a comparative project on the history of deindustrialisation. Haapala is Vice Chair of the Council of Culture and Society at the Academy of Finland.

Gernot Heiss is Professor of Austrian History in the Department of History, University of Vienna, Austria. He has published widely on early modern history, particularly the history of noble estates and the history of education, on twentieth century historiography and cultural history, and on the history of the cinema. His publications include 'Von Österreichs deutscher Vergangenheit und Aufgabe. Die Wiener Schule der Geschichtswissenschaft und der Nationalsozialismus', in G. Heiss, S. Mattl, S. Meissl, E. Saurer, K. Stuhlpfarrer (eds), *Willfährige Wissenschaft: Die Universität Wien 1938–1945* (Wien 1989); 'Pan-Germans, Better Germans, Austrians. Austrian Historians on National Identity from the First to the Second Republic', *German Studies Review*, 16 (1993), pp. 411–33; and 'Im

"Reich der Unbegreiflichkeiten". Historiker als Konstrukteure Österreichs', *Öster-reichische Zeitschrift für Geschichtswissenschaft*, 7, 4 (1996), pp. 455–78.

Maciej Janowski is Visiting Associate Professor at the Central European University, Budapest, Hungary and Associate Professor at the Institute of History of the Polish Academy of Sciences. He has published widely on Polish modern history, particularly the development of liberal thought. His books include *Polish Liberal Thought before 1918* (2004).

Bernard Eric Jensen is Associate Professor of History and History Didactics at School of Education at Aarhus University, Denmark. He has been head of an interdisciplinary research project on the ways in which history is represented and used in Danish society today. The results of this project are summarised in *At formidle historie – vilkår, kendetegn, formål* (1999). He has done extensive research on the history of historical scholarship in Denmark as well as Germany. His publications include *Danmarkshistorier – en erindringspolitisk slagmark* (1997) and *Historie – livsverden og fag* (2003).

Stefan Jordan is a research fellow at the Historische Kommission bei der Bayerischen Akademie der Wissenschaften; he also teaches at the Ludwig-Maximilians-Universität München, Germany. He is the author of *Deutschspra-chige Geschichtstheorie in der ersten Hälfte des 19. Jahrhunderts* (1999) and *Einführung in das Geschichtsstudium* (2005). His research interests are in the theory and history of historiography. with Hugo Frey, Jordan is working on a comparative project on French and German historiography.

James Kennedy is Professor of Dutch History at the University of Amsterdam, the Netherlands, having served from 2003 to 2007 as Professor of Contemporary History at the Vrije Universiteit of Amsterdam. He is principally a specialist in Dutch postwar history, having written books on the history of the 1960s and of euthanasia policy in the Netherlands. He has also written extensively on religious developments in the Netherlands, and is currently working on *A Concise History of the Netherlands*.

Árpád v. Klimó, is Research Fellow at the Zentrum für Zeithistorische Forschung Potsdam, and was Visiting Professor at Vienna University in 2007. From autumn 2008 he is Visiting Professor at the University of Pittsburg. His main publications include *Nation, Konfession, Geschichte. Zur nationalen Geschichtskultur Ungarns im europäischen Kontext: 1860–1948* (2003); and (co-edited with Malte Rolf) *Rausch und Diktatur. Inszenierung, Mobilisierung und Kontrolle in totalitären Systemen* (2006).

Pavel Kolář is a research fellow at Zentrum für Zeithistorische Forschung Potsdam. His interests include the history of historiography and historical culture and the history of Communist dictatorships in East Central Europe. He is the author of *Geschichtswissenschaft in Zentraheuropia. Die Universitäten Prag, Wien und Berlin um 1900* (Leipzig: Akademische Verlagsanstalt, forthcoming).

Dušan Kováč is Professor and Vice-President of the Slovak Academy of Sciences in Bratislava, Slovakia. Between 1990 and 1998, he was director of the Institute of Historical Studies (SAS), and from 1998 to 2005 he was Secretary General of the SAS. His main fields of research include the history of the Slovak historiography and the history of the Central Europe in the late nineteenth and early twentieth centuries. His most important recent publications include *How Slovak Historiography is Coming to Terms with a 'Dual Past'* (2006); *Slovakia in the 20th century, vol. 1: On the Beginning of the Century* (2004); (with Robert Evans and Edita Ivaničková) *Great Britain and Central Europe* (2002); and *Paradoxa und Dilemmata der postkommunistischen Geschichtsschreibung* (2002).

Joep Leerssen has been Professor of European Studies at the University of Amsterdam, the Netherlands since 1991. He works on three related fields of interest: 'imagology', the critical study of cross-cultural stereotyping and of images of national characterisation; Irish literary and cultural history, especially the representation of Ireland in English and Gaelic literature, mainly in the eighteenth and nineteenth centuries; and the international history of cultural nationalism in Europe in the nineteenth century, especially the role of networks of scholars and intellectuals. In all these fields he has published monographs, edited collections and articles in journals such as *Journal of the History of Ideas, Poetics Today, Field Day Review* and *Nations and Nationalism*.

Chris Lorenz is Professor of Philosophy of History at the Free University of Amsterdam, the Netherlands. He is also team leader of the ESF research programme 'Representations of the Past: The Writing of National Histories in Europe' (NHIST, 2003–8). Relevant publications include: 'Beyond Good and Evil? The Second German Empire of 1871 and Modern German Historiography', *Journal of Contemporary History* 30 (1995), pp. 729–65; *Konstruktion der Vergangenheit. Eine Einführung in die Geschichtstheorie* (1997); 'Comparative Historiography: Problems and Perspectives', *History and Theory* 39, 1 (1999), pp. 25–39; 'Border Crossings. Some Reflections on Recent Debates in German History', in Michman, D. (ed.), *Remembering the Holocaust in Germany 1945–1999* (2001); 'Towards a Theoretical Framework for Comparing Historiographies: Some Preliminary Considerations', in Seixas, P. (ed.), *Theorizing Historical Consciousness* (2004).

Benoît Majerus is a research assistant at the Fonds National de Recherche Scientifique, Université libre de Bruxelles, Belgium. He has recently co-edited *Les lieux de mémoire au Luxembourg. Usages du passé et construction nationale, Luxembourg* (2007).

Jitka Malečková Between 2004 and 2008 Jitka Malečková was Program Officer at the Russell Sage Foundation in New York, and from October 2008 will return to Charles University Prague, where she worked as Associate Professor in the Department of Middle Eastern Studies until 2004. She is author of *Úrodná půda: Žena ve službách národa* (2002). She writes on nationalism and gender in Central and Eastern Europe, modern Ottoman history and terrorism. Recent publications include 'The Emancipation of Women for the Benefit of the Nation: The Czech Women's Movement', in Paletschek, S. and Pietrow-Ennker, B. (eds), *Women's Emancipation Movements in the 19th Century: A European Perspective* (Stanford, 2004), and 'Terrorists and the Societies from which they Come', in Victoroff, J. (ed.), *Tangled Roots: Social and Psychological Factors in the Genesis of Terrorism* (2006).

Guy P. Marchal studied in Basel and Paris, and was professor at the University of Basel, Switzerland, 1976–93 and Professor of General and Swiss History at the University of Lucerne, Switzerland, 1989–2003. He is a medievalist with special interests in the histoire des mentalités, historical anthropology, and historiography and the history of traditions. He is co-chair of the five-year European Science Foundation programme on 'Representations of the Past: Writing National Histories in Nineteenth and Twentieth Century Europe' (2003–8) and one of the series editors of the Palgrave Macmillan series accompanying the programme. His main works include *Die frommen Schweden in Schwyz. Das 'Herkommen der Schwyzer und Oberhasler' als Quelle zum schwyzerischen Selbstverständnis im 15. und 16. Jahrhundert* (1976); *Geschichte der Schweiz und der Schweizer* (1983); and *Schweizer Gebrauchsgeschichte. Geschichtsbilder, Mythenbildung und nationale Identität* (2006).

Sérgio Campos Matos is Professor of Contemporary History at the University of Lisbon, Portugal since 1985. He is the author of *História, mitologia, imaginário nacional (1895–1939)* (1990), *Historiografia e memória nacional no Portugal do século XIX* (1998 and *Consciência historica e nacionalismo Portugal nos séculos XIX e* (forthcoming)). He is currently researching on Portuguese and Spanish historical and political cultures in a wider context.

Hercules Millas has a PhD in political science and a BSc in civil engineering. He has taught Greek and Turkish literature and cultural history in various universities in Turkey and Greece. Presently he teaches at the University of Athens,

Greece. In addition to some 15 volumes of translations of poetry and many journal and newspaper articles, his main publications involve historiography, inter-ethnic images and perceptions in textbooks, novels and history writing, in all cases focusing on the Greek-Turkish case.

Keith Robbins is Emeritus Vice-Chancellor of the University of Wales Lampeter, having previously been Professor of History at the University of Wales, Bangor and the University of Glasgow, Scotland. He has been president of the Historical Association and editor of its journal, *History*. He is general editor of many series, including Inventing the Nation (Arnold), Religion, Society and Politics in Britain (Pearson Education), Britain and Europe (Arnold) and Profiles in Power (Pearson Education). He has written widely on British foreign policy, domestic politics, international history, war and church history. His many books include *Nineteenth-Century Britain: Integration and Diversity* (1988); *History, Religion and Identity in Modern Britain* (1993); and *Great Britain: Identities, Institutions and the Idea of Britishness* (1998) and *England, Ireland, Scotland, Wales: The Christian Church 1900–20* (2008).

Krijn Thijs is a postdoctoral researcher at the Center of Language and Identity at the University of Leiden, the Netherlands. He obtained his PhD from the Vrije Universiteit Amsterdam in 2006 for his dissertation written as a guest-researcher at the Zentrum für Zeithistorische Forschung, Potsdam: *Drei Geschichten, eine Stadt. Die Berliner Stadtjubiläen 1937 und 1987* (Köln und Weimar, 2008). In cooperation with the Duitsland Instituut Amsterdam, he co-edited (with P. Dassen and T. Nijhuis) *Duitsers als slachtoffers. Het einde van een taboe?* (2007). He is currently working on a research project on the continuities in German memory culture since the 1980s.

Marius Turda is RCUK Academic Fellow in 20th Century Central and Eastern European Bio-Medicine at Oxford Brookes University, England. He is the author of *The Idea of National Superiority in Central Europe, 1880-1918* (2005), co-editor (with Paul J. Weindling) of *'Blood and Homeland': Eugenics and Racial Nationalism in Central and Southeast Europe, 1900–1940* (2007) and co-editor (with Matt Feldman) of *'Clerical Fascism' in Interwar Europe* (2008).

Anna Veronika Wendland is a researcher at Ludwig-Maximilians-Universität, Department of History, Munich, Germany. She completed her PhD thesis in 1998 and was a researcher at the Centre for History and Culture of East Central Europe in Leipzig, Germany between 1997 and 2003. She was awarded the Fritz Theodor Epstein Prize of the German Association of Historians of Eastern Europe. Principal research interests include the eastern and western borderlands of Austria-Hungary and Russia, specifically those territories now belonging to the Baltic states, Poland, Belarus and Ukraine; the social and cultural history of national movements in East-Central and Eastern Europe; Eastern Central European urban and regional history; the history of political ideas and historical narratives in Poland, Lithuania and the Ukraine. Her current project is a monograph on urban identity and national integration in Lviv and Vilnius, 1890–1960.

Thomas Welskopp is Professor of the History of Modern Societies at Bielefeld University, Germany. He was 2003/4 fellow at the Center for Advanced Study in the Behavioral Sciences, Stanford, CA. He is the author of *Das Banner der Brüderlichkeit. Die deutsche Sozialdemokratie vom Vormärz bis zum Sozialistengesetz* (2000), and *Arbeit und Macht im Hüttenwerk. Die deutsche und amerikanische Eisen- und Stahlindustrie von den 1860er bis zu den 1930er Jahren* (1994). He is co-editor (with Thomas Mergel) of *Geschichte zwischen Kultur und Gesellschaft. Beiträge zur Theoriedebatte* (1997) and (with Katja Girschik and Albrecht Ritschl) of *Der Migros-Kosmos. Zur Geschichte eines außergewöhnlichen Schweizer Unternehmens* (2003).

Ulrich Wyrwa is Associate Lecturer at the University of Potsdam, Germany and head of a research group on Anti-Semitism in Europe (1879–1914) at the Centre for Research on Anti-Semitism at the Technical University, Berlin, Germany. His fields of research are European Jewish history and the history of anti-Semitism primarily in nineteenth-century Italy and Germany, and the history of Jewish historiography in Europe. He is editor of *Judentum und Historismus. Zur Entstehung der jüdischen Geschichtswissenschaft in Europa* (2003), and author of 'Das Bild von Europa in der jüdischen Geschichtsschreibung des 19. und frühen 20. Jahrhunderts', in K. Armborst and W.F. Schäufele (eds.), *Der Wert 'Europa' und die Geschichte. Auf dem Weg zu einem europäischen Geschichtsbewusstsein* Mainz 2007 (Veröffentlichungen des Instituts für Europäische Geschichte Mainz, Beiheft onhne 2) ss. 74–93. www.ieg_mainz.de/vieg_onhne_beheifte/02-2007.html.

Acknowledgements

This volume is the result of a truly cooperative effort by scholars from many different national historiographical traditions, who, over the course of three years, have met three times (in Cardiff, Budapest and Munich) and discussed their contributions to this volume, revising and refining them after each meeting. As editors, we are, above all, immensely grateful to our contributors and thank them for the time and effort they have put into making this volume work. We are also indebted to the local organisers of these meetings who made our stays in various European cities so memorable. We would furthermore like to express our thanks to two subsequent NHIST programme coordinators, Andrew Mycock and Sven de Roode, who were of invaluable help in preparing the chapters for publication and liaising with authors and publisher. At the publishing house, we would like to thank Michael Strang, Ruth Ireland and Ruth Willats for their patience and assistance in the publication of this the volume and the *Writing the Nation* series, in which it appears.

This is volume 3 of the *Writing the Nation* series, which is the main outcome of the five-year European Science Foundation Programme entitled 'Representations of the Past: The Writing of National Histories in Nineteenth- and Twentieth-Century Europe' (2003–2008) (see www.uni-leipzig.de/zhsesf) It has been planned and executed in close collaboration with the editors of the other volumes, and we would like to take the opportunity to thank Ilaria Porciani, Lutz Raphael, Jo Tollebeek, Matthias Middell, Lluis Roura, Frank Hadler and Tibor Frank for their input into this volume. We are also grateful to the European Science Foundation and its unstinting support. We also want to thank the local organizers for organizing our workshops in Cardiff, Budapest, Munich and Prague. In particular we would like to thank the general editors Chistoph Conrad and Guy P. Marchal for their helpful comments and their advice throughout the duration of the programme. We also thank the Alexander von Humboldt Foundation for financing Chris Lorenz's stay at the Berliner Kolleg für Vergleichende Geschichte Europas in spring 2007 and Arnd Bauernkämper for his hospitality at the BKVGE. Last but not least, we would like to thank Merle Read at blackbord editorial services for her work on the texts written by authors whose native language is not English.

The maps in this volume have been put together by the historical cartography project at the University of Trier and we are grateful to Lutz Raphael and Michael Grün for letting us use them.

As always, any shortcomings in this volume are the sole responsibility of the editors.

Stefan Berger, *Disley*
Chris Lorenz, *Amsterdam*

Maps of Europe 1789–2005

1: *Map of Europe 1789*

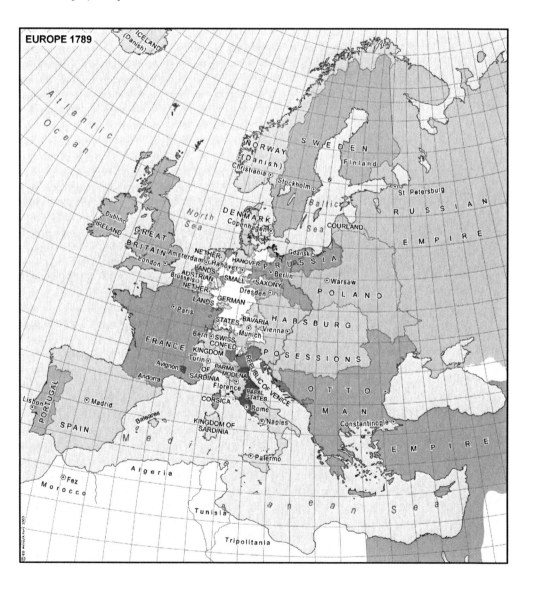

2: Map of Europe 1830

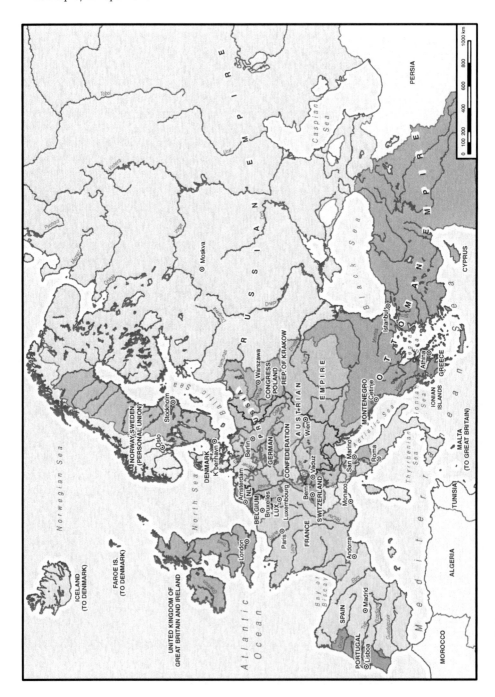

3: *Map of Europe 1875*

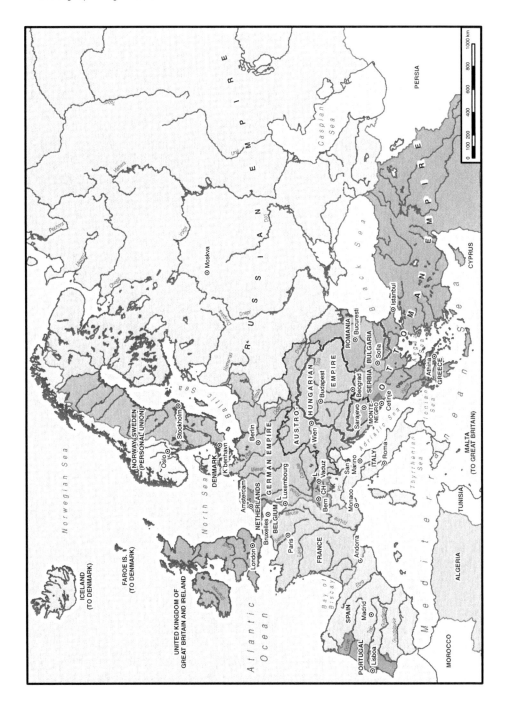

4: *Map of Europe 1928*

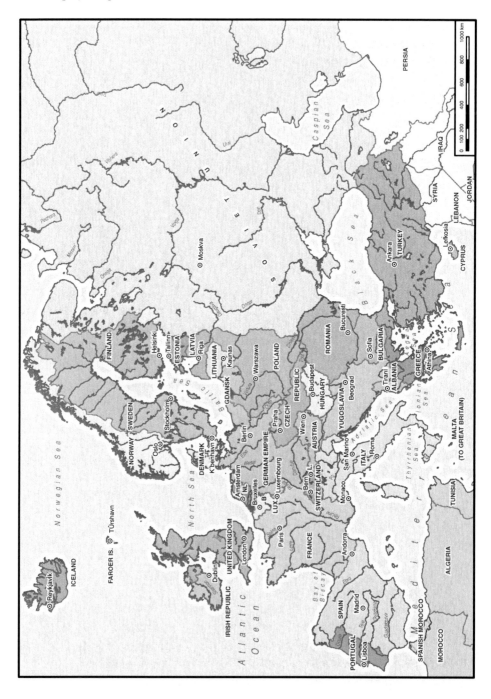

5: *Map of Europe 1955*

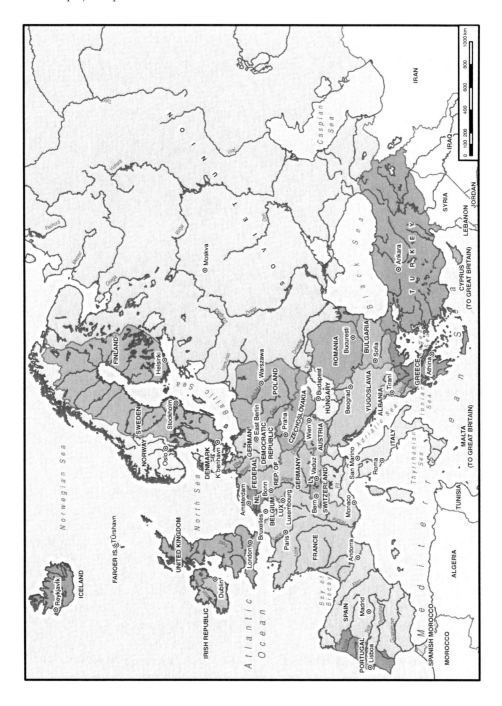

6: *Map of Europe 2005*

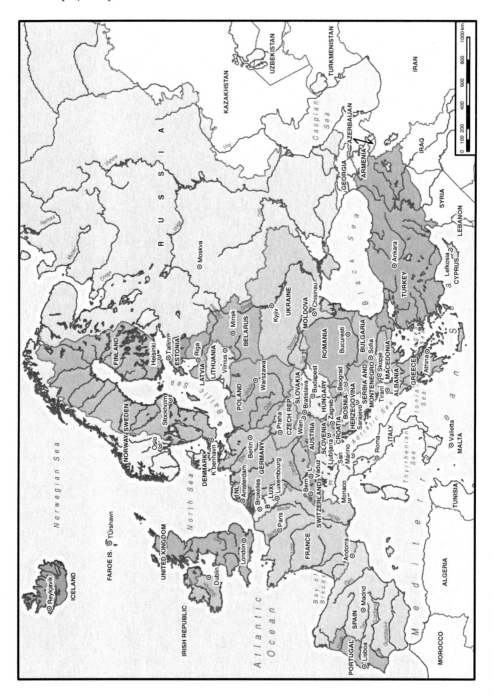

1
Introduction: National History Writing in Europe in a Global Age

Stefan Berger and Chris Lorenz

National history has been a dominant genre of history writing in Europe for almost two centuries and it no doubt still is an important – if not the *most* important – type of historical text also outside Europe. Most collectivities who identified themselves as (existing or would-be) 'nations' have produced a bewildering variety of national histories over time, which were not only in competition with other histories of the 'same' nation, but simultaneously in competition with histories of other 'nations'. Consequently, intertextuality has been a fundamental characteristic of national histories, and since historical texts belong to the genre of narratives, narration has played a vital role in constructions of national histories. What Ann Rigney has observed in relation to the historiography of the French Revolution also holds for national historiography in general: 'the starting point [of historiography] is not silence, but what has been said already', 'revisionist works are intertextually linked to the works they seek to displace'. As a consequence of this intertextuality, historical representation possesses an 'agonistic dimension' that is crucial to its understanding. Historians 'do write regularly in the negative mode, the assertion of what happened going hand in glove with the denial of what did not happen, what was certainly not the case or only partially so.'[1]

This volume seeks to provide some answers to the question of how national historians have framed their national narratives in a variety of different national contexts across Europe and how these narratives have been interconnected. These interconnections are analysed at two levels; first, at an *inter*-national level, that is at a level where the interactions between at least the historiographical traditions of two nations are concerned (for instance, the interaction between French and German national historiographies); and second, at a level where, *within* a national tradition, constructions of the nation are connected to

---

[1]See A. Rigney, 'Time for Visions and Revisions: Interpretative Conflict from a Communicative Perspective', *Storia della Storiografia*, 22 (1992), 86–91.

competing conceptions of collective identity of a *trans*national character (the so-called Others of the nation). In this volume we focus on religion, class, ethnicity/race and gender as the Others of the nation, while in volume 4, regions and empires are dealt with as alternatives in competition with the nation. The rationale for this distinction is that while regions and empires are *spatial* alternatives to the nation, religion, class, ethnicity/race and gender lack this primary spatial dimension. Therefore, they are labelled the 'non-spatial Others' of the nation in this volume; narratives focusing on these other identities we have called 'master narratives', competing with the master narrative of the nation.

The contributors to this volume were specifically asked to investigate the relationship between national histories and histories of these Others. Where and under what conditions did they have the power to develop into *trans*national rivals of nation – for example, in religious or class histories? Where and under what conditions did they challenge national histories, and where and under what conditions were they subsumed and integrated into national narratives?

Geographically, our discussions are restricted to Europe, although we are cognisant of the fact that national history writing was not exclusively a European phenomenon. In fact, national histories can be described as one of the most successful exports of Europe in the imperial age. In Africa, where no sense of nation existed before the colonial encounters, it was to structure the post-independent national narratives, and in India and China, where indigenous concepts of nation existed, these changed significantly under the impact of the encounter with European national narratives.[2] Last but not least, the 'New Nations' outside Europe were all modelled on the European national model.[3]

By focusing on Europe in this volume – and we consciously embraced a 'broad' conception of Europe to include both Turkey and the successor states of the Soviet Union west of the Urals – we aimed at incorporating comparative and transnational perspectives from the start and not to leave the comparison to the reader.[4] This raised the question of comparative clustering – which

[2]For an attempt to avoid Eurocentrism and develop global perspectives on the writing of national histories, see S. Berger (ed.), *Writing the Nation: Towards Global Perspectives* (Basingstoke, 2007).
[3]See G. Bouchard, *The Making of the Nations and Cultures of the New World: An Essay in Comparative History*, (Montreal, 2008).
[4]On the importance of comparative and transnational approaches to historical writing, see in particular, S. Berger, 'Comparative History', in idem, H. Feldner and K. Passmore (eds), *Writing History. Theory and Practice* (London, 2003), pp. 161–82, and C. Lorenz, 'Comparative Historiography: Problems and Perspectives', in *History and Theory*, 38, 1 (1999), 25–39; C. Lorenz, 'Towards a Theoretical Framework of Comparing Historiographies: Some Preliminary Considerations', in P. Seixas (ed.), *Theorizing Historical Consciousness* (Toronto, 2004), pp. 25–48; D. Cohen and M. O'Connor (eds), *Comparison and History: Europe in Cross-National Perspective* (London, 2004) includes references to other important literature on the topics of comparative history, the history of cultural transfers and transnational history.

national narratives were to be compared with which other national narratives? In this volume we thus presuppose the existence of our basic unit of comparison, which is national traditions of history writing and the possibility of their mutual transfer.[5]

The criterion for the selection of cases for comparison has been a geographical one, meaning proximity and thus acknowledging the fundamental importance of space in history. Nevertheless, we have been very aware of the possibility of alternative ways of clustering the national historiographical traditions (for example, comparing German to Russian and not French historiography). The arguments for our selection therefore can only be judged on the basis of the quality of the individual chapters, so we will leave it at that and wait for the readers' verdict.

The structure of the volume is as follows. We start with a chapter by Chris Lorenz which deals with a conceptual clarification of the notion of identity – the very basis of thinking in terms of Others – and with a conceptual history of the notions of ethnicity/race, class, gender and religion. Following a chapter on the central concept of 'master narrative' by Krijn Thijs, four broad survey chapters discuss the relationship of national narratives to narratives of ethnicity/race, religion, class and gender. Joep Leerssen, in his contribution on nation and ethnicity/race, locates the roots of national narratives in the Romantic period around 1800 and argues that ideas about 'the nation' in Europe usually derived from 'historist nationalism'.[6] According to Leerssen, the notions of ethnicity, nation, race and people were used indiscriminately in the nineteenth century, both in the historical and the 'para- historical' disciplines, and the idea of an ethnic foundation of the nation survives in latent form today.

Surveying the relationship between nation and religion, James Kennedy distinguishes between two patterns; first, the supersession of religion by nation and, second, the merging of religion with nation. According to the first pattern, the

---

[5]M. Werner and B. Zimmermann, 'Beyond Comparison: *Histoire croisée* and the Challenge of Reflexivity', *History and Theory,* 45, 1 (2006), 30–50, point to this problem: 'In the case of transnational exchanges, these points of departure and arrival are generally located within the national societies and cultures that are in contact. Consequently, the original situation and the situation resulting from the transfer are apprehended through stable national references that are presumed known: for example, 'German' or 'French' historiography'.

[6]We use the word historism (*Historismus*) and not historicism (*Historizismus*) to note a crucial difference between the idea of *Historismus*, frequently attributed to Leopold von Ranke, that everything has developed historically and can only be understood in particular historical contexts, and the idea of *Historizismus*, coined by Karl Popper, of the teleological 'law-like' development of the historical process (attributed by him to both Marxist and Nazi thinkers). Popper single-handedly created this conceptual confusion in the Anglo-Saxon world in his book *The Poverty of Historicism* (London, 1957).

'objective' national viewpoint simply transcends the 'partisan' religious views on the past. According to the second, the 'holy nation' eventually transforms the cult of the nation into 'political religion'. This sacralisation of the nation has been widespread in Europe. Kennedy traces the changes of these two patterns over the last two centuries, emphasising the ever-changing and contested character of the relationship between ideas of the nation and religion.

In their contribution on nation and class, Thomas Welskopp and Gita Deneckere consider class to be an historical category that is central to social history rather than national history. Even if one cannot speak unambiguously of a 'counter-historiography' opposing the hegemonic historiographical representation of the national past, the 'scientific' status of this tradition has always been contested. The equation 'history equals national history' could also be read as 'national history equals scientific, i.e. true, history' whereas alternative class histories have traditionally been stamped as ideological, Marxist, partisan and hence 'unscientific'. Even now that 'scientific' historians have been unmasked as producers of historical myths *par excellence*, the 'truth' of the class histories is still embattled in academic historiography.[7]

Jitka Malečková discusses the problematic field of nation and gender. She points out that the interest that both men and (particularly) women historians have paid to women has undoubtedly been connected with the women's movement, resulting in the two heydays of women's history in the late nineteenth and late twentieth centuries. However, the writing of women's history was rarely national history and often exerted little influence on how national histories continued to be gendered in specific ways. One could say that women were included in master narratives only when it served the interests of the nation in the view of the hegemonic male historians. Women were 'added' to the existing national master narratives, rather than new narratives being elaborated, revising the periodisation of national history or including new domains of life.

The second part of the volume consists of specific country comparisons. In particular, the editors asked all contributors to address the following issues in the national historiographies, most of which are directly connected to the notion of 'historical identity' (see below): First, how are origins, foundational events and personalities narrated? Second, what role did 'rise and decline' narratives play and how were 'golden ages' as well as catastrophic events portrayed? Third, how were the key national heroes and villains cast? Fourth, how was the issue of continuity or discontinuity of the nation addressed? Fifth, how was the uniqueness and special character of the nation established?

---

[7]On 'mythmaking' in national history, see C. Lorenz, 'Drawing the Line: "Scientific" History between Myth-making and Myth-breaking', in: Stefan Berger, Linas Eriksonas and Andrew Mycock (eds), *Narrating the Nation. Representations in History, Media and the Arts*, New York/Oxford 2008, 35–55.

Sixth, which Others were excluded and how were such exclusions dealt with in narrative terms? Seventh, what place did wars and battle narratives have in national histories? Eighth, how was the nation gendered? Finally, ninth, how was Christianity nationalised and the nation sacralised across Europe?

The country comparisons start with Hugo Frey's and Stefan Jordan's comparison of Germany and France. The authors argue that different relationships pertain between the master narratives in these two historiographies. Whereas in secular France, religion and state/nation were considered to be two completely separate spheres, in Germany they were closely connected. Further differences between France and Germany are located in the use of the term 'class' in both historiographies. Whilst in France this category could be related to the nation, in Germany it remained for far longer a counter-discourse to the national narrative outside the borders of 'scientific' history.

'Big' national historiographies such as the French and German examples, which interacted in manifold ways with other national historiographies across Europe, could be compared to a whole range of other national historiographies. The reader of this volume will observe how key German and French historians and historical institutions figure in a number of the chapters. The clustering in this volume is therefore neither exclusive nor necessarily the only one that makes sense. However, we believe that it sheds important light on the development of national historical narratives and widens the horizon to the diverse ways in which those narratives were being constructed across different national contexts.

Guy Marchal's chapter on Switzerland provides valuable comparative outlooks on German, French and also Belgian historiographies, reflecting the intellectual proclivities of diverse linguistic communities in Switzerland. Marchal comments in particular on the importance of confessionalism in diverse national master narratives, the narrative technique of projecting history backwards in order to achieve continuities, the marginality of racial definitions of the Swiss nation and the early participation of women in the writing of Swiss national history.

Another nation in Europe with distinct linguistic groups which tended to orient themselves towards linguistic groups in neighbouring countries is Belgium – with the Flemish historians more oriented towards Germany and the Netherlands and the Walloon ones more towards France. In his contribution, Marnix Beyen concentrates on a comparison of Belgium with the Netherlands. His main conclusion is that national history writing is threatened far more by the Other in Belgium than in the Netherlands, where national history writing remains the dominant professional genre. By comparison, national history writing in Belgium has been reduced to an amateur genre. Benoit Majerus adds some sections on Luxembourg to Beyen's chapter. Majerus devotes special attention to the circumstance that no academic history writing existed in Luxembourg until the foundation of the University of Luxembourg in 2003. This different institutional context had, he argues, the effect of weakening the links between nationalism and history writing – which in an indirect way confirms the 'normal' direct link between nation-building and the academic institutionalisation of history writing in Europe.

The German model was also hugely influential throughout Scandinavia and Finland. This becomes apparent in the chapter co-written by Peter Aronsson, Narve Fulsås, Pertti Haapala and Bernard Erik Jensen, although it deals largely with intra-Scandinavian comparisons (including the case of Finland). They conclude that, with regard to professional history, Sweden and Finland experienced the greatest difficulties in constructing a stable national master narrative with the active participation of professional historians. However, the difficulties had different causes: in Finland it was its stateless past, while in Sweden it was its imperial past and the problems connecting this past to a social-democratic present. Denmark adjusted earlier and more decisively to a new national framework as a consequence of the collapse of the conglomerate Danish state in 1864. In Norway the tradition of national history writing seems to have been the most continuous and least interrupted of the Nordic countries.

In their contribution on Spain and Portugal, Sergio Campos Matos and David Mota Alvarez represent the case of the Iberian peninsula, where French influence was marked. They argue that in Spanish and Portuguese historiographies historist ideas of the peninsular nations tended to dominate, organised around the idea of ethnic origins. They were informed by organicist conceptions of decadence and progress – typical for historism in its classical form – and by an obsession with identifying (and exorcising) those responsible for decline.[8] After the 1960s, this obsession was superseded by a more distanced concern with understanding economic backwardness in a comparative perspective. Interestingly, the two authors also reach the conclusion that Portuguese and Spanish historians hardly ever took note of each other, developing strong individual and autonomous national traditions of history writing.

The decline of the Spanish empire throughout the nineteenth century led Spanish historians further cause to lament the alleged national decay. In the case of the Habsburg empire, there was not even a nationalising strategy of an imperial core after the greater German solution had been ruled out in 1866/1871. Gernot Heiss, Árpád von Klimó, Pavel Kolář and Dušan Kováč examine the case of the former Habsburg Empire and the later successor nations of Austria, Hungary, Czechoslovakia and the Czech and Slovak Republics. The authors highlight the fact that German-Austrian historiographical nationalism was concentrated on the imperial monarchy, from which other ethnic groups within the

---

[8]On the origins of historism, see G. Iggers, *The German Conception of History: The National Tradition of Historical Thought from Herder to the Present*, 2nd rev. edn (Middletown, CT, 1983).

empire constructed national historiographies which sought to reject or gain as much autonomy as possible. While the historiography of the empire united diverse ethnic national narratives, national historiographies divided them.

With a particular focus on Poland and the Czech lands, Maciej Janowski widens the perspective of the volume further to Eastern European nations. The dominant controversy in historical debates in East-Central Europe involves theories of endogenous and exogenous national development, which include the question of how different or similar their national trajectories have been from 'the West'. This confirms Rigney's argument that history writing is not only about what happened, but simultaneously about what did *not* happen. It also confirms that implicit ideas about 'normal' developments form the background of all claims to national *Sonderwege*.[9] Janowski's chapter sheds light on these debates, whilst also highlighting the revisionism of positivist historiographies in both countries *vis-à-vis* their Romantic forefathers.

Going further east, Vero Wendland deals with Russia and some of its western neighbours, namely Ukraine and the Baltic states. They were all once part of the Russian empire and, with the exception of the Baltic states in the interwar period, also of the Soviet empire. Hence the Russian, Ukranian and Baltic national narratives were strongly interrelated, making for interesting processes of transfer but also stark dichotomies and rejections. After discussing the construction of 'peasant nations' *vis-à-vis* an imperial core, Wendland analyses popular challenges to the hegemonic national narratives and considers the impact of both ethnocentrism and communism on all of these national histories.

Marius Turda continues the trawl through Eastern Europe by comparing national historiographies in the Balkans, focusing in particular on Romania. His chapter traces the diverse ways in which national historians of the Balkans sought to overcome both the Ottoman legacy and the claim by many Western historians that theirs were 'unhistorical' nations. He draws attention to the crucial importance of discourses of historical rights and historical continuities, and pays due attention to the excessive forms of politicisation in the Balkan national historiographies before, during and after communism.

Hercules Millas emphasises similar roots of the national master narratives of Greece and Turkey. Both national historiographies negated the Ottoman empire; Greece rejected the Ottoman legacy altogether, while Turkey transformed it. Greek nation-building preceded Turkey's by about a century and Millas argues that this explains why the Greeks were on the offensive and the Turks on the defensive, both representing the other nation as its key Other.

Such a geographical *tour de force* leaves us with a medium-sized island group on the western margins of Europe – home to Great Britain and Ireland. Keith

---

[9]See Lorenz, 'Comparative Historiography'.

Robbins argues that constitutionalism and freedom have been crucial for the construction of what were largely English (and some Scottish) histories of these Isles. Empire broadened that story-line considerably in the late nineteenth and early twentieth centuries. Robbins also comments on the implications of the development of a separate Irish national history both before and after the emergence of the Free State. He considers the notions of Britain as a Protestant and Ireland as a Catholic nation and looks at the early integration of class narratives into the national paradigm. Overall, the comparative isolation of British debates on national history took place in is striking, although the dialogue with and reception of German historiography in particular could be strong at certain times and places.

Finally, in Ulrich Wyrwa's contribution on Jewish historiographies in different European nation-states – included in the volume as an early example of transnational history – four types of narrative are distinguished: 1) the universal-historical narrative; 2) the regional- or local-historical narrative; 3) the narrative based on the idea of a liberal national state, in which Jews and non-Jews were integrated; and 4) the Zionist narrative. Wyrwa is particularly good at providing tantalising glimpses of the tensions between these historians' national commitments and their transnational orientations as Jewish historians. Only Zionism did not suffer from it, but this came at the expense of much subtlety and the espousal of more straightforward nationalist narratives.[10]

In terms of chronology, the editors asked all contributors to write survey articles dealing with the period from the early nineteenth to the early twenty-first centuries. However, this does not imply that national histories were not being written much earlier than the nineteenth century; therefore, the analysis could easily be extended backwards. In some cases, notably England, notions of nation entered historical works (for example, those of William of Malmesbury and Geoffrey of Monmouth) in the twelfth century.[11] Certainly, European humanists combined their rediscovery of some of the classical texts from antiquity with notions of national character and national identity. Tacitus' *De Germania*, for example, was identified by the Italian humanists as example

---

[10]The historiographical development in Italy in a comparative perspective is sadly missing in this volume. Three scholars have successively promised to write this chapter during the last five years, but each failed to deliver what was required. The editors deeply regret this and can only hope that this omission will be remedied in a second edition.

[11]A. Bues and R. Rexheuser (eds), *Mittelalterliche nationes – neuzeitliche Nationen. Probleme der Nationenbildung in Europa* (Wiesbaden, 2003); J. Gillingham, 'Civilizing the English? The English Histories of William of Malmesbury and David Hume', *Historical Research*, 124 (2001), 17–43.

of the superiority of Roman/Italian over Teutonic/Germanic culture, whereas the same text served to prove the opposite for German humanists.[12] In the Reformation and Counter-Reformation of the sixteenth and seventeenth centuries, national history underpinned anti-Catholic identities in many of the Protestant nations of Europe.[13] In some respects one might say that many of the tropes and ideas of national history were well established before the onset of modernity.

And yet, it was not pure pragmatism which made NHIST focus on the modern period. Arguably, something important changed in the writing of national histories between 1750 and 1850. For a start, history became an institutionalised and academic profession legitimating itself by a discourse of 'scientificity'.[14] The historians' scientificity allegedly gave them privileged access to the past and, on the basis of this epistemological superiority, they successfully claimed practical superiority too: that is, to be the most important pedagogues of the nation.[15]

The very meaning of 'nation' also underwent significant transformations between the mid-eighteenth and mid-nineteenth centuries. It became tied more firmly to notions of citizenship and attempted to encompass all people in a given territory rather than only certain elites, as had usually been the case

---

[12]C. Hirschli, 'Das humanistische Nationskonstrukt vor dem Hintergrund modernistischer Nationalismustheorien', *Historisches Jahrbuch*, 122 (2002), 355–96; R. Stauber, 'Nationalismus vor dem Nationalismus? Eine Bestandsaufnahme der Forschung zu "Nation" und "Nationalismus" in der frühen Neuzeit', *Geschichte in Wissenschaft und Unterricht*, 47 (1996), 139–65; J. Helmrath, U. Muhlack and G. Walther (eds), *Diffusion des Humanismus: Studien zur nationalen Geschichtsschreibung europäischer Humanisten* (Göttingen, 2002).

[13]H. Schilling, 'Nationale Identität und Konfession in der europäischen Neuzeit', in B. Giesen (ed.), *Nationale und kulturelle Identität: Studien zur Entwicklung des kollektiven Bewußtseins in der Neuzeit* (Frankfurt/Main, 1991), pp. 192–252.

[14]For the professionalisation and institutionalisation of history, see R. Thorstendahl and I. Veit-Brause (eds), *History-Making. The Intellectual and Social Formation of a Discipline*, (Stockholm, 1996); P. den Boer, *History as a Profession: The Study of History in France, 1818–1914* (Princeton, NJ, 1998); W. Weber, *Priester der Klio: historisch-sozialwissenschaftliche Studien zu Herkunft und Karriere deutscher Historiker und zur Geschichte der Geschichtswissenschaft 1800–1970* (Frankfurt/M., 1987); M. Bentley, *Modernizing England's Past. English Historiography in the Age of Modernism 1870–1970* (Cambridge, 2005); G. Lingelbach, *Klio macht Karriere. Die Institutionalisierung der Geschichtswissenschaft in Frankreich und in den USA in der zweiten Hälfte des 19. Jahrhunderts* (Göttingen, 2003). For the ideas of 'scientificity', see C. Lorenz, 'Scientific/Critical History', in A. Tucker (ed.), *Blackwell Companion to Historiography and Philosophies of History* (Cambridge, 2008), and H. Feldner, 'The New Scientificity in Historical Writing around 1800', in Berger, Feldner and Passmore (eds), *Writing History*, pp. 3–22.

[15]See G. Scholz, *Zwischen Wissenschaftsanspruch und Orientierungsbedürfnis, Zu Grundlage und Wandel der Geisteswissenschaften*, (Frankfurt/M., 1991).

in medieval and early modern discourses about the nation. Hence, the modern discourse about nation – roughly starting with the French Revolution – was qualitatively different from the pre-modern one, which also justifies our decision to begin with the establishment of modern national histories.

An increasing claim of 'scientificity' also meant that academic history writing was increasingly portrayed as a superior form of history writing – not only superior to other genres such as the historical novel,[16] but also to amateur national history. However, this process of academic history pushing other forms of history writing to the margins of the public discourse about the nation's past occurred at different times in different regions of Europe and was never entirely successful in replacing more popular presentations of national history. In panoramas, dioramas, funfairs and through the full arsenal of 'banal nationalism', forms of popular and often 'spectacular' national history remained alive and sometimes challenged the more authoritative academic versions of the national past.[17] The asynchronicity of the appearance of academic national master narratives in history writing across Europe made it imperative for many authors to take into consideration important national histories which were not written by professional historians – exemplifying intertextuality over the borders of different historical genres. Hence amateur and professional historical narratives are considered in the subsequent pages – and also because female historians for a long time were not included in the history profession and thus remained 'amateurs' by definition.[18] During the nineteenth century in particular, many important historical texts, which cemented national master narratives, were not written by professional historians.

However, before embarking on this venture, one preliminary task must be dealt with in the remainder of this introduction. Since both history writing and the writing of historiography have lost their 'epistemological innocence', we shall be as self-reflexive as possible. We shall do this by tracing the problem of historical representation – no doubt, NHIST's core problem – in the recent discussions about history and memory. By thus locating our project in the historiographical landscape, we put ourselves 'on the map', so to speak. So we agree with Michael Werner and Bénédicte Zimmermann that self-reflexivity,

---

[16]On the presentation of national history in other genres than historiography, see S. Berger, L. Eriksonas and A. Mycock (eds), *Narrating the Nation: The Representation of National Narratives in Different Genres* (Oxford, 2007).
[17]B. Melman, *The Culture of History. English Uses of the Past* (Oxford, 2006); also M. Samuels, *The Spectacular Past. Popular History and the Novel in Nineteenth-Century France* (New York, 2004). On banal nationalism, see M. Billig, *Banal Nationalism* (London, 1995).
[18]See B. Smith, *The Gender of History: Men, Women, and Historical Practice* (Cambridge, MA, 1998).

including self-reflexivity in the form of historicisation of the categories (see chapter 2), is the only way to go about in comparative and transfer history.[19]

The origins of the problem of representation in national history: some reflections on time, the nation and historiography

Given the constitutive significance of the categories of time and space for 'scientific' history it is tantalising to see how little energy historians have invested in reflection on them. The intuitive ideas that time is identical with change, and that distance in time is the necessary condition for 'scientific' history writing, were usually taken for granted and not seen as in need of further analysis or justification from the nineteenth century onwards. Interested 'partisanship' – religious, political or otherwise – simply needed time in order to disappear and give way to supra-partisan 'objectivity'.[20]

In the same period, the nation-state turned into the self-evident spatial unit of the professional historian, not in need of any further justification. This situation lasted well into the twentieth century and arguably into the twenty-first century too.[21] It is only quite recently that the constructed character of all temporal and spatial units, and frames of historians, have been recognised and theorised – and even then only by a small minority of historians inclined to reflexivity.[22]

However this may be, the astonishing growth of interest in 'the nation' among European historians since 1989 is undoubtedly connected to time. It is

---

[19]See Werner and Zimmermann, 'Beyond Comparison', p. 32, where they characterise their approach by 'a threefold process of historicisation: through the object, the categories of analysis, and the relationships between the researcher and object'.

[20]See M. Phillips, 'Distance and Historical Representation', *History Workshop Journal*, 57 (2004), 123–41; M. Phillips, 'History, Memory and Historical Distance', in P. Seixas (ed.), *Theorizing Historical Consciousness* (Toronto, 2004), pp. 86–109. See further, B. Taylor, 'Introduction: How Far, How Near: Distance and Proximity in the Historical Imagination', *History Workshop Journal*, 57 (2004), 117–22.

[21]On the intimate relationship between history and nationalism, see D. Woolf, 'Of Nations, Nationalism, and National Identity: Reflections on the Historiographic Organization of the Past', in Q. E. Wang and F. L. Fillafer (eds), *The Many Faces of Clio: Cross-cultural Approaches to Historiography* (Oxford, 2007), pp. 71–104; S. Berger, 'A Return to the National Paradigm? National History Writing in Germany, Italy, France, and Britain from 1945 to the Present', in *Journal of Modern History*, 77 (2005), 629–78.

[22]On the constructedness of history in general, see C. Lorenz, *Konstruktion der Vergangenheit* (Vienna and Cologne, 1997).

related to the discourse on a united Europe and to the unexpected comeback of the nation in East-Central Europe in the wake of the fall of the Berlin Wall.[23] Since 1989, an economically and politically 'United Europe' is often represented in political discourse as Europe's inescapable destiny. The same problematisation of the nation-state is being produced by the discourse on 'globalisation', because whatever meaning is attributed to the term, it is clearly meant to indicate a movement *beyond* the nation-state.[24] The same holds for the new discourse on 'regionalisation'.[25] Charles Maier's recent introduction of the concept of 'regimes of territoriality' in history is therefore very 'timely', although no doubt also inspired by François Hartog's introduction of the concept of 'regimes of historicity'.[26] The fact that similar discussions have been rampant in 'global', 'world' and 'transnational' history has certainly added momentum to this 'decentring of the nation-state'.[27]

This burgeoning interest since 1989 in the nation has its own historiographical irony, as national history had already been declared dead a couple of times in the twentieth century, beginning in the aftermath of the First World War and repeatedly in the 1960s and 1970s (although *de facto* most history since the nineteenth century has remained the political history of nation-states).[28] This identification appeared almost 'natural', while history was

---

[23]Some of the classic texts of nationalism studies, including Gellner's, Anderson's and Hobsbawm's influential books, were published in the 1980s, but it is still true to say that interest in this area grew exponentially after 1989. In addition, some areas of Europe saw blatantly nationalist histories aiming to establish anew or strengthen national(ist) master narratives, which is entirely different from the scholarly books of nationalims published in the 1980s.

[24]See J. Osterhammel and N. Petersson, *Die Geschichte der Globalisierung* (Munich, 2003), pp. 12–15.

[25]See C. Applegate, 'A Europe of Regions: Reflections on the Historiography of Sub-national Spaces in Modern Times', *American Historical Review* 104, 4 (1999), 1157–82.

[26]C. S. Maier, 'Transformations of Territoriality 1600–2000', in G. Budde, S. Conrad and O. Janz (eds), *Transnationale Geschichte. Themen, Tendenzen und Theorien* (Göttingen, 2006), pp. 32-56; F. Hartog, *Régimes d'historicité. Presentisme et expériences du temps* (Paris, 2003); F. Hartog, 'Time and Heritage', *Museum International*, 57, 227 (2005), 7–18.

[27]See, for example, U. Frevert and D. Blackbourn, 'Europeanizing German History', *Bulletin of the German Historical Institute, Washington D.*, 36 (2005), 9–33. For the discussions in global history, see the overview by P. O'Brien, 'Historiographical Traditions and Modern Imperatives for the Restoration of Global History', *Journal of Global History*, 1 (2006), 3–39; and A. Dirlik, 'Performing the World: Reality and Representation in the Making of World History(ies)', *Bulletin of the German Historical Institute, Washington DC*, 37 (2005), 9–27.

[28]For the nineteenth century, see T. N. Baker, 'National History in the Age of Michelet, Macauly, and Bancroft', in L. Kramer and S. Mah (eds), *A Companion to Western Historical Thought* (Oxford, 2002), pp. 185–201. Also Woolf, 'Of Nations, Nationalism, and National Identity'.

professionalising and attaching itself to the nation-state both institutionally and financially from the nineteenth century onwards. Both the state elites and the majority of professional historians presupposed that education in (national) history was essential for 'nation-building' and for 'responsible' citizenship. This meant that the practical function of history was conceived of as *indirect*, through individual and collective identity formation, rather than as direct, through *exempla*, as had been the case under the 'classical' regime of historicity. Similar ideas are now circulating concerning the role of 'European' history in constructing a 'United Europe'.[29]

Both Koselleck and Hartog have argued that the 'classical' regime of historicity, captured by Cicero's formula *historia magistra vitae*, has given way to the 'modern' regime of historicity from the late eighteenth century onwards. Instead of the past being authoritative for the present in the form of practical exempla, after the French Revolution the future became the point of practical orientation in the form of a *telos* in the making, especially 'the nation' and its 'special mission' (and later, for some, 'the classless society'). This change of the regimes of historicity implied a fundamental change in the relationship between the three dimensions of time: past, present and future. As far as the 'lessons of history' under the 'modern' regime of historicity are concerned, Hartog has argued, 'If there is any lesson, it comes, so to speak, from the future, no longer from the past.'[30] It would take the two world wars and the Holocaust before the future and thus the 'modern' regime of historicity became a serious problem, including the identification of history with the progressive development of nation-states.

Some students of historiography, such as Pierre Nora, locate the first cracks in the 'modern' regime of historicity in the 1930s, whilst others, like Hartog, locate its end more precisely in '1989'. Both regard the 'memory boom' and the 'heritage boom' of the last two decades – the replacement of 'history' by 'memory' and 'heritage' or 'patrimony' – as a clear sign that our relationship to the past in Europe has changed fundamentally. Both argue that this means that the 'modern' regime of historicity has given way to a new regime, which Hartog calls the *'presentist' regime of historicity* beginning in '1989' and circumscribed as follows:

> *Historia magistra* presented history, or supposedly did so, from the point of view of the past. On the contrary, in the modern regime, history was written,

---

[29]See Dominic Sachsenmaier, 'Recent Trends in European History – The World Beyond Europe and Alternative Historical Spaces', *Journal of Modern European History*, 7 (2009), nr. 1, 5–25.

[30]F. Hartog, 'Time, History and the Writing of History: the Order of Time', in Thorstendahl and Veit-Brause (eds), *History-Making*, pp. 85–113, 97.

teleologically, from the point of view of the future. Presentism implies that the point of view is explicitly and only that of the present.[31]

As both also argue that this change from the 'modern' to the 'presentist' regime of historicity is directly connected to the demise of the nation-state and of national history, we will take a closer look at their arguments in turn. Since Nora argues that the decline of the nation in history writing and the rise of historiographical reflection are directly related, we will need to address his argument first. Jay Winter's argument that memory has now taken the place in historical studies formerly held by the notions of race, class and gender is a further incentive to reflect on the history vs. memory issue in this introduction.[32] We shall address Hartog's thesis after this, as he builds on Nora's line of argument.

The loss of the 'memory-nation' and the rise of 'scientific' history

In the tradition of Maurice Halbwachs, Nora regards history and memory as opposites:

> Memory and history, far from being synonymous, appear now to be in fundamental opposition.[–]. Memory is a perpetually actual phenomenon, a bond tying us to the eternal present; history is a representation of the past. … Memory is blind to all but the group it binds – which is to say, as Maurice Halbwachs has said, that there are as many memories as there are groups, that memory is by nature multiple and yet specific: collective, plural, and yet individual. History, on the other hand, belongs to everyone and to no one, whence it claims universal authority … at the heart of history is a critical discourse that is antithetical to spontaneous memory. History is perpetually suspicious of memory, and its true mission is to suppress and destroy it.[33]

According to Nora, this opposition between memory and history went unremarked as long as history was predominantly *national* history; that is as long as the communities carrying memory and history coincided in 'the

[31]Hartog, 'Time, History and the Writing of History', 109.
[32]J. Winter, 'The Generation of Memory: Reflections on the "Memory boom" in Contemporary Historical Studies', *Bulletin of the German Historical Institute Washington DC*, 27 (2006), 69–92.
[33]P. Nora, 'Between Memory and History: *les Lieux de Mémoire*', *Representations*, 26 (1989), 7–25, esp. 8–9. For general overviews of the field of memory studies, see A. Assmann, 'History and Memory', in N. Smelser and P. Baltus (eds), *International Encyclopedia of the Social & Behavioral Sciences*, vol. 10 (Oxford 2001), pp. 6822–9; P. Hutton, 'Recent Scholarship on Memory and History', *The History Teacher*, 33, 4 (2000), 533–48.

nation'. Characteristic for this temporary 'symbiosis' of history and memory beginning in the nineteenth century was 'a tone of national responsibility assigned to the historian – half preacher, half soldier. ... The holy nation thus acquired a holy history: through the nation our memory continued to rest upon a sacred foundation.'[34]

Hutton develops a similar argument centred on the intimate relationship between the focus on the nation and nineteenth-century historicism:

> Historicists tended to emphasise the interplay between memory and history. From Jules Michelet in the early nineteenth century to R.G. Collingwood in the early twentieth, collective memory, construed as the living imagination of the historical actors of the past, was perceived to be the subject matter of historical understanding. Often sympathising with the political traditions they studied, particularly that vaunted the nation-state as an instrument of progress, historicists regarded history as an evocation of memory's insights. They studied history so as to recreate in the present the past as it had originally been imagined. In evoking the images in which the world was once conceived, they taught that historians could re-enter that mental universe and so recover the presence of those times. The relationship between memory and history was fluid and uncomplicated.[35]

The historians' task was to construct a continuous story-line between the nation's holy origins and the present state of the nation. In France, it was only the crisis of the 1930s that forced a break between the historians and 'their' nation. According to Nora, when 'society' replaced 'the nation' as the object of history, the historian's actual 'mission' was lost:

> This 'uncoupling' of history and the nation meant that (national) history also abandoned its claim to bearing coherent meaning and consequently lost its pedagogical authority to transmit values. ... No longer a cause, the nation has become a given. ...history is now a social science, memory a purely private phenomenon. ... The memory-nation was thus the last incarnation of the unification of history and memory.[36]

Therefore, according to Nora, history does not supply groups with an identity, only memory does, and 'historical identity' only existed as long as (national) history coincided with (national) memory.

---

[34]Nora, 'Between Memory and History', 11.
[35]Hutton, 'Recent Scholarship on Memory and History', 535.
[36]Nora, 'Between Memory and History', 11.

We will argue from a fundamentally different position below, because we use a different, multidimensional notion of 'historical identity' which recognises other 'codes of difference' in historiography alongside the 'code of nationality'. Typically, the conservative Nora treats the nation as the *only* historiographical relevant 'code of difference' and thus remains embedded in the very historiographical tradition he sets out to analyse.

After history and the 'memory-nation' parted company, according to Nora, memory resurfaced in its plural form of the *lieux de mémoire*, once tied to the *milieux de mémoire*, but now disappearing; 'There are *lieux de mémoire*, sites of memory, because there are no longer *milieux de mémoire*, real environments of history.'[37] Hutton argues that, in Nora's scheme, the relationship between history and memory is reversed following the disintegration of the 'memory nation' (i.e. the master narrative of the nation). Since then history has lacked a backbone – the nation – and is disintegrating:

> The grand narrative of modern French history is broken up into particular narratives, each relocated at a different site of memory. These places of memory are only loosely connected, if at all. Memories are unbound from their fixed places in a grand narrative to become simultaneous reference points for historians reconstructing their cultural heritage ... History becomes an art of locating these memories.[38]

Again, in Nora's eyes, 'the nation' is the only possible 'master narrative' in historiography; once 'the nation' no longer exists, its only alternative is 'fragmentation'. This view is not restricted to conservative thinkers in France.[39]

What we confront in Halbwachs', Nora's and Hartog's thinking is a *spatial* conception of historical time. According to this view, the past and present exist simultaneously *next to* each other: 'Places of memory inspire creative thinking about history. In that sense, memory makes the past live again.'[40] This spatial conception of historical time contrasts with the *temporal* conception of historical time as developed by Sigmund Freud, who affirmed the power of the existential reality of the past *in* the present. As Hutton notes, 'We have no choice but to remember that past. Only by working through repressed memory will we be empowered to liberate ourselves from it.'[41]

---

[37]Nora, 'Between Memory and History', 7.

[38]Hutton, 'Recent Scholarship on Memory and History', 538–9.

[39]For a comparison with the US, see A. Megill, 'Fragmentation and the Future of Historiography', in *American Historical Review*, 96, 3, (1991), 693–8.

[40]Hutton, 'Recent Scholarship on Memory and History', 539. On the spatial conception of time, see also K. E. Till, *The New Berlin. Memory, Politics, Place* (Minnesota, 2005).

[41]Hutton, 'Recent Scholarship on Memory and History', 539–40.

Just like the conservative German philosophers of history Joachim Ritter, Odo Marquard and Hermann Lübbe, Nora posits a direct link between the 'acceleration of change' in modern nineteenth- and twentieth-century history, resulting in the erosion of the tradition or 'living memory', and the rise of 'cold', 'scientific' history as a 'compensation' for 'lost memory'.[42] Cold 'scientific' history, by criticising 'living' national tradition, is undermining it, but offers nothing in return – except itself. Consequently, Nora diagnoses the rise of the history of *historiography* – of history making *itself* into its own object – as a consequence of its 'splitting off' from its 'natural' *milieu de mémoire* of the 'memory-nation'. He notes, 'Perhaps the most tangible sign of the split between history and memory has been the emergence of a history of history, the awakening, quite recently in France, of a historiographical consciousness.' In a Nietzschean vein, Nora is critical of this 'split' of history from 'living memory'– what Nietzsche calls 'life' – by turning towards itself:

> By questioning its own traditional structure, its own conceptual and material resources, its operating procedures and social means of distribution, the entire discipline of history has entered its historiographical age, consummating its dissociation from memory – which in turn has become a possible object of history.

Therefore, Nora likens practising historiography with 'running a knife between the tree of memory and the bark of history'.[43]

After successfully performing this act, history, however, has cut off both itself and memory from their roots 'in life' (read, the nation) and thus is left without a practical basis or a practical goal. History, after cutting itself loose from the 'memory-nation' in its historiograpical (or 'epistemological') stage, could only transform itself and the history of memory into its new objects of investigation. The result is the (self-reflexive) study of historiography on the one side and the 'memory boom' we have experienced for more than two decades on the other.

Presentism and the 'memory boom'

Characteristic of the present memory boom, according to Nora, is 'the obsession with the archive that marks our age, attempting at once the complete conservation of the present as well as the total preservation of the past', visible in the explosive development of archives, museums and monuments – including archives consisting of recorded oral testimonies. As the real *milieux de mémoire*

---

[42]Nora, 'Between Memory and History', 7, 18.
[43]Nora, 'Between Memory and History', 10.

have dissolved, and with them 'true' memories in Nora's view, *everything* is archived. The task of the 'archive-memory' is 'to record: delegating to the archive the responsibility of remembering'.[44] Steven Spielberg's initiative to record the testimonies of *all* the survivors of the Holocaust is a good example of this phenomenon.

The recent trend for 'heritage' and 'patrimony' is interpreted by Hartog in the same vein as Nora as a symptom of the same 'presentist' regime of historicity; not knowing what to preserve one tries to preserve almost everything.[45] The result of the displacement of traditional memory by 'archive-memory' is paradoxical; by storing the traces of the present indiscriminately, it becomes progressively unclear what they are traces *of*.[46] According to Nora, since the nation and its origins no longer confer unity and continuity on the past, nor a *telos* in the future, history under the 'presentist' regime of historicity tends towards *dis*continuity. In fact, he argues, the relationship between the present and the past, and between the present and the future, shows a structural similarity. When the relationship between the present and the past gets blurred so does the relationship between the present and the future. When the continuity of history dissolves and discontinuity takes over, continuity dissolves in *both* temporal directions:

> Progress and decadence, the two great themes of historical intelligibility at least since modern times, both aptly express this cult of continuity, the confident assumption of knowing to whom and to what we owe our existence – whence the importance of the idea of 'origins', an already profane version of the mythological narrative, but one that contributed to giving meaning and a sense of the sacred to a society engaged in a nationwide process of secularisation. The greater the origins, the more they magnified our greatness. Through the past we venerated above all ourselves. It is this relation which has been broken.

Nora implies that this occurs simultaneously with the dissolution of the memory-nation.[47] Instead of the search for identity in the continuity between 'us' and our 'forefathers', which characterised the 'modern' regime of historicity, the *search for alterity* in the *discontinuity* between the present and the past is characteristic of the 'presentist' regime of historicity now in place. 'Given to us as radically other, the past has become a world apart.'[48]

---

[44]Nora, 'Between Memory and History', 13.
[45]See Hartog, 'Time and Heritage', 12–14.
[46]Nora, 'Between Memory and History', 14.
[47]Nora, 'Between Memory and History', 16.
[48]Nora, 'Between Memory and History', 17. However, Nora does not use Hartog's terms 'regime of historicity' or 'presentism'.

The genres of micro-history and of history of everyday life are characteristic of this 'presentist' consciousness of the alterity of the past. This is, Nora suggests, a consciousness of alterity paradoxically clothed in the garb of directness (oral literature, quoting informants to render intelligible their voices being the characteristic of these two historical genres).[49] 'It is no longer genesis that we seek but instead the decipherment of what we are in the light of what we are no longer.'[50]

Presentism and the centrality of the notion of representation

Characteristic of the 'presentist' regime of historicity, according to Nora, is the total abandonment of the ideal of 'resurrecting the past' and, as the 'epistemological' consequence, the central place occupied by the notion of *representation*.[51] Hutton also connects the renewed interest in narrative – including grand narrative – to this self-reflective, 'representational' stage of historiography. This stage starts with Hayden White's *Metahistory*, published in 1973, manifesting the end of the traditional trust in the 'transparency' of narrative and of the 'uncritical faith of historians in the neutrality of historical narrative, a faith whose bedrock was fact'.[52]

The result of the acknowledgement of the fact that our relation to the past is inevitably shaped by our present modes of representation has been what Hartog has dubbed the 'presentist' regime of historicity. Presentism is the result of the gradual 'forgetting' of the past *and* of the future in the second half of the twentieth century, according to Hartog, with the *omnipresence of 'the present'* the result. 'Presentism' pretends to be its own horizon and it tries to shape both the future and the past according to its own image, so to speak, as atemporal replicas of itself.[53]

---

[49]Nora's diagnosis and imagery of the present state of history is also found in F. Ankersmit, 'History and Postmodernism', in F. Ankersmit, *History and Tropology: The Rise and Fall of Metaphor*, (Berkeley, CA,1994), pp. 162–82; more precisely in Ankersmit's comparison of 'modern' or 'essentialist' history with a tree and 'postmodern' history with its leaves (pp. 175–6), and in his identification of history of everyday life and micro-history as the typical 'present' (or 'postmodern') genres of history (pp. 174–7).

[50]Nora, 'Between Memory and History', 17-18. Here too we find the same idea in F. Ankersmit, 'The Sublime Dissociation of the Past: Or How to Be(come) What One is No Longer', in *History and Theory*, 40, 3 (2001), 295–323.

[51]Nora, 'Between Memory and History', 17.

[52]Hutton, 'Recent Scholarship on Memory and History', 535. For the background, see also A. Rigney, 'Narrativity and Historical Representation', *Poetics Today*, 12, 3 (1991), 591–605, and A. Megill, '"Grand Narrative" and the Discipline of History', in F. Ankersmit and H. Kellner (eds), *A New Philosophy of History* (London, 1995), pp. 151–74. For Hayden White, see H. Paul, *Masks of Meaning. Existentialist Humanism in Hayden Whites Philosophy of History*, (Groningen, 2006).

[53]Hartog, 'Time, History and the Writing of History', 106.

Hartog exemplifies the 'presentist' condition in the transition from the 'monument' to the 'memorial', 'as less of a monument and more a place of memory, where we endeavour to make memory live on, keeping it vivid and handing it on'.[54] Under the 'presentist' regime of historicity, the nation-state is no longer the central custodian of 'history-memory', because its definition of 'national history memory' is 'rivalled and contested in the name of partial, sectoral or particular memories (groups, associations, enterprises, communities, which all wish to be recognised as legitimate, equally legitimate, or even more legitimate)'.[55] So, if Hartog is right, the Others of the nation seem to be gaining the upper hand at the end of the twentieth century.

Characteristic of the 'presentist' condition is the circumstance that, for the associations, 'the value of the objects that they elect is found partially in the fact that they have sought their recognition. Overall it is more a question of local patrimony, joining memory and territory with operations aimed at producing territory and continuity *for those who live there today*' [emphasis added].[56] So, paradoxically, the 'memory' being referred to under the 'presentist' regime of historicity is no 'real' memory at all: 'Heritage associations demonstrate the construction of a memory that is not given, and therefore not lost. They work toward the constitution of a symbolic universe. Heritage should not be studied from the past but rather from the present and concerning the present.'[57]

'Presentism', however, as a mode of temporal thinking has serious flaws, according to Hartog, which manifest themselves in a kind of return of the 'repressed' temporal dimensions of the past and the future in the present. In this respect, his diagnosis is more refined than Nora's. Symptomatic of the 'return' of the past in the present is the tendency to view the present (in the making) with the eye of history 'as a present, which has *not yet* completely happened and has *already* past. As a present that would be for itself its own past.'[58] An example is the tendency of the media to produce 'historical events' almost every day.

The 'return' of the future in the present is signalled by Hartog in the media's characteristic obsession with predictions and polls: 'The poll is a tool to forecast the future without, so to speak, moving out of the present. It is a photograph, which in a way suppresses time.'[59] Concern for the future can also be

[54]Hartog, 'Time and Heritage', 14.
[55]Hartog, 'Time and Heritage', 14.
[56]Hartog, 'Time and Heritage', 14.
[57]H. Glevarec and G. Saez, *Le Patrimonie saisi par les associations*, 263, quoted by Hartog, 'Time and Heritage', 14.
[58]Hartog, 'Time, History and the Writing of History', 108.
[59]Hartog, 'Time, History and the Writing of History', 108–9. Another 'presentist' symptom is the extreme valorisation of youth – a futile attempt to stop time.

detected in the preoccupation with conservation and in the environmental movement. From the mid-1970s onwards, the 'leak' of 'presentism' into the past has also manifested itself in the anxiety about identity and its characteristic search for roots, and its worries about what has been 'forgotten' (especially in relation to the Second World War).[60]

Last but not least, Hartog argues that '1989' and its aftermath present strong arguments that the past really *does* penetrate the present – *pace* Sartre and postmodernism – pointing at the problems of the presentist 'museified gaze'. Hartog illustrates these problems with the illuminating example of the Berlin Wall; as soon as the wall came down, its museification began, as well as its immediate merchandising.[61]

So, although triumphant in the twenty-first century, 'presentism' seems fundamentally insecure of itself: 'The past is knocking at the door, the future at the window and the present discovers that it has no floor to stand on.'[62] Like Nora, Hartog interprets the craze for memory and heritage as a sign *not* of continuity between the present and the past, but as a sign of *rupture* and of *discontinuity* due to the acceleration of change: 'Heritage is one way of experiencing ruptures, of recognising them and reducing them, by locating, selecting, and producing semaphores. ... Heritage is a recourse in times of crisis'.[63]

At the end of the twentieth century, under the 'presentist' condition, memory and patrimony appear to be the clear winners in their competition with history. After two centuries, distance – the ultimate virtue of the 'professional' historian and the precondition of writing 'scientific' history – apparently has left very little to recommend itself. As Hartog observes: 'The past attracts more than history; the presence of the past, the evocation and the emotions win out over keeping a distance and mediation.'[64] So, after the catastrophes of the first half of the twentieth century and finally after '1989', both the past and the future have collapsed simultaneously, so to speak, and we are condemned to the present.[65] What historians have left is – the history of historiography. The only sensible thing historians can do under the 'presentist' condition, according to Hartog, is to reflect on

[60]Hartog, 'Time, History and the Writing of History', 109.
[61]Hartog, 'Time and Heritage', 14.
[62]Hartog, 'Time, History and the Writing of History', 110.
[63]Hartog, 'Time and Heritage', 15.
[64]Hartog, 'Time and Heritage', 16.
[65]See also J. Torpey, 'The Future of the Past: A Polemical Perspective', in Seixas (ed.), *Theorizing Historical Consciousness*, pp. 240–55, esp. p. 250; 'The discrediting of the twin forces that dominated the twentieth-century history – namely, nationalism and socialism/communism – has promoted a pervasive ‚consciousness of catastrophe' among the educated segments of Euro-Atlantic society.'

their own temporal position in a comparative way and to argue for it explicitly – in fact, an argument similar to that developed by Werner and Zimmermann.[66] This does not, of course, 'cure' their temporal condition, but makes it at least self-reflexive.[67]

Interestingly, Hartog ends his reflections on historiography by returning to the problem of national historiography:

> How should we write national history without reactivating the patterns of nineteenth century historiography: that is to say, the close association of progress and the nation (the nation as progress and history as progress of the nation), or without presenting the nation as a paradise lost? It is here that it would be especially useful to be able to reopen the past, and look at it as a set of possible pasts which were at one time possible future and to show how the way of the national state, with its national or nationalist historiography, generally won out.[68]

Hartog does not indicate what the alternatives for national histories would look like, nor is he specific about the form that historiographical self-reflexivity should take. Our volume, however, does exactly that by conceptualising the alternatives for national history in a systematic way by tracing these alternative master narratives over time in their competition and struggle with national histories. In this way, our volume is pursuing the same objectives that Arif Dirlik has set out for world history, essentially reconstructing and deconstructing the conceptual and political wars waged in the nineteenth and twentieth centuries between alternative conceptions of history. What Dirlik states for the spatial alternatives to national history holds for its non-spatial alternatives as well:

> My rehearsal of the historicity, boundary instabilities, and internal differences – if not fragmentations – of nations, civilisations, and continents is intended to underline the historiographically problematic nature of [world] histories organised around such units. These entities are products of efforts to bring political or conceptual order to the world – political and conceptual strategies of containment, so to speak. This order is achieved only at the cost of suppressing alternative spatialities and temporalities, however, as well as covering over processes that went into their making. A

---

[66]Werner and Zimmermann, 'Beyond Comparison'.
[67]Hartog, 'Time, History and the Writing of History', 111.
[68]Hartog, 'Time, History and the Writing of History', 112.

[world] history organised around these entities itself inevitably partakes of these same suppressions and cover-ups.[69]

This volume represents our systematic attempt to uncover the 'cover-ups' of national histories in Europe throughout the nineteenth and twentieth centuries. Whether we are successful is for the readers to judge, but the attempt is in any way worth making.

---

[69]Dirlik, 'Performing the World', 18–19.

2
Representations of Identity: Ethnicity, Race, Class, Gender and Religion. An Introduction to Conceptual History

Chris Lorenz[1]

Prior to considering the relationships between the different constructions or markers of collective identities of ethnicity, religion, class and gender in European historiographies, some conceptual clarification is needed on the concept of identity in general and of *historical* identity in particular. In the case of identity this clarification is particularly important as the use of this notion has grown exponentially since the 1980s and with it a growing ambiguity in its meaning.[2] The first section of this chapter will therefore present a conceptual analysis of identity. In the second a short history will be presented of the concepts of ethnicity, race, class, gender and religion – the fundamental concepts of this volume. They will be analysed as 'essentially contested concepts' and their histories will clarify some of the interconnections between these 'codes of difference'. These histories will explain why these contested categories have such notorious fuzzy boundaries. This second section will also identify a common development in the discussions about the concepts of ethnicity, race, class, gender and religion; that is, a change from 'essentialism' to 'social constructivism'. This development is highlighted as it is essential for an understanding of the current debate about 'The Nation and its Others', and thus for the present volume.

The concept of historical identity

When we talk of the identity of individuals and collectives, we refer to the properties that make them different from each other in a particular frame of

[1]With thanks for the financial support of the Alexander von Humboldt Stiftung and for the hospitality of the Berliner Kolleg für Vergleichende Geschichte Europas in spring 2007.
[2]Fundamental is E. Angehrn, *Geschichte und Identität* (Berlin and New York, 1985). For the inflationary use of 'identity' in the social sciences, R. Brubaker and F. Cooper, 'Beyond "Identity"', *Theory and Society* 29 (2000), 1–47.

reference. It is on the basis of their particular set of properties that we can identify them *as* individuals or collectives within specific sets and thus distinguish
them. Identity and difference, sameness and otherness, are therefore reciprocally
related; without identity there is no difference, and without difference there is no
identity. For example, the notion of personal identity or a Self presupposes the
notion of a non-Self or an Other. Therefore, there can be no Other in any
absolute sense, because the concepts of Self and Other are conceptually related.[3]
This provides a solid argument to frame the chapters of this volume in the form
of comparisons. On closer analysis, identity and difference thus turn out to be
fundamentally *relational* concepts. *Essentialist* notions of identity, which, for
example, imply that nationhood and ethnicity are pure and invariant essences,
are thus based on conceptual confusion, although this does not lessen the practical consequences of such essentialist confusion (e.g. ethnic cleansing).[4]

This relational quality of identity also holds for the notion of *collective identity*.
We can identify an 'in-group' – a 'we' – only *in relation to* an 'out-group' – 'they'.
As the Greeks in antiquity were aware, there were only Greeks in relation to barbarians, and there was only an Orient in relation to an Occident. There can only
be *inclusion* in a collective if there is at the same time *exclusion*.

In history, we can observe the relational character of collective identity con-
cretely because we can trace the demarcations of in-groups from out-groups
in statu nascendi. The discourses on ethnic and national identities are a case in
point, as Joep Leersen highlights in his chapter on 'historicist nationalism' in
this volume. For instance, the discourse on German national identity in the early
nineteenth century was conducted by opposing characteristics of the Germans
to characteristics of the French and Slavs. Similar observations pertain to the
discourse on the Greek identity, where the Turks often functioned as the identity *ex negativo*, and vice versa. So we can observe that representation of collective identity is closely related to particular *other* collective identities in a
negative way.[5] As Spinoza, Hegel and Foucault have argued, this is the case
because identity is constructed by negation. This also holds for the special
cases in which a new identity is constructed by negating one's own former
identity. This phenomenon is not unusual in the aftermath of traumatic experiences: both individuals and collectives may try to start a 'new life' by adopting another identity. This transformation is usually accompanied by publicly
acknowledging past 'mistakes' and by trying to make up for them. The Federal

---

[3]S. G. Crowell, 'There *is* no Other. Notes on the Logical Place of a Concept', *Paideuma* 44
(1998), 13–29.
[4]See N. Naimark, *Fires of Hatred. Ethnic Cleansing in Twentieth-Century Europe* (Harvard,
MA, 2001).
[5]See C. Koller, *Fremdherrschaft. Ein politischer Kampfbegriff im Zeitalter des Nationalismus*,
(Frankfurt/M., 2005).

Republic of Germany offers a clear historical example because it defined itself politically as the democratic negation of totalitarian Nazi Germany while simultaneously negating 'the other German state' – the GDR – as simply another brand of totalitarian rule. All post-communist states and post-dictatorial states could furnish other examples.

In history, this negative bond between collective identities is often connected to some sense of being under threat and is therefore embedded in power struggles. In the early nineteenth century the Germans, for instance, had recent negative experiences with Napoleonic France. This is also true for many of the Slavonic nations in East-Central Europe *vis-à-vis* both their German (including Habsburg-German) and Russian neighbours during the nineteenth and twentieth centuries. This negative bond between different collective identities – the need of a 'negation' in articulating one's own identity – also helps to explain another important historical phenomenon in the process of nation-building: the collective exclusion of minorities by majorities – ranging from discrimination to expulsion and annihilation – especially in periods of crisis. During crises, linguistic, cultural or religious minorities are usually represented as *aliens* or *strangers*, who pose a threat to the very identity of those who are represented as a (typically homogeneous) 'majority'.[6] The simultaneous rise of nationalism and of popular anti-Semitism in the nineteenth and twentieth centuries illustrates this, with anti-Semitism particularly virulent in regions with suppressed forms of nationalism, such as East-Central Europe.

Exclusion, necessary for the construction of collective identity, thus turns into a practical danger when the demarcation between an in-group and an out-group develops into a moral demarcation that excludes the out-group. According to Jan Assmann, this has been the case since monotheisms displaced polytheistic religions in antiquity. Religious monism has, as such, unwittingly fostered moral intolerance by introducing the notion of 'false gods'; this is the price we pay, so to speak, for monotheism. By linking the demarcation between the in-group of true believers and the out-group of believers in 'false gods' to moral demarcations, monotheistic religions have paved the way for the 'immoral' practices of nationalism, including 'ethnic cleansing':

The distinction ... is the one between true and false in religion .... Once this distinction is drawn, there is no end of re-entries or sub-distinctions.

---

[6]E. Balibar, 'Fictive Ethnicity and Ideal Nations', in J. Hutchinson and A. D. Smith (eds), *Ethnicity* (Oxford 1996), pp. 162–8 asserts that the idea of (ethnic) homogeneity of 'nations' is a 'fabrication' of states when they nationalise their populations, a position also represented by Eric Hobsbawm in *Nations and Nationalism since 1780* (Cambridge, 1990). Within the discourse of 'The Nation' there is no space for 'overlapping' national identities.

These cultural or intellectual distinctions construct a universe that is full not only of meaning, identity, and orientation but also of conflict, intolerance and violence.[7]

So there is a profound analogy between religion and nationalism as forms of collective identity, especially according to those who interpret nationalism as a secular religion.

Before we turn to the concept of *historical* identity, it is important to bear in mind that it is just one type of identity. Individuals can also be identified through their *biological* identity – their fingerprints, DNA profile or iris scan. Similarly, in a not so distant past, serious attempts were made to identify collectives in terms of racial or class identities, when race was seen as an atemporal, biological category and class as a quasi atemporal one (at least between 'primitive communism' and 'real communism') . Therefore the identification of individuals and collectives in terms of *historical* identity is not self-evident and requires explanation.[8]

What is specific for the *historical* identity of individuals and collectives is that this type of identity is defined by its development in time. The paradigm case of historical identity since the nineteenth century has therefore been conceived on the model of personal identity, although we must be very careful not to attribute the properties of individuals to collectives.[9] The historical identity of a subject consists of the set of distinct characteristics which are developed over time through interaction with a particular environment . In the case of individuals we usually call this *personal identity* – their 'personality' or 'character'. However, in the case of collectives we usually call it *historical identity*, although in the past the term 'character' has also been used in national contexts (as in 'national character') and to define a national 'soul' or 'spirit' (*Volksgeist*).[10]

This set of characteristics is not random, and must relate to important characteristics developed over time. Personal and historical identity does not mean just telling individuals and collectives apart from each other (i.e. describing their *numerical* identity); rather, it means a characterisation of their *individuality*

---

[7]J. Assmann, 'The Mosaic Distinction: Israel, Egypt, and the Invention of Paganism', *Representations* 56 (1996), 48–67, 48.

[8]For an exploration of the various functions and justification of history, see C. Lorenz, 'History, Forms of Representation and Functions', in N. Smelser and P. Baltus (eds), *International Encyclopedia of the Social & Behavioral Sciences* vol. 10 (Oxford, 2001), pp. 6835–42.

[9]On the many pitfalls of constructions of collective identity, see L. Niethammer, *Kollektive Identität. Heimliche Quellen einer unheimlichen Konjunktur* (Reinbek, 2000).

[10]See J. Bos, *Reading the Soul. The Transformation of the Classical Discourse on Character, 1550–1750* (Leiden, 2003).

(i.e. describing their *qualitative* identity). It is no accident, then, that the bio-graphy, in which an individual develops a personal identity in time – its defining characteristics *as a person* – has often been regarded as the paradigm of doing history as such (by Wilhelm Dilthey, for instance). On closer ana-lysis, historical identity thus has a paradoxical quality because it is identity through *change in time*. When we are referring to the historical identity of Ger-many or Poland, for instance, we are referring to a (national) collective, which *retained a* particular identity over time in its interactions with its environ-ment, although both also changed at the same time. The assumption that history equates to change thus presupposes that the subject of history – of change – remains stable and therefore at the same time retains its identity. As such, history simultaneously presupposes *absence* of change, a quality usually associated with *myth*; the historical presupposes the unhistorical. Historical identity is essentially *persistence through change* or the *identity of identity and non-identity*, to quote the apt Hegelian formulation of Odo Marquard.[11]

Since historical identity is persistence through change in time, it is con-ceptually linked to the notions of origins and continuity – two constitutive concepts of history as a 'discipline' and very present in national history. We expect that a history of the German or French nation will inform us about where the Germans or French came from. Historians achieve this by iden-tifying their origins in time and by showing how these origins are linked to later developmental forms of the German or French nation by constructing lines of continuity. However, the question 'where did the German nation or French nation come from and how did it develop?', as we have seen, pre-supposes what must be clarified: the *existence* of a German and a French nation. This is the 'unhistorical' or 'mythical' aspect of 'scientific' history, also identified by Pierre Nora.

Temporal continuity in histories can be constructed in three forms. First, in the form of a *cycle*, where the subject of history after a period of time returns to its original state. This was the dominant temporal structure in classical antiquity. Second, in the form of linear *progress*, where the subject of history develops towards an ideal end-state. This is the temporal structure of Christian and Enlightenment thinking, which is basically a secularised version of the Christian view of history.[12] Third, in the form of linear *decadence*, where the subject of history develops towards a state of dissolution. This temporal struc-ture is exemplified by histories of empires in decline. Most national histories are typically histories of progress, although episodes of decadence – due to

---

[11]O. Marquard, *Apologie des Zufälligen* (Stuttgart 1986), p. 361.
[12]See J. K. Wright, 'Historical Thought in the Era of the Enlightenment', in L. Kramer and S. Maza (eds), *A Companion to Western Historical Thought* (Oxford, 2002), pp. 123–43.

catastrophic events – are usually interwoven in the 'progressive' story-line, such like histories of nations with former empires (e.g. Spain).

Typically, national historians have not, to any significant extent, reflected on the temporal structure of their histories or on the 'mythical', 'unhistorical' component of historical thinking. Harold Mah has traced this symptomatic blind spot back to the origins of *Historismus* in Herder and Möser, noting that their:

> historicist histories required the assumption of a mythical past. A mythical event or development functioned for them as a privileged origin establishing a standard whose continuous influence was then perceived to be disseminated throughout the rest of history, so that subsequent events or developments could be measured against it or legitimated by it. That originating event or development thus overshadowed what came after it; it reduced or even cancelled out the historical significance of subsequent events. German tribalism thus defined the truly German, while the French culture that many of Germany's rulers had adopted in the eighteenth century was rejected as alien or anti-German. … Historism [= *Historismus*], in other words, can paradoxically be seen as the expression of a desire to overcome history, whether it was the cosmopolitan influence of French culture or other undesirable developments and political life …. The importance of this ahistorical classical thinking in a deeply historicising philosophy is a paradox that suggests the same motive that is suggested in historicist myths of origin – namely, that one attends to historical development in its most elaborate way in order to overcome history, to transcend its contradictions, transience, and mortality.[13]

Hence, although 'scientific' national history, based on *Historismus*, claimed to 'historise' the whole past, it has refrained stubbornly from 'historising' *itself*, from analysing its own origins and from reflecting on the motives behind its 'historicising' drive.[14] On closer analysis, paradoxically, these motives turn out

---

[13]H. Mah, 'German Historical Thought in the Age of Herder, Kant, and Hegel', in Kramer and Mah (eds), *A Companion to Western Historical Thought*, pp. 143–66, esp. pp. 160–1. Compare Mark Phillips' similar observations concerning the authoritative formulation of historism in the Anglo-Saxon sphere in Collingwood's *Idea of History* in Phillips, 'Distance and Historical Representation', esp. pp. 135–8. Michel Foucault has therefore proposed to supplant history by 'genealogy', see T. Flynn, 'Foucault's Mapping of History', in G. Gutting (ed.), *The Cambridge Companion to Foucault* (Cambridge, 2005), pp. 29–48.

[14]This blind-spot of 'scientific' history also is found in the very marginal position of historiography within the profession. Historiography as a specialisation only originated in the late nineteenth century and is typically not regarded as 'real' history.

not to be so different from the motives of the ancient Greeks to prefer 'poetry' over history, critiques of 'ahistorical' thinking from antiquity to the Enlightenment notwithstanding, to get some existential foothold in this transient world of mortal souls in the form of general truths.[15] The main difference between the mindset of the ancient Greeks and the 'scientific' historians since the nineteenth century is that the former were candid about their desire for general truths while the latter prefer to cloak their desire for 'lessons of history' in the form of 'the origins' and 'the catastrophic events' of their nations.[16] Therefore, the difference between the 'pre-national', ancient 'regime of historicity' – based on the idea of *Historia magistra vitæ* – and the modern, 'national' 'regime of historicity' – based on the idea that the future gives meaning to the past – may not be so rigid in their practical aspect after all.[17]

After clarifying the concept of historical identity in general we can now turn to the concepts of collective identity specific to this volume.

Ethnicity/race, class, religion and gender as essentially contested concepts

Like 'the nation', ethnicity, race, class, religion and gender belong to the type of notions W. B. Gallie has called 'essentially contested concepts'. As such, a characteristic of these concepts is that there are always equally plausible rival interpretations that ensure consensus cannot be established. Debates concerning the ('right') meaning and definition are therefore ongoing and sustained by respectable arguments and evidence. All the basic concepts of political discourse and of social scientific and historical discourse belong to this category. Gallie illustrates his argument on the basis of notions such as 'freedom' and 'democracy', but nation, ethnicity, class and race would have sufficed (as would 'tradition', 'community' and 'citizenship' which are not accidentally related to the discourse on the nation).[18]

All these concepts are used as both *analytic categories* of social scientific and of historical analysis and as what Pierre Bourdieu has called *categories of*

---

[15] See M. Finley, 'Myth, Memory and History', in *History and Theory*, 4, 3 (1965), 281–302.
[16] See E. Runia, 'Presence', in *History and Theory*, 45, 1 (2006), 1–30. Runia signals the discourse of trauma as the dominant present form in which meaning is mobilised in historiography without making this explicit (p. 4).
[17] See also, R. Koselleck, '*Historia Magistra Vitae*: The Dissolution of the Topos into the Perspective of a Modernized Historical Process', in R. Koselleck, *Futures Past: On the Semantics of Historical Time* (Cambridge, MA, 1985), pp. 21–38, esp. p. 32.
[18] W. B. Gallie, 'Essentially Contested Concepts', in idem, *Philosophy and Historical Understanding* (New York, 1964), pp. 157–91.

practice, that is categories in which 'lay' actors represent themselves in order to identify with others and undertake social and political action.[19] So, in these cases there is a very close connection between the first-order concepts of social actors and the second-order concepts of social scientists and historians, to use another useful distinction made by Alfred Schütz.[20]

Moreover, the second-order concepts of social scientists and historians can be and are regularly transformed into first-order concepts in which social actors interpret themselves as groups *vis-à-vis* others.[21] This transformation process can be located on an axis with 'completely forced' and 'completely voluntary' as its poles, dependent on whether the codes of difference are adopted voluntarily by the actors themselves ('group identification') or are imposed by others ('social categorisation'). The latter was, for example, the case with 'the gypsies' (who identified themselves as 'Sinti' or 'Roma') and with the assimilated Jews in Europe during the Nazi period, who used to identify themselves in terms of their nationality, but who were classified according to their 'race'.

In short, concepts like nation, ethnicity, race, class, religion and gender are used as collective 'codes of difference', both as *self*-representations of what social actors regard as their relevant collective identities and as representations of collective identities *by others*, not least by states, social scientists and historians.[22] In both sorts of representation 'codes of difference' identify '*a difference that makes a difference*', but the two kinds of representation do not necessarily coincide, as the history of nationalism amply testifies. As Hegel long ago and Charles Taylor more recently have argued, representations of identity have to be *recognised* by others in order to be socially 'effective'.[23] This

---

[19]See for this distinction, Brubaker and Cooper, 'Beyond "Identity"', esp. pp. 4–6.

[20]A. Schütz, 'Concept and Theory-formation in the Social Sciences', in idem, *Collected Papers*, vol. 1 (The Hague, 1973), pp. 48–67.

[21]As to the concepts of 'group' and 'collective' or 'group identity', we follow the anthropologist Frederick Barth's basic definition of social groups: 'If a group maintains its identity when members interact with others, this entails criteria for determining membership and ways of signalling membership and exclusion'. See F. Barth, 'Ethnic Groups and Boundaries', in Hutchinson and Smith (eds), *Ethnicity*, p. 79.

[22]R. Kastoryano, 'Définir l'Autre en France, en Allemagne et aux États-Unis', in R. Kastoryano et al. (eds), *Les Codes de la Différence. Race, Origine, Religion. France, Allemagne, Etats-Unis.* (Paris, 2005), p. 14. He notes 'Définir l'Autre c'est surtout dessiner des frontières réelles ou symboliques. Ces frontières conduisent à des différenciations internes par catégories sociales, culturelles et morales'.

[23]C. Taylor, *Multiculturalism and the Politics of Recognition* (Princeton, NJ, 1992). See also Kastoryano, 'Définir l'Autre', 16: '[–] la question se pose est de savoir quelle identité devient légitime pour une reconnaissance publique [–] Bien entendu, toute relation dans l'altérité n'implique pas nécessairement le conflit, mais elle traduit de fait une relation de pouvoir qui génère souvent des conflits'. Also see J. Leerssen, 'The Politics of National Identity', in idem, *National Thought in Europe. A Cultural History* (Amsterdam, 2006), pp. 105–73.

recognition can be and regularly was/is denied – all 'ethnic' groups that have failed to be recognised as a 'nation' (such as the Kurds in Turkey and Iraq or the Catalans in Spain) are a case in point. Therefore, all representations of collective identity are embedded in a *politics* of recognition. This helps to explain why all codes of difference have been related to political movements and to political struggles, and why they keep being 'contested' in both political practices and the social sciences.[24]

With the help of Michel Foucault we could characterise ethnicity, race, class, religion and gender as a *discursive field*, the field of the non-spatial Others of the nation or of the non-spatial collective identities (which, as discussed below, does not mean that these concepts lack spatial *aspects*). In this discursive field we can also locate other related 'codes of difference', or Others, which we will not deal with explicitly in depth. Before we elaborate on the issues discussed already, we shall briefly address the other 'codes of difference' not yet identified in order to prevent false expectations. All history is necessarily selective and all we can do is to make our choices explicit; this also holds for the analytical kind of history we have been pursuing in this volume.

First, we have not been explicitly dealing with the distinction between coloniser and colonised, because in NHIST this distinction has been classified as a spatial distinction, dealt with in the context of the (colonial) empire as a (spatial) alternative to the nation.[25] Of course, there is also 'internal colonisation' *within* the framework of the nation – Irish and Baltic histories are cases in point – but this phenomenon enters our field of vision only if it is relevant from the viewpoint of ethnicity. As a consequence, we will neither deal with the interesting interrelationship between the racial construction of (European) whiteness and (colonial) colouredness,[26] nor go into the related distinctions between (European) 'civilisation' and ('primitive' or 'uncivilised') 'barbarism'.[27]

---

[24]See M. Castells, *The Power of Identity. The Information Age: Economy, Society and Culture. Volume II* (Oxford, 1997).

[25]See, for the example of the Habsburg Empire, J. Feichtinger (ed.), *Habsburg Postcolonial: Machtstrukturen und kollektive Gedächtnis* (Innsbruck, 2003). See, for an overview of the postcolonial themes, 'Postcolonial Studies', in G. Bolaffi et al. (eds), *Dictionary of Race, Ethnicity and Culture* (London 2003), pp. 222–7.

[26]For an overview of whiteness studies, see D. Dworkin, *Class Struggles* (Series History: Concepts, Theories and Practice) (Harlow, 2007), pp. 162–89. For further reading, see G. Lerner, 'Gender, Class, Race, and Ethnicity, Social Construction of', in N. Smelser and P. Baltus (eds), *International Encyclopedia of the Social & Behavioral Sciences* vol. 10, (Oxford, 2001), p. 5989.

[27]For the notion of 'civilisation', see Jürgen Osterhammel, *Europe, the 'West', and the Civilizing Mission* (London 2006). See, for claims to civilisational superiority outside Europe, especially in China, P. O'Brien, 'Historiographical Traditions and Modern Imperatives for the Restoration of Global History', *Journal of Global History*, 1 (2006), 3–39.

Last but not least, we will leave aside the issues of 'multiculturalism' and the 'new ethnicities'. This volume thus remains 'Eurocentric' in an old-fashioned sense, because it does not deal with the entanglements of Europe and the rest of the world, including Europe's colonial legacies and the legacies of the former colonies in Europe.[28]

Second, we do not deal with *all* aspects of gender in history. The construction of masculinity and femininity – both important in national histories – will not receive any significant systematic attention as we choose to focus only on the analysis of the gendered nature of national *narratives*. Nor will we deal with the construction of heterosexuality and homosexuality in national histories or with the gender relations in the colonial setting for the very same reasons. This is also the case for the question of whether or not gender is a more fundamental code of difference in comparison to class, race and ethnicity. We subscribe to Kathleen Canning's argument that 'the use of gender as an analytical tool does not *per se* connote a primacy of gender relative to other forms of inequality, such as race, class or ethnicity; rather it suggests the inextricable links between gender and other social identities and categories of difference'.[29]

Third, we do not deal with the distinction between patriotism and nationalism, including the question of whether a distinction between a 'legitimate' and 'healthy' measure of nationalism called 'patriotism' and 'unhealthy' variants called 'nationalistic' exists. Of course, the question of 'constitutional patriotism' enters our field of vision through the lens of 'civic nationalism', but this is the only exploration of this issue in this volume. We also approach the related distinction between ethnocentrism and ethnicity, and racism and race, in a similar manner.[30]

So this is what we will *not* do. Now we will elaborate on what we will do, thereby introducing the concepts to be explored and their interrelationships. Thus we hope to clarify why the codes of difference we are dealing with have very permeable boundaries of meaning and why most of them have been sliding into one another. The key to this problem lies in the history of these concepts.

---

[28]For a fundamental critique of Eurocentrism in European history, see D. Sachsenmaier, 'Recent Trends in European History: The World Beyond', *Journal of Modern History* (forthcoming 2008).

[29]K. Canning, 'Gender History', in Smelser and Baltus (eds), *International Encyclopedia of the Social & Behavioral Sciences* vol. 10, p. 6009; K. Canning, *Gender history in Practice: Historical Perspectives on Bodies, Class, and Citizenship* (Ithaca, NY, 2006); Dworkin, *Class Struggles*, pp. 137–62.

[30]See R. A. LeVine, 'Ethnocentrism'; G. M. Frederickson, 'Racism, History of', in Smelser and Baltus (eds), *International Encyclopedia of the Social & Behavioral Sciences* vol. 10, pp. 4852–5 and pp. 12716–20; B. Isaac, *The Invention of Racism in Classical Antiquity*, (Princeton, NJ, 2004), pp. 15–39.

Ethnicity/race, class, religion and gender: a short conceptual history

Having labelled our key concepts as 'essentially contested', the observation that they all lack an unambiguous definition will come as no great surprise. As a consequence, their interrelationships have also been contested and sliding – to the point where some have argued that *all* our codes of difference are 'intersectional', meaning that they cannot be established independently of each other because they are interacting and mutually constitutive. According to this argument, gender and race are mutually constitutive, for instance, because unitary categories like 'woman/women', 'man/men' and 'black/blacks' conceal actual heterogeneity.[31] The gender ideal of 'womanhood', embodying purity and dependency on male protection, was long defined exclusively for *white* women only, while women of colour were represented as economically self-supporting and open to sexual access by white men. The reverse was true for the black male in the Antebellum South; the black man was represented as economically dependent on his white owner and as sexually craving for white women. Gender and racial codes of difference must therefore be analysed as 'intersectional'. The same arguments have been developed for gender and class.[32]

According to the same argument, nationality and religion are interdependent and not codes of difference *in themselves*. Whether a Jewish German emigrating to the United States was classified as a German or a Jew varied with the socio-political context; during the mid-nineteenth century s/he was categorised as a German and in the 1930s as a Jew. Similar arguments apply to Jamaicans, who were classified as 'white' in Jamaica but as 'coloured' in England.[33] This complexity does not of course mean that these concepts are meaningless in themselves, but only that they acquire their concrete meaning in varying socio-political contexts. So, in analysing codes of difference, it is

---

[31]Canning, 'Gender History', p. 6006. See also Stuart Hall, 'The New Ethnicities', in Hutchinson and Smith (eds), *Ethnicity*, pp. 161–2.

[32]B. Robnett, 'Race and Gender Intersections', Smelser and Baltes (eds), *International Encyclopedia of the Social & Behavioral Sciences* vol. 10, pp. 12681–4; R. Crompton, 'Social Class and Gender', in Smelser and Baltes (eds), *International Encyclopedia of the Social & Behavioral Sciences* vol. 10, pp. 14233–8; Dworkin, *Class Struggles*, pp. 135–212; 'Ethnicity and Race' and 'Religion and Ethnic Conflicts', in G. Bolaffi et al. (eds.), *Dictionary of Race, Ethnicity and Culture*, (London, 2003), pp. 99–102 and 283–90.

[33]Lerner, 'Gender, Class, Race, and Ethnicity, Social Construction of', pp. 5984–9; G-A. Knapp, 'Traveling Theories: Anmerkungen zur neueren Diskussion über "Race, Class, and Gender"', *Österreichische Zeitschrift für Geschichtswissenschaften* 16, 1 (2005), 88–111.

necessary to relate them to their specific contexts, as is usual in the history of ideas and in intellectual history.[34]

Ethnicity and race

The 'contested' quality of 'codes of difference' has recently been confirmed by R. M. Williams in relation to ethnicity: 'Struggles over definitions in this field have a long and complex history. Because the objects of interest are inherently complex, the search for the One True Definition will evidently fail.'[35] Williams notes (as does Joep Leerssen in this volume) that 'the term has been used variously to signify "nation", "race", "religion", or "people", but the general generic meaning is that of collective cultural distinctiveness', usually linked to ideas of common descent and of shared history. Therefore, 'An ethnie here is a culturally distinctive collectivity, larger than a kinship unit, whose members claim common origin or descent.'[36]

J. Hutchinson and A. Smith also emphasise the idea of common cultural or biological characteristics of an ethnie and its 'medium-sized' scale, somewhere between the local and the national. They describe 'ethnies' with the help of six ideal-typical characteristics:

1 a common *proper name*, to identify and express the 'essence' of the community;
2 a myth of *common ancestry*, including a myth of a common origin in time and place, which gives an ethnie a sense of fictive kinship – a kind of 'super-family' (this family model also holds for 'the nation');
3 shared *historical memories*, or better, shared memories of a common past or pasts, including heroes, events and their commemoration;
4 one or more *elements of common culture*, which need not be specified but normally include religion, customs, or language;
5 a link with a *homeland*, not necessarily its physical occupation by the *ethnie*, only its symbolic attachment to the ancestral land, as with diaspora peoples;

---

[34]See R. Kastoryano, 'Définir l'Autre en France, en Allemagne et aux États-Unis', pp. 20–1: 'La question est de savoir comment sont construites ses catégories [of difference], et à quoi elles correspondent. La tâche est difficile, car les concepts varient dans le temps, s'appliquent à des populations diverses et impliquent des interactions spécifiques entre les groupes et le pouvoir'. For intellectual history, see F. Oz-Salzberger, 'Intellectual History', in Smelser and Baltus (eds), *International Encyclopedia of the Social & Behavioral Sciences* vol. 10, pp. 7605–12; Q. Skinner, 'Meaning and Understanding in the History of Ideas', in idem, *Visions of Politics, Vol. 1: Regarding Method* (Cambridge, 2002), pp. 57–90.
[35]R. M.Williams, 'Ethnic Conflicts', in: Smelser and Baltus (eds), *International Encyclopedia of the Social & Behavioral Sciences* vol. 10, p. 4806.
[36]Williams, 'Ethnic Conflicts', p. 4806.

6 a *sense of solidarity* on the part of at least some sections of the ethnie's population.[37]

Through the idea of a 'homeland', an ethnie also has a clear spatial dimension. Barth too emphasises this spatial aspect.[38] Many ethnies claim to be nations, but this is not necessarily the case. Moreover, for many nations, claims have been made that they originate in multiple ethnies; the Dutch nation, for example, has been represented as descending from three ethnic groups: the Frisians, Saxons and Franks. The Swiss and the Belgian cases are other obvious examples of multi-ethnic nations.

Hutchinson and Smith argue that ethnicity is typically a code of difference applied to others and is not used for self-representation. This usage goes back to the Greeks, who used the term *ethnos* for others and not for themselves:

This dichotomy between a non-ethnic 'us' and ethnic 'others' has continued to dog the concepts in the field of ethnicity and nationalism. We find it reproduced in the ways in which the Latin *natio* applied to distant, barbarian peoples, whereas the Roman term for themselves was *populus*. We find it also in the English and American (White Anglo-Saxon Protestant) tendency to reserve the term 'nation' for themselves and 'ethnic' for immigrant peoples, as in the frequently used term of 'ethnic minorities'.[39]

Given the contemporary omnipresence of the notion of 'ethnicity', it is surprising that the term was a latecomer, first making a regular appearance in English dictionaries in the 1950s and replacing the notion of race in the social sciences only from the 1960s.[40] The English term 'ethnic', however, goes back to the Middle Ages, derived from the Greek *ethnikos*, which in turn was a translation of the Hebrew *goy*.[41] Its meaning shifted from 'non-Israelite, gentile' to 'non-Christian and non-Jewish' pagan; hence originally ethnic was a religious code of difference. Only from mid-nineteenth century did the current meaning of 'ethnic' to refer to a secular group of people emerge.[42]

---

[37]Hutchinson and Smith (eds), *Ethnicity*, pp. 6–7.
[38]Barth, 'Ethnic Groups and Boundaries', p. 79.
[39]Hutchinson and Smith (eds), *Ethnicity*, p. 4; S. Olzak, 'Ethnic Groups/Ethnicity: Historical Aspects', in Smelser and Baltus (eds), *International Encyclopedia of the Social & Behavioral Sciences*, vol. 10, p. 4814.
[40]D. Schnapper, 'Race: History of the Concept', in Smelser and Baltus (eds), *International Encyclopedia of the Social & Behavioral Sciences*, vol. 10, p. 12702; Olzak, 'Ethnic Groups/Ethnicity: Historical Aspects', p. 4814, remarks, however, that the English word ethnicity was first recorded in 1772 in the sense of 'heathenish superstition'.
[41]Olzak, 'Ethnic Groups/Ethnicity: Historical Aspects', p. 4813.
[42]Hutchinson and Smith (eds), *Ethnicity*, p. 4; Olzak, 'Ethnic Groups/Ethnicity: Historical Aspects', p. 4814.

Max Weber used the term 'ethnic' as interchangeable with 'racial'; ethnic groups were

> those human groups that entertain a subjective belief in their common descent because of similarities of physical type or of customs or of both, or because of memories of colonisation and migration; this belief must be important for the propagation of group formation; conversely, it does not matter whether objective blood relationship exists.[43]

Weber also discussed ethnic groups under the term 'nationalities', so the notion of 'ethnic' – originally a religious distinction – has slid in the direction of both 'race' and 'nation'.[44] With his emphasis on 'subjective beliefs' as constitutive for 'ethnic/racial' groups, Weber anticipated what later became known as 'social constructivism' (see below).

A typical example of the semantic slippage between the ethnic and national codes of difference is that only since the 1980s have archaeologists – under the influence of anthropology – started to use the concept of ethnicity where they formerly used nation or people. However, in anthropology, 'ethnic group' was a relative newcomer as until 1945 anthropologists used the notion of 'race', tribe' and 'culture'. 'Race' was only dropped after 1945 and, because of the colonial taint, the notion of 'tribe' was increasingly replaced by 'ethnicity' from the 1960s onwards.[45]

The rising popularity of 'ethnicity' after the Second World War was directly connected to the sudden unpopularity of the other concept used interchangeably with ethnicity in this discursive field – 'race'. Ethnicity only made its appearance in a world where Hitler had given racism a bad name. Therefore Jürgen Habermas, Daniel Levy and Nathan Sznaider argue that 1945 has been the real watershed in the twentieth century. The question, then, is in which respect are the codes of difference 'ethnic' and 'racial' identical and in which are they different? In order to answer this we need to trace the history of the concept of 'race'.[46]

---

[43]Olzak, 'Ethnic Groups/Ethnicity: Historical Aspects', p. 4815.
[44]Also see C. Calhoun, 'Ethnonationalism: Cultural Concerns', in Smelser and Baltus (eds.), *International Encyclopedia of the Social & Behavioral Sciences* Vol. 10, pp. 4870–4.
[45]See Jenkins, 'Ethnicity: Anthropological Aspects', p. 4824.
[46]See J. Habermas, 'Geschichtsbewußtsein und posttraditionelle Identität. Die Westorientierung der Bundesrepublik', in idem, *Eine Art Schadensabwicklung Kleine Politische Essays VI*, (Frankfurt/M. 1987), p. 165: 'Auschwitz hat die Bedingungen für die Kontinuierung geschichtlicher Lebenszusammenhänge verändert – und nicht nur in Deutschland'. Habermas therefore argues that 'Auschwitz' has become 'zur Signatur eines ganzen Zeitalters'; In translation in J. Habermas, *The Postcolonial Condition. Political Essays*, (Cambridge, MA, 2001). Also see D. Levy and N. Sznaider, *The Holocaust and Memory in a Global Age* (Philadelphia, 2005); Kastoryano, 'Définir l'Autre', p. 21: 'l'ethnicité apparaît comme une invention en réaction à la "race"'.

Although 'proto-racist' practices go back to antiquity – when blacks were already stigmatised – the origins of the modern idea of race can more plausibly be traced to Spain at the end of the fifteenth century.[47] During the *Reconquista*, for the first time a *social* categorisation was introduced on a supposedly *biological* basis when 'pure-blooded' Old Christians were set apart from New Christians of 'impure blood', by which was implied recent converts to Catholicism of Muslim and Jewish origin. This 'impure blood' could not be erased and was thus hereditary. The idea that the biological determined the social would remain the distinctive feature of racial thinking, as was the idea of racial hierarchy. So, just like the idea of 'ethnicity', the idea of 'race' was a code of difference with a religious origin before it was transformed into an autonomous code of difference from the sixteenth century onwards. Therefore, the history of race and of racism is often linked to the history of anti-Semitism (although anti-Semites did not necessarily refer to the 'Jewish race'), going back to the Europe-wide discrimination against and demonisation of the Jews by the Christian Church from the late Middle Ages onwards.[48]

This new idea of 'race' would also produce the justification of black slavery for Christians. Although the standard Christian justification for enslaving Africans was that they were 'heathens' and that enslavement would make heaven accessible to them, converted slaves were kept in bondage because of their 'heathen ancestry': 'Like with the doctrine of the purity of blood in Spain descent rather than performance became the basis for determining the qualifications for membership in a community that was still theoretically based on a shared Christian faith.'[49]

From the sixteenth century, the English- and German-speaking regions increasingly interpreted their histories in terms of 'race'. The British claimed that their political superiority was due to their Saxon 'blood ties' and the superiority of the liberty-loving 'Germanic race', as Tacitus had described them in Roman antiquity. The same *topos* led in France to the myth of two 'peoples' – the aristocracy claimed superior Germanic 'blood ties', while the rest of the French descended from the Gauls, who had been defeated by the German invaders.[50] So in the British case the meaning of 'race' slipped into that of 'nation' while in the French case it slipped into that of 'estate' – a social category.[51]

---

[47]Frederickson, 'Racism, History of', p. 12716. For 'proto-racism' in antiquity, see Isaac, *The Invention of Racism*.

[48]Frederickson, 'Racism, History of', p. 12716. The Jews were represented by the Christian Church as having a pact with the devil and plotting the destruction of Christianity; Hutchinson and Smith (eds.), *Ethnicity*, pp. 238–78.

[49]Frederickson, 'Racism, History of', p. 12717.

[50]Schnapper, 'Race: History of the Concept', p. 12701; Frederickson, 'Racism, History of', p. 12717; 'Race', in Bolaffi et al. (eds), *Dictionary of Race, Ethnicity and Culture*, pp. 239–45.

[51]In the nineteenth century, however, in France too the term 'race' was often used synonymously with 'nation'. See Kastoryano, 'Définir l'Autre', p. 19.

From the eighteenth century onwards, with the ever-growing European expansion over the rest of the globe, ethnologists started to think of human beings as part of the natural world and to subdivide man into (usually three to five) races. The term race came to designate constant human types which not only described but also explained human diversity: 'people who look different belong to different races, and they are different because they belong to different races. That view is still widespread.'[52] So the racial codes of difference are based on a set of presumably typical physical features, primarily skin colour, shape of skull and of nose, eye fold and hair texture. Significantly, no genes determining these morphological features have ever been identified, and if the existence of one significant genetic difference were the criterion for defining races, 'every village would be occupied by a different race'.[53]

The biological taxonomy of nature in classes introduced by Karl Linnaeus (1707–78) was the foundational event in the history of racial thinking as he was the pioneer in defining the concept of 'race' as applied to humans. Within *homo sapiens* he distinguished four categories: *Americanus*, *Asiaticus*, *Africanus* and *Europeanus*. They were first based on place of origin, and later on skin colour, mediated by the concept of climate. This link between climate and geography anchored 'race' in space; each 'race' supposedly occupied a distinct geographical territory. So, like ethnicity, race has its spatial aspects.[54] Each race had certain characteristics, caused by the climatic environment and having become hereditary, that were endemic to individuals belonging to it. Linnaeus' races were clearly skewed in favour of Europeans, so his work represents the theoretical origin of racial hierarchies in which Europeans always were at the top.[55] Elites in Europe used this hierarchical classification to justify their conquering or subjugation of members of the 'lower' races, including the institution of slavery. So thinking in races implied thinking in racial hierarchies. This is perhaps not strange given the fact that the term 'race' was used for people sharing the same 'blood', that is, to genealogically related individuals, especially those of *noble* families. Only in the 1930s did biologists start to criticise the notion of human 'races' in the plural.[56]

---

[52]G. Barbujani, 'Race: Genetic Aspects', in Smelser and Baltus (eds), *International Encyclopedia of the Social & Behavioral Sciences*, vol. 10, pp. 12694–700, 12695.

[53]Barbujani, 'Race: Genetic Aspects', p. 12699. See also T. Duster, 'Race Identity', in Smelser and Baltus (eds), *International Encyclopedia of the Social & Behavioral Sciences*, vol. 10, pp. 12703–6, esp. p. 12704: 'the biological concept of race as applied to humans has no legitimate place in biological science'.

[54]Barbujani, 'Race: Genetic Aspects', p. 12695.

[55]Isaac, *The Invention of Racism*, p. 12, argues that this tradition to regard one's own people as 'the best' goes back to Greek and Roman Antiquity.

[56]Schnapper, 'Race: History of the Concept', p. 12701.

This *polygenetic* view meant a breach with the *monogenetic* Christian insist-
ence on the essential unity and homogeneity of the human race and its
collective elevation above the animal kingdom based on the Bible. This
Christian view did not necessarily have egalitarian or emancipatory implications, although it had this potential too, as was later exemplified by the movement for the abolition of slavery. Indeed, most Christian thinkers held that
white was the original or 'real' colour of humanity and that blackness and
brownness resulted from a process of degeneration caused by climate and conditions, as Georges Louis Buffon (1707–88) had argued in his *La Dégénération
des animaux* (1766). Buffon's book is also considered as a starting point of
modern racism because he considered the black 'race' to be a degenerate form
of the white 'race', just as he regarded apes to be degenerate men. Although he
acknowledged that all human 'subspecies' belonged to the same race, like
Linnaeus he posited a definitive hierarchy in which some are closer to animals
than others.[57]

From the end of the eighteenth century full-fledged variants of racial thinking
developed until, from the 1870s, Social Darwinism was established as 'the
science of race'. Feeding on Romantic ideas of cultural or 'ethnic' nationalism,
implying, for example, that only individuals of 'Germanic', Teutonic', 'Aryan' or
'Nordic' ancestry were part of the 'German race', alias the 'German nation',
ethnic nationalism and racism became hard to distinguish for some time and
not only in the German lands. Exclusion of those labelled as belonging to other
'races' – 'the Jews' and 'the gypsies' for instance – thus became only 'natural'.

The same obsession with 'purity' – with 'pure' ancestry and 'pure' legacy –
could be found in Great Britain, the US (where it manifested itself in discrimination against native Americans, blacks and later immigrants from eastern
and southern Europe) and France (where it manifested itself in overt anti-
Semitism). It was no coincidence that a French thinker, J. A. de Gobineau, in
1853 was the first to postulate the 'natural' hostility of the human 'races' and
who warned that their 'intermingling' by marriage would lead to 'impurity',
followed by inevitable 'decline'. The risks of 'impurity' made quite a few racial
thinkers wary of the colonial enterprise, although this did not inhibit the
British from using the myth of the 'Aryan race' to legitimise their domination
of 'the empire'.

Another French thinker, Gustav LeBon, postulated in 1894 that 'distinct races
are unable to feel, think and act in the same manner, and subsequently are also

---

[57]Isaac, *The Invention of Racism*, pp. 8–10. Isaac also points to thinkers in the fifteenth and
sixteenth centuries, ranging from Paracelsus to Giordano Bruno, who *identified* for instance
Indians and pygmies with animals, denying them humanity; Frederickson, 'Racism, History
of', p. 12718. See also Barbujani, 'Race: Genetic Aspects', for the varying number of human
'races' 'discovered', as between 3 and 53, during the period 1735–1962.

unable to understand one another'. Race thus developed into a category explaining all historical phenomena. De Gobineau, for example, explained the political revolutions of 1848 in terms of race.[58] This idea that biological 'race' determines the social and cultural – turning the racial code of difference into the ultimate, foundational one – would eventually lead to the idea and the practices of 'racial hygiene' and of 'eugenics' in the twentieth century, culminating in the genocide of the 'Jewish race' in Europe by Nazi Germany. The concept of 'racism', however, in 1910 had not yet made it into the *Oxford English Dictionary* – it only originated in the 1930s.[59] Characteristically, the 'Jewish race' was an invention based on the transformation of a religious code of difference into a (biological) 'racial' one. Maybe it is one of the ironies of twentieth-century history that although 'race' as a code of difference outlasted the Holocaust – in the US well into the 1960s and in South Africa into the 1990s – 'scientific racism' did not.

Ethnicity and race after 1945: from essentialism to social constructivism

With the downfall of 'race' as a scientifically and morally acceptable code of difference after 1945 and the rise of 'ethnicity', their discursive field also changed gradually but fundamentally. This was mainly the consequence of growing awareness that 'race' represented a *social* – relational – rather than a *biological* code of difference. Social scientists drove the message home that racial thinking had constructed and *produced* 'races' and not the other way round. This constituted little less than a Copernican Revolution. Conceptualising 'races', 'ethnies' and 'nations' as objective entities, 'out there', which can be defined in terms of racial, ethnic and national essences gave way to conceptualising them in terms of the social construction of codes of difference of Selfs in relation to Others. Essentialism or primordialism thus also gave way to relationism, social constructivism, instrumentalism or situationalism; positions associated with Eric Hobsbawm in history and with Benedict Anderson in anthropology.[60] With the benefit of hindsight it can be concluded that the 'trick' of essentialism had been to naturalise (codes of) differences which were no more than historically, culturally and politically contingent.

One of the consequences of this move from essentialism to social constructivism was that in the social sciences the study of 'races' gave way to the study of 'race relations'. Another was that now race had evaporated as a category

---

[58]Schnapper, 'Race: History of the Concept', p. 12702.
[59]Isaac, *The Invention of Racism*, p. 1; http://www.answers.com/topic/racism?cat=health (accessed 6 July 2007)
[60]Hutchinson and Smith (eds), *Ethnicity*, pp. 7–10; Leerssen, *National Thought in Europe*.

with 'objective' (biological) characteristics, its distinction with ethnicity had to be rethought. In the US context, the distinction between ethnicity and race has recently been located in their distinctive *assimilationist potential*, primarily related to state policies. Where (white) ethnic identities have developed into 'an option rather than an imperative' (e.g. the 'ethnic cuisine'), 'boundaries between racial groups were tenaciously maintained by social institutions, sanctioned by state policies and legitimised by racial ideologies'. While (white) ethnic identity, according to some, has tendentially transformed into an issue of self-definition (e.g. 'Irish-American' or 'German-American'), this 'voluntary' character is missing in coloured racial identities (e.g. 'Black-American' or 'Native American').[61] As a consequence, although claims to racial identity are identical in form to claims to ethnical identity – and both have proved to be malleable and related to political movements – 'race' has proved to be the more 'inflexible' code of distinction than 'ethnicity'.[62]

'Ethnicity' as a code of difference was also rethought in the social sciences in constructivist ways from the 1960s onwards. Instead of looking for 'essential' characteristics of an 'ethnie' and its distinct 'culture', as Hutchinson and Smith did, the anthropologist Frederick Barth warned against the presumption that social reality is made up of 'distinct named groups' – of 'islands' – with fixed characteristics, such as cultural difference, social separation and language barriers: 'while purporting to give an ideal type model of a recurring empirical form, it implies a preconceived view of what are the significant factors in the genesis, structure and function of such groups' . Instead, Barth insisted that ethnic identity was produced and reproduced in routine social interaction and social practices, in which boundaries between Self and Others are constructed. Instead of taking boundaries between 'ethnic groups' as givens, Barth focuses on *boundary construction* and *boundary maintenance*.[63] In socio-

[61]Hutchinson and Smith (eds), *Ethnicity*, p. 12, who refer to anti-essentialist social scientists who argue 'not only that all ethnic communities are deeply divided, but also that ethnicity itself is an optional identity and is often overshadowed by other (gender, class, regional) identities'. See also Jenkins, 'Ethnicity: Anthropological Aspects', p. 4827, who argues that in the 'modern' world 'the contours and contents of national identity, and the contexts of its uses and justifications, may be more visible than ethnicity'.
[62]'Ethnicity and Race', in: Bolaffi et al. (eds), *Dictionary of Race, Ethnicity and Culture,*, p. 101. An example of the interrelatedness of racial categories and politics is M. Adhikari, *Not White Enough, Not Black Enough: Racial Identity in the South African Coloured Community* (Athens, OH, 2005).
[63]Barth, 'Ethnic Groups and Boundaries', pp. 75–82.
[64]E. Goffmann, *The Presentation of Self in Everyday Life* (New York and London, 1959); P. L. Berger and T. Luckmann. *The Social Construction of Reality* (New York , 1966).

logy, similar ideas were simultaneously developed by Ervin Goffman, Peter Berger and Thomas Luckman among others.[64]

Jenkins has summarised Barth's social constructivist approach of 'ethnicity' in six points:

> First, the analysis of ethnicity starts from the definition of the situation held by the social actors. Second, the focus of attention then becomes how ethnic boundaries are maintained or changed in the structured interaction between 'us' and 'them' which takes place across boundaries. Third, the ethnicity of actors is not necessarily fixed: it is defined situational. Fourth, the ethnic identity depends on ascription, by members of the ethnic group in question and by outsiders with whom they interact. Fifth, ethnicity is not a matter of 'real' cultural differentiation; differences are in the eye of the beholder, the 'cultural stuff' which had hitherto believed to determine group identification is somewhat irrelevant. Finally, ecological issues are influential in producing and reproducing ethnic identity: economic competition for scarce resources plays an important role in the generation of ethnicity.[65]

A similar development from essentialism to relationism and social constructivism has characterised the code of difference of 'gender', to which we turn now.

From 'women' to 'gender'

The conceptual history of 'gender' is much shorter and therefore somewhat simpler than those of 'race' and 'ethnicity'. The word 'gender' comes from the medieval English *gendre*, which comes from the Latin *genus*, all meaning 'kind', 'sort' or 'type'.[66] In French, it is related to the *genre*, as in type or kind. The term 'gender' was first introduced in its modern meaning by the psychologist and sexologist John Money in 1955 to describe the behaviour of 'intersexual' persons (also known as hermaphrodites), that is, people who lack a clear physical sexual identity as male or female, but who nevertheless have an unambiguous representation of their sexual identity: 'He used the term *gender role* to signify all those things that a person says or does to disclose himself

---

[65]Jenkins, 'Ethnicity: Anthropological Aspects', p. 4825.
[66]According to the *Middle English Compendium*, 'gendre'/'gender' means: 1. (a) A class or kind of individuals or things sharing certain traits [sometimes distinguished from *species*, which denotes a class based upon different criteria]; (b) a race or nation; (c) a sex; (d) ~ *of wilde swin*, a herd of wild swine [cp. *gendren* v.]; 2. *Gram*. (a) The category of gender in the morphology of nouns and pronouns; (b) the category of voice in the morphology of the verb. See http://ets.umdl.umich.edu/cgi/m/mec/med-idx?size=First+100&type=headword& q1= gendre&rgxp=constrained (accessed 1 May 2007).

or herself as having the status of boy or man, girl or woman, respectively. It includes, but is not restricted to, sexuality in the sense of eroticism.'[67]

Such representations had been labelled under 'sex role' or 'sex identity', but in the 'intersexual' cases these terms lack a clear meaning because the 'sex' of the persons in question cannot be determined on the basis of the identifying physical counterparts. It is essentially this meaning of the term 'gender' that has been adopted by 'gender historians' from the 1980s, who substituted 'gender' for 'women' as the object of their specialisation. As Canning notes, 'Gender is a category of social analysis which denotes the social and cultural, as opposed to natural or biological, relations of the sexes.' Later, 'gender' came to include 'the symbolic system or signifier of relations of power in which men and women are positioned differently'.[68] So 'gender'– unlike 'race', 'class', 'religion' and 'nation' – is *not* both an analytic category and a category of social practice (in Pierre Bourdieu's terms), but only an analytic category. This sets gender as a code of difference apart from the others.

Basically, the rise of 'gender' and the disappearance of the distinction 'woman/man' – which was and is a category of social practice – as the fundamental code of difference in the study of the sexes represented the same *transformation of 'essentialism' to 'relationism' and 'social constructivism'* we have signalled above in the study of 'race' and 'ethnicity' – and 'nation' for that matter. Instead of taking the differences between men and women as a given, rooted in nature, from now on the differences between the two sexes were seen as the outcome of social, cultural and political relations and processes in which the differences between 'femininity' and 'masculinity' are discursively produced. The historian Joan Scott is usually credited with this transformation with her essay 'Gender: A Useful Category of Historical Analysis' (1986), although she referred to others using the gender notion, such as Natalie Davies.[69]

This transformation implied not only a break with (biological) 'essentialism', but also *with the concept of class* which had been important in 'women's history'. In the 1960s and 1970s, sex and class had often been represented as

[67]See 'Gender', http://www2.hu-berlin.de/sexology/GESUND/ARCHIV/SEN/CH11.HTM #b3-GENDER (accessed 1 May 2007).
[68]K. Canning, 'Gender History', p. 6006; J. Scott, *Gender and the Politics of History*, (New York, 1988), pp. 28–31.
[69]See Scott, *Gender and the Politics of History*, pp. 28–50, esp. p. 32: '"Gender" as a substitute for "women" is also used to suggest that information about women is necessarily information about men, that one implies the study of the other'. For the transformation of women's history into gender history, see also R. Habermas, 'Frauen- und Geschlechtergeschichte', in J. Eibach and G. Lottes (eds), *Kompass der Geschichtswissenschaft* (Göttingen, 2002), pp. 231–45.

parallel forms of oppression; the female sex was often viewed as a subordinate class, subjugated by a dominant class of men. The transformation of 'women' into 'gender' also implied a break with the unitary view on 'women' and 'men', often based on the notion of 'experience', and a break with the history of the 'oppression' of 'women' by 'men' that overlooked differences in race, class, ethnicity and sexual preference.[70] Class analysis was criticised heavily by feminist historians because it was usually based on the male 'breadwinner model' of the division of labour whereby the class position of women was identified with the position of their male 'breadwinner'. This thus effectively excluded women from class analysis. Moreover, this model became increasingly inadequate as more women entered the labour market as well as with the increasing number of single households, although class theorists have developed several counter-arguments in order to adapt to this type of critique.[71]

From the 1990s, the analysis of gender as a code of difference however came more into line with the constructivist analysis of race, as sex and sexuality too came to be seen by some as discursively constructed and no longer the biological basis of gender (just as in racial analysis 'colour lines' – that is, differences in colour – were no longer seen as the biological basis for distinctions between 'races', but as socially constructed). Gender theorists like Judith Butler no longer posit a fixed relationship between sex and gender, and criticise this presupposition as a hangover of thinking in the 'unitary' and 'binary codes' of heterosexuality:

> Gender can denote a *unity* of experience, of sex, gender, and desire, only when sex can be understood in some sense to necessitate gender – where gender is a psychic and/or cultural designation of the self – and desire – where desire is heterosexual and therefore differentiates itself through an oppositional relation to that other gender it desires. The internal coherence or unity of either gender, man or woman, thereby requires both a stable and oppositional heterosexuality.[72]

Given the existence of non-heterosexuality (in several varieties), the 'discursivation' of sex and gender, and of the body (transforming the body into

---

[70]K. Canning, 'Gender History', p. 6006; Lerner, 'Gender, Class, Race, and Ethnicity, Social Construction of', pp. 5984–9.
[71]Scott, *Gender and the Politics of History*, pp. 53–93; Canning, *Gender History in Practice*, pp. 123–39; Crompton, 'Social Class and Gender', p. 14235.
[72]Therefore, Butler argues that 'traditional' feminism and gender theory stayed within 'the epistemic regime of presumptive heterosexuality' and 'heterosexism'. See J. Butler, *Gender Trouble. Feminism and the Subversion of Identity* (New York and London, 1999), pp. 30–1.

'processes of *embodiment*') basically *detaches* sex and gender from notions of physical difference. It thus takes the fundamental ambiguity of the 'inter-sexual condition' as the general model of gender analysis. This may be a plausible point of departure for some, but for others it is clearly a 'bridge too far'. Crompton, for instance, argues that 'to recognise the biological roots of gender, however, is not to collapse into a biological determinism or essentialism'.[73]

Following Butler, the fundamentally gendered *and* ambiguous nature of rep-resentations of the nation has become an important topic of gender history. While the nation as a place of origin and source of being is often represented in female terms – from 'Mother Russia' to '*la patrie*' in France – the nation as an active subject is simultaneously represented in male terms – as a 'band of brothers' or 'Founding Fathers'. The trope of the 'rape of the nation' is also heavily and ambiguously gendered; in war the female nation is threatened by foreign men. When men are asked to 'sacrifice' themselves in war for the nation they are actually asked to protect their women and children. Like ethnicity, nationhood is thus represented on the model of the family. So the relationship between warfare and nation-building has also been analysed from a gender perspective. The equation of the bearing of arms with masculinity and citizen-ship in any case explains the less than full inclusion of women in many nations, as is manifested by their late and often incomplete admission to full citizenship rights.[74]

The rise and fall of class

It is not uncommon to connect the spectacular rise of ethnicity/race and gender as codes of difference with the same spectacular fall (or even 'death') of class as a code of difference in history and in the social sciences, especially after 1990.[75] There is ample evidence to support this thesis directly related to the disintegration of the labour movement and of socialism in the West, although Marxism has simultaneously been inspiring new avenues of social analyses.[76] The word 'class' derives from the Latin *classis*, which could mean a

---

[73]Crompton, 'Social Class and Gender', p. 14234.
[74]A. M. Alonso, 'Nation-states, Nationalism and Gender', in Smelser and Baltus (eds), *International Encyclopedia of the Social & Behavioral Sciences* vol. 10, pp. 10376–80; Canning, *Gender History in Practice*, pp. 192–239.
[75]Dworkin, *Class Struggles*, p. 76, however rightly observes that class analysis 'has a history of being pronounced dead, something that should be kept in mind when considering its current obituaries'.
[76]See Dworkin, *Class Struggles*. Any comparison of the number of entries containing the word 'class' with those containing the word 'ethnic' and 'gender' underscores the picture of the former's 'fall'.

'fleet', an 'army' or a 'division' in school (= school class).[77] Next to these meanings, the word is used only in the formal sense of a 'division' from the sixteenth to the eighteenth centuries to indicate a set of objects identified by specific formal criteria (e.g. 'species', 'genus' and 'type').

The first social 'filling' of the concept of 'class' goes back to Livy, who described the division of the Roman people by Servius Tullius into six 'classes' according to their military function and property. In the eighteenth century, this social 'filling' returned as the word 'class' was regularly used to indicate a subcategory of an 'order' (*Stand*; *état*) – the traditional social 'code of difference' in Europe before the French Revolution.[78] The concept of 'class' was first introduced as an analytical social category by the French physiocratic economist François Quesnay, who developed an economic model of society in 1758–9 in which he divided the population into three 'classes' on the basis of their economic activity: 'the productive class' (the tenants), 'the class of landowners' and 'the sterile class' – in Quesnay's view all those who work outside the domain of agriculture. Alongside these three classes he distinguished those 'who just work and consume'. This was the majority of the population, but they did not fit into Quesnay's class scheme based on ownership of land and on agricultural labour – the only productive sector according to physiocratic theory.

The first transition from physiocratic theory to 'modern' class analyses – that is, to Marx's theory of 'class' – is represented by the work of the Scottish economist Adam Smith. In his famous *Inquiry into the Nature and Causes of the Wealth of Nations* (1776) he argues that all labour, not just agricultural labour, is productive and distinguishes three 'orders of people' based on their source of income: wages, profits and rent of land. So although Smith still uses the concept of 'order', this is distinct from the traditional meaning of 'order' based on notions of 'honour', 'birth', 'dignity' and 'loyalty'. 'Order', according to Smith, is already defined in economic terms and therefore pre-dates Marx's economic concept of 'class'. Occasionally, Smith uses the term 'class' itself, but less often than his use of 'order'. Social analysts in the nineteenth century would continue using both 'order' and 'class' next to each other – in the German *lands* often synonymously – although 'class' in general became more prevalent in the course of time.[79]

A second transition to Marx's theory of class is represented by the economist David Ricardo (1817) in *On the Principles of Political Economy and Taxation*. In contrast to Smith, Ricardo argued that the interests of the three classes dis-

---

[77]R. Walter, 'Stand, Klasse', in O. Brunner, W. Conze and R. Koselleck (eds), *Geschichtliche Grundbegriffe. Historisches Lexikon zur politisch-sozialen Sprache in Deutschland*, vol. 6 (Stuttgart, 1990), pp. 218–19.
[78]Walter, 'Stand, Klasse', pp. 218–21.
[79]Walter, 'Stand, Klasse', pp. 227–8. See also the chapter on nation and class below.

tinguished by Smith were not only *contradictory* but in fact *irreconcilable* – anticipating Marx's notion of 'opposite class interests' and 'class antagonism'. Moreover, unlike Smith, he regarded the 'class' that lived off rent as 'not working' and 'parasitic', thus introducing an antagonistic two-class scheme. This scheme was explicitly specified by William Thompson in *An Inquiry into the Principles of the Distribution of Wealth Most Conducive to Human Happiness* (1824), where he distinguished two 'classes': the 'producer and the non-producer', i.e. 'the owners of labour on one side and the owners of the means of labouring on the other'. They did not form homogeneous blocs, but were multi-fractured along lines of occupation, income, etc. Thompson also developed the view that economic class antagonism reproduced itself on the political level in the opposition between the 'governing classes' and 'the majority of the productive classes' who lacked political influence. Therefore, decades before Marx, the connection to productive labour was represented as the basis of 'classes' and of class antagonism, in the spheres of economics and politics. Indeed, France Sismondi had done just that in 1818.[80]

According to E. P. Thompson the explanation for the development of class theory around this time is simple: it is the circumstance that the English working class was 'making itself' and was thus 'in the making' at the end of the eighteenth and in the first decades of the nineteenth centuries.[81] So, unlike the later anti-Marxist critique that 'classes' had only been an 'invention' of the Marxist tradition, it was 'the social question' that had produced 'social' and 'socialist' thinking in terms of 'classes'. In this respect there is a huge difference between 'class' and 'race' as codes of difference, although, of course, both 'class' and 'race' are discursively constructed.

This is not the place to go into the extensive and wide-ranging debates about Marx's theory of class in all its complexity, or into the wide variety of its applications to history. Marx's own statements remained rudimentary and the relationship between his theoretical formulations and historical analyses is strained.[82] We will summarise the essentials of Marx's concept of 'class' here in five points:

1 Although different classes have different levels of income and different lifestyles, the crucial determinant of class is ownership or non-ownership of the means of production. This view of 'class' distinguishes Marxist concepts of 'class' fundamentally from Max Weber and the Weberian tradition in

[80]Walter, 'Stand, Klasse', pp. 250–3.
[81]E. P. Thompson, *The Making of the English Working Class* (London, 1963).
[82]For a systematic overview and analyses of Marx own writings on 'class', see D. McLellan, *The Thought of Karl Marx: An Introduction* (New York, 1971); for the recent debates, see Dworkin, *Class Struggles*.

sociology (although Weber also subscribed to the view that property and lack of property are the basis of all class situations).

2 Class is not just a 'position' which individuals occupy in society, but the structural relationship of the group of owners of the means of production to the group of non-owners. The class relationship between labour and capital is one of exploitation and therefore is *antagonistic*. Class analysis thus is always a form of *relationism*. You cannot have one class in a society because in class relationships it takes (at least) two to tango.

3 Class is not just an analytical category developed by social scientists and historians; class relations exist in reality and exert 'objective', causal effects on those who 'occupy' the class positions, whether they are conscious of it or not. For Weber, groups – including 'classes' – exist only if groups of individuals share common ideas about their group membership. From the mid-nineteenth century, class also became a category of social practice.

4 Class struggle is a feature of every society since the development of settled agriculture, and also where social divisions seem to be based on factors other than the ownership or non-ownership of the means of production (e.g. in caste societies or in feudal societies). Class struggle is thus an inherent feature of all class societies and is the 'motor' of history. This is an *essentialist* idea about how history as a process is structured and differs fundamentally from Weber's nominalism and his rejection of any one-sided materialist philosophy of history.

5 Class struggle under capitalism will lead to a polarising relationship between the class of owners and the working class, eventually leading to a revolution in which capitalism will be supplanted by socialism.[83]

Although each of these characteristics – individually or taken together – has been criticised and/or abandoned by most later Marxists, the combination of *essentialism*, *relationism* and *antagonism* can be seen as the kernel of Marx's own analyses of classes. Furthermore, just like race, ethnicity and gender, essentialism in class analysis has clashed with social constructivism since the 1980s. As – in the case of Marxist class analysis – essentialism was a form of relationism from the start – in contrast to the *non*-relational essentialism of race and ethnicity – the abandonment of essentialism could not consist of a transformation to relationism, as had been the case with race, ethnicity and gender. The problem for class analysis was this: all forms of essentialism imply determinism – that is, determination of

---

[83]See P. Saunders, 'Class, Social', in Smelser and Baltus (eds), *International Encyclopedia of the Social & Behavioral Sciences* vol. 10, p. 1934. For an extended argument, see Dworkin, *Class Struggles*. Eric Hobsbawm (1917–) is probably the most famous living Marxist historian, who has also been subscribing to its Leninist amendments. See E. Hobsbawm, *On History* (London, 1998).

collective identities like ethnies, races and sexes by their supposed essences. This also holds for the relationist form of essentialism – in the Marxist case the determination of (the working) class by its relation to the other (capital-owning) class.[84] The essence of Marx's form of class analysis was that it posited a determining antagonistic relation between the (economically defined) classes, independent of the 'subjective' ideas and 'subjective' political and cultural experiences of the 'incumbents' of the 'class positions'. This had created the notorious problem of 'false consciousness', a tenet that would continue to haunt Marxists and explicitly be dropped by the later 'cultural' brands of Marxism, starting with Antonio Gramsci and E. P. Thompson who expanded on Marx's notion of ideology. According to Thompson, the working class had 'made' itself as much as it had been made by capitalism during the early Industrial Revolution, and as far as it was 'class consciousness', this was the product of their own political and cultural experiences.[85]

Since, according to Marx, essentialism was internally linked to antagonism, simultaneously with essentialism another pillar of Marxist class analysis was undermined. The strong internal coherence of Marx's class theory also made it vulnerable when confronted with fundamental critique. This may help explain why, from a theoretical point of view, Marxist class analysis was hit harder by the 'constructivist turn' than traditional conceptions of ethnicity, race and gender. As soon as 'class' and 'class interest' were represented as a (historically contingent) product of 'class discourses' and 'the language of class', class changed into something that was in need of an explanation instead of representing the explanation itself. In the words of Gareth Stedman Jones:

> Language disrupts any single notion of the determination of consciousness by any social being because it is itself part of social being. We cannot therefore decode political language to reach a primal and material expression of interest since it is the discursive structure of political language which conceives and defines interest in the first place. What we must study therefore is the production of interest, identification, grievance and aspiration within political languages themselves.[86]

However, as soon as class changed from being the *explanans* to being the *explanandum*, the questions 'What's the point of class analysis?' and 'What

---

[84]Essentialism had been one of the constitutive ideas of the Aristotelian concept of science: relationism was one of the core ideas of classical mechanics. See E. J. Dijksterhuis, *Mechanization of the World Picture* (Oxford, 1961).

[85]Thompson criticised the modern 'structuralist' variants of Marx class analysis (Louis Althusser, Nicos Poulantzas, Perry Anderson) in *The Poverty of Theory and Other Essays* (London, 1978).

[86]Quoted in Dworkin, *Class Struggles*, p. 113.

remains of Marx?' were unavoidable. From the 1980s, they were acknowledged by historians such as Stedman Jones and Patrick Joyce who had formerly subscribed to class analysis and who had been 'Marxists'. The 'discursive
turn' in class analysis was sometimes also seen as a form of 'class treason' as it
more or less implied the 'burial' if not 'the death' of class. This postmodern
version of Marxism, however, did not make many converts.

The absence of a visible growth in antagonism between the working class
and the capitalist class in the West, also evidenced in the ever-growing 'middle
classes', seemed to undermine the basis of Marx's class analysis in time. This
was furthered by the fundamental change from an industrial to a service
economy – continuously eroding the classical industrial 'proletariat' – and the
ideological hegemony of neoliberalism since the 1980s. The conversion of Western social democracy to a neoliberal worldview after 1990, the critique of class
analysis by gender and postcolonial studies and, last but not least, the implosion
of 'real socialism' did not make the attraction of class analysis greater. The net
result is that after 1990 class analysis, and social history based on this notion,
looks to many as outdated as religion did to most in the 1970s. As a consequence, a 'new' cultural history has taken centre stage, although there is already
a counter-movement against the 'excesses' of culturalism.

This takeover was accelerated by those postmodern critics, such as Jean
Baudrillard and Zygmunt Baumann, who argued that the notions of 'society' –
the object of sociology and of 'the social' and thus class as a useful code of
difference – were limited to the era of 'modernity' and of the nation-state.
Seen from this perspective the semantic sliding between the notions of 'class'
and of 'nation', as identified by Welskopp and Deneckere in this volume, was
far from accidental. According to these critics, class has simply outlived its
legitimate lifespan in the era of 'postmodernity' and 'globalisation'.

The critique of class as a code of difference also received impetus from postcolonial theorists who criticised the hidden spatial dimension of class. They
argued that Marxism and class analysis are fundamentally 'Eurocentric' as
they are based on the history of Europe, especially in its Enlightenment
version.[87] This 'Eurocentric' version of world history had from its very beginning turned a blind eye to the *racial* character of capitalism, denying the
fundamental role of slavery in the genesis of capitalism and of the 'Black

---

[87]In this respect Marxism belongs to the family of modernisation theories originating in
the Enlightenment and shares its fundamental problems. See C. Lorenz, '"Won't you tell
me where have all the good times gone?" On the Advantages and Disadvantages of Modernization Theory for History', in Q. E. Wang and F. L. Fillafer (eds), *The Many Faces of Clio:
Cross-cultural Approaches to Historiography* (New York and Oxford, 2007), pp. 104–27.

Atlantic'.[88] Geoff Eley, therefore, has argued that a new analysis of capitalism
and its origins is called for that takes both the postcolonial and the gender
critique of classical Marxism seriously – and thus the role of slave labour and
female labour beyond wage labour (especially servant labour).[89]

From religion to religion?

As a genuine contested concept, the concept of religion has been discussed for
more than 150 years and is still lacking the most basic consensus. In contrast
to 'race', 'ethnicity' and 'class', even the etymology of the word 'religion' is
uncertain and has been the object of discussion for almost two centuries. The
English word clearly derives from the Latin *religio*, 'reverence (for the gods)' or
'conscientiousness'. The origins of *religio*, however, are obscure. The most
important etymological interpretations are:

1 From Latin *religare*, reconnection to the divine – referring to the ritual
   duties in Roman religion. This was Cicero's (106–43 BC) interpretation.
2 From Latin *religere* – treating carefully or considering carefully. This was
   Lactantius' (*c.* 250–*c.* 325) interpretation.
3 From *religare*, re-connection to the divine – from Latin *re* (again) + *ligare*
   (connect, as in English ligament). Since the eighteenth century 'religion' first
   only referred to Christianity and later on also to other societies of believers.

Given the lack of agreement on the etymology of *religio*, it will come as
no surprise that the definitions of religion also vary widely.[91] Byrne distinguishes four basic types, while O'Toole mentions the first two only:

1 *substantive definitions* define religion in terms of the typical content of its
   beliefs. A classic example is Tylor's definition of religion as 'belief in spiritual beings'. Modern examples focus on such elusive phenomena as the
   sacred, the transcendent, the supernatural or the superempirical;

[88]For a summary of the debate and the literature see Dworkin, *Class Struggles*, pp. 85–133; J.
M. Bryant, 'The West and the Rest Revisited: Debating Capitalist Origins, European Colonialism, and the Advent of Modernity', *Canadian Journal of Sociology*, 31 (2006), 403–44.
[89]G. Eley, 'Historicizing the Global, Politicizing Capital: Giving the Present a Name',
History Workshop Journal, 1 (2007) 154–88.
[90]See Karl-Heinz Ohlig, 'Religion', in Alf Christophersen and Stefan Jordan (2008)
Lexikon Theologie. Hundert Grundbegriffe (Stuttgart, 2008), pp. 258–61.
[91]See Daniel Pals, 'Is Religion a sui generis Phenomenon? *Journal of the American Academy
of Religion 55* (2) 1951), 259–84. See also R. O'Toole, 'Religion, Sociology of', in Smelser
and Baltes (eds), *International Encyclopedia of the Social & Behavioral Sciences* vol. 10,
pp. 13106–12, esp. p. 13109, where O'Toole observes that 'scholars are travelling in all
directions at once and that every assertion eventually evokes its exact opposite'.

2 *functional definitions* define religion by reference to the role religion plays in personal and social life or the structure of religious thought and action. A celebrated example is Durkheim's definition of religion in terms of a symbol system based on and enforcing a distinction between the 'sacred' and the 'profane' reality which unites members of society into a moral community by providing answers to questions concerning the meaning of existence;

3 *experiential definitions* demarcate religion by reference to a putative common, or core experience religious actors participate in.[92] An example is Müller's definition that religion amounts to an ability to experience the infinite in the finite;

4 *family resemblance definitions* reject the search for the necessary and sufficient conditions for the classification of an institution as religious. There is no attribute or set of attributes common to all things we call 'religious' because they form a loose set; there is merely a network of overlapping similarities and there is no common 'essence' to all religions. Definitions of religion, as with the other codes of difference, thus move from essentialist definitions (1–3) to social constructivism (4).

Although definitions of religion usually do not specify special spatial markers, *institutionalised* religions usually do have 'holy' or 'sacred' places. Some are related to the life and death of their founder(s), others to places of worship (temples, churches), places of conservation (of relics and corpses), sites of commemoration and places of pilgrimage. Therefore religion too, although treated in this volume as a 'non-spatial' Other of the nation, has its spatial aspects. The scholarly interest in the study of religion was, like race, also one of the consequences of Europe's encounter with the non-European Other, although intellectual reflection on religion(s) can be traced back to scholars in Greek and Roman antiquity and was also heavily conditioned by

---

[92]P. Byrne, 'Religion: Definition and Explanation', in Smelser and Baltus (eds), *International Encyclopedia of the Social & Behavioral Sciences* vol. 10, pp. 13061–2; O'Toole, 'Religion, Sociology of', pp. 13107–8; also D. Silver, 'Religion without Instrumentalisation', *Archives européennes de sociologie*, 47, 3 (2006), 421–34. On religious experience, see F. Watts, 'Religion, Psychology of', in Smelser and Baltus (eds), *International Encyclopedia of the Social & Behavioral Sciences* vol. 10, pp. 13102–6. Cf. D. Pollack, 'Sacred and Secular', *Archives européennes de sociologie* 47, 3 (2006), 417, who states that 'more and more social scientists presume that religion is indefinable by definition, that categories cannot be applied universally, but rather need to be placed in specific historical contexts ...'. The same position is argued by Timothy Fitzgerald, 'Critique of Religion as a Cross-cultured Category', in *Method and Theory in the Study of Religion*, 9.2 (1997), 91–110.

the Reformation. Fundamental topics of this field of knowledge, such as the critique of religion, theories of the origin of religion and its social functions, and the comparison between polytheism and monotheism, find their origin in these ancient writings, so thematically there is a remarkable continuity in the reflection on religion.[93]

The Latin term *historia religionis* first appeared in the sixteenth century and was used alongside terms like *historia ecclesiastica* as titles of chronicles of important events in church history. It was also applied to religions other than Christianity.[94] The birth of a critical study of religion understood as textual criticism of biblical texts, based on Jean Mabillon's treatise on the 'historico-philological method' in *De re diplomatica* of 1681 and starting with Richard Simon's *Histoire critique de l'Ancien Testament* in 1678, came only after Christianity was split by the Reformation and after the religious wars of the seventeenth century had destroyed the Christian 'culture of unity'. Textual criticism of biblical texts also produced the distinction between the theological and historical study of religion, which did not mean that all or most historians of religion displaced Christian apologetics. Within the critical study of religion one can see a distinction between historians who continued to postulate divine providence in human history, such as Jacques-Bénigne Bossuet in his *Discours sur l'histoire universelle* (1681), up to Leopold von Ranke in the nineteenth century, and historians who postulated that there was no place in human history for providence, as Montesquieu did in his *De l'esprit des lois* (1748) as well as Voltaire.

Montesquieu acknowledged religion as one of the factors alongside climate, laws, customs and traditions conditioning the intellectual character of a nation and its underlying 'spirit'. Voltaire, however, regarded religion as only a 'phase' in the history of civilisation that would be superseded by the phase of 'reason', an idea systematised into a full-blown stage theory by the marquis de Condorcet and Auguste Comte in the nineteenth century.[95] Voltaire formulated a religio-critical stance that originated in the 'radical' Enlightenment thinkers like Baruch Spinoza (1632–77) and would be characteristic of eighteenth- and nineteenth-century materialists from baron d'Holbach and Claude Helvetius to Ludwig

---

[93]See H. G. Kippenberg, *Die Entdeckung der Religionsgeschichte. Religionswissenschaft und Moderne* (Munich, 1997).

[94]F. W. Graf and A. Reuter, 'Religion, History of', in Smelser and Baltus (eds), *International Encyclopedia of the Social & Behavioral Sciences* vol.10, pp. 13071–2.

[95]See J. Israel, *The Radical Enlightenment: Philosophy and the Making of Modernity*, (Oxford, 2001); A-N de Condorcet, 'The Progress of the Human Mind', in Patrick Gardiner (ed.), *Theories of History: Readings from Classical and Contemporary Sources* (New York, 1959), pp. 49–58; A. Comte, 'The Positive Philosophy and the Study of Society' , in Gardiner (ed.), *Theories of History*, pp. 73–82.

Feuerbach and Karl Marx. According to this view, religion must be understood as a consequence of fear and ignorance and as a projection of the ideal characteristics of mankind on (a) transcendent creature(s). This perspective was subsequently extended by non-materialists like Friedrich Nietzsche and Sigmund Freud. The (psychological) idea that reason would eventually overcome the need for religion, based on irrational emotions such as fear and hope, had also been expressed by David Hume in *The Natural History of Religion* (1757). In its nineteenth-century liberal versions this evolutionary vision would lead to the idea that religion would in time be superseded by nationalism as the dominant form of collective identity – a key idea discussed by James Kennedy in his contribution to this volume.[96] During the twentieth century, this evolutionary idea of 'supersession' was also known as the 'secularisation thesis' which equates modernisation with a general decline of the social significance of religion.[97]

Next to the religio-critical stance, there were also historians who rejected the idea of the 'supersession' of religion and who developed a positive religio-historical position. They viewed religion as an integral part of the 'progressive' history of civilisation. This position was formulated, for example, by Christoph Meiner in *Grundriß der Geschichte aller Religionen* (1787). The critique of progressive stage-theory thinking concerning religion developed simultaneously with this theory itself. Most famously, Jean-Jacques Rousseau argued that religion as part of culture had been in steady decline. Religion had degenerated from an honest 'affair of the heart' into an institutionally depraved ecclesiasticism no longer capable of integrating the community. In his *Du Contrat social ou principes du droit politique* (1762) he therefore pleaded for the establishment of a new 'civil religion'.[98]

Another type of influential critique of progressive stage-theory thinking is found in Johann Gottfried Herder, who supplanted stage-theories of history

---

[96]See also A. D. Smith, 'Religion: Nationalism and Identity', in Smelser and Baltus (eds.), *International Encyclopedia of the Social & Behavioral Sciences* vol. 10, pp. 13085-13090, for a discussion on nationalism as a form of 'political religion'.

[97]For the meaning of the secularisation thesis, see esp. D. Yamane, 'Secularization on Trial: In Defense of a Neosecularization Paradigm', *Journal for the Scientific Study of Religion*, 36, 1 (1997), 109–22, esp. 115, where he argues that 'secularisation 'is best understood not as the decline of religion, but as the declining *scope* of religious authority'; R. N. Bellah, 'Religion: Evolution and Development', Smelser and Baltus (eds), *International Encyclopedia of the Social & Behavioral Sciences* vol. 10, pp. 13062-6, and O'Toole, 'Religion, Sociology of', pp. 13106–12. O'Toole signals that the recent critiques of the secularization thesis are also based on 'an increasingly broad conception of religion', exemplified by the New Religious Movements (p. 13110).

[98]Graf and Reuter, 'Religion, History of',p. 13073.

with the idea of organic growth of historical entities in his *Ideen zur Philosophie der Geschichte der Menschheit* (1803). History is actually the unfolding of individual cultural units, which were usually taken to consist of 'peoples' or 'nations', each with a specific 'national character' or 'spirit'.[99] Herder viewed religion as the older, and therefore more 'basic', form of culture and solidarity in comparison to nationalism.[100] In the nineteenth century, Herder's ideas about 'national character' became a crystallisation point of nationalist thinking.

The debates on religion in the nineteenth and twentieth centuries were enriched by comparative research, especially concerning India and Persia and their relationship to European languages and mythologies, and anthropological research undertaken among 'primitive' tribes and societies outside Europe. Edward Burnett Tylor, in *Primitive Culture* (1871), argued that religions in tribal societies represented the beginnings of religious history and therefore needed careful examination. His thesis that animism – the attribution of a living soul to plants, inanimate objects and natural phenomena – was the primal form of religion was soon challenged by William Robertson Smith in *The Religion of the Semites* (1890) and by Emile Durkheim in *Les Formes élémentaires de la vie religieuse* (1912). They both argued that totemism (the worship of ancestors symbolised by totemic emblems of plants) represented the origin of religion. Evolutionary ideas about religion also informed James George Frazier's *opus magnum The Golden Bough. A Study in Magic and Religion* (1890–1915) in which he argued that everywhere in human mental evolution a belief in magic preceded religion, which in turn was followed in the West by science. (This was strongly reminiscent of Comte's 'law of the three stages'.) In the first stage, a false causality was seen to exist between rituals and natural events. Religion appeared in the second stage and the third stage was science. Customs deriving from earlier periods persisted into later ages where they were frequently reinterpreted according to the dominant mode of thought. The argument for nationalism as a 'political religion' would furnish an interesting example of this latter phenomenon (although it does not fit in the transition of stage 2 to 3).[101]

Whilst in most states the study of religion by historians was encapsulated in the specialisation of church history, limiting the history of religion to the

---

[99]H. Mah, 'German Historical Thought in the Age of Herder, Kant, and Hegel', in Kramer and S. Mah (eds), *A Companion to Western Historical Thought*, pp. 143–66; J. G. Herder, 'Ideas Toward a Philosophy of the History of Man', in Gardiner (ed.), *Theories of History*, pp. 34–49.

[100]See Herders section IX.5 'Religion ist die älteste und heiligste Tradition der Erde' of his *Ideen zur Philosophie der Geschichte der Menschheit*, vol. 2, book 9 (1803).

[101]See Smith, 'Religion: Nationalism and Identity'.

history of the church(es), the most important discussions in the first half of the twentieth century took place among sociologists and anthropologists. Starting with Weber's study of the relationship between Protestantism and the origins of capitalism in *Die protestantische Ethik und der Geist des Kapitalismus* (1904–5) and Ernst Troeltsch's *Die Soziallehren der christlichen Kirchen und Gruppen* (1912), a discussion started about the role of religion in 'modern' societies, including those not located in Europe and North America. While religion was more or less eliminated as an interesting domain of culture for historians during the dominance of social history from the late 1960s to the early 1980s, it made a comeback through the history of mentalities propagated by the second generation of *Annales* historians after 1980. In this *Annales* framework, the study of religion, exemplified by Philippe Ariès, Michel Vovelle, Jacques LeGoff and Jean Delumeau, is cut loose from the traditional 'great thinkers' and 'great text' type of history. Religious history came to be seen as a history of religious consciousness whose carriers remain for the most part anonymous. Its themes and questions often were derived from anthropology: the attitudes towards birth and childhood, mortality and death, corporeality and sexuality, nature and environment, God and the Church, heaven and hell.[102]

From the 1960s onwards methodical renewal also mainly came through anthropology, especially in the UK and the US. This was predicated on two new developments, one historical the other disciplinary, and although they are directly related, they must be analytically kept distinct. The first, historical, development was the massive decline in institutional religion in the late 1960s and into the 1970s; the adherents of the 'secularisation thesis' experienced their finest hour when institutionalised Christianity faced an unparalleled crisis. The former believers simply turned their backs *en masse* on the church pews and never returned. Any critique of the 'modernisation thesis' must face and explain this fundamental fact.

From the 1970s onwards, however, the critics of the 'secularisation thesis' claim a strong tail wind. First, after the 'fall' of institutionalised (church) religion, the rise of the 'New Religious Movements' (NMR) is presented as a 'falsification' of the aforementioned thesis (while its supporters continue to point to their very marginal and floating character and syncretic character). Scientologists, Unificationists, Rajneeshis, Transcendental Meditationists, Hare Krishnas and Astrologists are probably the best known examples of the NMRs. Second, the worldwide rise of religiously inspired political movements (the

---

[102]See Graf and Reuter, 'Religion, History of', pp. 13075–6; P. Burke, *The French Historical Revolution: The Annales School 1929–1989* (Stanford, CA, 1991).

Iranian Revolution, Solidarity in Poland, liberation theology in Latin America) and the rise of religious fundamentalism (Christian, Islam, Hindu) is often presented as a 'falsification' of the 'secularisation' thesis.[103]

However the weights of the secularising and de-secularising forces are measured it is beyond reasonable doubt that the character of 'modern' religiosity in the West has changed fundamentally in comparison with the situation before the 1960s. 'Modern' religiosity has, 'instead of living in terms of authoritative orders', 'very much to do with the sphere of consciousness' and is 'very much in the hands of the experiencing subject. It largely operates beyond tradition: that is to say, autonomous subjects – not traditions – are authoritative, subjects developing their own religiosities by way of the test of their own life requirements'.[104] 'Modern' religiosity, therefore, is no longer essentialist because typical 'modern' religious individuals do not live according to 'essential' religious rules and texts, but construct their own 'personal' religions tailored to their personal needs. The broad religious trends are individualisation, privatisation, fragmentation and bricolage, thus testifying to their essentially postmodern character. Having a 'belief without belonging' is the mode of religious commitment typical of this condition. As a consequence, rational choice theory has been widely adopted as an explanatory model in religious studies.[105]

Alongside this 'real historical' development from essentialist to constructivist conceptions of religion and religiosity from the 1970s onwards there has been a similar development in the disciplinary study of religion. Inspired by anthropology, the study of religion followed the 'constructive turn', also

---

[103]For the secularisation debate, see Yamane, 'Secularization on Trial'; S. Bruce, *God is Dead: Secularization in the West* (Oxford, 2002); H. McLeod and W. Ustorf (eds), *The Decline of Christendom in Western Europe: 1750–2000* (Cambridge, 2002); Pippa Norris and Ronald Inglehart, *Sacred and Secular: Religion and Politics Worldwide* (Cambridge, 2004); O. Blaschke, 'Abschied von der Säkularisierungslegende. Daten zur Karrierekurve der Religion [1800–1970] im zweiten konfessionellen Zeitalter: eine Parabel', *Zeitenblicke* 5, 1 (2006), http://www.zeitenblicke.de/2006/1/Blaschke/dippArticle.pdf (accessed 3 July 2007); Silver, 'Religion without instrumentalisation'.
[104]P. Heelas, 'Religiosity: Modern', p. 13112; Yamane, 'Secularization on Trial', p. 116, argues that the 'privatization' of religion supports the secularisation thesis.
[105]O'Toole, 'Religion, Sociology of', pp. 13109, 13111; L. Young (ed.), *Rational Choice Theory and Religion: Summary and Assessment*, (New York, 1997); S. Bruce, *Choice and Religion: A Critique of Rational Choice Theory* (Oxford, 1999); J. M. Bryant, 'Cost-Benefit Accounting and the Piety Business: Is Homo Religiosus, at Bottom, a Homo Economicus?', *Method & Theory in the Study of Religion*, 12, 4 (2000), 520–48.

emphasising the constructive character of notions of the Self and Other. The focus on the social constructedness of religious communities has, of course, been at the very heart of the study of collective religious rituals.[106] Since then themes such as gender, race and the religious forms of minority groups have played an important role in (especially American) historiography of religion.[107] So, all in all, the recent trends, as far as religion as a code of difference is concerned, are similar to those in the field of ethnicity, race, gender and class.

---

[106]D. Eickelman, 'Transnational Religious Identities (Islam, Catholicism, and Judaism): Cultural Concerns', in Smelser and Baltus (eds), *International Encyclopedia of the Social & Behavioral Sciences* vol. 10, p. 15862: 'Transnational religious identities, like other personal and collective identities, are socially constructed'.

[107]See M. Rosado Nunes, 'Religion and Gender', in Smelser and Baltes (eds.), *International Encyclopedia of the Social & Behavioral Sciences* vol. 10, pp. 13034–7.

3
The Metaphor of the Master: 'Narrative Hierarchy' in National Historical Cultures of Europe

Krijn Thijs

The connection between historical interpretation and social control has for long been an undisputed fact; it constitutes the starting point of many recent studies about historical legitimisation, memory cultures and professional historiography. A term frequently encountered in these studies is 'master narrative', the 'big story' told by the dominant group in a given society. Master narratives relate mythical origins of the group (nation, class, religion, race), define the identity of the we-community as well as that of its enemies, structure the way in which time is experienced, and justify the social and political reality around which the group is organised. By interpreting the world and its history, master narratives convey social power.

On closer inspection, however, the definition and meaning of master narratives are less clear than is implied by their everyday usage. Sometimes they refer to the *meta-récits* defined by Jean-François Lyotard: the big ideals of modernity which were used to legitimise the foundations of western civilisations until well into the 1960s.[1] Master narratives, as outlined by Claude Lévi-Strauss, can also refer to the stories of colonial rulers who justify their power by repressing the histories of their slaves.[2] But when master narratives are adopted as a research category in historiographical investigations, they are mostly used to indicate historiographical paradigms. Master narratives, then, refer to dominant accounts of the past which define the historical identity of a community. In this sense, master narratives come under discussion in Europe, for example, when we talk about displacing national

---

[1] J-F. Lyotard, *La Condition postmoderne: rapport sur le savoir* (Paris, 1979).
[2] C. Lévi-Strauss, *Tristes tropiques* (Paris, 1955).

histories with a 'European master narrative', or when this process encounters criticism.[3]

Although the various interpretations of the concept are closely interrelated, the lack of agreement on its specific application has made many people wary of using it. The reason for this lies, I believe, in the lack of thought given to the criteria underlying 'master'-narratives, which distinguish them from 'normal' ones. This chapter, therefore, should contribute to clarification of this concept by examining more closely the status of 'master' within master narratives. I will begin by briefly recapitulating the introduction of the term to the field of historical research during the 1980s. Next, I will study more closely the 'master' metaphor itself. My main argument is that there are at least three possible readings of this which may lead to very different variants of the master narrative concept. I will conclude by developing an understanding of master narratives in terms of the (intertextual) power they have over other narratives. To this end, I will introduce the term 'narrative hierarchy' and develop some tools to study this phenomenon in national historical cultures.

Synthesis in history

There is no doubt that French thinkers such as Lévi-Strauss and Lyotard have had an enormous influence on the category of master narrative – the former in his anthropological studies about 'people without history', the latter in his philosophical critique of the legitimisation of knowledge. Although no one would dispute this direct derivation, it nevertheless does overlook an intermediary stage of reception which is more familiar to the professional *historian*. This is because the influence of anthropology and philosophy made its mark on historical studies within methodical debates, which had relatively autonomous roots in history writing itself. The term 'master narrative', along with its derivatives 'grand narrative' and 'meta-narrative', entered professional history during discussions about 'coherence' and 'synthesis' in Anglo-Saxon historiography. These debates were initiated not by radical pioneers of post-modernity, but rather by moderate critics concerned about the future of their discipline. Lawrence Stone wrote a well-known plea for the revival of 'narrative' in history. In 1986 Thomas Bender called for a new 'synthesis' of the fragmented history of the United States, while in 1988 Peter Novick outlined

---

[3]C. Conrad and S. Conrad (eds), *Die Nation schreiben: Geschichtswissenschaft im internationalen Vergleich* (Göttingen, 2002); M. Middell, 'Europäische Geschichte oder *Global History – Master-narratives* oder Fragmentierung?', in K. Jarausch and M. Sabrow (eds), *Die historische Meistererzählung: Deutungslinien der deutschen Nationalgeschichte* (Göttingen, 2002), pp. 214–52.

the gradual demise of the 'ideal of objectivity' in American historiography.[4] These authors expressed growing scepticism towards the hyper-specialisation and increasing relativism in history.

Despite this, their diagnoses and suggestions did not result in a new, all-embracing consensus, but, on the contrary, in a confirmation of the fragmented nature of the discipline. Bender, for example, proposed a way of rethinking the American notion of nationhood, focusing on the development of public culture. This renewal was meant not to cancel out the fragments conveyed by sub-discourses, but to integrate them. They were meant to be geared to the narrative core, Bender explained: 'Monographic studies of various groups need to be consciously oriented to the largest historical process of interaction in the formation of public culture.'[5] His venture initially met with public approval, but soon critical voices made themselves heard. 'I hesitate to join the ranks of those demanding synthesis for its own sake,' Nell Irvin Painter announced. 'Not only do I still remember the 1950s and retain a distrust of illusory synthesis, I also believe that the new histories have taught us a great deal about United States society.'[6] Painter spoke on behalf of a group of historians with a shared scepticism towards the general desire for new and simplifying narratives in American history.[7] They mostly used the terms 'master narrative' or 'grand narrative' in their writings instead of 'narrative synthesis', as Bender did. However, their arguments were formulated in reference to Bender's discussion, whereby the content of master narrative in historical studies evolved in conjunction with these debates about coherence. In this respect, 'narrative synthesis' and 'master narrative' were closely related.

However, this conceptual shift was more than just terminological juggling, for it implied some significant changes in the object of discussion and in the attitude of historians. First, the new concepts were rarely used in direct reference to an anticipated text or to a real 'story' that a historian would be able to 'write'. Grand narratives, rather, were thought 'behind' or 'above' historical representations. Thus, 'real' texts written by historians tend to degenerate

---

[4]L. Stone, 'The Revival of Narrative', *Past and Present*, 85 (1979), 3–24; T. Bender, 'Wholes and Parts: The Need for Synthesis in American History', *Journal of American History*, 73 (1986), 120–36; P. Novick, *That Noble Dream: The 'Objectivity Quest' and the American Historical Profession* (Cambridge, 1988).

[5]Bender, 'Wholes and Parts', p. 131.

[6]N. I. Painter, 'Bias and Synthesis in History', *Journal of American History*, 74 (1987), 109–12, 111.

[7]See R. Rosenzweig, 'What *Is* the Matter with History?', *Journal of American History*, 74 (1987), 117–22; A. Megill, 'Fragmentation and the Future of Historiography', *American Historical Review*, 96 (1991), 693–8.

from independent and autonomous stories into *manifestations* of bigger narratives. Second, the term 'master narrative' pointed towards aspects of historical synthesis that conveyed political legitimacy, social power and cultural hegemony. It discovered processes of *exclusion* and *homogenisation*. For Painter, 'the purposed synthesis of the 1950s ... claimed to encompass all the American people but spoke only of a small segment, white, male elites, presenting an illusion of synthesis that was no synthesis at all'. This argument reveals the influence of the French intellectuals mentioned above, and some critics accused Bender of constructing a new master narrative that would produce new 'victims'.[8]

Third, the term 'master narrative' implied a *distinct detachment* from the affirmative discussions about syntheses. Although the sceptics' aversion to the grand narratives was in fact no less normative, it nonetheless resulted in their *historicisation*. In this way, the debates about synthesis were largely suspended, because the big story of the national past now changed from the former objective of history writing ('narrative synthesis') to an object of research itself ('master narrative'). Dorothy Ross, for example, identified different grand narratives in American historiography and investigated their literary structures. She concluded that grand narratives followed each other in slow but steady succession, starting with a romantic narrative of Western progress and American exceptionalism, and ending in an uncertain and ironic present.[9] In similar fashion, Allan Megill investigated the regulative influence of grand narratives on scientific research. He assumed that every single historical work is tied to a conception of a general history, in other words, 'big-H History'.[10]

Following studies such as those by Ross and Megill, the category of the master narrative found its way into historical research. It is nevertheless characteristic that, while Ross and Megill both refer to grand narratives, they approach the subject from different angles. Their conceptions are certainly comparable: Ross uses the term 'to mean the story (with beginning, middle, and end) of all humanity', while Megill means 'the story that the world would tell if the world itself could tell its history'.[11] In practice, however, Ross uses the concept in reference to (American) national history. She analyses major historical works and debates in which the national story-forms come to the fore, and which reveal its changes and transformations, while Megill focuses

---

[8]Painter, 'Bias and Synthesis', pp. 110–11.
[9]D. Ross, 'Grand Narrative in American Historical Writing: From Romance to Uncertainty', *American Historical Review*, 100 (1995), 651–77.
[10]A. Megill, '"Grand Narrative" and the Discipline of History', in F. R. Ankersmit and H. Kellner (eds), *A New Philosophy of History* (London, 1995), pp. 151–73, 153.
[11]Ross, 'Grand Narrative', p. 651; Megill, 'Fragmentation', p. 696.

on historiographical developments in the complete Western world and thereby points to even bigger – universal – grand narratives.

Even today it remains unclear which version, if any, is the 'proper' one, on what level grand narratives operate and how they relate to meta- or master-narratives. While postmodern prophets continue to preach about paradise 'Beyond the Great Story', and freedom fighters still search for contemporary 'master narratives',[12] there are no generally accepted definitions of the specific concepts or the differences between them.[13] The fact that leading theorists of narrative, such as Paul Ricoeur and Hayden White, ignored the term is also a sign that its sponginess has not altered. When Bender recently reconsidered the controversy he had sparked off in 1986, he once again expressed his distrust of poststructuralism in cultural and literary studies: 'It is to this body of theory that we owe the commonplace use and misuse of the epithet "master narrative".'[14]

But despite their lack of clear meaning, the above survey of the 'meta-', 'master-' and 'grand' narrative concepts as they emerged from the 1980s nevertheless revealed some persistent characteristics, albeit ones that amount to a refinement rather than to specific definitions. First, although this family of concepts is conceived of in terms of separate levels, it is consistently abstracted from specific texts in the form of printed books. Second, it emerged from a French intellectual heritage of critic and emancipation. Third, it is used sometimes in an accusatory, sometimes a historicising, but rarely an affirmative manner.

The metaphor of the master

The transfer of the category from American criticism of the 1980s to present-day research on the construction of national histories in Europe is not taking place unimpeded. If we are to apply master narratives as a meaningful research concept to national historiographies, similar to Ross's application in the US, it becomes obvious that European history – because of its many nations and frequent caesuras – also provides the context for a considerable number of national grand narratives. And even the national historiographies contain within them various narrative forms, as in Germany, for example, where very different historical narratives were constructed by the Third Reich, the Federal

---

[12]R. F. Berkhofer, *Beyond the Great Story: History as Text and Discourse* (Cambridge, MA, 1995); J. Cox (ed.), *Contesting the Master-narrative* (Iowa, 1998).

[13]As far as I know, only Megill has proposed a classification. See his 'Grand Narrative', pp. 152–3.

[14]T. Bender, 'Strategies of Narrative Synthesis in American History', *American Historical Review*, 107 (2002), 129–53, 132.

Republic of Germany (FRG) and the German Democratic Republic (GDR), even though the national paradigm was adhered to in each case. And whereas in the US it remains unclear on which level master narratives are to be located – that is, whether they are fundamental categories of historical understanding (such as 'development' or 'progress') or, on a lower level, particular myths of the nation – it seems clear that the concept can advance our understanding of national historiographies within Europe only if it is conceived of on one of these lower levels.[15]

This brings me to the question of the status of a master narrative in the national historical traditions in Europe. Which criteria distinguish master narratives from other narratives? First of all, the concept is based on a metaphor. By qualifying a historical mode of thought with the defining metaphor 'master', we refer to a historical culture that is marked by a specific *hierarchy*, at the top of which stands the 'master'. At the same time, this concept alone prescribes neither the *direction* of this hierarchy nor the quality that distinguishes a master narrative from other stories. Is this their public dominance? Or the social power of their representatives? Or their intertextual influence? Their literary quality? As a result, their conceptual opposite remains unclear as well: are these to be defined as 'local' or 'normal' narratives, or still as so-called 'counter-narratives'? The understanding of this metaphor is crucial for research involving the concept. Its polyphonic usage can, I believe, be traced back to three different (generally implicit) interpretations of this metaphor. The notion of 'master' is generally understood variously as a master in contrast to slaves, as a maestro standing before an audience or as an original copy as opposed to a reproduction, although the final and perhaps most promising interpretation is rarely ever used.

Master–slave

The first reading of the master narrative metaphor is perhaps the most common, both in its original context in the US and now also in Europe. It may be understood as an expression of extreme, polarised social relations between rulers and ruled. In this sense, a master narrative is literally one governed by masters, as opposed to the histories of 'slaves', 'savages' or 'the excluded'. This understanding of the master metaphor stands for the normative rejection of master narratives such as those encountered in the synthesis debates of the 1980s, and, as Kerwin Lee Klein has demonstrated, this understanding is the

---

[15]C. Conrad and S. Conrad, 'Wie vergleicht man Historiographien?', in idem, *Die Nation Schreiben*, pp. 11–45, 30.

result of a long historical and philosophical tradition.[16] Typical of the polarisation of the master and slave is the connection between narrative, metaphysics and totalitarian rule. Klein traces this variant back to the early works of Lyotard, who originally understood 'meta-narratives' as the dominant narratives in modern (communist) dictatorships. According to Lyotard, dissidents in Budapest, Beijing and the Soviet Gulags were therefore archetypal representatives of counter-narratives. Klein shows how this image became largely universalised in Lyotard's better-known work *La Condition postmoderne* (1979), in which now fundamental – ahistorical – ideals, such as education, freedom and wealth, operated as meta-narratives. However, this extended definition evidently has little in common with the master narratives that historians today aim to explore within the context of national historiographies.[17] Klein, therefore, suggests that historians 'would be better served by recognising that narrative mastery comes not from "meta" form, but from social situation. ... Master narratives are simply those that hold the positions of dominance.'[18] In this line of thinking, these dominant positions are socially conditioned: master narratives repress the slave stories of socially marginalised people, legitimise this social reality and thereby reproduce it.

This is how the concept came to be used by minority and gender historians, and such usage of master narrative in relation to the notion of emancipation is perhaps the most original and frequent.[19] I would like, however, to make three objections to this tailoring of the 'master' metaphor, because of the limitations threatened in the scope of its research. The first objection concerns the ruler–slave metaphor itself. Although this metaphor certainly captured the relations between Western colonialists and native cultures as depicted in Lévi-Strauss's studies on 'peoples without history', it appears to be less suited to research focusing on European nations in the nineteenth and twentieth centuries. For the power relations suggested by the concepts of 'master' and 'slave' are too simplistic to add to our knowledge even of modern dictatorships, not to mention democracies. The master–slave metaphor tends to overemphasise dichotomies between perpetrators and victims which recent research has largely dispensed with. When applied to complex societies of the

---

[16]K. L. Klein, 'In Search of Narrative Mastery: Postmodernism and the People without History', *History and Theory*, 34 (1995), 275–98.

[17]K. H. Jarausch and M. Geyer, *Shattered Past: Reconstructing German Histories* (Princeton, NJ, 2003), p. 5.

[18]Klein, 'In Search of Narrative Mastery', p. 297.

[19]Cf., for example J. Appleby, L. Hunt and M. Jacob, *Telling the Truth about History* (New York, 1994); K. Hausen, 'Die Nicht-Einheit der Geschichte als historiographische Herausforderung: zur historischen Relevanz und Anstößigkeit der Geschlechtergeschichte', in H. Medick and A-C. Trepp (eds), *Geschlechtergeschichte und Allgemeine Geschichte: Herausforderungen und Perspektiven* (Göttingen, 1998), pp. 17–55.

twentieth century, therefore, this metaphor seems to be too crude. Second, the universal historical scope of this metaphor hardly seems applicable to the limited context of (European) nations. The power relations evoked by this understanding of master narratives correspond to civilisations rather than to nations. This makes the task of comparing historiographies on a transnational level in Europe very difficult indeed, for how can we distinguish between them if they are all pervaded by the same narratives of masters and slaves? And in a more contrived way, a third objection could point to the strict condemnation of master narratives, which of course accompanies the thinking in terms of masters and slaves, but which also runs the risk of narrowing our perception. Rather than critical historical research into the development and function of master narratives, as well as the processes by which they are adopted and adapted, this approach almost inevitably leads to a normative search for possibilities of escaping or overcoming them. Such an approach is often tied to ethical or political counter-narratives and runs the risk of serving as a means of legitimising alternative programmes, rather than providing an independent epistemological basis for historical research.

The understanding of the hierarchy of mastery in terms of masters and slaves nonetheless exposes an essential component of master narratives consisting of social dominance and its potential exclusion of others. This is not the only interpretation of the concept, however. There are at least another two meanings which can be read into the master metaphor, each of which entails a distinct type of hierarchy.

Master–audience

The second version of this concept is used far less frequently than the first. Rather than applying the notion of 'master' metaphorically as a 'ruler' over 'slaves', it evokes the idea of a virtuoso 'author' faced with a mute 'audience'. In view of the fact that the origins of the concept stem from the emancipatory critique of power as outlined above, this interpretation of the master as a maestro is of comparatively less importance and could be dismissed as a misunderstanding. Nonetheless, the maestro reading of the master is prevalent in some contexts and especially in languages other than English. For example, the translation of master narrative as *Meistererzählung* caused many misunderstandings in Germany, since this new term was already in use (it traditionally refers to the literary works by masters of art). Here, the concept of master narrative was subjected to semantic transformations in which it became charged with new meanings.[20]

---

[20]For a more detailed account on this, see my 'Vom "Master-narrative" zur "Meister-erzählung"? Überlegungen für ein Konzept von "narrativer Hierarchie"', in M. Winkler and A. Kliems (eds), *Sinnstiftung durch Narration in Ost-Mittel-Europa: Geschichte – Literatur – Film* (Leipzig, 2005).

It is remarkable how contradictory the interpretation of the master in terms of the maestro is to the American and French master narratives. 'Maestro' focuses attention on the master of art, while the invisible master narrative originally prevailed in the background. While the maestro shines by artistic or expert virtuosity, a master narrative rules by framing and prefiguring. And whereas the maestro stands individually as the champion of a 'poetic competition', a master narrative is a subtle expression of struggles for socio-political hegemony. When the master narrative is personified in terms of maestro and used for historical study, the author (the master) and his skills (the narrative) dominate the scene. This is (to stay with our example) why attempts to apply *Meistererzählungen* as a category of historiographical study prove to be problematic in Germany. Here, master narratives are often identified with popular books on history, and they thereby degenerate from a hegemonic narrative framework (which can at least *manifest* itself in printed works) into the virtuoso story of a single 'maestro'. According to this interpretation, there are as many master narratives as there are narrating masters. The maestro understanding of the master metaphor tends to think of narrative as an individual achievement connected to a single author, rather than as a powerful frame connected to a culture, society or system of rule.[21]

Master–copy

A third interpretation of the metaphor develops the hierarchy of masterliness on an *intertextual* level by locating the power of master narratives in their characteristically dominant relation to other narratives. Analogous to printing or film technology, in which an original record is called a 'master' from which copies are made, this metaphor indicates that such a copy always retains the structure of the 'master' original. It does not suggest that the master presupposes repressive rule over slaves or performs before an audience, but that it is an 'original' whose 'reproductions' retain the same structure (although nothing prevents one version from existing alongside another). In this understanding, master narratives dictate their narrative framework to numerous partial stories, and therefore both integrate them and lend them legitimacy. As a result, we could understand the master narrative as an ideal typical 'narrative frame' whose pattern is repeated, reproduced and confirmed by highly diverse historical practices.

According to this understanding of master narratives, the status of mastery is also based on social dominance. Yet it does not enquire into the foundations of this 'position of dominance' but on the contrary into its means of

---

[21]Similar ambiguities occasionally also arise in English: cf. J. Sperber, 'Master-narratives of Nineteenth-Century German History', *Central European History*, 24 (1991), 69–91.

expression. By understanding master narratives as frames or models we may gain insight into their power and compare them on the basis of their manifestations, that is, the numerous 'smaller' histories whose narrative structures are – with varying degrees of liberty or constraint – modelled on that of the main narrative. Dorothy Ross's approach involved exploring the various narrative patterns of national historiography shared by several monographs and historical overviews in the US. Allan Megill likewise approached master narratives by enquiring into the cognitive structures underlying historical writings. Both deal with neither repressed 'peoples without history' nor the storytelling virtuosity of individuals, but rather with overarching narrative structures representing history. They both enquire into the way in which history is related to 'bigger stories' and in which specific works share common narrative frames.

If we think of master narratives as frameworks in terms of the research themes currently being pursued on a transnational level in Europe, it follows that they signify (as before) a version of the national past which is dominant and meaningful at a specific moment in time. Yet its dominance as a narrative can no longer be understood merely in terms of the social power of its supporting groups (a class, race or religion), but rather in terms of the influence it has on other 'local' narratives. These refer to partial histories: those that cover a short time-scale (eras, dynasties, revolutions), limited spaces (regions, cities) or specific social groups. But these smaller narratives also refer to other historical practices, such as museums, celebrations, anniversaries or monuments. Such 'official' forms of historical practice are dependent on the master narrative, which is thus situated at the top of a *narrative hierarchy*. Its function as a source of meaning and of discipline, its tendency to legitimise 'local' histories and its power to exclude differing narratives which do not copy its structure and meaning ensure that this hierarchy is both a product and a producer of social reality.

Narrative hierarchy

I begin by elucidating the conception of a 'narrative hierarchy', ranging from abstract major narrative frames to concrete, told histories, with two examples. Ann Rigney has studied storytelling in the classic works on the French Revolution by Lamartine, Michelet and Blanc. According to Rigney, the characteristics common to their stories (which transport very different political implications) mark the contours of a basic narrative pattern:

> For all the differences between the three histories in length, in the degree of detail with which they treat particular episodes, and in the particular links they establish between them, each one is structured around these canonical events, these areas of common historical ground. Their common

narrative skeleton is manifest in the titles of different chapters and sub-sections of the individual histories.

Even Lamartine's book, which recounts only the history of the Girondists, is organised according to this pattern: 'It falls back, as it were, into the tracks of the master narrative.'[22] These 'tracks of the master narrative' embody the integrative power of the dominant historical interpretation – or, the other way around, the prevailing doctrine from which dissidents, innovators and opponents try to free themselves.

James Wertsch defines another approach to narrative hierarchy which addresses the question of collective memory. He distinguishes between fundamental 'schematic narrative templates', which represent nothing more than an empty narrative form or literary motif, and 'specific narratives', which build on these narrative patterns and fill them with meaning. 'The notion of template is involved because these abstract structures can underlie several different specific narratives, each of which has a particular setting, cast of characters, dates and so forth.' A characteristic example of such a narrative scheme occurs in the figure 'Victory over foreign powers', as Wertsch demonstrates in his case study of Russia, where this narrative template is deeply rooted in the national culture and repeatedly used in interpretations of the past. In other words, the narrative template 'Victory over foreign powers' models several 'specific narratives' of the past in Russia, from the Mongolian invasion of the thirteenth century to the Second World War. It welded together a 'we-community' and thereby built cultural continuity in defiance of historical caesuras.[23]

Approaches such as those of Rigney or Wertsch support an idea of narrative hierarchy which often appears to be missing from the concept of master narratives in comparative historiographical research. Whereas comparative studies hitherto concentrated generally on identifying various master narratives within national contexts themselves, the notion of narrative hierarchy draws our attention primarily to their sphere of influence, to their status as *master narratives*. To this end, attention should be focused on the *manifestations* of the master narratives by examining concrete and smaller stories, and asking for their shared narrative framework ('common narrative skeleton'; 'schematic narrative template'), which is delivered from and thereby reproduces the master narrative. This common narrative skeleton may be identified by a

---

[22]A. Rigney, *The Rhetoric of Historical Representation: Three Narrative Histories of the French Revolution* (Cambridge, 1990), pp. 36–7.
[23]J. V. Wertsch, *Voices of Collective Remembering* (Cambridge, 2002), p. 62 (quotation) and pp. 87–116.

relatively abstract set of core narrative elements, which could be derived from structural narratology for example, and which are suitable for describing the narrative structure of dominant story-lines. For the analysis of form and content of national historical narratives this set may encompass elements such as:

1 The central *actors* of the story: which historical figures represent the centre or the core of the nation? On what grounds is the nation constituted, and who is identified as its main agents?
2 The central *antagonists* or *enemies* of the nation: which historical groups or forces are identified as the main threat to the nation? How are their origins explained, and are these forces already excluded or defeated in the narrating present, or is liberation from them a promise for the future? Or are these Others simply not spoken of; are they even excluded from the story of the past, and present only by absence?
3 The overarching idea of *progress of history*: master narratives inform concrete histories about the process of the passing of time in general, and of the decisive forces of history. Is history, including national history, supposed to be cyclical, progressive or contingent?
4 The *periodisation* of national history: where are the national origins of the nation located? Which events, wars, victories or sufferings marked the main turning points in the national past? And, closely related:
5 The *time economy*: many narratives define a historical period of glory which is or is promised to be revived by the present. Is this golden age a long ago and mythical era or a real remembered period in the past? (By which forces or events was it lost?) Or is it located in a utopian future? Are any dark ages contrasted to these times of glory? And are there any historical periods or events of suffering and trauma, which are cannot be told at all, and which therefore occur as blank spots, as ellipses?

Such an approach lends itself well to comparative study, for two reasons. First, narratives of different nations can be compared on their narrative structures and on the transnational import and export of specific narrative elements – for example, on their copying or inverting of the role of historical figures or events. The same goes for different narratives of a single national past, which can be compared on the shifts they establish in contrast to each other, for example, in changing the main protagonists of the nation or in inverting the golden and dark ages. These are common questions about the images of the past, the form and content of narratives, their ideological implications and their political functions.

   However, second, the notion of a narrative hierarchy allows the study of these narrative structures in their possible function of master narratives as well. In this understanding, a master narrative defines a more or less loose set of narrative elements as described above, which functions as a main framework for concrete stories of (part of) the national past. This narrative 'original' or frame manifests itself – and can therefore be deciphered – in numerous historical moments that give sense and meaning to the community, such as historiography, official memory culture, museums and anniversaries. In this way the master narrative is adopted, 'practised' and reproduced in many satellite narratives, as soon as they adopt its main framework. Those local narratives that do not adopt, or even explicitly reject, the narrative structure of the common framework will develop the status of counter-narratives. Therefore, master narratives mark borders of legitimacy: they define a bandwidth in which one can legitimately tell (parts of) national history. They enable a broad rangeof possible versions of history to exist alongside each other, all of which are based on the same actors, periodisation and set of events. It is only when the changes within the vision of history transgress the permitted range that the master narrative loses credibility and makes way for new narrative forms.

In other words, during a period of relative historical calm, a master narrative embodies what is generally considered to be the most natural version of the past, and conveys general historical knowledge of a society that is repeatedly echoed in the work of historians, political scientists and journalists. But this common narrative framework – structured around a set of narrative elements – is nevertheless subject to constant and subtle, though relatively limited, change. The hierarchy existing between the master and local narratives is invariably prone to a degree of 'bottom-up' movement. So the intertextual understanding of the master metaphor ('original' and 'reproduction') promises to avoid the strict dichotomisation of 'rulers' and 'slaves' mentioned earlier. Although both interpretations have in common the idea that the dominance of master narratives goes hand in hand with the social dominance of those who support them (and with the exclusion of those who oppose them), the intertextual approach is receptive to processes of adoption and appropriation by means of which a narrative framework secures, defends and even loses its dominant status. The master narrative is dependent on the continuous reproduction of its narrative template in order to maintain its 'master' status.

Different master narratives thus can be compared on the basis of their manifestations in various temporal and spatial contexts: in relation to their zone of influence, to their coherence or to the social and institutional basis on which they rely for support. Questions may be asked about the stability of their hegemonic position, supposing that their masterliness increases in direct proportion to the number of its reproductions: the monographs, monuments or speeches which adopt its story-line and meaning. During how long a period was the narrative frame able to inform historical practices? What were the specific historical themes that were researched in the domain of this master narrative? What counter-narratives circulated, and how and by whom were they suppressed? Another field of comparison may be the 'openness' or 'tightness' of the narrative framework itself, supposing that a master narrative is narrower (*geschlossener*) the smaller the narrative range is which it defines – in other words, the more precisely it fills in its own narrative structure and the less it allows any deviations. To what degree do different master narratives allow pluralism in their sphere of influence? Do they exclude and suppress all deviating stories? Or are they able to integrate certain aspects of them and so transform over time to maintain their position of dominance? After all, the reproduction of the narrative master-pattern takes place not only at the centre of the social base of those in power, but above all in the periphery of society, in the remote spheres of historical culture. It is for this reason that we should also pay attention to intertextual, 'bottom-up' processes, such as the potential undermining of the dominant narrative template by 'smaller' narratives, the battle between central and local identities to establish control over meaning, and the challenge posed to master narratives by new events, research findings or political power struggles. Precisely these asymmetrical and inter-narrative relations could play a decisive role in studying the establishing, maintaining and border-crossing transfers of master narratives in European national histories.

Summary

The ambiguous usage of the master narrative concept may, I believe, be traced back to different interpretations of the master metaphor, which understand the category variously as 'maestro narrative', 'ruler narrative' or 'narrative frame'. I have argued that the concerns of contemporary historiographical research in Europe are best served if we understand master narratives as 'narrative frames'. For a reading of master narratives in terms of literary achievements of single historians is based on a misunderstanding. The original interpretation of master narratives merely as the stories of rulers is also of little benefit to comparative historiography in Europe, because it leads to excessive polarisation and implies a universal historical scale.

Therefore, I have defended the third version and opted for the concept of 'narrative hierarchy'. In this sense, master narratives are understood as schematic 'narrative frameworks'. They prefigure concrete histories and thereby lend them structure, meaning and legitimacy. They are powerful because they stamp their story-lines on smaller narratives and because they exclude those other stories that do not adopt their narrative structures. Leading narrative patterns become reproduced within and thereby legitimised by local narratives, or, alternatively, can be denied or rejected and thus stripped of legitimacy. In order to do justice to the mutual, dynamic, but also asymmetrical interdependence of narratives about the past, a concept of 'narrative hierarchy', at the intertextual summit of which stands the master narrative, appears to be indispensable.

Translated by Peter Carrier

4
Nation and Ethnicity

Joep Leerssen

In 1828 Amédée Thierry published his *Histoire des Gaulois depuis les temps les plus reculés jusqu'à l'entière soumission de la Gaule à la domination romaine*. As a history it was something of a novelty, and Thierry accordingly felt the need to tell his readers what to expect, and what not:

> Do not expect to find in these pages either the philosophical interest of the progressive development of a single, great and operative fact, or the picturesque interest that lies in the successive destinies of a single territory, the fixed theatre of a thousand changing, varied scenes. The facts in this history are numerous and diverse, and their setting is the entire ancient world ... nonetheless all is dominated by a strong unity. This is a biography which for its hero has one of those collective personalities, called *peoples*, which together constitute the great family of mankind.[1]

Other historians had made nations the collective actors and heroes of their historical narrative. Augustin Thierry, Amédée's brother, had three years previously begun to publish his *Histoire de la conquête de l'Angleterre par les Normands*; in Germany, Leopold von Ranke had in 1824 given his work on French–Habsburg rivalry in Italy the title *Geschichte der romanischen und germanischen Völker von 1494 bis 1514*. The preface to that work is famous for formulating the fundamental maxim of Ranke's historicism, that the past was to be studied within its own and proper (*eigentlich*) frame of reference. The work's less famous introduction was no less portentous in that it posited ethnicity as the proper taxonomical category for the study of history. The introductory 'Outline towards a Treatise on the Unity of the Romance and Germanic Peoples and on Their Common

[1]A. Thierry, *Histoire des Gaulois depuis les temps les plus reculés jusqu'à l'entière soumission de la Gaule à la domination romaine* (Paris, 1828), I, p. ii (author's trans.); further references in the text are to this edition.

Development' (*Umriss einer Abhandlung von der Einheit der romanischen und germanischen Völker und von ihrer gemeinschaftlichen Entwicklung*) posited the idea that in all European nations either a Romance or a Germanic element was paramount, and that this political-temperamental DNA was a determining influence in European history.

Ethnicity thus becomes a fundamental organising principle for focusing historical experience and grouping historical knowledge. Peoples are distinct and distinctive entities with a specific character generating a recognisable role pattern in the vicissitudes of history. That, too, is what Thierry found when he sacrificed thematic or territorial unity as his organising principle for the sake of an ethnic focus.

> As I progressed in my writing task, I sensed an increasingly strong philosophical concern, I seemed to discern something individual, something constant and unchanging, emerging from all these diverse occurrences, which took place in so many different places and in such different social settings – just as in the history of a single man, across all the most dramatic incidents of life, one sees the outline of invariant traits: the hero's character.

There is a poetic agenda of sorts here. Thierry is a true Romantic, a contemporary of Sir Walter Scott and Honoré de Balzac, in that his narration dispenses with classical poetic cohesion (what in neo-Aristotelian terms would have been the unity of time, place and incident) for the sake of psychological interest in a motivating and unifying *character*. 'Character', in other words, is no longer the sum total of salient features which sets off a given individual or aggregate from its peers, it becomes (in true Romantic fashion) the spiritual essence, temperament and psychological base-modality which motivates a certain individual and that individual's behaviour, almost like his *Geist* in a Hegelian sense. The history of a nation, therefore, will tend to extrapolate from the vicissitudes of incident towards the fixed base-modality of the nation's character.[2] That, too, is how Thierry concludes his work:

> My task, then, is accomplished. I had undertaken to delineate the destinies of the Gaulish race and I have gradually reached the historical periods in which its individuality disappeared into the patterns of a superimposed

---

[2]On 'the nation' as the collective heroic actor in romantic history writing: A. Rigney, *The Rhetoric of Historical Representation: Three Narrative Histories of the French Revolution* (Cambridge, 1990). On the characterological metaphor in Thierry: A. Rigney, 'Mixed Metaphors and the Writing of History', *Storia della Storiografia*, 24 (1993), pp. 149–59. On the shifting meaning of 'character': L. Van Delft, *Littérature et anthropologie: caractère et nature humaine à l'âge classique* (Paris, 1993).

civilisation, when its history became an episode in a different history. Over the course of seventeen years I have followed it, step by step, across the periods of its adventurous, richly fulfilled life; and at each step, I have demonstrated it to have been the same: intelligent, spiritual, brave, ardent, but little capable of constancy and order, vain, divided by pride.

(III, p. 508)

History considered as a form of national psychology? Indeed, the history of the Gaulish substratum in French history did take on anthropological overtones. In the wake of Thierry's work, the French-English physician W. F. Edwards (author of a volume of *Recherches sur les langues celtiques* and member of the Société Ethnologique of Paris) took cranial measurements to collect physical evidence for the ethnic background of the French population and its ambiguous (Celtic-Gaulish or Germanic-Frankish) descent.[3] Edwards published his findings in an open letter to Thierry entitled *Des caractères physiologiques des races humaines considérés dans leur rapports avec l'histoire* (1829).

Although Thierry calls this a *philosophical* interest, it must be distinguished from what his Enlightenment predecessors might have called by the same name. Bolingbroke had already called history *philosophy teaching by example*, and even among the Enlightenment philosophical historians of a century earlier we can discern an interest in national characters. We may say of David Hume and Montesquieu that they applied two modes of philosophical comparison, one diachronic the other synchronic, the former leading to the study of history, the latter to the study of national character. Montesquieu's *Esprit des lois* (1748) is predicated on the differences between nations, and Hume turned to the topic in his 1743 essay 'Of National Characters'. The title of Voltaire's *Essai sur les mœurs* (1756), it will be recalled, is a truncated form of the fuller *Essai sur l'histoire générale et sur les mœurs et l'esprit des nations*, with the subtitle *sur les principaux faits de l'histoire depuis Charlemagne jusqu'à Louis XIII*. Likewise, Giambattista Vico's *Scienza nuova* (1725) stipulates in its subtitle that it is about the 'common nature of nations' (*d'intorno alla comune natura delle nazioni*). The early eighteenth century is replete with such cross-national,

---

[3]On Gaulish ancestry debates in modern France, see K. Pomian, 'Francs et gaulois', in P. Nora (ed.), *Les Lieux de mémoire*, 2 (Paris, 1997), pp. 2245–300, and P. Viallaneix and J. Ehrard (eds), *Nos ancêtres les Gaulois: actes du colloque international de Clermont-Ferrand* (Clermont-Ferrand, 1982), esp. C. Lacoste, 'Les Gaulois d'Amédée Thierry', pp. 203–10. Also, A. Jourdan, 'The Image of Gaul during the French Revolution: between Charlemagne and Ossian', in T. Brown (ed.), *Celticism* (Amsterdam, 1996), pp. 183–206, and J. Leerssen, 'Outer and Inner Others: The Auto-image of French Identity from Mme de Staël to Eugène Sue', *Yearbook of European Studies*, 2 (1989), 35–52.

characterological comparisons,[4] and history is often dovetailed with anthropology in order to arrive at a 'philosophical' study of these variations in mankind.

To that extent, then, the 'philosophical' interest of ethnically oriented history writing in the style of the Thierry brothers and Ranke is not a complete novelty. They had their source traditions too: from the Renaissance onwards, many European nations had assiduously cultivated origin myths and invoked the heritage of primitive tribal forebears, especially if mentioned by Roman authors as stalwart defenders of their local liberties. The Gaulish ancestry myth in France takes shape as a democratic counter-narrative to the aristocratic cult of Frankish genealogies; in Germany, the cult of Arminius the Cheruscan (of the battle of the Teutoburg Forest) is due to his applicability to the Lutheran Reformation; the Low Countries invoked the historical memories of the Belgic tribes and leaders such as Ambiorix, and the Batavians and their leader Civilis, for reasons of their value as moral-political exempla; and the same may be said of the cult of the Goths in seventeenth-century Sweden, of the British tribes (Caractacus, Boadicea) and of the Anglo-Saxons in seventeenth- and eighteenth-century England.[5]

---

[4]See J. G. Hayman, 'Notions of National Characters in the Eighteenth Century', *Huntington Library Quarterly*, 35 (1971), 1–17; J. Leerssen, *National Thought in Europe: A Cultural History* (Amsterdam, 2006), pp. 52–70, and 'The Rhetoric of National Character: A Programmatic Survey', *Poetics Today*, 21, 2 (2000), 267–92. Also, F. K. Stanzel, 'Das Nationalitätenschema in der Literatur und seine Entstehung zu Beginn der Neuzeit', in G. Blaicher (ed.), *Erstarrtes Denken: Studien zu Klischee, Stereotyp und Vorurteil in englischsprachiger Literatur* (Tübingen, 1987), 84–96, and F. K. Stanzel et al. (eds), *Europäischer Völkerspiegel: Imagologischethnographische Studien zu den Völkertafeln des frühen 18. Jahrhunderts* (Heidelberg, 1999).

[5] Each of these late medieval and early modern national ancestry myths has generated a sizeable body of critical literature. Much is contained in the huge survey by A. Borst, *Der Turmbau von Babel: Geschichte der Meinungen über Ursprung und Vielfalt der Sprachen und Völker*, 4 vols in 6 (München, 1995). I mention further, by way of example, J. Juaristi, *El bosque originario: genealogías míticas de los pueblos de Europa* (Madrid, 2000), and L. Poliakov, *Le Mythe aryen: essai sur les sources du racisme et des nationalismes*, new edn (Bruxelles, 1987). Specifically on Germany, see F. L. Borchardt, *German Antiquity in Renaissance Myth* (Baltimore, MD, 1971); R. Kuehnemund, *Arminius, or The Rise of a National Symbol in Literature* (Chapel Hill, NC, 1953); K. von See, *Barbar Germane Arier: die Suche nach der Identität der Deutschen* (Heidelberg, 1994). On Britain, see S. Kliger, *The Goths in England: A Study in Seventeenth and Eighteenth Century Thought* (Cambridge, MA, 1952); S. Smiles, *The Image of Antiquity: Ancient Britain and the Romantic Imagination* (New Haven, CT, 1994); A. J. Frantzen and J. D. Niles (eds), *Anglo-Saxonism and the Construction of Social Identity* (Florida, 1997). On the Netherlands: I. Schöffer, 'The Batavian Myth during the Sixteenth and Seventeenth Centuries', in J. S. Bromley and E. H. Kossmann (eds), *Britain and The Netherlands*, 5 (The Hague, 1975), pp. 78–101; A. van der Woud, *De Bataafse hut: verschuivingen in het beeld van de geschiedenis (1750–1850)* (Amsterdam, 1990). Also, for a comparative perspective involving Sweden, see O. Mörke, 'Bataver, Eidgenossen und Goten: Gründungs- und Begründungsmythen in den Niederlanden, der Schweiz, und Schweden in der frühen Neuzeit', in H. Berding (ed.), *Mythos und Nation: Studien zur Entwicklung des kollektiven Bewußtseins in der Neuzeit*, 3 (Frankfurt, 1996), pp. 104–32.

Nonetheless, there is something novel in Thierry's characterological approach. His narrative focusing on the temperamental blueprint of a collective-ethnic protagonist is qualitatively different from earlier observations on 'national character'. Nationality, for him, constitutes not just a subordinate variable within the human type-at-large (such as temperament or astrological sign), but rather a separate category in itself. Enlightenment anthropology had still been universalist, much like Enlightenment linguistics. Anthropology up to and including Immanuel Kant had been about human identity in general, 'man' as in Alexander Pope's dictum concerning 'the proper study of mankind'. Similarly, eighteenth-century notions concerning the origin of language had taken their topic as a universalist, undifferentiated abstract principle of linguistic capacity. However, after Johann Gottfried Herder had turned the question inside out (in that he was concerned not with the origin of human language, but with the mainspring of the proliferation of different human languages), anthropology too had become concerned with the differences among human societies rather than with the universal, fundamental qualities that made mankind human. The Humboldts had fielded a plan for a *comparative anthropology* and had gone on to place linguistic difference in the centre of a taxonomy of ethno-national differentiation:

> Most circumstances attending a nation's life (place, climate, religion, political constitution, manners and customs) can somehow be seen separate from it, and so too can we factor out (even in the case of intense mutual exchange) what they received and imparted by way of learning. But one thing is of a different order altogether; it is the breath, the very soul of the nation, accompanies it at every step, and (whether it be seen as a cause or as an effect) always sets the horizon for any analysis: its language.[6]

Small wonder that the new science of comparative linguistics (in which Alexander von Humboldt played a formative part) was seen by some as a sister discipline to comparative anthropology. Nicholas Wiseman spoke in 1835 of the 'sister sciences' of 'philological and physiognomical ethnography', meaning that the diversity of the human race could be established either by physical analysis (for example, cranial measurements) or by linguistic comparison (for example, etymology). The paradigm was clinched in August Schleicher's *Compendium der vergleichenden Grammatik der indogermanischen Sprachen* (1861–2), which aligned the 'family tree' structure of the Indo-European languages with the similar 'family tree' structure of Darwinian biology and the human races. In combining Hegel's historical philosophy (Schleicher had become a Hegelian adept while a

---

[6] *Latium und Hellas* (1806) (trans. JL); cf. Leerssen, *National Thought*, pp. 206–7.

student at Tübingen) with Darwin's phylogenetic comparatism and principle of 'natural selection', he summarised an alignment between race and culture that had been in the air since Humboldt.[7]

Much as language and linguistic philology were pulled into a racial-comparative paradigm, history writing too was increasingly drawn to physical anthropology. The fact that Thierry's study of France's Gaulish ancestry should lead to a racial-comparative measurement of the physical typology of its inhabitants is not alone. In a similar pattern, the long-standing awareness that British history was a compound of Celtic, Anglo-Saxon, Danish and Norman incursions and settlements led straight to the physical anthropology of Sir John Beddoe (*The Races of Britain*, 1885), while the philologist Robert Gordon Latham could with equal ease write on English language and literature and on *The Ethnology of Europe* (1852).[8] In the Low Countries, a scheme was established which replaced the older 'Batavian myth' with a racial-ethnic originary compound of Frisians, Saxons and Franks.[9] As European historians turned towards national histories (rather than the history of a territory, an idea or successive reigns) they embedded that nation's identity increasingly in tribal roots and cultures, matters investigated also by archaeologists and linguists. Historians became the avant-garde of racial thought. Arthur de Gobineau, whom we know mainly as the author of the fateful *Essai sur l'inégalité des races humaines* (1853), the blue-print of European racism in the late nineteenth and early twentieth centuries, owed most of his contemporary standing to his highly regarded works on Persian history and on the European Renaissance.

*

The idea of nationality, national character and race came to historians from a variety of source traditions and was accordingly burdened with great conceptual and terminological vagueness. What are the entities and aggregates of which we speak? Nations, peoples, races? Little distinction was made between the words or indeed the concepts. The various terms are near-synonyms, between which a great degree of phraseological and semantic slippage occurs. Nineteenth-century discourse does not rigidly distinguish between human aggregates held together by language, by culture, by descent, by shared historical

[7]B. Dayrat, 'The Roots of Phylogeny: How Did Haeckel Build His Tree?', *Systematic Biology*, 52, 4 (2003), 515–27.

[8]For the influence of Thierry/Edwards-style ethnographic history, including Beddoe, see F. E. Faverty, *Matthew Arnold the Ethnologist* (New York, [1951] 1968), pp. 36–40.

[9]M. Beyen, 'A Tribal Trinity: The Rise and Fall of the Franks, the Frisians and the Saxons in the Historical Consciousness of the Netherlands since 1850', *European History Quarterly*, 40, 4 (2000), 493–532.

experience, by social intercourse or by physical resemblance. For any of these the word *race* can be used, or the word *people* or the word *nation*. Indeed, it is the very slippage between these terms which may have rendered biological essentialism and cultural determinism such a protean and unquestioned presence in nineteenth-century national thought. In his famous preface to the *Histoire de la littérature anglaise* (1863), Hippolyte Taine listed three determinants for a given culture: race, environment and stage of development (*race, milieu, moment*). Ernest Renan (who had blithely given a racialist poetics in his *La Poésie des races celtiques* of 1854) was still at pains to sort out the conceptual mess in his *Qu'est-ce qu'une nation?* of 1881. Nineteenth-century historians habitually trace the histories of present-day nations (a predominantly social concept, organised by polity) back to prehistoric tribes (a racial-ethnic concept). Poland traces itself back to the ancient Sarmatians; Romanians discover the Dacians; the modern Greeks call themselves Hellenes rather than any modern name. In each case, historians and philologists see it as their appointed task to establish the continuity from ancient tribal origins to the modern nation: Joachim Lelewel for Poland, Bogdan Petriceicu Hasdeu for Romania, Konstantinos Paparregopoulos for Greece. Linguists, for their part, will call languages by a nomenclature referring to territories or modern nations: *Spanish, Polish, Bulgarian, Icelandic*; but the superimposed categories of language families will bear the names of ancient tribes and races: *Slavic, Celtic, Germanic, Semitic, Aryan*. In each case, the social and the racial aggregates are almost wilfully *not* distinguished, made to shade into each other.

The case of Germany is both instructive (for present-day readers) and influential (in its own day). It begins with Johann Gottlieb Fichte's blueprint for European ethnic nationalism, the *Reden an die deutsche Nation* (1808). The term *Nation* is portentous. At first sight one might expect that he would eschew it, for it is a term redolent of the political jargon of the French Revolution; indeed, Fichte's lofty, philosophical *Reden* are vituperatively anti-revolutionary, influenced by more activist street-fighting authors such as Ernst Moritz Arndt and Friedrich Jahn, who prefer the nomenclature of *Stamm* or *Volk* (witness Jahn's *Deutsches Volkstum* of 1810). Yet on closer scrutiny Fichte's term is both deliberate and apt. He gives his *Reden* under the shadow of the millennial trauma of the abolition of the Holy Roman Empire (1806), the empire being vested in the 'German nation' in the official name of that thousand-year-old institution: *Das Heilige Römische Reich deutscher Nation.* Fichte's implication is that, although the empire no longer exists, its constituent *Nation* still does, bereft of its sovereign incorporation but alive in its substance.

In the course of his lectures, Fichte then celebrates this enduring German nation as possessing a true and anthropologically authentic identity, in that it never abandoned the language of its ancestral origins. This introduction of linguistic-ethnic roots into present-day socio-political analysis is typical and was to prove highly influential. Ernst Moritz Arndt had a similar penchant for an ethno-linguistically morphed geopolitics, easily alternating between tribal archaeology and current affairs, and in the next generation Jacob Grimm was to spell out Fichte's point in more detail. In the view as propounded by Arndt, Fichte and Grimm, all of Europe following the *Völkerwanderung* had been dominated by the Germanic tribes, from Goths to Anglo-Saxons. Some of these, however, allowed themselves to become estranged from their origins (*entartet*, degenerate) by adopting the Latin idiom of the regions they subdued. This applies to the Italian Ostrogoths and Longobards, to the Spanish Visigoths and to the French Burgundians and Franks. Ever since, Europe has been a theatre of conflict between the Germanic tribes who had remained true to their ethnic-linguistic roots (Germans proper, Scandinavians, Dutch, Anglo-Saxons in Britain and even America) and the degenerate Latinised tribes of the south. Here, of course, lies also the foundation of Ranke's ethnographic vision in the *Geschichten der romanischen und germanischen Völker*.

Fichte provided his fellow intellectuals with a moral philosophy of *Deutschtum*. It was picked up in various disciplines, the legal sciences foremost among them. Legal historians such as Friedrich Karl von Savigny had already been habituated to the distinction between *Germanisten* and *Romanisten*: specialists in native German customary law and Roman institutional and canon law, respectively; we should be aware too that the origins of historicism must probably be sought among legal scholars like him.[10] The legal sciences had always, before Napoleon's codification, relied on a scrupulous accumulation of jurisprudential sources, and legal source editions in many European countries from Muratori onwards (Blackstone in England, Schlyter in Sweden) taught a lesson or two to both historians and philologists. (Vico's own *Scienza nuova*, which indirectly formed the basis for the philological turn in the human sciences, was itself intended for a new *sistema del diritto naturale delle genti*, as the subtitle puts it.)[11] What is more, men such as Savigny had in the course of

---

[10]On Savigny, see the useful sketch by I. Denneler, *Friedrich Karl von Savigny* (Berlin, 1985), which also lists further sources. On Savigny's influence on Grimm's historicism, see J. Leerssen, 'Literary Historicism: Romanticism, Philologists, and the Presence of the Past', *Modern Language Quarterly*, 65, 2 (2004), 221–43.

[11]The standard work on the influence of Vico is still I. Berlin, *Vico and Herder* (1960), reissued as part of Berlin's *Three Critics of the Enlightenment: Vico, Hamann, Herder*, ed. Henry Hardy (London, 2000). The conduit by which Vico's thought spread to affect Romantic historians and philologists is still obscure – ironically, most people seem by 1800 to have forgotten that it was Vico who coined the term *philology* in its modern sense, encompassing, significantly, the various culture-anthropological fields of language, literature, myth, history and legal institutions. It seems that the main disseminator was his pupil Cesarotti with his influential Vico-inspired comments on Homer and Ossian.

such legal-historical work come to hold the firm belief that any culture is a diachronic process of growth and adaptation, and that any cultural understanding must therefore trace growth processes rather than merely their outcome. This habit of thought was taught by Savigny to men such as Ranke and Grimm (who started off as Savigny's assistant and maintained a lifelong legal-historical vocation), and may well constitute the beginning of historicism in Europe. As Grimm himself declared, he owed:

> a lifetime's debt to his mentor Savigny for every scholarly impulse. Inductive research he had learned from him, and the recourse to true and pure sources. In particular, Savigny had taught him the historical analysis of legal institutions; it was here that he had learned, as they say, to understand *what is* in terms of *how it had become*.[12]

Is it surprising to see, when Grimm called an international conference of *Germanisten* in Frankfurt in 1846, that he should include under that appellation not only philologists (linguists and textual scholars) and legal scholars, but also historians such as Ranke? On that occasion, Grimm not only gave his famous definition of a *Volk* as 'the totality of persons speaking a common language', but also a long speech on the unity of the three disciplines, all of which aimed to elucidate *Deutschtum*, the nature and character of the German people, through the analysis of its language, literature, myths and stories, manners and customs, legal institutions – and history.[13] Grimm's *Germanistenversammlung* of 1846 is usually seen as a warm-up exercise for the *Nationalversammlung* of 1848, which was held at the same venue (Frankfurt's Paulskirche), with many delegates present on both occasions. As such, it is surely one of the key events (along with the similar, but opposed, Pan-Slavic Congress held at Prague in 1848) in the relations between culture and politics in the mid-nineteenth century. The most important legacy from the cultural to the political arena was perhaps this: that the fundamental status given to German ethnicity in the cultural field favoured the Prussian-oriented wing in politics, which rejected Austrian leadership in a new German empire because of the large, non-Germanic population under the Habsburg Crown.

---

[12]Wilhelm Scherer's notice on Grimm (trans. JL) in *Allgemeine deutsche Biographie. Auf Veranlassung und mit Unterstützung seiner Majestät des Königs von Bayern herausgegeben durch die Commission der Königl. Akademie der Wissenschaften*, 56 vols (Leipzig, 1875–1912).

[13]J. Grimm, *Kleinere Schriften*, 8 vols (Berlin/Gütersloh, 1864–90), vol. 7, pp. 556–63. F. Fürbeth et al. (eds), *Zur Geschichte und Problematik der Nationalphilologien in Europa: 150 Jahre Erste Germanistenversammlung in Frankfurt am Main (1846–1996)* (Tübingen, 1999).

History in this context becomes part of an investigation into nationality. That nationality can be a tribal-racial concept, a linguistic-cultural one, a legal-institutional or a moral-social one, as the case requires. Not only is the nation the main hero of the historical narrative, the narrative is also an attempt to characterise the nation, its particular vocation in world history and in humankind. Michelet's *Histoire de France* is a good case in point. At every turn, certain events are singled out (to the exclusion or marginalisation of others) as being representative of a true, eternal Frenchness carried across the generations by the French nation. National character thus becomes a transcendent principle in human affairs. The philosophy of Fichte, Schelling and Hegel had seen the nation or *Volk* as a secular form of eternal life for the individual. Nationality binds history together by the natural solidarity between generations, anchored in human virtues such as filial piety for our ancestors, or parental solicitude for our posterity. The nation counts as the manifestation and carrier of grand historical destinies and spiritual principles in human affairs. This transcendent, Platonic notion of a collective and permanent anthropo-spiritual presence, the *Volkstum* or *Volksgeist* so important to Fichte and Hegel, so influential with Michelet and the Romantic historians, sets the nineteenth century apart from the Enlightenment. Its abstraction embraces, and loftily rises above, various possible historical manifestations in human aggregation, such as nation, society, people, citizenry and race, rendering distinctions between those concepts superfluous.

*

In tracing the ethnic-national charge of history writing in the nineteenth century, we should place it in its proper context: as a literary and discursive genre barely distinct from its social and discursive environment. Historians (contrary to what their twentieth-century successors would like to believe) did not work in the isolation of an autonomous, discrete discipline. That discipline was only beginning to emerge as such: the craft of history writing was crystallising out of a source tradition of belles-lettres and antiquarianism, in a process of professionalisation and academic institutionalisation of which the nineteenth century saw the mere beginning. Historians gained employment and source access at newly founded institutions such as state archives, libraries and universities; they were initially glorified archivists, librarians or *littérateurs*. Historians wrote moral essays, like Michelet, or novels, like the Portuguese Alexandre Herculano. Frequently, their historical work went in tandem with the *imaginaire* of culture at large, in that historians investigated the topics which creative writers were to develop as potent cultural myths. Social and literary myths, such as Robin Hood (King Arthur, King Alfred) in England, Jeanne d'Arc in France, El Cid in Spain, were all developments and spin-offs of sources made available or accessible by historians.

The border between history and philology was particularly narrow.[14] It is no anomaly to see Ranke included with legal and literary historians as a *Germanist*. 'Literary history' as it came to be practised in the nineteenth century was very close to 'cultural history as expressed in written texts', and often tended towards an investigation of the written track-record of the nation's characteristic 'genius'.[15] There was a lively tradition of hybrid social-cum-literary histories which are the forerunners of both cultural history and comparative literature: for instance, Henry Thomas Buckle's *History of Civilisation in Europe* of 1858.[16] The emergence of medieval studies was sustained jointly by historians and philologists. G. G. Gervinus' *Geschichte der poetischen Nationalliteratur der Deutschen* (5 vols, 1835–42), Anders Fryxell's *Bidrag till Sveriges literatur-historia* (9 vols, 1860–69), Francesco De Sanctis' *Storia della literatura italiana* (1870–71), Teophilo Braga's *Theoria/Manual da historia da litteratura portugueza* (1872/75) and Alexandros Rizos Rangavis' *Histoire littéraire de la Grèce moderne* (1877) are as important for the articulation of notions of national character and national identity as Taine's (previously mentioned) *Histoire de la littérature anglaise*. When Emile Chasles published a *Histoire nationale de la littérature française* in 1870, we can see the repercussions of Thierry's racial-characterological approach in the headings of its various sections: *Origines. Le Génie Gaulois, ou la race. Les Gallo-Romains et la civilisation. Les Gallo-Francs et l'épopée. Les Gallo-Bretons et l'esprit romanesque.*

Thus, political and social history was woven with a thousand threads into a wider warp and woof of writing about the past. As such, historians formed part of the great nineteenth-century process of the nationalisation of the European mental landscape. They did not invent it, still less did they resist it; they were increasingly authoritative voices in the general post-Romantic, philologically inspired climate that saw culture and society as anthropological categories of ethnic units defined and determined by language and descent.

---

[14]A single example from the institutional field: the first chair of national history in the Netherlands, at Leiden University, was split off from a chair for rhetoric and belles-lettres; when the incumbent, Matthias de Vries, found that philological matters took up too much of his time to take proper care of the teaching of historical courses, he applied for a subsidiary fissional chair which was to be filled in 1859–60 by Robert Fruin, the father of Dutch national history. L. van Driel and J. Noordegraaf, *De Vries en Te Winkel: een duografie* (Den Haag, 1998), 134.

[15]M. Spiering (ed.), *Nation Building and Writing Literary History* (Amsterdam, 1999).

[16]Interestingly, such cultural or intellectual histories (one might add Guizot's *Histoire de la civilization en Europe*, 1828, and H. Hallam's *Introduction to the Literature of Europe*, 1837–9) tended to be more transnational in scope.

All the same, these intellectual currents had an immediate, and sizeable, effect on society at large. It is no surprise to find that historians played a prominent role in the process of state formation.[17] The importance of national historical education and even indoctrination for the legitimation of the nineteenth-century state is well known[18] and can be measured both institutionally and culturally: from the way in which both national history and national literary history were enshrined as compulsory school subjects, and from the great boom in juvenile national-historical fiction in the later nineteenth century. Equally prominent is the role played by historians of national politics and in the great offices of state: François Guizot in France, Johan Rudolf Thorbecke in the Netherlands.[19]

However, the professionalisation of history writing not only reflected state-sponsored institutionalisation; state initiatives, such as the organisation of national libraries and archives, historical chairs and institutes, such as the Ecole des Chartes, or the coordination of ambitious national-historical documentary source editions (the *Monumenta Germaniae Historica*, the Rolls Series) meant that the Romantic-ethnic views of mid-nineteenth-century historians were incorporated into the official, 'national' historical institutions.

Thus, the institutionalisation and professionalisation of history was, above all, a nationalisation of history. Even today, we find that historians, when they reflect on their craft and responsibilities, see themselves (their position and the topic of their investigation) primarily and automatically within the boundaries of their own nation and society. Lucian of Samosata's second-century exhortation that the historian should be 'stateless, a foreigner amidst books', was buried in the process.[20]

*

Thus far I have concentrated mainly on the role of historians in long-established 'old states' (Britain, France, the Netherlands) or (in the case of Germany) countries with a firmly established culture-institutional basis. One

---

[17]Generally S. Berger et al. (eds), *Writing National Histories: Western Europe since 1800* (London, 1999).

[18]P. den Boer, *Geschiedenis als beroep: de professionalisering van de geschiedbeoefening in Frankrijk (1818–1914)* (Nijmegen, 1987).

[19]Laurent Theis, 'Guizot et les institutions de mémoire: un historien au pouvoir', in P. Nora (ed.), *Les Lieux de mémoire*, 3 vols (Paris, 1997), vol. 1, pp. 1575–97; Charles O. Carbonell, 'Guizot, homme d'état, et le mouvement historiographique français du XIXe siècle', in *Actes du colloque François Guizot (Paris, 22–25 octobre 1974)* (Paris, 1976), pp. 219–37.

[20]Lucian's sentiment ('xenos en tois bibliois kai apolis') is in his *Pōs dei historian syngraphein* ('How to write history'), c. 164 AD.

may add that in Russia too the nationalisation of its culture was materially indebted to advances in historical learning. Karamzin and Pushkin undertook important historical source-research and spread their knowledge not only in history writing, but also in history-based fictional writing: Nikolai Karamzin's *Marfa* (1803) and Alexander Pushkin's *Captain's Daughter* (1837) and *Boris Godunov* (1831) are based on these authors' earlier historiographical research, which in turn laid the basis for subsequent national-historical activities such as Mikhail Glinka's operas and the development of a musical 'Russian School'. Indeed, the fact that Tsar Alexander III was to enshrine *narodnost'* (nationality) as one of the three pillars of his empire[21] would have been unthinkable but for this historiographical preparatory fieldwork.

However, the trends signalled in these cases of established realms were also operative in the subaltern regions of Europe, and possibly with even more public impact. In *Qu'est-ce qu'une nation?* Ernest Renan pointed out that the advances in the historical sciences might bring to light ancient conflicts best forgotten, and that this might even threaten the fabric of national cohesion by reminding marginalised minorities of their ancient grievances. That prediction has proved to be all too true. Within France the discovery of subaltern 'lost histories' (such as the Albigensians and Cathars around Albi and Montségur, or the Camisards in the Cevennes) was already underway – typically, in a combination of historical source-research and literary-imaginative treatment. Elsewhere in Europe this type of historical recuperation was to fan the flames of outright separatist nationalism.

The case of Ireland may stand as an example.[22] Its Gaelic culture with its attendant sources was made available to mainstream academic and interested audiences in the period from 1780 onwards and proved a central catalyst in the development of separatist nationalism. An anthology of seditious, anti-English Jacobite poetry written in the eighteenth century appeared in 1831 (James Hardiman's *Irish Minstrelsy*); literary genres such as the national tale (an early, activist form of historical novel) and nationalistic poetry became steeped in antiquarian and historical themes and references; and one of the most influential national poets, Thomas Moore, author of national verse and song (*Irish Melodies*), wrote a *History of Ireland* in 1835–45, based on sources made accessible over the previous decades. His successors in the Young Ireland

---

[21]Count Sergey Semionovic Uvarov, in a report to the tsar in 1833, had declared that education must be based on the principles of orthodoxy, autocracy and nationality (*pravoslavie, samoderzhavie, i narodnost'*). Alexander's intolerance of minority cultures within his empire was to reflect the last of these three.

[22]Cf. generally J. Leerssen, *Remembrance and Imagination: Patterns in the Historical and Literary Representation of Ireland in the Nineteenth Century* (Cork, 1996).

movement (Thomas Davis foremost among them) followed in this dual poetic and historiographical agenda. Their narrative-historical surveys and treatises, often reprinted best-sellers, were long arguments for Irish independence and against British supremacy; their verse was replete with historical references to the ancient glories of the Irish nation and British-inflicted oppression (indeed, the title of their newspaper was *The Nation,* and a best-selling anthology of their verse was entitled *The Spirit of the Nation*). Crucial in Davis's thought was the distinction between region (or province) and nation; the distinction lay precisely in the absence or presence of history. A land without history was a mere province; a land with its own history was a nation deserving of self-determination. In the event, this historicist separatism was to form the launch pad for the Irish insurrectionary drive for independence in the early twentieth century. It was formulated most clearly by Douglas Hyde, a language activist, who recuperated the cultural heritage of Gaelic Ireland in his *Literary History of Ireland, from Earliest Times to the Present Day* (1899). It was dedicated to his fellow workers in a Gaelic language revival movement on the basis of their shared understanding 'that Ireland has a past, has a history, has a literature', and on their shared agenda of seeking 'to render the present a rational continuation of the past'.[23] One of the workers so addressed was to lead the insurrection of 1916. Hyde himself was to become the first president of Ireland in 1938.

A few general trends and patterns can be singled out from this case. A historicist imagination, based on previous archival recuperation, flourished in Romantic narrative histories alongside the genres of narrative fiction and verse; its political-separatist rhetoric hinged on the invocation of persistent nationhood and national identity transcending the record of oppression; the authors involved placed culture and national cultural specificity at the centre of their focus, and frequently crossed from the realm of writing into the arena of political action, one foreshadowing and facilitating the other.

Specifically in the subaltern regions of Europe, ethnicity was, for historians, practically the only category in which a 'national' history could be conceived. Histories of France or of Denmark had the institutional framework of a long-standing kingdom with all the trappings of statehood to fall back on: the archive of reigns and administered politics. To some extent, that institutional framework was still available for those who wanted to write the histories of erstwhile kingdoms such as Poland, Hungary or Scotland: although the country was no longer an independent state, there was at least the vestige and

[23]Cf. J. Leerssen, 'À la recherche d'une littérature perdue: Literary history, Irish identity and Douglas Hyde', *Yearbook of European Studies,* 12 (1998), 95–108.

remembrance of sovereign existence, which could give focus to historical treatment. Typically, such histories (or historical novels or historical epics) would evoke the glory that once was, and then, following the loss of sovereignty and the advent of foreign rule, claim that the principle of national identity, though lost in its constitutional embodiment, was still alive as a spiritual principle within the members of the nation – in other words, a 'national' history of a non-state or erstwhile state could conveniently shift its focus from the nation-as-state to the nation-as-ethnicity. In lieu of an institutionally permanent state, the national history is then presented in terms of the ongoing manifestation of a collective ethnic volition. Witness the following sentiment from a popularising separatist Irish source:

> Let me tell you the story of Ireland. It is not a history. When we speak of the history of a nation, we mean the biographies of its kings: the line of monarchs forming a spinal column from which historical events seem to spring laterally. The history of Ireland is invertebrate. It has no such royal backbone. ... The efforts of the Irish race to regain their country present a monotonous record of bloodshed extending over seven centuries, even to our own day: the last of these massacres occurred eighty-three years ago. These convulsions are the only reigns into which the story of Ireland can be perspicuously divided. They might be called Reigns of Terror.[24]

In histories from the subaltern parts of Europe, the sovereign, constitutional incorporation of the nation's collective individuality, is, then, not to be found in the past, or at best only in a remote past, a paradise lost (the medieval Serbian and Bulgarian monarchies, Greece before the Turks, Poland before the partitions, Hungary before the battle of Mohács, Ireland before Strongbow's invasion, and so on). The carrier of the nation's permanence in the more recent past is the ethnic collectivity of the people themselves, and they manifest their presence through idealism, rebellion and culture. The thrust of such histories is that the incorporation of the ethnic nation into a *Staatsnation* is a matter for the future. Such histories portentously stretch 'from antiquity to the present day' and often conclude with a perspective for future action. It is here, perhaps, that Rankean historicism meets the type of ideological historicism that was criticised by Karl Popper:

---

[24]D. Boucicault, *The Fireside Story of Ireland* (London, 1882).

the idea that we can influence the future by learning the lessons of history.

*

It is well known that scholars and intellectuals are often in the vanguard of national emancipation movements.[25] This pattern is obvious not only in Western European minority nations such as Ireland,[26] but particularly noticeably so in Central and Eastern Europe, where we shall now turn our gaze (acknowledging, in doing so, with special gratitude the many excellent national case studies referred to in the respective footnotes).

Although 'nation-building' intellectuals can be folklorists, linguists or poets, historians and historical philologists form an important element among them.[27] The Polish historian Joachim Lelewel, author of *Considérations sur l'état politique de l'ancienne Pologne et sur l'histoire de son peuple* and many other historical works, is a case in point.[28] He started his career as librarian-professor in Warsaw, obtained a chair in Wilna from which he was dismissed for political reasons in 1824, and subsequently became a liberal Slavic-nationalist activist. He participated prominently in the doomed Polish uprising of 1830, perhaps the one crisis in Metternich Europe which marked the adoption of Romantic philosophy by nationalist insurgents[29] (exported as it was to be by exiled Poles such as Chopin, Lelewel himself and above all Lelewel's poetic comrade-in-arms Adam Mickiewicz). The Warsaw slogan 'For our liberty and yours' is said to have been coined by Lelewel. At the same time, liberalism and emancipation, or the right to self-determination, were not the only driving forces in these events and developments. A firm belief in ethnic individualism was the cognitive precondition on

---

[25]The most systematic analysis has been given by M. Hroch: *Die Vorkämpfer der nationalen Bewegung bei den kleinen Völkern Europas: eine vergleichende Analyse zur gesellschaftlichen Schichtung der patriotischen Gruppen* (Praha, 1968); 'Programme und Forderungen nationaler Bewegungen: ein europäischer Vergleich', in H. Timmermann (ed.), *Entwicklung der Nationalbewegungen in Europa, 1850–1914* (Berlin, 1998), pp. 17–29. Also: R. Grigor Suny and M. D. Kennedy (eds), *Intellectuals and the Articulation of the Nation* (Ann Arbor, MI, 1999).

[26]The Basque case is elucidated by Jon Juaristi, *El linaje de Aitor* (Madrid, 2000). The cases of Catalan and Icelandic historicist nationalism present no striking exception to the pattern.

[27]Cf. D. Deletant and H. Hanak (eds), *Historians as Nation-Builders: Central and South-East Europe* (London, 1988).

[28]J. S. Skurnowicz, *Romantic Nationalism and Liberalism: Joachim Lelewel and the Polish National Idea* (Boulder, CO, 1981).

[29]Cf. H. Kohn, *Pan-Slavism, Its History and Ideology* (New York, 1960), pp. 39–40. More generally, A. Walicki, *Philosophy and Romantic Nationalism: The Case of Poland*, new edn (Notre Dame, IN, 1994).

which these claims were based. Thus, during the Warsaw uprising, the poet, folk-song collector and professor of Polish literature Kazimierz Brodziński delivered a lecture to the Warsaw Society of Friends of Science on the principles of Polish nationality, *O narodowości Polaków*, defining its spiritual/characterological essence.

In other words, all historiographical nationalism in East-Central Europe invokes, more or less explicitly, the axiom of ethnic specificity and individuality. This was the categorical starting point for the agenda of national emancipation. Liberty for the nation was sought as a matter of political justice, as a fair distribution of power and status; but it was sought for the *nation*, and that group was always an aggregate of shared culture and common descent, an ethnicity. Here as elsewhere among minority nations the tendency was that, owing to the absence of an institutional archive, historians gravitated towards the register of cultural and informal history; and owing to this cultural-historical slant, the 'national'-collective protagonist of their historical narratives was mainly 'the nation', understood as an ethnic whole.

A brief *tour d'horizon* of the Slavic complex further substantiates this. All Slavic national initiatives are developed on the inheritance of a set of philosophical, philological and poetic ideas concerning the ethnicity and character of 'the Slavs'. Herder's ideas on the peaceful Slavic temperament and its Messianic role for the future are one factor. Jan Kollár's poetic cycle *Slavý dcera* (1824), widely current in Central and Eastern Europe, was another, as well as his rousing essay on 'Slav interconnectedness'. And a philological framework had been given to 'the Slavs' by the linguistic antiquaries Josef Dobrovský and Jernej Kopitar, from Bohemia and Slovenia, respectively. Dobrovský above all was instrumental in giving the Slavic cultures a firm historical presence (*Über die ältesten Sitze der Slawen in Europa und ihre Verbreitung seit dem sechsten Jahrhundert*, 1788). With the help of Kopitar (a philologist employed at the Imperial Court Library of Vienna), Dobrovský established a comparative grammar of Old Church Slavonic and the Ur-form of the Slavic languages (1822), and charted the civilising missions of SS. Cyril and Methodius as founders of a Slavic Christianity (1824). The Slavic nations gleaned from Dobrovský's work a sense of historicity which was indispensable to contemporary claims to national enfranchisement.[30] These claims circulated among and between various Slavic nationalities, from Bulgaria to Ukraine, and were often inspired by an encompassing, pan-Slavic sense of common descent and ethnicity. Instrumental in the spread of such Slav ethnic nationalism were the Czech historian František Palacký (1798–1876) and the Slovak antiquarian/historian Pavel Šafařík (1795–1861). The latter acted as a go-between between Central Europe and the Balkans, in that, Slovak by birth, he

---

[30]M. Wirtz, *Josef Dobrovský und die Literatur: frühe bohemistische Forschung zwischen Wissenschaft und nationalem Auftrag* (Dresden, 1999).

taught and worked at the Lyceum of Novi Sad, in Habsburg-controlled Serb Voivodina. His *Slovanské starožitnosti* ('Slavic Antiquities) of 1836 was particularly influential.[31] Palacký, for his part, is a celebrated actor in Czech national history.[32] His career is typical: he started as an archivist, became editor of a learned journal, published a history of Bohemia in 1836 and was propelled into the political arena in 1848; what Lelewel was for 1830 Poland, Palacký was for 1848 Czechia. In his later life he became influential with his federalist ideas for a Slavic federation under the Habsburg Imperial Crown; it was he above all who formulated the notion that Czechia was a westward-looking nation, based on Enlightenment values, and as such different from the eastern Slavdom, Russian-style – a national self-image which has continued to reverberate among Czech intellectuals from Masaryk to the present. All the same, Palacký himself developed this liberal programme on the basis of a firm belief in Slavic ethnicity – witness his role as convener and president of Prague's Pan-Slavic Congress of 1848.

Ukrainian historians for their part underwent influences not only from the tsarist realm within which they functioned, but also from the remains of Polish 1830s-style liberalism and Slovak-imported pan-Slavism. Historians such as Mykola Kostomarov and Panteleimon Kulish followed the pattern of a Romantic return to ethnic roots (which in the case of Ukraine frequently meant a celebration of their Cossack ancestry), and around 1848 participated in a liberal, pan-Slavic initiative, the 'Brotherhood of Saints Cyril and Methodius'. Although that Brotherhood was quickly disbanded by the tsar's secret police, the idea of a separate Ukrainian nationality and historical experience was cautiously maintained through the following decades in Kostomarov's and Kulish's historical work, in their historical novels and in the historically inspired poetry of Taras Shevchenko, Ukraine's 'national poet'.[33]

---

[31]Generally, Kohn, *Pan-Slavism*. The correspondence between Šafařík and Palacký has been edited: *Korespondence Pavla Josefa Šafaříka s Františkem Palackým*, ed. Venceslava Bechynová and Zoe Hauptová (Praha, 1961).

[32]M. E. H. N. Mout, '"Vader van de natie": František Palacký (1798–1872)', in M. P. Bossenbroek, M. E. H. N. Mout and C. Musterd (eds), *Historici in de politiek* (Leiden, 1996), pp. 55–76; Jiří Štaif, 'František Palacký a česká historická pamět' (jublieum r. 1898)', in M. Řezník and I. Sleváková (eds), *Nations, Identities, Historical Consciousness: Volume Dedicated to Prof. Miroslav Hroch* (Prague, Charles University, 1997), pp. 229–50; J. F. Zacek, *Palacký: The Historian as Scholar and Nationalist* (The Hague, 1970). Alongside Palacký there is, of course, the no less arresting figure of Josef Jungmann (1773–1847), lexicographer and activist, author of a literary history (*Historie literatury i jazyka českého*, 1825; 2nd edn, 1849).

[33]G. S. N. Luckyj, *Panteleimon Kulish: A Sketch of His Life and Times* (New York, 1983). T. M. Prymak, *Mykola Kostomarov: A Biography* (Toronto, 1996). The importance of Kostomarov and Kulish as 'nation-builders' can be gauged from R. Lindheim and G. S. N. Luckyj (eds.), *Towards an Intellectual History of Ukraine: An Anthology of Ukrainian Thought from 1710 to 1995* (Toronto, 1996).

In the Ottoman Balkans, historians as nation-builders play a less prominent part. There is the Michelet-influenced Romanian rebel-historian Nicolae Bălcescu, who romantically spread the national myth of the great Romanian Prince Mihai the Brave;[34] the myth of the battlefield of Kosovo, so powerful in Serb nation-building, was likewise reinvigorated under Romantic inspiration; Bulgarian nationalism would have been unthinkable without the Ukrainian-born antiquary Juri Venelin, who practically invented (or at least was the first to identify) the Bulgarian nation in a series of 'historical-critical researches' (Moscow, 1829–41) on 'The Ancient and Present-day Bulgarians in Their Political, Ethnographic and Religious Relationship to the Russians'. Greece, of course, had a powerful school of national historians (exemplified by the name of Konstantinos Paparregopoulos) asserting the continuity of the Greek nation from classical times to the anti-Ottoman insurrection.[35]

Indeed, there was no corner of Europe unaffected by historicist nationalism and by nationalist historians. In the Baltic states we see the career of Jonas Basanavicius (1851–1927), author of a speculative antiquarian work on the Thracian roots of the Lithuanian nation, follow a pattern that uncannily mirrors the trajectory of Ireland's Douglas Hyde, from national cultural activism to political prominence.[36] In Finland the nationalist historian Georg Zacharias Forsman (1830–1903), author of a large Finnish national history (*Suomen kansan historia*, 1869–72) went as far as to Finnicise his family name

[34]On Bălcescu and the Mihai theme, see L. Boia, *History and Myth in Romanian Consciousness* (Budapest, 2001), and V. Stan, *Nicolae Bălcescu, 1819–1852* (București, 1977). On Bălcescu's successors as historian-politicians, see B. Jelavich, 'Mihail Kogalniceanu: Historian as Foreign Minister, 1876–8', pp. 87–105, and M. Pearton, 'Nicolae Iorga as Historian and Politician', pp. 157–73, bothj in Deletant and Hanak, *Historians as Nation-Builders*.
[35]E. Gazi, *Scientific National History: The Greek Case in Comparative Perspective (1850–1920)* (Frankfurt, 2000); K. S. Brown and Y. Hamilakis (eds), *The Usable Past: Greek Metahistories* (Lanham, MD, 2003); D. Kohler, 'Naissance de l'historiographie grecque moderne: auteur de l'*Histoire du peuple grec* (1861–1875) de Constantin Paparrigopoulos (1815–1891)', in M. Espagne and M. Werner (eds), *Philologiques, I: Contribution à l'histoire des disciplines littéraires en France et en Allemagne au XIXe siècle* (Paris, 1990), 279–309.
[36]A. E. Senn, *Jonas Basanavicius: The Patriarch of the Lithuanian National Renaissance* (Newtonville, MA, 1980); see also Senn's 'The Lithuanian Intelligentsia of the Nineteenth Century', in *National Movements in the Baltic Countries during the Nineteenth Century*, ed. A. Loit (Uppsala, 1985), pp. 311–15. For Lithuania, one should also mention Simanas Daukantas (1793–1864) and his idealistic *Istorija zemaitiska* ('History of Samogitia': written before 1838 and first published in serial form in a US Lithuanian newspaper, 1891–96). An excellent study of the historicist nationalism in Lithuania is V. Krapauskas, *Nationalism and Historiography: The Case of Nineteenth-Century Lithuanian Historicism* (New York, 2000).

to Yrjö Koskinen. He too turned to politics, as leader of an Old Finnish party dominating the Finnish senate.[37]

*

What does this *tour d'horizon* show us? Nineteenth-century historians across Europe took a prominent role in confirming or articulating their nation's identity. There is no nation in Europe that does not owe its sense of identity or even its existence to a historicist *prise de conscience*. Examples can be found from Iceland to Bulgaria and from Portugal to Finland. What is more, this historicist charge in so much national self-positioning and self-fashioning, universally prevalent as it is in Europe, seems far less salient in state formation beyond Europe. Romantic historicism may be a distinguishing feature that sets off European nationalism (culture-based, historicist) from national movements and nation-building in other parts of the world. Audacious and globalising as that extrapolation may be, it seems to be warranted by the close parallels between the many cases surveyed at least as a working hypothesis.

But the structural similarity between these many, very disparate cases also presents an intriguing challenge. How, indeed, can we account for these close and largely synchronous parallels within Europe, across such vast differences as exist between old, established states such as Portugal and Britain and newly emerging national aggregates such as Bulgaria and Finland, between modernised societies such as France and the Netherlands and pre-industrial, premodern societies such as Lithuania and Iceland?

A definitive answer must draw on a mass of comparative work yet to be undertaken: a charting of cross-border traffic and influences and further comparative national or regional case-typologies. By way of a first suggestion, one may venture the hypothesis that the spread of historicist nationalism and ethnic history writing follows an epidemic pattern, a contagion of ideas where notions, programmes, agendas and examples spread from origin to audience, which, once 'infected' with these ideas as 'receivers', can in turn spread them further by transmitting them to a second-order audience (and so on). Such an epidemiological spread of ideas (which can be defined as any communication

---

[37]Their anti-Swedish cultural agenda drove them into complicity with Russian rule. On Finland, see Aira Kemiläinen, 'Fiction and Reality in Writing of National History in Finland from the 19th Century on', in M. Řezník and I. Sleváková (eds), *Nations, Identities, Historical Consciousness: Volume Dedicated to Prof. Miroslav Hroch* (Prague, 1997), pp. 29–52. Generally for Finland and the Baltic region, see also M. Branch (ed.), *National History and Identity: Approaches to the Writing of National History in the North-East Baltic Region, Nineteenth and Twentieth Centuries* (Helsinki, 1999).

which turns the receiver of a message into a transmitting relay)[38] would ensure a very rapid dissemination of an historiographical or philological attitude across a primary network of scholars maintaining mutual contacts, thence across the second-order network of scholars with whom one's contacts maintain contact, and so on. The existence of such networks, and the exponentially increasing catchment potential and density from first-order (immediate) contacts to second-order contacts-of-contacts to third- and fourth-order meta-contacts, stands to reason and can be demonstrated by indicators such as correspondence, reviews of and references to each other's work, translations, citations, etc. The institutional infrastructure of modernisation may have affected Europe at different moments over the course of the nineteenth and twentieth centuries, but scholarly and literary networks spanned and linked countries and regions at different stages of their infrastructural development.

A case in point is a French translation (used by the Sorbonne professor Claude Fauriel) of Serb folksongs collected by the folklorist and 'nation-builder' Vuk Karadžić. The material in question reached Fauriel through a relay network involving a French translator (Elise Voiart) translating a German translation (by Therese von Jacob) based on Karadžić's texts as sponsored in Germany by Jernej Kopitar and encrusted with philological comments by Jacob Grimm and a historical disquisition by Leopold von Ranke. Voiart's translation was dedicated to François Guizot, sponsor of Fauriel's Sorbonne professorship.[39]

It was probably through reverberations, networks and relays like these that historians such as Ranke (and historian-politicians such as Guizot) became enmeshed in the cultural nationalism of activists such as Karadžić, literary writers such as Voiart and Von Jacob, and philologists such as Kopitar, Grimm and Fauriel. Much work, I repeat, is yet to be done to chart these networks and the communication flows across them, but it is obvious that all of Europe (old states and new, sovereign states and marginal regions, modernised and 'backward'), and all of Europe's historical profession and craft, were infected by a coherent set of ideas linking ethnic individuality and historical presence.

---

[38]D. Sperber, 'The Epidemiology of Beliefs', *Explaining Culture* (Oxford, 1996), ch. 4. Cf. also Sperber's *La Contagion des idées* (Paris, 1996).

[39]V. S. Karadžić, *Chants populaires des Serviens, recueillis par Wuk Stéphanowitsch* (Paris, 1834). See also M. Ibrovac, *Claude Fauriel et la fortune européenne des poésies populaires grecque et serbe: étude d'histoire romantique, suivie du Cours de Fauriel professé en Sorbonne (1831–1832)* (Paris, 1966).

Romantic as these ideas were in their provenance, they proved to have great penetrative power in politics and state formation.

*

Much as the notion of nationality and ethnicity could refer to many different types of ties that link a group into a collective whole (ties such as language, perceived descent, social intercourse, political system, shared territory), so too the historical investigation of 'the nation' could be undertaken by the most diverse branches of scholarship. Alongside social and political history writing, the collective past was investigated in other erudite endeavours such as archaeology, mythology, historical linguistics, historical geography, ethnographic history and literary history – endeavours which I will here designate as 'para-historical'. As we have seen, ethnic thought proliferated and ramified across all these specialisms and endeavours, but twentieth-century developments suggest that it maintained a more stubborn currency in the para-historical disciplines than in the type of social and political history writing that had become academically institutionalised by the late 1870s.

Some of the patterns outlined here seem, to some extent at least, peculiar to the nineteenth century. They arise as part of the scholarly climate of Romanticism, and unfold their greatest potential and appeal in the vogue of Romantic nationalism. In the period 1870–1914, the ethnic approach to national history is to be found among the popularisers and populist historians. By that time the academically established, professionalised section of the craft abandons the tendency towards ethnic generalisations. In Britain the mid-Victorian school that had glorified the Anglo-Saxon roots of the English nation (Froude, Kemble, Freeman, Greene)[40] dwindled without successors. Even in the fervently anti-German, revanchist climate of post-1871 France, a figure such as Camille Jullian is an exception. A Celtic archaeologist and pupil of Fustel de Coulanges, he was to gain a seat on the Académie française on the basis of his eight-volume *Histoire de Gaule*; but he was quite willing to use Gaulish antiquity for contemporary war propaganda and to see France as a continuation of Gaulish ethnicity in his wartime propaganda – witness publications such as *Le Rhin gaulois, le Rhin français* (1915), *Pas de paix avec Hohenzollern: à un ami du front* (1918), *La Guerre pour la patrie* (1919) and *De la Gaule à la France: nos origines historiques* (1920), books that show the

---

[40]H. A. MacDougall, *Racial Myth in English History: Trojans, Teutons, and Anglo-Saxons* (Hanover, NH, 1982); N. Stepan, *The Idea of Race in Science: Great Britain, 1800–1860* (London and Oxford, 1982).

imprint of the populist *gauloiserie* of Henri Martin and, ultimately, the legacy of Thierry.

It was into the fields of historical linguistics, archaeology and other para-historical disciplines that ethnic thought retreated.[41] Historians such as Huizinga might occasionally issue essays on 'the Dutch national character', the emphasis usually on explaining national patterns from historical circumstances rather than explaining historical patterns from national circumstances – the ethnic determinism, in other words, which had been so prominent a century previously, was receding. Not so, however, in the historical fields where non-written evidence predominated. In archaeology, the use of tribal categories such as 'Celtic', 'Romance/Latin', 'Slavic' and 'Germanic' remained operative; likewise in historical linguistics and philology. Maps were used to make inventories of the etymology of place names or the prevalence of certain linguistic patterns, and thence to extrapolate whether a given area had in earlier times been settled by tribe X or tribe Y, and what sediments had been left by the historical flux and reflux of conquering Celts, Romans and Germans. Cultural artefacts and grave-finds were habitually taken as a marker of a tribe's 'ownership', 'conquest' or 'occupation' of the site in question – never as a possible sign of trading traffic or gift exchange. Dialectologists drew military-style maps in which the arrows (signalling competing linguistic influences) clashed like armies on a battlefield; processes of linguistic influence were habitually described in terms of 'penetration', 'expansion' and 'resistance'. In a bilingual country such as Belgium, such matters had acute political relevance: whereas the historian Henri Pirenne saw Belgium's destiny as a perennial crossroads of 'Romance' and 'Germanic' Europe, his philological colleague Godefroid Kurth investigated the competing forces of westward-pushing Franks and an eastward-pushing Latinity; debates around the linguistic frontier in Belgium were directly influenced by such scholarly antiquarianism.[42] The contemporary political investment of debates over ancient tribal settlements and conquests is reflected in the contemporary issue of Macedonian antiquity, so strenuously contested by Athens and Skopje.

Nor was the persistence of ethnic historicism (such as it was) uniform across Europe. By the late nineteenth century, historical scholarship as academically

---

[41]There is by now a substantial body of research tracing the impact of ethnic essentialism in late nineteenth- and twentieth-century folklore, archaeology, and so on as practised in various European countries. To list these studies separately would offer interesting illustrative material for the European history of national and ethnic thought, but that is beyond the scope of this chapter.

[42]Cf. D. Lamarcq and M. Rogge, *De taalgrens: van de oude tot de nieuwe Belgen* (Leuven, 1996).

established was above all a history of the modern nation-state; it therefore tended to concentrate on patterns of state formation, on political and social developments. Ethnicity in the nineteenth century had forced itself on the historians' agenda largely as one of the fault-lines across Europe's multi-ethnic *ancient régime* states. Ethnicity meant, in other words, the extent to which Irish, Breton, Catalan, Czech, Finnish or Greek did not form part of Britain, France, Spain or the Habsburg, Russian or Ottoman empires. Ethnicity was a marker of exceptionalism; in the new nation-states as they had emerged between 1830 and 1918 it largely lost that function. Ironically, if we want to trace the twentieth-century survival of ethnic history – or of pronounced ethnicising trends in national history writing – we may have to look for them in the countries for whom the 1918 treaties constituted a national dismemberment (interwar Germany and Austria, Hungary, Russia and Turkey) and to some extent the former Ottoman countries which had seen traumatic territorial fluctuations between 1911 and 1922 (Bulgaria, Serbia, Greece, Turkey).[43]

In this context, a particular ethno-historical specialism has become known by its German appellation of *Volksgeschichte*. It was a type of archaeological geopolitics that flourished most egregiously in the climate of National Socialism – which itself did not, of course, emerge out of the blue in 1933 but had its roots into the Wilhelminian period and before. We can trace a manic Nazi farrago like Rosenberg's *Mythus des 20. Jahrhunderts* (1930) back to the *Grundlagen des neunzehnten Jahrhunderts* (1899) by Wagner's son-in-law, the English-born Houston Stewart Chamberlain, who in turn betrays the influence of Gobineau. Writings like those of Rosenberg and Chamberlain are not, of course, serious history. At best they are forms of cultural criticism trying to underpin an ideological *parti pris* with references to 'the past' and as such fit in with other quasi-historical lucubrations such as Max Nordau's *Entartung* (1892), Charles Maurras' *L'Avenir de l'intelligence* and Oswald Spengler's *Untergang des Abendlandes* (1918–22, grandiosely styled in its subtitle to contain 'Umrisse einer Morphologie der Weltgeschichte'). It was in sweeping disquisitions like these that the tendency was continued to see Europe as a battlefield of competing tribes and nations over the centuries. The genre flourished most outside the academy, or at least outside the academic history departments: among philologists and representatives of

---

[43]Cf. S. Berger, 'How Historians Tell Their Tales: Towards a Happy Eclecticism', *German History*, 23, 2 (2005), 397–404, esp. 402: 'where national historiographies were centred around the state, a particular territory or politics, there *Volksgeschichte* tended to be weak. It is not by chance that *Volksgeschichte* was particularly prominent in many of the newly founded states or eastern Europe'.

new fields of interest such as *Wesenskunde* and *Völkerpsychologie*;[44] and it infected, of course, the historical academic history writing as it underwent Nazi *Gleichschaltung* after 1933.

The National Socialist idea of nationality is more or less *sui generis*, and one had best call it by its self-styled appellation: *völkisch*. The nation in *völkisch* terms is a biological community, a race (though the concept *Volk* is narrower than *Rasse*: a *Volk* might be seen as the socio-political manifestation of a race). The history of the *Volk* is thoroughly determined in its larger patterns by its innate and cultivated temperament and by its purity and collective solidarity, and in its crises, by the willpower of its leaders and their capacity to understand the patterns and necessities of the historical juncture. Thus, the *völkisch* historical vision often concentrates on single, powerful historical figures and their entourage (Thomas Carlyle's biography of Frederick the Great of Prussia was one of Hitler's favourites), while there is also a tendency to go into large geo-anthropological abstractions. Karl Haushofer's notorious *Geopolitik* correlated national destinies with the geomorphological features of their areas of settlement and *Lebensraum*.[45] Similarly, the most typical exponent of *völkisch* history writing, the pursuit of *Volksgeschichte*, tended towards an historical geography of national settlements and migrations. The nomenclature of its specific applications tellingly links the principle of ethnicity to the equally ahistorical framework of space. *Volkstum-* and *Deutschtumforschung* (the study of nationality and Germanness) were really diachronic extensions to a national *Völkerpsychologie*; other branches hinged on the concepts of *Volk* and *Raum* (landscape-space): *Raumforschung, Volks- und Raumgeschichte*.

---

[44]*Völkerpsychologie* was established in 1860 through the *Zeitschrift für Völkerpsychologie* of Moritz Lazarus and Heymann Steinthal; it influenced later practitioners such as Wilhelm Wundt, author of a massive, ten-volume *Völkerpsychologie: Eine Untersuchung der Entwicklungsgesetze von Sprache, Mythus und Sitte* (1900–1920). Wundt also did his bit for the national cause with wartime propaganda such as *Über den wahrhaften Krieg* (1914) and *Die Nationen und ihre Philosophie: Ein Kapitel zum Weltkrieg* (1915). The legacy of this 'ethnic psychology' was taken into American anthropology by Franz Boas and can still be felt in the ethnic determinism that has continued to exist in the social sciences from Geoffrey Gorer to Geert Hofstede. Cf. I. Kalmar, 'The Völkerpsychologie of Lazarus and Steinthal and the Modern Concept of Culture', *Journal of the History of Ideas*, 48 (1987), 671–90; G. Welz, 'Die soziale Organisation kultureller Differenz: zur Kritik des Ethnosbegriffs in der anglo-amerikanischen Kulturanthropologie', in H. Berding (ed.), *Nationales Bewußtsein und kollektive Identität: Studien zur Entwicklung des kollektiven Bewußtseins in der Neuzeit*, 2 (Frankfurt, 1994), 66–81.
[45]F. Ebeling, *Geopolitik: Karl Haushofer und seine Raumwissenschaft, 1919–1945* (Berlin, 1994). D. T. Murphy, *The Heroic Earth: Geopolitical Thought in Weimar Germany, 1918–1933* (Kent, OH, 1997).

These pursuits were of enormous importance in determining and abetting the policies of the Third Reich. Annexationist thought *vis-à-vis* the Netherlands or Belgium, or the policies of ethnic cleansing and colonial implantation in the Reich's conquered territories in the East, were academically legitimised by the treatises that came out of *Volksgeschichte*.[46] The importance of their political impact is, however, strangely counterbalanced by the obvious intrinsic worthlessness of these pseudo-scientific pursuits. *Volksgeschichte* was a dead-end, a deadweight, in the development of the human sciences: the hothouse flower of an intellectual climate where speculation could rampage freely, driven by fanatical ethnic chauvinism, and safeguarded from sceptical critique by the totalitarian state whose interests it served. The writings of the *völkisch* historians are of interest mainly for the light they shed on the intellectual climate of the Third Reich and the corruptibility of the academy.[47] But although the name and most extreme exponent of *Volksgeschichte* are German, its tendency to infuse ethnicism with a sense of historical geography was not. Manfred Hettling, in the introduction to a European survey, lists a number of elements which together configure the profile of *Volksgeschichte* and which separately were present in most European countries; whether or not something like *Volksgeschichte* emerged is to a large extent a matter of contingency: the presence of alternative socio-political institutions or perspectives. Italy, Poland and France were, for different reasons, unaffected by this form of history writing; it was more prominently present in Serbia and especially in Hungary;[48] in other countries, forms of historical ethnocentrism made themselves felt in different form. Again, when studying the methodology of workers in the field of *Westraumforschung* such as Franz Petri,[49] one must note that his tenets and tendencies are less derived from historical training or examples

[46]Cf. H. Derks, *Deutsche Westforschung: Ideologie und Praxis im 20. Jahrhundert* (Leipzig, 2001). The impact of *Volksgeschichte* in the Netherlands has been thematized in a special issue of the *Tijdschrift voor geschiedenis*, 118, 2 (2005), ed. B. Henkes and A. Knotter: *De Westforschung en Nederland*.
[47]W. Oberkrone, *Volksgeschichte: Methodische Innovation und völkische Ideologisierung in der deutschen Geschichtswissenschaft, 1918–1945* (Göttingen, 1993).
[48]M. Hettling (ed.), *Volksgeschichten im Europa der Zwischenkriegszeit* (Göttingen, 2003). The Hungarian case (not represented in Hettling's collection, but involving important representatives such as Bálint Hóman and Elemér Mályusz) is treated by Á. von Klimó, 'Volksgeschichte in Ungarn (1939–1945): Chancen Schwierigkeiten und Folgen eines "deutschen" Projekts', in M. Middell and U. Sommer (eds), *Historische West- und Ostforschung in Zentraleuropa zwischen dem Ersten und dem Zweiten Weltkrieg: Verflechtung und Vergleich* (Leipzig, 2004), pp. 151–78.
[49]K. Ditt, 'Die Kulturraumforschung zwischen Wissenschaft und Politik: das Beispiel Franz Petri (1903–1993)', *Westfälische Forschungen*, 46 (1996), 73–176.

than from philology: the mode in which Petri works comes straight from Romantic philologists such as Ernst Moritz Arndt and Jacob Grimm.

Volksgeschichte lost all intellectual credit after 1945, although in some instances it morphed into something calling itself *Strukturgeschichte*: an historical geography stressing social rather than ethnic patterns.[50]

*

Ethnic nationalism everywhere in Europe did entail, of course, a nationalist historiography imbued with the discourse and rhetoric of blood, race and descent. A complex case in point is 'Greater Netherlandism'. This ideology, which argued that, despite differences in religion and historical track-record, there remained a fundamental unity between Flanders and the Netherlands in the factor of a shared language, was encountered in ethnicist form among fascist movements such as the Dutch Nationaal-Socialistische Beweging and the Flemish Verdinaso, but also informed Catholic activists in the Netherlands who were inimical to fascism, such as Anton van Duinkerken, and the work of one prominent Dutch historian, Pieter Geyl, who was a staunch and outspoken anti-fascist. His *Geschiedenis van de Nederlandsche stam* (3 vols, 1930–59) broke the prevailing tendency to organise 'national' histories on the basis of state formation and instead chose to encompass the Netherlandic nation as a 'lineage', that is, on an ethnic rather than political basis. As this case shows, the legacy of ethnic thought in twentieth-century national history writing was not restricted to the extreme right, although it was found there in greater and more obnoxious density. Ethnicism was continued into the twentieth century also in those states which had found their independence or definitive outline only after 1918: in such cases 'nationhood' was still the overriding *telos* and guiding principle of history and historiography.

That is not to say that in such cases the term 'nation' was always necessarily used in an ethnic sense – we encounter it, rather, as a sort of trans-generational extension of the concept of society. In the terminology and discourse of twentieth-century history writing, the words 'society' and 'nation' appear to stand in a synchronic–diachronic relationship. The collectivity of a country's inhabitants at a given moment constitutes its *society*; the same collectivity maintained over a period of time is called the *nation*. Only in some cases, such as the

---

[50]The Austrian historian Otto Brunner (1898–1982) is a case in point. Cf. L. Raphael, *Von der Volksgeschichte zur Strukturgeschichte: die Anfänge der westdeutschen Sozialgeschichte, 1945–1968* (Leipzig, 2002).

Baltic countries or Greece, do we continue to encounter a prominent, anthropological sense of ethnicity in the writing of national histories.[51]

Apart, then, from the outgrowth of *Volksgeschichte* (and perhaps also in reaction to it), history writing in the twentieth century on the whole shows a retreat from the ethnicism of the previous century. For their research to some extent historians sought alternative frameworks to the national one. With the rise of cultural history and *Geistesgeschichte*, the emphasis had moved from the national context to thematic work on intellectual climates and currents; then, with the rise of the *Annales* school, the emphasis shifted again, but again tended to eschew the framework of nationality; finally, the rise of the new cultural history of Ginzburg, Darnton and Le Roy Ladurie has continued to explore studiously a-national modes of focusing their research interests.

It should not be forgotten that much of Europe was under communist rule for a considerable part of the twentieth century. While the communist notion of nationhood or *narodnost'* never completely expunged ethnicity from its rhetoric (the cultivation and presentation of folklore was, after all, part of communist propaganda, both for internal and external purposes), communist historiography naturally worked in socio-economic rather than ethnic terms. Marxist anti-nationalism also affected the very important tradition of left-wing historiography in Western Europe. Following the impact of structuralism and poststructuralism in the 1960s, identities such as nationality and ethnicity came to be seen not as extra-historical categories, but as constructs, which the historian should deconstruct rather than take for granted. Ernest Gellner's idea that national identity was the product, not the precondition, of the nationalist ideology was echoed by historians, who in the 1970s and 1980s demonstrated time and again the invented and constructed nature of traditions and nationalities.

All this might seem to indicate that the ethnic mode of national history writing formed part of Romantic nationalism, dwindled by the end of the nineteenth century and survived into the twentieth century only in (a) the 'new states', which owed their existence and sovereignty to nineteenth-century nationalist movements, (b) the deranged continuation of Nazi *Volksgeschichte*, and (c) the verbal trappings of an ingrained ethnic discourse (the clichéd vocabulary of race, blood and lineage) which maintained, for a while, a threadbare and not very meaningful currency – until it was tabooed by its associations with National Socialism.

[51]A. Kemiläinen, *Finns in the Shadow of the 'Aryans': Race Theories and Racism* (Helsinki, 1998); R. Clogg, 'The Greeks and Their Past', in Deletant and Hanak, *Historians as Nation-builders*, pp. 15–31.

Nonetheless, some vestiges of ethnic thought remain, sometimes latently. There is still a natural assumption on the part of many historians that their natural constituency is their own nation. The viewpoints collected in *Historians and Social Values*[52] show that historians tend to see their role and responsibility primarily as accounting for their own nation's past for the benefit of their compatriots. That a British historian such as John Julius Norwich or Owen Chadwick might write the history of Byzantium, Venice or the papacy seems almost like a singularity, an exception to the historian's default preoccupation with his or her national history.

Moreover, the deconstructive nature of historians' preoccupations with national traditions and nationality seems of late to have shifted somewhat. Following Nora's epoch-making *Les Lieux de mémoire*, the trappings of identity formation at the level of symbolism and remembrance have become a topic in history that is studied increasingly sympathetically. The acerbic denunciations of counterfactual fraud that we saw in Hobsbawm and Ranger's *The Invention of Tradition*[53] have made way for a more mellow, appreciative and only slightly ironical interest in the way in which human societies shape their memories and their past in a creative and almost poetical process of remembrance. Ethnicity is now automatically understood to be a construct, no longer needs to be denounced or deconstructed as such, and under the proviso of its constructed nature the concept is gaining new legitimacy as an operative factor in history. If the popularity of historical exhibitions and collections on nineteenth-century nationalist culture and kitsch are anything to go by,[54] we may be entering, in other words, a post-deconstructive phase where, informed by identity politics, the topic of 'ethnicity as a human construct' may come to enjoy quite as much appeal as did the topic of 'ethnicity as a human category' a century and a half ago.

---

[52]J. Leerssen and A. Rigney (eds), *Historians and Social Values* (Amsterdam, 2001).
[53]E. J. Hobsbawm and T. Ranger (eds), *The Invention of Tradition* (Cambridge, 1983).
[54]For example, M. Flacke (ed.), *Mythen der Nationen: ein europäisches Panorama* (München and Berlin, 1998); J. Blokker et al., *Het voorouder-gevoel: de vaderlandse geschiedenis met schoolplaten van J. H. Isings* (Amsterdam, 2005).

5
Religion, Nation and European Representations of the Past

James C. Kennedy

'When the Napoleonic adventure was at an end,' wrote Benedetto Croce (1866–1952) in his *History of Europe in the Nineteenth Century*, 'among all the peoples hopes were flaming up and demands were being made for independence and liberty.' In Europe and elsewhere 'oppressed nations' began to resist foreign rulers, and in countries such as England too, pressure mounted for 'a general modernisation and rationalisation' that would 'ensure a freer and more generous way of life and of progress'. All these national developments were 'linked in a single chain' inspired, as Croce argued, by 'the religion of liberty'. Many testified to the truth of the new ideal: 'poets, theorists, orators, publicists, propagandists, apostles and martyrs'. Across the barricades and battlefields of Europe, 'the "missionaries" of liberty had as companions the "crusaders" of liberty'.[1] The new religion set itself against the old religions, but also 'summed them up in itself and went further'. As the religion of liberty ascended it was as if the age of the spirit – that Third Age prophesied by Gioacchino da Fiore in the thirteenth century – had been born.[2]

Croce did not deny the fact that 'opposing religious faiths', although now 'surpassed', continued to constitute 'important historical realities' in the nineteenth century. And it was the Catholic Church that loomed particularly large as an antagonist for the Italian historian. However, Croce knew that the future did not

---

[1]But the new religion, according to Croce, did not include 'personifications, myths, legends, dogmas, rites, propitiations, expiations, priestly classes, pontifical robes', since such elements 'do not belong to the intrinsic, and are taken out from particular religions and set up as requirements for every religion with ill effect': B. Croce, *History of Europe in the Nineteenth Century*, trans. Henry Furst (New York and Burlingame, 1963 [1933]), p. 18. For Croce, liberty was a universal spirit that required no such external manifestations. This is a rather startling contrast with the prevailing view today of historians, who concern themselves with political religion and the 'sacralisation' of nations.

[2]Croce, *History of Europe in the Nineteenth Century*, pp. 3–19.

lie with the Church: 'thought and science continued to slip from her ... her womb was stricken with sterility as if by divine punishment for having sinned against the spirit'. This was particularly true, he held, of Catholic efforts to represent the past:

> Above all, the historiography of Catholic sympathisers when compared to that of the liberal side revealed in manifest fashion the poverty to which Catholic thought had been reduced, and even its triviality and puerility ... [I]t is well known that the Church considered the entire course of modern history as nothing but horrible perversion, and attributed the authorship and the guilt of so much evil to the Luthers and the Calvins, the Voltaires and the Rousseaus, and other 'corrupters', and to 'sects', which, she said, by weaving secretly a web of intrigues, had gained a temporary and diabolical triumph. In short, instead of history, she busied herself with telling fairy stories of ogres to frighten children.[3]

There is much one could say about this text, and not least about Croce's particular understanding of religion, defined by him simply as 'a conception of reality'.[4] The Italian intellectual believed that 'lay religion' must find its meaning not in transcendence but, as Edmund Jacobetti summarised it, 'in man, in his society, and his nation'.[5] But I find the passages compelling because in them Croce helps us frame important patterns concerning the ways in which nineteenth- and twentieth-century European historians (defined here as professional historians, as well as historically engaged intellectuals and public figures who have sought to contribute discursively to a public understanding of the past) have chosen to represent the relationship between religion and nation.

The first pattern concerns the extent and ways in which religion in the modern period ceased to constitute by itself an important part of the master narrative of nation – that it is no longer, as Croce implied, part of the real story. In a word, it is the question of to what extent traditional religion – typically a once privileged confession or church – was 'disestablished' and placed in a subordinate position to the 'real' master narrative of the nation, which now claimed to be more universal in scope than the mere 'sectarian' character of confession. Religion might yet be respected as an important and even positive historical force – as with Hegel, Croce's sense of *Aufhebung* included an

---

[3]Croce, *History of Europe in the Nineteenth Century*, p. 23.
[4]Croce, *History of Europe in the Nineteenth Century*, p. 27.
[5]E. E. Jacobetti, *Revolutionary Humanism and Historicism in Modern Italy* (New Haven and London, 1981), p. 120.

appreciation of religion's past achievements – but it was vital to recognise that traditional religion now had become secondary to a grander narrative, that is, to the 'transconfessional master narratives' of nation.[6] This process in which historians regarded the nation as superseding conventional religious and ecclesiastical boundaries often corresponded closely with the professionalisation of historians, whose own emerging standards of objectivity were partly defined by bracketing religious commitments in favour of the 'scientific' codes that ostensibly marked scholarly communities. Thus accounts of the past in which religion functioned as the central force became, if not exactly 'fairy tales', at least secondary or even marginal contributions to the telling of the (national) past. In this way, the surpassing of religion by nation effectively led over time to the 'secularisation' of many national narratives, in which religion was partly or wholly excluded from the main story.

The marginalisation and, increasingly in the course of the twentieth century, the exclusion of religion from the national master narrative is a complex issue for several reasons. In the first place, representations of the past are not produced only by historical professions, but by a variety of historically minded actors whose construction of the national past has sometimes been less 'secular' than the professionals. In the second place, the degree to which marginalisation took place depends in part on where one looks. Specifically, the 'rediscovery' of religion as a constitutive element in nation-building typically has been accompanied by a new interest in national commemorative cultures rather than in the academy itself, though the boundary between the two has hardly been absolute. The 'religious' has, for obvious reasons, often been more visible at the ceremonies and shrines of the nation-state than on the pages of much professional historical writing. In this sense, the shift in intellectual focus in recent years from 'history' to 'memory' (to use the well-worn distinction) has made the past seem more religious than it once appeared. Third, the current tendency to define religion as a fluid form of identification rather than as a fixed subscription to 'dogma' has problematised the notion of 'secularisation' by transforming religion into a more ubiquitous presence in European societies than earlier definitions had permitted.[7] Contemporary historians thus are more likely to see the religious assumptions and contours of ideas and practices once considered 'secular.' Finally, the variations in national experience and in the construction of national historiographies, from Turkey to Iceland, must give anyone pause in maintaining, as Croce did, that religion

---

[6]See Heiss et al., this volume (chapter 14).
[7]For a description of this general turn, see U. Altermatt, *Katholizismus und Moderne: zur Sozial- und Mentalitätsgeschichte der Schweizer Katholiken im 19. und 20. Jahrhundert* (Zurich, 1989), pp. 90–1.

has been in decline in Europe since the Napoleonic age. We must be careful, in summary, to heed the observation of Peter van der Veer that the assumptions about the interrelatedness of 'secularisation' and 'modernisation' are above all a reflection of the hopes of many secular intellectuals since the nineteenth century.[8] But it is also for that reason that we must take seriously that important strand in historiography in which religion was portrayed as no longer central to representations of the nation. To what extent, since the nineteenth century, and in which European countries, did new kinds of historical consciousness, particularly among historians, result in the eclipse of religion from master narratives of the nation?

This leads to a second related pattern: if historians could downplay, even ignore, traditional religion in order to narrate the nation, they could also amplify or transform religion in order to magnify it. In other words, we also need to focus on the way that representations of the past forged a symbiotic relationship between religion and nation that resulted in a 'holy nation'. In extreme cases, some have argued, this led to a wholly immanentised 'political religion' that served a 'deified nation' – most infamously in Hitler's Germany or Mussolini's Italy.[9] But in less extreme cases, too, the nation was 'sacralised', and religion 'nationalised', generating historical visions that underscored, in varying ways, the 'elect' character and calling of a nation. Croce's identification with 'the religion of liberty' restrained him from direct sympathy for any narrow 'cult of nationalism';[10] his *History*, after all, was composed in fascist Italy, under a regime for which he had no affection. But his willingness to conceive of modern ideology as a 'religion' is indicative of a recurring pattern in European historiography that has interpreted ostensibly secular political movements and national ideologies as religious expressions, 'civil', 'political' or otherwise. The focus here includes those historians who have analysed this phenomenon but also those engaged in this sacralising process: how did they contribute, within the contexts of their various countries, to the sacralisation of nation? And, I think it is important to add, how did historians and other intellectuals consciously seek to contribute to the 'desacralisation' of the nation? This has been an important historiographical trend in some countries since 1918, but especially since 1945.

---

[8]P. van der Veer, *Islam en het 'beschaafde Westen'* (Amsterdam, 2002), p. 65.

[9]Cf. the Irish intellectual C. C. O'Brien's tripartite distinction between increasingly dangerous forms of nationalism (chosen people, holy nation, deified nation) in *God Land: Reflections on Religion and Nationalism* (Cambridge, MA and London, 1988), pp. 41–2. The term 'political religion' was first worked out by Eric Voegelin in the late 1930s with his *Die politischen Religionen* and has enjoyed a modest renaissance in recent years; see later in the chapter.

[10]Croce, *History of Europe in the Nineteenth Century*, p. 16.

A third issue focuses on the extent to which the rise of the nation generated spaces in which the religious meanings of that nation were contested. Croce's 'important historical realities' – chiefly the persistence of political Catholicism – were more important than he believed. Indeed, nineteenth-century Europe was a 'second confessional age',[11] where traditional religious belief played an important role in how the nation – and its past – should be constituted.[12] The creation of the nation-state not only was shaped by older theological debates but actually intensified – not weakened – traditional religious commitments.[13] Religion was, therefore, by no means a plastic, pre-modern substance that proponents of the modern nation could mould or discard at will. Rather, historians and the arbiters of memory contended with their fellow citizens – and with their fellow believers – over the religious meaning of the nation, and did this for longer (arguably from well before Napoleon until well into the twentieth century, even to the present day) than is often assumed.

In summary, then, this chapter will offer an overview by means of the interrelationship between representations of the past and constructions of both nation and religion. It does so by asking three questions:

1 How and when did historians understand the nation (or later, 'society') as surpassing traditional religion in their efforts to narrate the nation and in their construction of the profession?
2 How did representations of the past attempt to reconstruct religion as an important means of sacralising the nation?
3 In what ways have historians disputed with each other over the ways in which religion and nation have been depicted?

Supersession, sacralisation, conflict: these are the issues that will frame this general survey of how historians have constructed the relationship between religion and nation. This short overview has the pretension of universality – of covering all the national historiographies of Europe – but such a claim will not bear full scrutiny. As an American specialising in postwar Dutch history my vistas are limited and my perspective privileges northern and western Europe. This limiting perspective includes the German-speaking countries of Europe,

---

[11]O. Blaschke, 'Das 19. Jahrhundert: Ein Zweites Konfessionelles Zeitalter?', *Geschichte und Gesellschaft*, 26 (2000), 38–75.

[12]See H-G, Haupt and D. Langewiesche (eds), *Nation und Religion in Europa: Mehrkonfessionelle Gesellschaften im 19. und 20. Jahrhundert* (Frankfurt, 2004), for the theme of religious conflict over the nation.

[13]For an example of how this proved to the case in late nineteenth-century Netherlands, see I. de Haan, *Het beginsel van leven en wasdom: de constitutie van de Nederlandse politiek in de negentiende eeuw* (Amsterdam, 2003).

where the relevant historiography is particularly rich. This chapter thus chooses to rely considerably on the specific insights of the national and regional specialists whose chapters make up most of this volume. Their insights make it possible for me to attempt an historiographical overview of the continent, an attempt which hopes to convey something of the richness and diversity that the place of religion has possessed in the construction of a nation, not least in the narratives of national historians in recent centuries.

Supersession

One year after the Catholic Emancipation Act of 1829, the English poet Samuel Taylor Coleridge published *On the Constitution of Church and State*, in which he outlined the distinction between the universal Christian Church and the 'national church'. The latter, as he envisaged it, was to be 'a great national guild of the learning professions', led by theology but including all the liberal arts and sciences. This learned group constituted the 'clerisy' of the nation, the 'true Church of England' which historically deserved the highest praise because of its learning and its toleration, as well as for its ecclesiastical traditions.[14]

Coleridge's idea that the 'national church' was something other than the Church Universal is illustrative of wider European patterns, especially in the nineteenth century, to create a non-sectarian though often Christian understanding of the nation. Historians often played an important role in the 'clerisy' of the 'national church', offering new interpretations of the nation and its religious identity. Indeed, one might say that during 'historiography's "Golden Age"' of the nineteenth century historians partially replaced philosophers and theologians in public influence.[15]

Nineteenth-century liberal narratives: religious inclusion

It remains striking how crucial European Protestant historians were in setting the tone for national historiographies of the nineteenth century. It was not only that their national (as opposed to the Catholic international) ecclesiology made it easier for them to function within a 'national church', but nineteenth-century bourgeois Protestantism, with its typical emphasis on both the inner spiritual life and public duties, arguably made it easier for them to reconcile broad religious

---

[14]S. C. Taylor, *On the Constitution of Church and State*, ed. John Colmer, *The Collected Works of Samuel Taylor Coleridge*, 10 (Princeton, NJ, 1976); C. Welch, *Protestant Thought in the Nineteenth Century*, vol. 1, *1799–1870* (New Haven, CT, 1972), pp. 121–3.
[15]E. Breisach, *Historiography, Ancient, Medieval and Modern* (Chicago, 1983), pp. 261–2.

sentiment with concrete national allegiances.[16] What is important to stress here is that these non-doctrinaire Protestant historians, as 'nation-building elites', sought to create a master narrative of the past that the whole nation could underwrite.[17] They did not see themselves chiefly as religious or political antagonists, but as impartial arbiters of historical truth.[18] And in part because they tended (by their own lights at least) to be less religiously doctrinaire, they sometimes considered their own history to be more objective and truthful than accounts rendered by more traditional religious observers. One of the key elements of this objectivity, in fact, was the ability to conceive of history in a way that consciously transcended 'sectarian' readings of the past. A good example of this mentality can be found in the Dutch liberal Protestant historian Robert Fruin. He made his mark in the late nineteenth-century Netherlands both by insisting that historical studies should be objective and impartial and by repudiating the earlier view that religion played the central role in the Dutch Revolt: rather, he said, it was a national struggle for liberty in which Catholics and Protestants alike had had a stake.

This consciously non-doctrinaire religious stance among Protestant historians took root in those countries where the Protestant 'clerisy' enjoyed a privileged social, cultural and political position, and felt largely secure over and against other religious groupings. It may be questioned whether historians of the Scandinavian countries are part of this pattern. Their collective outlook was often liberal, politically and religiously, but the nearly monolithic position of just one confession, Lutheranism, rendered the need to transcend confessional religion for the sake of building the nation-state much less pressing. Rather, it was Protestant historians who enjoyed a privileged place in religiously mixed countries who typically expressed this attitude, namely, those active in Great Britain, Germany, the Netherlands and Switzerland. In Britain, a mild-mannered religious outlook determined the historical views of the mostly Christian, mostly Anglican, 'Whig' historians throughout the nineteenth century. In the German-speaking world, Ranke, Droysen and Burckhardt had as students each studied at Protestant theological faculties and this would have profound effects on the contours of what emerged as historicism. Some (Ranke, Sybel and Droysen) would still point to Providence ('the finger of God') in

---

[16]See P. van Rooden, 'History, the Nation and Religion: The Transformations of the Dutch Religious Past', http://www.xs4all.nl/~pvrooden/Peter/publicaties/1999a.htm.
[17]This phrase is used by Oliver Zimmer in relation to the Swiss situation: Zimmer, *A Contested Nation: History, Memory and Nationalism in Switzerland, 1761–1891* (Cambridge, 2003), pp. 210–11.
[18]See also G. G. Iggers, 'Nationalism and Historiography, 1789–1996: The German Example in Historical Perspective', in S. Berger, M. Donovan and K. Passmore (eds), *Writing National Histories* (London, 1999), p. 19.

history, and this was not accidental; as Thomas Albert Howard has pointed out, people such as Hegel and Ranke softened the intellectual crisis of Christian orthodoxy by 'attributing [to] historical immanence a religious character' – an insight that helps explain the central importance of (national) history writing for well-educated and often pious Protestants, who in earlier times might have ended up as clergymen.[19] In any event, it was Protestants who dominated the German historical profession until the 1960s, when the last high-profile exponent of this tradition, Gerhard Ritter, went into retirement.[20] In Switzerland and the Netherlands, Protestant historians with a consciously non-doctrinaire mentality set the tone for their respective national historiographies in universities such as Leiden or the new 'national' university in Zurich. But in Protestant-minority regions, too, Protestant historians sometimes took a key role, at least for a time, in establishing a religiously irenic narrative of the nation. In France the chief proponent of this vision was Guizot. In the years before 1848 he linked the history of France with the story of liberty (which he believed found its origins in Protestantism), and at the same time articulated a broad religious identity for France that was neither authoritarian Catholic nor anticlerical.[21]

Even in countries where Protestant minorities were less well established, Protestant historians still sometimes played an important role in developing a collective national narrative that was trans-confessional in character. In Slovakia historians – drawn disproportionately from the Lutheran minority – constructed an irenic vision of the nation's past, often with the approval of their counterpart Catholics, who felt a common cause with Slovakian Protestants in defining a national identity against external forces.[22] In what became Latvia, it was another group of Protestants – the Moravians – who were over-represented among the historians. In a religiously mixed country where the majority Lutheranism was too closely tied to the Baltic German elites, it is perhaps not surprising that historians stemming from this pietistic, non-doctrinaire sect figured so prominently in the writing of Latvian national history.[23]

---

[19]M. Bentley, *Modern Historiography: An Introduction* (London, 1999), p. 65; T. A. Howard, *Religion and the Rise of Historicism: W.M.L. de Wette, Jacob Burckhardt and the Theological Origins of Nineteenth-Century Historical Consciousness* (Cambridge, 2000), pp. 5, 9.

[20]See Frey and Jordan, this volume (chapter 8); Iggers, 'Nationalism and Historiography', pp. 19–20, 28.

[21]G. Lefebvre, *La Naissance de l'historiographie moderne* (Paris, 1971), pp. 182–3; C. Crossley, 'History as a Principle of Legitimation in France (1830–1848)', in Berger et al., *Writing National Histories*, pp. 49–56.

[22]See analysis presented in Heiss et al., this volume (chapter 14).

[23]D. Hanovs, 'Latvia', paper prepared for Representations of the Past: The Writing of National Histories in Europe. Glamorgan, Wales, 21 May 2004.

It is therefore important to note the striking role that Protestant historians played in the development of both the historical profession and in the great national narratives of the nineteenth century. But the Protestant contribution in creating a consciously trans-confessional master narrative should not be overstressed. In the first place, nineteenth-century Protestant historians could also develop a more confessionally combative stance, focused not on the transcendence of religion but on asserting a consciously Protestant view of the nation. I shall say more about this in the next two sections, but suffice it here to say that German Protestant historians consisted not only of the likes of Ranke but also of Treitschke, who in the wake of the *Kulturkampf* was anything but vaguely inclusive. Similarly, Fruin in the Netherlands had his counterpart in the historian Groen van Prinsterer, who insisted, in contrast to Fruin, that the Netherlands was a Protestant (or more precisely, a Calvinist) country. And if Slovakian Protestant historiography was religiously irenic, this was much less true of the Protestant-dominant historical professions in the neighbouring Czech lands and in Hungary, where anti-Catholic, anti-Austrian and anti-Habsburg sentiment was strong.[24]

In the second place, it is vital to note that historiographical impulses which stressed the desirability of creed and traditional religious commitments were hardly restricted to Protestant historians alone. In a parallel vein, Jewish historiographers of the nineteenth and early twentieth centuries, from Jost to Philippson, told the story of the emancipation of the Jewish nation without placing much emphasis on religious traditions.[25] Furthermore, a less confessional interpretation of the nation also had its Orthodox and Catholic proponents. This pattern was perhaps most influential in the early nineteenth century, before the ethnicisation of religion had reached its zenith, and before the clerical/anticlerical conflict made non-doctrinaire Christianity more problematic as a unifying concept. In Greece this non-sectarian impulse was articulated at the very end of the eighteenth century by the Jacobin historian Rigas Velestinlis, who articulated a trans-confessional vision of Greece. The early nineteenth-century Serbian reformer and intellectual Vuk Karadžić had attempted to unite Serbia on the basis of language, not religion. Bishop and historian Josip Juraj Strossmayer of Djakovo in Croatia, whose long life extended across most of the nineteenth century, believed, even as he fought for Croatian rights within the Habsburg empire, that Serb and Croat, Orthodoxy and Catholicism, could be united in true nationalism and true Christianity.[26] One of Kossuth's associates in the mid-

---

[24]Heiss et al., this volume (chapter 14).
[25]See Wyrwa, this volume (chapter 19).
[26]See C Millas, this volume (chapter 18); S. Alexander, 'Religion and National Identity in Yugoslavia', in S. Mews (ed.), *Religion and National Identity* (Oxford, 1982), p. 597.

nineteenth century, the important Hungarian historian and bishop Mihály Horváth, also held to a Hungarian freedom that included the emancipation of Jews, even as he defined Hungarian religiosity over and against the Orthodox East.[27] In Western Europe the renowned British historian Lord Acton managed to combine his Catholicism with a liberal view of the nation during the last decades of the nineteenth century.[28]

As in Protestant countries, liberal historians in Catholic-dominant nations, even those with an anticlerical slant, often did not exclude religion from the national story, but sought to relativise its absolute claims by making religion merely part of their national narratives. The younger Michelet included Catholicism as part of the story of France, before a *volte-face* in the 1840s. Some Spanish liberal historians stressed the positive contributions of Catholicism; others, like Altamira, admired the sophistication of Islamic culture in Iberia, and understood Spanish history as the distillation of Christian, Islamic and Jewish influences.[29] By the 1880s, Spanish historiography was in the hands of secularly minded historians, some of whom made the religious history of Spain an integral part of the wider national narrative they were telling. Anticlerical historians who dominated the historical profession in France by the Second Empire and Spain by the 1880s could also make use of the religious past to construct a consciously secular narrative of the nation. As Croce noted, the liberal ideal could not reject its own 'historical genesis', and demonstrated 'an attitude of impartiality, regard, respect and even reverence' for the Catholicism which it had 'surpassed'.[30] Religion as such did not need to be rejected while representing the past, but dogmatism and clericalism had to be opposed because their own proprietary claims on the past conflicted with the no less proprietary claims of national liberal historians.

For many historians, whether in Protestant, Catholic or Orthodox countries, nations as political agents had surpassed doctrinaire religious faith as the motor of history. The eminent Anglo-Irish historian W. E. H. Lecky observed in the 1860s that the Christian nations of Europe had opted to side with the Islamic Ottoman empire rather than with Christian Russia, which he interpreted as a sign that religion no longer set the agenda in the age of nations.[31] Religion might yet play a role in national life (as it indisputably had in the past), but as a part, within a larger narrative. And by placing religion within

---

[27]See I. Deák, 'Historiography of the Countries of Eastern Europe: Hungary', *American Historical Review* (October 1992), 1046; Heiss et al., this volume (chapter 14).

[28]Drawn from R. Hill, *Lord Acton* (New Haven, 2000).

[29]Drawn from Matos and Álvarez, this volume (chapter 13).

[30]Croce, *History of Europe in the Nineteenth Century*, p. 25.

[31]Cited in O. Chadwick, *The Secularization of the European Mind in the Nineteenth Century* (Cambridge, 1976), p. 135.

the framework of the question *Qu'est-ce qu'une nation?* historians such as Renan – himself a former seminarian – made religion subservient to the story of the nation itself.

One might conclude by observing that the rise of nationally minded clerisies across Europe – and more specifically, of nationally minded historians – had at least a couple of effects on the way that historical research was ordered in respect to religion. In constructing the nation as a supra-confessional entity (however implicitly confessional such aspirations may have remained), it offered, to varying degrees, an opportunity for religious minorities (or underrepresented majorities) to participate in the master national-narrative and in national institutions, and to participate more fully in intellectual life. By the early twentieth century, for example, many Hungarian historians were of Jewish origin.[32] But this process took a long time – in many countries, it was well into the twentieth century before religious background played no role in determining the professional history cadres of a nation.

At the same time, the primacy of *national* history, and often of the political history of the nation, tended to define religious history down to a narrower sub-field: as Keith Robbins notes in this volume, church history in the British Isles was a field tangential to national history writing.[33] Self-consciously confessional historians also did not participate as equals in the national paradigm; the 'clerisy' of the 'national church', often liberal in religious orientation or those without professed religion, set the standards of the profession, and hence, to an important degree, the definitions of the nation.

Twentieth-century secular historiographies: the marginalisation of religion

Over the long run religion, now relegated to a constituent part of the nation, faded from view as the 'clerisy' of the 'national church' – including professional historians – immanentised its theological assumptions and set its sights on the things below. Secularly minded historians, such as the late nineteenth-century Frenchman Taine, saw a place reserved for the intellect of a 'secular clergy' which might guide modern democracies.[34] As organised religion seemed to lose its grip

---

[32]Deák, 'Historiography', p. 1048.
[33]See Robbins, this volume (chapter 9); K. Robbins, 'Institutions and Illusions: The Dilemma of the Modern Ecclesiastical Historian', in,idem, *History, Religion and Identity in Modern Britain* (London and Rio Grande, 1993), pp. 75–83.
[34]S. Jones, 'Taine and the Nation-State', in Berger et al., *Writing National Histories*, pp. 92–3. Given Coleridge's views it is interesting to note, as Jones does, that Taine admired the Church of England as an institution which generated the kind of clergy of whom he approved.

on public life, and as society became more religiously pluralistic, professional historians, themselves shaped by a consciously 'scientific' mindset, no longer saw religion as an essential component of history, or at least of national history. This trend was evident in Western Europe in countries such as Britain, France and Germany by the end of the nineteenth century, and more virulently in Soviet-dominated Eastern Europe after 1945.

There are, in fact, three distinct paths in which the marginalisation of religion developed within European historiographies in the course of the last century. In the first, *laicist historians determined to reject, downplay or ignore the role of religion in the national past*. This trend was already apparent in some anticlerical historians in Catholic Europe in the nineteenth century, but was most notable in some of the officially atheistic communist regimes of Eastern Europe, at least in those countries where religion was seen as a real threat to the nation as constructed by the communists. Some historians of communist Yugoslavia, perhaps most notably the Serb historian Milorad Ekmečić, castigated religion in general and Catholicism in particular for the failure of the Yugoslav nation to unite before 1918.[35] But anti-religious laicism in national history writing was confined neither to Catholic-dominant nor communist-dominated Europe; under laicist regimes such as that post-1923, official Turkish historiography endeavoured to find non-religious origins of the Turkish nation, whether in emphasising a pre-Islamic Central Asian past or a multi-religious 'Anatolian' one.[36]

A second path emerged in a number of Protestant-dominant countries where the tensions between religion and nation were less profound. In these societies with relatively little religious competition and little social and political mobilisation along religious lines, historians increasingly tended to ignore religion as unimportant, as opposed to consciously opposing or suppressing it. In Britain, however, the nation came to be understood in ostensibly inclusive secular values that went 'beyond' religious identity, a trend that went hand in hand with a tendency among British historians to take a reductionist view of religion.[37] In Norwegian historiography, which worked within the context of a virtually mono-confessional culture, the history of religion and church history 'received next to no attention' in the period after the Second World War.[38]

Finally, there was the path most typical of, though not restricted to, the mixed-confessional nations of Western Europe, in which religious history was

---

[35] I. Banac, 'Historiography of the Countries of Eastern Europe: Yugoslavia', *American Historical Review* (October 1992), 1090–1, 1102.
[36] See Millas, this volume (chapter 18).
[37] See Robbins, this volume (chapter 9).
[38] J. Simensen, 'National and Transnational History: The National Determinant in Norwegian Historiography', in F. Meyer and J. E. Myhre (eds), *Nordic Historiography in the 20th Century* (Oslo, 2000), p. 103.

essentially relegated, alongside church history, to those historians who maintained a strong identification with a particular religious community. This was the choice faced by Jewish historians in Germany – remain outsiders or abandon the aspects of their public activities, including the writing of history, which revealed their Jewish identity.[39] For the groups choosing to maintain their religious identity, perhaps the most common approach was to construct their own histories of what were now effectively 'subcultures' within a national framework. In Western Europe this was chiefly the fate of Catholic historiographies. In Switzerland, Catholics responded to the dominance of liberal Protestant historiography in part by developing supporting national narratives, and Dutch Catholics, for example, felt obliged to honour William the Silent, the founder of the Protestant state.[40] Participation in the nation-state could also mean, as was apparently the case of Italian Catholic historians after 1945, ignoring the difficulties of the past between church and state.[41]

Although it is helpful to note that there were three distinct paths by which religion was pushed to the margins of national historiographies, these static categories might suggest that professional historians continued to play in the twentieth century the same role in the national clerisy – and in national narratives – as they had in the nineteenth. This was not necessarily the case, however. In the first place, the clerisy as defined in a way that Coleridge would have recognised did survive, at least in many countries, well into the twentieth century. The most important development perhaps is the process of professionalisation, in which historians, increasingly trained as specialists (and thus reducing themselves to 'simple erudition', thought Croce),[42] became less interested in conceiving of themselves as part of a clerisy with high

[39]The place of Jews as outsiders in German history is widely contextualised in H-G. Haupt and D. Langewiesche (eds), *Nation und Religion in der Deutschen Nation* (Frankfurt, 2001).

[40]See, for example, the case of Belgium and the Netherlands in the contribution of F. Metzger, 'Die Reformation in der Schweiz zwischen 1850 und 1950', in Haupt and Langewiesche, *Nation und Religion in Europa*, and Beyen and Majerus, this volume (chapter 11). The Dutch Catholic historian L. J. Rogier remarked on the 'double loyalty' of Catholics to fatherland and the Catholic Church: see J. A. Bornewasser, 'Prof. dr. L. J. Rogier (1894–1974)', in P. A. M. Geurts and A. E. M. Janssen, *Geschiedschrijving in Nederland*, vol. 1 (The Hague, 1981), p. 375; reprinted from *Bijdragen en Mededelingen betreffende de Geschiedenis der Nederlanden*, 90 (1975), pp. 71–80.

[41]C. Pavone, 'Italy: Trends and Problems', *Journal of Contemporary History*, 2 (1967), 58–9; see also M. Clark, 'Gioacchino Volpe and Fascist Historiography in Italy', and R. Vivarelli, 'A Neglected Question', both in Berger et al., *Writing National Histories*, pp. 189–90 and 231–3.

[42]Croce, *History of Europe in the Nineteenth Century*, p. 258.

responsibilities to the nation-state. This was most true in the ethnically homogeneous nations of Western Europe whose existence or identity was not perceived as threatened, and where often the specialisation in the production of knowledge was most advanced. Speaking to the nation on any subject, religious or otherwise, seemed out of place in a Weberian world of 'intellectualisation' and 'rationalisation'.[43] Until the earlier twentieth century, for example, popular and professional history in Denmark had both been driven to tell the national story of Denmark, influenced in part by the national vision of the Lutheran clergyman Grundtvig expressed chiefly in the folk high schools. After that, however, the divide between profession and public widened, in part because professional historians consciously became more interested in debunking 'Nordic and national mythologies' than in creating grand national narratives.[44] It is not necessarily the case that professional historians completely lost their wider public function, or that the task of nation-building through (religiously shaped) national master narratives disappeared. In most countries with highly professionalised academies, prominent historians often continued to constitute part of a visible national elite. But in some nations at least, professional historians often did so with greater detachment, often leaving the grand national narratives, with or without a religious dimension, to the non-professionals.[45] In summary, consciously secularised, professionalised and frequently anti-nationalist historians were not particularly inclined to write narratives with a strong interest in either religion or nation, but were increasingly focused on the research agenda of a profession oriented to other questions.

This relates to a second factor in the decline of the 'national church:' the move in the early and mid-twentieth century away from both the nation and religion to the 'social', defined by Talal Asad as 'secular space, distinct from both state and religion', and the ostensible locus of 'real human life'.[46] The development of the *Annales* school in France at the end of the 1920s is a

---

[43]For a response to this characterisation of modernity, see H. Lehmann, 'Über die Varianten einer komplementären Relation: Die Säkularisierung der Religion und die Sakralisierung der Nation in 20. Jahrhundert', in Lehmann, *Protestantisches Christentum im Prozeß der Säkularisierung* (Göttingen, 2001), p. 81.

[44]F. Meyer, 'Social Structure, State Building and the Fields of History in Scandinavia', and C. T. Nielsen, 'Between Art and Scholarship: Danish Scholarly and Popular History in the 19th and 20th Centuries', both in Meyer and Myhre, *Nordic Historiography*, pp. 43–5 and 306–14.

[45]P. Kennedy, 'The Decline of Nationalistic History in the West, 1900–1970', in W. Laqueur and G. L. Mosse, *Historians in Politics* (London and Beverly Hills, CA, 1974), pp. 329–52.

[46]T. Asad, *Formations of the Secular: Christianity, Islam, Modernity* (Stanford, CA, 2003), p. 191.

famous example of this move (though it must be said that a later emphasis on mentalities opened up space again for religion as an important cultural factor). The *Annales* school's social orientation was truly transnational in scope, but 'society' in various national historiographies effectively served as a synonym for the 'nation-state'. In postwar Nordic historiography more generally and in Swedish history writing more specifically, 'society', for example, functioned as an implicitly normative statement about the superiority of a secularised, post-nationalist welfare state.[47] Similarly, the trend in Germany since the 1960s among left-of-centre historians, including the prominent Hans-Ulrich Wehler, towards social history also constituted national history in a new form. Here religion played a marginal historical role. In Jewish historiography up to the Second World War, the social story of emancipation was strongly emphasised by some historians. Furthermore, Marxist concerns for 'the social', an important current in postwar historiographies in many European countries, further consolidated this trend. This emphasis on the social in the postwar period – whether national or transnational in orientation – seemed often to be constructed on the assumptions of a secularisation thesis in which religion long had faded away in modern Western societies.

This development did not mean that these social historians necessarily abandoned all the aspirations of the nineteenth-century clerisy. For example, the *Historikerstreit* enjoined by Wehler and other progressive German social and political historians in the 1980s attempted to change the German public's understanding of German national history. Similarly, progressive revisionists in other countries also sought to reach the public by offering an alternative vision of their own nation's history. In defining this public task for themselves these historians resembled Coleridge's clerisy, however ambivalent or hostile they stood in relation to the nation-state, and however their professionalised orientation and style effectively cut them off from a wider public. In any event, religion seldom played an important role in these histories.

The 1980s and after: the return of the gods in European national historiographies?

Several developments in the last two decades point to a reversal of this trend towards marginalisation. In a very general way, the persistence of both religion and nation prompted not only historians to reinvestigate and reappraise the place of nation, religion and the relationship between the two. Here two broad trends have been noticeable. In the post-communist states of Eastern Europe, historians and the creators of public memory reconstituted national clerisies that seized new opportunities to reconstruct the national past, forging

---

[47]See Aronsson et al., this volume (chapter 10).

new narratives that in countries such as Hungary included a new role for religion as a force of resistance against Soviet domination.[48] In Western Europe broader research fields in the history of religion, initially from social sciences such as sociology, can be traced back to as early as the 1950s in France, when scholars of religion themselves began to define religion more broadly, and often, as in the case of Goff and Rémond, within a national framework.[49] And of course, there were always professional historians, such as the conservative German Thomas Nipperdey (the brother of the well-known theologian Dorothee Sölle), who distinguished himself from Wehler in the 1980s in part because of the relatively large role he assigned to religion in the German past.[50] A renewed interest in the constituent parts of the nation-state in part prompted non-confessional historians to develop multi-volume studies on religious subcultures in countries such as the Netherlands by the 1990s.[51] But perhaps above all, the appearance of many immigrants from many parts of the world – who often brought with them their own religious traditions – prompted many scholars, including historians, to understand (national) history less in terms of secularisation and more in terms of religious pluralisation. The new emphasis on the persistence of multiple religious voices in the national past – evident in some contributions to this volume – arguably bears some resemblance to some of the religiously irenic, nineteenth-century historians who interpreted national history in a transconfessional mode. Religion as an historical force is now, more than a quarter century on, part of the master narrative, but for many historians it remains a factor that is chiefly important for its contribution to a larger whole, whether 'the nation' or 'society'.

Sacralisation

This rediscovery of the importance of religion outlined above has enabled contemporary historians to see that religion was hardly absent from representations of the national past, and the secularisation that occurred probably happened later, and less thoroughly, than some have supposed. 'Faith and religion always have been constituent elements of European nations,' concluded one scholar in analysing an exhibition of nineteenth-century paint-

---

[48]One striking example of this is the role religion plays in depicting both Hungarian resistance and the oppression of the Soviet era in Budapest's Terror Háza, a museum housed in the former headquarters of the secret police.

[49]J. Le Goff and René Rémond, 'Préface', *Histoire de la France religieuse*, vol. 1 (Paris, 1988), p. 9; Rémond, 'France: Work in Progress', *Journal of Contemporary History*, 2/1 (1967), 35–48.

[50]See Frey and Jordan, this volume (chapter 8).

[51]See, for example, the concluding volume of the project: J. C. H. Blom and J. Talsma, *De verzuiling voorbij: godsdienst, stand en natie in de lange negentiende eeuw* (Amsterdam, 2000).

ings on the nation. Fully a quarter of the collection presented contained either direct or indirect references to Christianity.[52] Indeed, religion often served to sacralise the nation, not least in historical representation, especially if we expand our definition of historical representation to include commemorative culture. But however scholars conceive of historical representation, a crucial question continues to divide them: how broadly should religion be defined when outlining the means by which the nation's history was sacralised?

Political religion, civil religion and secular uses of a religious past

That nations, national ideologies and national representations of the past sometimes exhibited at least a quasi-religious character has been remarked on by various observers. By the mid-nineteenth century French historians such as de Tocqueville and Michelet perceived the religious dimensions of the French Revolution, and the latter thought that in the revolution 'the God of the nations has spoken through France'.[53] But it was not until the twentieth century that historians and political theorists began to conceive of nationalisms and ideologies as 'political religions'. This was in the 1930s and 1940s in particular, with the rise of the Third Reich and to a lesser extent because of developments in Soviet Russia. Friedrich Meinecke's *Die Deutsche Katastrophe* (1946) spoke of 'Hitlerreligion' and deemed both 'Hitlerism' and Marxism 'new beliefs'.[54] After a long period in which secular-minded historians ignored the concept, 'political religion' has re-emerged in recent years partly through the demonstrated potency of nationalism during the 1990s.

Whether 'political religion' is useful as a concept is a matter of some debate. An author in this volume, Árpád von Klimó, has, among others, vigorously challenged the very concept,[55] questioning whether religion in a wholly this-worldly form does not make the definition of religion so diffuse as to render it

---

[52]M. Flacke (ed.), *Mythen der Nationen: ein Europäisches Panorama* (2000), p. 15; E. François and H. Schulze, 'Das emotionale Fundament der Nationen', in Flacke, *Mythen*, p. 24.

[53]Cited in P. Geyl, *Debates with Historians* (Glasgow, 1955), p. 78; see also Chadwick, *Secularization*, p. 200; A. de Tocqueville, *The Old Regime and the French Revolution* (New York, 1983), pp. 10–14. It should be noted that for both men (but more for de Tocqueville) it was the *universal* features of the revolution, rather than its national ones, that gave it its religious qualities.

[54]F. Meinecke, *Die Deutsche Katastrophe* (Zürich and Wiesbaden, 1946), p. 121.

[55]Á. von Klimó, 'Das Ende der Nationalismusforschung? Bemerkungen zu einigen Neuerscheinungen zu "Politische Religion", "Fest" und "Erinnerung"', *Neue Politische Literatur*, 48 (2003), 271–91; and his review, 'Hildebrand, Klaus (Hrsg.): *Zwischen Politik und Religion. Studien zur Entstehung, Existenz und Wirkung des Totalitarismus*' (München, 2003), H-Soz-u-Kult, 28.10.2004, http://hsozkult.geschichte.huberlin.de/rezensionen/id=4870&count=5485&recno=15&type=rezbuecher&sort=titel&order=down. See also S. Stowers, 'The Concepts of "Religion", "Political Religion" and the Study of Nazism', *Journal of Contemporary History*, 42/1 (2007), 9–24.

fruitless for research.[56] Some historians who use the concept, such as Emilio Gentile, have restricted the definition of political religion to totalitarian movements and regimes, where rituals and religious feeling are orchestrated as if they constituted the only true faith. Under such conditions, political religion served to fill the vacuum left by traditional religion, at once making use of some its elements while at the same time opposing conventional religion as a competitor.[57] Fascist Italy and Nazi Germany have figured most prominently in the historiography making use of political religion, but communist regimes have been included as well.

Gentile does make a helpful distinction between 'political' and 'civil' religion, quite common in freer societies, where religious elements, sometimes clearly grounded in a particular faith, sometimes trans-confessional in nature, served to 'sacralise' the nation.[58] Historians such as Michelet, in abandoning his earlier view that Christianity and the revolution had shaped the past in favour of an interpretation that set the two against each other, could effectively 'nationalise' religious symbols such as Joan of Arc to powerful effect in his histories of France.[59] Such civil-religious impulses have clearly been evident in constructing national memory, as evidenced, for instance, by the efforts by various European countries to sacralise their war dead in the wake of the First World War.[60]

Whatever their limitations, concepts such as 'political' and 'civic' religion do perhaps help historians see that laicist states and movements made inventive use of the religious past in order to 'sacralise' nations that had effectively banished traditional religion from the public sphere. Nations with strong formal or informal ties to the churches very obviously manifested civil religion, but so too did secularist nations. Indeed, some laicist regimes attempted *to make new and active use of the religious past in the nation's history*. The Czechoslovakian government made the religious reformer Jan Hus, burned at the stake by the Catholic Church in 1415, a national figure. This was true for the periods both before and

---

[56]My own sensibilities on this issue coincide with those of Rüdiger Safranski, who makes the distinction between religion, which maintains the mysterious and inexplicable nature of the world, and ideology, which does not, however religious the expression might be; see Safranski, *Das Böse oder Das Drama der Freiheit* (München, 1997), ch. 17.

[57]E. Gentile, *The Sacralization of Politics in Fascist Italy* (Cambridge, MA, 1996); M. Burleigh, *Earthly Powers: The Clash of Religion and Politics in Europe, from the French Revolution to the Great War* (New York, 2006); and also P. Burrin, 'Political Religion', *History and Memory*, 9 (1997), 321–49.

[58]E. Gentile, *Politics as Religion* (Princeton, 2001), pp. 139–41; see also R. N. Bellah and P. E. Hammond, *Varieties of Civil Religion* (San Francisco, 1980).

[59]J. Michelet, *Le Moyen Age: histoire de France* (Paris, 1869/1998), p. 740.

[60]S. O. Müller, 'Tod und Verklärung. Denkmale des Krieges in Großbritannien nach 1918', in Haupt and Langewiesche, *Nation und Religion in Europa*, pp. 173–201.

after the Second World War.[61] There is much literature on how the East German government, despite its refusal to see churches as important forces in history,[62] came to make use of Luther in the forging of an identity for its republic. By the 1950s the regime had also made use of the sixteenth-century religious radical Thomas Müntzer. Such efforts to include religious figures, however, often led to contradictions that undermined the myths the regime was attempting to make.[63]

Furthermore, laicising ideologies and states not only made use of past religious figures but *developed their own symbols and rituals*, in countries such as Belgium, France and Italy, with 'civil religion' serving a form of laicity.[64] These forms of commemoration hardly precluded a borrowing from religious language and materials – Lenin's tomb and the Paris Panthéon drew directly on Orthodox and Catholic religious traditions, respectively, and East German communists honoured the life of the fallen leader Ernst Thälmann (executed by the Nazis in 1944) as immortal, 'the Holy One'.[65] Perhaps none of this constituted a full-scale 'political religion', but a strong religious undercurrent is unmistakable. In some cases, *religious commitments contributed directly to the civil religious quality of laicist regimes* – one leading French Jew of the late nineteenth century could speak of 1789 as 'our admirable and messianic revolution', and Protestantism and republicanism were, as in the American case, seen as mutually supportive.[66] In countries such as France and Italy, national Catholicism and laicism were reconciled to a certain degree in sacralising the nation's life-and-death struggle in the First World War.[67] No laicist state, however, went as far as communist Albania in this respect. In the nineteenth century, Albanian intellectuals had been troubled by

[61]Heiss et al., this volume (chapter 14); Martin Schulze Wessel, 'Die Konfessionalisierung der tschechischen Nation', in Haupt and Langewiesche, *Nation und Religion in Europa*, pp. 148–9.

[62]R. Richter, 'Über evangelische Kirchen in der DDR, Religion und Geschichtsschreibung: Beobachtungen, Erfahrungen und Erkenntnisse', in A. Loesdau and H. Meier (eds), *Zur Geschichte der Historiographie nach 1945. Beiträge eines Kolloquiums zum 75. Geburtstag von Gerhard Lozek* (Berlin, 2001), p. 203.

[63]H. Lehmann, 'Die 15 Thesen der SED über Martin Luther', in Lehmann, *Protestantisches Christentum*, pp. 102ff.; R. Walinski-Kiehl, 'Reformation History and Political Mythology in the German Democratic Republic', *European History Quarterly*, 34 (2004), 43–67.

[64]See contributions on these countries in Haupt and Langewiesche, *Nation und Religion in Europa*.

[65]Richter, 'Über evangelische Kirchen', p. 202.

[66]Cited in P. Nord, *The Republican Moment: Struggles for Democracy in Nineteenth-Century France* (Cambridge, MA, 1995), pp. 81, 109.

[67]See, for example, J. de Fabrègues, 'The Re-establishment of Relations between France and the Vatican in 1921', *Journal of Modern History*, 2 (1967), 163–82; R. Rémond, *L'Anticléricalisme en France de 1815 à nos jours* (Paris, 1976), pp. 236–7; O. Janz, 'Konflikt, Koexistenz und Symbiose: nationale und religiöse Symbolik in Italien vom Risorgimento bis zum Faschismus', in Haupt and Langewiesche, *Nation und Religion in Europa*, pp. 231–52.

the fragmenting effect of Albania's many 'foreign' religions, prompting some to support the assertion of the poet Pashko Vasa that 'The religion of Albanians is Albanianism'. The proclamation in 1967 of the 'world's first atheist state', in which all religions were banned in the communist country, may be seen as the implementation of 'Albanianism' under the xenophobic leadership of Enver Hoxha.[68] Thus laicist regimes demonstrated a wide range of strategies to incorporate religion into the history of the nation, from opportunistic use of religious figures, to the rituals of civil religion, to examples in which the distinction between the religious on the one hand and the national and the political on the other were obliterated.

Confessional modes of sacralisation and the ethnicisation of religion

But however much laicist regimes may have utilised religion or the religious past to sacralise the nation, it should be stressed that in most European representations of the past, traditional religion did not dissolve into the nation or replace it, but both remained distinct entities, however great the symbiosis. In other words, traditional religion played a more dominant role in constructing the nation – and a view of its past – than a focus on political or even civil religion alone can allow. Here, too, several patterns within Europe are evident.

Perhaps the most obvious is that in which a *dominant confessional identity became nearly coextensive with the nation itself, effectuating the ethnicisation of religion.* 'We are Orthodox because we are Romanian, and we are Romanian because we are Orthodox,' wrote the philosophy professor Nae Ionescu during the interwar period. The rise of 'Orthodoxism' stemmed a conflict between Europeanists (or 'synchronists') who saw no alternative but to modernise along European lines and intellectuals (there were few historians among them) who saw Romania's identity in an agrarian society, spiritually oriented towards the Byzantine East, and who regarded Catholic–Protestant Europe as the antithesis of this ideal.[69] This impulse within Romania was not only a reflection of a wider pattern within Orthodoxy, with the pre-1917 national histories of Russia and Ukraine also interpreting Orthodoxy as an extension of their respective ethnicities, and, in Greece, with ethnicity and religion being conceptually synonymous.[70] It also reflected a wider sentiment among intellectuals in southeast Europe, who often sought to define the special quality of their Christianity (whether Catholic or Orthodox) *vis-à-vis* the East or West,

---

[68]A. Young, *Religion and Society in Present-Day Albania*, Working Paper, 97.3, Institute for European Studies (April 1997).

[69]K. Hitchins, 'Historiography of the Countries of Eastern Europe: Romania', *American Historical Review* (October 1992), 1071–5.

[70] See Wendland, this volume (chapter 15) and Millas, this volume (chapter 18).

or both.[71] But the effort of Romanian intellectuals is a particularly tragic example of how a 'sacralised' identification of a particular confession with a particular nation could help set the context for mass murder. As Robert Paxton has recently noted, the 'religious messianism' of the Legion of the Archangel Michael was 'the most ecstatically religious of all fascist parties and one of the readiest to murder Jews and bourgeois politicians'.[72] Confessional definitions of the nation, in which Muslims (in Catholic Spain) or Jews (in interwar Austria) were defined as foreign or as an *innere Feind*, may serve as parallel examples.[73]

Not all nations with a developed confessional sense of national identity descended into such barbarities, and not all national-confessional identities were fed by a strong sense of opposition. In some cases, the perception of a 'natural' relationship between a particular religion and a particular nation were seen as so self-evident that they generated little historical controversy or polemics against a religious Other. In the Nordic countries, state, folk and religion were seen as constituting a unity that largely went unquestioned. The 'natural' connection between religion and national or regional identity is illustrated by the example of the mid-twentieth-century Finnish historian Pentti Renvall, who labelled Catholicism 'as foreign to Nordic thinking'.[74] This did not mean, however, that the historiography of these regionally isolated, overwhelmingly Lutheran countries placed much stress on the religious divide that they mostly took for granted. Similarly, in an overwhelmingly Catholic country such as Luxembourg, with relatively weak anticlerical traditions and no university of its own until 2003, Catholicism was an uncontested identity among the country's lay historians, essentially unthreatened by external or internal foes.[75] In these cases, sacralisation of the nation through its identification with a particular religion was the result of a more implicit than explicit commitment.

In most cases, however, the presence of religious enemies, real or imagined, generated sustained efforts by historians to identity religion with nation. The best-known example of this tendency was the efforts to define the Germany of the Second Empire as in essence a Protestant nation, defined over and against the French Revolution, (southern German) Roman Catholicism and, in part because of the influence of Treitschke from the 1880s on, the Jews. King Gustavus

---

[71]M-L. Murgescu, 'National Histories and Their "Other" in Southeastern Europe', paper presented at the workshop Narrating National Histories in Europe, European Science Foundation/NHIST Scientific Programme. Budapest, 24 October 2004.
[72]R. O. Paxton, *The Anatomy of Fascism* (New York, 2004), pp. 20, 97, 203.
[73]See Matos and Álvarez, this volume (chapter 13) and Heiss et al., this volume (chapter 14).
[74]Renvall, cited in Meyer and Myhre, *Nordic Historiography*, p. 59.
[75]Benoit Majerus, presentation at ESF Workshop, Representations of the Past: The Writing of National Histories in Europe, Munich, 24 October 2005.

Adolphus, for example, was memorialised not only in Sweden, but in Protestant Germany as well – 'that hero of the North of glorious memory', as Hegel hailed him.[76] But it was Luther as 'national prophet', of course, who was interpreted by many Protestant historians, such as Droysen and Sybel, as the spiritual founder of the German nation.[77] This trend was strongly evident in the late nineteenth century (most notably the celebration of Luther's 400th birthday in 1883), but also in the period from 1917 (the 400th anniversary of the Reformation) to 1933, when the 'back to Luther' movement was an important current in Protestant circles.[78] Both the creation of a multi-confessional empire in 1871 and the collapse of that empire prompted the majority religious group in Germany to underscore the essentially Protestant idea of the nation. This was not, of course, only a German phenomenon: in emulation of the way German Protestants honoured Luther, Swiss Protestant historians of the late nineteenth and early twentieth centuries assigned a central place to Zwingli in the history of a nation which was culturally dominated by Protestants, but included a very large minority of Catholics.[79] Nor was this pattern confined to Protestant-dominant countries alone. Russian historians regarded Orthodoxy as 'one of the constitutive [features], often the constitutive feature', of the Russian nation, set over and against Catholic and, more ambiguously, Protestant Europe.[80] More generally, various countries in Europe that had had contacts with the Muslim world depicted Islam as a danger, thus reifying the Christian identity of the nation.[81] In summary, the perceived presence of religious rivals – both domestic and foreign – served to intensify a confessional-based sense of nationality.

An important component of these forms of confessional identification with the nation was often a sense of religious, or quasi-religious, national mission. 'Spain, evangeliser of half the globe; Spain hammer of heretics, light of Trent, sword of Rome, cradle of Saint Ignatius ... that is our greatness and our unity: we have no other' is how Marcelino Menéndez y Pelayo articulated Spain's mission in the 1880s, even as he harboured doubts about the durability of Spain's traditional identity.[82] As the citation from Menéndez y Pelayo shows, the sites of

---

[76]François and Schulze, 'Das emotionale Fundament', pp. 24–5; G. W. F. Hegel, *The Philosophy of History*, in C. J. Friedrich (ed.), *The Philosophy of Hegel* (New York, 1954), p. 137.

[77]Iggers, 'Nationalism and Historiography', p. 15.

[78]K. Kaupisch, 'The "Luther Renaissance"', *Journal of Contemporary History*, 2, 4 (1967), 29–49.

[79]Metzger, 'Die Reformation'.

[80]A. Miller, 'Russia', paper prepared for the ESF's Representations of the Past: The Writing of National Histories in Europe. Glamorgan, Wales, 21 May 2004.

[81]François and Schulze, 'Das emotionale Fundament', p. 25.

[82]In M. y Pelayo, *Historia de los Herterodoxos Españoles*, cited in Frances Lannon, 'Modern Spain: The Project of a National Catholicism', in Mews, *Religion and National Identity*, p. 567.

national mission varied considerably. For Denmark, a sense of national mission was primarily an internal, spiritual one, informed by a collective Lutheran identity, in the wake of its military defeat in 1864.[83] Romanov Russia developed a religiously informed sense of historical mission.[84] In Portugal, whose Catholic writers shared with their Spanish counterparts the sense of 'evangelising mission', the nation was interpreted in the nineteenth century as a bulwark against the Ottomans.[85] This view found parallel expression in much of Greek historiography, influenced by the Greek Orthodox Church and often irredentist in its national-religious aspirations, especially before 1922.[86] The colonial experience shaped religious identities in both the colonising and colonised countries, intensifying the religious element in national identity for both colonisers and colonised, in part through missionary efforts of European Christian churches.[87] The many various expressions of national mission, across and within nations, a sense often enhanced by religious identification, are extensively illustrated in this volume.

In countries where political independence was not possible, the sacralisation of the nation could be furthered by *the church itself serving as the representative of the nation.* Overwhelmingly Catholic Lithuania lost its national independence in the 1940s, but the sense of nationhood was kept alive in part by the transmission of *The Chronicle of the Catholic Church in Lithuania*, which highlighted the persecution of clerics and others in the Lithuanian SSR.[88] The nation, enslaved, found its national and international expression in the church. It would probably have been harder to preserve a sense of Lithuania's national identity had it not been that the centre of the church lay in Rome, not Vilnius. This example also illustrates an important pattern that went along with the sacralisation of nation – the 'nationalisation' of the church. Religious bodies were themselves transformed by their identification with the nation, as religious life itself underwent a 'regime' change within the context of the nation-state.[89]

The perceived importance of religion for national identity is perhaps most evident in the strategies of those *who sought to create new religious identities for nations, particularly but not exclusively in Eastern Europe, where the predominant religion was considered of little use in maintaining a vital national identity.* In

---

[83]Meyer and Myhre, *Nordic Historiography*, pp. 41–5.
[84]Miller, 'Russia'.
[85]See Matos and Álvarez, this volume (chapter 13).
[86]Millas, this volume (chapter 18).
[87]Van der Veer, *Islam en het 'beschaafde Westen'*, pp. 56–7.
[88]*The Chronicle of the Catholic Church in Lithuania* (Brooklyn, 1975–87), itself a translation of the original *Lietuvos katalika baznycios kronika*.
[89]P. van Rooden, *Religieuze regimes: over godsdienst en maatschappij in Nederland, 1570–1990* (Amsterdam, 1996).

Hungary, historians hostile to Austria and the Habsburgs generated or in some cases forged, as István Deák has put it, 'the cult of the Protestant Transylvanian tradition'. Though not long followed by professional historians, the Protestant story of Hungarian resistance to the Catholic Habsburgs was found useful by the Stalinists ruling Hungary in the 1950s.[90] In Latvia, double domination by the Russian Orthodox government and the Lutheran Baltic-German *Herrenvolk* made it more difficult to historicise the nation in religious terms. In the 1920s the Latvian nationalist and self-taught ethnographer Ernests Brastins sought on the basis of old folk songs to 'restore' Latvia's ancient religion, Dievturiba, rejecting the internationalism of both Christianity and Europe. Its influence was apparently greater than its number of adherents would suggest.[91]

Desacralisation and resacralisation

The emphasis of current historiography is very much on processes of sacralisation and 'nationalisation'. This obscures the fact that there have been various efforts by historians, other intellectuals and religious figures and institutions to 'desacralise' and demythologise the nation and to 'denationalise' religious bodies – sometimes with lasting results in parts of (especially) post-Second World War Europe.

In the first place, it must be noted that not all historians, religious or otherwise, understood the primary narrative as that of the nation, and resisted efforts to link a particular religion with a particular nation. Throughout the nineteenth century, for example, 'universal history' of a Christian or often more specifically Catholic pedigree placed the focus of history not on the nation but on the unfolding history of the universal church.[92] Since the eighteenth century the papacy had been suspicious of the pretensions of the centralised nation-state, and Catholic experience in the nineteenth century did not invariably render them enthusiastic adherents of the new national states. In specific instances, as in Italy in the decades after 1870, Catholic historians (not to mention socialists and communists) rejected the nation-state of the *Risorgimento* as a topic worth investigating.[93] For the British Catholic historian Christopher Dawson, Europe, not Britain, was the focus of historical interest.[94]

---

[90]Deák, 'Historiography', pp. 1047, 1052.
[91]A. Putelis, 'Folklore and Identity: The Situation in Latvia', *Novo Religion*, 3, 1 (1999), 119–36.
[92]Roland Stromberg in this respect cites the project of Lord Acton and his Bavarian mentor and colleague Ignaz Döllinger: *European Intellectual History* (Englewood Cliffs, NJ, 1986), pp. 99–100; Breisach, *Historiography*, pp. 271, 320.
[93]R. Vivarelli, 'A Neglected Question', in Berger et al., *Writing National Histories*, p. 231.
[94]See K. Robbins, 'National Identity and History: Past, Present, Future', in Robbins, *History*, pp. 32–3.

In short, historiographical traditions certainly existed which resisted sacralising the nation through religion and through the nationalisation of religion.

In the course of the twentieth century, additionally, there arose a counter-trend among historians and other historically minded intellectuals against the sacralisation of the nation. In Britain the First World War precipitated efforts to seek new identities – for H. G. Wells, in the concluding chapter of his *Outline of History*, it meant throwing out the gods of nationalism and moving towards a religion of humanity.[95] Perhaps the most ambitious of all efforts to reconceive of history beyond the nation was the work of yet another British historian, Arnold Toynbee, who stressed the centrality of 'civilisations', and later of world religions, as the shapers of history. All these examples were part of a longer trend, furthered by the crisis of 'the national principle' after 1945. Perhaps this was most poignantly evident in German-Jewish historiography, where the Holocaust rendered any close association between German national identity and Judaism extremely difficult, triggering a 'denationalisation of faith'.[96] The experience with the mass violence of the twentieth century prompted historians (Pieter Geyl warned against the 'total allegiance' demanded by the nation-state[97]), theologians (from Barth to Teilhard de Chardin) and other public figures to call in effect for the 'desacralisation' of the nation. A new wave of religious self-reflection generated by the changes of the Second World War and cultural developments since the 1960s prompted many religiously inspired historians to adopt a more critical approach to (among other matters) the relationship between religion and nation.[98] These processes also took place in Iberia, though the presence of right-wing dictatorships until the mid-1970s meant that these discussions took place later. The religiously informed narrative of the *Reconquista*, so prevalent in much of Portuguese and Spanish historiography, began to lose its force after the 1960s, as Iberian historians questioned the moral validity of this vision of history.[99] In many Western European countries a wariness among historians about the claims of the nation went hand in hand with hostility to traditional religion, a force which was now seen, more than ever, as contributing to the unfortunate processes of sacralisation.

These trends towards a conscious rejection of a sacralised nation, particularly after 1945, do not gainsay countervailing developments, of course, least of all efforts to renew the ties of a particular faith to a particular nation. Postwar

---

[95]H. G. Wells, *The Outline of History*, vol. 4 (New York, 1925), p. 1290.
[96]See Wyrwa, this volume (chapter 19).
[97]Geyl, *Debates with Historians*, pp. 232–3.
[98]Campos Matos and Mota Álvarez, this volume (chapter 13) make note of a new 'Catholic self-reflection' in recent Catholic historiography.
[99]Ibid.

Zionist historiography – itself a reaction to the nationalisation of Judaism in various European countries – is arguably an example of this trend.[100] But it is more clearly evident in post-Soviet Eastern Europe, where dominant confessions, whether Catholic or Orthodox, have again played an express role in defining – and sacralising – the nation in countries such as Serbia, Croatia, Bulgaria and Romania in the 1990s.[101]

The examples from Eastern Europe are relatively easy to identify, perhaps. But in other European countries, where the strong identification of a particular faith with a nation was more problematic, it must be asked to what extent alternative, spiritually infused and ostensibly transnational entities were constructed to replace, or at least partly supplant, the nation as a source of moral authority. 'Scandinavianism'? The Christian West? Europe? The global community? Scientific authority? One journalist-historian has suggested that 'Auschwitz' has in effect functioned as a 'public religion' in the Netherlands, in which the public rituals of memory construct a sacralised understanding of the Dutch nation.[102] It is not at all clear that the sacralisation of the nation is over, even in Western Europe, where the nation seems to have been rediscovered as *the* basis for community.

Using a religious metaphor, some historians recently warned: 'Historians today would do well not to continue the unholy alliance with government and states in constructing diverse forms of national identities.'[103] But what understandings of 'the holy', implicit and explicit, have enabled historians in the various countries of Europe to detach themselves, in whole or in part, from sacralising the nation?[104] And to what extent have they really succeeded in breaking with a process many historians have to regard as dangerous?

Conflict

The emphasis on supersession and on sacralisation may suggest that representations of the past in each nation occurred univocally, without much difference of vision. And indeed, the previous two sections have tended to focus, if not exclusively, on trends within dominant or highly influential groups that defined the historical relationship between religion and nation. Or they have indicated how some religious groups cooperated, or at least coexisted, while contributing to a common national identity based on a more or less common

---

[100] Wyrwa, this volume (chapter 19).
[101] Murgescu, 'National Histories'.
[102] J. Oegema, *Een vreemd geluk: de publieke religie rond Auschwitz* (Amsterdam, 2003).
[103] S. Berger, M. Donovan and K. Passmore, 'Apologies for the Nation-State', in Berger et al., *Writing National Histories*, pp. 11–13.
[104] Meyer and Myhre, *Nordic Historiography*, p. 94.

past. Franziska Metzger convincingly notes that Catholics contested, concurred with and adopted alternative identities in Protestant-dominated Switzerland.[105] But recognition of this complexity must certainly not occlude the fact that historians with diverging religious convictions and diverging interpretations of the nation often stood arrayed against each other, competing with each for influence in determining the proper historical relationship between religion and the nation.[106] Religion's role in the nation generated many forms of conflict, as a recent edition of Haupt and Langewiesche has demonstrated.[107] This conflict was sometimes already apparent in the eighteenth century; as Oliver Zimmer has recently noted about late eighteenth- and nineteenth-century Switzerland, regions, localities, and political and religious groups 'began to compete for status, prestige and recognition' within the framework of the nation.[108] The competition and the subsequent disagreements over the proper relationship between religion and nation were hardly confined to Switzerland, nor were they restricted to the nineteenth century, when the religious mobilisation of the 'second confessional age' and the construction of the nation-state often reinforced one another. Indeed, debates over the role of religion in the nation did not suddenly begin in 1789, but were rooted, in least in the German-speaking world, in early modern times. Furthermore, I would argue, the debates over the place of religion in the nation did not disappear, at least in most European countries, after European states 'secularised' in the postwar period. Religion often remained a central component in the conflict between the dominant cultural forces and more marginalised groups who protested against the prevailing conceptions of the nation.

This does not mean, of course, that competing historical visions of the nation and its religious character always led to headlong conflict. As Metzger has shown in the case of Swiss Catholics, open conflict was only one strategy employed. They also sometimes developed historical visions of the nation that largely converged with the dominant Protestant vision – a tendency noted in the first section. And they also developed alternative, regionally based histories, in which the question about the nation's religious heritage was not directly answered.[109] But conflict – now broadly defined – remained in all of these strategies an underlying current, and it is worth outlining briefly which patterns such conflicts formed.

---

[105]F. Metzger, 'Geschichten der Nation in Deutschland und der Schweiz: Überlagerung von Diskurs- und Erinnerungsgemeinschaften', paper prepared for the ESF's Representations of the Past: The Writing of National Histories in Europe. Budapest, Hungary, 21–3 October 2004.
[106]See, for France, P. Nora et al., *Realms of Memory: The Construction of the French Past*, vol. 1, *Conflicts and Divisions* (New York, 1996).
[107]Haupt and Langewiesche, *Nation und Religion in Europa*.
[108]Zimmer, *Contested Nation*, pp. 14–15.
[109]Metzger, 'Die Reformation'.

Inter-confessional and intra-confessional conflict

At first glance, it would seem that the most abiding examples of conflicts over representations of the past have come from Europe's multi-confessional states. Not surprisingly, the conflict between Catholic and Protestant interpretations of the nation could generate sharp divergence of opinion within countries with sizeable percentages of either group. 'The nineteenth century recreated a Pope who could make the mighty afraid,' Owen Chadwick has written, and the sharpness with which Protestants and anticlericals could define the nation in an anti-Catholic way was a reflection of this.[110] In Poland, for example, national historians of the nineteenth century took a critical stance towards the historical role of the Jesuits in their national narratives.[111] Similarly, both Protestants and Catholics found ways to confessionalise the founding myths of the Swiss nation, effectively excluding each other – and Jews – from the nation's history.[112]

But it is not as if non-dominant religious groups were merely passive or reactive to these attacks. Jewish historians constructed the narrative of Jewish suffering in the midst of a predominantly hostile world, which offered a counter-narrative to the predominant national narratives.[113] In Germany, too, Catholics constructed their own cults (to St Boniface) and shrines within the context of the new German state, marking out in part what it meant to be a Catholic German. The essentially contested nature of the national past and its religious dimensions thus came to the fore. The conflict within Germany between Catholics and Protestants over the identity of the German nation was apparently strongest between the mid-nineteenth century and the First World War. And late nineteenth-century Ireland was the battleground between conflicting historiographical visions of St Patrick's legacy, Protestant and Catholic.[114]

But it was not as if the Protestant/Catholic or Jewish/Christian divide within national communities was always invariably the hardest to bridge: on the contrary. The often bitter conflict between Catholic and anticlerical historians was often more intense than between Protestants and Catholics.[115] For

---

[110]Chadwick, *Secularization*, p. 139.

[111]See Janowski, this volume (chapter 16).

[112]Metzger, 'Die Reformation', pp. 92–3, 96–8.

[113]See Wyrwa, this volume (chapter 19).

[114]O. MacDonagh, 'Time's Revenge and Revenge's Time: A View of Anglo-Irish Relations', *Anglo-Irish Studies*, 4 (1979), 1–19; B. Stuchtey, 'Literature, Liberty and Life of the Nation: British Historiography from Macaulay to Trevelyan', in Berger et al., *Writing National Histories*, pp. 34–5.

[115]For an overview of these conflicts, see C. Clark and W. Kaiser (eds), *Culture Wars: Secular – Catholic Conflict in Nineteenth-Century Europe* (Cambridge, 2003).

example, Belgian Catholics and liberals, deeply opposed to each other, found it impossible to construct a common 'historical myth', whereas less polarised Dutch Protestants and Catholics (in the context of a longer-established state) shared to a large extent the same historical vision.[116] Spain also serves as a good example of this conflict, as illustrated in this volume. In the decades prior to the First World War, anticlericals in France competed vigorously for the historical symbols of the nation, and in Italy a similar conflict took place. As Croce himself illustrates, the clerical/anticlerical conflict over the direction and meaning of the past could be in Catholic Europe just as potent as any conflict in multi-confessional states.

However, the conflicts over the significance of religion and the nation were hardly restricted to the conflicts between confessions, or between ideologies. Within confessions, too, divergent visions of the nation emerged, sometimes just as or more polarised than the conflict between religions. To use Germany as an example again, Catholics in the mid-nineteenth century, and Jews in the early twentieth century, disagreed among themselves about how they as communities stood in relation to the German nation. Protestant historians in the Netherlands and Germany disagreed among each other about just how Protestant the nation was, and to what extent the nation surpassed religious categories. In recent decades, Muslims in Western European countries have defined, in various ways, their own loyalty to the nation in the light of the fact that these nations have not been historically Muslim.[117] In these cases one cannot speak of a static, univocal strategy of a single confession, but of processes of internal conflict and permutation. Confessions did not constitute monoliths from which a nation's past was constructed, though the parameters of belief clearly delimited what visions of the national past were available.

Recent conflicts in the multi-religious public square

Much of the research on how religion has had an impact on conflicting visions of the nation has focused on the conflict between confessions, and within confessions, and mostly in the period prior to the Second World War. Indeed, the period after the war remains relatively under-researched, either because religion and/or nationalism are assumed to have disappeared as significant factors in historical representation, or because religious pluralism and the 'hybridisation' of memory (Pierre Nora) has made it difficult to create and sustain stable constructions of the nation. Certainly the decline of grand national narrative in historiography and the solemn rites of commemoration

---

[116]See Beyen and Majerus, this volume (chapter 11).
[117]J. Malik, 'Nationale und religiöse fremd- und Selbstbilder: Muslime in Deutschland', in Haupt and Langewiesche, *Nation und Religion in Europa*, pp. 283–302.

that characterised national identity in Europe up to the mid-twentieth century have made it more difficult to define and interpret the intersection of religion and nation. But that does not mean that the link between the two disappeared in the postwar period, or that conflicts within postwar European nations have.

In the first place, the reconstruction of postwar states led to renewed discussion over the religious identity of the (new) nation. For example, the dissolution of Prussia in 1947 and the creation of the Federal Republic in Germany two years later effectively put an end to Germany as a Protestant nation, with the Catholic Konrad Adenauer now governing a country with almost equal numbers of Protestants and Catholics. Some Protestants suspected, however, that Adenauer's Catholicism made him none too eager in seeking reunification with Protestant East Germany. Forty years later the dissolution of the German Democratic Republic led to intensive research and debate about the role of the East German Protestant Church in the events of 1989, and hence in the reunification of the German nation. In Poland, the fall of communism led to the contested move to make Catholicism an integrative part of Poland's new identity, as manifest in the discussion of whether the cross should be displayed at Auschwitz, and how the Polish nation should be remembered.[118] Sometimes, too, the persistence of disagreement about the place of religion in the nation prompted the antagonists not to amplify the conflict but to suspend the debate. In postwar Austria, for example, Social Democrats and Catholics, unwilling to renew earlier enmities but unable to forge a consensual vision of Catholicism's role in the nation's identity, let the matter drop as a public issue. Austria's national identity thus became 'stuck' over the lack of consensus about religion.[119]

In the second place, both the perceived decline and the return of religion prompted much soul-searching and debate about how the nation (or society) should be defined. In 1972, for example, two intellectuals proclaimed the end of the Netherlands as a 'Christian' nation, and the 'death' of Christian Britain, too, was a topic of historiographical discussion across the North Sea.[120] The

---

[118]G. Zubrzycki, 'The Broken Monolith: The Catholic Church and the "War of the Crosses at Auschwitz" (1998–99)', in M. Geyer and H. Lehmann (eds), *Religion und Nation: Beiträge zu einer unbewältigten Geschichte / Nation and Religion: An Unfinished History* (Göttingen, 2003).
[119]This thesis was advanced at a European Social Science History Conference in March 2004: The Relations between Politics and Religion and the Narratives on National Identity in 20th-Century Austria.
[120]M. van Amerongen and I. Cornelissen, *Tegen de revolutie: het evangelie! Het kerkvolk in de Nederlandse politiek of: het einde van een christelijke natie* (Amsterdam, 1972); C. G. Brown, *The Death of Christian Britain* (London, 2000).

disestablishment of Sweden's Lutheran Church in 2000 was a public redefin-
ition of what it meant to be a nation. Meanwhile, intellectuals across various
European countries disagreed fiercely with each other about whether the existence of the 'multi-religious public square'[121] constituted an unacceptable threat
to the nation. This was a debate among Yugoslav historians in the 1980s, and
also in France in recent years, where Alain Finkielkraut maintained that the
alliance of Jews, Gentiles, Muslims and anti-racists was going to turn France
into another Lebanon, a fragmented country of fissiparous religious divides.[122]
In particular, the migration of Muslims and other 'non-Western' faiths to various
countries in Western Europe prompted many intellectuals and public figures to
debate whether the nation should be understood as laicist, (Judeo-)Christian or
multi-religious. The Prince of Wales, for example, generated controversy when
he said that he envisaged himself as *Fiderum Defensor*, 'defender of faiths', rather
than *Fidei Defensor*, 'Defender of the Faith', now the title of British monarchs.

   The diffusion and reconstitution of religious belief and practice in the 'postmodern' world has rendered the ties between religion and the nation more
difficult to define. And the development of the pluralistic, multi-confessional
societies in Europe in the last half-century may have inhibited efforts in most
nations to sacralise the nation along explicitly mono-confessional lines. But it
has hardly ended the debate over how the nation should be religiously constituted, either in laicist states, such as France, or states where the public influence
of religion traditionally has been encouraged, as in Germany. The public role
of symbols particular to one religion is of course one major issue, as is the
(historic) role of religiously derived 'values' in determining the moral contours
of a nation. In turn, many professional historians, perhaps in part to underwrite the religious pluralism of the present, have stressed the religious pluralism of the past, showing both historical diversity and the unfortunate effects
of repressing such diversity. It is a laudable effort in a time when religious
intolerance is on the rise in many European countries. But are historians
in doing so rising above the fray over the old battle of the place of religion in
the nation, or are they too protagonists in that long battle to determine the
proper role of religion in society, and in the nation?

[121]D. Eck, 'The Multireligious Public Square', in M. Gerber and R. L. Walkowitz (eds),
One Nation under God? Religion and American Culture (Cambridge, MA, 1999), pp. 3–20.
[122]J. Jackson, 'Historians and the Nation in Contemporary France', in Berger et al., *Writing
National Histories*, pp. 245–6.

6

The 'Nation' and 'Class': European National Master Narratives and Their Social 'Other'

Gita Deneckere and Thomas Welskopp

Introduction

From the outset, 'class' was a potential threat to harmonising tales of the 'nation'. If not synonymous with 'the people' in revolutionary episodes that served as founding myths for the nation, class by nature defied the very claims to unity, cultural conformity and territorial integrity that national master narratives set out to establish. As well as being identified with a revolutionary threat, class also stood for the unruliness of the masses, internal conflict and the contention of the existing social and political order. Yet it was not only the characterisation of class as a divisive force that made it represent a haunting danger: it also offered an alternative, organising and mobilising principle for a different kind of unity, that of 'solidarity'. Thus, it carried dual meanings: an internal struggle against other ruling groups in society ('class struggle'), and transcendence of national boundary lines ('internationalism').[1]

The advent of class interpretations of contemporary societies and their histories roughly followed the triumph of national historiography. Hence, it appears worthwhile to investigate systematically how national master narratives came to terms with the problem of class. Did evolving class ideologies aspire to generate an alternative, competing master narrative of their own? Consequently, can the relationship between the two be characterised as an ongoing struggle between two master-discourses for hegemony? Did class histories succeed in challenging histories of the nation by creating a powerful counter-discourse? Or were national historiographies flexible and tolerant enough to integrate the social groups that stood for the 'dangerous classes' into a broadened vision of their national past? Also, from the reverse perspective, did members of those classes attempt to and succeed in inscribing a chronicle of class into the national master narrative? If so, was this symptomatic of an act of emancipation or of selling out revolutionary

---

[1] P. Calvert, *The Concept of Class: An Historical Introduction* (London, 1982), pp. 11ff.

radicalism to a subordinate place in the nation? Finally, did this mean that the role of class in its relation to the nation was a sub-discourse rather than a contentious counter-discourse?

This chapter will try to answer these questions by comparing five Western European historiographies (those of France, Britain, Germany, Belgium and Switzerland), which cover the French Revolution to the early 1990s (with a sidestep into the historiography of East European state socialist countries from the time of the Russian Revolution to the disintegration of the Communist Bloc). Across Europe, 'national' histories followed widely diverging modes of emplotment. They varied from unfolding development from a mythical past ('origin') to the apogee claimed to be reached in the present time or in the future ('progress'), over cycles and stages; alternatively, they presented a harmonious rise from a cathartic moment such as a foundational myth ('revolutionary tradition') to a loss of former achievements ('decline'), coupled with a political agenda to regain and surpass losses in the future ('rebirth').[2] Repeatedly, critical events caused a substantive re-emplotment of national histories. In any case, we can assume that the respective emplotment of a national history says a great deal about the very preconditions that a 'class' history had to meet to gain any traction. Since the emplotment of class histories generally depends on national contexts, they might also be just as diverse.

Another frustration for our undertaking is that a number of strands of 'national' historiography seem to ignore or openly deny the issue of 'class'. At first, we tried to resolve this problem of bypassing or 'silencing' by concentrating on revolutionary episodes, believing that although class may be ignored, a revolution cannot. However, further into our research we found that the relations between class and revolution were as complex as those between class and nation. In fact, we can now identify a *triangle* of semantic ties, in which nation, class *and* revolution form the corners (and 'the people' perhaps occupy the middle ground between them).

Finally, we have followed all this complexity over the course of nearly two centuries. The chapter covers a lot of ground and takes into account widely diverse developments in the countries whose historiographies we investigated. Nevertheless, we can establish that they converged in some common patterns: the growth of the welfare state and industrial corporatism, the ascent of labour parties to political power, the rise and fall of the Communist Bloc in Eastern Europe, and the establishment of (a sometimes Marxist) social history

---

[2]S. Berger, 'Geschichten von der Nation: einige vergleichende Thesen zur deutschen, englischen, französischen und italienischen Nationalgeschichtsschreibung seit 1800', in C. Conrad and S. Conrad (eds), *Die Nation schreiben: Geschichtswissenschaft im internationalen Vergleich* (Göttingen, 2002), pp. 51–6.

as an academic discipline that itself aspires to act as the custodian of the national past. Therefore, over time, we can expect multiple patterns of change in the relations between 'nation' and 'class', and this calls for a relatively chronological argumentative strategy.

The French Revolution

Evidently, the French Revolution was *the* great founding event in the making of the modern nation and the revolutionary rupture on which the new world was founded.[3] French historians from Guizot to Michelet perceived their nation to be the champion of 'liberté, égalité, fraternité', and believed that France would spread revolutionary values to the rest of Europe and the whole world. In their view, the third estate became 'the nation'. The greatest historian of the revolution, Jules Michelet, being a republican, also celebrated the heroism of the *sans-culottes* who fought for *la patrie*, though.[4] For Michelet, 'la France' merged with '*la patrie*' and '*le peuple*', 'the people' being a mythic whole at the centre of his romantic narratives.[5] For him, the superiority of France over other nations was due to its tradition of 'fraternal equality', which extended back to the Middle Ages, making the history of France the history of mankind.

However, the French Revolution with all its paradoxes also posed fundamental problems to the national bourgeois state set up in its aftermath, generating a conflict that threatened national stability and unity. The liberal historical project of '*le juste milieu*', of which Augustin Thierry and François Guizot were representatives, had to come to terms with the potentially destructive energies of the dangerous classes. In their eyes, the July Revolution of 1830 was the culminating point in French history, the logical outcome of the historical process in which conflict was finally resolved, balance achieved and reason made triumphant. The social reality of France in the 1830s and 1840s, however, was marked by new forms of conflict, generated by industrialisation and economic liberalism. Democracy became synonymous with egalitarianism and the social and political demands of the 'fourth estate', for whom the revolution also meant a promise of equality and a privileged form of change.[6] The internal dynamics of Jacobinism challenged the very institutions through which French society of 1789 attempted to fix its own history. This can

---

[3]F. Furet, 'La Révolution française est terminée', *Penser la Révolution française* (Paris, 1978), p. 14.

[4]J. Michelet, *Histoire de la Révolution française* (Paris, 1939 [1st edn, 1847–53]).

[5]J. Michelet, *Le Peuple* (Paris, 1974 [1846]), p. 236.

[6]Furet, *Penser la Révolution française*, p. 18.

be seen in the reiterated revolutionary episodes which marked nineteenth-century French history: riots and upheavals until 1834, a latent revolutionary spirit which came to the fore in February and June 1848, and the Paris Commune of 1871. Thus, it can be seen that the French nation oscillated endlessly between the need to terminate the revolution and the urge to revive it again.

Consequently, the complex question of whether or not it is possible to dissociate the events of 1793 from those of 1789 marks and divides nineteenth-century historiography.[7] Naturally, conservatives such as Joseph de Maistre believed that this was not possible, but liberal thinkers such as Guizot, Benjamin Constant and Mme de Staël tried to trace back the revolution to its 'truth' of 1789 and to separate it from the despotic sequences that were incompatible with the idea of liberty: the Terror, Robespierre and Napoleon. Their texts justified 1789 but repudiated 1793, portraying the Terror as a deviation from the triumphal road the French nation took in 1789, a provisional perversion in the name of '*le salut public*'. Owing to historical necessity the revolution was categorised as being entirely liberal and was purged of its terrible Other. Jacobinism was seen to be a by-product of the counter-revolution – an '*accident de parcours*'.[8] Republican historians such as Michelet and Edgar Quinet abhorred the Terror and the dictatorship of Robespierre and Napoleon as much as did the liberals, and found similar ways of forcing these episodes out of their narratives. Quinet saw the revolutionary tradition to be complicit with absolutism and reaction, tracing this back to Byzantinism, the victory of Caesar over the Gauls, the elimination of the Albigensians in the thirteenth century, St Bartholomew and the defeat of the Reformation, the return of Louis XI, Richelieu and Louis XIV, and so on. In this dialectic Jacobinism was another incarnation of royalism.[9]

The Paris Commune of 1871 further complicated the matter. Whereas Michelet sympathised with 'the people', for Hippolyte Taine 'the masses' only represented regression, danger and madness. Taine was one of the exponents of the growing professionalisation of French historiography that took the superiority of German critical research (especially in philology) as an example in a period marked by defeat in the war of 1870.[10] Taine's *Origines de la France contemporaine*, published in six volumes (1878), was inspired by the events

[7]Furet, *Penser la Révolution française*; idem, *La Révolution en débat* (Paris, 1999).
[8]F. A. Mignet, *Histoire de la Révolution française* (Paris, 1833).
[9]F. Furet, 'La Gauche et la Révolution au XIXe siècle', *Edgar Quinet et la question du jacobinisme 1865–1870* (Paris, 1986).
[10]P. den Boer, *Geschiedenis als beroep: de professionalisering van de geschiedbeoefening in Frankrijk 1818–1914* (Nijmegen, 1987); J. Tollebeek, 'Een Burke, getekend door Tocqueville: Taines periodisering van de Franse geschiedenis', in J. Tollebeek, G. Verbeeck and T. Verschaffel, *De lectuur van het verleden* (Leuven, 1998), pp. 487–505.

of the Paris Commune, which shocked the French elite. Politicians and the majority of the intelligentsia ranging from Thiers to Flaubert denounced the destructiveness of the masses. Taine, expressing his disgust, emphasised the pathological nature of 'the populace' also perceived by him in the revolutionary events of 1789. He criticised the idyllic view of Michelet that the bourgeoisie had made the revolution and had led the people to victory. By arguing that historiography should be based on psychology in order to understand the mental state of the people more thoroughly, Taine contributed decisively to the emergence of the field of political psychology, and in particular to crowd psychology. For him, the new revolutionary upsurge of the urban working class seemed to prove that something was thoroughly wrong with the national character of the French that let them lose their heads so easily.[11]

Socialist historians gave 1871 a proper place in their revolutionary timeline, which ran parallel to the national narratives of liberals and republicans, although it also acknowledged the events of 1793. For *'quatre-vingt-neuvistes'* the spirit of the revolution was betrayed by subsequent events, whereas the *'quatre-vingt-treizistes'* saw the promise in the dynamics of the revolution as a whole. In the vein of Louis Blanc, socialist historians saw the republic as a necessary condition for socialism to follow, but viewed it as just an historical phase that had to be surpassed by the dynamics of equality. They saw in *l'An II*, with its use of terror for the sake of the *salut public*, the revelation of the real essence of the revolution and the pronouncement of revolutions to come. They believed that whereas individualism had triumphed between 1789 and 1791, the year II anticipated the reign of fraternity. For them, 1793 was the accomplishment of the failed revolution of 1789; Robespierre anticipated socialism, Jacobinism was the prefiguration of the triumph of labour over capital, and the bourgeois revolution of Voltaire had to be surpassed by the people's revolution of Rousseau. This teleological vision of the revolution in the search for the origins of socialism started with Louis Blanc in 1847[12] and was subsequently adopted by communist historiography. Albert Soboul studied the archives of the Parisian *sans-culotterie*, organised in 48 sections, to stress the importance and specificity of the 'popular revolution' of 1793–4. He did not avoid idealising this period of Jacobin dictatorship.[13]

Socialist historiography constructed a linear vision of human emancipation, portraying 1789 as its first stage and the socialist revolution as the final, future

---

[11]J. van Ginneken, *Crowds, Psychology and Politics, 1871–1899* (Cambridge, 1992), pp. 20–51; S. Jones, 'Taine and the Nation-State', in S. Berger, M. Donovan and K. Passmore (eds), *Writing National Histories: Western Europe since 1800* (London and New York, 1999), pp. 85–96.
[12]L. Blanc, *Histoire de la Révolution française* (Paris, 1847).
[13]A. Soboul, *Les Sans-culottes parisiens de l'An II* (Paris, 1979 [1958]), p. 3.

stage. This vision was expressed in an overtly nationalistic and patriotic mould. Like Jean Jaurès, who in his *Histoire socialiste de la Révolution française* had sought to blend a non-revolutionary version of Marxism with the patriotic historiographical tradition, many socialist historians were intoxicated by the idea of the French nation as the bearer of the torch of mankind, and their work can be read as a pedagogy of progress. However, France lost its pioneering role in the history of mankind with the Russian Revolution of 1917. The Marxist historiography of the French Revolution was marked by it on the rebound, and after 1917 French Jacobins were represented as the ancestors of the Russian Bolsheviks.

Despite all the linear simplifications and justifications, the focus on the popular classes and their role in the revolution[14] has enlarged historical knowledge of the peasantry and the urban lower class in a considerable way, thus paving the way for 'history from below'. Georges Lefebvre's seminal work on the French peasantry[15] is a case in point: his studies show that the French Revolution was a more complicated social phenomenon than just a radical break with traditional society opening up the capitalist era. This is precisely what revisionists such as Alfred Cobban[16] and François Furet questioned in the 1970s, the 'orthodox' view that the French Revolution represented the breakthrough of capitalism and the coming of the bourgeoisie, seen in an anachronistic manner. Marxist historiography (not Marx himself[17]) was denounced for its myth of the revolutionary break – before, feudality; after, capitalism; before, the nobility; after, the bourgeoisie. The paradox is that militant historians such as Lefebvre opened up new fields of research and a social history that stressed the continuity between the *ancien régime* and the modern nation, but failed to question the radicalism of the revolutionary changes themselves.

National grand narratives in relation to class and its revolutionary Other

It is interesting to see how the national master narratives of countries that did not experience a great revolution in the eighteenth or nineteenth century nevertheless related to France and its revolutionary tradition as the Other that is denied in their own histories. In these narratives, 'class' is barely given a

---

[14]Cf. A. Mathiez, *La vie chère et le mouvement social sous la Terreur* (Paris, 1927); D. Guérin, *Les luttes de classes sous la Première République*, 2 vols (Paris, 1946).

[15]G. Lefebvre, *Les Paysans du nord pendant la Révolution française* (Paris and Lille, 1924); idem, *Quatre-vingt-neuf* (Paris, 1939); idem, *La Grande Peur* (Paris, 1953); idem, *Etudes sur la Révolution française* (Paris, 1954).

[16]A. Cobban, *Historians and the Causes of the French Revolution* (s.l., 1970).

[17]F. Furet, *Marx and the French Revolution* (Chicago and London, 1988) [first published in French in 1986].

mention or is simply bypassed in a story-line that methodologically brackets off 'class' and instead focuses on diplomacy, politics, war and powerful rulers. This silencing of class issues may even represent a denial of class – though perhaps not of its present existence, but certainly of its legitimacy as a political reference point for revolutionary movements and its inevitability as a structural reality in future society.

In Britain the myth of the Whig interpretation of history, denounced by Herbert Butterfield as early as 1931,[18] marked historiography from Macaulay to Trevelyan. British national history was a parliamentary and constitutional narrative that reached back to the Magna Carta (1215) and culminated in the Glorious Revolution (1688). This long tradition of parliamentarism and the absence of major disruptions nourished the idea that Britain, as 'the mother of parliaments', had to fulfil a 'civilising' mission in the rest of the world. This grand narrative dominated national histories in their conservative, liberal and Marxist variations well after 1945. It also meant that conservative British historians endorsed the progressive electoral reform of the first half of the nineteenth century, even if Chartism did pose a threat to established institutions similar to that of the 1848 revolution in France.[19] The fear provoked by Chartism and the revolutions of 1848 motivated Thomas Babington Macaulay to write an historical account describing how reform at the correct time would make revolution unnecessary and provide national stability, which was the creed of the Whigs in the nineteenth century. Against the excesses of the French Revolution, English historians presented the peaceful outcome of the Glorious Revolution as a milestone in the success story of the English people. They also portrayed parliamentary liberty as intertwined with this peaceful tradition.

The fact that Britain was spared the revolutionary consequences of the upheavals that France suffered was seen to be a mark of identity and a good reason for admiration from other countries. Historians exhibited a tendency to focus on the seventeenth century, a period of struggle between monarchy, aristocracy and parliament (won by the latter), writing a teleological history that culminated in the present. Thus, for the English, there was no starting point for a new history comparable with the year 1789 in France; the Reform Bill of 1832 was the outcome of what had been initiated in 1688, and not a new beginning. Macaulay argued that: 'The history of England is emphatically the history of progress', and the present also supplied the standard for judging

---

[18]H. Butterfield, *The Whig Interpretation of History* (London, 1965 [1931]); A. Wilson and T. G. Ashplant, 'Whig History and Present-Centered History', *Historical Journal*, 31 (1988), 1–16.

[19]J. Hamburger, *Macaulay and the Whig Tradition* (Chicago, 1976); P. M. B. Blaas, *Continuity and Anachronism: Parliamentary and Constitutional Development in Whig Historiography and the Anti-Whig Reaction between 1890 and 1930* (The Hague, 1978).

the past. English historians saw their history as a continuous line of civilisation undisrupted by traumatic events, which strengthened their sense of national superiority. George Macaulay Trevelyan was the last great representative of this conservative Whig historiography. He also demonstrated a Victorian concern for social matters and a fear of twentieth- century mass society, which he saw as a threat to English values and institutions.[20]

In Germany, with its national unification in 1870/1, the problem of 'class' and internal conflict was rendered differently, but the reference to France is comparable with British historiography. As national unification was a predominantly bourgeois project, the projected nation-state was clearly presented as a promised 'healer'. On the one hand, it would provide a unified market in which future economic growth would take place and eventually end all social problems. On the other, it attributed to statehood an almost mystic quality which would elevate the entire nation – rich and poor alike – to an unprecedented cultural and ethical stage of development.[21] In this vision, the state as both the product and agent of statehood was capable of forging a higher unity in a people traditionally divided into hostile denominations of regional 'tribes' (*Stämme*), estates (*Stände*) and 'classes'.[22] The rise of the 'social question' specifically occurred in a period when the process of unification, as heralded by national historiography, finally seemed to have prevailed over traditional forces of division. The reaction to this new source of tension and struggle, therefore, tended either to place 'class' in the revolutionary tradition emanating from France (despite Friedrich Engels' 'class' analysis of England,[23] historians continued to point to France when referring to the threat represented by the 'dangerous classes') – thus, treating 'class' as another French export, followed quickly by 'internationalism' – or to neglect 'class' altogether as a phenomenon inherent to the unfolding new social order.

In German *Historism* the main narrative used the theme of the nation's repeated periods of decline (from the late Middle Ages, with a low point around

---

[20]B. Stuchtey, 'Literature, Liberty and Life of the Nation: British Historiography from Macaulay to Trevelyan', in Berger et al., *Writing National Histories*, pp. 30–2; J. Kenyon, *The History Men: The Historical Profession in England since the Renaissance* (London, 1983); J. Clive, *Macaulay: The Shaping of the Historian* (Cambridge, 1987); D. Cannadine, *G. M. Trevelyan: A Life in History* (London, 1993).

[21]H. von Treitschke, *Deutsche Geschichte im Neunzehnten Jahrhundert*, Erster Teil, *Bis zum zweiten Pariser Frieden*, 9th edn (Leipzig, 1913), pp. vi, v.

[22]H. von Treitschke, *Politik: Vorlesungen gehalten an der Universität zu Berlin*, ed. M. Cornicelius, vol. 1, 5th edn (Leipzig, 1922), p. 9.

[23]F. Engels, 'Die Lage der arbeitenden Klasse in England: nach eigener Anschauung und authentischen Quellen' (1845), in *Marx-Engels-Werke*, vol. 18 (Berlin, GDR, 1973), pp. 209–87.

the end of the Thirty Years War, and then the breakdown of the old empire under the onslaught of Napoleon's armies), followed by immense struggles to regain national identity during the Reformation and the 'wars of liberation' against Napoleon. There was a sequence of dividing forces that each time had to be overcome for Germany to reach an as yet incomplete national unification: first, there was noble sectarianism, then there was denominational strife between Protestants and Catholics which opened up the German territories to the influences of foreign powers, turning the nation into a theatre of dreadful war (1618–48). Finally, there was revolutionary France, which exported the 'un-German' spirit of revolution and turned Germany into a victim of imperialistic wars.[24]

The British and German cases reveal that it is precisely when 'class' is pushed into historiographical oblivion that it becomes omnipresent in tales of national identity and unification. The 'nation' appears as the answer to 'class' in reaction to an absent (because omitted) Other, which is silenced precisely by the discursive power unfolded by national historiography. Class tensions from within the nation were suppressed in the national narrative by projecting and exporting 'revolutionary evil' to the external enemy, France, thereby transforming the threat posed by 'class' into an antagonism between nation-states.

Representations of 'the people' as the true nation

As Hobsbawm has stressed, the original revolutionary-popular idea of patriotism signified the sovereign people constituting 'the nation' and had no ethnic connotations whatsoever.[25] The concept of 'the people' politicised claims to citizenship rights on an egalitarian basis. Thus, 'the people' entered the political stage not as an exploited collectivity but as an association of 'common men' (typically men). Labour movements in different countries adapted to the discourse of *la patrie* and the promise of *liberté, égalité, fraternité* to claim the civil rights denied to the working classes. This led to varying interpretations and representations of the role of 'the people' in revolutionary episodes, as we saw earlier in the case of the French Revolution(s). In Belgian historiography also, the ongoing debate around the 1830 revolution shows (besides disputes over the communitarian division) diverging judgements about the proletarian character of the event that founded the 'artificial' state of Belgium. However,

---

[24]L. von Ranke, *Geschichte der romanischen und germanischen Völker von 1494 bis 1514*, 3rd edn (Leipzig, 1885), pp. v–viii; idem, 'Idee der Universalhistorie' (1831), *Vorlesungseinleitungen*, ed. Volker Dotterweich and Walther Peter Fuchs (Vienna, 1975), pp. 72–89.
[25]E. J. Hobsbawm, *Nations and Nationalism since 1780: Programme, Myth, Reality* (Cambridge, 1991 [1990]), pp. 87–91.

144 *Gita Deneckere and Thomas Welskopp*

these national and socialist narratives are not as mutually exclusive as it may seem. The ethnic concept of *das Volk*, which came to the fore in the 1920s, was very much opposed to 'modern' patriotic and socialist visions of *le peuple*, and nourished explicit counter-narratives to 'class' and conflict.

Histories in 'republican' or 'democratic' traditions (in their late eighteenth- and nineteenth-century meanings), such as those of France and Belgium, used revolutions as foundational myths without denying their social underpinnings by definition. Within these traditions 'the people' rose to nationhood through revolutionary action against foreign or domestic oppressors. 'The people' were then considered to be the actual, 'true' nation. While 'class' may lie at the core of this notion of 'the people', the latter was a much more openly political term which implied the inclusion of the overwhelming majority of the population, whereas oppressing social groups formed only a tiny minority. The 'majority factor' was crucial for successfully certifying that revolutionary action was justified and would not lead to new injustice, disorder or internal divisions, but to solidarity and unity on an unprecedented scale.

For the key Belgian historian Henri Pirenne, the independence achieved by the Belgian people in 1830 had to be conserved at all costs; the aggression of neighbours that had used Belgian territory as a battlefield for so long had to be resisted.[26] In Pirenne's vision, very much like Michelet's *peuple*, 'la Belgique' merged with 'the Belgian people', which from ancient times existed with a particular identity and national character. Since the end of the Middle Ages, the Belgian nation appeared at the front line of Roman and German culture, deeply rooted in social and economic developments and strengthened by the Burgundian unification of the fifteenth century (this national unity existed long before the establishment of the Belgian nation-state in 1830). In his monumental *Histoire de Belgique*, Pirenne demonstrated the unity of Belgian history and the inevitability of revolution in an unprecedented way, convincing a large public through the factuality, clarity and epic qualities of his work. When Belgium celebrated its centennial in 1930, Pirenne was still accorded the highest esteem and became something of a national symbol.[27]

[26]H. Pirenne, *Histoire de Belgique des origines à nos jours*, tome 3, *De la fin du régime espagnol à la Révolution belge* (Brussels, 1950 [1st edn, 1926]), p. 530.
[27]H. Hasquin, *Historiographie et politique: Essai sur l'histoire de Belgique et la Wallonie* (Charleroi, 1981), pp. 52–69; J. Stengers, 'La Révolution de 1830', *Les Grands Mythes de l'histoire de Belgique*, ed. A. Morelli (Brussels, 1995), pp. 144–6; Jo Tollebeek, 'Het gevoelige punt van Europa: Huizinga, Pirenne en de plaats van het vaderland', *De ekster en de kooi: Nieuwe opstellen over de geschiedschrijving* (Amsterdam, 1996), pp. 225–47; A. van der Lem, 'Het nationale epos', *De palimpsest: Geschiedschrijving in de Nederlanden 1500–2000*, ed. J. Tollebeek, T. Verschaffel, and L. H. M. Wessels (Hilversum, 2002), pp. 186–90.

The work of Pirenne, because of its Marxist undertones and focus on socio-economic factors, was also much appreciated in socialist circles.[28] A translation of the *Histoire de Belgique* was published by the Ghent socialist *Volksdrukkerij*. Prominent leaders participated in a homage to Pirenne in 1912 and attended his funeral in 1935. Nevertheless, the patriotic view of the 1830 revolution had been criticised by Belgian socialists since the 1880s. Léon Defuisseaux, Edward Anseele, Louis Bertrand and others believed that the essentially proletarian character of the revolution was 'confiscated' by the bourgeoisie, who denied the real heroes of the barricades the right to vote. Research into the social origins of the September 1830 revolutionaries proved that they were workers and artisans, 'real' people that were excluded from politics by way of reward.[29] In his *Histoire de la démocratie et du socialisme en Belgique*, Bertrand listed 'the martyrs' of 1830 as an empirical illustration.[30] The 1930 case of Bertrand – who in the meantime had become minister of state, charged with a chapter in the official and prestigious *Livre d'Or du peuple belge* in which he reiterated the socialist interpretation of the revolution – provides an interesting example of the integration and compatibility of national and socialist narratives.[31] In 1929 Maurice Bologne included a sociological examination of the victims of the revolution in his *L'Insurrection prolétarienne de 1830 en Belgique*. These anonymous heroes, who had gained their rights in the struggle for emancipation, were presented as the forerunners of the social democrat labour movement.[32]

In this context Swiss historiography provides us with an exception that proves the rule (referring to the above-mentioned patterns of integrating 'class' history into the national meta-narrative). Of the four most popular national historians writing around 1900, only Karl Dändliker explicitly included the 'proletariat' in his patriotic definition of the 'Swiss people' (*das Schweizervolk*). For him even the socialists were foremost Swiss patriots. He presented their socialism as being of a recognisable Swiss variety, clearly distinguishable from foreign organisations: '[t]he doctrines of the complete equalisation of property and violent uprising

---

[28]Cf. G. Vanschoenbeek, 'Socialisten: gezellen zonder vaderland? De Belgische Werklieden-partij en haar verhouding tot het "vaderland België", 1885–1940', *Bijdragen tot de Eigentijdse Geschiedenis / Cahiers d'Histoire du Temps Présent*, 3 (1997), 240–5.

[29]L. Defuisseaux, *Les hontes du suffrage universel* (Brussels, s.d.); E. Anseele, *De omwenteling van 1830: historische roman* (Gent, 1882); L. Bertrand, L. de Brouckère, and C. Huysmans, *1830–1905: 75 années de domination bourgeoise* (Brussels, 1905).

[30]L. Bertrand, *Histoire de la démocratie et du socialisme en Belgique depuis 1830* (Brussels, 1906), p. 27.

[31]L. Bertrand, 'Le Parti socialiste belge', *Centenaire de l'Indépendance, Livre d'Or du peuple belge* (Brussels, Antwerp, 1930), pp. 105–10.

[32]M. Bologne, *L'Insurrection prolétarienne de 1830 en Belgique* (Liège, 1929), with a preface by Emile Vandervelde. This small book was translated in Dutch and reprinted in 1979 by the Flemish editor Kritak.

... do not appeal to and contradict the practical sense of the Swiss population,' he argued. 'Thus the *Zürcher Arbeiterzeitung* ['Zurich working men's journal'] only expressed the general mood when it gave [the following] declaration to the *International*: "We want to be and remain *Eidgenossen* in the first place and honour devotion and faithfulness to the fatherland as the first political duty of a Swiss [citizen]".'[33] Dändliker rehabilitated the revolutionary episode of the peasant wars (which most other national historians condemned as an aberration retarding national unity), portraying them as a part of the underprivileged majority's struggle for independence, and thereby established that economic conflict and patriotic solidarity were not necessarily mutually exclusive.

From the 1920s onward, 'histories of the people' (*Volksgeschichten*) became popular throughout most of Europe. Yet although the boundaries of this genre remained blurred (English 'people's history' could mean, in Trevelyan's case, a social history of the working class, and the language and cultural studies of the French *Annales* did not jettison the notion of 'the people' as a revolutionary subject), the thrust of most *Volksgeschichten* formed radical counter-narratives to 'class' and 'revolution'. This was particularly evident in Germany, where the *Volksgeschichte*, apart from the early, mildly Marxist social histories of young German historians such as Eckart Kehr or Hans Rosenberg during the 1930s, presented itself as a more superior counter-history to Marxism and liberalism than what the individualistic *Historism* (itself of liberal origin) had been able to put forward as the authoritative national history. Here, 'the people' (*Volk*) positively signified a direct opposition to 'society', a term that had all the negative connotations of class division and internal struggle. Thinking in terms of 'society' was charged with opening up opportunities for socialism to take root and to agitate for 'social revolution'. Particularly under National Socialism, the notion of *Volk* took on an openly racist meaning and placed an assumedly shared genetic heritage at the centre of national identity.[34]

Revolutions and revolutionary episodes in national narratives

National narratives differ markedly in the way that their historiographies handle revolutions or revolutionary episodes. In some European countries, 'revolution' provides something like a foundational myth, and a virtual starting point for national history. In Switzerland the Tell and Winkelried tales and the 'union

---

[33]Quote in S. Buchbinder, *Der Wille zur Geschichte. Schweizergeschichte um 1900: die Werke von Wilhelm Oechsli, Johannes Dierauer und Karl Dändliker* (Zurich, 2002), p. 223.
[34]Cf. M. Hettling, 'Volk und Volksgeschichten in Europa', pp. 7–37; W. Oberkrome, 'Entwicklungen und Varianten der deutschen Volksgeschichte (1900–1960)', pp. 65–95; both in M. Hettling (ed.), *Volksgeschichten im Europa der Zwischenkriegszeit* (Göttingen 2003).

oath' of 1291 were depicted as the mythical origins of the Swiss Confederation. In the nineteenth century, national-liberal historiography, as envisaged by Carl Hilty and elaborated by Johannes Dierauer and Karl Dändliker, drew a teleological line from the uprising against Habsburg rule to the contemporary Swiss Federation, implying that the original 'comrades under oath' and the current community of Swiss citizens shared one and the same identity. Significantly, the 'tradition of liberation' heralded in this historiography was completely insulated from later revolutionary events; national tradition was not to be contaminated by current political affairs. By including the founding myths in its 'tradition of liberation', nineteenth-century historiography is said to have 'frozen in time' Swiss national history.[35] At the end of the nineteenth century, popular historians set out to overcome the confessional fault-lines within the Swiss bourgeoisie with their narratives of identity and unity. This explains their harmonious character, which, on the other hand, came with sharp exclusionary tendencies against other parts of the population, most markedly the working class. Swiss national historiography did everything to deny that social movements could verify their goals by alluding to the legitimacy of the Tell tradition. However, the peasant uprisings of the early seventeenth century explicitly tried to do the same, and the Swiss labour movement two centuries later also repeatedly aimed to root the public memory of the peasants' struggle (and thereby their own struggle) in this shared Swiss tradition.[36]

The 1918 general strike in Switzerland, which became known as the *Landesstreik*, as well as other strike movements in 1919, was not acknowledged in Swiss historiography until the 1960s.[37] An exhaustive treatment did not appear until 1968, when the still authoritative study by Willi Gautschi was published.[38] The rare references that were made to the strike still glossed over the fact that the *Landesstreik* had involved more of a 'class struggle' from above (from the anti-liberal right), and there was a tendency to portray the conflict as a left-wing conspiracy set in motion by the Soviet embassy.[39] 'Class conflict' and revolutionary tendencies were considered to be 'un-Swiss' and

---

[35]Buchbinder, *Wille zur Geschichte*, p. 232; G. P. Marchal, 'Les Traditions nationales dans l'historiographie de la Suisse', in W. Blockmans and J. Philippe Genet (eds), *Visions sur le développement des états européens: théories et historiographies de l'état moderne* (Rome, 1993), pp. 271–96; 276ff.

[36]Marchal, 'Traditions', pp. 297f.

[37]B. Degen, 'Arbeiterbewegung und Politik in der Geschichtsschreibung', in B. Studer and F. Vallotton (eds), *Histoire sociale et mouvement ouvrier: un bilan historiographique 1848–1998 / Sozialgeschichte und Arbeiterbewegung: eine historiographische Bilanz 1848–1998* (Zurich 1997), pp. 33–60.

[38]W. Gautschi, *Der Landesstreik 1918* (Zurich 1968).

[39]M. Hettling et al., *Eine kleine Geschichte der Schweiz: der Bundesstaat und seine Traditionen* (Frankfurt am Main, 1998), pp. 40ff.

outside the national tradition.[40] During periods of social tension, for instance in the 1930s or the late 1960s, public and political debate repeatedly referred to the *Landesstreik* in a cautionary tone. A revolutionary episode such as this, a *second* general strike, had to be avoided at all costs. Yet since the actual account of past events was not represented in national historiography, public memory treated it like a phantom, an imaginary anomaly within Swiss history, which pragmatic politics and social concessions to the unions would help prevent from recurring. 'Revolution' in Swiss mainstream history, therefore, had to be a unique event, one that was long past and widely stripped of any social content. The legitimacy of 'liberation' was to be reserved for resistance against external alien forces.

In other national histories, as we have seen in relation to the Belgian Revolution (but presumably most significantly in Germany), revolutions were downplayed, denied or had their social aspects pushed into the background. The failed revolution of 1848 was seen as an aberration and the revolution of 1918/19 as the machination of foreign powers. Instead, positive references to German national history highlighted a tradition of 'liberation' and 'emancipation' (not in an individualistic or liberal, but in a collective, national sense) through war. In the line of continuity constructed to legitimise the German unification of 1871, the 'wars of liberation' against Napoleonic dominance appeared as the direct prelude to Bismarck's 'wars of unification' in 1848–66 and 1870/1, while the revolution of 1848 was virtually bypassed. Class and revolution on the one hand, and liberation and war on the other, represented opposites: the former carried the negative sense of internal division and conflict, the other stood for the positive values of forging national solidarity and unity.

The rich tradition of nineteenth- and twentieth-century collective action in Belgium was likewise erased from collective memory and historiography. The last 'real' revolution occurred at its creation, but the country had since been familiarised with a recurring pattern of protest and reform. Owing to their fear of revolution, the authorities repeatedly made concessions, but publicly denied their motivation.[41] In official discourse, of which political historiography was part, the significance of 1848 was downplayed despite its important role in the consolidation of the Belgian state. The traumatic influence of the European revolutions and their ramifications for Belgium were never recognised.[42]

Thus, from different points of departure, European national histories arrived at a strikingly similar degree of denying 'class' and revolutionary episodes in their

---

[40]Comité pour une Nouvelle Histoire de la Suisse (ed.), *Geschichte der Schweiz und der Schweizer*, 3rd edn (Basel, 2004), pp. 765ff.

[41]Cf. G. Deneckere, *Sire, het volk mort: sociaal protest in België 1831–1918* (Antwerp, 1997).

[42]G. Deneckere, '(Dis)remembering the 1848 Revolution in Belgium: How an Important Historical Rupture Got Forgotten', in C. Tacke (ed.), *1848: Memory and Oblivion in Europe* (Brussels, 2000), pp. 57–78.

overarching meta-narratives. Furthermore, it has become evident that national historiography privileged the national over the social aspects of any revolutionary episode that actually occurred. Those that heralded a cultural or political notion of the 'nation' perhaps would include the social side, yet most likely not with 'class' in a Marxist sense but as a synonym for the 'common people'.

Alternative class narratives outside the academic sphere: labour movement history

In order to give voice to the workers and claim a place for them in history, the historiography of the working classes and the labour movement was almost everywhere in Europe pioneered by the socialist movement itself. The proliferation of 'class' narratives outside the academic discipline of history was caused by the degree to which the respective hegemonic mainstream excluded alternative, or complementary, meta-narratives. Germany once more might represent the most radical case. *Historism* militantly safeguarded its near-monopoly, not only from potential subversion by 'class' and revolutionary accounts, but also from all attempts to broaden the methodological scope of the historiography by ventures into social or cultural histories. Even the conservative political economists who were reform-minded and initiated the 'historical school' of economics in Germany found themselves discredited as 'lecture hall socialists' (*Kathedersozialisten*).

We propose, therefore, that the richness of 'class' and revolutionary historiography, which took shape within the ranks of the labour movement, developed in proportion to the degree of its political isolation and exclusion from academic history. Consequently, historical writing in the German labour movement appeared especially diverse, although the situation in Switzerland was very similar. Intellectual circles in German and Swiss social democracy remained sharply isolated, their 'class' and revolutionary histories written for a similarly isolated milieu of potential readers. Intellectuals such as the British Fabians, who bridged the gulf between socialism and academia, could not flourish in Germany and Switzerland; the greater and earlier openness to social history in Britain, and also in France and Belgium, was obviously related to an earlier political democratisation and to the integration of labour parties within the institutions of the nation-state. The work of Beatrice and Sidney Webb, founders of the renowned London School of Economics, and R. H. Tawney and G. D. H. Cole, who occupied high positions in Oxford, received academic recognition from the outset.[43]

These pioneering authors did not construct a 'counter-class' narrative, but broadened the definition of the 'nation' to include the working classes.

---

[43]Cf. Berger, 'Geschichten von der Nation', p. 63.

Significantly, Cole called them 'the common people', whose full working-class consciousness was awakened between 1832 and 1848, during the general trade union, factory, anti-Poor Law and Chartist agitations.[44] It is likely that the 'social question' and 'class' would be able to successfully claim a role in national historiography in cases where the nation-state could already look back on a long, continuous history, and remained uncontested in its geographical boundaries. This may have prepared the ground for a more tolerant atmosphere within the discipline, although social history in Britain developed in the rather peripheral sub-field of economic history and much later than the mainstream of national historiography.

Political factors may have contributed to pushing for an integrative angle on 'class' history. Unlike in Germany, where the labour movement remained politically isolated, in Britain from the 1860s onwards liberals profited from the collaboration with organised labour. Thus, a 'liberal' social history (albeit taking a social-democratic turn early in the twentieth century) was logical, since it could provide a narrative that depicted the integration (rather than the emancipation) of the working class into the British nation and could appeal to an inclusive rather than an oppositional patriotism on the workers' side. 'Invented traditions', like that of the 'freeborn Englishman', prepared the way for the image of a nation embracing its self-conscious plebeian majority. Inclusive 'class' history, on the other hand, could serve as a political argument within the established social order. Without completely denouncing the class divisions within industrial society or propagating the socialist system as an alternative, the Fabian social democrat Tawney, for example, was able to attack the British class system for its long-standing excessive class privileges, as well as its added rigidity, which were likely to have hindered social progress and stifle individualism.[45]

It may be the case that the integration of class into academic history came at the price of separating class and revolution. This is vividly demonstrated by Trevelyan's well-known definition of social history as 'a history of the people with the politics left out'.[46] In this vein, the initial establishment that a social class can exist despite there being no trace of 'revolutionary class-consciousness' among the workers seems to be a precondition for Tawney's social democratic 'nationalisation' of class.[47]

In general, historical accounts of class and its relationship to revolution and the nation, written by authors from the intellectual fringes of the labour movement, appear to fall into four (albeit frequently blurred) categories. The

---

[44]S. and B. Webb, *The History of Trade Unionism* (London, 1911); G. D. H. Cole and R. Postgate, *The Common People, 1746–1946* (London, 1946).
[45]Calvert, *Concept of Class*, p. 106.
[46]G. M. Trevelyan, *Illustrated English Social History* (London, 1942).
[47]Cf. Calvert, *Concept of Class*, p. 106.

first is 'class' history as a counter-national, 'internationalist' narrative. Evidently, the pioneers in this genre were Karl Marx and Friedrich Engels with their *Communist Manifesto*.[48] In Germany they had successors among members of the social democratic labour movement. Franz Mehring's books, most notably his monumental *History of German Social Democracy* (1897–8), stood in the tradition of Marx and Engels and provided, in a literary *tour de force*, a combined history of the German working class and the social democratic labour movement since its formation. This contribution's internationalist perspective and revolutionary optimism distinguished it as a clear-cut alternative to the *Historist* tales of national unification. Mehring's *Lessing Legend* (1893) openly defied nationalist myths of Prussia's advancement of culture and especially the role of Frederick II in the promotion of the arts and sciences. However, even taking Mehring's case as an example, it becomes obvious that alternative approaches to history do not necessarily have to take on an internationalist perspective. Instead, his *German History since the End of the Middle Ages* represented an attempt at a *national* counter-history.[49] The treatment of revolutions in this line of historiography was marked by a sustained revolutionary optimism: whereas the true, decisive revolution was portrayed as yet to come, past revolutionary episodes were classed by the degree of their relative failure or 'maturity'. For the German case, it is striking that counter-national history privileged the events of the Paris Commune over the revolution of 1848. Whereas the first represented the 'dawn of a new age', and a foreboding of the promised socialist revolution, the latter was seen as 'the fatal cramp in the agony of the *ancien régime*'. The responsibility for failed revolutions was frequently assigned to the subversion of 'traitors', for instance, the bourgeoisie's actions in 1848/9, and those of the moderate Social Democrats in the revolution of 1918/19.

The second category is class narratives as 'contentious' histories. These differed from the type above in that they criticised the existing order more from an integrationist and emancipatory perspective than from an 'internationalist' or revolutionary one. Claims for emancipation were directed at the existing nation-state. The Social Democrats' leader, Robert Grimm, was a major exponent of this form of narrative for Switzerland.[50] He adopted the hegemonic liberal view of Swiss history and simply reformulated its narrative in a dialectical Marxist idiom. Instead of progress originating out of the 'tradition of liberation',

[48]K. Marx and F. Engels, *Manifest der Kommunistischen Parte* (London, 1848).
[49]F. Mehring, *Geschichte der deutschen Sozialdemokratie*, 2nd edn (1903–4) (= *Gesammelte Schriften*, vols 1 and 2) (Berlin, GDR, 1960); idem, *Lessing-Legende: zur Geschichte und zur Kritik des preußischen Despotismus und der klassischen Literatur* (Berlin, 1893); idem, *Deutsche Geschichte vom Ausgange des Mittelalters*, 2 vols (Berlin, 1910–11).
[50]R. Grimm, *Geschichte der Schweiz in ihren Klassenkämpfen* (Zurich, 1976 [1920]); idem, *Geschichte der sozialistischen Ideen in der Schweiz* (Zurich, 1978 [1931]).

for Grimm the class struggle was the prime moving factor in Swiss history. He thus drew an equally teleological line, which connected Tell to the peasant uprisings of early modern times and to the labour movement of his day.[51] In Germany the works of Eduard Bernstein provide an excellent example. A social democratic revisionist, he concluded his *History of the Labour Movement in Berlin* (1907), an ardent accusation of the ruling classes in Germany who denied German workers an appropriate position and voice in the nation-state, with an explicit homage to English constitutionalism and parliamentarianism.[52] In such accounts, the depiction of revolutionary episodes changed from being optimistic and aggressive to defensive in tone. Revolutions were presented as working people's last resort to defend themselves against irresponsible, intransigent elites, whose failures and neglect had provoked the uprising of the masses.

The third category is class narratives as claims of 'respectable' integration into the nation. Countless accounts of the German labour parties' linear progress and organisational success fall into this category. Progressive trade union histories chronicling the achievements of the respective association complemented this genre. Louis Bertrand in his *Histoire de la démocratie et du socialisme en Belgique* (1906–7), which was splendidly illustrated, combined the characteristics of the former category with a strong inclination to convince the bourgeoisie of the respectability of the workers (as represented by the organised labour movement). The treatment of wildcat strikes, insurrections and riots, and the 'pre-socialist' phase in the making of the labour movement, only served to highlight the superiority of the disciplined and 'mature' organisation of the present. Last but not least, from the late nineteenth century a number of important biographies and autobiographies of labour leaders appeared. Much of this 'class history' as labour movement history either fulfilled self-legitimising purposes, or fought the battles of the past again on contemporary historiographical ground. It is notable, however, that from a methodological point of view, this 'class history' reproduced a mirror image of the nationalist meta-narrative of ideas and great men, albeit in a socialist key. Thus in Germany, what the historian Vaughn Davis Bornet had called for as an appropriate 'New Labor History' for the US in 1955 – a history based on the 'official and personal correspondence files of union leaders' and amounting to a generous 'diplomatic history' of 'our union statesmen' – became reality.[53] This

---

[51]Cf. Marchal, 'Traditions', pp. 279f.

[52]E. Bernstein, *Die Geschichte der Berliner Arbeiterbewegung*, 3 vols (Berlin, 1907; reprinted Glashütten/Taunus, 1972).

[53]V. Davis Bornet, 'The New Labor History: A Challenge for American Historians', *The Historian*, 18 (1955), 1–21ff., quoted in R. Rosenzweig, 'Sources of Stability and Seeds of Subversion: David Brody and the Making of the "New" Labor History', *Labor History*, 34 (1993), 503–9, p. 503.

class history did not simply remain firmly rooted in a national framework: contributions often explicitly used a wider, more egalitarian and democratic nation as their point of reference. The political thrust of this historiography was reform-minded yet anti-revolutionary. Indeed, parties, unions and their respective leaders boasted of themselves as respectable, responsible political bodies whose 'true patriotism' was expressed through moderation. In this line of reasoning, revolutions were not condemned completely, but were seen as justified only in acts of resistance against unjust provocation. In other circumstances, episodes were criticised as 'immature aberrations' set in motion by conspiracies from competing, more radical factions of the labour movement. Thus, the status of revolutions was diminished to a part in the 'learning curve' that the moderate labour movement had to go through.

The fourth category is 'class' and revolutionary history as a narrative of national counter-culture. In Germany this form of 'ethnographic' historiography became popular in ultra-leftist groupings of the Social Democrat Party, especially after their separation into a radical minority and a moderate majority during and after the First World War. Histories of this kind were designed to provide the nascent communist parties with a tradition of their own, which was rooted in a more radical, primordial working-class culture, and which the established organisations of the labour movement presumably did not (or no longer) represent. The 'true proletariat' was seen as culturally rich, diverse, uncorrupted and anti-authoritarian in outlook, but for the present (between 1914 and 1924) still in thrall to 'bourgeois culture'. The traditional labour movement was accused of 'embourgeoisement'. Although the beginnings of this counter-historiography as an alternative to traditional labour movement history were eventually stamped out by Stalinisation, it somewhat resurfaced in academic circles which sympathised with the radical Marxist groupings of the 'New Left' in the 1960s.[54]

Communist and state socialist narratives of class and nation after 1917

Historiographical accounts of the Russian Revolution of 1917 started years after the event itself. The inner power circles of the new Bolshevik regime felt a pressing need for historical legitimation. Yet a prolonged Marxist account of Russia's long-term development, with a heroic tale of the victorious

---

[54]The most notable practitioner of this kind of history in Germany was Otto Rühle (1874–1943): O. Rühle, *Illustrierte Kultur- und Sittengeschichte des Proletariats*, vol. 1 (Berlin, 1930), vol. 2 (Gießen, 1977). Cf. H. Groschopp, 'Otto Rühle: zum Arbeiterbild in der ultralinken deutschen Arbeiterbewegung der zwanziger Jahre', in K. Tenfelde (ed.), *Arbeiter im 20 Jahrhundert* (Stuttgart, 1991), pp. 299–320.

revolutionary uprising as its shining *telos*, could obviously not fulfil this purpose. Early Soviet historiography did not portray the revolutionary episode as the necessary leap onto the stage where history would be fulfilled. Rather, the young regime had to cope with two major problems of legitimation. On the one hand, it still appeared difficult to explain why a socialist revolution had succeeded in a nation so clearly backwards from the point of view of a Marxist 'objective' class analysis. On the other, a savage civil war was still raging, and thus for retaining (or winning back) public support against the internationally reinforced 'White' enemy, it seemed essential to demonstrate that the revolution was in fact the act of the Russian people as a self-conscious whole.

Leo Trotsky's *History of the Russian Revolution*, written in the late 1920s when he was already in Turkish exile from Stalin's persecution, reacted to this twofold dilemma. His account attempted to depict the armed struggles in the Petrograd of October 1917 and the larger 'objective' revolutionary forces in the nation as complementary elements of one and the same overarching and irresistible revolutionary process.[55] Trotsky resorted to the terminology of thermodynamics in order to connect the local uprisings to the revolutionary mood in the countryside.[56]

Thus, by alluding to the laws of physics, Trotsky made the case that the decisive military conquest of the Winter Palace by the Bolsheviks was a logical final step in an almost mechanically determined revolutionary process, and not the isolated *coup d'état* of a well-organised militant minority. Trotsky also argued that just as the actual uprising embodied only the decisive, yet inevitably partial and localised final drama of this process, so the Bolsheviks themselves represented – in his rhetoric – a much larger entity, assuming the role of a revolutionary avant-garde.

Using the same metonymical logic, Trotsky constructed the revolutionary subject as a 'class' in a backward nation. In this construction the Bolsheviks, as the revolutionary avant-garde, appeared not as a militant minority forcing untimely tactics onto an otherwise passive peasant majority, but as a crucial part in forging a class that united a small, industrial proletariat and a grudging but isolated peasantry into an active revolutionary force. The voluntarism of the armed coup finally appeared to be restrained by underlying 'objective' revolutionary conditions. The coup – in Trotsky's thermodynamic metaphor – had only added the required excess temperature to a bowl of simmering liquid ready to boil.[57]

---

[55]J. Baberowski, *Der Sinn der Geschichte: Geschichtstheorien von Hegel bis Foucault* (Munich, 2005), s. 11f.

[56]L. Trotskij, *Geschichte der russischen Revolution*, 3rd edn (Frankfurt/M, 1982), pp. 921f.

[57]Trotskij, *Geschichte der russischen Revolution*, pp. 933–8.

Whereas the concept of 'nation' did not play an explicit role in early post-revolutionary Soviet historiography, the notion of 'people' (as embodied in the term 'the working people', or 'workers' and 'peasants') did assume prominence. It is not difficult to discern in this the rhetorical strategy of merging 'class' and 'nation' in a powerful icon, thus lending legitimacy to the communists both as 'class leaders' and as patriotic agents of unification. In a sense, the Russian peasantry provided the folkloristic element that coloured the modernist and internationalist revolutionary avant-garde in a picturesque ethnic pattern. During the 1920s, however, this ethnic colouring of 'class' retained nothing of its initial subtlety. Ethnic histories composed of class language became a prime propaganda weapon both in international and domestic discourses.[58]

The internationalist offensive of Soviet communism provided communist parties all over Europe with a role model and also a new perspective on their own national histories which could be utilised for self-legitimising functions. Popular uprisings such as the 'peasant wars' and other social movements in medieval and early modern Europe could consequently be interpreted as forerunners of present-day class struggles, and their heroes heralded as revolutionary activists *avant la lettre*. Since most of the newly founded nation-states in Central and Eastern Europe in the 1920s claimed a tradition of prevailing in insurrections against ethnic oppression that reached back for centuries, the young communist parties worked hard to appropriate these revolts as early expressions of class struggle and to present themselves as legitimate heirs to their cause. Competition arose between nationalist and class interpretations of past ethnic conflicts, and the strength or weakness of the communists in the respective new nation-state often decided between historiographical hegemony and marginalisation.[59]

Communist class narratives, however, were largely nothing other than national ethnic narratives in a revolutionary disguise. This became especially salient in Soviet domestic affairs. From the civil war that ensued after 1917, communist propaganda and historiography began to depict internal adversaries such as the tsarist nobility or 'unwanted' social groups such as the well-off farmers (kulaks) as class enemies and ethnically defined 'outcasts'. In the case of the Baltic noblemen, who were leading activists in the counter-revolutionary wars, class lines and ethnic segregation neatly coincided. Since the mid-1920s it mattered less and less if a group was declared to be 'outcast' (also being stripped of the right to vote) for reasons of having an 'exploitative lifestyle' or of belonging to a non-Russian nationality, or of other forms of 'un-Soviet

---

[58]E. Oberländer, *Sowjetpatriotismus und Geschichte: Dokumentation* (Cologne, 1967), pp. 248f.
[59]For Hungary, see Á. von Klimó, *Nation, Konfession, Geschichte: zur nationalen Geschichtskultur Ungarns im europäischen Kontext (1860–1948)* (Munich, 2003), pp. 158ff.

behaviour'. Disqualifications on the grounds of class hostility and ethnic background became interchangeable, and the party pushed the definitions of putative enemies to unimaginable limits, utilising historical arguments to justify their physical extermination. Even prior to Stalinisation, the Soviet leadership proclaimed that the 'New Soviet Man' did not only have specific class qualities but also distinct ethnic attributes; he was decidedly Russian.[60]

With the enforcement of Stalin's personality cult in the aftermath of his fiftieth birthday (1929), the 'nationalisation' of communist class historiography made a further qualitative leap.[61] The new course was canonised in the first edition of the *History of the Communist Party of the Soviet Union (Bolsheviks)* (1938) and its abbreviated version, the *Short Course*, which laid down the party doctrine for communist satellite parties all over Europe.[62] Under Stalin's regime the nationalisation of historical narratives accompanied violent and bloody social restructuring policies such as the completion of agricultural collectivisation around 1933 and the forced industrialisation prescribed in the second five-year plan (1933–7).[63] Stalin exalted the 'State of Workers and Peasants' in the 1936 constitution, and Stalinist historiography filled this phrase with a new 'Soviet patriotism' that increasingly drew on older forms of Russian nationalism. On the one hand, this tacit rehabilitation of pre-revolutionary ideas served as a reassuring ideological compensation for the ruptures brought about by Stalin's policies; on the other, 'Soviet patriotism' became a sharp ideological weapon that forced loyalty on those affected by reforms. Stalinist historiography took the defamation of dissident social and ethnic groups to extremes. Although still employing class terminology, the construction of the alien Other under Stalinism no longer took pains to unmask its class position according to Marxist-Leninist theory. Arguing against the immorality of 'un-Soviet behaviour' and drawing on ethnic stereotypes, Stalinist historiography created the utterly villainous figure of an 'enemy of the people'. In reverse perspective this meant that the Stalinist Soviet Union now addressed a new 'Soviet people'. This concept merged 'class' and nationalism in an even more blatant way than earlier versions of the idea during the 1920s, and, furthermore, deflated 'class' to the meaning of an unflinching loyalty to the regime.[64]

---

[60]G. Alexopoulos, *Stalin's Outcasts: Aliens, Citizens, and the Soviet State, 1926–1936* (New York, 2003).

[61]M. Hildermeier, *Geschichte der Sowjetunion 1917–1991* (Munich, 1998), pp. 554–60.

[62]The *Geschichte der Kommunistischen Partei (Bolschewiki), Kurzer Lehrgang* (Berlin, GDR, 1946) covered the history of the Communist Party in Russia and the Soviet Union from 1883 to 1937.

[63]Von Klimó, *Nation*, pp. 302f.

[64]Cf. Hildermeier, *Geschichte der Sowjetunion*, pp. 554–60.

Internationally, the Comintern proceeded to 'Stalinise' European communist parties in order to bring them firmly into line with the Moscow regime. This had the paradoxical effect, as Árpád von Klimó has noted for Hungary, that communist parties grew increasingly nationalist the more they became 'Stalinised' and dependent on the Soviet Union.[65] On the one hand, this move was programmatic, and Georgi Dimitroff justified it as a necessary counter-reaction to the unqualified reclamation of national histories by Europe's fascist parties.[66] On the other hand, the nationalisation of class narratives appeared as an adequate way for communist satellite parties to follow the example set by the Soviet Union, as nationalised class narratives could justify the domestic implementation of political structures which the 'fatherland of all working people' (the Soviet Union) already possessed.[67]

The 1930s saw the emergence of a pattern that would remain prominent in communist historiography until the demise of the Soviet empire. The nationalisation of class histories reached a new stage with the 'externalisation' of class distinctions. The language of class struggle was now applied to the conflicts between nation-states (to be more precise, between communist and noncommunist nations). The basic concept that the 'fatherland of all working people' had to defend itself against the onslaught of capitalist, imperialist and, as the 1930s drew on, fascist aggressors, and that communist parties in those countries had the duty to contribute to the defence of the communist 'fatherland', radicalised the nationalisation of class histories to a phenomenon of foreign affairs. Once more, the socioeconomic meaning and analytical precision of the signification of 'class' was deflated, and descriptions of the respective alien 'class enemies' had ethnic and racial overtones. The emptiness of the remaining class rhetoric became especially prominent when the Comintern abruptly oscillated between its isolationist 'social fascism', the doctrine of the late 1920s, and its opportunist 'people's front' policies of the late 1930s. Whereas the charge of 'social fascism' was directed against all noncommunist political groupings (for instance, the Social Democratic Party in Weimar Germany), the notion of the 'people's front' included all the 'progressive' political fractions willing to take on a common enemy. Therefore, the spectrum of the 'people's front' contained non-communist and even nonsocialist groups as well as nationalist currents, if they were not fascist or rightwing authoritarian.

---

[65]Von Klimó, *Nation*, p. 302.
[66]W. Pieck, G. Dimitroff, and P. Togliatti, *Die Offensive des Faschismus und die Aufgaben der Kommunisten im Kampf für die Volksfront gegen Krieg und Faschismus* (Berlin, GDR, 1960), p. 161.
[67]Pieck, Dimitroff, and Togliatti, *Die Offensive des Faschismu*, p. 166.

The Second World War brought the identification of purely politically conceived class rhetoric with the nation state to its apogee, embodied in the pronouncement of the conflict as the 'Great Patriotic War'. In Soviet historiography, the terms 'fascist' and 'German' became fully synonymous. Yet whereas there were remnants of class allusions still present in the word 'fascist', the racial connotations of the expression 'brutal Germanic hordes' clearly dominated.

During the Cold War the 'internationalisation' of nationalised class histories provided the backbone of 'bloc' thinking. At this time, the Communist Bloc saw itself as being on the defensive against the capitalist and imperialist powers of the Western hemisphere. Interestingly enough, 'bloc' rhetoric came with a diminishment of racist nationalism. Yet its 'empty' class content did inform many historical narratives and liberation movements all over the world, constructed in order to legitimise their struggles against colonial powers or, after decolonisation, against American or Western hegemony. This was again a paradoxical effect, since most of these 'invented traditions' of class struggle against a colonial oppressor actually described traditional ethnic and nationalist lines of conflict.

In retrospect it is not surprising that class history in communist and state socialist nations did not produce a rich social history of inequality. Rather, earlier conflicts that were ethnic or national in nature were depicted as class struggles, albeit more in the mode of political (party) history than that of social history. The overarching class rhetoric, stripped of its original roots in Marxist-Leninist class analysis, was profoundly nationalised and party politicised. This empty class language resonated with ethnic, racial and nationalist implications. This might have been the reason why major strands of historiography in some post-communist countries made a rapid, yet smooth, turn from stale party orthodoxy to overt and radical nationalism. Some of these historiographies, like those of Poland, were previously 'nationalistic' in varying degrees, under the guise of orthodox class rhetoric. Others, however, did not follow the nationalist trend, for instance, those in the Czech Republic, or in the former GDR (which of course presents a special case).

'Class', revolutions and the 'nation' in the social history of the late twentieth century

In the 1950s in Germany, former practitioners of *Volksgeschichte* acted as forerunners to the establishment of social history as a respected field within mainstream academic historiography. They achieved recognition by jointly returning to the essential premises of *Historism*, especially reformulating the ideas of historical 'individuality' for the analysis of modern society and by developing a form of social history that nevertheless remained staunch in its anti-Marxism. This social history, promoted foremost by Werner Conze and Theodor Schieder, became known as 'structural history' (*Strukturgeschichte*).[68] Conze in particular renounced his former focus on agrarian society and called for a comprehensive analysis of the 'industrial world', although still avoiding the term 'society', which for him was contaminated by Marxism. Conze inspired extensive research into the working and living conditions of 'the labouring estates' from the nineteenth century to the present. This was done precisely to show that German workers never formed a 'class' in the Marxist sense. He tried to demonstrate that German workers had always been diverse, embedded in long-standing traditions and taken care of by state and entrepreneurial welfare policies, in their true core displaying a rather conservative and patriotic character.

However, Conze still had to explain the unprecedented rise of a revolutionary labour party as well as the revolutionary episodes that did occur in Germany. Here again his illuminating work depicted the 'revolution' as an omnipresent and frightening – if largely implicit – threat that loomed over a nation-state in the process of coming into being. For Conze, the revolution of 1848 represented the monarch's and bourgeoisie's fateful failure to arrive at a compromise that would have taken the proletariat on board the national ship before it lost control.[69] Subsequently to this, he held the German state and the industrialists responsible for the continuous exclusion of the workers and their self-conscious isolation within a social democratic milieu. It is only this exclusion that explained for Conze the fact that German workers refused to acknowledge the notable economic gains they achieved during the *Kaiserreich*, and only this dissatisfaction made German workers susceptible to the inflammatory agitation of a handful of fanatical labour ideologues. Thus, Conze argued that it was not 'class formation' according to the Marxist model, but the German workers' denial of their appropriate position within the nation that lay at the roots of their latent revolutionary potential.[70]

Only the second-generation social historians in Germany, from the late 1960s onwards, openly committed themselves to the category of 'class'. This meant a determined step towards the internationalisation of social historical research, since social history elsewhere (the US, UK, France, and so on) had discovered 'class' as an analytical tool for the historical interpretation of modern society much earlier, regardless of whether it was Marxist or non-Marxist in

---

[68]Cf. T. Welskopp, 'Social History', in S. Berger, H. Feldner and K. Passmore (eds), *Writing History: Theory and Practice* (London, 2003), pp. 203–22; 208f.

[69]W. Conze, 'Vom Pöbel zum Proletariat: Sozialgeschichtliche Voraussetzungen für den Sozialismus in Deutschland' (1954), in H-U. Wehler (ed.), *Moderne deutsche Sozialgeschichte*, 5th edn (Cologne, 1976), pp. 111–36.

[70]W. Conze, *Die Strukturgeschichte des technisch-industriellen Zeitalters als Aufgabe für Forschung und Unterricht* (Cologne and Opladen, 1957).

ideological orientation. 'Class' histories during this time aimed to criticise the existing social order and its political establishment. The thrust of this criticism ranged from revolutionary radicalism to welfare-state reformism. As far as a certain opposition to hegemonic Whig-narratives of national histories was concerned, this critical vantage point gave the social history of the 1960s and 1970s an outspoken, anti-national twist. Social history presented itself as the critical progressive alternative to political narratives of the nation's past in which 'great old men' – kings, politicians, generals – figured as the uncontested heroes of national conservatism.

The transnational diffusion of class concepts and the widespread oppositional stance against national histories which excluded the 'ordinary people' did not, however, produce a truly *international* social history. Quite distinct from Anglo-American historical sociology with its typical sweeping multi-case comparisons and reliance on universalist macro-sociological modernisation models, most social histories remained confined by national boundaries. This was precisely because they had to fight for existence in rather peculiar national disciplinary contexts, their critical impetus was aimed at peculiar political systems on the level of nation states, and they failed to escape, even in their criticism, the national histories they claimed to be part of and strove to contest. Therefore, seen as a whole, social history was never able to resolve the underlying tensions between the universalist concepts and methodologies it promoted and its desire to narrate an alternative but nevertheless coherent national history which was superior to traditional political narratives of a national past.

Two seminal collections of essays from the late 1970s and early 1980s on the international phenomenon of working-class formation in nineteenth-century Europe and North America illustrate the effects of these tensions. Both volumes, one entitled *Working-Class Formation*, edited by Ira Katznelson and Aristide R. Zolberg, and the other *Klassen in der europäischen Sozialgeschichte*, edited by Hans-Ulrich Wehler, consisted of a series of national case-studies. These not only failed to develop any comparative perspective of their own, but by and large also failed to adhere to the common theoretical model as outlined in the editors' introductory remarks. Thus, national peculiarities had a profound influence on even the conceptual level of how the case-studies could talk about 'class'. Parochial 'class languages' rather than explainable variations on a common theoretical model coloured the different stories of working-class formation. The latter, in consequence, appeared as a series of national exceptionalisms, as a set of individualised development paths hardly comparable to each other.[71]

---

[71] I. Katznelson and A. R. Zolberg (eds), *Working-Class Formation: Nineteenth-Century Patterns in Western Europe and the United States* (Princeton, NJ, 1986); H-U. Wehler (ed.), *Klassen in der europäischen Sozialgeschichte* (Göttingen, 1979).

This example highlights the crucial fact that when class narratives made substantial inroads into academic social history, they came to dominate the vastly expanding field of labour and labour movement history. At least until social history discovered the *Bürgertum* (the bourgeois middle classes) in the mid-1980s, class narratives and histories of the working class were treated as synonymous. This caused many academic class histories to resume traditions that the earlier labour movement histories, written by protagonists within those movements, had carved out. Some of this relapse occurred because contemporary political positions now served as historical authorisations of current debates among conflicting wings of academic socialism, which had gained a foothold on university campuses since the late 1960s.

This was not only true for labour movement history in the narrow sense of the history of organisations and political ideas where past heroes were mobilised for present-day causes, or once defeated and forgotten ideological currents were rehabilitated for very much the same purpose. Across the board, the social history of workers and the working classes inherited the tensions that arose between the focus on 'class' as a transnational phenomenon and the desire to place the class narratives it tried to establish within a national context. Like the older 'class' histories from outside the academic sphere, we can identify five overlapping modes that academic social history employed in order to place their 'class' accounts within a wider, national historical master narrative. These modes bear some resemblance to the aforementioned categories, but differ in three important respects. First, academic social history explicitly made the *methodology* of 'class' analysis and sociological 'class' concepts a part of its narrative of the working classes. Second, contemporary interpretations of the labour movement's own history became points of historical reference in their own right and added another level to their ideological, as well as narrative, complexity. Finally, the emancipation of the workers, whether as fully entitled political citizens and consumers or as profiteers of their labour unions' and parties' integration into the welfare states and national governments, had in most Western countries become an historical fact. Academic 'class' narratives, whether affirmative or critical, hence were often commentaries on this twentieth-century development.

Historical 'wars of succession'

'Class' histories in academic social history emerged early on in the process of broadening the older organisational and ideological histories from the context of the labour movement itself. Their defining trait was that they in turn did not venture far into the economic, social and cultural living conditions of ordinary workers. Rather, 'class' was introduced as a formal category of Marxist origin. Furthermore, these formulations of 'class' did not attempt to meet the more sophisticated theoretical standards of the sociological debate. They actually represented normative premises about what a 'true' working class must look like, who 'truly' belonged to the working class, and what the proper political outlook and activity of working-class organisations should be.[72] The catchword in studies of this structure was the notion of an ostensible 'elementary labour movement', a popular version of Marx's phrase that in his own usage was already purely ideological. The 'elementary labour movement' was supposed to originate from the midst of the labouring masses themselves (from the bottom upwards) as the only authentic expression of 'class consciousness' not filtered or manipulated by treacherous, opportunistic or power-hungry labour organisations.

Against this normative background that also pointed to ideological self-positioning, social historians at this point judged the deeds and ideas of specific persons or organisations in terms of being more or less 'true' representations of 'class'.[73] It is easy to see that most of those histories were still occupied with disentangling the contemporary maze of factionalism and ideological sophistry. They were the most direct continuation of the older labour movement's internal histories, to which references to 'class' now added some theoretical depth and, therefore, academic respectability.

'Class' histories of this type served a wide range of political purposes, and their respective instrumental function decided on the relation of 'class' to 'nation'. Orthodox Marxist class history, as practised in state socialist academia, mainly tried to identify the historical, legitimate forerunners of existing socialist nations. The degree of 'true classness' that these histories ascribed or denied historical agents resounded with the meaning of 'socialist patriotism'. The selective political appropriation of the labour movement's history remained the main theme of state socialist 'class history', and this explains why, with few exceptions, this historiography did not produce much social history proper.[74]

Class histories of this type also flourished during the post-1968 rebellion and the resurgence of academic Marxism. The reason why the highly ideological debates of this time promoted historical 'wars of succession' is easy to single out: the historical points of reference that the protagonists in these debates either claimed for themselves or repudiated served as symbolic markers

---

[72]Cf. E. Foner, 'Why is There No Socialism in the U.S.?', *History Workshop*, 17 (1984), 57–80; R. McKibbin, 'Why Was There No Marxism in Great Britain?', *English Historical Review*, 99 (1984), 297–331.

[73]A recent example is C. Gotthardt, *Industrialisierung, bürgerliche Politik und proletarische Autonomie: Voraussetzungen und Varianten sozialistischer Klassenorganisationen in Nordwestdeutschland 1863 bis 1875* (Bonn, 1992). For a conservative criticism cf. A. Kraditor, *The Radical Persuasion* (Baton Rouge, 1981).

[74]Both a notable exception to state socialist orthodoxy and a forerunner of the genre of 'working-class formation' studies characterised below is H. Zwahr, *Zur Konstituierung des Proletariats als Klasse: Strukturuntersuchung des Leipziger Proletariats während der industriellen Revolution* (Berlin, GDR, 1978).

for their own degree of radicalism. These claims and repudiations did not remain confined to national boundaries, yet the introspective nature of these ideological discourses acted as a kind of national counterweight.

Radical romanticism

Post-orthodox labour histories in the UK, and only a little later in the US, covered a wide range of topics and approaches, but converged in their common desire to restore to historical workers and their organisations a 'voice of their own'. From the outset the study of workers' organisations was already deemed to be a 'history from below', expressing solidarity with the labour movement.[75] Quickly both methodological sophistication and the project of a 'political peda- gogy' called for research designs much more open to the statements and agency of the workers themselves.[76] 'Class' history became the history of ordinary workers at their workplaces, in their life-worlds and in their arenas of sociability, which endowed the historical subjects with a sense of 'heroic agency'. Defeated or curbed movements, tragic rebellions, fallen heroes and their forgotten home- made philosophies[77] eminently moved towards the centre of attention. This was regardless of whether the historical study remained a local micro-history or, like E. P. Thompson's groundbreaking *Making of the English Working Class*, presented the grand narrative of an entire 'class' movement created from the experience of individual agents over a long time.[78]

The 'radical romanticists' among the labour historians searched for past and lost radicalisms in order to give colour to the otherwise anonymous 'faces in the crowd'. They were looking to build historical identity through identifying with the heroes of the past. Not surprisingly, British Marxist historians were themselves active in the labour movement. After 1956 most of them were dissi- dent communists and frequently on the margins of the major British university scene. They practised adult education and kept close contacts with unionists and labour politicians, particularly through the History Workshop Movement, which succeeded in drawing non-academic 'ordinary people' into historical research.[79]

For our purposes it is essential to note that class histories of this background fought a battle on two fronts: on the one hand, they tried to re-establish the subjectivity and cultural richness of actual workers from the past against an

---

[75]An example is V. L. Lidtke, *The Outlawed Party: Social Democracy in Germany, 1878–1890* (Princeton, NJ, 1966).

[76]G. Eley, 'Marxist Historiography', in Berger, Feldner, and Passmore, *Writing History: Theory and Practice*, pp. 63–82; 71.

[77]For example, I. Prothero, *Artisans and Politics in Early Nineteenth-Century London: John Gast and His Times* (London, 1981).

[78]E. P. Thompson, *The Making of the English Working Class* (Harmondsworth, 1963).

[79]For details see Eley, 'Marxist Historiography', pp. 72–4.

abstract, structuralist, and determinist Marxism. This meant to pitch an agency-oriented concept of 'class' against a reified notion of Marxist orthodoxy. More-over, it also proposed a vigorous promotion of 'class'. On the other hand, 'subjectification' called for almost folkloristic references to cultural idiosyncrasies which, in the British case, took the form of national peculiarities. The culturally colourful 'class' was nationalised, as these 'romantic' class histories saw in them visions of an alternative, more democratic national past. Thompson and others 'sought to recuperate the national past in a self-consciously oppositional and democratic fashion, wresting control of the national story from conservative opinion-makers of all kinds and rewriting it around the struggles of ordinary people in a still unfinished democratic project'.[80]

In the American case, the national focus of 'romantic' class histories remained much more dispersed. Although David Montgomery's *Fall of the House of Labor* (1987) came closest to Thompson's undertaking, it is significant that he did not call his book *The Making of the American Working Class*.[81] This was because American labour history had more to tell than the national story of 'class'; it appeared fragmented and discontinuous, criss-crossed by ethnic, religious and gender lines. The combination of the categories of class, race and gender became the methodological tool with which American labour history came to terms with this diversity. The effect, however, was that identity-building by class historiography often took smaller ethnic, religious or gendered entities (only loosely bound by an American tradition of gradually assimilating into a 'national' culture, generation by generation) for its point of reference, rather than the national level.[82]

Social democratic enlightenment

'Working-class formation' became a paradigm in international labour history in the late 1970s and early 1980s. Formation analyses formed, on the one hand, a more structuralist reaction to Thompson's heroic tale, and, on the other, a response to Hartmut Zwahr's *Konstituierung des Leipziger Proletariats als Klasse* (1978), which represented the first social historical account of class formation within GDR historiography. Although Zwahr's study was criticised for being too deterministic – it culminated in the founding of the wing of the Social Democratic Party in 1869 that first embraced Marx's theory – it was obviously

[80]Eley, 'Marxist Historiography', p. 72.
[81]D. Montgomery, *The Fall of the House of Labor: The Workplace, the State, and American Labor Activism, 1865–1925* (Cambridge, MA, 1987).
[82]The most prominent example, besides the oral histories compiled by Studs Terkel, is H. G. Gutman, *Work, Culture, and Society in Industrializing America: Essays in American Working-Class and Social History* (New York, 1976); idem, *Power & Culture: Essays on the American Working Class*, ed. Ira Berlin (New York, 1987).

not deterministic enough in its social scientific mobility parts to escape chicanery by GDR party officials.

The 'working-class formation' approach attempted to link labour and labour movement history in order to explain workers' organisations and ideological development by studying the social conditions that employees were working and living under. Their common design was to turn the core concept of an 'economic base' determining an 'ideological superstructure' into a sequence of levels causally linked to each other and representing a progression from the advent of capitalism, via the spread of wage work and capitalist management regimes, to the founding of trade unions and socialist parties.[83]

'Working-class formation' histories failed to bridge the gap between the social history of workers and an adequate explanation for the ascent of the labour movement in its timing, organisational forms and ideological orientations. Yet they succeeded in writing 'class' history into a more progressive version of the national narrative. By focusing on the nineteenth century and eschewing Germany's difficult period of 1917–45, which witnessed the separation of the communist and social democratic labour movements, class history could be portrayed critically but also as a bygone phenomenon. Whereas the argument that class tensions were particularly strong in Germany became instrumental for the hypothesis of a German *Sonderweg* into the National Socialist catastrophe, social democratic participation in government, the successful establishment of a corporate system of industrial relations and the rise of a strong welfare state all pointed to a national success story after 1945.[84] Liberal democratic social historians provided a critical but conciliatory reassessment of history, portraying it as a cathartic act of political pedagogy that aimed at further democratisation. 'Working-class formation' histories, therefore, presented a collectivist equivalent to the nineteenth-century psychological novel. Their 'happy end' was that the labour organisations that were founded in conflict-ridden times had meanwhile matured, gained full respectability and contributed successfully to the complete integration of the working class into welfare democracy.

Again, this optimistic nationalisation of class history did not work for cases such as the US, where the labour movement was fragmented, discontinuous and overall rather weak. Here, 'working-class formation' studies either told a story of ultimate failure, or constructed, as David Montgomery did, an epic tale of a repeatedly crushed, but ever resurgent labour activism. Yet it was the

---

[83]Cf. Welskopp, 'Social History', p. 213.
[84]Jürgen Kocka speaks of 'class devolution' in the second half of the twentieth century: J. Kocka, 'Problems of Working-Class Formation in Germany: The Early Years, 1800–1875', in Katznelson and Zolberg, *Working-Class Formation*, pp. 279–351; idem, *Lohnarbeit und Klassenbildung: Arbeiter und Arbeiterbewegung in Deutschland 1800–1875* (Berlin, 1983).

impossibility of a neat fit between class formation as analysed on a structural level and the organisational and ideological expressions of class in a Marxist sense that inspired in both the US and the UK a search for reasons why socialism had failed in their countries, and the embrace of more local radicalisms as found in certain ethnic groups and other role models for identity-building.

'Whig' histories of class

Modernisation theory, especially as promoted by American economists, sociologists and political scientists since the 1950s, preceded and influenced the 'working-class formation' paradigm. Yet intrinsically, historical applications of modernisation theory often served to counter Marxist accounts of the past, and consequently class histories fell into the other four categories. It is not misleading to interpret modernisation histories as Whig narratives of the historical Western triumph over class. In their long-term analyses of developments in the social structure of modernising societies, such histories either downplayed the historical role of class divisions or concentrated on their erosion by economic growth and social progress. Studies of social mobility attempted to demonstrate that class lines were never as rigid as postulated in Marxist theory. They asserted that if there were class privileges, they were only dominant in earlier periods of a society's history, a time preceding thorough modernisation which enabled social advancement and pluralism. Not only in quantitative studies but also in theoretical tracts, modernisation history emptied 'class' of its political content as a category of conflict and, when not replacing 'class' with the more neutral term 'stratum', reduced it to a gradual statistical classification.

Although social mobility studies in particular at times resembled histories of 'working-class formation' (or rather, the latter emulating the former), modernisation histories were not interested in social processes as preconditions for and promoters of (successful) labour organisations. On the contrary, they focused on the ability of capitalist societies to integrate workers into a pluralistic welfare economy and on the capacity of democratic regimes to absorb 'class' tensions.[85] In a sense modernisation theory produced the most affirmative class histories, which replaced conflict with a liberal-conservative consensus interpretation of the past. Modernisation theory was not confined to national boundaries, but created a national model, the US, which served as the norm and example for other nations.

---

[85]A Marxist variation used mobility studies, however, in a critical sense, since it argued with modernization processes to explain the absence of a class-conscious labour movement or its failure to embrace a theoretically expected degree of radicalism. As examples see A. Dawley, *Class and Community: The Industrial Revolution in Lynn* (Cambridge, MA, 1976); D. F. Crew, *Town in the Ruhr: A Social History of Bochum, 1860–1914* (New York, 1979).

Fordist demonology

The 'labour process debate' of the late 1970s produced what can probably be termed the most 'international' mode of class history, although this neo-Marxist narrative started in and with the US for obvious reasons. 'Labour process' theorists painted a thoroughly pessimistic picture of American labour history. During much of the nineteenth century, American workers in the skilled trades still held a great deal of control over their workplace conditions. They were able to defend their status by militant labour practices at the point of production and effective trade union organisation.[86] Yet during the Second Industrial Revolution, the growth of corporations combined with cost-cutting imperatives and new technologies to promote a new managerial ideology that called for complete hegemony over the workforce. In the late nineteenth and early twentieth centuries, managers used Taylorism and Fordism to wrest technical knowledge from the workers, deskill labour and subordinate it to corporate capitalism. By means of both autocratic control and the promise of consumerism, the capitalist management rendered the workforce helpless and politically passive. Ethnic diversity played into the hands of management and ensured the lasting fragmentation of the workforce.[87]

This American story was exported with the rise of neo-Marxism throughout Europe. Historians took the contemporary reception of Frederick W. Taylor's and Henry Ford's ideas in their respective countries as a foreboding that a similar development of the labour regime as that which had already become reality in the US was under way. Yet the strength of the labour movement and the participation of social democratic parties in many Western European countries reduced the 'labour process' theory's persuasive power for European conditions. However, the view of management as an internationally active conspirator against the working class, and the new twist of anti-Americanism that it added to neo-Marxist anti-capitalism, retained some charm during the 1980s. In Germany, neo-Marxist historians adopted the 'labour process' approach for a left-wing criticism of the established labour movement and its historical forerunners. According to their interpretation, Fordism in Germany produced the 'mass worker' who was not helplessly victimised by management, but became the core

---

[86]D. Montgomery, *Workers' Control in America: Studies in the History of Work, Technology, and Labor Struggles*, 2nd edn (Cambridge, MA, 1981).

[87]H. Braverman, *Labor and Monopoly Capitalism: The Degradation of Work in the Twentieth Century* (New York and London, 1974); R. C. Edwards, *Contested Terrain: The Transformation of the Workplace in the Twentieth Century* (New York, 1979); D. M. Gordon, R. C. Edwards and M. Reich, *Segmented Work, Divided Workers: The Historical Transformation of Labor in the United States* (Cambridge, MA, 1982).

of 'a different kind' of labour radicalism – the 'true' representation of class consciousness that the union and party establishment had betrayed.[88]

*

Finally, a more recent development in German historiography does not fit into any of the above-mentioned categories, although it once originated under categories one and three. It was a phenomenon of the 1990s and of the reunified German nation-state that the smooth 'nationalisation' of Social Democracy became possible. Social Democracy now appeared as a factor in national integration and unification rather than as an expression of class tensions. The revolution of 1918/19 played a crucial role in this narrative. The new interpretation tried to end the ongoing debates between Marxist and non-Marxist positions on whether or not the revolution was a failure and why. This was of major importance since some positions hypothesised that the lacking radicalism and stamina of Social Democrats during the revolution (in fact, their crackdown on revolutionaries with the help of right-wing militias) eventually helped bring about the fall of the Weimar Republic. The revisionist national history conceded that a more thorough exchange of elites during the first phase of the revolution would have been possible and that a socialisation of the basic industries could have been an alternative to the return to private capitalism. Yet a 'social revolution'as postulated by contemporary leftists and radical social historians remained a structural impossibility in a society as highly developed and complex as Germany's. A 'social revolution' of the Russian type was thus 'externalised' from a national narrative that had finally integrated Social Democracy and 'class'.[89]

Conclusion

Our analysis has shown that the relation between 'nation' and 'class' in European historiographies from the early nineteenth century to the present has not been one of competing master narratives, one constructed around the rise

[88]Examples are K. H. Roth and Elisabeth Behrens, *Die 'andere' Arbeiterbewegung und die Entwicklung der kapitalistischen Repression von 1880 bis zur Gegenwart: ein Beitrag zum Neuverständnis der Klassengeschichte in Deutschland* (Munich, 1974); E. Brockhaus, *Zusammensetzung und Neustrukturierung der Arbeiterklasse vor dem Ersten Weltkrieg: zur Krise der professionellen Arbeiterbewegung* (Munich, 1975); E. Lucas, *Zwei Formen des Radikalismus in der deutschen Arbeiterbewegung* (Frankfurt/M, 1976).
[89]H. August Winkler, *Der lange Weg nach Westen*, vol. 1, *Deutsche Geschichte vom Ende des Alten Reiches bis zum Untergang der Weimarer Republik*; vol. 2, *Deutsche Geschichte vom 'Dritten Reich' bis zur Wiedervereinigung*, 4th edn (Munich, 2002), vol. 1, pp. 380f.

of the nation-state, the other tracing the rise of the working class across all national borders. In fact, the national master narrative has proved to be the stronger paradigm, taking on and defending the role of the hegemon, whereas 'class', at least in historiography, failed to organise a coherent alternative master narrative altogether. In this sense, the historical discipline confirmed that its rise and development were intricately bound up with the national project. It was an essential part of the advancing nation-state, and was sometimes used as a weapon to fend off social claims – be it to revolutionary alternatives or to the emancipation of the 'dangerous classes'.

This discursive superiority revealed itself foremost in the fact that the national master narrative could afford, at least under specific circumstances, to ignore 'class', while almost no class history could ignore the 'nation'. Even where 'class' was invoked to dispute the harmonising and Whig claims of national history, they remained present in the evolving narrative if only as a negative foil against which the counter-narrative unfolded. The 'nation' nevertheless structured these contentious accounts and provided their frame of reference. This was not true in the reverse case. 'Class' and revolutionary episodes could be conspicuously absent from many national history accounts. They frequently played the role of an 'absent Other' that national historiography necessarily fought, but by means of denying their existence or passing over them in silence.

German *Historism* represented the extreme case of a historiography that seemed almost intentionally invented for this purpose. It was a means of ideologically bridging the social ruptures and divisions in society that stood in the way of national unification, and which after unification threatened the new nation's integrity. Other European historiographies, as time went on, learned to integrate the working people of their countries into a master narrative of the nation, although at the cost of downplaying revolutionary episodes or isolating them in a mythical past (in the case of Switzerland). 'Class' thereby became 'nationalised' and stripped of any revolutionary content.

Counter-histories from the left failed to break out of national boundaries (if they intended to do so in the first place) and were by no means automatically 'internationalist' in outlook. On the contrary, they often represented attempts to write the working classes and labour movement into the dominating national account. This altered its accentuation but still reformulated the storyline as a national narrative. The reason for this more or less voluntary integration may lie in the fact that labour movements, albeit structurally similar phenomena across Europe, acted within the institutional environment of their respective nation-states and had to look to the national level if they aspired to political power. Even the new social history of the 1960s and beyond remained fixated on the national frame of reference. In the German case, a social democratic version of national history was its latest product.

Finally, the historiography of the state socialist regimes before 1989 presented a case of 'class' degenerating to a hollow formula which more or less openly disguised ethnic hegemonies, nationalist ambitions or national interests in a Cold War world. The rapid transition from Marxist-Leninist orthodoxy to a new, frequently racist, nationalist historiography in some eastern European countries during the 1990s confirmed just that.

Our comparative, long-term analysis thus has shown that class played the role of a sub-discourse to the national master narrative rather than that of a contentious counter-discourse. Of the two discursive constructions, the one with a superior potential for essentialising social relations prevailed and colonised the Other. The nation ruled in European historiography, and class, if acknowledged at all, served the nation.

7
Where Are Women in National Histories?

Jitka Malečková

This chapter examines how national histories – and particularly master-narratives – have been gendered.[1] In recent decades we have learned a lot about the relationships between gender and nationalism, nationalism and the writing of history, and gender and history. Studies of women's participation in national movements and of women's history writing have considerably enriched our knowledge of the role of women in national pasts.[2] Little attention has been paid to the intersections among nationalism, gender and historiography, especially the gendering of national master narratives.[3] Feminist historians put women, or more recently gender, and not the nation, at the centre of analysis. Gender history appeared just when postmodernism challenged national master narratives, further reducing their appeal for those interested in the place of women in history. If we do not study how gender was treated in the writing of national history, however, we may be restricting our understanding of gender roles, nationalism and historiography, and denying women a past – at least as long as national history remains the prevailing framework of thinking and writing about history.

---

[1]I would like to thank Ida Bloom, Geoff Eley, Ira Katznelson, Mary O'Dowd and Ilaria Porciani for their comments on earlier drafts; Atina Grossman, Peter Lambert and Susan Zimmerman for suggesting literature; and James Lancaster, Alane Rollings and Jeremy Weinberg for helpful edits.

[2]See, for example, I. Blom, K. Hagemann and C. Hall (eds), *Gendered Nations: Nationalisms and Gender Order in the Long Nineteenth Century* (Oxford and New York, 2000); B. Smith, *The Gender of History: Men, Women, and Historical Practice* (Cambridge, MA and London, 1998); and J. Wallach Scott's revised *Gender and the Politics of History* (New York, 1999).

[3]The exceptions include B. Melman, 'Gender, History and Memory: The Invention of Women's Past in the Nineteenth and Early Twentieth Centuries', *History and Memory*, 5 (1993), 5–41, focusing on English-speaking histories, and I. Porciani and M. O'Dowd (eds), 'History Women', special issue of *Storia della storiografia*, 46 (2004), focusing on women historians.

This chapter traces some of the ways in which mainstream national histories were gendered. There is a lot we do not know about histories written by women. While women often supported and spread national master narratives, mainstream national histories, including those analysed here, were mostly written by men. There is also a lot that we do not know about the construction of masculinity in national histories. Yet history has been largely written as a history of (abstract) men, implicitly considered to represent the experience of 'humankind'. Men can hardly be considered the nation's Other, which is the topic of this volume. Writing about men was a default. The explicit interest in gender was expressed first as an interest in women. Therefore, this chapter concentrates on how national master narratives incorporated – or did not incorporate – women.

A brief chapter on such an extensive and under-studied subject is necessarily selective and sometimes speculative. It focuses on three periods to show how gender was treated in national histories. Each of the three sections pays special attention to the region (or national situation) that seems most characteristic of the period described, although for comparison's sake developments in other parts of Europe are also mentioned. The first section deals with the constitutive period of nationalism when not only the major concepts of national histories but also many enduring gender stereotypes were constructed. The focus is on Central and Eastern Europe where nationalism and its expressions in historiography were particularly prominent in the nineteenth century. The second section, devoted to the interwar period and the Second World War, with a marked emphasis on the rise of fascism in Germany, examines the impact of extreme manifestations of nationalism on the place of women/gender in national histories. The third section concentrates on the intersection between the writing of national and women's histories in the 'post-national' period in the wake of the second wave of feminism.[4] The emphasis is on Western European historiographies, which led the field of women's history and were the first in Europe to turn to gender history. The section explores how the emergence of women's history as a discipline affected the writing of national histories.

---

[4]Michelle Perrot mentions three reasons for the emergence of women's history in the 1960s and 1970s – scientific (both within history and other disciplines in the West), sociological (women in academia) and political (the women's liberation movement): M. Perrot, *Les Femmes ou les silences de l'histoire* (Paris, 1998), pp. vii–viii. Also other historians emphasise the convergence of political and historiographical factors: when political concern for women's rights coincided with historiographical traditions encouraging research on classes and everyday life, it resulted in a flurry of scholarship in the last half of the nineteenth century and the last quarter of the twentieth century. B. Hanawalt, 'Golden Ages for the History of Medieval English Women', in S. Mosher Stuard (ed.), *Women in Medieval History and Historiography* (Philadelphia, 1987), p. 2.

Construction of national histories in the nineteenth century

All national histories were constructed in gendered terms, both in the emphases they placed and in their omissions. The first professional historians essentially wrote a history of men: national history equalled political history, and that in turn meant diplomacy and wars – the deeds of men. The inclusion of women in national histories was not guaranteed. When women figured in master-narratives, as this section shows, it was because historians saw a purpose in including them.

To be sure, women appeared in historical works from the very beginning of historiography. Leaving aside women rulers and saints, attention to women *as a group* is associated particularly with two periods of national histories: first, early national history, the mythical origins of the nation, and, second (in the historiography of the late nineteenth and twentieth centuries), the more recent period of revolutions, national movements and wars of unification. The early period of national history, which is the focus here, provides particularly fertile soil for comparative analysis: the origins of the nation were necessarily addressed in all concepts of national histories, and this period was often connected with the 'national' images of womanhood.

When historians in the nineteenth century described the life of women among their ancient ancestors, they often drew on older sources. At the same time, nineteenth-century historians elevated only some images as a part of the national past, while condemning others to oblivion, and often used the same sources to support opposing claims. The way in which historians selected and interpreted images of women, as the following pages will show, was inspired by specific national concerns.

Women often had an important place in historical works celebrating a golden age in national history, especially in those societies whose current state made a glorious past particularly attractive, such as those in Eastern Europe that lacked national independence. Historians realised that early history belonged to the sphere of myths, yet they interpreted these myths as a reflection of the principles on which the early societies had been based. They tried to enhance national pride and identity by showing how advanced even women had been among their ancestors. 'Because the relationship between the women's sex and the men's sex and their behaviour towards one another in a nation is a measure of national education,' a Czech historian wrote, 'the evidence about the moral qualities of our women, their equality with men at home and in public life, and their equality in legislation presents a clear proof of the noble character and spiritual advancement of our nation.'[5] Historians presented the habits and character

---

[5] F. Dvorský, *Staré písemné památky žen a dcer českých* (Praha, 1869), p. vii.

of their ancestors, and especially of women, as proof of the superior qualities of the nation in its original, pure form. The original idyll was only later corrupted by the interference of an external force.

Slovak intellectuals tried to defend their nation from criticism of its lack of political institutions and political history, that is, of a historical medieval state. They cited the peaceful character of the Slovaks and the centrality of the family (which, according to some, impeded their interest in public life). They claimed that, among their early pagan ancestors, women were faithful and virtuous, and enjoyed great freedom. Slovak historians held the expansionist Germans responsible for the decline of their society. The Germans had destroyed the Great Moravian empire – presented as a Slovak state – and introduced their own values, including patriarchal family relations.[6]

The Czech construction of national history closely connects women to the constitutionalist myth in the story of Princess Libuše, founder of the ruling dynasty, and the war of the Czech Amazons: ancient Czechs had a judge who had no sons, but three exceptionally talented daughters. When he died, the youngest, the prophetess Libuše, was elected princess. She married and founded the medieval Czech ruling dynasty, the Přemyslids. Under her rule, so the legend goes, women enjoyed special privileges. When she died, they revolted against male dominance and, led by Vlasta, launched a successful war against men, like the Amazons. In the end, men defeated them with a trick: they invited them to a feast to celebrate the truce, then each of them abducted one woman.

Starting with Pelcel in the late eighteenth century, Czech historians referred to the exceptional education and other qualities of Libuše and her two sisters.[7] In the nineteenth century, Libuše and even Vlasta, leader of the women's revolt against men, were used as national symbols. The most influential Czech historian, František Palacký, emphasised that Libuše was elected because of her qualities, despite being a woman and the youngest of the three sisters. He described family mores and the position of women among the pagan Czechs in the most positive terms, and suggested that this proved that democratic principles prevailed among the ancient Slavs, unlike the Germans.[8] In 1868 J. E. Vocel took this idea further. In the German family, he wrote, the father was an absolute ruler. Women could never be independent, but were bought

---

[6]F. V. Sasinek, *Dejiny drievnych národov na území terajšieho Uhorska*, 2nd edn (Turč. Sv. Martin, 1878); B. P. Červenák, *Zrcadlo Slovenska* (Pešť, 1844). Červenák tends to blame the Magyars rather than the Germans.
[7]F. M. Pelcel, *Nová kronika česká*, 1 (Praha, 1791), pp. 90–3.
[8]F. Palacký, *Dějiny národu českého v Čechách a v Moravě*, 1/1 (Praha, 1848), pp. 81, 188–94 and 218–21.

and treated as objects. The Slavic family, in contrast, was based on the principle of equality, of rights and of duties, and on mutual love. The democracy and equality among the Slavs thus was demonstrated by their attitude to women.[9]

The Czech inclusion of ancient female heroines (as real historical figures) in national history contrasts with Polish historiography. The Poles, too, have a myth connected with early history: after the death of Krak, founder of Krakow, one of his sons murdered his brother and was expelled; thus their sister, Wanda, became princess. She dedicated herself to the gods and refused to marry a German prince. In order to save her nation from a German attack she committed suicide. Polish historians almost unanimously described this story as a mere myth.

This major difference between Czech and Polish historians may be partly explained by the Polish historians' more critical approach to the sources. Polish historians, since Joachim Lelewel in the 1820s,[10] were critical of the myths about their history. Moreover, the myth about Wanda is not connected with the origins of the ruling dynasty, which made it easier to ridicule. Polish historians did not unanimously emphasise a golden age in Polish history, but alternated between the progress-oriented and golden age approaches. Women figured less prominently in nineteenth-century Polish histories, at least in influential mainstream works.[11] It seems that given their more confident attitude to the past, nineteenth-century Polish historians did not need to use women to defend their national history and stimulate national pride as their Czech counterparts did.

While the golden age found little expression among mainstream Russian historians, since the 1850s some (male) historians critical of the official historiography dealt with the history of Russian women and celebrated pagan Russian society for the freedom of its women. These women were brave and virtuous, had substantial property rights and could participate in public affairs. Russian historians of women blamed their subsequent decline on Byzantium, namely on the adoption of Christianity from the east. Along with Christianity, various Byzantine practices, such as asceticism, were adopted by the Russians. Byzantine views on women as the source of sin were also taken on, so that women were gradually expelled from public life, secluded and enslaved. This development was then intensified by Tartar rule.[12]

---

[9]J. E. Vocel, *Pravěk země české* (Praha, 1868), p. 354.

[10]J. Lelewel, *Dzieje Polski potocznym sposobem opowiedziane* (Warszawa, [1829] 1961), pp. 39–46.

[11]There were some historians, such as J. I. Kraszewski, who celebrated the golden age in pagan Polish prehistory and women's position in that period.

[12]V. Shul'gin, *O sostoyanii zhenshchin v Rossii do Petra Velikago: istoricheskoe issledovanie* (Kiev, 1850), p. xxv; S.S. Shashkov, *Istoriya russkoi zhenshchiny*, 2nd edn (S. Peterburg, 1879), pp. 1–23; I.E. Zabelin, *Domashnii byt russkikh tsarits v XVI i XVII stoletiyakh* (Novosibirsk, [1901] 1992), pp. 8–9.

Different views on the place of women in the early national past often reflected intellectual debates about the current state and future development of the nation. Historians who emphasised progress in their national past used the example of women as proof that historical development brought advancement for the whole society, improving the low status of women. In Eastern Europe this approach prevailed among mainstream Russian historians. From Karamzin in the late eighteenth century to Solov'ev and Pogodin in the second half of the nineteenth century, they followed the medieval chronicle of Nestor in describing the pagan Russians as savages – with the exception of the Poliane, who were monogamous and whose women were virtuous.[13] Solov'ev's view is typical: the prevalence of brute strength could not create favourable conditions for respecting the fair sex. Individual women, however, could play an important role, as shown by Princess Olga, the smartest person of the pre-Christian period, who ruled in the name of her son.[14] Yet it was only the Christian Church that brought Russian society into civilisation and increased women's status, making the mother equal to the father. The advancement of the position of women was another proof that the Russian nation was heading, throughout its history, towards civilisation.

Such debates were not limited to Eastern Europe. Jane Rendall points out how the golden age and the progress-oriented histories in Scottish historiography of the second half of the eighteenth century expressed different views on the position of Scotland in Great Britain. Both those who turned to a golden age in history (Germanic or Celtic) and those who looked to the future, modern civic society, connected with Britain, used Tacitus' references to women to support their views. Descriptions of the position of women among ancient Germanic tribes thus served both for the defence of old liberties (in contrast to the present) and as a (negative) contrast to progress, represented by contemporary Britain.[15]

Nineteenth-century Italian historians, like their Russian counterparts, were divided by their views on the impact of the Church on the nation's history, though in the Italian case both sides favoured a progress-oriented approach to history. Catholic historians of the mid-nineteenth century claimed that the Italian papacy was superior to ancient Rome, at least in part because it had defended Italian independence against Germanic tribes. Their opponents saw

---

[13]N. M. Karamzin, *Istoriya gosudarstva rossiiskago*, 1, 5th edn (Sanktpeterburg, 1842), pp. 97–108; S. M. Solov'ev, *Istoriya Rossii s drevneishikh vremen*, 1 (Moskva, [1851] 1959), pp. 247–61; M. M. Pogodin, *Drevnyaya russkaya istoriya do mongol'skago iga* (Moskva, 1871), pp. 2–10.

[14]Solov'ev, *Istoriya*, p. 247.

[15]J. Rendall, 'Tacitus Engendered: "Gothic Feminism" and British Histories, c. 1750–1800', in G. Cubitt (ed.), *Imagining Nations* (Manchester and New York, 1998), pp. 57–74.

the progressive line of Italian history from the Roman empire to the Lombards as a force that contributed to the unification of Italy. While both groups were more concerned with the medieval period, some historians in each group referred to women in Rome and the Italic tribes, the Etruscans or the Sabines.

Atto Vannucci mentioned the high position of women among the pre-Roman peoples of Italy and described Rome, the centre of the world, as the embodiment of all virtues. Although Roman principles brought order and greatness to the empire, they were still barbaric, because of the tyrannical power given to the father over the life of women and children. Only later developments, with Christianity, brought freedom to all and prevented fathers from treating women and children as slaves and possessions.[16] In the latter part of the century, Pasquale Villari, in a work significantly called *L'Italia e la civiltà*, while appreciating the greatness of the Roman empire, tried to show that the Lombards who took over Italy were not savages. He demonstrated this using the example of women, who, according to him, had more personal freedom than in Rome. Though always dependent and protected, they enjoyed legal rights and a certain respect.[17]

Women among Germanic tribes, referred to in various European historiographies (especially East European ones), were of primary concern to German historians. Karl Lamprecht, for example, suggested the existence of matriarchy among the old German ancestors.[18] Treitschke's views are particularly interesting: he believed that ancient Germans, or at least their leaders, were polygamous, while he considered matriarchy an open question. Although women were worshipped, they were not equal, 'because the respect for woman cannot but be the outcome of a long development in civilisation'.[19] Christianity added to the old Germanic worship of women a real respect for women, which later degenerated into the unmanly service of the troubadours. At the same time, a 'wardship' was exercised by the male sex over the female, and men exacted a heavy payment for their protection. Treitschke saw some centuries of German history as 'feminine' and others as 'masculine': in the heroic tenth century, when the Saxon kings were at the peak of their power, women appeared to have no importance. In contrast, the century of the Hohenstaufen, with its gallantry and the minnesingers, was quite distinctly feminine in its universal attempt to adorn itself with womanly graces.[20]

---

[16]A. Vannucci, *Storia dell'Italia antica*, 3rd edn (Milano, 1873), vol. 1, p. 761 and passim.
[17]P. Villari, *L'Italia e la civiltà* (Milano, 1925), pp. 14–20.
[18]K. Lamprecht, *Deutsche Geschichte: Zur jüngsten deutschen Vergangenheit*, 2/1 (Freiburg im Breisgau, 1903), p. 17.
[19]H. von Treitschke, *Politics*, 1, trans. Arthur James Balfour (New York, 1916), pp. 239.
[20]Treitschke, *Politics*, pp. 243–6. On the position of women in early German history, see also G. Buschan, *Leben und Treiben der deutschen Frau in der Urzeit* (Hamburg, 1893).

With the spread of critical positivist historiography, the myths, with their heroines, lost importance. Yet, some issues of the nineteenth-century debates kept reappearing. Idealised images of women in the past often implied a criticism of the present position of women, and could be invoked as proof that women's equality was both useful and possible. Shashkov, the Russian historian of women, wrote explicitly to contribute to the emancipation of women. Images created by historians of the high status and freedom of women in the early periods of national history were later used by proponents of women's rights. Male and female Czech advocates of women's emancipation in the second half of the nineteenth century claimed that Czech women had always enjoyed the rights that Western women had started to achieve only in more recent, enlightened times.[21] Later, debates concerning the position of women among ancient Germans gained prominence in Nazi Germany.

While historians' works served as a source for current debates, they also reflected contemporary values, including views on women, femininity and masculinity. Karen Offen notes that the most influential among the intellectuals who wrote on women, such as Proudhon and Michelet in France, Schopenhauer and Riehl in Germany, Maine in England and Bachofen in Switzerland, expressed anti-feminist views.[22] Interestingly, their works have been interpreted in contradictory ways.[23]

The concept of a golden age of women's rights, which appeared in many national histories, would seem to be inspired by Bachofen's claim that human history was first matriarchal. But many of the historical works praising a golden age were written before the influential *Mother Right* was published in 1861. Bachofen called extreme forms of matriarchy 'Amazonism'. He believed that matriarchy, with women dominant in society as well as among the gods, replaced a primitive promiscuity and in turn gave way to the more progressive patriarchy.[24] Bachofen's work, which had a strong impact on historians in the

---

[21]K. Jonáš, *Žena ve společnosti lidské, zvláště v Anglii a v Americe* (Praha, 1872), p. 109; Dvorský, *Staré písemné památky*, pp. v–viii; E. Krásnohorská, *Ženská otázka česká* (Praha, 1881), pp. 4–6.

[22]K. Offen, '"Woman Has to Set her Stamp on Science, Philosophy, Justice, and Politics": A Look at Gender Politics in the "Knowledge Wars" of the European Past', in C. Bosshart-Pfluger, D. Grisard and C. Späti (eds), *Geschlecht und Wissen/Genre et Savoir – Gender and Knowledge: Beiträge der 10. Schweizerischen Historikerinnentagung 2002* (Zürich, 2004), pp. 384–6.

[23]For views differing from Offen's, see e.g. D. Partenheimer, Introduction to *An English Translation of Bachofen's Mutterrecht (Mother Right) (1861): A Study of the Religious and Juridical Aspects of Gynecocracy in the Ancient World* (Lewiston, Queenston and Lampeter, 2003), pp. iii–vii; M. Ozouf, *Les Mots des femmes: essai sur la singularité française* (Paris, 1995), pp. 323–97.

[24]See J. J. Bachofen, *Myth, Religion, and Mother Right*, trans. Ralph Manheim (Princeton, 1967), pp. 69–120.

late nineteenth century and into the twentieth century, thus could be interpreted quite differently from feminist and anti-feminist positions.

Michelet's ideas on women, still quoted in French historiography, were
influential throughout nineteenth-century Europe. In *Women of the Revolution*,
Michelet identified women's sentiments and passion with the most terrible
period of the French Revolution, contrasting it with the eighteenth century,
when *l'esprit* of the encyclopedists dominated society.[25] In other works, men
symbolise for Michelet activity, energy, will and fertility, and women the
annihilation of will and sterility – hence male superiority over women.[26] At the
same time, unlike many other historians, Michelet acknowledged women's
power and (to some extent) agency. In the France of the *ancien régime*, he
claimed, women ruled by sentiment, passion and the superiority of their initiative. 'Men made 14 July; women, 6 October.'[27] Most importantly, Michelet connected women with patriotism: he wrote that women, less spoiled by scholastic
habits, were more capable of caring for the country,[28] and that Jeanne d'Arc was
a manifestation of both the Virgin and the country (*la patrie*).[29]

Heroines such as Joan of Arc were often contradictory. Generally, what could
be interpreted as a masculine quality or behaviour in women was viewed negatively. Women could bear masculine features and be praised for them only in
extreme situations, such as wars, or if they were exceptional, elite heroines. A
striking example of gender ambiguity is provided by women fighters, such as the
Czech (or Swedish)[30] Amazons. In Russian history the exceptional figure of
Princess Olga was sometimes interpreted as an embodiment of both masculinity
and femininity. Zabelin presented in Olga a symbol of ideal pagan Russian womanhood. She did what a prince would do – took revenge on her enemies, fought,
collected taxes and administered her territory. Although she fulfilled 'male' roles,
her contemporaries did not find it strange because she behaved as a widow-
mother and housewife on her property. Courage and manliness were the

---

[25]J. Michelet, *Les Femmes de la Révolution*, in J. Michelet, *Œuvres complètes*, 39 (Paris,
n.d.), p. 17.
[26]J. Michelet, *La Femme* (Paris, 1860), pp. 379–80; J. Calo, *La Création de la femme chez
Michelet* (Paris, 1975), p. 144.
[27] Michelet, *Les Femmes de la Révolution*, pp. 17 and 19.
[28] Michelet, *Les Femmes de la Révolution*, p. 15.
[29]J. Michelet, *Histoire de France au Moyen Age*, 6 (Paris, n.d.), p. 288.
[30]Swedish historians inherited a seventeenth- and eighteenth-century myth of 'Gothicism',
celebrating the golden age in the distant past of Gothic migrations. Virtues such as manliness, courage and trustworthiness were emphasised. Women, too, were strong and used to
warfare like the men. While waiting for their husbands to return home, they became like
Amazons, highly praised in martial deeds, 'the bravest warriors ever seen in the world'.
P. Hall, *The Social Construction of Nationalism: Sweden as an Example* (Lund, 1998), pp. 42–6.
I would like to thank Charlotte Tornbjer for bringing this work to my attention.

demands of the day. Yet, the ancient image of Olga also expressed the stereotype of womanhood, connected with cunning and almost supernatural wisdom. In the following seven centuries, writes Zabelin, the 'masculine' example of Olga was not upheld as Christianity had changed the ideal of womanhood; women were not independent actors any more.[31]

Compared to this late nineteenth-century Russian historian, Victorian historians, including women, seem surprisingly traditional. They celebrated the femininity of past heroines while showing ambivalent attitudes to women who did not fit the nineteenth-century ideal of womanhood. Thus, as Maitzen points out, Mary, the Catholic Queen of Scotland, who was perceived as more feminine than Queen Elizabeth, was also the more popular of the two, among both female and male historians.[32]

In the countries where many women were writing history, the attention male historians paid to women could be seen as part of the struggle for intellectual dominance in the discipline. This is the way contemporaries saw the situation in Great Britain.[33] In Eastern Europe, and on the continent more generally, women often figured prominently among authors of historical novels, but they did not venture into non-fiction history (at least not 'serious', 'high' history) in sufficient numbers to be seen as rivals in the newly established discipline. Women did write history, but often chose different topics – history of women, social life and culture,[34] biography, autobiography, family history, arts or customs.[35] Such works are usually excluded from accounts of national historiography. As a result, we know little about the relationship of many women writing on history to national master narratives.

Women seem to have contributed to the dissemination more than to the construction of national histories. Their often very popular biographies and historical novels helped to spread national master narratives among wider groups of the population in ways that professional (male) historians' extensive volumes could not have achieved. Yet women have done more than that. According to Ilaria Porciani and Mary O'Dowd, historians of women con-

[31]Zabelin, *Domashnii byt*, pp. 41–6.
[32]R. A. Maitzen, *Gender, Genre, and Victorian Historical Writing* (New York and London, 1998), pp. 164–96; see also A. Strickland, *The Life of Queen Elizabeth* (London, 1906 [1910]), p. 712.
[33]See Dr Doran, *Lives of the Queens of England of the House of Hanover*, 1 (London, 1855), p. vi.
[34]Smith, *Gender of History*, p. 157.
[35]See A. Epple, *Empfindsame Geschichtsschreibung: eine Geschlechtergeschichte der Historiographie zwischen Aufklärung und Historismus* (Köln, Weimar, Wien, 2003); Porciani and O'Dowd, *History Women*, pp. 10–11; M. P. Casalena, 'La Participation cachée des femmes à la construction de l'histoire nationale en Italie et en France (1800–1848)', in Porciani and O'Dowd (eds), *History Women*, pp. 42–3.

tributed to national historiography by celebrating the role of women in the national past.[36] Ragna Nielsen's 1904 work, comparing the situation of nine-teenth-century Norwegian women to the strong Viking women of the sagas, was quoted with respect by one of the most prominent male historians, Halvdan Koht, who, unlike Nielsen, saw women as agents in history.[37] In Italy, as Porciani notes, female historians participated in laying the foundations of national history and memory, although their contribution has been forgotten.[38]

Ireland presents a particularly interesting example of the role of women in the construction of a national past: Mary O'Dowd shows how female scholars contributed to the creation of an image of a golden age for women in early medieval Ireland by the Gaelic literary revival, which influenced the popular belief in the high status of women in Irish society before the English conquest.[39] 'One cannot read the Annals of Ireland', Mary Aikenhead wrote in 1879, 'without observing how important was the position occupied by women in Erin.' She linked the status of women in early Ireland to the situation of the society as a whole, making it relevant for late nineteenth-century Ireland as well.[40]

As early as the late eighteenth century, women sometimes wrote on more 'general' topics, common among mainstream male historians.[41] Harriet Mar-tineau's *History of England during the Thirty Years' Peace* shows how a woman his-torian could appropriate such a topic. Martineau continued a standard political history started by a man. In sections on the lives, achievements and obituaries of exemplary ancestors, however, Martineau discusses women alongside men, making her concern with gender quite clear.[42]

Generally, it seems that women's works tended to be in agreement with national master narratives. More research is needed to confirm this state-ment. However, instead of challenging mainstream historians' claims, women could choose subtle diversions from or subversions of the master narrative. Maitzen suggests that in Victorian Britain, women such as Agnes Strickland

---

[36]Porciani and O'Dowd, *History Women*, p. 32.

[37]I. Blom, 'Women in Norwegian and Danish Historiography, c.1900–c.1960', in Porciani and O'Dowd (eds), *History Women*, pp. 135–7.

[38]I. Porciani, 'Les Historiennes et le Risorgimento', *Mélanges de l'École française de Rome: Italie et Méditerranée* 112 (2000), p. 326.

[39]M. O'Dowd, 'Interpreting the Past: Women's History and Women Historians, 1840–1945', in A. Bourke et al. (eds), *The Field Day Anthology of Irish Writing*, 5 (New York, 2002), p. 1104.

[40]Bourke et al., *The Field Day Anthology of Irish Writing*, p. 1110.

[41]See, for example, C. Macaulay, *The History of England from the Accession of James I to the Elevation of the House of Hanover*, 1–5 (London, 1769–72); Baronne de Staël, *Considér-ations sur les principaux évènemens de la Révolution française*, 1–3 (Paris, 1818).

[42]See, for example, H. Martineau, *The History of England during the Thirty Years' Peace, 1816–1846*, 1 (London, 1849), pp. 588–92.

took 'advantage of instabilities in existing models of history … to broaden the range of meanings that could be articulated'.[43]

In earlier works on women, gender identity did not overshadow national identity. It is not surprising that male historians, both in non-dominant nations[44] and established nation-states, used their works to further national interests and pride even when dealing with women in general European history. René de Maulde La Clavière intended his *Women of the Renaissance* to show the superiority of French legislation and practices concerning women over those of the English.[45] The situation was not too different among women historians: in 1828 Fanny Mongellas devoted her attention to women all around the world; however, the experience depicted is limited to Christian women and contrasted with the fate of women in other, particularly Muslim, societies.[46] An 1894 book on famous Czech women by Tereza Nováková, a leader of the Czech women's movement, celebrated the moderate character of Slavic women. It criticised the elitist noblewoman Polyxena not for her well-known conspicuous consumption, but for her lack of interest in national issues.[47] The book had a clear national agenda. Yet, like works of other nineteenth-century female authors, it also included women in national history.

Fascism and the historiography of the interwar period

After the First World War the interest in women's history in Europe is thought to have waned as a result of the decline of women's movements following the war.[48] Was this the case in mainstream national histories as well? At first sight, a divide appears between Western and Eastern Europe. While in France and Britain concern with women in historical works seemed to have ebbed somewhat, Central and East European countries often witnessed an increasing attention paid to women in the national past. It is possible to argue that the contrast reflects two types of national situation: the well-established nation-states such as Britain or France, on the one hand, and the new nation-states or those states

---

[43]Maitzen, *Gender*, p. xiii.

[44]E.g. Jonáš, *Žena ve společnosti lidské*.

[45]R. de Maulde La Clavière, *The Women of the Renaissance: A Study of Feminism*, trans. George Herbert Ely (London, 1900), pp. 1–5.

[46]F. Mongellas, *De l'influence des femmes sur les moeurs et les destinées des nations; sur leurs familles et la société, et de l'influence des moeurs sur le bonheur de la vie*, 1 (Paris, 1828), p. x.

[47]T. Nováková, *Slavín žen českých*, 1, *Od nejstarších dob do znovuzrození národa českého* (Praha, 1894), pp. 307–28.

[48]Unlike, for example, Hanawalt ('Golden Ages', pp. 11–12), Melman ('Gender, History and Memory', pp. 32–3) attributes the decline in the later 1930s mainly to the development within the historical discipline.

where nationalism played an important role in the interwar period, on the other. In the latter – though only when it fitted the perceived national interests – women tended to be more integrated into national history.

This section will consider the impact of three different national situations on the inclusion of women in (or their exclusion from) master narratives. It will briefly look at the historiography of the established nation-states in Western Europe and the new states that emerged as a result of national movements and the dissolution of empires after the war, and concentrate on historiography under fascism.

The inclusion of women in history could take various forms. Billie Melman distinguishes two types of English-language historical works: one 'seeking to incorporate women in the national history, or history of a class, and educate them as citizens of the empire-state, and the relativist women's history, which emphasized the specificity of gender experience in history and which had rejected the nationalist framework altogether'.[49]

Despite the perceived decline, important works on women were published in Britain and France between the wars, including ground-breaking studies that are seen as predecessors of the late twentieth-century feminist historiography.[50] In Britain the role of the London School of Economics in encouraging women's history deserves to be mentioned here. The involvement of LSE-linked historians with national history was far from uniform: sometimes, like Lilian Knowles, they were even fervent supporters of British imperialism.[51] Others focused on the experience of women: Alice Clark's *Life of Women in the Seventeenth Century* presented a particularly influential reinterpretation of national history from the perspective of women, comparing the situation of women in modern Britain unfavourably with their conditions in the pre-industrial period.

Only exceptionally, however, were women included in national master narratives of that time. Representatives of the most progressive historical movement, the emerging *Annales* school in France, which radicalised the history of man, were surprisingly conservative concerning women. They rarely dealt with the subject, and when they did, they wrote traditional, event-oriented, positivist

---

[49]Melman, 'Gender, History and Memory', p. 34.

[50]Natalie Zemon Davis gives as an example of the best of these studies, Alice Clark's *Life of Women in the Seventeenth Century* from 1919 and Léon Abensour's *La Femme et le féminisme en France avant la Révolution* from 1923. See N. Z. Davis, '"Women's History" in Transition: The European Case', *Feminist Studies*, 3 (spring/summer, 1976), p. 85. Other often quoted contributions include Eileen Power's works, M. Thibert's *Le Féminisme dans le socialisme français de 1830 à 1850* from 1926, and I. Pinchbeck's *Women Workers and the Industrial Revolution (1750–1850)* from 1930.

[51]G. Pomata, 'Rejoinder to Pygmalion: The Origins of Women's History at the London School of Economics', in Porciani and O'Dowd (eds), *History Women*, pp. 88–9.

history.[52] In Britain, George Macaulay Trevelyan's influential *English Social History*, published during the Second World War, did a better job including descriptions of women's life, work, education, entertainment and family life, alongside men's. Unlike many other intellectuals, Trevelyan appreciated the independence women gained with employment, even in factories.[53]

In the new nation-states established in the nineteenth century or after the First World War, an increasing number of professional women historians dealt both with traditional topics of their respective historiographies, and with women in national histories. Irish women historians, inspired by Irish nationalism and other political views, wrote studies on political history and history textbooks, some of which have become very popular. Dorothy Macardle's *The Irish Republic* was 'one of the major works on contemporary Irish history to appear during the Free State period', and Mary Hayden's textbook was recommended to students in the National University of Ireland system.[54] While Hayden wrote articles on women's history her major work on Irish history did not pay particular attention to the role of women in the Irish past.[55] Women historians in Finland tried to incorporate women in the Finnish national past. Katri Laine emphasised the importance of the household and women's work at home, while preserving the framework of mainstream Finnish national history.[56]

In the 1920s Rosa Imvrioti interpreted the history of ancient Greece and Byzantium from a feminist perspective that also fitted the prevalent paradigm of Greek national history.[57] The 1930s brought Łucja Charewiczowa's pioneering works on Polish women's history and historiography, connecting feminist and patriotic aims.[58] Male historians also studied women, though often as objects rather than subjects of Polish history.[59] In interwar Czechoslovakia,

---

[52]See S. M. Stuard, 'Fashion's Captives: Medieval Women in French Historiography', in Stuard (ed.), *Women in Medieval History*, p. 69.

[53]G. M. Trevelyan, *English Social History: A Survey of Six Centuries. Chaucer to Queen Victoria* (London, New York, Toronto, [1942] 1946), pp. 486–8.

[54]N. C. Smith, *Irish Women Historians, 1900–1950*, in Porciani and O'Dowd (eds.), *History Women*, pp. 71–5.

[55]O'Dowd, 'Interpreting the Past', pp. 1118–21.

[56]See M. Kaarninen and T. Kinnunen, '"Hardly Any Women at All": Finnish Historiography Revisited', in Porciani and O'Dowd (eds.), *History Women*, p. 161.

[57]See E. Gazi, 'Engendering the Writing and Teaching of History in Mid-War Greece', in Porciani and O'Dowd (eds.), *History Women*, pp. 119–29.

[58]A. Kusiak, 'Łucja Charewiczowa: inicjatorka badań nad przeszłością kobiet polskich', in A. Żarnowska and A. Szwarc (eds), *Kobieta i kultura: kobiety wśród twórców kultury intelektualnej i artystycznej w dobie rozbiorów i w niepodległym państwie polskim*, 4 (Warszawa, 1996), pp. 99–103.

[59]For example, S. Wasylewski, *Portret kobiecy w Polsce XVIII wieku* (Warszawa, 1926); K. Szajnocha's *War for the Honour of a Woman* [*Wojna o cześć kobiety*: Wspomnienie historyczne z czasów Kazimierza W., *Rozprawy naukowe* 1886, 22, pp. 1–29] is interesting for the author's comments on the inferior position of women in medieval Poland. *pub det*

famous male intellectuals Arne Novák and Stanislav Kostka Neumann wrote extensive works on women's history.[60] And women sometimes made it into history and literary history textbooks.

During the Second World War, when European nations were endangered, historians sometimes turned with renewed vigour to the role of women in the fate of the country. The Czech example is quite striking. In 1940 a prominent Czech historian, Karel Stloukal, edited a 600-page volume on Czech women's history, with contributions by 28 scholars, men as well as women. In the introduction, he wrote:

> The participation of women in our history is so important that it truly deserves more attention than has been devoted to it till now. Only in the most recent times has the effort to evaluate the contribution of Czech women to our national culture started to revive, and an interest in this new topic has made its way also to the wider public.[61]

Other jointly produced works on Czech women's history were published in the same year.[62]

The Czech case was not unique: Ida Blom points out that a striking number of books and articles on women's history, written by professional women historians, were published in both Norway and Denmark in the late 1930s and early 1940s.[63] A mainstream (male) Polish historian, Władysław Konopczyński, who had not been otherwise interested in women's history, wrote a (rather conservative) book on the role of women in Polish political life.[64] The attention paid to women definitely did not increase everywhere. However, it seems that in at least some of the new nation-states, women participated in national histories as both authors and subjects, especially when nationalism was on the rise during the war.

History writing under fascism both confirms and complicates the pattern connecting nationalism with an interest in the women's past. It is necessary to note that while gender under Nazism is a burgeoning topic in today's German historical studies, we still lack analyses of the ways Nazi historians (or historians in the Nazi era) incorporated women in their historical works.

---

[60]A. Novák, *Podobizny žen* (Praha, Brno, [1918] 1940); S. K. Neumann, *Dějiny ženy: populární kapitoly sociologické, etnologické a kulturně historické*, 1–4 (Praha, 1931–2).

[61]K. Stloukal (ed.), *Královny, kněžny a velké ženy české* (Praha, 1940), p. 7.

[62]R. Bednaříková-Turnwaldová, A. Birnbaumová, M. Tumlířová and B. Veselá (eds), *Česká žena v dějinách národa* (Praha, 1940); *Žena v českém umění dramatickém* (Praha, 1940). Both these works emphasized the contribution of women to the progress of the Czech nation.

[63]Blom, 'Women in Norwegian and Danish Historiography', p. 148.

[64]W. Konopczyński, *Kiedy nami rządziły kobiety* (London, 1960).

In historiography, as in other areas, fascism did not bring about a clean break with the past, but either strengthened earlier tendencies or developed them to extremes. It is possible to distinguish three interconnected trends. First, earlier debates on women among the pagan Germanic tribes, including the questions of polygamy, the habit of buying brides and to a lesser extent matriarchy, acquired a new relevance, as the polygamy and 'promiscuity' of the old Germans had to be refuted in the name of the new German virtues. Second, motherhood, which had an important place in and was (ab)used by Nazi ideology, attracted the attention of historians as well. Under Nazism, historians were often concerned with the origins of the Nordic race and with racial issues more generally, and women as mothers were attributed an essential role in preserving racial purity. Third, following Hitler's speeches,[65] Nazi ideologists and historians emphasised the importance of women in the resurrection of the German nation, using examples from history to support their appeals.

Both historians and ideologists often quoted the work of Gustav Neckel, an expert in ancient Nordic sagas and early German history. In 1932 Neckel published a defence of the ancient German family built on love. He claimed that among the ancient German tribes, marriage was not based on violence and subjugation of women; that monogamous relationships prevailed while promiscuity and polygamy were mere exceptions; and that the buying of brides was just a theory, as it was mentioned only in legal sources.[66]

The legal historian Herbert Meyer wrote in a similar spirit in 1932, as well as in his 1940 book on marriage among ancient Germans. Arguing with the critics of the old Germanic family habits and position of women, he emphasised that in early German history, women were not inferior to men, and gave examples of their high position. He used Tacitus and references from Germanic law to disprove the thesis about polygamy and particularly the buying of wives among ancient Germans. He claimed that a woman was not sold, but given to marriage, just as a man gave himself to his wife. Marriage was a community of free will, not a woman's subjugation to the will of the stronger. Woman was man's comrade and mistress of the household. Her adultery was punished more strictly not because her status was lower than man's, but because it allowed the influx of foreign blood to the tribe.[67]

---

[65]See H. P. Bleuel, *Sex and Society in Nazi Germany* (Philadelphia and New York, 1973), pp. 54–5.

[66]G. Neckel, *Liebe und Ehe bei den vorchristlichen Germanen* (Leipzig and Berlin, 1932), esp. pp. 1–6.

[67]H. Meyer, *Ehe und Eheauffassung der Germanen* (Weimar, 1940), passim. See also H. Meyer, 'Die Eheschließung im *Ruodlieb* und das Eheschwert', *Zeitschrift der Savigny-Stiftung für Rechtsgeschichte*, 52 (1932), 276–93.

Perhaps surprisingly, well-established mainstream historians also occasionally mentioned the position of women among the Germanic tribes. The Tübingen professor emeritus Johannes Haller wrote in 1939 about women's active participation in early Germanic society: women were men's partners, helping and encouraging them, and sometimes even fighting at their side. Individual women seers seem to have been more respected and influential than male priests. Marriage was sacred and polygamy was limited to the elites, according to Haller.[68]

Works on women and gender relations drew on an earlier tradition, though the interest in 'German blood' and race increased under Nazism. Women were used to show the racial superiority of the Germans. *The Myth of the Twentieth Century*, a theory of history based on race, written by the influential Nazi ideologist Alfred Rosenberg in 1930 and re-edited several times in the 1930s and 1940s, is among the most fascinating examples. Although the book was intended as a guide for the future, the future was grounded in arguments from history. Questions of masculinity and femininity played an important role in these arguments. Man was, according to Rosenberg, superior to woman in all respects of creation and power. Male spirit gave birth to a world order against (female) chaos. Most importantly, men created the state, which is therefore a men's state – and can never be anything else. The Nordic man was characterised by great firmness and toughness, and embodied all the virtues of a master.

Rosenberg mentioned that among the ancient Germanic tribes, women were respected, but he denied the hypothesis about matriarchy. Unlike Treitschke, who did not see 'feminine centuries' in German history as a decline, Rosenberg considered women's power in history a sign of degeneration, which leads to chaos. He identified women's prominence with promiscuity and connected women's emancipation with the emancipation of Jews (or elsewhere with Marxism, communism or liberalism), all of which he viewed as similarly dangerous. In the past, emancipation of women and militarism were in direct contrast; whenever women gained more rights, it weakened militarism, and vice versa. In present-day Germany, he wrote, women are necessary for the salvation of the nation and preservation of the race, but only if they are chaste and know their right place.[69]

---

[68]J. Haller, *Der Eintritt der Germanen in die Geschichte* (Berlin, 1939), pp. 21–3. I would like to thank Peter Lambert for bringing this text and particular passage to my attention.
[69]See A. Rosenberg, *The Myth of the Twentieth Century: An Evaluation of the Spiritual-Intellectual Confrontations of Our Age* (Newport Beach, CA, 1982), pp. 2–79 and 300–26; R. Pois (ed.), *Race and Race History and Other Essays by Alfred Rosenberg* (New York, Evanston, San Francisco and London, 1970), pp. 33–99. On the scholarship of the Nazi period, see W. Jacobeit, H. Lixfeld and O. Bockhorn (eds), *Völkische Wissenschaft: Gestalten und Tendenzen der deutschen und österreichischen Volkskunde in der ersten Hälfte des 20. Jahrhunderts* (Wien, Köln and Weimar, 1994).

Rosenberg inspired many scholars, including Fritz Arlt, who in his dissertation, published in 1936, compared women in Old Icelandic sagas with women in the Old Testament.[70] Arlt claimed that the value of women in the sagas was derived primarily from their role as bearers of tradition and of the transcendental – through blood and the power relations of their kin. Apart from their kin, women's value was based on their behaviour, ability to work and motherly qualities. While the emphasis on blood and the transcendental came from Rosenberg, Arlt presented a very different image of the Old Icelandic women: strong mistresses, rational, proud, dominant, brave, independent, sometimes manly and, regardless of what some authors say, also virtuous. Women were free, equal to men and participated in decision-making. Arlt mentioned the purchase of brides only in passing, quoting experts such as Neckel, in order to show that when it happened, it was a mere exception, not the norm.

Arlt's study of women in ancient sources served to show the superiority of the Germans over the Jews. Arlt depicted women of the Old Testament as collective beings in the harems of their husbands, seen as unclean and as man's property, whose value is based on their ability to give birth and to work. Interestingly, in the case of women of the Nordic sagas, motherhood was self-understood, but women's value was 'the modern biological concept of blood value'.[71] While in the sagas woman was free and equal, a beloved companion for whom man cared, in the Old Testament, woman was man's servant, valued only as a fertile and working property of her husband. According to Arlt these differences cannot be explained by climate and other factors of geography, but by race.

Yet another image of motherhood is presented by Herman Wirth, one of the most fascinating figures of the Nazi discourse on women. Wirth was editor (and, according to some, author) of the *Ura Linda Chronicle*, a forgery on which many Nazi historical claims were based.[72] Dedicated 'to my German mothers', the text and particularly Wirth's extensive commentaries paid substantial attention to women, especially to *Volksmutter* (Folk Mother), the highest authority in the old Germanic matriarchal society. In his detailed study of Old German language and symbols of Germanness,[73] Wirth wrote that women

---

[70]F. Arlt, *Die Frauen der altisländischen Bauernsagen und die Frauen der vorexilischen Bücher des Alten Testaments, verglichen nach ihren Handlungswerten, ihrer Bewertung, ihrer Erscheinungsweise, ihrer Behandlung: Ein Beitrag zur Rassenpsychologie* (Leipzig, 1936). I would like to thank Frank Mecklenburg for bringing this text to my attention.

[71]Arlt, *Die Frauen der altisländischen Bauernsagen*, p. 57.

[72]*Die Ura Linda Chronik: Übersetzt und mit einer einführenden geschichtlichen Untersuchung herausgegeben von Herman Wirth* (Leipzig, 1933).

[73]H. Wirth, *Was heißt deutsch? Ein urgeistesgeschichtlicher Rückblick zur Selbstbesinnung und Selbstbestimmung*, 2nd edn (Jena, 1934).

had once been the bearers and guardians of sacred values, 'our Germanness', and *Volksmütter* had been the last refuge of Nordic religiosity and freedom. The path to Germanness had to go via the *Volksmütter* – the godly and the eternal that would make the Germans free and noble once again. Like Rosenberg, Wirth criticised liberalism, democracy and Marxism, under whose impact the women's movement took a wrong turn, towards masculinisation. The work concluded with an appeal, emphasising that without women and their godly motherhood, all men's efforts would be in vain and the resurrection of Germany impossible.

While German historians under Nazism often referred to past women both in their defences of German national qualities and in their historical lessons for the resurrection of the German *Volk*, they also explicitly expressed their opinion, that German history was masculine. This was different from the implicit treatment of history as male that we find in all historiographies, where 'abstract' men are a 'default', but stand for all humanity. Rosenberg wrote about the masculine, military character of German history as embody-ing important Nordic values – honour and duty. Only men were the basis of this history, the germ cells of the state, which can only be theirs; women and the family were added later or were excluded.[74] Leonhard Franz, in his schol-arly analysis of prehistoric female statues, goddesses and symbols of fertility, set apart the Nordic territory (which included the German ancestors), where views about fertility seem to have been given a masculine form.[75]

Women joined this historical discourse, and, as in other areas, sometimes accepted and promoted Nazi ideology, including Nazi ideas on women.[76] While some women historians treated women in German history as a schol-arly topic and perhaps an occasion to write on women,[77] others did more than just write in the framework of the ideology of the time. In *Images of Germanic Women's Life*, Gisela Wenz-Hartmann wanted to show German women their ancestors in order to awaken the heritage of pride, morality and courage. She emphasised that women have always had an important place among the Germans because the tribe needed strong and proud women alongside strong, proud men, to educate free sons and daughters. These women possessed great pride, which lay in their Nordic-Germanic blood, honour and motherhood. Although women worked for patriotic purposes, Wenz-Hartmann wrote, their arena was not the whole country, but the family. The tasks of the German

---

[74]Rosenberg, *Myth of the Twentieth Century*, pp. 304–12.
[75]L. Franz, *Die Muttergöttin im Vorderen Orient und in Europa* (Leipzig, 1937), p. 24.
[76]Bleuel, *Sex and Society*, pp. 54–68.
[77]See, for example, G. Bäumer, *Adelheid, Mutter der Königreiche* (Tübingen, 1936).

woman in the Third Reich were to serve the future, to be mother of the people and to preserve its blood.[78]

In Italy, larger numbers of women entered the historical discipline under fascism, and some even had prominent careers. As Ilaria Porciani shows, this, paradoxically, happened exactly when the *riforma Gentile* prohibited women from becoming professors of philosophy and history. Fascism brought increasing attention to the traditionally popular topics of Italian historiography: mother of Mazzini, mothers of heroes and, after the First World War, the cult of the soldier's mother.[79]

Ideas on women during the fascist era, Lucia Re points out, were not limited to the new Italian woman as exemplary wife and mother.[80] They changed over time, and several competing discourses on women and sexual differences existed side by side. The contradictions were embodied in the work of one person – the influential philosopher and ideologue of the Italian fascist regime, Giovanni Gentile. In a 1934 essay, including an emotional essentialist celebration of motherhood, Gentile rejected women's emancipation and used historical arguments from 'the virile ages of antiquity' to show that women's place was in the home.[81]

Interestingly, in Gentile's *Genesis and Structure of Society*, a philosophy of history, women are conspicuously absent.[82] The section on 'Understanding and Loving' deals with the Christian commandment to love one's neighbour, and then goes on to speak about 'brothers'. Even more striking is the section on the 'Family', where women are not mentioned at all, only children and the institution of family, specifically inheritance and the family as a continuation of men's lives and hopes. History is 'a story of man'. The striking absence of women, accompanied by references to fascism as 'the cult of Man: the cult of the power', makes the book essentially masculine.

Gentile was also general editor of the *Enciclopedia italiana di scienze, lettere ed arti*. Under the heading 'Woman', this major encyclopedia published under the fascist regime gives an account of women's position in various societies in history, with particular attention paid to ancient civilisations. Women appear active in this text, though their impact is not always seen as positive. Jewish and Arabic civilisations, for example, gave women fewer legal rights than did earlier Oriental civilisations, but were in fact under a stronger feminine influence. Ancient Romans felt deeply the attraction of family life and made wives the com-

---

[78]G. Wenz-Hartmann, *Lebensbilder germanischer Frauen* (Leipzig, 1940), pp. 3–5.
[79]Porciani, 'Les Historiennes', pp. 354–5.
[80]L. Re, 'Fascist Theories of "Woman" and the Construction of Gender', in R. Pickering-Iazzi (ed.), *Mothers of Invention: Women, Italian Fascism, and Culture* (Minneapolis and London, 1995), pp. 76–99.
[81]Re, 'Fascist Theories of "Woman" and the Construction of Gender', pp. 81–5.
[82]G. Gentile, *Genesis and Structure of Society* (Urbana and London, 1966) [written in 1944].

panions and collaborators of their husbands. The dark side of women's freedom was, according to this account, that some women by their intrigues and political ambitions destroyed their husbands.[83]

Fascism thus continued in the line of works that incorporated women in national histories within the framework and serving the purpose of nationalism. Although the emphasis on blood and race was more extreme than at other times and in other nationalist histories, it was not unique. Historians of the fascist era were far from unified in their views on women and therefore did not present one image of women's position and roles that could be translated into current policy.

Women, gender and national history since the 1970s

Although historians of women since the late 1960s increasingly abandoned the national framework of history, women's/gender history is inseparable from the study of gender in national master narratives. A lot has been written about the failure of mainstream histories in Europe to incorporate women's experiences.[84] It is worth asking, however, how the unprecedented number of works on women's and later gender history published in the late twentieth century, including widely read and path-breaking works, influenced the way mainstream national histories have treated gender. Moreover, with the fragmentation of national master narratives under the impact of postmodernism, which coincided with a shift to gender, gender history has become one of the potential heirs of the national master narrative.

This section examines the relationship between women's and national histories, focusing primarily on Western Europe, where most substantial and innovative changes in approaches to the study of women/gender in history occurred. It asks how mainstream national histories have responded to the rise of women's history and whether the emergence of gender history changed this relationship: has gender created a master narrative of its own?

Bonnie Smith argues that when women wrote about the past from a feminist perspective, they were excluded from professional history, which claimed to be objective and non-partisan, except when it defended imperialism and nationalism.[85] Has women's history become more acceptable, then, and been

---

[83] *Enciclopedia italiana di scienze, lettere ed arti*, 10 (Roma, 1932), pp. 146–52.

[84] See C. Hall, *White, Male and Middle-Class: Explorations in Feminism and History* (Cambridge, 1992), p. 34; F. Thébaud, *Écrire l'histoire des femmes* (Fontenay-aux-Roses, 1998), p. 19; M. Riot-Sarcey, 'The Difficulties of Gender in France: Reflections on a Concept', *Gender and History*, 11 (1999), p. 496; Perrot, *Les Femmes*, p. xvii; K. Canning, *Languages of Labor and Gender: Female Factory Work in Germany, 1850–1914* (Ithaca and London, 1996), pp. 6–7; K. Canning, *Gender History in Practice: Historical Perspectives on Bodies, Class, and Citizenship* (Ithaca, NY and London, 2006), pp. 48–53.

[85] Smith, *Gender of History*, pp. 173 and 181.

included in mainstream national historiography, when the authors work within the prevailing paradigm of national history and emphasise national specificity?

Women's history, which appeared between the late 1960s and late 1970s as an autonomous field of historical research all around Western Europe, was typically supranational. The authors contributing to edited volumes devoted to women in various (Western) European countries were increasingly in dialogue with each other, rather than with their colleagues in respective national histories.[86] The by-product of this situation (undoubtedly inspiring for women's history) was that, on the one hand, historians of women were mostly uninterested in rewriting national histories or viewing history in terms of national categories, and on the other hand, women's history was easily ignored by mainstream national histories. Yet there were differences among individual national historiographies.

Women were not completely ignored in large historical projects on national histories. It is surprising, however, to read in the mid-1980s *Cambridge Historical Encyclopedia of Great Britain* about the Victorian age and philanthropy and to find hardly any references to women and the relevance of gender.[87] Even the extensive *Cambridge Social History of Britain* from 1990 contains no separate entry on women or gender, other than a valuable chapter on 'the family'.[88]

Women historians have had to position themselves around the dominant historical discourses, including the traditions of their national histories and their (mostly male) teachers. As a rule, women's history presented a challenge to traditional national history, and the writing of women's history thus sometimes appeared as a revolt of daughters against their fathers. Catherine Hall explicitly mentions how young women historians decided to 'reject our fathers', Marxist teachers who presented class as gender-blind.[89] British feminist historians nevertheless share mainstream British history's focus on 'class', which seems to be a much more salient category of analysis in British women's history than 'nation'.

West German women's history followed the development of mainstream national history with its focus on the Nazi past. Women historians did not

---

[86]See, for example, K. Offen, R. Roach Pierson and J. Rendall (eds), *Writing Women's History: International Perspectives* (Bloomington, IN, 1991).

[87]C. Haigh (ed.), *The Cambridge Historical Encyclopedia of Great Britain and Ireland* (Cambridge, 1985), pp. 276–86.

[88]See G. Eley, 'Playing it Safe. Or: How is Social History Represented? The New *Cambridge Social History of Britain*', *History Workshop*, 35 (1993), p. 216. In the late 1990s the encyclopedia of medieval England (P. E. Szarmach, M. T. Tavormina and J. T. Rosenthal (eds), *Medieval England: An Encyclopedia*, New York and London, 1998) attempted to give women agency and provided more information on women's experiences than the 1999 *Blackwell Encyclopaedia of Anglo-Saxon England*, M. Lapidge, J. Blair, S. Keynes and D. Scragg (eds.).

[89]Hall, *White, Male and Middle-Class*, p. 11.

challenge only their teachers, but also their own fathers, asking about their role in supporting the Nazi regime. They also had to come to terms with the past of their mothers. The so-called *Historikerinnenstreit* addressed the support of women for Nazism and the limits of women's ability to resist the very regime which disempowered them.[90] The debates around these questions were followed by a wide public of historians,[91] perhaps because they touch on deep sensitivities of German national history with its idealisation of motherhood.

Mainstream German national history, nevertheless, is not particularly welcoming to women's or gender history. Jürgen Kocka's 1973 *German Social History* included information on the economic and social conditions of working-class women,[92] yet his later work has not incorporated the results of women's history.[93] The third volume of Hans-Ulrich Wehler's comprehensive *Deutsche Geselschaftsgeschichte* pays more attention to women than the previous parts,[94] but the descriptions of the women's movement or educational opportunities reflect little of the debates in women's history.

Nor is the major enterprise on French national history, *Les Lieux de mémoire*, edited by Pierre Nora, particularly concerned with women or gender. A gender perspective is missing in Mona Ozouf's chapter 'Liberty, Equality, Fraternity', though not only the topic but also the accompanying illustrations call for it.[95] Apart from passing references to the women's movement, women's rights or motherhood, the three volumes which have been translated into English include a few chapters with more sophisticated gender analyses. Michel Winock shows how the memory of Jeanne d'Arc reflects the conflicts and divisions (and maybe also the unifying factor) of French society.[96] Women are often connected to the realm of the symbolic: continuing in the tradition of Maurice Agulhon's

---

[90]Canning, *Gender History in Practice*, pp. 49–51. Two particularly influential books – C. Koonz's *Mothers in the Fatherland: Women, the Family and Nazi Politics* (New York, 1987) and R. Bridenthal, A. Grossmann and M. Kaplan (eds.), *When Biology Became Destiny: Women in Weimar and Nazi Germany*, (New York, 1984) – were written or edited largely by 'foreign' historians. See also A. Grossmann, 'Feminist Debates about Women and National Socialism', *Gender and History*, 3 (1991), pp. 350–8.

[91]Canning, *Gender History in Practice*, p. 50.

[92]J. Kocka, *Klassengesellschaft im Krieg: Deutsche Sozialgeschichte, 1914–1918* (Göttingen, 1973).

[93]On Kocka's attitude towards women's history, see I. Hull, 'Feminist and Gender History through the Literary Looking Glass: German Historiography in Postmodern Times', *Central European History*, 22 (1989), 282–3.

[94] For a criticism of the first two volumes, see Canning, *Languages of Labor and Gender*, pp. 7–8 n. 16; Hull, 'Feminist and Gender History', p. 294.

[95]M. Ozouf, 'Liberty, Equality, Fraternity', in P. Nora (ed.), *Realms of Memory: The Construction of the French Past*, 3, *Symbols* (New York, 1998), pp. 77–114.

[96]M. Winock, 'Joan of Arc', in Nora, *Realms of Memory*, 3, pp. 433–80.

influential *Marianne au combat* from 1979, authors analyse how women represent France and appear on monuments or as national symbols.

The fact that some of the most prominent French historians, like Duby, wrote on women and the family is significant in promoting women's history in France and bringing women's lives to the general historical consciousness.[97] While not trying to write from a 'women's perspective', Duby is sensitive to aspects of women's lives. He served as co-editor of the comprehensive *Histoire des femmes en Occident*. This work, for which French historians of women are probably best known, is international both in its authorship and scope, and was inspired by an Italian publisher, but French historians of women tend to focus on French national history.

The interest in national history is clearly expressed in references to French specificity. The most striking example is undoubtedly Mona Ozouf's controversial *Paroles des femmes*, including a nationalist polemic on American feminism. This text is particularly noteworthy due to the author's position in mainstream French historiography. Ozouf points out equality in education that started with the culture of the salons, women's civilising role and the Enlightenment, and led to a belief that all human beings are equal. Therefore, Ozouf claims, it was not necessary to emphasise special women's rights, that relations between men and women were non-confrontational, and that, unlike American women, French women could enjoy difference without making it into a political issue. Ozouf quotes George Sand, who said that there is only one sex, as well as Montesquieu, who wrote, 'in spirit we are all women', suggesting that the French are in fact a feminine nation.[98] Interestingly, even Françoise Thébaud, who criticises the *génie national* to which Ozouf attributes the French gender harmony, tends to refer to a 'French specificity'.

One such specificity is French historians' reluctance to accept the concept of gender.[99] While some, like Michelle Perrot, acknowledge the usefulness of gender as a tool of historical analysis, in practice, French historians until recently preferred to present their work as a part of women's history; sometimes they saw these two as equivalent.[100] According to Thébaud, French his-

---

[97]See G. Duby, *The Knight, the Lady and the Priest: The Making of Modern Marriage in Medieval France*, trans. Barbara Bray (New York, 1983); G. Duby, *Love and Marriage in the Middle Ages*, trans. Jane Dunnett (Chicago, 1994). See also B. Lepetit, 'Histoire des femmes, histoire sociale: présentation', *Annales*, 48 (1993), pp. 997–8.

[98]Ozouf, *Les Mots des femmes*, pp. 323–97, esp. 329.

[99]Riot-Sarcey, 'Difficulties of Gender', p. 494.

[100]There is more interest in gender and specifically masculinity among the young generation and in recent years. See, for example, A. Rauch, *L'Identité masculine à l'ombre des femmes: de la Grande Guerre à la Gay Pride* (Paris, 2004); O. Roynette, 'La Construction du masculin de la fin du XIXe siècle aux années 1930', *Vingtième siècle: revue d'histoire*, 75 (2002), 85–96.

torians rejected gender because they did not want to separate themselves from mainstream studies.[101]

For exactly the same reason, scholars in post-communist Eastern Europe interested in women's studies often preferred the term gender, which they found more inclusive. With the exception of Yugoslavia, women's/gender studies in Eastern Europe did not emerge as a result of women's movements, but were directly inspired by Western feminist scholarship. Under communism, 'class' shadowed 'nation' in postwar national histories. Works on women written in this period were either intended to prove the superiority of socialism over capitalism, or presented as somewhat exotic. Women's experiences were often made into 'human' experiences,[102] and women were generally absent in master narratives.

The rise of nationalism in Eastern Europe after 1989 did not lead to the incorporation of women in mainstream national histories. Master narratives continue to be written in 'all-human' (rather than explicitly and consciously male) terms. Noteworthy among the exceptions is Boris Mironov's meticulously researched and documented *Social History of Imperial Russia*.[103] Although under-theorised, the wealth of information it contains on women's lives and gender relations in all strata of Russian society is truly striking. Among women's histories, a unique enterprise is the extensive series on nineteenth- and twentieth-century Polish women's history (including education, politics, culture, everyday life, etc.), edited by Anna Żarnowska and Andrzej Szwarc, with contributions by a number of (female and male) historians of different generations.[104]

It seems that women's/gender history throughout Europe largely has been developing parallel to mainstream national history, rather than as its integral part. Their relationship was often marked by a mutual lack of interest, though historians of women and gender, out of necessity, had to take into consideration the paradigms of national history.

It is symptomatic that the most influential and respected works dealing with women are not written by feminist historians. Linda Colley, author of *Britons: Forging the Nation, 1707–1837*, is not an historian of women, but

---

[101]Thébaud, *Écrire l'histoire*, p. 88.

[102]See J. Malečková, 'Gender, Nation and Scholarship: Reflections on Gender/Women's Studies in the Czech Republic', in M. Maynard and J. Purvis (eds), *New Frontiers in Women's Studies: Knowledge, Identity and Nationalism* (London, 1996), pp. 100–1.

[103]B. N. Mironov (with Ben Eklof), *The Social History of Imperial Russia, 1700–1917*, 1–2 (Boulder, CO, 1999–2000).

[104]A. Żarnowska and A. Szwarc (eds), *Kobieta i społeczeństwo na ziemiach polskich w XIX wieku* (Warszawa, 1995); *Kobieta i edukacja na ziemiach polskich w XIX i XX wieku*, 1–2 (Warszawa, 1995), etc.

gender has an important place in her book. She (like British historians of women) shows how a conservative ideology of separate spheres could be used to defend the position of women and legitimise their intervention in the public sphere.[105] Although not unanimously acclaimed and remaining controversial, her book was able to make an impact on British historical scholarship. It is interesting to note that the highly praised recent work of Catherine Hall, the renowned historian of women, on the British colony and metropole, is not on women's history, but it weaves gender into a postcolonial national history.[106]

In France it is common even among critical historians of women, such as Michelle Perrot and Françoise Thébaud, to point out a 'specific' French path to feminism. Yet Mona Ozouf, who has written on women without presenting herself as a historian of women, and on the French 'national genius' that has led to the singularity of gender relations in France, seems to be most integrated in mainstream French historiography. In Czech historiography, the best example is Milena Lenderová's *To Sin and to Pray: Woman in the Last Century*, a mosaic of information on Czech women's lives in the nineteenth century, written in the framework of Czech national history and explicitly distancing itself from feminism.[107] It got very positive reviews in both scholarly journals and popular magazines – exactly because it tames the potentially dangerous concept of gender.

Yet women's/gender and national histories do intersect, resulting in some remarkable contributions to national history. In northern Europe, for example, we find both efforts by mainstream male historians to include gender experiences in their narratives, and women historians reinterpreting national histories. In his *Woman and Slave* from 1971 and its unfinished sequel, published posthumously, a respected male historian, Niels Skyum-Nielsen, attempted to incorporate women as a marginalised group in Danish history. In 1999 Norwegian historians of women published an extensive volume that covers and interprets the entire Norwegian history from a gender perspective.[108] Irma Sulkunen introduced a concept of dual citizenship to modern Finnish history, approached through gender. Women's early suffrage in Finland resulted, according to Sulkunen, from the fact that the country was lagging behind and

---

[105]L. Colley, *Britons: Forging the Nation, 1707–1837* (New Haven, CT, 1992), pp. 237–81.
[106]C. Hall, *Civilising Subjects: Colony and Metropole in the English Imagination, 1830–1867* (Chicago and London, 2002).
[107]M. Lenderová, *K hříchu i k modlitbě: žena v minulém století* (Praha, 1999).
[108]See Fulsås et al., this volume (chapter 10). I am grateful to Narve Fulsås and Bernard Jensen for bringing these works to my attention.

the concepts of private sphere and conservative motherhood had not yet reached the Finland of the early twentieth century.[109]

Women's history has contributed to national history in various ways: including women's/gender experiences in the national past, reinterpreting national history from a women's perspective and reshaping the study of the history of nationalism. All the major (historically anchored) theories of nationalism that revolutionised nationalism studies in the 1980s were gender-blind.[110] Works that followed, in contrast, have convincingly shown that the 'imagined communities' were constructed as gendered. Numerous studies have analysed the participation of women in national movements, women's national(ist) writings, the impact of war on gender relations, gendered symbols and myths, and the construction of masculinity, to name just some of the topics.[111] Most of these contributions appeared in edited volumes, collecting chapters on individual national cases or devoted to the past of one nation. *Home/Front*, edited by Karen Hagemann and Stefanie Schüler-Springorum, for example, showed the construction of masculinities and femininities in Germany in the time of and between the two world wars.[112] The emphasis on multiple gender experiences is symptomatic of the intersection between gender and national history at the beginning of the twenty-first century.

The interest in the concept of gender and in gender history, which shares common points of reference in the (variously understood) works of Joan Scott and Michel Foucault, has undoubtedly increased all around Europe. Nevertheless, I believe that in European national histories, gender did not create a master narrative that could replace 'nation' and be comparable to 'class' as central to constructing a single dominant account of the past. The turn to gender occurred just at the time when master narratives in general, and those centred on the nation in particular, were shattered. Single-author syntheses of national history, even when they are not influenced by postmodernism, tend to be replaced by edited volumes, representing various sub-fields of history, groups of population and areas of life. It is hard to imagine a 'gender history'

---

[109]Kaarninen and Kinnunen, 'Hardly Any Women at All', p. 167.

[110]See B. Anderson, *Imagined Communities: Reflections on the Origins and Spread of Nationalism* (London, 1983); E. Gellner, *Nations and Nationalism* (Ithaca, NY and London, 1983); A. Smith, *The Ethnic Origins of Nations* (Oxford, 1986); J. Breuilly, *Nationalism and the State* (Manchester, 1982).

[111]See, for example, Blom et al., *Gendered Nations*; C. Hall, K. McClelland and J. Rendall (eds), *Defining the Victorian Nation: Class, Race, Gender and the British Reform Act of 1867* (Cambridge, 2000); T. Mayer (ed.), *Gender Ironies of Nationalism: Sexing the Nation* (London and New York, 2000).

[112]K. Hagemann and S. Schüler-Springorum (eds), *Home/Front: The Military, War and Gender in Twentieth-Century Germany* (New York and Oxford, 2002).

of England or France presenting a unified master narrative, without the necessary fragmentation brought by the different experiences of women and men, rich and poor, young and old, women of colour, lesbians, and so on.

Conclusion

Since the emergence of modern national historiographies in the nineteenth century, women as a group generally have been incorporated in master narratives in order to serve the perceived needs of the nation, especially to buttress national consciousness and self-esteem. Stronger nationalism did not necessarily mean more attention was paid to women in history, but national concern can help explain why mainstream male historians in the nineteenth and up to the mid-twentieth centuries included women in their stories. The inclusion of women in national histories could confirm – and not only disrupt, as is sometimes claimed – the prevailing historical arguments and concepts.

In the constitutive period of nationalism, references to the position and qualities of women in the golden age of national history, or the improvement of women's status with the nation's progress, reflected the debates over the current state of the nation. Historians often pointed to women when they wrote about national character and habits, while political histories dealt with individual women, namely queens, more than with women's experiences more generally. In the interwar period, historians tried to incorporate women in the national past particularly when the past had to be redefined in a new nation-state or from a new ideological perspective, such as fascism. Historians under fascism drew on earlier traditions, adding or increasing the concern with blood, racial purity and masculinity. The way they used images of women resembled the way other nationalist historiographies employed them: to prove the superiority of their nation.

Postwar nationalism, which has become more subtle than in the past, has done less to affect the attention paid to women in national histories than did the more explicit nationalism of previous periods. Yet the acceptance of historians such as Linda Colley and Mona Ozouf suggests that those works addressing women/gender (but not considered feminist) that are written in the framework of national history (even if in a rather non-traditional way) may have a chance of being included in mainstream national historiography. Catherine Hall's recent works on 'general' national history, while informed by her long-term studies of women, present a somewhat different example of this model.

Generally, however, mainstream national histories still fail to incorporate women's experiences and to respond to the challenges to periodisation and narrative frameworks posed by historians of women and gender. Gender is a somewhat tamer concept in continental Europe than in the Anglo-American context, less connected either with race or with class. Explicitly viewing history as fragmented and challenging national master narratives, gender has not created a master narrative of its own. Even this concept of gender seems to be only slowly making its way into European national histories. Yet there are signs of a change occurring since the late 1990s: we may just be beginning to see the impact of the earlier efforts by historians of women and gender to incorporate gender experiences into national histories.

8

National Historians and the Discourse of the Other: France and Germany

Hugo Frey and Stefan Jordan

It is widely accepted that in the modern period French and German historiography was profoundly shaped by nationalism. In both states the process was circular. Historians' arguments were marked by the nationalist mood, and then these writers contributed further by discovering patriotic meaning in the past. This chapter invites the reader to look again at the above picture and we will present an argument that is partly sceptical of the exclusivity of the nationalism–historiography synthesis. Other social narratives of identity – class, religion and race – also played a relatively significant role. Famous historians, patriots such as Jules Michelet and Leopold von Ranke, were influenced by political ideas that were transnational in character. Nationalist historiography did not completely erase pre-existing or new transnational ideas. Instead, the case-study of the French and German historians highlights how they integrated the Other concepts into their work. We conclude by underlining that only the transnational idea of gender is problematic, and perhaps uniquely hostile, to the writing of national histories.

Understanding nationhood

A sense of 'national sentiment' is evident in the French dynastic space from at least the fifteenth century.[1] However, most scholars identify the 1789 revolution as the moment when the idea of the nation was fully elaborated. The word nation may have existed in the language before then but it had little meaning in the consciousness of the people.[2] It was only through the social

---

[1] A. D. Smith, *Chosen Peoples: Sacred Sources of National Identity* (Oxford, 2003), pp. 106–14.
[2] N. Hampson, 'The Idea of Nation in Revolutionary France', in A. Forrest and P. Jones (eds), *Reshaping France: Town, Country and Region during the French Revolution* (Manchester, 1991), pp. 13–25.

turmoil of the 1780s and 1790s that the modern, republican, meaning of the nation was created. As Michel Winock explains, nationhood, *'made in France'*, was founded on the revolution and the popular democratic, legal will.[3] To be a citizen of the republic was to be French, and vice versa. In parallel to this assertion, counter-revolutionaries, including historians, imagined a second, very different, country. They rejected republicanism on the grounds that it was an *anti-French* development. In its place they envisaged an organic, ethno-cultural rather than civic definition of France.[4] Ironically, republicanism and royalist visions of nationhood shared some racist undercurrents. Republicans demanded civic loyalty from regional groups with little if any connection to the elite culture and, from the 1870s onwards, established modern colonial rule overseas. Royalist nationalism was no benign force either. Its vision of France was differentialist on cultural and racist grounds.[5] Infamously, by the 1930s prominent supporters of the royalist Action Française drifted towards fascism and later sympathised with pro-Nazi collaborationist parties.

The formation of the modern idea of Germany is very different. Repeatedly over the last 200 years, intellectuals, politicians and historians have contributed a series of definitions of the fatherland. The stability of the republican/counter-revolutionary division in France is missing from view. In its place we find changing nationalist conceptions that placed different weight on a variety of national identity markers: language, culture, the dynastic house, the *Volk* community, civic life. In the first instance, intellectual attitudes to the nation-state were determined by positive or negative interpretations of 1789. However, this ambiguity was soon replaced by an original conception. For example, in 1815 Barthold Georg Niebuhr asserted: 'The community of nationality is more than a political situation in which people of one and the same tribe are separated and combined.'[6] Thus, by the 1820s Romantic intellectuals posited that Germanness was a given of nature. This 'German-style' national identity relied on cultural-linguistic and folkloric markers. After the failed revolution of 1848, and even more so after unification in 1871, intellectuals asserted a further definition that looked to Prussia and was closely linked to Prussianism. It was also presented in close proximity to the dominant religion, Protestantism. By the

---

[3]M. Winock, 'Qu'est qu'une nation?', *L'Histoire*, 201 (1996), 8.
[4]For example, J. de Maître, *Considérations sur la France* (Basil, 1797; repr. 1814); L. de Bonald, *Oeuvres* (Paris; originally edited 1854). See also S. Mellon, *The Political Uses of History* (Stanford, CA, 1958), pp. 31–60; R. Gildea, *The Past in French History* (New Haven, CT and London, 1996), pp. 26–31, 227–9, 298–339.
[5]P. Birnbaum, *'La France aux Français': histoire des haines nationalistes* (Paris, 1993).
[6]Cited in F. Schnabel, 'Der Ursprung der vaterländischen Studien', *Blätter für deutsche Landesgeschichte*, 88 (1951), 6.

end of the century, intellectuals who celebrated the concept of *Volk* identity fash-
ioned another interpretation of being German. The idea of *Volk* gave the nation
an essential core: a cultural–biological–folkloric essence. The historian Johann
Gustav Droysen captured the concept in his writings, where he explained:

> The idea of *Volk* is a result of history, and it organises its own existence; it
> builds up the national body from human beings, which are only a unit in
> this idea. Without the idea human existence would not have an essential
> direction. The idea of *Volk* is the constant, unifying, form-giving force, but
> it is not original, it is built on historical development. It does not remain
> the same, it is moving in history.[7]

Völkisch theory was popularised by journalists and antiquarians, and these
völkisch-oriented groups created their own field, *Volksgemeinschaft*, which soon
found common ground with racist doctrine.[8] Ultimately, it was this revised
version of Germanness that became a characteristic of Nazism. After 1945 any
discussion of *völkisch* identity patterns was expelled to the neo-Nazi fringe.
However, the search for a new national self-consciousness was not free from
elements of the former ideology. For this reason one must speak of a patchy
pattern of continuity. Postwar historians, writers and intellectuals attempted
to think of Germany in complete opposition to the former Nazi ideology, yet
many had themselves been shaped by Nazi ideas and structures. The main difference in the postwar period was, however, that the new way of thinking
about West German national identity was primarily based on civic, economic,
social and cultural markers, as opposed to overtly 'political' phenomena. In
addition, when politicians and intellectuals looked towards political concepts
they favoured European federalism, and by the late 1980s there was a serious
intellectual debate on the question of post-national identity.[9]

　To sum up, for the French the national idea was the subject of a bipolar
left–right confrontation that continued almost unchanged for 200 years, and
in which the interpretation of the revolution profoundly influenced cultural and
political life. Historical arguments around the legitimacy or illegitimacy of 1789
made writers of history a core group who were consistently drawn to contribute
to definitions of France. In comparison, the German picture is composed of
successive episodes of nation-building. Repeatedly, one mode of thinking Germanness supplanted the next, and on each occasion the historical profession

[7]J. G. Droysen, *Historik*, ed. Peter Leyh (Stuttgart, 1977), p. 305.
[8]For example, A. Rosenberg, *Der Mythos des 20. Jahrhunderts: eine Wertung der seelisch-
geistigen Gestaltenkämpfe unserer Zeit* (München, 1930).
[9]For example, J. Lenoble and N. Dewandre (eds), *L'Europe au soir du siècle* (Paris, 1992).

contributed. For example, Romantic historians, ironically initially influenced by a Swiss work, Johannes von Müller's *Geschichten schweizerischer Eidgenossenschaft,* helped imagine the original pattern of Germanness.[10] Karl von Rotteck's and Heinrich Luden's studies followed that template of national historiography, and their publications proved to be significant works for the early nationalist movement.[11] Later generations of historians assisted in the various redraftings of the essence of Germanness.

In comparison, French divisions over political identity (republican vs. royalist orientation) created some long-term stability, establishing a single – stable – core debate. In Germany, no such debate is sustained over 200 years. Only recognition of Germany's need to face Nazism as a fundamental event in national history after 1945 approaches a scenario close to France's stable but divided relationship with 1789.

The fundamental variations in core conceptions of nationhood greatly influenced how historians encountered Other discourses. Historians associated with the French republican tradition interpreted the past in a distinctive mode from the counter-revolutionaries or German nationalists. Notably, these writers' treatments of the idea of class are unique. Republican civic secularism also adopted an original position on religion. Nevertheless, it is reductive to think that the republican patriotic historiography split France completely apart from wider trends. As we will discuss further below, when it came to integrating race/racism into national historiography similarities link writers in France with members of the profession in Germany.

The integration and expulsion of class from the national idea

Theoretically, class loyalty can separate an historian from the national idea. Notably within anarchist and pacifist intellectual traditions, such a disposition is a strong possibility. However, two different and distinctive attitudes towards class developed in our test nations. In France, republican historians frequently integrated the ideas of socialism, class and patriotism in their work. In Germany nationalist historians expelled notions of class from their mindset altogether. It was only in the GDR (German Democratic Republic), aligned to Marxist-Leninism, that class was associated with a patriotism.

French republicans searched for the 'real people' who had made the revolution. Writers from this current of interpretation found and glorified the

---

[10]J. von Müller, *Geschichten schweizerischer Eidgenossenschaft,* 5 vols (Leipzig, 1786–1808).
[11]H. Luden, *Allgemeine Geschichte der Völker und Staaten,* 2 vols (Jena, 1819–22); K. von Rotteck, *Allgemeine Weltgeschichte für alle Stände, von den frühesten Zeiten bis zum Jahre 1831,* 4 vols (Stuttgart, 1831–2).

peasants, small artisans and soldiers of the revolutionary armies. For example, in the 1820s and 1830s, Augustin Thierry explicitly researched the common people whom he identified as the authors of national history.[12] Other Romantic historians gave notions of class – the people, the third estate – an active role in their reconstructions. François Guizot preoccupied himself with the bourgeoisie who had made the revolution.[13] For him all history was about class struggle and the eventual triumph of the third estate. Later, Michelet located the popular classes, peasants, weavers, industrial workers, as being more or less representative of an eternal national community.[14] After 1870 the drama of the Paris Commune kept the idea of the revolutionary spirit alive.[15] Above all, more than anywhere else in Europe, left-republican historians aligned social justice, attention to class conflict and class identities with a pride in national destiny.

Early social history writing that recovered authentic workers' voices was similarly tinged with nationalism. Encouraged by middle-class intellectuals (George Sand, Victor Hugo and Michelet among them) a romanticised notion of working-class and peasant life was popularised in the 1840s. In 1839 Agricol Perdiguier published his *Livre du compagnonnage*, which was followed by *Mémoires d'un compagnon* in 1855. These semi-ethnological works, personal memoirs, illustrate how a sense of class consciousness was integrated into the patriotic republican vision of history. Michelle Perrot, whose brilliant work we are drawing on here, explains that early historical reconstruction of working-class experience was shaped by a deferential and defensive respect for the nation. She explains Perdiguier's specific discourse: 'Man of unity, worker and nationalist, he dreamt of a peaceful working class, well policed ... disciplined, moral, clean, sober in its pastimes and integrated into the Nation.'[16]

A synthesis of class discourse and nationalism recurred in communist writings. After liberation in 1944 the party identified itself as the embodiment of the national resistance movement. The central myth was that party leader Maurice

---

[12]A. Thierry, *Dix ans d'études historiques* in *Oeuvres complètes* (Paris, 1867); cited in C. Delacroix, F. Dosse and P. Garcia (eds), *Les Courants historiques en France 19e–20e siècle* (Paris, 2005), p. 15.

[13]F. Guizot, *Cours d'histoire moderne: histoire de la civilisation en Europe* (1985 [1828]), cited in Delacroix et al., *Courants*, pp. 20–1.

[14]J. Michelet, *Histoire de la Révolution française*, 7 vols (Paris, 1847–53; repr. 1980); J. Michelet, *Le Peuple* (Paris, 1846; repr. 1974); for further analysis of Michelet the starting point is P. Viallaneix, *La Voie royale* (Paris, 1959); pertinent analysis on 'people' and 'class' is contributed in J. S. McClelland, *The Crowd and the Mob* (London, 1989), pp. 121–7.

[15]Gildea, *Past*, pp. 44–8.

[16]'Homme de l'unité, ouvrière et nationale, il rêve d'une classe ouvrière pacifique, policée ... disciplinée, morale et propre, sobre en ses plaisirs et integrée dans la Nation.' Michelle Perrot, 'La Vie ouvrière', in P. Nora (ed.), *Les Lieux de mémoire*, vol. 3, *Les Frances*, 3, *De l'archive à l'emblème* (Paris, 1992), pp. 87–129.

Thorez and all of the Parti communiste français had dedicated themselves to the good of the nation throughout the war. The Hitler–Stalin pact (1939–41) was explained as an irrelevant tactical decision. Everyone else was suspected of class treachery or national disgrace. No-one escaped interrogation. Former Pétainist intellectuals were challenged, but so too were Gaullists, with even de Gaulle being criticised for serving the bourgeoisie and not all of France. Professional historians who had not followed strict Marxist-Leninist practice were targeted, and Annie Kriegel denounced the heritage of Marc Bloch and the *Annales*.[17] That Bloch and the *Annales* school were influenced by Marx was insufficient. To be communist was to be patriotic, and to be ambivalent towards Marxism was to be anti-national. That was the rhetorical grid that dominated everything.[18]

However, there were ambiguities in the party's historiography. For that group nationalism had to be woven into the dominant Marxist-Leninist dialectical theory of history that was a global concept. For example, Thorez explained fascism and communism as being representative of the long-term forces of counter-revolution and revolution.[19] For him the resistance had been part of the later tradition, and world history was moving ever closer to its next phase because of the role it had played. In this fashion Thorez's patriotic resistance myth-making was blended with a Marxist theory of world historical development. This is an intriguing rhetorical device because it underlines how communist historiography was double-edged and not purely nationalistic. Contemporary historical events were celebrated along conventional patriotic lines. But the communists then used their philosophy of history to reshape these concepts further. For Thorez the resistance movement was important not only because it was French but also because it was part of a preordained teleological vision of world class conflict. Anti-fascism was part of an international class war, not only a defence of sovereignty. Indeed, glancing through Albert Soboul's famous interpretations of the revolution of 1789, some similar ambiguities are evidenced. To paraphrase, Soboul portrayed the French social revolutionaries as an advanced guard of class struggle. He knew they were national heroes, but also indicated that they were actors in a world historical dramaturgy.[20]

---

[17]O. Dumoulin, *Marc Bloch* (Paris, 2000), p. 165; referring to A. Bessie (Kriegel), 'La grande pitié de l'histoire officielle', *La Nouvelle critique*, 26 (1951). For a further example of the mode, see J. Bruhat, 'Ecrire et faire l'histoire en combattant', *Cahiers du communisme*, 1 (1950), 96–108.
[18]See M. Thorez's (ghost-written) autobiography, *Fils du peuple* (Paris, 1949, new and rev. postwar edn). There are numerous studies of French communist historiography: see J. Verdès-Leroux, *Au service du parti* (Paris, 1983); G. Lavau, *A quoi sert le Parti communiste français* (Paris, 1981); and M-C. Lavabre, 'Histoire, mémoire, et politique: le cas du PCF', thèse de doctorat d' Etat, Institut d'études politique, Paris, 1992.
[19]Thorez, *Fils*, p. 65.
[20]A. Soboul, *Précis d'histoire de la Révolution française* (Paris, 1962).

Although at the turn of the eighteenth century there had been a German fashion for publishing workers' memoirs, the ideas of class and national identity were only rarely integrated.[21] By the 1860s, especially at the time of the Prussian-Austrian war, when nationalist feelings were increasing, concepts such as 'international class alignment', 'class struggle' or 'international class unity' were not at all important for the university elite. This rejectionist attitude to class remained dominant until the 1960s, when social history finally made its mark, partly under the influence of the *Annales* school. For long periods of German history writing the idea of class was banished to the counter-culture.[22] With no revolution, or revolutionary tradition, to analyse or debate, the elite university historians saw no significance in class as an explanatory term. The relatively significant position of the idea in French social thought and historiography (Thierry, Guizot, Michelet), and obviously in Marx and Engels's work, simply pushed nationalist intellectuals away from it altogether. For the conservative scholars class represented a foreign danger (France) and/or social revolution (Marx and Marxism).[23] Even those few bourgeois theorists such as Max Weber, who tried to make it a systematic analytical category, employed the following definition: '"Class" means all persons in the same class situation. (a) A "property class" ..., (b) A "commercial class" ..., (c) A "social class" makes up the totality of those class situations within which individual and generational mobility is easy and typical.'[24]

When considering social structures the nineteenth-century theorists and historians preferred the term *Stand* (rank), and later in the federal republic, *Schicht* (stratum), to *Klasse*. Ranke's use of *Stand* is representative of the stance taken by many others.[25] He viewed Germany as a union between legal sovereigns and the naturally ordered *Ständen*. This union of collective harmony

---

[21]See A. Kelly (ed.), *The German Worker: Working Class Autobiography from the Age of Industrialization* (Berkeley, CA and London, 1988).

[22]See T. Kössler, 'Zwischen Milieu und Markt: die populöre Geschichtsschreibung der sozialistischen Arbeiterbewegung, 1890–1933', in W. Hardtwig and E. Schütz (eds), *Geschichte für Leser: Populäre Geschichtsschreibung in Deutschland im 20. Jahrhundert* (Stuttgart, 2005), pp. 259–85.

[23]See H-O. Sieburg, *Deutschland und Frankreich in der Geschichtsschreibung des 19. Jahrhunderts (1848–1871)* (Wiesbaden, 1958), notably ch. 3.

[24]M. Weber, *Economy and Society* (Berkeley and London, 1979), p. 302. '"Klasse" soll jede in einer gleichen Klassenlage befindliche Gruppe von Menschen heißen. a) Besitzklasse ..., b) Erwerbsklasse ..., c) Soziale Klasse soll die Gesamtheit derjenigen Klassenlagen heißen, zwischen denen ein Wechsel aa) persönlich, bb) in der Generationenfolge leicht möglich ist und typisch stattzufinden pflegt.' Max Weber, *Wirtschaft und Gesellschaft* (Tübingen, 1922), p. 177.

[25]L. Ranke, 'Frankreich und Deutschland' [1832] in L. Ranke, *Geschichte und Politik* (Leipzig, 1936), p. 60.

had been established as the timeless historical-political constitution of Germany. For Ranke the different social strata were bound together by a collective sense of *Treue und Pflicht* (faith and duty) to the whole. As these terms imply, as well as the use of the terminology of social 'orders' there was a nostalgic retention of medieval notions held up against the modern, politically unstable idea of classes – perspectives quite similar to those favoured by nineteenth-century royalist historians in France who also glorified medieval social organisations as part of 'a golden age' and used patriotism to repress social tension between the classes.[26]

The expulsion of class from national historiography partly changed in the Federal Republic of Germany with the *68er-Bewegung* (student movement of 1968) which introduced the term in connection with left-wing analysis of society. Now, it was an acceptable category among historians, but they were no longer very nationalistic people. With the demise of this movement at the end of the 1970s, the number of historical publications using class theory diminished. Of course, in the GDR *Klasse* was an important basis for the indoctrination of historical materialism. There, as with French communists, it was a fundamental category for explaining all world historical processes. Efforts were made to people history with exemplary class warriors whom the citizens of the GDR could learn from and emulate. But, as Mary Fulbrook remarks: 'The political message was so blindingly obvious, the propagandistic element of most historical accounts intended for popular consumption so blatantly transparent, that it failed to achieve its intended effect. As Ernst Engelberg ruefully noted … tales of class heroes could seem just a shade dull.'[27] Nonetheless, in a more negative rhetorical style, this over-investment in German class heroes deflected public attention away from much meaningful consideration of the legacy of Nazism and the Holocaust.

So, French and German historians' attitude to nation and class was at a significant variance. The French case provides prominent examples of inter-relation and synthesis between the concepts. Republicanism, and especially left-republicanism, wove class and nation together in a coherent discourse. As Herman Lebovics has argued, 'the workers' were part of one of the two visions of a 'true France' being contested from the 1880s to the 1940s.[28] In Germany

---

[26]S. Wilson, 'A View of the Past: Action Française Historiography and its Socio-Political Function', *Historical Journal*, 19 (1976), 145, 149–50.

[27]M. Fulbrook, 'Dividing the Past, Defining the Present: Historians and National Identity in the Two Germanies', in S. Berger, M. Donovan and K. Passmore (eds), *Writing National Histories* (London, 1999), pp. 224–5; see also B. Wolf, *Sprache in der DDR* (Berlin and New York, 2000), p. 121.

[28]H. Lebovics, *True France: The Wars over Cultural Identity, 1900–1945* (Ithaca, NY, 1992), pp. 138–9.

it is striking that for much of the time national historians rejected class from their work altogether. Liberal historians such as Ranke did not see class as being significant in building a peaceful community of nations. Nor did a nationalist writer such as Heinrich von Treitschke give it any credence.[29] It took 1960s radicalism or GDR state power to position class inside national historiography.

We should also highlight here that communist historians, in France, the FRG or the GDR, attempted to integrate glorifications of the working class into nationalist poses. However, there was always an intellectual difficulty for scholars working within this school of thought. The overarching philosophical framework, the belief in international class conflict and world revolution, tempered the discourse. There were imbalances and the sources of this type read as if the historians were using nationalism for their own ulterior motives.

Religion

Religious thinking and belief mark the historical communities of the two states. This claim suggests a structural similarity. It is nevertheless important to be cautious before drawing this conclusion. In France, because of the republican tradition, no single religious belief system dominated nationalist historiography. There were of course strong links between Catholicism and royalism, but they represented only one strand of the historical divide over the meaning of 1789. Below we will hypothesise that the French picture is more fluid than the German where Protestant theological training was synonymous with the birth of German historical studies in the nineteenth century.

As Delacroix, Dosse and Garcia explain, in the late nineteenth century in Paris, in Gustave Monod's journal *Revue historique*, the idea of scientific method went hand in hand with a vision of republican and secular national progress.[30] For Monod it was the professional historian's task to piece together historical developments and identify continuity and disjuncture. The past was irreversible and the historian's duty was to piece it together. Republicanism and scientific method were in perfect harmony because both were on the side

---

[29]H. von Treitschke, *Was fordern wir von Frankreich?* [1870], in H. von Treitschke, *Aufsätze, Reden und Briefe*, vol. 3 (Meersburg, 1929), pp. 450–89.
[30]Delacroix et al., *Courants*, pp. 67–9.

of reason and progress. For the republican professionalisers of the discipline of history, men such as Monod or Seignobos, telling the story of the past according to a thorough rational method meant the national history that emerged was better, more thorough and more rigorous, as a result. The idea of 'history as science' allowed for the composition of a complete picture of the national heritage, slowly revealed by the work of the historians. The history of revolutions, the different bickering 'peoples' that made up the French story, would all finally be brought together in a single scientific narrative that would let the *patrie* know itself and be united. This was an historical narrative that rejected religion and unreason as forces that simply confused any rational understanding of national history.

The threat of republican scientific, secular historiography was not lost on Catholic historians and intellectuals. Thinkers such as R. K. Huysmans, or the historians-cum-journalists Massis and Tarde, saw the new empiricism as an unfortunate trend.[31] The new history that was fashionable in the faculty at Sorbonne, its claim to methodological rigour, the fact-gathering, the card indexes, were all idiotic developments. That approach entirely missed the point of writing a French history. Historiography for Catholic revival intellectuals (1871–1914) was not about methodological precision. For them that idea had been foolishly imported from Protestant Germany. Instead, for this group, French history was about spirit, meaning and God – a Catholic God, that is. Intelligence, talent and spirituality were the sure guides to understanding France's role and place in the grand scheme of things. Method was no substitute for that.[32]

The micro-debate between republican-scientific national historiography and Catholic spiritual historiography that punctuated the 1880s is illustrative of the wider intersection between 'nationalism–historiography–religion'. Religion surely played an important role in both republican and counter-revolutionary currents of historical interpretation. However, the legacies of the revolution shaped every perspective, creating divisions and multiple currents of interpretation. To generalise, for the republicans, often supported by Protestants, national history would take into account religious identities but map them onto a story of the long progress to the triumph of republican rationalism. The tradition was proud to celebrate aspects of the secularising past: for example, the life and work of Voltaire, the Enlightenment and the early revolutionary period. The crimes of the Church – notably the counter-Reformation, the Inquisition – were highlighted to remind readers of the dangers of clericalism. In short, republican

---

[31]H. Massis and A. de Tarde wrote together under the pseudonym 'Agathon'; see their *L'Esprit de la nouvelle Sorbonne* (Paris, 1911).
[32]R. Griffiths, *The Reactionary Revolution: The Catholic Revival in French Literature, 1870/1914* (London, 1966), p. 48.

nationalism would celebrate its own historical development, sometimes taking in the Reformation as an antecedent to the revolution. Conversely, the historical crimes of the clergy were condemned and rhetorically noted to justify the anticlerical terror. No historian probably ever put it that bluntly, but that was, shall we say, the spirit of this current of historiography. As Robert Gildea argues, there was also an effort to mend fences and take a respectful view of the Catholic faith to bring it into a more united national republican family. Instead of taking on religion *per se,* republicans 'tended to attack the Church not in general but only on exposed outworks, such as the Jesuits'.[33]

For the royalist right-wing, Catholic identity and counter-revolutionary nationalism were linked, and remain so today in some dusty corners of the Front National.[34] For this tradition of interpretation, the special nature of France was its role as the first daughter of the Church. Its national history was a spiritual and not a secular matter; 1789 was a catastrophe, a divine act of punishment and the republican era a passing phase of expiation for former sins. As Gildea explains: for the Catholic right-wing patriot, all national disasters could be modelled on this narrative pattern: 1870, 1940, 1954 (Dien Bien Phu) or 1962 (the loss of Algeria).[35] The suffering of the nation was a long history of punishment, but this was divine will. In this school of thought the modern world, the Reformation and the revolution were seen as either fundamental errors or divine retribution.

Over the years, variations within republicanism and Catholic royalism have produced an array of more complex theologically informed intersections with nationalist historiography. In the early period of Romantic historiography, writers were marked with a sense of spiritualism. Sometimes this was a confused search for a special unity around the idea of a national secular community (Jules Michelet's contribution in some of his writings), and on other occasions more elaborate para-theological ideas were asserted – one thinks of the famous case of Saint-Simon.[36] In the later period, after 1918, social-Catholicism, the strand of theological doctrine *personnalisme,* splintered from the Catholic counter-revolutionary tradition to search out social-spiritual alliances between priests and workers. Since at least the 1980s, that group's house journal, *Esprit,* has published historiographic articles and contributed to collective national debates on history and collective memory. It is, however, not a repository for national-religious rhetoric. Today, the journal is a publication where leading historians feed their research into wider intellectual debate in which the majority of historiography is written in the secular, neo-scientific mode.

[33]Gildea, *Past,* p. 215.
[34]See, for example, the integrist newspaper *Présent.*
[35]Gildea, *Past,* pp. 225–30.
[36]C. Crossley, *French Historians and Romanticism* (London, 1993), pp. 105–33.

The German experience was quite different. The first generation of modern German historians was in large part composed of children of Protestant priests who had started their careers by following in their fathers' footsteps to read theology. These historians (e.g. Ranke, Droysen) saw themselves as men empowered to document God's deeds by their historiographical praxis. The early historical profession therefore was defined as the *Priester der Klio* ('Clio's priests'). As such it was the historian's task to identify 'leading ideas' in history that were quite directly linked to God's thoughts and God's historical plan for humankind. In turn, the historian could reflect on the elected *Große Persönlichkeiten* ('great people') who had acted as 'God's agents' in world history. Historians were the narrators of the destiny of the world and their task was to tell that story with due reverence and methodological accuracy.[37]

The ingrained Protestant theological outlook was closely tied to nationalist aspirations. After 1848 the so-called *Preußisch-kleindeutsche Schule* (Prussian Small-German school), including Theodor Mommsen, Droysen and Heinrich von Sybel, identified Protestant Prussia as the *Machtstaat* of a future unified Germany. Historical writing, Protestant self-confidence and Prussian power went hand in hand. Moreover, the Prussian Protestant historians built on an intellectual heritage. Thus, it is difficult to consider German historiography's role in imagining the nation without accounting for the underlying influence of Protestantism. Theoretically this transnational religious belief might have, could have, opened the way to a liberal national identity, admiring of England like François Guizot's Romantic liberal position during the July Monarchy (1830–48). But, as we know, Prussian Protestantism did not take this path. Instead, it was bound closely to faith in the monarchy and to the continuation of a bourgeois intellectual culture.

By the 1880s this school of interpretation was gradually being marginalised. In particular the early twentieth-century German cultural fashion for 'technology' (technics) left many of the more old-fashioned Protestant historians at a loss. Furthermore, by the 1930s the centre of power had changed completely: the race–*Volk* national identity combination was the dominant force and the Protestant historical tradition went along with the mood, or temporarily became silent. It is, however, a testimony to the sway Protestantism once held that its impact partly recurred in the 1950s. Gerhard Ritter's continued influence is one of the famous postwar examples. His attempt to explain Hitler as an aberration is illustrative. Thus, in his *Europa und die deutsche Frage* (1948) he reuses the national-Protestant synthesis as a form of post-Nazi self-defence. His argument ran: Allied propaganda had oversimplified contemporary history and was demonising the German past. Luther and Bismarck

---

[37]Droysen, *Historik*, p. 30.

were not to be seen as phantoms of the Hitlerism to come. Pierre Ayçoberry summarises: Ritter was the 'fosterer of Germany with a virgin past which merely succumbed to an accidental temptation'.[38] In the 1960s the historicist focus on religious aspects of historical development became unpopular. Certainly, after the establishment of social history as the leading theoretical paradigm in historical studies, and the installing of *Gesellschaft* (society) as a new leading mode of thinking about the past, far less attention was paid to religion. A materialistic concept of history, which was focusing on economic and social processes, inspired by Weber and the *Annales* school, displaced the role once played by religion. The typically German *Ideenlehre* was replaced by the materialist notion of 'society'. The university faculties, which had been staffed nearly exclusively by Protestants, now began to include Catholic or non-religious historians. For left-of-centre professional historians 'religion and nation' were dead as a synthetic master narrative, a point of view that is not so clearly true for right-wing self-publicists. The contrast between left and right historiography that emerged is most strikingly illustrated by comparing the two major projects of German history undertaken by Hans-Ulrich Wehler and Thomas Nipperdey. Wehler's *Deutsche Gesellschaftsgeschichte* (at least in the first three volumes) overlooked religion, church and belief. Conversely, the conservative Nipperdey gave it significant space.[39]

More recently the left's new-found interest in culture and ideas has reintroduced religion and nation as subjects for research.[40] In the late 1990s both terms were used by left-wing historians more intensively than in the previous 20 years. However, more often than not, the approach is to deconstruct these notions or to explore their discursive form, instead of reproducing the original discourse.

To draw together the comparison: Germany witnessed a long history of Protestant-nationalist writings and few if any examples of a Catholic-nationalist synthesis. Although there were ultramontane writers, their work did not play an identifiable role and the tradition produced no single important 'national'

[38]G. Ritter, *Europa und die Deutsche Frage* (Munich, 1948); see P. Ayçoberry, *The Nazi Question: An Essay on the Interpretations of National Socialism* (London, 1981), p. 119.
[39]See P. Nolte, 'Darstellungsweisen deutscher Geschichte: Erzählstrukturen und 'Master Narratives' bei Nipperdey und Wehler', in C. Conrad and S. Conrad (eds), *Die Nation schreiben* (Göttingen, 2002), pp. 236–70; G. Besier, *Religion, Nation, Kultur* (Neukirchen-Vluyn, 1992), pp. 182–6.
[40]See G. Hübinger, 'Kulturgeschichte', in S. Jordan (ed.), *Lexikon Geschichtswissenschaft: Hundert Grundbegriffe* (Stuttgart, 2002), pp. 198–202; S. Jordan, 'Literaturbericht: Theorie und Geschichte der Geschichtswissenschaft', in *Geschichte in Wissenschaft und Unterricht*, 56 (2005), pp. 426–38.

text.[41] The position is very different in Paris, where multiple strands of inter-pretation did develop. Specifically, the divisions between secular and Catholic historians produced two different national narratives in which the idea of God played different roles. Catholic patriotic historiography elevated France as the first daughter of the Church, and revelled in ideas of the sins of the modern world and the glories of the medieval period. Needless to say, the republicans saw things differently. They identified religion with dynastic tyranny and out-dated conservatism. Nevertheless, when the *patrie* was threatened in 1914, his-torians from either side of the religious divide supported the *Union sacré* against Germany. French republican sympathy for Protestantism never extended to a transnational affinity for German Protestantism, or vice versa.

Finally, late nineteenth-century French Catholic patriotic historiography and the German Protestant school of thought shared simple structural features. Both groups of historians asserted that their nation had a unique role to play in God's grand design. Both groups understood it to be the role of intellectuals, including historians, to decipher those processes. Nationhood, religious belief and the his-torian's task were conflated. However, German Protestantism valorised empirical historical method, at least on paper, if never fully in practice. In sharp contra-diction, the French Catholic current of thought denounced that approach as an offshoot of Enlightenment thinking, religious failing and foreign contamination.

Origins, tribes and bloodlines: race in national historiography

Historians from both states meshed patriotic ideology and transnational racist doctrine together in their *oeuvres*. However, this was an ambiguous business and subject to inconsistency. History writing was a different mode of expres-sion from 'scientific' race theorising, and so historians were always more likely implicitly or unwittingly to use terms such as race in their work without giving much of an explanation or extended theorisation to their meaning. Nonetheless, the concept did feature in and affect a great deal of national historiography – so much so that for long periods in the nineteenth century, and up to the 1960s, there is a repeated alignment between historical discourses of national pride with an implied ethno-racist superiority. Historians from both states were shaped by the idea of race, but in bringing it into their national narratives they blurred it with that overriding concept.

In France early royalist historiography had a tendency to slide into race theory. At the turn of the eighteenth century the royalist exile Montlosier

[41]See S. Weichlein, 'Meine Peitsche ist die Feder: populäre katholische Geschichts-schreibung im 19. und 20. Jahrhundert', in Hardtwig and Schütz, *Geschichte für Leser*, pp. 227–57.

attacked the revolutionaries through a more or less explicit use of the term 'race'. Condemning the republicans, he asserted that they had 'risen from slaves (a mixture) of all races and all time'.[42] For Montlosier ethno-racist purity belonged to the nobility, whereas race and degeneration were aligned to the 'people' who had brought down the *ancien régime*. Furthermore, international agreements could be made on the basis of this interpretation. For royalists, such as Montlosier, the ancient tribal Franks were the source-point of his social caste, the nobility, and so association with Germanic aristocracy was an alliance that could be founded on authentic 'blood ties' and used against inauthentic republicanism. Moreover, since from Montlosier's perspective France had degenerated into republican anarchy, it was obvious that his Germanic tribe was superior. Hannah Arendt commented: 'Paradoxical as it sounds, the fact is that Frenchmen earlier than Germans or Englishmen were to insist on this *idée fixe* of Germanic superiority.'[43] Thus, a tradition of royalist historiography that scanned the tribal communities of ancient Europe for racial groupings, that explained 1789 and that pointed to possible aristocratic alliances with the Germanic nobility on race-heritage grounds, was born. This was one strong implication of the conte de Gobineau's own infamous writings which led him to abandon any sympathy for contemporary France because it had degenerated too far to be redeemed.[44] Other counter-revolutionaries retained a measure of sympathy for France but they locked this allegiance into a race mythology of the destiny of the Franks and the Gauls. Or later, writers such as the royalist leader Charles Maurras looked to Roman-Latin strengths against the barbarism of the Germanic Franks.[45]

Royalist historiography introduced and perpetuated other prejudicial attitudes that were racially coded. Abbé Barruel's five-volume *Mémoire pour servir à l'histoire du jacobinisme* (1797) contains the first modern conspiracy theory of history.[46] Barruel blames the revolution on a secret Masonic conspiracy. He does not make mention of any 'Jewish conspiracy', but within a decade that claim was articulated and slowly made popular alongside the anti-Masonic

---

[42]Count de Montlosier, cited in H. Arendt, 'Race Thinking before Racism', *Review of Politics*, 6 (1944), 46.

[43]Arendt, 'Race Thinking', p. 46.

[44]Count de Gobineau, *Essai sur l'inégalité des races humaines*, 2 vols [1853–5], 2nd edn (Mesnil, 1884). See also M. Biddiss, *Father of Racist Ideology: The Social and Political Thought of Count Gobineau* (London, 1970).

[45]See C. Maurras, *Devant l'Allemagne éternelle* (Paris, 1937). Action Française historiography was attacked by republicans for its ethno-racist definition of national identity: see, e.g., J. Reboul, *M. Bainville contre l'histoire de France* (Paris, 1925).

[46]A. Augustin Barruel, *Mémoires pour servir à l'histoire du jacobinisme*, 4 vols (Paris, 1973; [London: 1797–84]); see N. Cohn, *Warrant for Genocide* (London, 1996 [1967]), pp. 30–6.

theses. Furthermore, the later nineteenth- and twentieth-century royalist historians would repeat that inference. As Stephen Wilson argues, Charles Maurras, Léon Daudet, Pierre Gaxotte and others articulated anti-Jewish conspiracy rhetoric in their writings. After the Dreyfus affair, royalist historiography classed the French Jewish community as being central to their mythology of an 'anti-France' also made up of republicans, Protestants, Freemasons and other 'foreigners'.[47] It is also worth underlining that patriotic republican writers such as Michelet were not immune to displays of anti-Semitism. For example, in much of *Le Peuple* Michelet contrasts the glories of the peasantry with the menace of international Jewish usury. There was even something of a fashion for this interpretation between the 1850s and 1870. In fact, the perspective never fully faded, with it recurring in snippets of 1950s communist historiography.[48]

In addition, some Romantic republican historians who were sympathetic to 1789 narrated the past to explain the social schism of revolution, with reference to race and ancestral tribal groups. Augustin Thierry's *Histoire de la conquête de l'Angleterre par les Normands* (1825) is one example of the latent and implicit use of race in this type of historiography.[49] Thierry implies that all European history is driven by conflict and that tribal victors of each conquest slowly but surely eliminate the culture of their predecessors. His treatment of the Norman Conquest suggests that, following the victory of 1066, Norman aristocratic culture supplanted Anglo-Saxon practices. The two warring parties – Norman and Anglo-Saxon, as well as the Celts of the western British Isles – are described as races. History is viewed as a narrative of confrontation, victory and defeat between these groupings. In addition, Thierry argues once-victorious races are susceptible to degeneration through miscegenation with defeated parties. Lessons and implications were extrapolated for contemporary France. Thierry inferred that, just like the mixing of the Anglo-Saxons and the Normans, the French had witnessed generation after generation of racial victory, inter-mixing and then further conflict. Close to the royalist position of Montlosier, Thierry saw the revolution as another battle fought between 'degenerating victors' and 'rising but once defeated race groups'. Quite distinct from Montlosier's thesis, Thierry celebrated 1789–93 because he understood it as a final moment of unity after centuries of division. The revolution was a positive

---

[47]Wilson, 'A View of the Past', pp. 146, 158–9.

[48]Michelet, *Le Peuple*, p. 141, is a violent expulsion of Jewishness from French national identity; see also some 100 years later, R. Garaudy, 'Silhouettes: Léon Blum, Paul Reynaud', *Cahiers du communisme*, 9 (1948), 9. See also Gildea, *Past*, pp. 305–6; Léon Poliakov, *Histoire de l'antisémitisme*, vol. 2 (Seuil, 1981), 286–7. Poliakov notes that until the late nineteenth century anti-Semitism was mainly located on the anti-clerical left of French politics.

[49]A. Thierry, *Histoire de la conquête de l'Angleterre par les Normands*, 3 vols (Paris, 1825).

national episode because it had brought unity after centuries of racial antagonism. However, as Martin Seliger underlines, the central axis of Thierry's historical theory was 'the political inequality created by conquest', an interpretation of
Thierry that is supported by Ceri Crossley, who comments: 'he did not advance a
theory of biological determinism in a consistent or rigorous manner'. Similarly,
Gossman suggests ambiguity rather than a fully developed race theory of
national historical development.[50]

The case of Augustin's brother, Amédée Thierry, is less ambiguous. His
Histoire des Gaulois depuis les temps refoulés (1844–5) focuses on racial identity
as a central feature in defining Frenchness.[51] It fully recognised pure race types
and suggested that Gallic peoples were unique and unaffected by the Frankish
invasion. The Gauls were the ethnic-racial core of the French people who
would seal the revolution against the aristocratic-foreign race of Franks. Indeed,
Amédée's retrospective association between Gaulish tribes and the republican
tradition announced a regular discursive mode that read the revolution as a
positive unifying experience of the previously divided ancient peoples of
France. For example, the novelist François-René de Chateaubriand claimed to
witness a blending process at work as a consequence of the revolution. Now,
after 1789, France could be formed of two mighty peoples (Gauls and Franks)
with complementary and intertwining cultures. Later, under the more nationalist Napoleonic Second Empire (1851–70), glorifications of the Roman and
Gallic origins of the French were juxtaposed with more negative readings of
Nordic or Germanic elements.[52]

For our purposes, the specific details of the 'Frank and Gaul' debate and the
variations of interpretation on race group origins are not directly relevant.
What is important is that some Romantic, republican, historians looked to
tribal-racial origins of nationhood. They narrated the past around processes of
'struggle' and 'degeneration', and interpreted 1789 as a unifying triumph that
brought closure. There was a great deal of imprecision and confusion in the

---

[50]Crossley, *French Historians*, p. 56; L. Gossman, *Between History and Literature* (Cambridge,
MA, 1990), pp. 100–1; M. Seliger, 'Race Thinking during the Restoration', *Journal of the
History of Ideas*, 19 (1958), pp. 273–82.
[51]A. Thierry, *Histoire des Gaulois depuis les temps les plus reculés jusqu'à l'entière soumission
de la Gaule à la domination romaine*, 3 vols (Paris, 1828). See C. Lacoste, 'Les Gaulois
d'Amédée Thierry', in P. Viallaneix and J. Éhard (eds), *Nos ancêtres les Gaulois* (Clermont
Ferrand, 1982), pp. 203–9.
[52]J. Barzun, *The French Race: Theories of its Origins and their Social and Political Implications
prior to the Revolution* (New York, 1932), pp. 256–62, where Edgar Quinet is cited as a key
figure in the reassertion of pro-Gaul interpretations under the Second Empire, a line later
restated in Action Française historiography, via the influence of Fustel de Coulanges.
Although Barzun's work is dated it still provides a clear summary of the various schools of
thought.

use of terms. Throughout the century the term race was used by well-known historians, if often only casually and without any full explanation of meaning or philosophical status. As Edward Gargan cautioned when reading Taine's use of race as a category of analysis in his *Histoire de la littérature anglaise* (1905): 'He undeniably thought heredity transmitted national traits and modes of historical behavior. But Taine also used the expression race in much the same way as historians who cannot be charged with Hitlerism. Winston Churchill, for example.'[53]

Since at least the 1950s, very few major scholarly works have bothered to explain any causal link between the contemporary period and the Gauls, Franks, Romans or Celts. All that remains of that tradition is neo-pagan theorisation that is associated with the Nouvelle Droite, an extreme right-wing intellectual group that claims to be concerned with promoting a 'European heritage', instead of adopting an overtly nationalist position. The anti-Semitic tradition (left-wing and right-wing variants) has however continued. In 1940 Vichy opened the floodgates to popular anti-Semitic and other conspiratorial historiography. Under the directorship of Bernhard Faÿ, the French National Library was briefly organised to search out anti-French conspiracies. Postwar, for several years, French historians never fully acknowledged or questioned the anti-Semitic heritage or Vichy's involvement in the Holocaust. Robert Aron's popular history of the regime, which in 1954 sold over 10,000 copies in its first edition, revealed some aspects of the anti-Semitic culture but was also careful to relativise Vichy's role so as to end internal political divisions. Similarly, René Rémond's famous work *La Droite en France* (1954) identifies 'fascism' as a foreign tradition, an ideological import from Italy and Germany. Novelists such as the anti-Semite Louis-Ferdinand Céline re-emerged as cult figures who attracted literary historians wishing to glamorise the aesthetic power of his modernism. However, the extreme case here is that of the ultra-right-wing writer and university professor of literature, Maurice Bardèche. His pamphlet *Nuremberg ou la terre promise* (1947) instigated Holocaust denial writing by arguing that good Frenchmen were being prosecuted by the Allies and de Gaulle, because there was a wider demonisation of Nazi war crimes.[54]

Let us recall, repeating Hannah Arendt, that it was French aristocrats who invented Germany as a racial construct, long before the German intellectual

---

[53]E. Gargan, 'Editor's Introduction', in H. A. Taine, *The Origins of Contemporary France* (Chicago, 1974), p. xxviii.

[54]R. Aron, with G. Elegy, *Histoire de Vichy* (Paris, 1954); René Remond, *La Droite en France, de 1815 à nos jours* (Paris, 1954); M. Bardèche, *Nuremberg ou la terre promise* (Paris, 1947). For Bardèche, see I. Barnes, 'Fascism and Technocratic Elitism: The Case of Maurice Bardèche', *Wiener Library Bulletin*, NS, 34/53–4 (1981), 36–40.

world came to that conclusion. Certainly, nineteenth-century German historical and intellectual circles were comparatively late to come to think about the idea of race. There were, however, some relatively minor discourses on 'wilderness' peoples, pre-civilised groups from the New World, but, to follow Susanne Zantop's research, these were more 'fantasies' or 'fairy tales' than elaborate modern race theories.[55] One can therefore place the beginning of a scientific discourse on race when the German term *Rasse* became part of the language as a loanword from the French in the middle of the eighteenth century.[56] Even so, as Arendt implied, the concept was not elaborated into its common modern meaning until some time later. Thus Herder, who not only in Germany had the most important influence on the development of a typology of peoples, rejected the term because he felt that it referred to a non-existent 'difference of evolution' in mankind.[57] Hegel, who had a stronger impact on the progress of historical thought in Germany than Herder, also rejected its use.[58] In his eyes a rationality inherent in each human being spoke against the use of race as a systematic category of social or historical analysis. In fact, race was not used as a common category in German thought (including historiography) until the end of the nineteenth century, and then its popularity followed international intellectual fashion rather than being part of a distinctive internal development. Before unification in 1871 the use of race to bolster national identity was unheard of because it was not a useful category to unite the German states. Instead, the concept of culture was the source that was consistently cited to help define nascent Germanness. Culture and precisely not race was viewed as the essential link that would bind together the separate German states into a nation. This choice was because any argumentation on race grounds was functionally unhelpful: for if Germany was conceived as a racial Germany, logic would suggest that it should extend to

[55]S. Zantop, *Colonial Fantasies: Conquest, Family, and Nation in Precolonial Germany, 1770–1870* (Durham, NC and London, 1997).

[56]For a historical overview of the concept, see S. Lorenz and W. Buselmaier, 'Rasse', in J. Ritter and K. Gründer (eds), *Historisches Wörterbuch der Philosophie*, vol. 8 (Basel, 1992), pp. 25–30; M. Weingarten, 'Rasse', in H. J. Sandkühler (ed.), *Europäische Enzyklopädie zu Philosophie und Wissenschaften*, vol. 4 (Hamburg, 1990), pp. 14–16.

[57]'Endlich wünschte ich auch die Unterscheidung, die man aus rühmlichem Eifer für die überschauende Wissenschaft dem Menschengeschlecht zwischengeschoben hat, nicht über die Grenzen erweitert. So haben Einige ... Abtheilungen desselben ... Racen zu nennen gewaget; ich sehe keine Ursache dieser Benennung. Race leitet auf eine Verschiedenheit der Abstammung, die hier ... gar nicht statt findet.' J. G. Herder, *Ideen zur Philosophie der Geschichte der Menschheit*, II, 7, 1 [1784], in his *Werke*, ed. H. Düntzer, vol. 10 (Berlin, [1864]), p. 42.

[58]G. W. F. Hegel, *Enzyklopädie der philosophischen Wissenschaften im Grundrisse* [1830], in *Werke*, vol. 10 (Frankfurt/M, 1986), pp. 393, 57f.

include *Angehörige germanischer Rassen* ('members of Germanic races'), the Austrians, the Swiss and possibly also peoples from the Low Countries. Thus, race was rejected and the ideas of *Kulturnation* and *Staatsnation* were seen as the more congruent markers through which to define the German nation. Moreover, the dominance of idealism over positivism in mid-nineteenth-century German intellectual life worked against any strong racial thinking blending with nationalism. The main category which the idealistic tradition referred to, and which was especially proclaimed by historical studies as the *Leitwissenschaft*, was the term *Volk*. In the pre-unification period (1850–70) that term pointed to cultural similarities and was not charged with a racist content. The viewpoint of Leopold Ranke is again a good example. Although he accepted a difference between Romanic and Germanic peoples, this was based on cultural specificities, typically language. It was linguistic unity that Ranke saw as a clear sign of a national unit and its potential collective unity.[59]

The idea of race did become fashionable in the late nineteenth century, and this development was especially based on the popularity of the work of Richard Wagner's son-in-law, the Englishman Houston Stewart Chamberlain.[60] In the light of his work and other popularising texts, *Volk*, which had once been seen through cultural and linguistic markers, became aligned to a racial codification. Now, German race thinking was increasingly integrated into intellectual life and society. Just as French national historians saw Germans as a barbaric race, German counterparts identified the French as a degenerate racial national enemy. Typically, Max Nordau punned on the very term *fin de siècle* by suggesting it should be replaced with *fin de race*,[61] a view that the anti-French Frenchman de Gobineau shared. Conspiracy theory anti-Semitism was likewise quite late to arrive in German popular culture and publishing. Whereas Abbé Barruel had sparked that discourse in France in the 1820s, it was not until the 1860s that the first German-language conspiracy text was published in the *Historisch-politische Blätter für das Katholische Deutschland*.[62] However, by the later part of the century the populist Treitschke was notorious for the anti-Semitic tone of some of his lectures. As Michael Burleigh has highlighted, populist historiography of the medieval period, published under Weimar, repeated racist assumptions

---

[59]See L. Ranke, *Geschichten der romanischen und germanischen Völker 1494 bis 1514* (Leipzig, 1824); Ranke, *Über die Epochen der neueren Geschichte*, ed. T. Schieder (München & Wien, 1971); Ranke, 'Zum Kriege 1870/71', in Ranke, *Geschichte und Politik*, p. 421.
[60]H. S. Chamberlain, *Die Grundlagen des Neunzehnten Jahrhunderts* [1899], 2 vols (Munich, 1938).
[61]M. Nordau, *Entartung* (Berlin, 1892), p. 5.
[62]Cohn, *Warrant*, p. 37.

about Jews, Slavs and Germans, an interpretation that is confirmed in Saul Friedländer's incisive assessment of German university elites and their response to Nazism. Quite obviously, then, the late arrival of race thinking and anti-Semitic conspiracy-mongering in Germany did not limit the long-term dissemination of the sentiment.[63]

The racism of official ideology in Nazi Germany is unique, even among other European nations' forms of colonial elitism and prejudice. Specific to that ideology was anti-Jewish racism and its close alignment to anti-democratic and anti-capitalist doctrine. For Nazi and proto-Nazi ideology *Das Judentum* (the Jewry) was identified with an imagined bourgeoisie building a global conspiracy, whose aim was to destroy the union and the values of the national community. Many German historians who later became prominent figures – one might think of Theodor Schieder's expertise on *Ostraumforschung* as an example – accepted or supported Nazi racism. Furthermore *Rasse* was even used by Nazi critics such as the historian Otto Vossler, who partly used it as a verbal concession to the Nazi system, and partly just as a popular, 'modern' term.[64] For a time the German profession was bound to a system of nationalist, racist, anti-Semitic persecution. Professors and their researchers sought to maximise gain from working in the Nazi system. The profession engaged with Nazism in ways that ranged from awkward silence when German Jewish students and scholars were expelled from the university to enthusiastic scholarly propagandising. Nazism carved out huge swathes of racially informed research topics: village names, ethnic groupings in Eastern Europe, 'Indo-Germanic studies', the 'Jewish question', and so on. There was no lack of historians working in these fields from 1933 onwards. After 1938, professors in history at the University of Vienna were additional enthusiastic fellow-travellers.[65]

After the war, silence reigned regarding the role of the profession in the previous twenty years. Historians failed to face their complicity with Nazism to any great extent. Compromises, great and small, were obligingly forgotten, and indi-

---

[63]M. Burleigh, 'The Knights, Nationalists and the Historians: Images of Medieval Prussia from the Enlightenment to 1945', *European History Quarterly*, 17 (1987), 35–55; S. Friedländer, *Nazi Germany and the Jews*, vol. 1, *The Years of Persecution, 1933–39* (London, 1998), pp. 49–55.

[64]See O. Vossler, *Der Nationalgedanke von Rousseau bis Ranke* (Munich and Berlin, 1937), p. 20.

[65]In addition to prior references, discussion of historians under National Socialism is found in W. Schulze and O. Gerhard Oexle (eds), *Deutsche Historiker im Nationalsozialismus* (Frankfurt/M, 1999); K. Schönwälder, 'The Fascination of Power: Historical Scholarship in Nazi Germany', *History Workshop Journal*, 43 (1997), pp. 133–55; H. Schleier, 'German Historiography under National Socialism', in Berger et al., *Writing National Histories*, pp. 176–89.

vidual scholars with ethically tainted careers returned to their university departments. A further consequence of this silence was that the idea of race was expelled from the German intellectual mind. Beneath that official stance, ideas once located in Nazi era *Volk* historical studies were reborn as local and social history, although, as Karen Schönwälader underlines, 'secret continuities' of Nazi *Volksgeschichte* in 1960s historiography should not be over-interpreted.[66] The dominant mode was to make a violent break with the past, a position encouraged by patterns of generational change.

Let us now draw back our focus to make comparative judgements. French national historians used race in their work earlier than their German counterparts. It became common for some royalist and Romantic writers to frame explanations of the revolution around a sense of competing tribal–racial groups (with either side favouring the preferred Gauls or the Franks). The narrative form of history writing meant that this material was far more subtle than in the fields of science – hard (biology) or soft (geography, archaeology, political science). Likewise, individual historians were often vague and contradictory. German historians' contributions to nation-building before 1871 were less influenced by ideas of race. *Volk*, in the pre-1871 period, was conceived as a cultural or linguistic concept. Likewise, the intellectual fashion for idealism meant that positivist racism was always likely to be less influential. This is not the time or place to offer a definitive account of the German historians' actions under the Third Reich. We will, however, simply note that it is increasingly evident that compromise was the norm and that support for the ideology of the regime was relatively commonplace.

After the war the Nazi experience meant that concepts of race were excluded from German scholarly history writing, only to be found implicitly in a more general way as everywhere else in Europe in the 1950s and 1960s. De Gaulle's liberation of France – or rather the perception that this had been the case – and his resistance myth-making prompted retaliation from nationalist Pétainist historians. Thus, as a consequence, a postwar anti-Semitism gained confidence sooner in France than in West Germany. As has been recently revealed through a public inquiry, even in the 1970s and 1980s one major university (Lyons III) employed scholars who advocated racist views and some of whose 'historiography' popularised anti-Semitic interpretations. There were no comparable controversies within the German university system.[67] However, Ernst Nolte's comments on the 'rational' nature of German anti-Semitism are uncomfortably knowing and polemical. We assume that these statements extend his earlier

---

[66]Schönwälder, 'Fascination', pp. 144–6.
[67]H. Rousso, *Le Dossier Lyon III* (Paris, 2005).

controversial theses that the Holocaust was a second 'Asiatic' crime which mimetically replicated Stalin's purges.[68]

Gender: towards a corrosion of national historiography

Gender stereotyping and the social construction of national identity through historiographical narratives was commonplace in nineteenth-century France and Germany. For example, in Germany the idea of the 'Mothers of the Nation' (*Mutter der Nation*) played an important role in some understandings of German-ness. Likewise, it was traditional to personify the nation as female – 'Germania', and so forth. In France much symbolic investment was always placed on the key female warrior figure, Jeanne d'Arc. Numerous other stereotypes and historical fantasies blended gender and national identities together in public and academic discourse. Often women were simply absent from the historical record alto-gether, invisible to the male historian's eyes. On other occasions it was through clichés that women were included in 'the past', although dominant political con-siderations did prove influential, as when French royalist historians defended the reputation of Marie Antoinette against republican insults.

In both countries the historiographical profession was a male-dominated elite. Before the 1970s there were few women writing history, let alone patriotic his-tory, and these cases were relatively marginal and marginalised, like the fascinat-ing story of Lucie Varga's 'lost' contribution to the *Annales* school.[69] Even when women had had a greater role to play, as in the German left wing during the Weimar Republic, they often did not write as 'women' or with a conscious elab-oration of gender in mind. Thus, communist women historiographers such as Rosa Luxemburg or Clara Zetkin did not develop a special female perspective on history. Bound to the ideology of Marxism, women's rights were a goal one had to fight for; but the struggle for those rights was seen as a part of the liberation of the whole working class. It was only in the 1960s and 1970s that both French and German professions adopted a radically different relationship to questions of gender. Now, rather than historians reproducing traditional stereotypes or operating within pre-existing male ideologies, they began to see it as their task to break down these models and fill the lacunae of male

---

[68]For recent examples of Ernst Nolte's provocations see his published letters with F. Furet, *Feindliche Nähe* (Munich, 1998), and *Der kausale Nexus: Revision und Revisionismus in der Geschichtswissenschaft* (Munich, 2002).

[69]P. Schöttler, 'Lucie Varga ou la face cachée des *Annales*', in *Femmes de culture et de pouvoir* (Bruxelles: 2000), pp. 227–45.

historiography. Next, we will analyse how, if at all, this new gender history writing has shaped the respective narratives of nationalism. We argue that the deconstructive tone of much gender historiography has in part undermined conventional essentialist understandings of nationhood. However, as we explain, there are a few counter-examples that seem so exceptional that they might well prove the rule.

The first major works of French historiography to discuss gender overtly via a women's history approach were published in the early 1970s. These pioneering pieces emerged from social history (the tradition in which Michelle Perrot was working) and sociology (for example, the publications of Yves Sullerot). Perhaps the core early text to legitimate the field as an area of historiographical interest was Pierre Grimal's *L'Histoire mondiale de la femme* (1965–7). In addition, the new women's history was influenced by two figures positioned on the fringe of the dominant *Annales* group: the royalist, journalist and 'amateur historian' Philippe Ariès and the radical philosopher Michel Foucault. Michelle Perrot, a leading proponent of women's historiography in France, recalls the importance of both men's work. She suggests that Ariès's *L'Enfant et la vie familiale sous l'ancien régime* dragged mainstream 1970s *nouvelle histoire* closer to the world of women's experiences. Equally, Foucault's work, his theorisations of power, oppression and sexuality, was a driving force. His vision legitimated the study of outsiders, placed in question the nature of scientific knowledge and continued the radical mood of May '68.[70] Women's history writing continued the spirit of those heady days, or as Perrot remembers: 'les bourgeoisie je les ai franchement détestés'.[71]

As Françoise Thébaud has explained, the first wave of women's history was mainly reconstructive and intended to bring women's lives into the historical frame. The school of interpretation was closely linked to social history's project to recover the lost voices of workers' lives. By the mid-1980s it had changed, becoming influenced by scholars working in the US (notably Joan Scott) and the interest in gender studies. However, gender did not become as common a term for French historians as it did elsewhere (notably the US, UK and Germany). In particular, 'gender' did not translate well into the rather unfamiliar 'genre'. Likewise, as Fabrice Virgili highlights when reviewing the field, it was always the case that 'women's history' made in France referred to interactions between women and men. The new women historians, writing on women, had -

---

[70]The best summary of women's history writing in France is offered in F. Thébaud, *Ecrire l'histoire des femmes* (Fontenay-aux-Roses, 1998); for an autobiographical discussion from a lead protagonist, see M. Perrot, 'L'Air du temps', in P. Nora (ed.), *Essais d'ego-histoire* (Paris, 1987), pp. 270–300.
[71]Perrot, 'L'Air', p. 290; besides teaching the first women's history courses at the Sorbonne, her contributions include the team-edited *Travaux de femmes dans la France du XIXe siècle* (Paris, 1978).

consistently wished also to explore relations between the genders, even if not explicitly theorising their work in that way. Virgili's example is Michelle Perrot and Georges Duby's multi-volume edited work, *L'Histoire de femme en Occident*. Its terms of reference were not tied to 'women alone' but aimed to account for 'humanité sexué' (humanity understood as two sexes). Indeed, according to Virgili, there was always a rational movement in French scholarship to develop the writing of women's experiences to questions of gender. Analyses of the oppression of women, exemplified in texts from the 1970s and 1980s, inevitably led to treatment of oppressive power, men and the ideology of masculinity.[72]

Did the new historiography contribute to supporting the national idea? In part, yes. As the debate on the use and translation of gender/genre indicates it was being written from a specific national educational, social, political and linguistic framework. Karen Offen sheds further light. She argues that even one of the best examples of French gender/women's history by Françoise Thébaud displays a tendency to look inwards to French language scholarship rather than to international debate and use excellent work published in Canada and the United States.[73] A more overt example of a national–gender history intersection is Mona Ozouf's *Les Mots des femmes: essai sur la singularité française*. Published in 1995, it asserts a very nationalist-sounding argument. To simplify, Ozouf explains that French women's lives have been far better because of the nature of French historical experience. In particular, the nature of gender roles in the *ancien régime* court worked to empower women in their relations with men. Furthermore, US political correctness and the idea of gender are divisive concepts that do little to enhance the experience of women or men. According to Ozouf, the French intellectuals Cixous or Irgaray might raise similar questions to those popular in the US, but they have the wisdom to position their work as sophisticated intellectual rhetoric and to avoid policy formation. For Ozouf, French women are historically more secure in their identity precisely because they have had a French experience.[74]

Notwithstanding Ozouf's arguments on the singularity of French experiences, women's history has not been closely associated with didactic patriotism. A quick glance at conservative patriotic history publications from the

---

[72]G. Duby and M. Perrot, *Histoire des femmes en Occident*, 5 vols (Paris, 1988–92; repr. 2002). For historiographic analysis see F. Virgili, 'L'Histoire des femmes et l'histoire des genres aujourd'hui', *Vingtième siècle*, 75 (2002), 5–14; G. Duby and M. Perrot (eds), *Femmes et histoire* (Paris, 1993).

[73]K. Offen, 'French Women's History, Retrospect (1789–1940) and Prospect', *French Historical Studies*, 26 (2003), 756–7. To be fair, Thébaud does highlight the major international influences on French women's history in her work. She might just not mention every text with which Offen is familiar.

[74]M. Ozouf, *Les Mots des femmes: essai sur la singularité française* (Paris, 1995); discussed in Thébaud, p. 16.

1960s to the 2000s shows a completely different world from the intellectual tradition of women's history. Magazines such as *Enquête sur l'histoire* or *La Nouvelle revue d'histoire* make no use of gender as an idea and mostly cover traditional male realms of historiography – military history, politics, colonialism. They recycle all the stereotypes of male national heroes and military triumphs. Limited if any attention is paid in these publications to women or gender as an analytical category.[75] In short, there are no famous examples of feminist, post-structuralist, patriotic historiography, besides Ozouf's republican 'singularity' thesis. Generally speaking, 'women, gender and history' sit near the internationalist left wing of social research and are most sceptical of nationalism. It is an area that has developed out of subcultures of political struggle for rights and resistance to orthodoxy, the spirit of May '68. It is a school of thought that has questioned the dominant discourses that have stereotyped and excluded women from historical view. It is a historiographical position that has cast doubt on 'male' epistemological assumptions and sought to rethink methodological practices. It is a highly reflexive field in which analysis of 'doing history' is more prominent than in most other areas.[76] In short, for France, women/gender is not a historiographical concept where one will find many links to classic nationalism, royalist or republican.

A relatively similar balance-sheet can be drawn up for the role of gender history in Germany. There too gender (usually again meaning women's history), emerged out of left-wing social history and social reformism of the 1960s. It arrived on the conceptual scene out of wider intellectual discourses of emancipation. Its development as a field of research and an optic through which to read the past was especially influenced by American trends in 'women's studies'. As in France, language influenced how the English term gender became part of the scholarly community. The German translation of gender – *Geschlecht* – developed two distinct scholarly meanings: sex and gender. Within the early historical writings this was clearly taken as a straightforward biological category, being used rather more like the English word 'sex'. Later, influenced by the linguistic turn and the 'history of perception', *Geschlecht* was defined as a cultural category closer to the English idea of gender construct.

The field developed successfully, with some important contributions from scholars such as Karin Hausen, Barbara Duden, Gisela Bock and Ute Frevert. Their work represents some of the best examples of the new historiographical

---

[75]Overviews of contemporary conservative/extreme right-wing history publishing are offered in H. Frey, 'Dominique Venner: Arms and the Man', *Modern and Contemporary France*, NS, 4.4 (1996), pp. 509–12, and C. Flood, 'The Politics of Counter-Memory on the French Extreme Right', *Journal of European Studies*, 35 (2005), 221–36.

[76]The strand of reflexive self-critique is exemplified in Perrot and Duby, *Femmes et histoire*.

focus on gender. However, it would be an exaggeration to suggest that all German history writing was refashioned as a consequence. But, one can confidently state that at least a second view on history – more open to the concept of gender – exists in parallel to other scholarship which remains insensitive to these issues. In particular German gender history facilitated new research questions and subjects which were previously unexplored. Liberal and socialist historians use the idea of gender as a means by which to start to question and deconstruct the old gender and national stereotypes.[77] In particular, notions of gender have opened up and significantly changed fields from medieval history to the present. Former traditional subjects, such as courtly chivalry or witchcraft, have been interpreted as key sites to use and to read gender codes. Angelika Epple offers exemplary work. Her special achievement is that she extends the concept of historiography itself to include discussion of forms of writing outside established academic scholarship. She highlights how women explored the past through private forms of writing, such as diaries and other biographical texts. Hence Epple finds an *empfindsame Geschichtsschreibung* ('sensitive historiography') in the past which was the typically female counterpart to male history publishing.[78]

Although gender history is sometimes firmly rooted inside national intellectual traditions, it strikes us that scholars who use this optic consistently question traditional parameters of nation and historiography. In both states gender history developed out of a radical tradition of resistance to conservatism and directly questioned male institutions, including the nation. Gender studies, in France blurring with women's history, has been shaped by international scholarship, and more often than not makes little overt rhetorical play with patriotism. It might be purely coincidental that the rise of gender history took place when ideas of national identity were in retreat (1970–90). Perhaps these two issues are by-products of internationalism, social reform and a rise in individualism. On the other hand, it is also possible to place gender history writing in both states as a force that actively deconstructs

---

[77]U. Planert, 'Vater Staat und Mutter Germania: zur Politisierung des weiblichen Geschlechts im 19. und 20. Jahrhundert', in Planert (ed.), *Nation, Politik und Geschlecht* (Frankfurt, 2000). See also G. L. Mosse, *Nationalismus und Sexualität* (Munich and Vienna, 1985); K. Hagemann, 'Nation, Krieg und Geschlechterordnung', *Geschichte und Gesellschaft*, 22 (1996), 562–91; U. Frevert, *Militär und Gesellschaft im 19. Jahrhundert* (Stuttgart, 1997); U. Frevert, 'Nation, Krieg und Geschlecht im 19. Jahrhundert', in Manfred Hettling and Paul Nolte (eds), *Nation und Gesellschaft in Deutschland* (Munich, 1996), p. 151; A. Schmidt, 'Kämpfende Männer – liebende Frauen: Geschlechterstereotype auf deutschen Propagandaplakaten des Ersten Weltkriegs', in S. Kemlein (ed.), *Geschlecht und Nationalismus in Mittel- und Osteuropa, 1848–1918* (Osnabrück, 2000), pp. 217–53.
[78]A. Epple, *Empfindsame Geschichtsschreibung* (Köln, 2003).

conventional notions of national history – scientific or popular.[79] This field overtly questions the nature of forms of human identity and experience; it poses questions about traditional methodology from within national traditions. As exemplified by Epple, it discovers new forms of writing on and in the past. It interprets and explains masculinist stereotypes, casting a critical eye over how the national idea has contributed to the oppression of half of its citizens. It raises episodes of sexism and locates them in the reordering of national-masculinist hierarchies. It is often aligned with anti-imperialist, anti-racist histories of resistance. Furthermore, each of these features places women-gender as a category in historical research that is in its very nature likely to be radical, to work against conventional conservative sexist notions of *patrie* or *Vaterland*. Finally, to nuance our argument a little, we recognise that women's history writing, gender studies, certainly does take place in specific places, usually the national scholarly communities, and that research findings are written in linguistic forms that are historically associated with national identities. We also accept that work such as Ozouf's study indicates that some national–gender-history syntheses are perfectly possible. In addition, there is a risk that when gender historians deconstruct traditional discourses from the past (nationalism or sexism, or combinations of the two) they might unintentionally replicate aspects of the original discourse, a risk which is shared equally by those historians seeking to write histories of racism.

Summary

The Catholic intellectual and patriot Charles Péguy highlights a fundamental problem with all historiography. He explained the eternal question of empirical scope: 'It would take me a week to write the history of a second. It would take me a year to write the history of a minute. It would take me a lifetime to write the history of an hour. I would need an eternity to write the history of the day.'[80] Péguy's solution was to write history by intuition, by divine mysticism. What intuitive final conclusions can we add to this pragmatic and secular review?

Important cross-national differences are an obvious first and predominant outcome. In particular for the French, 1789 and the republican tradition instigated a civic notion of national identity that proved more open to

---

[79]The radical methodological implications of women's history/gender history are frequently highlighted in L. L. Downs, *Writing Gender History* (London, 2004); also in the impressive new collection: S. Morgan (ed.), *The Feminist History Reader* (London, 2006). We would like to thank Sue Morgan (University of Chichester) for her generous bibliographic suggestions on women's history writing.
[80]Charles Péguy cited in Griffiths, *Reactionary Revolution*, p. 44.

exploring social rights and social history. German identity did not develop in that fashion, and mainstream German historians were for most of the last 200 years unwilling to integrate class in their work. Similarly, the secularism of republicanism meant that religion figured less in France than in the solidly Protestant German profession. These are significant differences that mattered a great deal. The historian's interpretations of Other concepts, in combination with nationalism, meant that the French and Germans diverged. In short, the historian's handling of notions of class, religion and race inside national narratives produced a potentially antagonistic mood between the nations. Numerous areas of Franco-German difference, and therefore possible confrontation, might be reprised: French republican sensitivity to class and the idea of revolution vs. German fear and rejection of the concept; French understanding of racial origins flagging sympathy for the 'Gauls' while denigrating the Germanic Franks or 'barbarians'; not to mention French-Catholic nationalist historiography and its rejection of foreign German-Protestant scientific method. Each micro-point of difference is but one link in a longer chain of cross-national tension. The depth of detail of these historiographical differences is a small testimony to the problematic nature of Franco-German relations for much of the period.

Nonetheless, we might now also highlight some underlying similarities. For example, there were comparable approaches in French-Catholic and German-Protestant rhetoric. These schools of thought both integrated religious beliefs with nationalism. They each identified the historian's task as a neo-religious explanation of God's plan. They identified their respective nation as being 'elect' in the eyes of their God. They attacked each other for being foreigners with alien religious practices. Without unpicking the details of the argument, which were different in each state, the general idea of race thinking and anti-Semitism was also part of nationalist writings in both states. Historians linked nationhood to notions of race, and provided seductive, empirically informed narratives on the question of ethno-cultural-racial origins. Whereas medical theorists or biologists wrote complex treatises or came to fantastical schemata and typographies, historians made race a topic that was integrated into patriotic narration. Emotive and dramatic subjects such as the origins of the people or their relative power *vis-à-vis* their neighbours were a part of national history writing on either side of the Rhine. The experience of the effect of gender as a research question and framework has also shaped French and German actors in comparable ways. Emerging on the historiographical scene in the 1960s the radical spirit of gender history did much to encourage a rethinking of the status of history *per se* and by implication also essentialist notions of nationhood.

We have also cast a sidelight on intellectual exchanges, direct cultural intersections, between the two national traditions of historiography. As we pointed out above, there were episodes of direct confrontation that produced oppositional reactions in each nation. For example, one thinks of French hostility to German Protestant method in the 1880s and 1890s, or of the consistent German hostility to French republican-socialism and distrust of revolution. Other patterns of exchange are also to be found, for instance de Gobineau's important influence on German race thinking and historiography. A similar case, but in the other direction, is the story of the influence of Marx and Marxism in France and in explanations of the national event of 1789. There was also often a more general grudging admiration between the historical communities in Paris and Berlin, especially in times of relative peace. But such periods of admiration had a propensity to slide into polemical disagreement when international relations grew tenser or after the bloodletting of war (1870, 1914). As one would expect when one studies nationalist writers, each community predominantly wishes to look to its own national tradition, to develop its own vision of the past. Only after 1945 did French-German cultural transfer became part of a balanced and official bi-national relationship, and this was a process often framed by more general efforts towards European integration.

There is also a more schematic summation to the chapter. Generally speaking, nationalist encounters with transnational ideas play out in four classic ways: *integration, recuperation, exploitation, repulsion*. French (Catholic) and German (Protestant) nationalists integrated theological worldviews into secular patriotic narration. Pre-existing religious belief systems were fused into the new sense of nation. The integrative encounter is when potentially contradictory ideas are fused into a harmonious discursive outcome. Recuperation is a more complex model. It characterises the case when national historians used transnational ideas to bolster their objectives but stopped short of full synthesis. This relationship is demonstrated where historians used race thinking and anti-Semitism to underscore their glorification of nation. It points to when an historian adopts perspectives from a different body of knowledge to use it for rhetorical advantage in the new context. Communist historiography in both France and Germany indicates a third relationship. Therein it is evident that class played a far greater shaping force than nationalism. However, communist historians wished also to speak for their home communities, to take pride in experiences such as resistance to foreign invasion and liberation. This is a relationship of rhetorical exploitation. To repel ideas that are disturbing or critical to one's own ideology is a fourth common process. National historians took this line: German nationalists ignore or argue against ideas of class, French civic republicans dismiss notions of race or cultural identity when defending their nation's civic rights to the territory of Alsace-Lorraine, and many nationalist writers expel the idea of feminism or gender in their writing.

Finally, we have revealed a historiography, in France and Germany, wherein the idea of the nation was at best of secondary, if any, importance. Racist historians, notably de Gobineau, prioritised race over national community, repelling this political idea altogether. Marxist internationalists recuperated patriotism, but mainly they served the idea of international class struggle. Similarly, feminist historians think of nation only as a shaping framework, a place of patriarchy to be deconstructed.

9
Ethnicity, Religion, Class and Gender and the 'Island Story/ies': Great Britain and Ireland

Keith Robbins

A constitutional nation

National 'master narratives' emerged in Europe in the late eighteenth and early nineteenth centuries, often as a direct response to the political crisis of the French Revolution.[1] In France, and in some quarters outside it, that revolution was hailed as constituting a new epoch in human history. The values at its heart, so it was claimed, were universal, or at least potentially so. They were not anchored in the particular structures and histories of individual states. It was possible for Englishmen, such as Joseph Priestley or Thomas Paine, to become citizens of the republic. The dream of universality, however, provoked a reaction, taking different forms in different countries, which emphasised particularity.

The antiquity of the English state – though not the United Kingdom – was such that the crystallisation of a 'master narrative' was not a necessary accompaniment of either state or nationality formation in a way that was often the case elsewhere in Europe. Nevertheless, implicitly if not explicitly, historiography in the British Isles reflected certain assumptions about ethnicity, religion, class and gender. This chapter explores how historians in and of the British Isles have handled such categories and considers the extent to which this identifiable but undefined 'master narrative' has been contested. The

---

[1] When 'nationalism' itself emerged, and what was there before that, did of course remain controversial. C. Kidd, *British Identities before Nationalism* (Cambridge, 1999); L. Brockliss and D. Eastwood (eds), *A Union of Multiple Identities: The British Isles c.1750–c.1850* (Manchester, 1997); K. Robbins, 'An Imperial and Multinational Polity: The "Scene from the Centre", 1832–1922', in A. Grant and K. Stringer (eds), *Uniting the Kingdom? The Making of British History* (London and New York, 1995), together with other essays in that volume.

solidarities which cluster around the abovementioned four categories can constitute 'the Other' over against a 'national' narrative. The circumstances in which this can happen have not been absent from the British Isles in the period under review. This chapter argues, however, that it is confusing to speak in terms of conflicting streams of historiography perceived as ethnic-, religious-, class- or gender-based which challenge the hegemony exercised by a 'master narrative' which is 'national'. Rather, it has been the case that where such historiographies have existed they have normally been concerned to 'redress the balance', as they perceive it, in the treatment of a story that remains, even so, 'national'. Yet, given that the scope of this chapter is 'Great Britain and Ireland', redressing the balance has had different consequences within the cultural-political communities of these islands, leading in some cases, and most clearly in the case of Ireland, to the construction of alternative narratives which are also presented as 'national' through a different reconfiguration of ethnicity, religion, class and gender in the 'master plan'. Although a comprehensive scrutiny of all historiography in the British Isles since the creation (and subsequent partial dissolution) of the United Kingdom of Great Britain and Ireland in 1801 would be desirable for such a purpose, our analysis must necessarily be summary. It can also only note the changing contexts in which historians wrote and the audiences they addressed since the institutionalisation and professionalisation of historiography is considered elsewhere in this project.

Putting it simply, eighteenth-century English historiography had not even purported to be 'above politics'. It had reflected the divide between Whigs and Tories. The national focus was a constitution focus. Historians dilated on the nature of the English constitution and whether or not the Stuarts had 'perverted' the 'freedom' allegedly inherent in the Tudor constitution. Henry Bolingbroke, excluded from politics by his flirtation with Jacobitism, had used historical examples in his *Remarks on the History of England* (1730–1) to show how Walpole's government was threatening England's ancient constitution. He asserted that the principles of the Saxon Commonwealth were 'very democratical'.[2]

However, David Hume (1711–77), in his eight-volume *History of England from the Invasion of Julius Caesar to the Revolution in 1688* (1754-62) took pride in his detachment from party, though commentators have sometimes not been convinced about its extent. His first volume had in fact covered the period 1604–49 and only in the last two did he cover the period from Julius Caesar to Henry VII. There are three aspects of Hume which merit comment, quite apart from the contents of these volumes: he was a Scot and wrote in Edinburgh, he served in

---

[2] I. Kramnick (ed.), *Lord Bolingbroke: Historical Writings* (Chicago, 1972).

Paris as a secretary to the British ambassador (1763–7) – he had studied privately in France (1734–7) and was lionised in French circles – and, finally, had initially seen himself as a philosopher and notably had written his *Treatise on Human Nature* (1739). Hume's *History* had a considerable afterlife, being continued by Smollett, and again in 1834–5. It continued to be published in different editions throughout the nineteenth century. The author cast a sceptical eye on 'rights' supposedly embodied in constitutional documents over the long English past and subsequently upheld or subverted. In this sense, he moved outside the arguments which had dominated the English political nation. Further, he was interested in 'human nature'. There was nothing, he supposed, which was intrinsically and quintessentially 'English' about English history. He had long concluded that human beings did not behave in terms of reason alone. Various 'passions' had been in play since 'the beginning of the world', and still were. It therefore followed that mankind was much the same, in all times and places. History 'informs us of nothing new or strange in this particular'. Its chief purpose was to discover 'the constant and universal principles of human nature'. By studying men in all varieties and circumstances one became acquainted with 'the regular springs of human action and behaviour'.[3] Hume himself lived in England for just a couple of years and its 'human nature' had been assessed by reading books in the fine library of the Faculty of Advocates in Edinburgh, of which he was at the time the keeper.

Such an approach, while clearly not discounting the intrinsic interest which English history possessed, did not endow the English as a 'race' with a unique capacity. Reading about the English (or the French) was a good idea, Hume thought, if one wanted to know the sentiments, inclinations and course of life of the Greeks and Romans. Such an enterprise could scarcely provide a national master narrative which told a 'unique' story. Yet, whatever the long-term influence of Hume's writing, the notion of 'constant and universal principles' did not entirely satisfy other historians. One might accept that mankind was much the same, but nevertheless particular societies did seem to arrange those common elements in different ways. The French Revolution was perhaps a case in point – it was 'very French'. It occurred, of course, after Hume's death, but its significance loomed large for his successors.[4] Edmund Burke excoriated abstract political notions which were not anchored in the self-understanding of particular societies. He drew strong comparisons between Britain and

---

[3]Cited and discussed in J. Hale (ed.), *The Evolution of British Historiography: From Bacon to Namier* (London, 1967), pp. 26–7: D. Forbes, *Hume's Philosophical Politics* (Cambridge, 1975).

[4]H. Ben-Israel, *English Historians on the French Revolution* (Cambridge, 1968) is the most comprehensive treatment.

France. The French in 1789, he thought, might have moved to a constitution like that of Great Britain, but the National Assembly had set its face against such a prospect and calamity had followed. The Glorious Revolution of 1688–9 in England, Burke believed, had set a constitutional pattern and produced over the ensuing century an 'improved domestic prosperity' in which all the energies of the country, particularly its commercial energies, had been awakened. The French Revolution, in contrast, had laid the axe to the root of all property and consequently, he believed, to the country's prosperity.[5] A Victorian pre-occupation with the import of the French Revolution is scarcely surprising.

Thomas Carlyle (1795–1881)'s *French Revolution* (1833–42) was a book which sold for more than a generation and firmly established itself as a Victorian classic. Here was another Scot, unlike Hume, one who lived in London. Historical pasts gave him the opportunity to exercise his own prophetic present. His translations from German and his *Life of Schiller* had not brought the desired fame. For Carlyle, everything which was blasted away in France in 1789–95 was a sham. He was engaged in identifying a Truth which would replace it. Carlyle read widely, but his was an oracular work. The Oxford editor of the *World's Classic* edition in 1907 argued that its genius was such that nine out of ten English men or women who had ever read anything on the French Revolution would only have read Carlyle. His mind was held to have been of the Hebrew, not the Greek, cast. He had been able to paint for his readers a picture of 'the spirit and feelings of a Latin race' from whose genius his own 'Teutonic genius' was as the poles asunder. In his subsequent pursuit of heroes Carlyle found himself captivated by Oliver Cromwell and Frederick the Great of Prussia. In the comments of this editor, as much as in Carlyle himself, are to be found expressions which presupposed 'national characters'. Carlyle's own observations were so explo-sive and his prescriptions so idiosyncratic, however, that it is difficult to see his *oeuvre* as constituting an endorsement of any particular 'national destiny'.

Victorian contemporaries had little difficulty in identifying the essence of Britain's greatness to lie in its 'regulated freedom'. The beneficial character of the constitutional change which had been achieved in 1689 became the charter of Whig historiography in the nineteenth century and beyond. It found its most celebrated expression in the *History of England from the Accession to James II* by Thomas Babington Macaulay (1800–59). An account which was to have extended to 1832 (the landmark being constituted by the parliamentary Reform Act of that year) only reached 1715. Crucial issues revolving around the respec-tive powers of monarchy, aristocracy and parliament had been 'settled' in the seventeenth century in a 'once for all' civil war. Englishmen had learned how to

---

[5]L. Mitchell (ed.), *The Writings and Speeches of Edmund Burke* vii *The French Revolution 1790–1794* (Oxford, 1989).

achieve reform over time, without resorting to violence. It had entered into the fibre of their being. Macaulay wrote to teach 'the causes of national prosperity and decay'. He had hit upon what he believed to be central to the story he narrated. Parliament, as the focus and forum of the nation, with the unenfranchised 'virtually represented', the institutional expression of a national commitment to structures which balanced liberty and order.[6] The English had learnt how to compromise. Here was the 'Whig interpretation' of English history.

The fundamental mid-Victorian question was whether this balance, upheld, transmitted and operated by a restricted 'political nation', could survive the steady transition to a more 'democratic' system, though one which was still to be exclusively in the hands of men until 1918, by means of further extensions of the franchise in 1867 and 1884. Archibald Alison (1792–1867), a Scottish Tory lawyer, wrote *A History of Europe from the Commencement of the French Revolution to the Restoration of the Bourbons* in the decade after 1833, a vast enterprise in many volumes which was frequently revised and reprinted. Alison was not averse to drawing what he considered to be appropriate lessons for British politics. When he surveyed events on the continent, he concluded that 'regulated freedom', as exemplified in the British constitution, was best. And indeed, the grand political myth continued to flourish. John Seeley (1834–95), who became Regius Professor at Cambridge in 1869, pronounced that history should be studied because it was 'the school of statesmanship'. Hard and dry facts were to be preferred to the writings of 'charlatans' like Macaulay or Carlyle. The national story was broadening into an imperial story and Seeley had a duty to inform his fellow countrymen of the implications of their absentmindedness in this regard.[7] The political constellations of Tory/Conservative and Whig/Liberal continued to dominate British national life until the early twentieth century. Neither party could afford to frame itself in clear-cut 'class' terms. The system could still be 'managed' through traditional institutions even though, in detail, the relative power of monarchy, aristocracy and 'democracy' was shifting.

Dealing with 'charlatans' became a preoccupation of English historiography. That historiography has recently been examined by Michael Bentley

---

[6]J. Clive, *Thomas Babington Macaulay: The Shaping of the Historian* (London, 1973); J. Hamburger, *Macaulay and the Whig Tradition* (Chicago, 1976); B. Stuchtey, 'Literature, Liberty and Life of the Nation: British Historiography from Macaulay to Trevelyan', in S. Berger, M. Donovan and K. Passmore (eds), *Writing National Histories: Western Europe since 1800* (London, 1999), pp. 30–46; J. Burrow, *A Liberal Descent: Victorian Historians and the English Past* (Cambridge, 1981).

[7]D. Wormell, *Sir John Seeley and the Uses of History* (Cambridge, 1980). Seeley wrote *The Expansion of England* (London, 1883) and *The Growth of British Policy* (Cambridge, 1895). It would be wrong, however, to endow Seeley with an exclusively insular perspective. His *The Life and Times of Stein* (Cambridge, 1878) demonstrated an unusual interest in Germany and he regarded himself as Rankean.

with a scope which cannot be repeated here (nor in a style which can be emulated). He plausibly identifies a century after 1870 in which 'modernised history' asserted itself. How this initiative was won can only adequately be followed by examining the strategies of major players in their academic environments and teasing out their assumptions, both written and unwritten. In different ways, the historians who are alluded to in what follows (and many, considered by Bentley, who are not) brought about a rash of new methodologies geared to a 'scientific age' in which they had to establish proper history's credentials. In the process, the inherited 'master narrative' was battered and bruised or simply ignored. Yet, even if largely outside the departmental laboratories of universities, 'old history' survived, though it was not to be taken seriously by the real masters, who did not like narratives. It is through the contrasting personalities, presuppositions and preoccupations of Sir Lewis Namier and Herbert Butterfield, whose work is sketched here, that the ramifications of this shift can now be most fully seen.[8]

Acton, who became Regius Professor in Cambridge in 1895, was no stranger to the intersection of the academic and political worlds, being a peer of the realm and having briefly served as a Liberal MP. Yet his seven-year tenure of the post brought into prominence a man whose intellectual, cultural and religious formation was substantially 'unEnglish'.[9] Acton's mother was a Rhinelander and he moved in a milieu that was European. History should not be a mere narrative of political transactions and historians themselves should demonstrate impartial reserve in their writing. Nevertheless, constitutional government was everywhere desirable and this friend of William Gladstone knew that there was much to admire in the British example. He hated autocracy. Their constitutional preoccupations had caused the British to sit lightly on definitions of nationality.

---

[8]M. Bentley, *Modernizing England's Past: English Historiography in the Age of Modernism 1870–1970* (Cambridge, 2005). It should be noted, however, from the point of view of its relevance to this chapter, that the book is indeed concerned with *English* historiography – that is to say, with historians who were domiciled in England. It was with England's past that they were chiefly concerned. How that past interacted with the past of the UK in which they lived rarely obtruded on their reflections.

[9]G. P. Gooch, *Under Six Reigns* (London, 1985), p. 44. Gooch, a historian who much admired Acton, found him 'profoundly English' in his passion for ordered liberty, but 'utterly un-English in his scorn of compromise'. Gooch too had paid great attention to European scholarship – particularly French and German – and in his *History and Historians in the Nineteenth Century* (London, 1913). 'If the purpose of history is to stir a nation to action,' Gooch concluded, 'Droysen, Sybel and Treitschke were among the greatest of historians. If its supreme aim is to discover truth and to interpret the movement of humanity' they should not be placed in the first class. Gooch, an independent scholar and, briefly, Liberal MP, preferred truth. Cited and discussed in F. Eyck, *G. P. Gooch: A Study in History and Politics* (London, 1982) p. 199.

The best states, he believed, were multi-ethnic. The 'History of Freedom', which Acton never succeeded in writing, could not be confined within a national strait-jacket.[10]

Acton's successor, J. B. Bury (1861–1927) was another insider-outsider. His father was a Church of Ireland clergyman and he spent the first 40 years of his life in Ireland. He came to Cambridge from Trinity College, Dublin where he had been professor of modern history since 1893. By the time of his death in post, in 1927, he had witnessed the partition of his native country and the separation of the Irish Free State from the United Kingdom. His primary field was the whole of Greek and Roman history from Minoan Crete to ninth-century Byzantium. He had no interest in a 'national narrative' and deplored what he considered to be nationalistic or religious intrusions on the establishment of objective truth.

Despite the perspectives stemming from the unusual provenance of these two men, the continuity of the constitutional conception of the essence of England was maintained into the twentieth century. G. M. Trevelyan (1876–1962), a great-nephew of Macaulay and son of Macaulay's biographer, kept the flame alight.[11] Trevelyan was lugubriously describing himself by 1939 as 'a mere survival' but he had proved himself to have been the most successful historian of his generation in Britain – if success is measured in terms of the sales of his books and the tokens of public esteem he received. He had exiled himself from academic Cambridge, disliking the 'scientific' approach exemplified in the Regius Professor, Bury. Ironically, following the success of his *British History in the Nineteenth Century* (1922) and his *History of England* (1926) Trevelyan returned in triumph to Cambridge as Bury's successor in 1927. The Whig tradition, exemplified personally and historiographically by Trevelyan, was, however, under attack from different quarters and was losing its hegemonic status. He himself, though with diminishing confidence, continued to praise 'the English tradition', which would always revolt against the notion that 'the other side' should be permanently suppressed.[12]

Lewis Namier (1888–1960) came to England from Russian Poland in 1908 and, over a period of decades, immersed himself in studying eighteenth-century politics.[13] His *The Structure of Politics at the Accession of George III* (1929) and other work seemed to undermine notions of party continuity and ideology. Namier

[10]R. Hill, *Lord Acton* (New Haven, CT and London, 2000); and O. Chadwick, *Acton and History* (Cambridge, 1998) are the latest of many studies of Acton.
[11]D. Cannadine, *G. M. Trevelyan: A Life in History* (London, 1992).
[12]V. Feske, *From Belloc to Churchill: Private Scholars, Public Culture and the Crisis of British Liberalism, 1900–1939* (Chapel Hill, NC and London, 1996), p. 182.
[13]J. Namier, *Lewis Namier: A Biography* (London, 1971).

himself did not disdain elegant prose and to this extent had 'gone native', but his destructive shafts undermined established constitutional certainties. Not that he had an alternative 'national vision' to offer. He described his adopted country in his 1948 lecture on 'Nationality and Liberty' as one in which the historical process had produced a 'British island nationality' comprising the English, Scots and Welsh (with Ulster 'adhering'). The political life of the British island community was centred on its parliament at Westminster, which represented 'men rooted in British soil'.[14] He found it gratifying that this 'island community' had apparently not had to agonise over issues of national identity.

The young Herbert Butterfield (1900–79) had made his name with *The Whig Interpretation of History* (1931). It was often supposed that Trevelyan was his target, though no name was mentioned and the relationship between the two men was not personally adversarial.[15] The crime Butterfield identified in the tradition was that of studying the past with a constant eye on the present. It was still possible, however, for Trevelyan's last major book, *English Social History* (1944), with its definition of social history as 'history with the politics left out', to have a major public impact (with sales of over 400,000 copies in five years). Ironically, too, notwithstanding his assault on 'the Whig interpretation', Butterfield himself in *The Englishman and His History* (1944) wrote an encomium of 'the reconciling mind'. There was an alliance of Englishmen with their history which prevented the uprooting of things that had been organic to the development of the country. The solid body of Englishmen had prudently waited to 'steal for the whole nation what they could appropriate in the traditions of monarchy, aristocracy, bourgeoisie and church'.[16] Indeed, at the conclusion of his subtle discussion of the battle between Namier and Butterfield for the 'ownership' of the 'new eighteenth century', Bentley argues that Butterfield remained a 'half-whig' and quotes him writing in his private journal in 1963 that he was 'precariously poised between the whig interpretation and the Namierite interpretation'. He wanted to see the study of eighteenth-century history function as a form of 'political education'. Whig historians had taken ideological pretensions too much at their face value and had been cavalier with sources, but men did not support the government merely

---

[14]L. B. Namier, *Vanished Supremacies* (London, 1962), p. 47.

[15]C. T. McIntire, *Herbert Butterfield: Historian as Dissenter* (New Haven, CT and London, 2004).

[16]H. Butterfield, *The Englishman and His History* (Cambridge, 1944), pp. 11 and 139. Reba N. Soffer 'British Conservative Historiography and the Second World War', in B. Stuchtey and P. Wende, (eds), *British and German Historiography, 1750–1950* (Oxford, 2000), pp. 373–99 characterises Butterfield as a Conservative, but C. T. McIntire, *Herbert Butterfield: Historian as Dissenter* (New Haven, CT and London, 2004) takes a different view. Butterfield, it appears, only voted Conservative once in his life.

because they enjoyed profits and places. Yet, on another view, it was not simply a matter of Namier 'not believing in ideas'. J. L. Talmon suggested that he was in fact frightened by their power to disturb and was inclined to regard them as 'traumatic visitations'. On this reading, Namier was perhaps insulating himself from their neurotic European manifestations by manifesting himself to the world as an over-assimilated Englishman.[17]

In 1836 the young Benjamin Disraeli had written that 'England has become great by her institutions'. When the Oxford History School was founded, it was felt that a large element of constitutional history would give the school the strength and dignity it might otherwise lack.[18] A century later, German-born Sir Geoffrey Elton, who had made his name as a historian of Tudor England, became Professor of Constitutional History at Cambridge and testified to the continuing centrality of his subject, notwithstanding other fashions in research. He succeeded to the Regius Chair in 1984. In 1992, two years before his death, he published a tribute to 'the country in which I ought to have been born'. He saw a greatly changed world but hoped that 'the English' would 'manage to preserve the one characteristic which they gained in the centuries of a strong monarchy and a powerful system of legal rights, the one characteristic which marked them out among the nations'. They would retain the ability to tolerate variety and come again to respect the rights of the individual. He referred to 'the rights not of Man but of English men and women'.[19] This emphasis on 'the constitutional nation' – though paradoxically one without a written constitution – was thus still robust in the late twentieth century. It appealed perhaps particularly to historians born abroad who made their distinguished careers in England[20] because their 'England' seemed so successfully to have subordinated, or made unattractive, narratives centred on religion, race or class of a kind which had caused them to flee their homelands. It would be misleading, however, to suppose that narratives which did have such emphases were completely absent.

Ethnicity

A kingdom that was united, by definition, incorporated multiple histories. The 'island story' had expanded into the story of the British people or British peoples. 'Britain' was also the story of multiple ethnicities, variously defined

---

[17]Bentley, *Modernizing England's Past,* pp. 151 and 163–7.
[18]For a discussion of constitutional historians, see J. Campbell, 'Stubbs, Maitland, and Constitutional History', in Stuchtey and Wende, *British and German Historiography, 1750–1950* (Oxford, 2000), pp. 99–122.
[19]G. Elton, *The English* (Oxford, 1992), p. 234.
[20]P. Alter (ed.), *Out of the Third Reich: Refugee Historians in Post-War Britain* (London, 1998).

(or invented) and experienced with fluctuating intensity and consequence. Whether, in particular, 'Ireland's story' was part of the 'British Isles' story was perceived differently in the two islands, though without unanimity in either. Only in the Irish case did the historiography of insular ethnicities turn into the historiography of an independent state which had extricated itself from the 'British' master narrative. It was, however, an independent state in a politically divided island, a partition which brought into sharp focus issues of ethnicity and religion and the relationships between them, all in the context of an acceptance or rejection of the 'British' master narrative.

The ambiguities all that this entailed for 'ethnicity' can be seen, by way of example, in a letter written in praise of Abraham Lincoln in 1915 by James Bryce, veteran historian, Liberal politician and former British ambassador to Washington.[21] Lincoln was described as a man who belonged 'to the Race, not merely as a man of pure English blood, but also because his qualities were those which Englishmen and Americans like to think of as their favourite ideal ...'[22] There was, of course, good reason in the early phase of the war to emphasise Anglo-American connections.[23] Bryce was a man who had travelled the world and was accustomed, in his observations, to remark on 'race'.[24] Bryce's incorporation of Lincoln in 'the English race', it might be thought, was an expansive gesture from a man who was not himself English. Bryce was born in Belfast and raised in Glasgow. He has been variously described by historians as a Scot, an Irishman or an Ulsterman. Such a background, with its potential for such differently allocated identities, was perhaps an ideal prelude to a lifetime's engagement with issues of federalism as he pursued 'the British race' in its various manifestations across the world. Its global trajectory in the nineteenth century meant that the story of 'the British race' was different from that of the United Kingdom of Great Britain and Ireland, 'the mother country'. In country after country of overseas settlement the incomers, over generations, were to move through successive refinements of what belonging

[21]He was the author of *The American Commonwealth* (London, 1888); H. Tulloch, *James Bryce's 'The American Commonwealth': The Anglo-American Background* (Woodbridge, 1988).
[22]Written on 15 April to Sir Harry Brittain and quoted in Brittain's *Happy Pilgrimage* (London, n.d.), pp. 289–90.
[23]K. Robbins, 'Lord Bryce and the First World War', *Historical Journal* 10, 2 (1967), pp. 255–77.
[24]In his *South America: Observations and Impressions* (London, 1912), for example, he devoted a whole chapter to 'The Relations of Races in South America' in a context in which the European nations had now 'partitioned out the whole world of savagery, barbarism, and semi-civilization among themselves', p. 452.

to 'the British race' meant. If 'the British race' had been coextensive with a super-state called 'Greater Britain', as advocates of 'imperial federation' in the final decades of the nineteenth century urged, then race, nation and state would have remained aligned. That was not to be. Nevertheless, 'race', along with a term like 'the English-speaking peoples', continued, at least in the first half of the twentieth century and the era of the two world wars, to be a term used by some historians, particularly those who, like Churchill, were active in politics, to indicate a British or Anglo-American affinity, even ethnicity, which still lay beneath the 'nations' which were now identifiable 'beyond the seas'.

Such an 'ethnicity' was neither stable nor precisely definable. Historians could not dispute that the 'English race' was inescapably hybrid. Even the 'happy revolution' of 1688–9 had brought a Dutch *Stadholder* to the throne. The race was to be ruled by German monarchs. Its continuing hybridity was held to lie in the very circumstances of the creation of the English state and its Norman consolidation. Mediaeval England was a bi- or trilingual Anglo-Norman polity.[25] Historians naturally differed in their estimate of how 'Saxon' and 'Norman' had interacted. The English language itself combined Germanic and Romance elements.[26] The 'stock' of England consisted of Angles and Saxons, Danes and Normans – their individual distinctive imprints could still be seen in the landscape, in place and personal names, and in dialect and speech patterns. Nevertheless, as the Victorian poet Alfred Tennyson proclaimed, in greeting a Danish princess come to England to marry the heir to the British throne, an ethnic 'we' had emerged from this protracted (and continuing) process of blending. 'The English' could be thought to have 'made' themselves in 'the Age of Shakespeare'.[27] There was already something peculiar about the 'individualism' of the English.[28] This ethnicity had absorbed, and was continuing to absorb, 'economic migrants' or 'asylum seekers' from the European mainland. The great majority of these incomers had been absorbed into it within a generation or two and made only occasional gestures towards their ancestral origins. The English themselves could be portrayed as a band of happy men in a land of foaming tankards and full bellies.[29]

English ethnicity might be constructed out of the mingling Angles and Saxons, Danes and Normans. British ethnicity could not. It had to embrace (or

---

[25]H. MacDougall, *Racial Myth in English History* (Montreal and Hanover, NH, 1982).

[26]T. Turville-Petre, *England the Nation: Language, Literature and National Identity, 1290–1340* (Oxford, 1996); D. Matthew, *Britain and the Continent, 1000–1300: The Impact of the Norman Conquest* (London, 2005).

[27]See Adrian Hastings' discussion of 'England' as prototype in his *The Construction of Nationhood: Ethnicity, Religion and Nationalism* (Cambridge, 1997), pp. 35–65.

[28]A. Macfarlane, *The Origins of English Individualism* (Oxford, 1978).

[29]R. Colls, *The Identity of England* (Oxford, 2002), pp. 22–3.

fail to embrace) 'the Celts' (and in the countries of overseas settlement 'Anglo-Saxons' and 'Celts' frequently lived alongside each other to a greater extent than they had done 'at home'). The alleged qualities (or their lack) and the characteristics of 'Anglo-Saxons' and 'Celts' were frequently compared and contrasted at both a 'popular' and scholarly level.[30] The 'British race', at least on some accounts, mixed both elements. Further, to speak of only two elements was recognised to be an oversimplification. Just as England was not 'Anglo-Saxon' *tout court*, so the non-English territories of the United Kingdom were not uniformly 'Celtic'. Indeed, whether the term 'Celtic' related to languages still spoken or once spoken within the British Isles (Cornish, Manx, Irish and Scottish Gaelic and Welsh) or whether it could be applied to a 'race' or 'races' was and has remained a matter of controversy.[31] It was not conspicuous that possession of a common Celtic ethnicity, supposing one to exist, expressed an underlying Celtic solidarity. Bryce himself, who lived most of his life in England when not travelling overseas, may have been relatively indifferent as to whether he was by ethnicity a Scotsman, an Irishman or an Ulsterman. In Belfast and Glasgow, however, it did matter. How the 'local', the 'regional' and the 'national' have been treated historiographically is, however, considered by this author in another place.

It can be said in summary here, however, that the existence of such ethnicities complicated the compilation of a united national master narrative of a United Kingdom. Ethnicity, however, was most frequently solved by being ignored, that is to say, by assuming that it only had a secondary significance within the overall 'British' story (though it was a central aspect of the British-Irish story, or the impossibility of such a story). All three political parties – Conservative, Liberal and Labour – were pan-British, though with distinct territorial strengths. Historiography therefore reflected the dominant 'unionist' mode in politics, which existed until the latter part of the twentieth century. Such unionism did not presuppose or entail the elimination of multi-ethnicity but neither was multi-ethnicity deemed to require substantial historiographical attention. It was a situation which only changed in that latter period when, both politically and historiographically, the multi-ethnic character of Britain (and, contentiously,

[30]L. P. Curtis, Jr., *Anglo-Saxons and Celts: A Study of Anglo-Irish Prejudices in Victorian England* (Bridgeport, 1968): R. F. Foster, *Paddy and Mr Punch: Connections in Irish and English History* (London, 1993).
[31]M. Chapman, *The Celts: The Construction of a Myth* (London, 1992); P. Sims-Williams, 'Celtomania and Celtoscepticism', *Cambrian Medieval Celtic Studies* 36 (1998), pp. 1–36; J. T. Koch, 'Celts, Britons, and Gaels – Names, Peoples, and Identities', *Transactions of the Honourable Society of Cymmrodorion 2002* New ser. 9 (2003), p. 41.

of Ireland) received increased attention and came increasingly to be portrayed, with or without political implications, not so much as a single national master narrative as a set of such narratives, intertwined no doubt, but sufficiently coherent to be distinguishable.

From the perspective of the early twenty-first century, however, the question of ethnicity has ceased to be a matter which concerns itself solely with the 'historic' elements in the population of the British Isles. The scale and diversity of immigration into the United Kingdom and even in the Irish Republic have produced a society variously described as multiracial or multi-ethnic living in different relationships to 'the national past' as conceived in the nineteenth and the first half of the twentieth centuries. The extent to which incoming ethnicities remain intact, whether ethnic 'minorities' will always persist, raise questions of lively contemporary debate and division. They do so too in a context in which incoming Asian ethnicities are linked to adherence to non-Christian religions which had in the past and to some extent in the present been identified as Others by Christians in the British Isles.[32]

Religion

The political reality was that by the beginning of the nineteenth century the churches of the British Isles had made their accommodations with the state in which they were situated. It follows, therefore, that while individual historians wrote from within (and often about) particular Christian denominational traditions and, in doing so, noted the extent to which they 'dissented' from the story of the state, historiography did not polarise comprehensively between 'Protestant' and 'Catholic' narratives, though this element was certainly not absent.[33] It is argued in what follows that a major reason for the lack of such a pervasive historiographical confrontation lies in the plurality of Protestantism in particular, but also, to some extent, of Catholicism, as manifested differently in territories and nations of the British Isles.

The master narrative of the 'constitutional nation' as considered in the first section of this chapter had been developed and elaborated by historians,

---

[32]Among the many works by historians and political scientists may be noted C. Holmes, *Immigration & British Society, 1871–1971* (London, 1988); I. R. G. Spencer, *British Immigration Policy: The Making of Multi-Racial Britain* (London, 1977); and P. Panayi, *Immigration, Ethnicity and Racism in Britain 1815–1945* (London, 1994).

[33]M. Bauman and M. I. Klauber, *Historians of the Christian Tradition: Their Methodology and Influence on Western Thought* (Nashville, TN, 1995) include William Cunningham, J. B. Lightfoot, Thomas Martin Lindsay, Christopher Dawson, Herbert Butterfield and Stephen Neill as British examples.

largely but not exclusively either English or English-domiciled. They recognised that this Great Britain was a Protestant state. That condition could be identified by historians who were sceptical (like Hume), were 'cultural Protestants' or were convinced Protestants. Some historians have recently re-emphasised the extent to which Protestantism was both 'absolutely central' to the religious life of Britain and constituted, in the eighteenth century, the core ideology of the state and its defining characteristic.[34] It has been argued that too much attention has been given to the divisions within Protestantism which, though abundant and serious, should not be equated with the division between Protestant and Catholic. The exclusion of Roman Catholics from voting, from membership of both houses of parliament and from state offices (and the monarchy which still remains), which lasted until 1829, was a clear indication that they constituted an Other. They had also been subject to other legal restrictions and discriminations – though in practice the legal provisions were probably not always enforced.

Anti-Catholicism, however, was not just a matter of legal exclusions. It was a powerful popular emotion and past deliverances from Catholic plotting were publicly celebrated – as, for example, the burning of bonfires on 'Guy Fawkes Night'. The political importance of this perspective was that it aligned Britain, all other things being equal, with 'Protestant' northern as against 'Catholic' southern Europe – though things were rarely ever 'equal'.[35] The growth of 'Anglo-Catholicism' in the Church of England – sometimes referred to by opponents as 'bastard Catholicism' – and conversions to Rome (by Newman and Manning, for example) threatened the Protestant-national national identity. Some historians rallied to its defence. J. A. Froude published a 12-volume *History of England from the Fall of Wolsey to the Defeat of the Spanish Armada* (1856–70), which became a bestseller. He was explicit about its purpose. It was to cleanse the English Reformation and the Anglican Church of the 'stains' which had been allowed to gather on them. The fact that it was a bestseller led some of his colleagues to conclude that it was not history. Such criticism did not prevent him from becoming Regius Professor at Oxford for the last two years of his life. Froude suspected that Catholicism had learnt nothing and forgotten nothing. Once it had a numerical majority behind it, it would

---

[34] L. Colley, *Britons: Forging the Nation, 1707–1837* (London, 1994), pp. 18–19. See also J. C. D. Clark, 'Protestantism, Nationalism and National Identity, 1660–1832', *The Historical Journal* 43:1 (2000).

[35] D. G. Paz, *Popular anti-Catholicism in mid-Victorian England* (Stanford, CA, 1992); E. R. Norman, *Anti-Catholicism in Victorian England* (London, 1968); W. L. Arnstein, *Protestant versus Catholic in Victorian England* (London, 1982).

reclaim its old authority.[36] For his part, Charles Kingsley did battle with Newman. Protestant England was in jeopardy.[37]

In the early decades of the century, John Lingard, (1771–1851) a Roman Catholic, had written a *History of England* which put that 'Protestant England' in a rather different context, composed as it was by a man with clerical contacts all over Europe. The entire work went through seven English editions up to 1883 and was also translated into Italian, French and German. Lingard, who spent years at the State Paper Office in the Tower of London, thought that Macaulay wrote claptrap of every description. However, while he made no attempt to disguise the fact that he was a Catholic priest, he did not set out to write an explicitly Catholic counter-history. It is interesting in this respect to note that his work was initially rejected by two Catholic publishers and the first three volumes were brought out by a Protestant one. Some Catholics supposed that Lingard only confirmed Protestants in their errors, but he made it his rule, so he said, 'to tell the truth whether it made for us or against us'. He knew that what he had to say about the Reformation would shock Protestant prejudices, but 'my only chance of being read by them depends on my having the reputation of a temperate writer'.[38] The fact that Lord Acton could be appointed to the Regius Chair when his Catholicism had barred him from admission to Cambridge as an undergraduate testified to the extent to which 'Protestant England' as defended so vigorously in the mid-Victorian period was itself slipping into history. Bury, Acton's successor, rather hoped that religion itself was slipping into history.

Since there never has been a single Protestant 'Church of Britain' or 'Church of the British Isles', Protestant historiography has not been in simple competition with Catholic historiography. The United Kingdom state recognised and recognises a church 'Establishment' in the case of England and Scotland, though it has ceased to do so in Wales and Ireland/Northern Ireland. Since the Churches of England and of Scotland were not in communion with each other, and since there has been substantial, if latterly diminished, Protestant Dissent, the national 'British' story could not be taken to be synonymous with

[36]J. A. Froude, 'The Condition and Prospects of Protestantism', in *Short Studies of Great Subjects* Second Series, (London, 1871) p. 146. W. H. Dunn, *James Anthony Froude: A Biography* (Oxford, 1961, 1963).

[37]J. P. von Arx, *Progress and Pessimism: Religion, Politics and History in Late Nineteenth-Century Britain* (Cambridge, MA, 1985).

[38]E. R. Norman, *The English Catholic Church in the Nineteenth Century* (Oxford, 1984), pp. 291–2.; E. Jones, *The English Nation: The Great Myth* (Stroud, 2003), pp. 208 and 258 cannot think of any other English historian who achieved as much as Lingard, but attributes substantial ignorance of his accomplishment to the fact that he had not been trained in English universities and worked as a parish priest.

that of any one particular church.[39] Religion was nevertheless a central element in the 'national questions' in all the territories of the British Isles.[40] The
narrative was one of a people who were in a general sense Christian, whatever
that precisely entailed in terms of belief and practice. It could appear at particular moments that this history served a providential purpose. In 1940, for
example, national history might embody the cause of 'Christian civilisation',
a civilisation whose mingled elements could also be attractive to those outside
the churches.[41] Bentley, considering a number of historians, has concluded
that 'there is nothing to suggest that the war heralded the end of a Christian
historical perspective about the British past' and goes further in suggesting a
rebirth in the 1950s. He notes that the successive holders of the Regius Chair in
Cambridge between 1943 and 1983 were an Anglican convert from Methodism,
a Benedictine monk, a Methodist/College Anglican and an Anglican priest.[42] Of
course, such a list does not reveal a uniform understanding of the bearing of religion on the national story, nor, by definition, does it constitute a comprehensive
picture of the position of British academic historiography of this era.

In a career largely outside 'the historical profession', but not without influence
among a reading public, Christopher Dawson (1889–1970) a Catholic convert,
was anxious to place English history in a European and Catholic context.[43] His
writing offered broad and sweeping interpretations of the inner content of civilisations and cultures. He had relatively little interest in 'constitutions' as he

---

[39]A resurgence of interest in denomination history began in the later nineteenth and early
twentieth centuries when historical societies – Wesleyan Methodist (1894), Congregation-
alist (1901), Baptist (1908), Presbyterian (1913) – all wished to assert that the Church
of England did not 'own' the national Protestant past, though they did so in a context
in which its Anglo-Catholic wing, to say the least, was uncomfortable with a national
Protestantism.
[40]See the 'Church, Chapel and the Fragmentation of Faith', in K. Robbins, *Nineteenth-
Century Britain: Integration and Diversity* (Oxford, 1988) pp. 63–96 and 'Religion and
Identity in Modern British History', in *History, Religion and Identity in Modern Britain*
(London, 1993), pp. 85–104; R. V. Comerford, M. Cullen, J. Hill and C. Lennon (eds),
Religion, Conflict and Co-Existence in Ireland (Dublin, 1990); R. V. Comerford, 'Religion',
in idem *Ireland* (London, 2003), pp. 110–20: D. Llywelyn, *Sacred Place, Chosen People:
Land and Identity in Welsh Spirituality* (Cardiff, 1999).
[41]Robbins, 'Britain, 1940 and Christian Civilization', in *History, Religion and Identity*,
pp. 195–214.
[42]Bentley, *Modernizing England's Past*, pp. 66–7. He is referring to Sir George Clark, Dom
David Knowles, Sir Herbert Butterfield and Owen Chadwick.
[43] C. Scott, *Christopher Dawson: A Historian and His World* (London, 1982); G. Caldecott
and J. Morrill (eds), *Eternity in Time: Chrisopher Dawson and the Catholic Idea of History*
(Edinburgh, 1997). Bentley, *Modernizing England's Past*, pp. 56–8 has a discussion of
Catholic writing. Among Dawson's writings are *The Making of Europe* (1932) and *Religion
and the Rise of Western Culture* (1934).

sought to discern the prevailing spiritual assumptions of European, indeed of global civilisations. When he talked about 'the European mind' he thought Englishmen shared one with their neighbours. A sentence such as 'The spirit of Christian humanism dominated the whole of the seventeenth century manifested itself alike in the Baroque art of Spain and Italy and central Europe, in the Jacobean and Caroline literature of England and in the classical culture of France' typifies his inclusive, transnational perspective.[44] He found Oswald Spengler's *The Decline of the West* 'arbitrary and subjective'. It could not throw light on the inner meaning of change. He could do better. His contemporary 'meta-historian', Arnold Toynbee (1889–1975), likewise a man whose career was not that of an 'academic historian', had also read Spengler (borrowing the book from Namier in 1920) and found him 'dogmatic and determinist'. In the ten volumes of *A Study of History* (1934–61) he thought he could do better.[45] Neither man, however, escaped criticism from their contemporaries – 'real historians' – that they were arbitrary, subjective, dogmatic and determinist. The fact that their ideas received 'serious discussion' on the continent demonstrated that they were 'outsiders' whose concerns were treated sceptically by the 'mainstream'.

It was in Ireland that the issue of 'religion' and 'nation' took its most highly charged and intractable course in the nineteenth and twentieth centuries. The status of the Catholic Church within the newly established Irish Free State/Republic apparently confirmed that the Irish were a 'Catholic people'. It seemed to be matched by the assertion that the new Northern Ireland, still within the United Kingdom, was a Protestant state for Protestant people.[46] Nationality, ethnicity, religion and class were in reality infinitely more complicated, in both entities, than might be assumed from such bold categorisations. How the one should be prioritised over the other as the 'driver' of identity has taxed historiography particularly in the Irish context, but also more generally in the British context.

It has remained the case, however, that 'ecclesiastical historiography' has largely remained at a tangent from the 'national history' in which it is set. Conversely, particularly in the latter decades of the twentieth century, 'religion' has frequently been marginalised, or subjected to reductionist treatment, by

---

[44]C. Dawson, *Christianity & The New Age* (London, 1931), pp. 96–7.

[45]Toynbee thought he had suffered because he had tried to give his fellow 'Franks' a 'bit of a jolt' in looking at the encounter between the world and the West through the eyes of the great non-Western majority of mankind. W. H. McNeill, *Arnold Toynbee: A Life* (Oxford, 199), p. 224. Toynbee also gave Gifford Lectures at Edinburgh in 1952 and 1953, published as *An Historian's Approach to Religion* (Oxford, 1956).

[46]P. Mitchel, *Evangelicalism and National Identity in Ulster 1921–1998* (Oxford, 2003).

historians of the nation.[47] The arrival of ecumenism, however fragile, has brought about a difference of tone and substance in the consideration of 'religion' and 'nation' from that which has been noted in the nineteenth century. The 'death' of Christian Britain (and Ireland), whatever that is taken to mean, together with the substantial presence of non-Christian religions, created in the second half of the twentieth century a context in which the history of 'religion' and 'nation', as it has existed and been written about over the period *c*.1800–*c*.1960 now appears 'distant'.[48] Yet, arguably, while the context has changed, religion as Other or as 'unifier', has not lost its significance as a topic in the contemporary historiography of the British Isles. It might not now occupy (or even want to occupy) a place in the national master narrative which it had been accorded in most of the period under review, but nor could it be completely marginalised by believers or by sceptics (for their differing reasons).

Class

Standard national histories written by men within the 'constitutional nation' did not suppose that the nation was without some kind of social cleavage. What vocabulary and categorisation which could be applied to those cleavages, however, was more problematic. Trevelyan, for example, had no difficulty in describing the politics of the 1832 Reform Bill in terms of 'class'. The followers of Grey, he wrote, were acting under 'the direct inspiration of middle-class opinion' and 'under the compelling fear of working-class revolt'. Power passed from the landed aristocracy to the commercial classes in the opinion of J. A. R. Marriott, a historian whose history of England since Waterloo ran through eleven editions between 1913 and 1936. Marriott, himself a Conservative MP, further believed that it had passed to the 'manual workers' from the 'bourgeoisie' at the beginning of the twentieth century. A Whiggish Cambridge historian, J. R. Butler, writing in 1914 on the subject of the 1832 Reform Bill, painted a scenario in which a ruling class – 'the upper 10,000' – was pitted against 'the nation' or 'the people'. Exactly what a 'class' was, however, did not excite much protracted discussion. Butler acknowledged

---

[47]K. Robbins, 'Institutions and Illusions: The Dilemma of the Modern Ecclesiastical Historian', in idem, *History, Religion and Identity*, pp. 75-84; E. Norman, 'The Changing Role of the Ecclesiastical Historian', in N. Aston (ed.), *Religious Change in Europe, 1650–1914* (Oxford, 1997). See further the lecture 'Church and State', in Bentley, *Modernizing England's Past*, pp. 45–69; and M. Cowling, *Religion and Public Doctrine in Modern England: Volume III Accommodations* (Cambridge, 2001).

[48]C. Brown, *The Death of Christian Britain* (London, 2001); R. Hooker and J. Sargent (eds), *Belonging to Britain: Christian Perspectives on Religion and Identity in a Plural Society* (London, 1991).

that 'the people' constituted a generous category and that the middle and working classes might have interests that conflicted as much as they coincided. There
was, therefore, some kind of a 'class struggle' at the heart of Britain as 'the first
industrial nation'. Defining the contours of the 'middle class', however, was
problematic. Was there a great divide between the 'commercial' and 'professional' middle classes? Historians noted that such great advocates of a coming
'bourgeois order' as the mid-nineteenth-century radicals John Bright and Richard
Cobden ultimately found it impossible to mould the 'middle class' to their
liking.[49] Even so, Trevelyan, writing in 1913, held that Bright had 'profoundly
modified English politics and the relations and balance of English classes'.[50]

It was no accident, however, that foreign observers, from Friedrich Engels
onwards, looking at England sometimes saw 'class' and 'nation' locked in mortal
combat. Established historiography, however, while, as has been noted, not dis-
missing 'class', identified relatively smooth 'transfers of power' whose effect was
to erode if not abolish the distinction between the 'political nation' and 'the
people'. One commentator has stressed the extent to which, in early twentieth-
century historiography, class was integrated into a national history which
was presented as consensual.[51] He instances accounts of social change in England
between 1760 and 1830 written by J. L. and Barbara Hammond – *The Village
Labourer, The Town Labourer* and *The Skilled Labourer* (1911–19). Academic reviewers largely ignored these volumes, but over subsequent decades they became the
starting point for debates on the standard of living in industrialising England.
The divorce of classes had been an outcome of 'the industrial revolution', but
there was no inherent necessity for it to read 'like a history of a civil war', in
the Hammonds' words. The Chartist Movement of the 1840s, as Beatrice Webb
put it, was the apotheosis of the working-class revolt against the misery and
humiliation brought about the by onset of that revolution. Other writers, such as
G. D. H. Cole, likewise took 'class' to be essentially a 'modern' phenomenon and
began their narratives accordingly.[52]

This focus came under criticism from two quarters. Economic historians
of the same era, notably Sir John Clapham, stressed how diverse was the
economic life of England in the eighteenth century. Technological change
was uneven. Indeed, how far one can speak of *the* industrial revolution has

[49]K. Robbins, 'John Bright and Middle-Class Politics', in J. Garrard, D. Jary, M. Goldsmith
and A. Oldfield, (eds), *The Middle Class in Politics* (Farnborough, 1978), pp. 14–34; A. Kidd
and D. Nicholls, *The Making of the British Middle Class* (Stroud, 1998).

[50]G.M. Trevelyan, *John Bright* (London, 1913), p. 4.

[51]D. Feldman, 'Class', in P. Burke (ed.), *History and Historians in the Twentieth Century*
(Oxford, 2002) p. 185. Our discussion is indebted to this chapter.

[52]G. D. H. Cole, *A Short History of the British Working Class Movement 1789–1927* (London,
1932).

continued to be a source of controversy over subsequent decades. For his part, R. H. Tawney, disputing that 'the fall of man' occurred in the reign of George III, looked at social divisions in the sixteenth and seventeenth centuries. Three hundred years after the 'English Revolution' of 1640 a young Oxford historian and Communist Party member, Christopher Hill, published a substantial essay in which he argued that it had brought into being a new capitalist social order. Over the next quarter of a century a group of Marxist historians, in particular, wrote widely on popular movements and class formation. There was an alternative 'English tradition', it was argued, which, from the time when 'Saxon rights' had been usurped by the Normans, 'the people' had been seeking to recover.[53] Talking about 'Saxons' and 'Normans' was another way of talking about the 'two nations' – the poor and the rich – as identified by Disraeli in the 1840s in his novel *Sybil*. In *The Common People, 1746–1946* (1949) G. D. H. Cole and Raymond Postgate argued that the 'two nations' still confronted each other, though not as starkly as in the days of the Chartists.

The publication of E. P. Thompson's *The Making of the English Working Class* in 1963 was a further landmark. He concerned himself with the emergence of a 'collective self-consciousness'. Class experience, in his view, was still something largely determined by the productive relations into which men were born or involuntarily entered. Class 'happened' when some men felt and articulated the identity of their interests as between themselves and as against other men whose interests were different from, and usually opposed to, theirs. Over the following decades a vigorous debate took place in which historians of different persuasions attempted to pin down the working-class experience and explain what 'making' meant.[54] Attention came increasingly to concentrate on class as 'discourse'.[55] It came to seem that the landscape was not occupied by the 'rise' or 'fall' of a working class (or a middle class) but rather by

---

[53]C. Hill (ed.), *The English Revolution 1640* (London, 1940); B. Schwarz, '"The People" in History: The Communist Party Historians Group, 1946–56', in R. Johnson, G. McLennan, B. Schwarz and D. Sutton (eds), *Making Histories: Studies in History-writing and Politics* (London, 1982); H. Kaye, *The British Marxist historians: An Introductory Analysis* (Cambridge, 1984); Bentley, *Modernizing England's Past*, pp. 180–2.

[54]J. Foster, *Class Struggle and the Industrial Revolution* (London, 1974); Paul Johnson, *Saving and Spending: The Working-class Economy in England 1870–1939* (Oxford, 1985); A. Briggs, 'The Language of "Class" in Early Nineteenth-Century England' and 'The Language of "Mass" And "the Masses" in Nineteenth-Century England', in *Collected Essays: Volume One: Words, Numbers, Places, People* (Brighton, 1985); D. Eastwood, 'History, Politics and Reputation: E.P. Thompson Reconsidered', *History* 85, 280 (October, 2000) pp. 634–54.

[55]G. S. Jones, *Languages of Class* (Cambridge, 1985); D. Cannadine, *Class in Britain* (London, 1998).

protean identities in constant process of definition and interaction. Some historians specifically set out, not without considerable success, to topple 'class' from the central place it had come to occupy in the historiography of nineteenth-century England.[56] Even those of a different disposition felt that it had become increasingly unclear what the 'point' of working-history was.[57] It is not surprising to find studies of particular parts of England which argue that 'at several points in working-class life, from the workplace to the ballot box, class, as an influence affecting the choices made, appears to have been secondary, at best'.[58]

The English working class, or working classes, therefore did indeed live 'a life apart', but even so that life was not itself so uniform and self-contained as to posit 'class' as an identity outside and indeed opposed to the 'nation'.[59] The peculiarities of the English working class were English. There was some awareness of and rhetorical allegiance to a 'class solidarity' which transcended state boundaries, but 'internationalism' proved a frail concept, particularly, of course, at moments of crisis.[60] It is true, however, that the 'party of the working class' emerged in the twentieth century as 'the Labour Party' rather than 'the Socialist Party'. Its growth was tardy and its period of power, before 1945, very limited.[61] Even after its triumph in 1945 it is argued that a social democratic definition of democracy had not entrenched itself in British civil society. The political settlement of 1945 depended on the survival of the industrial working class – which in the nature of things was not likely to last indefinitely.[62] In short, Labour had not 'captured' the nation and was not sure whether it wanted to. 'Red Flag' and 'Union Jack' continued in ambivalent juxtaposition.[63]

Class and ethnicity, however, did come into play within the UK. The Labour Party which emerged at the beginning of the twentieth century was a *British* party. It aspired to represent the interests of the working class across Britain. Rhetoric to this end was normal. Early leadership came conspicuously from Scots

---

[56]P. Joyce, *Visions of the People: Industrial England and the Question of Class, 1848–1914* (Cambridge, 1991).

[57]M. Savage and A. Miles (eds), *The Remaking of the British Working Class 1840–1940* (London, 1994), p. ix; P. Joyce (ed.), *Class* (Oxford, 1995).

[58]T. Griffiths, *The Lancashire Working Classes c.1880–1930* (Oxford, 2001), p. 331.

[59]S. Meacham, *A Life Apart: The English Working Class 1890–1914* (London, 1977).

[60]D. J. Newton, *British Labour, European Socialism and the Struggle for Peace, 1889–1914* (Oxford, 1985); M. Donald, 'Workers of the World Unite? Exploring the Enigma of the Second International', in M. H. Geyer and J. Paulmann (eds.), *The Mechanics of Internationalism* (Oxford, 2001), pp. 177–204.

[61]K. Robbins, 'Labouring the Point', *Historical Journal*, 47, 3 (2004), 775–84.

[62]R. McKibbin, *Classes and Cultures: England 1918–1951* (Oxford, 1998), p. 536.

[63]P. Ward, *Red Flag and Union Jack: Englishness, Patriotism and the British Left, 1881–1924* (Woodbridge, 1998).

(J. R. Macdonald, Keir Hardie, even Arthur Henderson) but who functioned outside Scotland. To some extent emphasis on the need for common action jostled for supremacy with a 'soft' nationalism which looked to 'Home Rule' within the territories of the UK. Keir Hardie came to represent the Welsh constituency of Merthyr Tydfil and favoured Welsh Home Rule – but such devolution should not jeopardise class unity. How 'class' related to the Welsh concept of 'the people' (the *Gwerin*) was not a straightforward matter. Putting it simply, although highly symbolically, the debate in Wales and Scotland was whether to speak of the 'Welsh Labour Party' or 'the Labour Party in Wales' (or Scotland).[64] At the end of the twentieth century, an accommodation was found, though after great difficulty and perhaps with continuing instability, between a class/ideology that operated at the level of 'the British people' and one that recognised the existence of nations.

Gender

The national story for most of this period has largely been written about primarily by men in a world in which what had been 'significant' in that story had been shaped by men.[65] They had controlled its procedures, institutions, structures and political values. Historiography was largely in their hands, with only a few exceptions, at least in institutional terms.[66] It was a bold step when the Historical Association, which had been founded in 1906, chose Alice Stopford Green, an Irish Protestant, as its president in 1915. She had sustained her husband, J. R. Green (1837–83), author of the best-selling *Short History of the English People* (1874). She had married Green in 1877. What animated her at the time, however, was not so much the question of gender but the question of Ireland. In the circumstances of 1916 she took the symbolic step of uprooting herself from London where she had lived for 40 years and returning to Dublin.[67] The Historical Association, perhaps in the light of this experience, waited for many decades before selecting another woman president.

---

[64]D. Tanner, C. Williams and D. Hopkin (eds), *The Labour Party in Wales, 1900–2000* (Cardiff, 2000).

[65]M. Berg, *A Woman in History: Eileen Power 1889–1940* (Cambridge, 1996). The subject was a rarity in her generation. B. Smith, *The Gender of History: Men, Women, and Historical Practice* (Cambridge, MA and London, 1998) takes this issue further.

[66]As is indicated in the title of J. P. Kenyon, *The History Men: The Historical Profession in England since the Renaissance* (London, 1983); Bentley, *Modernizing England's Past*, pp. 122–5.

[67]R. B. McDowell, *Alice Stopford Green: A Passionate Historian* (Dublin, 1967); K. Robbins, 'History, the Historical Association and the "National Past"', reprinted in idem, *History, Religion and Identity in Modern Britain* (London, 1993).

Yet both for long periods in the nineteenth and again from the second half of the twentieth century the monarch, as the embodiment of the nation, has been a woman. Queen Victoria reigned, with not insignificant constitutional power, becoming the first and the last 'Empress of India' at a time when women had no vote in the affairs of the nation and no role in the military or naval expression of its might. She was also, of course, Supreme Governor of the Church of England.[68] The ambiguities of her position have begun to receive attention.[69] They were, of course, exceptional in scale, but how the roles of men and women, at various social levels, related to each other continue to be explored.[70]

'Britannia' was the formal personification, though 'John Bull' was an informal competitor.[71] Her defiant pose did not seem to suggest ready confinement to a 'separate sphere'.[72] There was, therefore, an unresolved tension on the question of 'owning' the nation – a tension evident in many spheres – as to whether the nation was a male preserve, thought of within a particular frame of 'masculinity', or whether it was equally (or for the most part unequally) accessible to men and women. Were women struggling to gain entry on equal terms to those structures and institutions which men dominated but with little or no intention to reshape their values or functions, or would parity inevitably entail their reconstruction?[73] There is, of course, a substantial literature on many of these matters and the general issues cannot be referred to here.[74] One can conclude,

---

[68]W. L. Arnstein, 'Queen Victoria and Religion', in G. Malmgreen (ed.), *Religion in the Lives of English Women* (Beckenham, 1986), pp. 88–128. The queen's willingness to receive the sacrament when worshipping in the Church of Scotland scandalised sections of English Anglican opinion. Brian Heeney, *The Women's Movement in the Church of England 1850–1930* (Oxford, 1988).

[69]D. Thompson, *Queen Victoria: Gender and Power* (London, 1990); E. Langland, 'Nation and Nationality: Queen Victoria and the Developing Narrative of Englishness', in M. Homans and A. Munich (eds), *Remaking Queen Victoria* (Cambridge, 1997); W. H. Kuhn, *Democratic Royalism: The Transformation of the British Monarchy, 1861–1914* (Basingstoke, 1996); J. Rendall, *The Origins of Modern Feminism: Women in Britain, France and the United States, 1780–1860* (London, 1985).

[70]K. D. Reynolds, *Aristocratic Women and Political Society in Victorian Britain* (Oxford, 1998), p. 221 concludes that aristocratic women did not operate in a 'separate sphere', nor were they rigidly defined by any notion of femininity – so intertwined were their public and private roles. Lady Bryce shared fully in her husband's travel and numerous activities.

[71]M. Taylor, 'John Bull and the Iconography of Public Opinion in England c.1712–1929', *Past & Present* 134 (February 1992), pp. 93–128.

[72]B. Harrison, *Separate Spheres: The Opposition to Women's Suffrage in Britain* (London, 1978).

[73]See essays in J. Rendall (ed.), *Equal or Different: Women's Politics, 1800–1914* (Oxford, 1987).

[74]L. Davidoff and C. Hall, *Family Fortunes: Men and Women of the English Middle Class 1780–1850* (London, 1987); J. Rendall, *The Origins of Modern Feminism: Women in Britain, France and the United States 1780–1860* (London, 1985); S. K. Kent, *Gender and Power in Britain, 1640–1990* (London and New York, 1999); D. Thompson (ed.), *Outsiders: Class, Gender and Power* (London, 1993).

however, that just as the symbolism was ambivalent, so were both men and women ambivalent about the gendered construction of the nation. In 1910 the former Conservative Prime Minister, A. J. Balfour, concluded that if there was 'no division on matters of general policy corresponding to the division between the sexes, the extension of the Suffrage would have no important effect either on legislation or administration'. Post-1919 there was a growing role for women in all of the party machines, but the *Woman's Leader* admitted in 1920 that 'women as women have no solidarity of opinion'.[75] Whether, subsequently, the first woman prime minister of the United Kingdom expressed or was still constrained by her circumstances from expressing any such solidarity remains contentious.

At a symbolic level, the mid-nineteenth-century statue at Westminster to the bellicose Queen Boadicea sits uncomfortably with the notion, to be found in some nineteenth-century literature, that the making and defending of nations was a peculiarly masculine responsibility.[76] Britannia was clearly able to look after herself. Whether Cathleen ni Houlihan (the feminine symbol of Ireland) could do so was less certain, as was whether women should take up arms to aid her It was sometimes supposed that 'Celts' were more courteous to women than 'Saxons' and that there was therefore some fundamental difference between England and the other territories but, rhetoric apart, there was little evidence to support such a contention.[77]

Gender therefore remains problematic in relation to the historiography of the British Isles. Although still outnumbered in their 'prominence' by men, women have not infrequently, in tackling such topics as politics and statecraft, normally controlled by men, indicated a personal disinclination to regard these topics as 'off limits'. 'Women's history', whether written by women or men, has established a territory of its own, though with contested boundaries. Yet the more fundamental question of the ways in which and the degree to which the national past as a whole has been historiographically gendered in the British Isles remains largely unexplored.

[75]Quotations cited in B. Harrison, *Prudent Revolutionaries: Portraits of British Feminists between the Wars* (Oxford, 1987), p. 308.

[76]I. F. W. Beckett, 'Women and Patronage in the Late Victorian Army', *History* 85, 279 (July 2000) pp. 463–80 argues that wives of four prominent soldiers played a significant role in the army's patronage system and were not confined by perceptions of 'separate spheres' and their 'incorporation' neither implied subordination nor constrained their ambition.

[77]P. Ward, *Britishness since 1870* (London, 2004), 'Gender and National Identity', pp. 37–54.

Conclusion

To conclude: ethnicity, religion, class and gender have all, to some degree, constituted Others in relation to the nation (or nations) of the British Isles in the period under review. These categories have all, though at different periods and for different purposes, attracted distinct attention from historians. Yet the narratives that have been constructed have rarely stood in direct antithesis to a historiography that was 'national'. The picture, rather, is one of a complex and shifting intertwining rather than of entrenched alternatives. The capacity and willingness to compromise, as reiterated in the master narrative of the 'constitutional nation', retold from generation to generation, was losing its grip. Except in the case of Ireland, however, it had succeeded in substantially absorbing or subordinating narratives centred on ethnicity, religion, class or gender. The fact that the constitution was not formally enshrined in a comprehensive document made it both opaque and flexible. It did represent, however, a constitutional story in which the UK was moulded according to the conventions of the English constitutional tradition as English historians had expounded it and to which historians outside England had had to adapt. Bentley argues that constitutional history, however, as a dominating historical discipline came to an end in the 1960s. This was partly a technical matter of a falling away of linguistic competence in Latin among historians. More fundamentally, however, it also yielded its supremacy before the new enthusiasm for 'social history'. It also gave way in the face of a political and historiographical mood, most strident outside England in the British Isles, which was increasingly disinclined to live in the shadow of the 'predominant partner' and its master narrative in thinking about their history. It was a shift also discernible, in relation to various periods, among historians writing in England, whether they counted themselves as English or not. How far 'New British History' (now not so new) was a response by historians to the political implications of British entry into the European Economic Community and the winding-down of the British Empire, and how far, in turn, it provided, sometimes implicitly and sometimes explicitly, a 'legitimising' underpinning of the political devolution which occurred at the end of the twentieth century, is difficult to determine. The political structure of the UK, hard though it now may be to define it, has moved beyond thinking that the English constitution offered a sufficient paradigm in considering its history.[78]

---

[78]These matters are discussed in K. Robbins, 'British History and the Generation of Change' (pp. 3–9) and by the other contributors to H. Brocklehurst and R. Phillips (eds), *History, Nationhood and the Question of Britain* (Basingstoke, 2004). J. G. A. Pocock has collected and reflected on pertinent articles he has written since 1974 in *The Discovery of Islands: Essays in British History* (Cambridge, 2005). See also Iain McLean and Alistair McMillan, *State of the Union: Unionism and the Alternatives in the United Kingdom since 1707* (Oxford, 2005).

10
Nordic National Histories

Peter Aronsson, Narve Fulsås, Pertti Haapala and Bernard Eric Jensen

At the beginning of the nineteenth century the Nordic region of Europe was governed by two large composite states. The Danish state included not only present-day Denmark, but also Norway and the two part-German duchies of Schleswig and Holstein. The kingdom of Sweden included present-day Finland. As a consequence of the Napoleonic Wars, however, these states experienced the loss of Norway and Finland respectively. Norway entered a new royal union with Sweden (1814–1905), whereas Finland became a grand duchy of the Russian Empire with a diet and government (1809–1917/18).

The Nordic countries represent the three main types of 'nation' in Europe in the nineteenth century. Denmark and Sweden had been states since medieval times; Norway was an 'historic nation' with an interrupted state history; Finland was a 'new nation' without any prior political independence. Denmark and Sweden gradually adjusted to their new borders. All these countries defined or redefined themselves as nations, trying thereby to adjust to or naturalise the new political realities. Their emerging national narratives show striking similarities in spite of the countries' highly different origins, a fact that raises the question of power of narrative strategies in relation to history proper. The history of a nation seems to have been the dominant idea, the master narrative, in Nordic historiography. Different pasts led to differences as to how the nation was to be defined, and they created different kinds of tensions within the different national histories.

In the twentieth century, experiences of war reinforced the national orientation of narratives, leaving the old conception of a common Scandinavian culture behind, except in Finland, where a cultural bulwark against the Soviet Union was in great demand. However, the narratives of a Nordic model were once again picked up in the heyday of the welfare state, and have been seen as a Nordic contribution to world history on a par with that of the Vikings a millennium earlier.[1]

Dissolving empires, emerging nations (1809–1905)

Intellectual impulses and basic concepts

One thing the four Nordic countries have had in common is the intellectual impulses that formed their historical consciousness in the nineteenth century. Their shared impulses were Germanic: Romantic, Hegelian and/or historicist. In all cases the impulses also seem to have been imported directly from Germany. Finland's 'national philosopher', J. V. Snellman (1806–81), studied in Germany and was an active proponent of Hegel. The Swedish historian E. G. Geijer (1783–1847) read both Schelling and Hegel. Denmark's anti-German national history was of an unmistakably German brand, as can be seen in N. F. S. Grundtvig's folk version of a philosophy of history, just as Norway's anti-Danish national history was: P. A. Munch quoted Niebuhr as his model and corresponded with Jacob Grimm.

The Scandinavian concept of *folk* had all the organic and teleological connotations of its German counterpart, *Volk* – a separate individuality expressing a unique folk spirit – and it became the central concept of history writing: the subject, the creator and the addressee of national histories. In Finnish the term was *kansa*, a word denoting at one and the same time nation, ethnicity and 'ordinary' people.[2] The Scandinavian *folk* have the same qualities – and ambiguities. Compared to the German *Volk* the Scandinavian concept was, however, more socially inclusive. In all four countries the national histories written from the 1830s had 'folk' in their titles: Geijer's *Svenska folkets historia* (1832–36), C. F. Allen's *Haandbog i Fædrelandets Historie med stadigt Henblik paa Folkets og Statens indre Utvikling* (1840), P. A. Munch's *Det norske Folks Historie* (1852–63), and *Oppikirja Suomen kansan historiassa* (in Swedish: *Finska folkets historia*, 1869) by Yrjö Koskinen (Georg Forsman).[3]

---

[1] Overall introductions to Nordic historiography in English include W. H. Hubbard, *Making a Historical Culture: Historiography in Norway* (Oslo, 1995); F. Meyer and J. E. Myhre (eds), *Nordic Historiography in the 20th Century* (Oslo, 2000); R. Torstendahl (ed.), *An Assessment of Twentieth-Century Historiography: Professionalism, Methodologies, Writings* (Stockholm, 2000); Max Engman, 'National Conceptions of History in Finland', in E. K. Lönnroth and R. Björk (eds), *Conceptions of National History: Proceedings of Nobel Symposium 78* (Berlin and New York, 1994), pp. 49–63; B. Stråth and Ø. Sørensen (eds), *The Cultural Construction of Norden* (Oslo, 1997).

[2] For the concept in Finnish and in Finland, see I. Liikanen, 'Kansa', in *Käsitteet liikkeessä* (Tampere, 2003), pp. 357–408.

[3] A critical reply to Koskinen by a Swedish-speaking professor was titled 'History of Finland', indicating his idea that there were two nations (*folk*) living in Finland, the Swedish and the Finnish: see M. G. Schybergson, *Finlands historia* (Helsingfors, 1887, 1889).

Behind the similarities, however, there were also significant differences in understanding the nature of a people. The Norwegian P. A. Munch made his intentions explicit in his preface:

> I have deliberately called this work the history of 'the Norwegian people', not of 'Norway', or of 'the Norwegian Empire' [*Rige*], or 'the Norwegian kings'. It was my intention to deliver as far as possible a true and complete exposition not only of the country's political or outward history, but of the people's inner history, of the people's life in its development and progress; not only of the monarchs' but also of the people's achievements.[4]

This tension and non-identity between *folk* and state was also found in Denmark. Danish history writing had traditionally had the Danish empire (*rige*), that is, the countries ruled by the Danish monarch, as its framework. Allen's history decisively challenged that tradition by having the concept of the Danish people as its overarching theme. And what constituted the Danish people, as opposed to the German citizens of the Danish state, was first and foremost language. According to this view, Denmark's natural border was between Schleswig and Holstein, not the border of the king's realm. And the establishment of a national state of Danish speakers became the conceived goal of history.

In Sweden, on the other hand, the *folk* became more or less tightly identified with the state in the narrative of leading historians. The king was seen as the primary expression of this collective being; the state was conceived as the culmination of the idea of nation. The history of the Swedish people was the history of the emergence and development of the central, royal power; it was the history of the kings, of their struggle for power, of the development of law and constitution. To Swedish historians, historical development was inconceivable without the state, long after the last officially appointed historian of the state had died, in 1834. Outside the discipline of history, however, a broad interpretation of people's lives and their history evolved through ethnological and literary enquiries into popular culture. Artefacts, habits and songs were seen as expressions of an unspoilt, primordial national culture.

Identifying national history with state history would have ruled out Finland as a member of the community of nations. In Finland 'folk culture' therefore had to take the state's place. In the eighteenth century H. G. Porthan (1739–1804) and his students (the Fennophiles) had conducted local studies, published in Latin, into the folklore, customs and habits of ordinary people,

---

[4]P. A. Munch, *Det norske Folks Historie*, Deel 1, Bind 1 (Christiania 1852), p. iv.

and this became the foundation of Finnish historiography. But well into the nineteenth century the Swedish identification of state and history still had its advocates in Finland. When Z. Topelius in 1843 posed the question: 'Do Finns have a history?' his answer had to be in the negative, because the Finns had had no state or political history of their own.[5] Many intellectuals disagreed, however, because they wanted Finland to have a history, and the publication in 1835 of the *Kalevala*, an anthology of poems drawn from heroic folklore, finally became Finland's passport to the family of civilised nations. It should be underlined that the identification of the nation with peasants and 'ordinary people' also made it possible to marginalise the linguistic differences between the Finnish-speaking majority and the Swedish-speaking inhabitants of the grand duchy. In this respect Finnish-ness became more a question of citizenship than of linguistic community. This was also due to the fact that, before the late nineteenth century, Finnish identity was primarily a creation of Swedish-speaking intellectuals, though of Finnish ethnic origin.

Origins and differentiating factors

How the *folk* were defined depended on who was perceived as the nation's Other. In Denmark it was Germany; in Sweden, Russia; in Finland, to some degree Sweden, but primarily Russia; and in Norway it was Denmark and Sweden. One result of having different kinds of enemies was that religion came to play a different role in the respective countries' self-identity. In Sweden and Finland, Lutheranism achieved a very important distinguishing quality as a result of these countries' relations with Russia. Swedish historians saw it as the destiny and mission of the Swedish state to be a Lutheran bulwark against Russian westward expansion. In Finland the Church remained Lutheran after 1809, and it became a national safeguard against the Russian Orthodoxy. Religion could not play the same distinguishing role in Denmark's rivalry with Germany or in Norway's rivalry with Denmark or Sweden. Even so, religion was an important component of national identity in all four countries. In Denmark the theologian–historian–author N. F. S. Grundtvig, who played a major role in the formation of the Danish national identity from the 1840s, saw religious and national awakening as two closely related phenomena, and joined the idea of the Danes as one of God's chosen peoples to his understanding of their particular mission in history.[6]

---

[5]For Topelius, see M. Klinge, *Idylli ja uhka: Topeliuksen aatteita ja politiikkaa* (Helsinki, 1998). For a critical analysis of the use of the *Kalevala* as evidence of the history of Finnish culture in the past, see I. Sulkunen, *Suomalaisen Kirjallisuuden Seura, 1831–1892* (Helsinki, 2004).
[6]O. Vind, *Grundtvigs historiefilosofi*, Skrifter/udgivet af Grundtvig-Selskabet, 32 (København, 1999).

None of the Nordic countries had any major religious divisions: the people constituted one Church. Therefore state, folk and religion could be more or less identified, and the churches were therefore conceived as state churches. The strength of the Lutheran identity can be illustrated by Norwegian national history. When the Reformation was introduced in Norway in 1536 it was imposed from Denmark and was accompanied by the elimination of the last remains of Norwegian independence. The last Norwegian archbishop, Olav Engelbriktsson, was also the last one who fought to uphold the power of the Norwegian 'Council of the Realm'. Even so, he never achieved the status of a hero in Norwegian national history. The concept of having missed the opportunity of becoming a Scandinavian Ireland was not entertained. Instead the Reformation was seen as inevitable, and beneficial in the long run. Although 1536 was the low point of Norwegian history, it was also a turning point. From now on Norway experienced demographic, social and economic progress, pointing inevitably towards new independence. Similar early threats to the Reformation were also part of the narrative in Denmark and Sweden, and associated again with foreign influences. In Finnish historiography the reformist Mikael Agricola became a hero, because he developed the written language of Finnish and thus combined the Lutheran Church with the idea of the Finnish people (*folk*) and their cultural identity.

The concept of the Other – external and internal – was also closely connected to ideas of origins. In all the Nordic countries the myth of a golden age of peasant freedom and equality played a crucial role. However, this myth was not an invention of the nineteenth century. In the seventeenth century it had been part of Swedish Gothicism, which linked the Nordic peoples to biblical legends and made them the foremost among Noah's descendants. In Denmark–Norway similar theories were formulated in the course of the eighteenth century, and Enlightenment thinkers such as Montesquieu and Justus Möser had also worked with a concept of Nordic freedom. Gradually it was turned into a specific Nordic-German property. Even in Finland peasant freedom seems to have been considered a Scandinavian import and not something originally Finnish: Koskinen saw 700 years of Swedish rule over Finland in positive terms because it had given the Finns Christianity and institutions based on peasant freedom.

The reception of Icelandic literature also played a significant role in the formation of this concept of the Nordic past. Danish and Swedish scholars viewed the sagas as expressions of a common Scandinavian culture. In Sweden this common past was seen as legitimising the union with Norway and paving the way for a possible expansion into the whole Nordic realm, thereby awakening memories of the medieval Union of Kalmar as a parallel to the ongoing German unification process, at the same time as meeting the possible threats to the Nordic realm from the east and the south.

To Norwegian historians, however, it became crucial to reject the notion that a common Nordic past was being reflected in Icelandic literature. For this purpose they had to develop a theory of migration.[7] This theory, based on archaeological and linguistic evidence, sought to demonstrate that the Norse tribes that had originally populated Norway (several hundred years BC) had followed a northern route from somewhere in Central Asia and had moved into an empty region. By contrast the tribes that had populated southern Scandinavia had moved into a region where other Germanic tribes were already settled, and they had had to conquer and mingle with these tribes. Norse culture, Norwegian historians asserted, was therefore the only one to survive in its pure form in the Nordic realm, and thus from the very beginning there had been three different Scandinavian nationalities. From Norway the Norse people had later colonised Iceland. The idea of a common Nordic past should therefore be considered a myth, Norwegian historians claimed, and the Icelandic sagas and the *Edda* seen only as a 'Norwegian-Icelandic' heritage, not a common Nordic one. It was similarly believed in Finland that the *Kalevala* proved that one could find an original archaic Finnish culture of eastern origin beneath the later Swedish layers. The Norwegian immigration theory was met with a hostile reaction in Denmark because it undermined the Danish claim to the existence of a clearly defined border between the realms of the Danish-Nordic and the German people. As of the 1860s, however, this theory was also abandoned in Norway,[8] and from then on theories of migration lost some of their significance in the national histories, except when marking out the origin of the Lapps and the original national appropriation of the territory after the last Ice Age. From that point the national past was extended backwards into the misty domains of prehistory, and national differences were explained as the product of a long and gradual process of interaction between the different peoples and the environments of their homelands.

Were national differences constructed in an essentialist or in a relational manner? It is not easy to give a clear-cut answer, because in the idea of *folk*, biology, or quasi-biology, politics and culture were mixed in very complex ways. We have seen that Finnish-ness was made a question of citizenship, such that political unity became more important than linguistic-cultural cleavages. At the same time the idea of the Finns having a distinct biological identity was never distant. 'Culture' was likewise a question of more than just language: it was associated with the concepts of 'national character' and

---

[7]Today's genetics dispute the migration theory. What remains unanswered is the distinctiveness of the Finnish language which belongs to the Uralian language family, as was correctly shown in the early nineteenth century.

[8]O. Dahl, *Norsk historieforskning i det 19. og 20. århundre* (Oslo, 1990), pp. 60–96.

historical destiny. The Danish–German border was not only a border between users of different languages; it was also considered a border separating one national habitus from another.

The most important distinguishing feature was history, and the national historians, particularly the historians of the new nations, were acutely aware of the hermeneutical character of their endeavour: how, by writing the nation's 'natural' history, they could contribute to the creation of the nation as a self-conscious, history-making subject. An example is the leading Norwegian historian of the late nineteenth century, Ernst Sars, who illustrated the complicated interrelatedness between 'natural', 'cultural' and 'historical' arguments. He was the first to write a comprehensive history of Norway, trying to demonstrate the unbroken continuity from the Viking era to the nineteenth century.[9] One of his main narrative strategies was to compare Norwegian, Danish and Swedish history in order to show how Norway was different from its neighbours. He claimed that these differences were ultimately rooted in nature, so that it was nature and history that had created three different Scandinavian nations. (Since Norway's written language was still Danish, he naturally played down the role of language as a differentiating factor.) Nations, he further claimed, were substantially divided: modern European nations lived together in peace, but were at the same time divided by significant differences in worldviews, preferences and characters. Primitive people, on the other hand, were divided only by superficial signs and appearances. Around the turn of the century Sars explicitly addressed the ideas of Gobineau and Chamberlain, and dismissed them on the ground that biologically or physically conceived differences had played no role in European history: the differences between Romans, Celts, Slavs and Germans were all of a historical-cultural-linguistic kind. At the same time he was convinced that mankind was divided into biologically different races, so different that they should not mingle. The Sami were seen as belonging to a different race. But how could Sars then consider Norway a homogeneous nation? This was no problem because he saw the Sami and other 'Ugrian-Chukchi' peoples as having no history, consequently they could be ignored. Thus, one can say that Denmark and Sweden here functioned as the 'significant Others' in the creation of a Norwegian historical identity. The Sami as a 'radical Other' were, on the other hand, suppressed and silenced, and by excluding them Sars did not have to confront the racist bias of his master narrative.[10] The same logic worked in Finnish historiography: it was known, or believed, that the Sami had populated the land before the Finns, but these primitive people withdrew when culture arrived and did not belong to the history of the nation.

---

[9]E. Sars, *Udsigt over den norske Historie*, 4 vols (Kristiania, 1873–91).

[10]N. Fulsås, *Historie og nasjon: Ernst Sars og striden om norsk kultur* (Oslo, 1999), pp. 99–102, 239–41.

Teleology and the internal other

Most national history writing in the nineteenth century was explicitly teleo-logical. History was considered to be incomprehensible without presupposing a purpose, goal or 'organic' development. The establishment of a peaceful world of homogeneous nation-states constituted the overarching *telos*. This implied a gendering of history whereby history was made by men, but was feminine by intent. The first step was the introduction of Christianity, which in the Nordic countries was seen as representing a feminine softening of the patriarchal, warlike, pagan spirit of the Vikings.

In Sweden, Denmark and Norway the starting point of the national master - narrative was an originally democratic society where free peasants chose their king. The people–king axis became the means of identifying the high and low points in the national history. Geijer founded a tradition in Sweden according to which the prosperous periods of national history were those during which landowning, self-governed peasants and the king had cooperated fruitfully. From a similar perspective Danish history, according to Allen, should be seen as U-shaped: starting from a high point where king and people had supported each other, and ending with those events that pointed towards a future intro-duction of a liberal constitution (that is, in 1849). In Norway national inde-pendence and the liberal constitution achieved in 1814 after 400 years of Danish rule were seen as the restoration of the freedom of medieval times. The chal-lenge during both periods was seen as being the same: to ground the state on a proper balance of power between king and people.

But how could Danish and Norwegian history, the history of an imperial power and a subjected people, of the coloniser and the colonised, employ the same narrative structure? It was achieved by making the nobility – and the Catholic Church – the internal Other in national histories of Denmark, just as it was in the Geijer version of Swedish history. The original, egalitarian Danish society had been deformed by the Church and nobility, and their hege-mony had first been challenged by the Reformation and the introduction of absolutism. Absolutism was seen as making once again all citizens equal before the law, and thereby as paving the way for the introduction of a free constitution.

In all four countries the nobility was not conceived of as being part of the *folk*. In Koskinen's Finnish history the nobility was foreign (Swedish) and it had exploited the Finnish peasantry. In Norway the nobility had been weak and unnational: it had pursued its material self-interest without regard to national concerns, and as a consequence the old Norwegian state had been taken over by its neighbours. In Denmark the nobility had repressed the ori-ginal freedom, and the nobility and Catholic hierarchy were seen as sources of unnational, particularistic policies and as vehicles of a growing foreign influence. The main impact of the Reformation had been to make the clergy again a part of the people. Sweden stood out in this respect, because the exclusion of the nobility did not occur without major protests. In response to Geijer, Anders Fryxell produced an influential narrative about the constitutional role and programme for political balance launched by the aristocracy, which caused a major debate in the 1840s whether it was justified to condemn the aristocracy and exclude them from the national narrative.[11]

In all the Nordic countries the teleological structure of the national master narrative seems to have been reformulated during the course of the nineteenth century. It moved away from a simple U-shaped model, where a democratic present was seen as being connected directly to a democratic past, towards more gradual schemes from the 1860s onwards. In Denmark it continued to be of a Germanic, idealist kind, whereas in Norway Ernst Sars, being also inspired by Buckle and Comte, preferred a rhetoric based on 'the laws of history'. He stated explicitly that teleology was a precondition for objectivity: only a historian with a firm grasp of the overall direction of history would be able to reconstruct it in a rational, objective manner by rising above the different partial perspectives. And only in light of history's development as a whole would it be possible to judge the proper role and contribution of the various historical actors. It thus maintained the concept of history as purposeful, and allowed for a more thorough integration of the various periods and forces into the master narrative. What had appeared as hindrances and repressions of nationality could be seen as having been beneficial in the longer run. In Norway the lack of a strong national nobility had made the state defenceless against Sweden and Denmark in late medieval times, but this turned out to be an asset when the age of democratic nation-states dawned. For Finland, Swedish rule had not only been oppressive, it had also prepared the ground for mature nationhood. Even Russian rule could be seen as a tool by which history separated Finland from Sweden – thereby pointing the way towards a fully independent Finnish nation-state. The words of Alexander I in 1809, when he annexed Finland to his realm, thus gained a new meaning: Finland was 'placed amongst the rank of nations'.[12]

Tensions

Behind these similarities each master narrative contained tensions that were specific to each of these countries and which sprang from their highly different pasts and their different, and arduous, roads towards a democratic present.

---

[11]A. Fryxell, *Om aristokrat-fördömandet i svenska historien jemnte granskning av tvenne blad i prof. Geijers trenne föreläsningar*, Häfte I–IV (Upsala, 1845–50).
[12]D. G. Kirby (ed.), *Finland and Russia, 1808–1920: A Selection of Documents* (London, 1975). See also Max Engman and David Kirby (eds), *Finland: People, Nation, State* (London, 1989).

In Sweden the identification of the history of the Swedish *folk* with the history of the Swedish state continued throughout the whole nineteenth century. This meant that national history remained connected to dynastic chronology and identified with political history. Two kinds of tensions played a role here. On the one hand there was a tension between an imperial perspective and a Swedish-national perspective. In a Swedish-national narrative the loss of Finland (1809) could be welcomed as a reduction of the Swedish state to 'Sweden proper', whereas in an imperial narrative it appeared very different since it indicated that the period of greatness belonged to the past. In the collectively produced *Sveriges historia från äldsta tid till våra dagar* ('The History of Sweden from the Oldest Times to the Present', 1877–81), volume 4 had the title *Sveriges storhetstid: från år 1611 till år 1718* ('Sweden's Days of Glory: From the Year 1611 to the Year 1718'), 1611 being the start of the reign of Gustav II Adolf and 1718 being the end of the reign of Karl XII. On the other hand there was also a tension between a purely political perspective and a perspective wanting to include society, culture and *folk* in the sense of 'ordinary people'. The leading historian of the late nineteenth century, Harald Hjärne, polemicised forcefully against the emerging 'cultural history', which had the effect of more or less excluding cultural history from the world of professional historiography. This gave Swedish historiography a rather conservative and exclusively academic character, which prevented academic history accommodating the growing demands of a democratic society. This is an interesting parallel to the effects of the Lamprecht controversy on German historiography. At the same time, however, in Sweden it left a space for popular amateur historians and novelists, such as August Strindberg.

It was not only professional and lay historians who wrote the master narratives. Other disciplines also played an important role, ethnology/folklore and archaeology being the most prominent. Swedish museums, such as the Nordiska muséet and the open-air Skansen, contributed, together with schools and popular culture, to the establishment of national master narratives. The role played by these cultural institutions furthered the establishment of a cultural identity with a distinct Scandinavian dimension, alive at least until 1905, when the dissolution of the Swedish–Norwegian union helped to re-establish a state-national narrative with a focus on Sweden's age of imperial greatness (the seventeenth century). Hence cultural differences within the country became depoliticised in order to further an integrative strategy, whereas in the new states of Norway and Finland the cultural heritage had to be integrated into the political and state-oriented narratives via an emphasis on either regional culture (Norway) or the state more directly (Finland). The political and social establishment in Sweden did not want to run the democratic risk of unleashing regional identification.

In Denmark things were different for two reasons. First, because of the conflict with Germany the *folk* had never become totally identified with the state: it was also defined by language. Therefore, there was a 'cultural' element present in national history from the start. Second, because Schleswig-Holstein was lost to Prussia/Austria in 1864, the Danish national framework introduced by Allen could easily become the taken-for-granted approach to Danish history. From that time academic historians began writing histories of Denmark to be read by the Danish people, and their work contributed to the maintenance and reworking of a Danish national identity. An influential example is A. D. Jørgensen's *Fyrretyve fortællinger af fædrelandets historie* ('Forty Stories of the History of the Fatherland', 1882), where the in-built teleology was directed at a future establishment of a border between Denmark and Germany in accordance with the national identities of the inhabitants of Schleswig. Around the turn of the century Danish historians published a collective *Danmarks Riges Historie* ('History of the Danish Empire', 1895–1906). This title, however, was somewhat paradoxical, since the prevailing perspective was Danish-national – that is, a history of Denmark inside those borders established in 1864. The traditional master narrative was challenged by K. Erslev, who employed a more materialist, conflict-oriented perspective, but it was not until after the First World War that this issue began to divide the history profession.

In Norway and Finland the idea of nation was founded on society and culture. The more or less imagined 'nationhood' was developed through peasant freedom, which had been preserved as the basic structure of the society. The main problem to be overcome was that because of their imperial histories the countries had become culturally divided. In Finland there was a minority of Swedish-speakers, including the nobles, most civil servants and burghers. Swedish was moreover the dominant language of administration and education until the 1880s. In Norway, Danish had become not only the written language but also the spoken language of business people and civil servants in the towns. In the countryside the peasants spoke Norwegian dialects, and during the 1850s a new Norwegian language was constructed by intellectuals with a rural-peasant background.

In both Finland and Norway these divisions resulted in different versions of national history. In Finland a straightforward Fennoman version of Finnish history was seen as too political, old-fashioned and discriminating, and was challenged both by 'Finnish-minded' historians doing 'people's history', inspired by Karl Lamprecht and German sociology, and by 'Swedish-minded' historians writing Finnish history from a Stockholm-centric perspective. Both took a more positive view on the 'Swedish period', at the same time as they identified themselves with the (imagined) Finnish state. Therefore they did not challenge the master narrative, but in contrast to the original Fennoman view insisted that Finnish national identity had to be seen as something relatively new, and should be based more on civic society and liberalism than on a conservative and loyalist mode of thinking. In Norway those historians who fought against democracy and identified themselves with the cultural heritage of the Danish period were also the ones to favour a strengthening of the union with Sweden, and they insisted that modern Norway should be seen as a result of seventeenth- and eighteenth-century developments. Those in favour of full national independence, foremost among them Sars, claimed that there was a line of continuity running from the old Norwegian kingdom through the union with Denmark and up to the present, and that such a connection had remained alive in Norwegian peasant society.

The introduction of democracy intensified these conflicts. In conjunction with the implementation of universal suffrage in Finland in 1907, which reduced the influence of the Swedish-speaking part of the population to its numerical strength, a more radical Swedish-nationalist version emerged, claiming that there were two nations in Finland. This group was partly successful in its efforts to have institutions, associations and journals divided along 'national' lines. In Norway the question was whether the linguistic-social division should be seen as a division between two nations – that is, between the descendants of the colonial power and the subjected population – or if Danish had become part of the national heritage so that the division was rather between 'two cultures' or 'two societies' within the same nation.

These questions were more or less resolved by later political developments. In Finland the struggle for democracy and the independence that was achieved in 1917 had the effect of strengthening the nationalistic Fennoman interpretation of Finnish history, with its long-term, teleological perspective. Norway's separation from Sweden in 1905 also stabilised the continuity perspective on Norwegian history. Whatever one might think of the mythical, constructed character of the national narratives, they were actually able to relate the past and the present to each other in ways that were not only perceived as meaningful, but which also appeared as realistic. The nation ended up as bilingual in both Finland and Norway: the former with Finnish-speakers and Swedish-speakers, and the latter with two written languages, New Norwegian and a 'Norwegianised' version of Danish.

The challenges of democracy and class (1905–1940)

Nordic societies modernised rapidly at the turn of the century, and it was no longer possible to write the histories of the emerging democratic societies without taking the existing class tensions into account. Social changes and conflicts were reflected in national histories. Yet, this did not amount to a serious challenge to the idea of a national history. The democratic nation-state needed an historical identity too, but the versions available had to be criticised, reworked and modified.

In all four Nordic countries a major challenge came from the labour movement and the intellectuals associated with it, some of whom were inspired by a Marxist interpretation of history. In Denmark and Norway a left-wing historiography with an emphasis on class became incorporated into the academic world, while in Sweden and Finland such approaches were rejected and expelled from an academic history which was preoccupied with the critical use of source material. Thus, in Sweden and Finland a class-based approach did not succeed in developing a new paradigm of national history. However, it was not totally absent in Sweden, but added a social dimension, especially through the new discipline of economic history. The leftist approach succeeded, however, in creating an alternative history culture among working-class people. In Finland this alternative kind of history was related to the experience of the civil war. The broader national context was not normally discussed, and if it was, the message was that a workers' history should not be excluded from the national history.

National or ethnic minorities did not become significant subjects of historical research in the Nordic countries before the Second World War. Their history was not totally neglected, but their place and role in national history was in the main ignored. That was the case with the Sami in Norway, Sweden and Finland, and the Eskimos in Danish historiography. The Sami became a subject of ethnographic research representing 'the internal Other' or 'the undeveloped' when compared to the dominant national culture and language. Though Nordic countries appeared progressive where women's rights and educational opportunities were concerned, women remained mostly absent in the academic world or were on the whole marginalised. It should, however, be mentioned that the first woman in the world to become a cabinet minister (1924) was the Danish historian Nina Bang. In Finland several women became academic historians, and one of them, Alma Söderhjelm (1870–1949), became professor of history in 1927. Those female historians with a doctorate, who specialised in 'male' subjects such as politics and technology, were accepted, but were also regarded as women with 'a man's mind'. Most women were supervised to study 'female' and less important issues of culture – history of art, manners, family and education.[13] At the same time female symbols (such as the Maiden of Finland and Mother Svea in Sweden) were actively employed by male historians and politicians in their representations of the past, especially in public history.[14]

---

[13]M. Kaarninen and T. Kinnunen, '"Hardly women at all"': Finnish Historiography Revisited', *Storia della Storiorafia*, 46 (2004), 152–70; E. Katainen et al. (eds), *Oma pöytä: naiset historiankirjoittajina Suomessa* ['A Table of One's Own: Women Writing History in Finland'] (Helsinki, 2005), includes statistical data on female students, masters, doctors and professors of history.

[14]J. Valenius, *Undressing the Maid: Gender, Sexuality and the Body in the Construction of the Finnish Nation*, Bibliotheca Historica, 85 (Helsinki, 2004).

People's history as national history

During the interwar period a significant number of national histories were published in all the Nordic countries. Some of these were conceived as 'histories
of the people' and were shaped along the lines of German *Volksgeschichte* or
Kulturgeschichte, but did not repeat their assumptions about the 'soul' of a nation.
One who played a significant role in some of the Nordic countries was the
German Karl Lamprecht, considered to be a founding father of the new cultural
history. However, many Nordic historians also found their main sources of inspiration in the other Nordic countries.

The general thrust of these national histories was to start to focus more attention on everyday life, and on the social and economic life of those classes who
together composed the common people, or now the nation. The development
story of the nation included the questions of how the Nordic countries were
populated, how modes of cultivation were spread and industries developed, and
how local communities were organised.

The character of this form of people's history varied in the Nordic countries.
During the interwar period some Danish historians began to challenge the traditional national master narrative. A major new history (*Europas Kulturhistoria*,
1928) was written by Hartvig Frisch, a socialist and later a minister. He sought
to incorporate the history of the Danes in the broader European tradition
in order to avoid a narrow national approach. The most prominent example,
however, was the history of Denmark which Erik Arup published in 1925 and
1932.[15] His approach was distinctly materialist, yet not of a Marxist kind, and
he had set himself the task of viewing the history of the peasantry as nothing
less than the backbone of Danish history: this was thus an early attempt to write
a national history viewed from below. It was not, Arup asserted, the history of
wars and kings that really counted, it was the peasants' slow, yet steady cultivation of the land and the selling and buying of goods that had made a significant difference in the long run. Arup's new history was an attempt to apply a
critical and positivist approach to Danish history, and its publication unleashed a
veritable history war in Danish society. Moreover, introducing a class perspective
on Danish history had the effect of splitting the history profession into two
opposing camps who openly fought each other for almost two decades.

In Norway the political centre of gravity in the historical profession after 1905
settled on the left of the political spectrum. The challenging of national history
on the basis of labour and class issues was personified by two of the leading historians, Halvdan Koht and Edvar Bull Sr., both of whom were labour politicians
and served as foreign ministers in Labour governments. For the younger Bull the
nation was not important: he wanted to study Norwegian 'society' rather than

---

[15]E. Arup, *Danmarks historie*, Bd. I–II (København, 1925–32).

the nation. It was symptomatic of the interests of Bull that he invited Marc Bloch and Alphonse Dopsch to Oslo in 1929 when a programme for 'Comparative studies in the cultural relations of peasant society' was to be inaugurated. Yet, despite his lack of interest in the nation, Bull ended his career as editor of a ten-volume *Det norske folks liv og historie* ('Life and History of the Norwegian People', 1930–35). Its periodisation, however, was based on a social and economic periodisation rather than on a conventional political chronology – with one significant exception, namely 1814, the year the modern nation-state came into being.

The older Koht saw it as his task to integrate nation and class, that is, Sars and Marx. He began to reinterpret medieval history in a class perspective – thereby destroying the traditional notion of solidarity between king and people – but insisted at the same time that class struggle and nation-building were not opposed processes: quite the contrary. Each time a new class had succeeded in gaining political power, the nation had become richer. The peasants had done so in the nineteenth century: now the turn had come for the working class to do something similar.[16]

In Finland cultural history achieved a strong position in the academic world without being connected to the labour movement. When the proponents of cultural history in 1904 founded the *Finnish Journal of History* (*Historiallinen Aikakauskirja*), they were inspired especially by Karl Lamprecht and Paul Barth (*Die Philosophie der Geschichte als Soziologie*, 1897). Another source of inspiration was the German historical school of economics and sociology – the works of Gustav Schmoller, Adolf Wagner, Lujo Brentano, Max Weber and Werner Sombart, who even visited Finland. But younger historians were also inspired by Finnish nationalism, and they were therefore welcomed by older professors and politicians. The new generation of historians and social scientists wanted to address the 'social question' in Finnish history. They took on a conscious role of nation-builders in the aftermath of the civil war. In the 1930s a comprehensive *Cultural History of Finland* was published. In fact it was a social history – a history of the population, industries, classes, everyday life and institutions. The last volume ('Age of Industrialism and National Rising') ends with chapters on education, civic activity and 'Finnish culture'.[17]

This history was written from the perspective of the 'people' (which in Finnish equals the 'nation'). It was a collective (holistic) history in the sense of Lamprecht attempting to fill the gap between a Finnish past without a state and the contemporary nation-state. The working class was integrated into

---

[16]O. Dahl, *Historisk materialisme: historieoppfatningen hos Edvard Bull og Ottar Dahl* (Oslo, 1974), pp. 71–9.
[17]*Suomen kulttuurihistoria*, I–IV (Helsinki, 1933–6).

the national history at the same time as it was integrated into the nation-state through reforms. One of the key figures of the Finnish school, Professor Väinö Voionmaa, was yet another Nordic cultural historian to become a minister in a national government.

The approach of cultural history broadened the subject and scope of national history, and hence redefined both actors and contexts. A typical novelty was the role of economic interest in history, but it was not understood as an outcome of man's selfish nature as in the nineteenth-century historiography, but as a normal function of social organisation and development. A similar emphasis was put on individuals and groups as actors, and on knowledge as a resource. This was clearly a self-image of the emerging modern society characterised by class divisions and social problems. Besides this more sociological approach, the new cultural history included a history of manners, feelings and cultural representations. Gunnar Suolahti, a Finnish student of Lamprecht, who was also influenced by the Danish historian T. Troels-Lund and the psychology of Wilhelm Wundt, developed a theory of cultural evolution which is surprisingly close to the analysis of the process of civilisation made by his contemporary, Norbert Elias.[18]

People's history in Sweden was of a very different kind. The field was early on dominated by histories which may be called 'popular history', namely history books written by others than professional historians and for a wide audience. Carl Grimberg's *Svenska folkets underbara öden* ('History of Sweden', 1913–24) became a best-seller. He was by training an historian, but not academically respected as a researcher. His narrative was a slightly modernised and democratised version of the old idealistic, anecdotal and state-oriented narrative. The bulk of Swedish professional historians, on the other hand, focused their work on highly specialised research. Their ideal of objective science, developed particularly by the Weibull School in Lund, was perhaps a victory for professional craftsmanship, but it also represented the eclipse of the historians' public role. Social issues and cultural studies were not totally ignored in Sweden, but they were mainly to be found outside academic history. Eli Heckscher was a professor in economics and was later given a chair in economic history. That became the starting point for a strong tradition in Sweden – economic history existed outside history departments, unlike in other Nordic countries. Cultural studies followed a similar pattern of professionalisation within such disciplines as ethnology, archaeology, cultural geography and sociology, in contrast especially to Finland, where cultural history was a joint effort of historians, social scientists, economists and ethnologists.

---

[18]For a detailed study on Suolahti, see P. Ahtiainen, *Gunnar Suolahti historiantutkijana* (Helsinki, 1991).

Another aspect of people's history was the way it was used politically. Though many historians were prominent political figures, particularly in Finland and Norway, their role in public discussion was determined by their political status, not by their scholarship. If socialist and moderate historians succeeded in launching social reforms, their rightist colleagues were more successful in influencing the public image of history. For instance, in Finland the common hostility towards Sweden and Russia gave a platform to a medieval historian, Jalmari Jaakkola, who repeated the old fantasies of the great past of Finnish peasant society. In wartime, historians 'did their bit' by writing justifications for national propaganda purposes.[19] In Denmark and Sweden a conservative nationalist historiography remained influential alongside the new cultural history. In all the Nordic countries the national master narratives had thus become politically divided.

A true novelty in the 1920s and 1930s was the rise of local history. Historical institutions (archives, museums, societies) were organised from state level to village level. There was a strong, nationally minded movement to make history everyone's property. Each family, village, community and county should write their history, and the hope was that these efforts would in the end make up a comprehensive national history. This view was shared by many academic historians too, and may be called an idea of an authentic people's history. It represented a peculiar combination of nationalism and democracy. Once again this tradition was introduced in Sweden outside the academic discipline of history, by local history societies, and was institutionalised only by a modest urban studies institute in Stockholm founded in 1919 by the Confederation of Swedish Towns. In Finland local history and traditional activities were organised on a national level. One could say that *national history was localised*, because the ideology of the movement was that the nation was a biological entity, and in the end national history consisted of the collected histories of tribes, families and individuals.

The Cold War and the welfare state (1945–72)

In the Scandinavian countries, as in the rest of Europe, the Second World War came to have a substantial impact on the national master narratives, but in different ways. Denmark and Norway could retrospectively produce a communal response to a comparatively light occupation, which in some respects strengthened the traditional master narrative. This was a more complicated issue in Finland because of its more complex experience of being aligned with

---

[19]See, among others, J. Jaakkola, *Suomen historian ääriviivat* ['Outline of Finnish History'] (Helsinki, 1940); and V. Auer and E. Jutikkala, *Finnlands Lebensraum* (Berlin, 1941).

Germany and the war with the Soviet Union (and hence the Allies). In Sweden the formal neutrality, which in reality had been an opportunistic orientation to the stronger side (first Germany and after 1943 the Allies), could not easily be used for an upsurge in national historical culture. The combination of bad conscience and rapid industrialisation prompted instead the emergence of a modernistic historical culture, underlining the difference between the past and the present.

The violence and distress of the interwar and war periods was on a general level met by a double response. The first was a return to a traditional political history, especially to medieval and early modern history, and its empiricist methodology. A greater emotional distance was created from earlier Scandinavian and European conflicts, which in turn could facilitate identification with the modern political community, at the same time as favouring a more timeless Scandinavian culture. This gave rise to the establishment of the new narrative associated with the Nordic welfare state – a model which gained international fame with *Sweden: The Middle Way*.[20]

The second response was to reinforce a social perspective on the past, through which the welfare state could be contrasted with the poverty of earlier times. Even if the same tendency also was at hand in other Nordic countries, the experiences of war and national resistance were able to feed a more positive version of the traditional master narrative in Denmark and Norway. In conclusion, there were three discernible others in the postwar historical discourses: hostile states, internal traitors and opponents of progress.

Finland had the most problematic war legacy, and the war had also to a large extent discredited the old national, Fennoman tradition of history writing. The complex experiences of civil war and the Second World War were treated only indirectly. It was done, for instance, through a discussion of the Cudgel War (*Klubbekriget*), a violent peasant rebellion in 1596–97. The first to deal directly with the history of the Second World War from the perspective of ordinary people was the author Väinö Linna. This can be considered both a symptom of and a contribution to an ongoing political marginalisation of Finnish historians, even on their home ground. Moreover, between the 1960s and the end of the twentieth century Linna's seminal contributions to the history of the civil war continue to set the agenda also for professional historians.[21]

Another symptom of the same trend was the publication of a new *Suomen historian käsikirja* ('Handbook of Finnish History', 1949). The delicate political issue of who should be responsible for editing it was solved by choosing an

---

[20]M. W. Childs, *Sweden: The Middle Way* (New Haven, CT, 1936).
[21]P. Haapala, 'Väinö Linnan historiasota', *Historiallinen Aikakauskirja* (2001), no. 1, 25–34; N-B. Stormbom, *Väinö Linna: kirjailijan tie* (Helsinki, 1963) (also in Swedish).

historian close to President Paasikivi. None of the contemporary professors was recruited. The professional historians focused their attention on meticulous research, emphasising the 'objective' nature of historical research, much as Swedish historians had done a generation earlier.

Because of Finland's delicate geopolitical situation, bordering on the Soviet Union, any controversial subjects had to be carefully scrutinised. The Swedish past could therefore become a resource also for Finnish-speaking researchers, since they wanted to emphasise the long-standing democratic and Western traditions of their fatherland.[22] The east–west conflict was toned down in favour of a more realistic-pragmatic understanding of the Soviet Union in order to achieve some degree of security.

Three different ways of handling the Danish master narrative were operative during the period 1945–72.[23] The first was an attempt to develop further Arup's approach to history. A group of young academic historians collaborated in the writing of a new popular history of Denmark – *Historikergruppens Danmarkshistorie* (1950–1) – in which they viewed Danish history as a process through which ordinary Danes had become more and more able to take responsibility for ruling their own country. Thus, the emergence of a democratically ruled nation-state was here presented as the overarching *telos* of Danish history. The second strategy sought to place Danish history in a somewhat new context. One of the aims of the next major history of Denmark – *Politikens Danmarkshistorie* (1962–6) – was to emphasise the gradual integration of Danish history into that of Europe, a process that had originally begun with the Christianisation of Denmark at the beginning of the Middle Ages, and which would be brought a decisive step closer if Denmark at some future date succeeded in joining the Common Market. Third, whereas *Politikens Danmarkshistorie* tended to stress the cooperative and harmonious nature of the Danish people, other historians began to view Danish history as being inherently conflict-ridden. At the beginning of the 1970s Niels Skyum-Nielsen, who saw himself as an upholder of the legacy left by Arup, began publishing a new history of Denmark. The aim was to bring into focus those groups that traditionally had been more or less completely left out of the standard histories of Denmark. The first volume appeared in 1971: it covered the period from 1085 until 1250 and was entitled *Kvinde og slave* ('Woman and Slave').

---

[22]Illuminating examples are popular books written by professional historians, *Suomalaisen kansanvallan kehitys* ['The Roots of Finnish Democracy'] (Helsinki, 1956); and E. Jutikkala, *Pohjoismaisen yhteiskunnan historiallisia juuria* ['Historical Roots of Nordic Society'] (Helsinki, 1965) (also in Swedish).

[23]B. E. Jensen, 'Danmarkshistorie: en genre i opløsning?', in idem et al., Danmarkshistorie: en erindringspolitisk slagmark (Copenhagen, 1997).

In Norway the war seems to have had a double impact. On the one hand it demonstrated the vulnerability of Norwegian independence, and thereby the contingent character of the nation. The last remains of national teleology had become undermined, and the national independence of 1814 had to be reinterpreted as an unexpected outcome of the Napoleonic Wars.[24] On the other hand the war also became a major source of national cohesion. The interconnectedness between liberal constitution, democracy and national independence that had characterised the events of 1814 and of 1905 had again been confirmed in 1940–45. National history had not lost its integrative capacity: where the Swedish welfare state was seen as a break with the past, its Norwegian counterpart was seen as a continuation of earlier generations' struggle for independence, democracy and social justice. As in the other Nordic countries the research ethos was underlined, but in Norway academic historians did not escape into specialised research and thereby withdraw from the public sphere. One of the foremost historians of the period, Sverre Steen, is an example. He published a multi-volume history of Norway in the nineteenth century, characterised by high standards of scholarship, dealing with politics, society and local government, and written in a highly readable, accessible and vivid prose.[25] Moreover, he addressed an even broader public in a series of radio lectures published under the romantic title *Langsomt ble landet vårt eget* ('The Country Slowly Became Our Own', 1967).

The Swedish master narrative slowly switched its focus from the Swedish state to Swedish society, and thus contributed to a merger of the two concepts. Henceforth a state-oriented history could readily be transformed into a national social history, reflecting the character of an ambitious integrative welfare state. Academic historians consequently began to move closer to contemporary society both methodologically and thematically. The history taught in schools should not be about ancient glory but should provide insight into the background to the development of the democratic system – and the totalitarian threat to it. The first – and only – significant attempt to publish a comprehensive academic history of Sweden after the Second World War was made in the 1960s. It was compiled by 98 historians who had agreed to write a consensus-oriented, richly illustrated, legitimate national history.[26] It has since been reprinted and abbreviated, but not followed up by other professional projects of this kind. On this point Swedish academic history represents the most extreme example, not only in a Scandinavian but in a European setting, of a professional group that had become extremely marginalised in

[24]J. A. Seip, *Utsikt over Norges historie*, vol. 1 (Oslo, 1974), p. 17.
[25]S. Steen, *Det frie Norge*, 8 vols (Oslo, 1951–73).
[26]S. Carlsson et al., *Den svenska historien*, Bd. I–X (Stockholm, 1966–8).

the historical culture at large. No doubt this in part had to do with Sweden's marginal position during the world wars and its progressive welfare policies. But partly it was also due to the fact that the national history mentioned had been organised thematically within larger epochal chapters, whereas the use of a chronological approach had been more pronounced in the other Nordic countries. This had furthered the production of strong chronological narratives in Denmark, Norway and Finland, where a historian had taken responsibility for a larger or a major period, whereas each Swedish scholar had a much more limited field of responsibility – which tended to undermine the idea of working within an overarching national plot, but rather regarded national history as an example of universal progress.

The presentation of a scientifically based and consensus-driven national narrative was the last time such a framework was reproduced in a naive or self-evident, hence unprecedentedly powerful, fashion, even in the context of Swedish 'unromantic nationalism'. The narrative emphasised the importance of history for understanding contemporary society, but also sought to be exciting and amusing to the general reader. Its scientific method and legitimacy were emphasised, but it also included many illustrations and made for easy reading. The format represented a compromise between market conditions and scholarly standards, yet the structure of this history was embedded in the century-old genres of topographical literature and national history. Through the frequent use of the term 'we' this history sought to appeal to a common identity and project it back in history: as the ice withdrew, our landscape had become populated by our ancestors, speaking Indo-European languages, and developing prehistoric societies. All this was presented as occurring within the setting of twentieth-century state borders, and it thereby naturalised the existence of the contemporary state and made its establishment the overarching goal of history – but without using the idealistic rhetoric of former times. Probably such a narrative was more powerful as it presented the whole history from the beginning to the present as one stressing basic continuity.

A functionalist view of society at large, influences from Anglo-American social science and an ongoing specialisation could be found throughout academic history in the Nordic countries, but this tendency was especially pronounced in Sweden with its combination of modernistic ideology and collective welfare-state solutions. On a political level history itself had become the Other, a narrative suitable mainly for highlighting the story of success brought to the nation through the successful negotiation between capital and labour, i.e. nationally oriented industrialists and the organised labour movement. The Swedish model was one example of the Nordic model – an approach which the other Scandinavian countries also subscribed to, and it could be seen as a new version of nineteenth-century Scandinavianism. 'The Other' in this perspective became continental Europe. This narrative suppressed the stories of centuries of wars and stressed the long period of peace, negotiation and democratic traditions from 1814 onwards.[27]

Academic historians had quite different positions in the Nordic countries. Swedish historians were marginalised first by their predominant affiliation to the conservative camp and later by their reluctance to participate in the production of public history, by their swift adaptation to a more analytical mode of history writing, and by preferring to communicate within the academic world rather than working as organic intellectuals. At the other extreme were the Norwegian historians who took an active part in forming public opinion. Especially in Denmark and in Sweden there was harsh criticism of the academic historians for their lack of public appeal since the times of Grundtvig and August Strindberg. In 1972 Vilhelm Moberg published *A History of the Swedish People*,[28] which represented a protest against academic historians' failure to interest themselves in the conditions and perspective of ordinary people. Parallel to this traditional contestation of academism a more profound Marxist criticism emerged, where the traditional narrative was criticised for its lack of theoretical consistency and naive objectivism. In Sweden this was done for the first time in the 1960s, while Norway had an early strand of radical history from the 1930s. In Denmark an older tradition of people's history was reinterpreted in *Dagligliv i Danmark* ('Everyday Life in Denmark, 1963–64). Such criticism of the established tradition, however, had trouble finding the source material it needed in order to write a new and revised history from below. It therefore tended to function more as a supplement rather than an alternative – filling out the gaps in the traditional national history.

National master narratives at the end of the twentieth century

During the last third of the twentieth century the cultural setting of Nordic history writing was significantly transformed by two major events. In 1972 referendums were held in Denmark and Norway on joining the European Community, but only Denmark became a member state at that point. Again in 1994 a majority of the Norwegian electorate rejected a proposal to join the European Union, whereas the electorates of Finland and Sweden opted to do so, thus making Norway the only major Nordic country to remain outside the EU. The relevance of this for the writing of history was threefold. First, the groups that were most opposed to joining the EU were also those that upheld traditional national master narratives. This history war was, however, mainly fought outside the institutions of academic history. Second, the populations

---

[27]Stråth and Sørensen, *Cultural Construction of Norden.*
[28]V. Moberg, *A History of the Swedish People* (New York, 1972).

of the Nordic countries were deeply divided when it came to identifying who or what was to be seen as the external Other when writing a national narrative. For the groups opposed to joining the EU it was mainly this union that came to represent the most powerful enemy of a national master narrative. Third, joining the EU also occasioned the publication of a series of new histories of Europe, thus establishing a new framework for the writing of national history.

In this period the Nordic countries also began to receive a significant number of immigrants and refugees from different parts of the world. The largest influx was to Sweden, the smallest to Finland. However, the political and cultural impact of such immigration was felt in all four countries. It not only occasioned – especially in Norway and Sweden – the writing of the histories of the entry of immigrants into the Nordic countries;[29] it also made it difficult to maintain the traditional notions of Denmark, Norway and Sweden as ethnically homogeneous societies, thus raising the issue of whether a future writing of history would have to be geared towards a multicultural society. During the same period there was a growing interest in the place of indigenous ethnic minorities in Nordic history, the most striking example being that of the Sami in Finnish, Norwegian and Swedish history. Other factors contributed to the transformation and pluralising of the national master narratives, most notably the growing interest in the new social history, gender history and local history. For the most part these new approaches were supplements to national history rather than challenging the key paradigms of national history.

Around 1970 the significance of local history had begun to change. Before then it had been mainly seen as part of an overarching national history; local studies had been a way of investigating at the micro-level problems of national history. After 1970 local history began to appear as an alternative to national history, since it was now being conducted for the sake of the local community and as part of local identity politics.

Women's history, having developed from the idea of an added dimension to a new paradigm of gendered history as a basic perspective on all history, has challenged the master narrative, demanding a paradigmatic shift in the Nordic countries.[30] The presence of women in history has its own history, following the waves of female emancipation. It has challenged the traditional

---

[29]K. Kjeldstadli (ed.), *Norsk innvandringshistorie*, 3 vols (Oslo, 2003); I. Svanberg and M. Tydén, *Tusen år av invandring: en svensk kulturhistoria* (Stockholm, 1998).
[30]A-S. Ohlander and U-B. Strömberg, *Tusen svenska kvinnoår: svensk kvinnohistoria från vikingatid till nutid* (Stockholm, 1996); I. Blom, 'Nationalism and Feminism in Europe', in H. Kaelble (ed.), *The European Way: European Societies during the Nineteenth and Twentieth Centuries* (Oxford and New York, 2004); I. Blom and S. Sogner (eds), *Med kjønnsperspektiv på norsk historie: fra vikingtid til 2000-årsskiftet* (Oslo, 1999/2005); A. Ljungh, *Sedd, eller osedd? Kvinnoskildringar i svensk historieforskning, mellan åren 1890 till 1995* (Lund, 1999).

master narrative, but is still most often integrated into it in various ways. In Finland *The Lady with the Bow* and many detailed studies have represented women as major contributors to civic society and hence of *national history and modernisation*. The role of modern women is associated with a centennial myth of the existence of a strong and free Nordic Woman. In Norway leading women's/ gender historians have produced a national history from a gender perspective. The major contribution of women's history in Scandinavia has not been to split national history (not even gendered reality), but to show how import- ant the birth of female citizenship has been for Nordic societies and their self-image – including history.[31]

There has been a notable difference between Sweden on the one hand, and Denmark, Finland and Norway on the other, when it comes to writing multi- volume national histories for a larger public. Academic historians or publish- ing houses in Sweden have not involved themselves in such a project, and it has thus been left to other professional writers to produce all-round histories of Sweden. The main reason why Swedish academic historians shunned such projects was a wish not to get involved in contemporary identity politics. This unwillingness stands in sharp contrast to their willingness to participate in rehabilitating less privileged groups. One might even say that the national inte- grative project changed from a focus on territory to groups such as workers, women, minorities and ethnic groups. The national ideology even in national cultural politics is identified as the Other, which should be met by empowerment of the local, regional and various group identities. Here, too, Sweden stands out among its Nordic neighbours and in its relationship with its public. Once again there are other, more traditional demands feeding the national response to inter- national and European challenges: the largest modern museum project, The Swedish History, was undertaken in the 1990s without professional historians being (invited to be) active participants.

In Denmark, Finland and Norway, however, the well-established tradition that academic historians cooperated in the writing of national histories has been upheld during the latter part of the twentieth century.[32] Yet, it is worth noting that the concept of *folk* which earlier played a very prominent role in the national master narratives no longer figured in the titles or subtitles of new national histories. This can be taken as indicating a change in the way national histories function in the context of contemporary identity politics. In

---

[31]P. Setälä and M. Manninen (eds), *The Lady with the Bow: The Story of Finnish Women* (Helsinki, 1990); Katainen et al., *Oma pöytä*; A. Wallette, *Sagans svenskar: synen på vikingati- den och de isländska sagorna under 300 år* (Malmö, 2004).
[32]K. Mykland (ed.), *Norges historie*, 15 vols (Oslo, 1976–80); K. Helle et al. (eds), *Aschehougs norgeshistorie*, 12 vols (Oslo, 1994–8).

contrast to what was happening in the first two-thirds of the twentieth century, academic historians no longer assume that the populations of Denmark, Finland or Norway can be considered as ethnically homogeneous. The traditional master narratives have been modified in other ways too. The new multi-volume national histories have frequently been the outcome of cooperation between a number of academic historians, each of whom was given significant freedom to shape the narrative structure of their own particular volume – thereby producing a national history in which there is no or little inner narrative coherence. There have even been instances where the periodisation of the history of the nation was completely arbitrary, and in such instances the maintenance of the framework of a national master narrative has become nothing more than an empty shell. This trend has been more marked in Denmark than in Finland and Norway.

Between 1965 and 2000 Finnish history was rewritten in dozens of major works from a revisionist perspective, especially exposing the national biases in the treatment of Sweden and Russia. The most important cases have been the reinterpretations of the civil war, the Second World War and the Russian period (1809–1917), which in current historiography is seen as a period of economic and social progress, a precondition of independence and the welfare state, and not as a period of Russian repression.[33] National history continues to be written from the perspective of a nation, but it is pursued in a more reflexive way than before.

It is only in Denmark that academic historians have begun to write what appear to be unequivocal counter-histories to the national master narratives. In 1996 Søren Mørch published *Den sidste Danmarkshistorie* ('The Last History of Denmark'), a history of the Danish nation-state beginning in 1848-9/1864 and ending in the last quarter of the twentieth century. The purpose of writing it was to explain to a Danish reading audience why it was no longer possible to write a national master narrative of Denmark. It had to be seen, it was pointed out, as a genre which now belonged to a bygone period. This frontal attack on the national master narrative was later followed up by Michael Bregnsbo and Kurt Villads Jensen's *Det dansk imperium: storhed og fald* ('The Danish Empire: Its Greatness and Decline', 2004). The history of Denmark until 1864 was not seen as a history of the Danish people, but of the Danish Empire and consequently as the history of a conglomerate state, and the history of Denmark between

---

[33]Especially interesting – and now largely accepted – is the reinterpretation of the nature of the Finnish state in the nineteenth century by O. Jussila and M. Klinge. See Osmo Jussila, *Maakunnasta valtioksi: Suomen valtion synty* (Porvoo, 1987), and *Suomen suuriruhtinaskunta, 1809–1919* (Helsinki, 2004); M. Klinge, *Keisarin Suomi* (Helsinki, 1997) (also available in Swedish). There is a wide consensus that Finland really was part of Sweden for 700 years and not a semi-independent proto-state.

1864 and 1973, when the population of the Danish state was ethnically homogeneous, was thus presented as the exception rather than the rule.

Conclusions

In very broad terms we may conclude that in all the Nordic countries the master narrative of historical representation has been an idea of the history of a nation. Historiography first flourished together with the rise of nationalism and nation-building. The twentieth century saw a more pragmatic and democratic attitude to the past. History was used to legitimise the ideas of Nordic democracy and the welfare state. It was therefore self-evident that national history became the history of all the people. Nordic historiography has always had an integrative task. This has led to the overemphasising of the homogeneity of society and the uniformity of historical experience. This may distinguish the Nordic countries from larger states and from oppressed nations. Nordic historiography strikingly often represents the past as a nation's success story – in the case of Finland a story of survival. This tone of history writing has allowed historians to concentrate more on the positive distinctiveness of their own nation and less on defining identity through the enemy.

Although the last decades of the twentieth century saw a disintegration of national history, it is striking how willingly the new social history, revisionist political history and women's history wanted to be integrated into the national history. Maybe that is the only possibility in a small – and equal – society which wants to safeguard its political consensus and identity.

The role of academic historians certainly varied in how they participated in creating Nordic understanding of history. In Sweden and Finland historians had more 'difficulties' in constructing a stable national master narrative, but for rather different reasons: Finland because of its stateless past and wartime experiences, Sweden because of its imperial past and difficulties in connecting this to a social-democratic present. The trouble for Sweden had started in the nineteenth century with the unresolved tension between a state/imperial and a national perspective. This was only solved when historians opted to become advocates of a self-sufficient research paradigm, underlining the discontinuity between past and present, and leaving living history to cultural heritage institutions, non-professional historians, television and other disciplines to produce national master narratives. Denmark adjusted earlier and more decisively to a new national framework in the wake of the collapse of the conglomerate Danish state in 1864. Since the 1970s the national framework has lost most of its former influence. In Norway the tradition of national history seems to have been the most continuous and least interrupted of Nordic countries. With a new liberal-democratic centre of gravity it has been able to serve as an integrative framework for understanding the country's modernisation over the

282 Peter Aronsson, Narve Fulsås, Pertti Haapala and Bernard Eric Jensen

last 200 years, and it has not had to meet the challenge of membership of the European Union. Creating an historical identity in a globalising context seems to be difficult in all the Nordic countries without also abandoning the idea of Nordic particularism. On the other hand, the example of the Nordic countries shows that the role of academic historians can be important in the construction of national identity.

11
Weak and Strong Nations in the Low Countries: National Historiography and its 'Others' in Belgium, Luxembourg and the Netherlands in the Nineteenth and Twentieth Centuries

Marnix Beyen and Benoît Majerus

During the Second World War, the most prominent historians in the Netherlands and Belgium decided to start a close collaboration with the aim of publishing a large-scale history of the Low Countries, which was to become the reference work in this field for several decades. In the history of national history writing, the project had a somewhat ambiguous character. On the one hand, it was a product of the feverish quest for national roots which began to express itself during the Second World War in both countries (and made publishers bold enough to risk such an undertaking); on the other hand, the choice of 'the Low Countries' as a geographical circumscription was a result of these historians' wish to break the chains of traditional, 'state-nationalistic' historiography. As such, it seemed at first sight to legitimise the new transnational entity which came into being during this period in the form of Benelux.

The undertaking resulted in the prestigious *Algemene Geschiedenis der Nederlanden*, which was published in twelve volumes between 1949 and 1958. Without a doubt, it remained the most important history of the Low Countries until the publication of the second edition in the late 1970s. From the outset, it was clear that this was not a genuine Benelux historiography, as the territory of Luxembourg, which had been part of 'the Low Countries' for centuries, was not systematically integrated into the narrative. Only the second edition included a short chapter on Luxembourg, written by Albert Calmes.

Regardless of this omission, the *Algemene Geschiedenis der Nederlanden* was soon under attack for offering 'two parallel national histories' rather than one integrated history of a 'transnational context'. A closer analysis of this lengthy work suggests that the tendency to remain within the boundaries of traditional national historiography pertained more to the Dutch than to the Belgian collaborators.[1]

This conclusion might, at first sight, appear to be surprising. During the early decades of the independent existence of the Dutch and Belgian nations, it seemed that the telling of national histories would be much easier for Belgian than for Dutch historians. The enthusiasm that was aroused by the Belgian Revolution was translated into a fairly coherent master narrative on national history. In this narrative Belgian history was presented as one long struggle to protect the medieval liberties of the Flemish and Brabant cities against the subsequent foreign conquests to which the country was subjugated. The Belgian Revolution appeared in this view as the final battle, in which this secular history had come to an end.[2]

In the Netherlands the revolution of 1830 was a traumatic experience far more than an occasion for self-glorification. It, therefore, implied a thorough rereading of the national past. On the one hand, it freed the Dutch from the need to give historical meaning to the United Kingdom of the Netherlands as it had been created in 1815, and therefore enabled them to return to the seventeenth century, the golden age of the Dutch republic, as an historical point of reference. On the other hand, they needed to come to terms with the fact that the glory of that golden age had now vanished, and that the Netherlands had definitively reverted to the position of a small nation.[3] This could result either in nostalgic reminiscences of seventeenth-century culture and society (combined with urges to restore this time of greatness) or in very critical enquiries into where it had all gone wrong. In particular, the confederalist state structure of the seventeenth century and the endless religious quarrels were blamed for the decline.[4] It was

---

[1] For the genesis of this project and for the critique it prompted, see J. Tollebeek, 'Uitgedaagd door historische gebondenheid: de belangstelling voor de (Noord-)Nederlandse geschiedenis in het Belgische onderwijs en onderzoek', in J. Tollebeek, *De ijkmeesters: opstellen over de geschiedschrijving in Nederland en België* (Amsterdam, 1994), pp. 17–35; M. Beyen, *Oorlog en Verleden: nationale geschiedenis in België en Nederland, 1938–1947* (Amsterdam, 2002), pp. 407–9.

[2] See J. Stengers, 'Le Mythe des dominations étrangères dans l'historiographie belge', *Revue Belge de Philologie et d'Histoire*, 59 (1981), 382–401; J. Tollebeek, 'Historical Representation and the Nation-state in Belgium, 1830–1850', *Journal of the History of Ideas*, 59 (1998), 329–53; E. Peeters, *Het labyrint van het verleden: natie, vrijheid en geweld in de Belgische geschiedschrijving, 1787–1850* (Leuven, 2003). This last author, however, stresses that the enthusiasm of the Romantic historians barely veiled a deeper sense of unease about their own time.

[3] See P. B. M. Blaas, 'De prikkelbaarheid van een kleine natie met een groot verleden: Fruins en Bloks nationale geschiedschrijving', *Theoretische Geschiedenis*, 9 (1982), 271–303.

[4] See P. B. M. Blaas, 'Het karakter van het vaderland: vaderlandse geschiedenis tussen Wagenaar en Fruin (1780–1840)', *De burgerlijke eeuw: over eeuwwenden, liberale burgerij en geschiedschrijving* (Hilversum, 2000), pp. 365–89.

not until the last decade of the nineteenth century, when the Netherlands experienced a 'second golden age', that a positive continuity between a great past and a great present could be restored.

But even if Belgian nationalism in the nineteenth century was more optimistic than its Dutch counterpart, it was no less problematic. Beneath the appearances of triumphalism a whole range of paradoxes seemed, much more than was the case in the Netherlands, to threaten the unity of the Belgian nation and its past. These paradoxes came to the fore during the first decades of the twentieth century, when the Ghent historian Henri Pirenne published his seven-volume *Histoire de Belgique*. Even if this *magnum opus* was internationally praised as a masterpiece and a model for other national histories, in Belgium itself its reception and legacy turned out to be extremely divisive – as we shall see. The great synthesis of Dutch history which appeared about that same time, P. J. Blok's *Geschiedenis van het Nederlandse Volk*, enjoyed the opposite reception: among historians, it was generally seen as a failed attempt to put Blok's own ideas about 'social history' into practice, but it nonetheless soon became the nearly undisputed point of reference in the conceptualisation of the Dutch national past.[5]

Whereas writing on the national past in Belgium turned out to be a potentially disruptive undertaking, in the Netherlands it fulfilled the unifying and pacifying role that Blok, like his predecessor and tutor Robert Fruin, attributed to it. Probably it was precisely that difference which accounted for the varying engagement of Dutch and Belgian historians in the *Algemene Geschiedenis der Nederlanden*. But even today, this difference seems to influence the way in which Dutch and Belgian historians tackle their national pasts.

In this chapter we will argue that this difference can be explained by the fact that in the history of national historiography in Belgium, the concurrence of alternative structuring principles has always been much stronger than in the Netherlands. We will illustrate this by dealing with the various Others as defined in the research programme. If the Grand Duchy of Luxembourg does play a rather secondary role in this chapter, this is not so much due to its size as to the totally different status of national history writing. First of all, a genuinely academic tradition of history writing did not exist until 2003, when the University of Luxembourg was created. In the context of this chapter, it is even more important to note that another precondition for writing national history, a national consciousness, seems to have been absent during much of the period considered in this chapter. Until the second half of the nineteenth century, few people in Luxembourg and even fewer outside believed in the

---

[5]J. Tollebeek, *De toga van Fruin: denken over geschiedenis in Nederland sinds 1860* (Amsterdam, 1990), pp. 93–5.

future of the country as an autonomous nation-state. There was not even a proto-nationalist current in the grand duchy. This was probably due to the political arrangement of the Congress of London of 1839. According to this, the ancient duchy was divided into two, one of which became a Belgian province, whereas the other became a semi-autonomous entity in union with the Netherlands: the King of the Netherlands was also Grand Duke of Luxembourg.

Hence, the grand duchy was detached from its ancient Southern Netherlandic set of references and set within an Orangeist framework. Even if none of the nineteenth-century Dutch monarchs showed much interest in Luxembourg, intellectuals such as Mathieu Lambert Schrobilgen and Jean Joris stayed within an Orangeism that retarded the development of an autonomous national historio-graphy.[6] The international crises of 1867 and 1870 bore witness to an awakening of a national awareness. It was only with the accession of a distinct branch of the Nassau dynasty in 1890, and the subsequent recognition of Luxembourg as an independent state, that historians partially liberated themselves from Orangeism. Within the discourse they developed on Luxembourgian national history, the theme of foreign domination became a classic element.

If the Grand Duchy of Luxembourg appears to be a separate case, it does nonetheless bear similarities to both Belgium – in terms of its Catholic roots and position straddling the linguistic frontier – and the Netherlands, in its dynastic ties and relatively late industrialisation. For this reason, it seems rele-vant to include Luxembourg within this comparative overview of the national historiography of 'the Low Countries'.

National histories and the confessional struggles of the nineteenth century

According to the generally accepted view, both Belgium and the Netherlands, in the course of the nineteenth century, were 'pillarised' – that is, divided along religious lines. A closer look, however, reveals that the character of the clerical-political struggle was totally different in the two countries. In the Netherlands, society had been characterised since the seventeenth century by a true religious diversity in which a highly heterogeneous (and to a certain degree secularised) Protestant majority lived with a large Catholic minority. The different religious groups strove for political and social recognition, but could never hope to become the sole political force dominating the Dutch

---

[6]C. Huberty, 'La Vie politique du XIXe siècle dans l'historiographie: bilan et perspectives', unpublished paper presented at the Premières Assises de l'historiographie luxembourgeoise, 10 December 2005.

state. Among the political and intellectual elites of the different groups, the quest for consensus and harmony overruled the religious battles.

Belgium, on the contrary, did not have a tradition of religious plurality, and therefore the process of 'pillarisation' was not so much the result of a search for balance between these groups. It was traditionally a homogeneously Catholic country, in which a struggle between two opposing ideals of state-building clashed directly: those who wanted to maintain the Catholic Church as a dominant political force were confronted with the advocates (often Catholic churchgoers themselves) of a clear separation between church and state. Pillarisation in Belgium, therefore, was a political battle between clericals and anti-clericals rather than a segmentation between different religious groups.

In both Belgium and the Netherlands the 'culture wars' between the religious groups implied diverging interpretations of the national past,[7] and prominent intellectuals within each were often historical narrators. For the representation of the national past, however, the aforementioned structural difference between the social–religious cleavages was crucial. Even if religious diversity in the Netherlands was more important than in Belgium, the accounts these different groups gave of national history were much more complementary than those of clericals and anti-clericals in Belgium.

The Dutch Catholics did in some instances fundamentally challenge the traditional Protestant account of historical facts. Thus, during the nineteenth and early twentieth centuries, they often referred to the episode of the 'martyrs of Gorcum', a group of monks crudely put to death by the so-called Watergeuzen (Protestant troops operating by water) in order to expose the excesses of the Dutch Revolt. Nevertheless, Dutch Catholics were not in favour of the sanctification of these martyrs in 1867, because they did not want to offend the Protestant majority.[8] Rather than fundamentally trying to change the dominant vision of national history, Dutch Catholics either reinterpreted the traditional narrative or tried to extend its boundaries in such a way that Catholic elements could be included.[9] Illustrative of this first strategy was the emphasis put by Catholic historians and intellectuals on the Erasmian rather than Protestant ideals of the Netherlands' central national hero, William of Orange. By doing

---

[7] From this we exclude the writing of the history of their own emancipating movement, as exercised among all the social-religious groups that are described here.

[8] H. de Valk, 'Nationale of pauselijke helden? De heiligverklaring van de martelaren van Gorcum in 1867', *Trajecta*, 6 (1997), 139–55.

[9] This view is corroborated by the recent biography of one of the most important nineteenth-century Catholic historians of the Netherlands, W. F. J. Nuyens: A. van der Zeijden, *Katholieke identiteit en historisch bewustzijn: W.F.J. Nuyens (1823–1894) en zijn 'nationale' geschiedschrijving* (Hilversum, 2002).

so, they felt entitled to participate fully, in 1933, in the great national celebrations surrounding the commemoration of William's 400th birthday.[10] Another instance of this strategy can be found in the efforts by Catholic intellectuals to direct the focus towards the conversion to Catholicism of the Netherlands' outstanding seventeenth-century poet, Joost van den Vondel.[11]

The second strategy mainly consisted of refocusing attention from the seventeenth century to the Middle Ages.[12] This, however, implied less a rejection of the Dutch nation as such than a rereading of its origins. The promotion of St Willibrord, the early medieval evangeliser of the Low Countries (and, therefore, a pre-Reformation figure), as a national hero was a clear manifestation of this 'widening' of the national historical narrative.[13] This extension of the national narrative was sympathetically received by Protestant historians (such as Johan Huizinga) even before the Second World War, and after the war gained full academic acceptance in the view of those historians who considered the bishopric of Utrecht (founded by Willibrord) as the prefiguration of the (northern) Netherlands.[14] On the other hand, the history professors appointed in 1922 at the newly founded Catholic University of Nijmegen turned out not to be active promoters of this medievalisation of the national past. One among them, J. D. M. Cornelissen, even dedicated important contributions to central icons of the liberal Protestant master narrative, such as Rembrandt and Johan De Witt.[15]

Even more than the Catholics, the so-called orthodox Protestants based their critique of the liberal Protestant model on a specific view of national history. In the work of their founding father, Guillaume Groen van Prinsterer,

[10]P. B. M. Blaas, 'Tussen twee herdenkingsjaren (1884–1933): het beeld van Willem van Oranje in de wetenschappelijke geschiedschrijving rond 1900', in E. O. G. Haitsma Mulier and A. E. M. Janssen (eds), *Willem van Oranje in de historie: vier eeuwen beeldvorming en geschiedschrijving* (Utrecht, 1984), pp. 137–60.

[11]See most recently M-T. Leuker, *Künstler als Helden und Heilige: nationale und konfessionelle Mythologie im Werk J.A. Alberdingk Thijms (1820–1889) und seiner Zeitgenossen* (Münster, 2001).

[12]P. Raedts, 'Katholieken op zoek naar een Nederlandse identiteit, 1814–1898', *Bijdragen en de Mededelingen betreffende de geschiedenis van de Nederlanden*, 107 (1992), 713–725; P. Raedts, 'Tussen Rome en Den Haag: de integratie van de Nederlandse katholieken in kerk en staat', in H. te Velde and F. Verhage (eds), *De eenheid en de delen: zuilvorming, onderwijs en natievorming in Nederland 1850–1900* (Amsterdam, 1996), pp. 29–44.

[13]Beyen, *Oorlog en Verleden*, pp. 67–8.

[14]See, among others, B. H. Slicher van Bath, 'Herschreven historie' [written 1945], *Herschreven Historie: schetsen en studiën op het gebied van der middeleeuwse geschiedenis* (Leiden, 1949), pp. 1–14, and, more elaborately, Jonathan Israel, *The Dutch Republic: Its Rise, Greatness and Fall, 1477–1806* (Oxford, 1995).

[15]J. D. M. Cornelissen, *Rembrandt: de eendracht van het land. Een historische studie* (Nijmegen, 1941); J. D. M. Cornelissen, *Johan de Witt en de vrijheid: rede uitgesproken op den 22sten dies natalis der R.K. universiteit te Nijmegen op 17 Oct. 1945* (Nijmegen, 1945).

historical research and political action were inextricably intertwined. Whereas the Catholic view of Dutch history had to be seen as an attempt to divert attention from the golden age, Groen's 'anti-revolutionary' view consisted, on the contrary, of an over-accentuation of the sixteenth and seventeenth centuries in the history of the nation. Structurally, therefore, it fitted well in the predominant master narrative. In Groen's interpretation, however, the Dutch glory of the seventeenth century was much less a triumph of tolerance and freedom than one of Calvinism. The success of the Dutch Revolt was described as proof that the Netherlands was a chosen nation, and Groen's sympathies lay unequivocally with those who had understood this fundamental truth: the Orange stadtholders and the Calvinist party. The so-called Statist party, on the contrary, was considered to have betrayed the national cause.

However antithetical this view was to the dominant master narrative, the bridges between them were never entirely burnt. Once more, reconciliation between them appeared to be possible through a common positive assessment of William of Orange. His biography allowed him to be considered as both a Calvinist revolutionary and an Erasmian reconciler, which enabled different religious groups to value him as the 'Father of the Fatherland'. The academically outstanding biography written in 1933 on the occasion of William's 400th anniversary, by the prominent Calvinist historian A. A. van Schelven, seemed to complete this process of reconciliation.[16] During that same period, however, orthodox Protestant and Catholic historians grew closer to each other in their struggle against what they considered to be the 'secularisation' of national history by liberal historians. Thus the dual antithesis between Protestant and Catholic, on the one hand, and between confessional and secularised, on the other, seemed to neutralise each other, and to facilitate the triumph of a pacifying interpretation of national history. This became particularly clear during the early days of the Second World War, when historians from the different groups tried to bolster the national mood by writing popularising national histories.[17]

Even if the dreams that were cherished by many historians during the war to 'de-pillarise' national historiography were not realised after the Second World War, the religious cleavages did not threaten the national master narrative.[18]

---

[16]A. A. van Schelven, *Willem van Oranje: een boek ter nagedachtenis van idealen en teleurstellingen* (Amsterdam, 1933).

[17]A good example is *Nederland, erfdeel en taak*, written in 1940 by the liberal historian Pieter Geyl, the orthodox Protestant historian A.A. van Schelven, the Catholic philosopher and historian Frederik Sassen and the liberal Protestant theologian Hendrik Kraemer. See, on the genesis and content of this book, Beyen, *Oorlog en Verleden*, pp. 74–5.

[18]See P. B. M. Blaas, 'Nederlandse geschiedschrijving na 1945', in W.W. Mijnhardt (ed.), *Kantelend geschiedbeeld: Nederlandse historiografie sinds 1945* (Utrecht/Amsterdam, 1983), pp. 9–47.

290 Marnix Beyen and Benoît Majerus

Histories written by Catholic and orthodox Protestant historians seemed to differ from those of their liberal counterparts only in terms of the attention they paid to the role of their own group in history. Only in the 1990s, with the accession of a new generation to the history chairs of Dutch universities, did even this difference seem to vanish.

In Belgium, on the contrary, the confessional tensions were soon translated into two separate master narratives of national history. The abovementioned account of the continuous struggle for freedom from foreign domination became a liberal, and therefore anti-clerical, monopoly. Since most of these foreign rulers had been Catholic monarchs, nineteenth-century Catholic historians were not keen to adopt this theme. The interpretation of the Dutch Revolt of the sixteenth century became one of the main battlefields where the Catholic and the liberal interpretations of the national past clashed.[19] While for the liberals sixteenth-century Protestantism was one of the main manifestations of the Belgian sense of freedom, the Catholics blamed it for having uprooted the Catholic character of the Belgian people (the origins of which they retraced to the early evangelisation of the country in the first centuries after the fall of Rome).[20] Protagonists in this battle, such as William of Orange and Marnix of Saint-Aldegond, were easily depicted as the devils in disguise.

The glorious rebirth of Catholic Belgium was situated by these Catholic historians during the reign of the Catholic Archdukes Albert and Isabella (1598–1621).[21] They had reigned over a pseudo-autonomous satellite state, and had made the Southern Netherlands into an epicentre of the Counter-Reformation. The two centuries of (first Spanish, then Austrian) Habsburg rule were seen by Catholic historians less as a period of foreign domination than as an epoch of sincere Catholic life. The only foreign domination that was recognised as such by the Catholic historians was that of the French revolutionaries (1794–1814), and the only modern revolt they glorified was the armed resistance, in 1798, of large parts of the Belgian countryside against the secularising and centralising policies of the French. It was with much more unease that the liberals gave to that same *Boerenkrijg* a place in their narrative about the succession of struggles for freedom. Only in periods when Belgium was

---

[19]See, for example, U. Vermeulen, 'Katholieken en liberalen tegenover de Gentse Pacificatiefeesten (1876)', *Handelingen der Maatschappij voor Geschiedenis en Oudheidkunde te Gent*, nieuwe reeks, 20 (1966), 167–85; H. Verschaffel, 'Marnix van Sint-Aldegonde, een symbool in de clerico-liberale strijd', *Spiegel Historiael*, 20 (1985), 190–95.
[20]See, for example, L. Van der Essen, *Le Siècle des saints (625–739): étude sur les origines de la Belgique chrétienne* (Brussels, 1943).
[21]See, for example, D. Diagre, 'Aartshertog Albrecht, modelheerser of engel des doods?', in A. Morelli (ed.), *De grote mythen van België, Wallonië en Vlaanderen* (Brussels, 1996), pp. 107–18.

threatened anew by French imperialism, notably during the reign of Napoleon III, did this reticence truly vanish.[22]

The liberal constitution of 1830 appeared in this Catholic picture not as the ultimate climax of the struggle for freedom, but only as an instrument to safeguard the Catholic 'national character' of Belgium against the Protestant despotism of William I. Much more than these constitutional rules (which, according to Catholics, were misused by the liberals to secularise Belgium), however, Catholics trusted the 'good monarchs', in the past and in the present, as guarantors of the Catholic integrity of the country.[23]

During the first decades of the twentieth century, this gap between the Catholic and the liberal vision of the national past was partly overcome, at least at the level of academic historiography. The 'scientification' of historiography was carried out by both liberal and Catholic historians, who found common ground in their quest for historical objectivity. Whereas the professor of national history in the French-speaking part of the Catholic University of Leuven, Charles Terlinden, stuck until after the Second War to his Catholic and fiercely monarchical view of the national past, his counterpart in the Dutch-speaking part, Léon Van der Essen, was a great admirer of the liberal Pirenne (who himself was a pupil of the ultramontane Catholic historian Godefroid Kurth). Even then, however, their respective views on national history remained largely coloured by their confessional backgrounds. Van der Essen's *magnum opus*, for which he was honoured with a laudatory foreword by Pirenne himself, dealt with Alexander Farnese, the military and political leader who was responsible for the fact that the Southern Netherlands had remained under the wings of Spain's Catholic monarch.[24]

During the second half of the twentieth century even this difference disappeared, although in the choice of topics the difference between historians of the Catholic universities (Leuven and Louvain-la-Neuve) on the one hand, and those of the state universities (Ghent, Liege) and of the 'liberal' universities (Brussels) on the other, remains important today. This evolution, however, was not only due to the diminished importance of the religious quarrels, but also to the fact that Belgian historians lost their appetite for national history. This in turn can be explained by the challenges which class and ethnicity as conceptual structuring devices for history mounted against national history.

---

[22]L. François, *De Boerenkrijg: twee eeuwen feit en fictie* (Leuven, 1998).

[23]See, among others, M. Beyen, 'Belgium: A Nation that Failed to Become Ethnic', in L. Eriksonas and L. Müller (eds), *Statehood before and beyond Ethnicity: Minor States in Northern and Eastern Europe* (Brussels, 2005), pp. 341–52.

[24]L. Van der Essen, *Alexandre Farnèse, prince de Parme, gouverneur général des Pays-Bas (1545–1592)*, 5 vols (Brussels, 1933–7).

As for the importance of Catholicism, the situation in Luxembourg was quite similar to that in Belgium, but the discursive power of the Catholic Church had been and still is far stronger. The anti-clerical movements had far more problems to produce an independent and audible narrative. In Luxembourg, even laicistic historians consider Catholicism as an essential component of national identity. The importance of Catholicism was often stressed as a positive force in the context of nation-building.[25] The religious minorities (Protestants and Jews) never tried (or failed) to offer a different version of history, their communities being far too small. Neither were anti-clerical movements such as the liberals or the socialists strong enough to enforce a competitive model. Even if Luxembourgian society is largely secularised today, there is still no coherent 'History of Luxembourg' with a critical apprehension of the role of the Catholic Church.[26]

Materialism and idealism: class as a variable threat

Just as the character of the confessional battles differed strongly in the three countries, the same can be said about the social struggle. Since Belgium was touched earlier and more fundamentally by large-scale industrialisation, and since this industrialisation was more strongly situated in heavy industry, socialism took shape at an earlier date, too. Being rooted in the experience of industrial labour (even if the first promoters of socialist ideals were bourgeois intellectuals rather than proletarians) made it very receptive to Marxist influences. This openness to Marxism was even enhanced by the fact that socialism in Belgium had to take its place in the existing antithesis between clericals and anti-clericals. Almost automatically, the socialist movement was embraced by the anti-clerical 'pillar'. Within this anti-clerical pillar, even among progressive liberal intellectuals, Marxism became a respectable line of thought.

In the Netherlands, on the contrary, the socialist movement was not only weaker (it would send its first representatives to Parliament only during the First World War), but it was also much less influenced by Marxism, or even by a strong class consciousness. If grassroots militancy by industrial factory workers did exist, Dutch socialism was dominated by intellectuals enamoured

---

[25]*Nos Cahiers*, 12/1 (1991): thematic edition dedicated to the relation between Catholicism and Luxembourg, with articles among others by P. Dostert, P. Margue and G. Trausch. *Nos Cahiers* is a Catholic cultural journal. Future studies will have to answer the question of whether the Catholic Church was not partly a counter-power to the nation-state in the nineteenth century. The above-mentioned conclusions are in any case much more valid for the twentieth than for the nineteenth century.

[26]After 1945 Luxembourgian historiography was largely dominated by generations of historians who can be more or less related to the Catholic milieu.

by the dream of reforming the whole of society without taking class consciousness as a starting point. Religious utopianism rather than fierce anticlericalism dominated the discourse of these intellectuals.

The implications of this difference for the way in which national historiography was conceptualised were immense. For one thing, Belgian socialist intellectuals before the First World War challenged Belgian national history radically by stressing that the Belgian Revolution of 1830, while originally born from a proletarian revolt, had been 'stolen' by the bourgeoisie. Among Flemish socialists, many of whom cherished Greater Dutch affinities, the Belgian uprising was even presented as a mistake from the start.[27] Even if this socialist revisionism with regard to the Belgian Revolution became less prominent after the First World War – when the Socialist party had been accepted into the political system of the country – it would nevertheless recur frequently throughout the twentieth century.[28] Dutch socialists before the First World War felt uneasy in their nation, too, but they never had an equally strong historical motif to legitimise their reticence. Moreover, they were too weak ever to threaten that Dutch nation.

The same can be said for Luxembourg. The leftist intellectuals did not have an historical event which they could use as a starting point for an alternative narrative. The *Klëppelkrich* (1798), a religious and agrarian uprising during the first years of the French republican regime, was profoundly counter-revolutionary, and the social disturbances of 1917–21 were only marginally exploited to build a new discourse over Luxembourgian history. The republican movement, which gained strength at the end of the First World War in the industrial south, did not survive the national and monarchical revival in the 1930s, which culminated in the centenary of the Congress of London, in 1939.[29] In the 1960s the communist historian Jean Kill tried to offer a coherent Marxist history of Luxembourg, stressing the importance of social history. However, he remained too strongly bound by the classical Luxembourgian master narrative to be considered really innovative.[30] The more

---

[27]M. Van Ginderachter, *Het rode vaderland: de vergeten geschiedenis van de communautaire spanningen in het Belgische socialisme voor WOI* (Tielt, 2005), pp. 275–81.

[28]Notably in the work of M. Bologne, *La Révolution prolétarienne de 1830* (Brussels, 1930), which would even be republished in 1980.

[29]C. Wey, 'Le Centenaire de l'Indépendance et sa commémoration en 1939', *Hémecht*, 41 (1989), pp. 29–53.

[30]J. Kill's book, *1000jähriges Luxemburg: woher? – wohin? Ein Beitrag zum besseren Verständnis der Geschichte des Luxemburger Landes* (Luxembourg, 1963), creates its structures by using the classic elements of Luxembourgian historiography, such as the foundation myth or the theme of foreign dominations (*Fremdherrschaften*), etc.

recent publications by Denis Scuto have not yet provided a comprehensive vision of the country's history.[31]

More important than the role of these partisan views on national history was the fact that Marxist influences penetrated Belgian historiography much more easily than the Dutch and Luxembourgian counterparts . This can be illustrated by comparing the aforementioned great syntheses of national history, those of P. J. Blok and Henri Pirenne. Whereas the former seemed to pay only secondary attention to economic factors, for the latter the origins of Belgium were closely linked to its role as the commercial crossroads of Europe. Even if this was a strong case for the antiquity of Belgium, the existence of the nation was not presented as an axiomatic fact but as the cultural and political result of contingent economic factors. Pirenne's view was less influenced by the Marxist view of historical materialism than by the economic history of the 'Catheder socialist' Gustav Schmoller. Nonetheless, the openness it created towards Marxist patterns of explanation would remain considerable among Pirenne's pupils of the 'Ghent school', which was strongly oriented to the French *Annales* (largely unknown in the Netherlands).[32] Because of their quest for economic and social explanations, they were little inclined to write national histories. This did not prevent Pirenne's direct spiritual 'children' (such as François-Louis Ganshof and Hans Van Werveke) from collaborating on different projects of national history (see below). It would be his most prominent spiritual heir, Jan Dhondt, who, in the 1960s, undertook one of the most radical attacks on the concept of national history as such.[33] By doing so, this overtly Marxist historian paradoxically drew the logical conclusion from the premises that had been at the basis of Pirenne's triumphalist national history. In the interpretation of the Belgian Revolution, Dhondt's heritage is visible even today: one of his most famous pupils, the influential Brussels historian Els Witte, proposes a class-based approach to that revolution, whereas the more 'idealistic' Leuven historians tend to stress its proto-nationalist basis and the fervour of cultural nationalism that erupted in its immediate wake.[34]

In this respect, the difference with the Dutch historian Jan Romein is very striking. Although very controversial because of his communist affiliation, he

---

[31]D. Scuto, *Sous le signe de la grande grève de mars 1921* (Esch-sur-Alzette, 1990).

[32]W. Prevenier, 'L'Ecole des "Annales" et l'historiographie néerlandaise', *Septentrion*, 7 (1978), 47–54.

[33]J. Dhondt, 'Henri Pirenne: historien des institutions urbaines' (1966), *Machten en mensen: de belangrijkste studies van Jan Dhondt over de geschiedenis van de negentiende en twintigste eeuw* (Gent, 1976), pp. 63–119. See in this respect also Beyen, *Oorlog en Verleden*, p. 404.

[34]On that difference, see M. Beyen, 'Een onafwendbaar toeval: de Belgisch-patriottische geschiedschrijving over de Belgische Revolutie', in P. Rietbergen and T. Verschaffel (eds), *De erfenis van 1830* (Louvain, 2006), pp. 75–89.

nevertheless became more and more interested during the 1930s in national history. Shortly before the Second World War he published, with his wife, Annie Romein, a four-volume series of short biographies of those whom he deemed the most important persons from Dutch history (*Erflaters van onze beschaving*). This would result during the Second World War in several pamphlets in which he tried to retrace the Dutch national 'soul' through history.[35] With this idealistic quest, he seemed far removed from a Marxist approach, and came very close to the grand narrative as it had been coined by historians such as Fruin, Blok and Huizinga. Marxist historians in the Netherlands who did not engage in writing national histories seemed to distance themselves from the historical establishment of their country. That was the case with Romein's Amsterdam colleague in economic history Nicolaas Posthumus. Although he gained an international reputation for his studies in the field of economic history and for his International Institute for Social History (created in 1935), he always remained somehow an outsider to the Dutch historical guild.[36]

Even in 1959 the Utrecht historian J. C. Boogman felt compelled to complain about the dominance of the national (or even patriotic) perspective in Dutch historiography, at the cost of, among other things, more internationally and economically oriented approaches to history.[37] However, a change was already starting to take place, and in the 1960s Dutch historiography diverged from the 'national and pillarised' perspective by which it had been dominated for more than half a century.[38] Even so, the weight of class as a structuring principle appears always to have remained lighter in the Netherlands than in Belgium, whereas cultural explanations of history have been far more important. A striking illustration of this difference can be found in the popularity in the Netherlands of the concept of 'political culture' as an organising principle for national history.[39] In Belgium the introduction of this concept

---

[35]See on Romein, among others, A. Otto, *Het Ruisen van de Tijd: over de Theoretische Geschiedenis van Jan Romein* (Amsterdam, 1998).

[36]On Posthumus, see L. Noordegraaf, 'Nicolaas Wilhelmus Posthumus (1880–1960): van gloeiend marxist tot entrepreneur', in: J.C.H. Blom (ed.), *Een brandpunt van geleerdheid in de hoofdstad: de Universiteit van Amsterdam rond 1900 in 15 portretten* (Hilversum/Amsterdam, 1992), pp. 287–312. On the genesis of the International Institute for Social History, see: M. Hunink, *De papieren van de revolutie: het Internationaal Instituut voor Sociale Geschiedenis, 1935–1947* (Amsterdam, 1986).

[37]J. C. Boogman, *Vaderlandse geschiedenis (na de middeleeuwen) in hedendaags perspectief: enige kanttekeningen en beschouwingen* (Groningen, 1959).

[38]Blaas, 'Nederlandse geschiedschrijving na 1945'. More specifically for the rise of economic history, see W. J. Wieringa, 'De ontplooiing van economische en sociale geschiedenis in Nederland', in H. Baudet and H. van der Meulen (eds), *Kernproblemen der economische geschiedenis* (Groningen, 1978), pp. 349–55.

[39]Most notably in R. Aerts, H. de Liagre Böhl, P. de Rooy and H. te Velde, *Land van kleine gebaren: een politieke geschiedenis van Nederland, 1780–1990* (Nijmegen, 1999).

has been impeded by the attachment of historians to social and economical concepts such as 'interest' and 'class'.

The litmus test of the nation: language and ethnicity

The one competing concept, however, that seriously threatened Belgian national history writing, while strengthening its Dutch and Luxembourgian counterparts, was that of ethnicity, taken as a concept referring to origin in a (more or less) biological sense. Since in the nineteenth century the importance of language as a marker of ethnicity became more important than ever, and ethnicity itself came to be seen as a criterion for defining a nation, writing a national history of a bilingual country such as Belgium became a highly problematic affair.[40] This was all the more true since the Belgian elites, deeply influenced by French centralism, clearly opted for unilingually French systems of justice, politics and higher education. The language of the Flemish, who constituted half of the Belgian population, was thus pushed back into the private sphere. Throughout the nineteenth century, several attempts were made by Belgian historians to deny that Belgian bilingualism was based on an ethnic dichotomy. For most of the nineteenth-century historians, such as Henri Moke, who wrote his *Histoire de Belgique* in the 1850s, it was evident that the ancestors of the Belgians were predominantly of Germanic stock. This genealogy fitted above all in the liberal narrative of a secular Belgian struggle for freedom, since the Germanic tribes had been, since the humanists, associated with the spirit of liberty.

By the 1860s, however, this assertion became ever more difficult to sustain. On the basis of his research into physical anthropology, the Brussels historian Léon Vanderkindere concluded that the Dutch-speaking Flemings descended, largely speaking, from Germanic tribes, whereas the French-speaking Walloons were of Celtic origin.[41] Although the progressive and francophone Vanderkindere was sympathetic to the aspirations of the Flemish movement, his scientific results were certainly not driven by the desire to create a schism within Belgium. If anything, Vanderkindere was a fierce Belgian nationalist for whom ethnic diversity was a trademark which made Belgium different from France, the country that was considered a threat by many Belgians during this period.

Vanderkindere's thesis with regard to Belgian ethnic origins would later be corroborated not only by other physical anthropologists, such as Emile Houzé, but

---

[40]See, for most of this paragraph, M. Beyen, 'Natural-born Nations? National Historiography in Belgium and the Netherlands between a "Tribal" and a Social-cultural Paradigm', *Storia della Storiografia*, 38 (2000), 17–22.

[41]See K. Wils, 'Tussen metafysica en antropometrie: het rasbegrip bij Léon Vanderkindere', in M. Beyen and G. Vanpaemel (eds), *Rasechte wetenschap? Het rasbegrip tussen wetenschap en politiek vóór de Tweede Wereldoorlog* (Leuven/Apeldoorn, 1998), pp. 81–99.

also by the Liège historian Godefroid Kurth, who tried to explain this ethnic difference historically. According to him, at the time of the Germanic migrations, a large forest (the so-called Charbon Forest) would have been situated at more or less the precise site of the actual linguistic border. This forest would have prevented the Germanic tribes from migrating *en masse* further south.

For Kurth's pupil Henri Pirenne the bi-ethnicity of Belgium was not something to be proved, but a simple fact. The whole challenge of his *Histoire de Belgique* was to prove that Belgium, in spite of this ethnic duality, was an historical nation. The evidence that he put forward to underpin his thesis was at one and the same time economic *and* cultural: as the central marketplace of north-western Europe, Belgium had since the Middle Ages become the crossroads of Latin and Germanic cultural influences and, therefore, the crossroads of Europe. This interpretation of national history was so successful that it definitively put an end to the nineteenth-century belief in the ethnic unity of Belgium – a belief that in the patriotic heyday of the late nineteenth and early twentieth centuries had led to the belief in the existence of a distinct 'Belgian soul'.[42] Only a fanatically patriotic historian such as Charles Terlinden would, until the Second World War, defend the thesis of the ethnic (Germanic) unity of Belgium. Ironically, he did so in an attempt to prevent the German occupiers from trying to divide the country on the basis of ethnic borders.[43]

The tragedy of Pirenne's national history was that, while trying to strengthen Belgian patriotism, it furthered the cause of the then radicalising Flemish, and to a lesser degree also that of Walloon nationalism. On the one hand, it corroborated the view that Belgium was ethnically divided (a view for which the Flemish nationalists had found evidence in the works of other Belgian patriots such as Vanderkindere and Kurth); on the other, it became, in the eyes of the Flamingants, an icon for the finalistic (and therefore anachronistic) view of national history cherished by the Belgian patriots. When the Flamingants, from the second decade of the twentieth century onwards, started constructing a Flemish national history on their own terms, this project was motivated in the first place as an attack on Pirenne.[44] For this, they found further ammunition in the Greater Dutch view of history (that is, the view which assumed a national affinity between all Dutch-speaking regions in the past) which found its main

---

[42]J. Stengers, 'Avant Pirenne: les preuves de l'ancienneté de la nation belge', *Bulletin de la Classe des Lettres et des Sciences Morales et Politiques de Belgique*, 6th ser., vol. 7 (1996), 551–72.

[43]Beyen, *Oorlog en Verleden*, pp. 125–6.

[44]In general on this construction of a Flemish vision of history, see L. Vos, 'Reconstructions of the Past in Belgium and Flanders', in B. Coppieters and M. Huysseune (eds), *Secession, History and the Social Sciences* (Brussels, 2002), pp. 179–206.

academic advocate during the interwar years in the flamboyant Utrecht historian Pieter Geyl.[45]

The construction of a Flemish national history was further aided by the fact that in the patriotic version of Belgian history – and notably in the works of Pirenne – the history of the County of Flanders and the Duchy of Brabant (the two principalities containing the core of modern Flanders) received the lion's share of attention. Many of the events and historical figures central to the patriotic version of history – such as the battle of the Golden Spurs and the popular leader Jacob of Artevelde – were easily fitted into the new Flemish national master narrative. Even the global theme of the succession of foreign domination (see above) was seamlessly recuperated by the Flemish national-ists. The only alteration they had to make was to add one more oppressor to the series: the Belgian state.[46]

Academic historians in Flanders reacted rather ambivalently to this. On the one hand, the most prominent among them were either pupils (such as Van Werveke and Ganshof in Ghent) or admirers (such as Van der Essen in Leuven) of Pirenne and showed enormous loyalty to their master. Participation in direct attacks on his vision of national history was, therefore, not to be expected. On the other hand, they showed very little inclination to defend his thesis. Several reasons can be given for this. First of all, as noted before, they were more interested in transnational social and economic evolutions than in the genesis of a national culture. They also actively participated in a process of emancipating Dutch-speaking culture in Flanders (and notably in the Dutchifying of Flemish universities), a process opposed by Pirenne. For these historians, it was unthinkable to be fully associated with an historical vision that, while recognising the ethnic diversity of Belgium, stressed its cultural and political unity.

The answer to the dilemma was a multi-layered national loyalty: these historians participated, as indicated earlier, in different projects of national

---

[45]On this Greater Dutch vision of history, see P. B. M. Blaas, 'De visie van de Groot-Nederlandse historiografen: aanleiding tot een nieuwe historiografie?', in J. Craeybeckx, F. Daeleman and F.G. Scheelings (eds), '*1585: Op gescheiden wegen ...*': *handelingen van het colloquium over de scheiding der Nederlanden, gehouden op 22–23 november 1985, te Brussel* (Leuven, 1988), pp. 197–218; L. Wils, 'De zogenaamde Groot-Nederlandse ges-chiedschrijving', *Vlaanderen, België, Groot-Nederland: historische opstellen, gebundeld en aangeboden aan de schrijver bij het bereiken van zijn emeritaat aan de K.U. Leuven* (Leuven, 1994), pp. 384–482.
[46]See, for this whole process, J. Tollebeek, 'De Guldensporenslag: de cultus van 1302 en de Vlaamse strijd', in A. Morelli (ed.), *De grote mythen uit de geschiedenis van België, Vlaanderen en Wallonië* (Berchem, 1996), pp. 191–202; S. Rottiers, 'Jacob van Artevelde, de Belgische Willem Tell?', in Morelli, *De grote mythen*, pp. 77–93; M. Beyen, *Held voor alle werk: de vele gedaanten van Tijl Uilenspiegel* (Antwerpen/Baarn, 1998).

history (without initiating these projects themselves), even if the projects were intended to promote contesting national loyalties. They also participated in Flemish nationalist as well as the Greater Dutch and the Belgian patriot historiography.[47] The 'Burgundian' view on Belgian history, the basis of the *Algemene Geschiedenis der Nederlanden*, was in essence an attempt to combine these different angles within one flexible view of national history. By stressing that the fifteenth- and sixteenth-century process of state-building contained the germs of a nation encompassing the whole of the Low Countries, these historians (among whom Van der Essen was the driving force) did not mutilate but extend the Belgian patriot interpretation. But in many respects, Pirenne had already done this himself.[48]

After the Second World War, Flemish historians would, to some degree, continue to hold this undecided position in the field of national historiography. Belgian history for them remained the natural object of their researches, but they very rarely engaged in synthetic views of national history as such. Equally few, however, were their attempts to undermine the Belgian perspective by presenting an alternative, Flemish vision of history. The fact that no course on Belgian or Flemish history was part of the history curricula of the Flemish universities undoubtedly contributed to this retreat from the domain of national history. After 1946 courses on Belgian history were replaced in both Leuven and Ghent by courses on the history of the Low Countries.[49] The 'Burgundian' view of history had become the 'official' way of writing national history in Flanders. The popularity of this was due less to the fact that it satisfied the needs of the newly created Benelux (which could hardly be named a new nation) than to its safe character: it allowed Flemish historians *not* to choose between a Belgian patriotic and a Flamingant interpretation of their national history. If the Belgian patriotic interpretation had become obsolete, the Flamingant one had rather become suspect since the collaboration of large parts of the Flemish movement during the Second World War. Significantly, the first large-scale postwar 'history of Flanders' was written in 1972 by Robert Van Roosbroeck, a historian who had been a prominent member (and probably co-founder) of the Flemish SS, and who therefore lived in exile in the Netherlands. The continuity between this three-volume *Geschiedenis van Vlaanderen* and the five-volume work of the same title published in the 1930s under the supervision

[47]See on this, M. Beyen, '"Een werk waarop ieder Vlaming fier kan zijn?" Het boek *100 Groote Vlamingen* als praalfaçade van het Vlaams-nationale geschiedenisbouwwerk', in J. Tollebeek, G. Verbeeck and T. Verschaffel (eds), *De lectuur van het verleden: opstellen over de geschiedenis aangeboden aan Reginald de Schryver* (Leuven, 1998), pp. 411–40; Beyen, *Oorlog en Verleden*, pp. 395–404.
[48]J. Tollebeek, 'Geyl en Van der Essen', *Ex officina*, 3 (1986) 139–51.
[49]Tollebeek, 'Uitgedaagd door historische gebondenheid'.

of the same Van Roosbroeck, was striking. This time, however, for obvious reasons there was no collaboration with prominent Flemish academic historians.

This lack of engagement with truly national historiography did not, however, prevented most of these Flemish academic historians from actively participating in Flamingant cultural organisations and collaborating in Flamingant historical initiatives, such as the *Encyclopedie van de Vlaamse Beweging* (1974–75). Overt statements against the Flamingant historiography were, until recently, made only by the Leuven historian Lode Wils, most notably in his *Van Clovis tot Happart*, a general overview of nation-building in the Low Countries, which first appeared in 1991 and recently reappeared under the title *Van Clovis tot Di Rupo*. From a much more deconstructivist point of view, the Ghent historian and journalist Marc Reynebeau came to an even more radical *démasqué* of Flemish nationalist historiography in his *Het klauwen van de Leeuw: Vlaamse identiteit van de 12de tot de 21ste eeuw* (1995). As a consequence of this growing disapproval with the militant manner of writing the history of Flanders, the urge was felt to write a new, thoroughly revisionist encyclopaedia of the Flemish movement. When this *Nieuwe Encyclopedie van de Vlaamse Beweging* appeared in 1998, it revealed the rather detached and 'constructivist' way in which Flemish academics were involved in the process of writing national history. This same constructivist perspective, together with the resurrection of an extreme right-wing Flemish nationalism, has contributed to the fact that some Flemish historians have recently found their way back, first to the history of Belgian patriotism, and later to that of Belgium itself.[50]

Since the francophone Belgians, generally speaking, maintained a stronger loyalty to the Belgian state than did their Dutch-speaking compatriots, Pirenne's theses met with much less opposition among them. With a few exceptions, such as Charles Terlinden, they remained as far removed from every form of patriotic single-mindedness as Pirenne himself had done, but nonetheless Belgium for them remained the logical framework for writing national history. Unlike their Flemish counterparts, francophone universities have continued to teach courses on Belgian history, and francophone historians received the *Algemene Geschiedenis der Nederlanden* with much less enthusiasm than did their Dutch-speaking colleagues. Even if some of them did collaborate on the project, many found it curious that the short time-span during which the '17 Provinces' had shown any unity was presented as the defining moment of national history.[51] The doubts of

[50] N. Beyens, 'Van nieuwe Belgen en vaderlandsloze beeldenstormers', in *Nieuwste Tijd: Kwartaalschrift voor eigentijdse geschiedenis*, 1 (2002), 71–86.
[51] Illustrative of this attitude was Jean Stengers, 'A propos de deux ouvrages de l'histoire néerlandaise: le "Geschiedenis van de Nederlandse stam" de M. Geyl et l'"Algemene Geschiedenis der Nederlanden", *Revue Belge de Philologie et de l'histoire*, 28 (1950), 309–21.

Flemish historians have always lingered with regard to the 'national inspiration' of the Belgian Revolution but seem to have been nearly absent from the works of their francophone counterparts. In particular, the Brussels historian Jean Stengers has repeatedly tried to prove this in an extremely erudite and magisterial manner.[52]

It is probably no coincidence that this same historian has been one of the first Belgian academics to tackle seriously the painful question of Belgium's colonial past. In his publications Stengers has always tried, by a painstakingly meticulous use of historical critique, to reject both the patriotic triumphalism about Belgium's colonial history and the debunking discourse in which Leopold II's involvement with Congo appears as a genocide.[53] Stengers' position has been defended by another francophone historian, Jean Vellut (of the University of Louvain-la-Neuve), who has become the leading expert in the field.[54] In Flanders, colonialism until recently has been nearly exclusively left to historians operating in the margins of the academic field.[55] If their position has been much more at the side of the debunkers, this probably once again reveals the weaker loyalty of Flemish historians to the Belgian state.

Within the francophone community, however, a Wallingant movement began to take shape in the last decades of the nineteenth century. If this movement only gained political momentum in its reaction to the claims of the Flemish movement, it nevertheless had its roots in a pre-existing Walloon regionalism. Before the First World War the large majority of the Walloon movement had already abandoned its hope for a unilingually francophone Belgium and opted for a federal solution, in which both linguistic communities would gain a high degree of autonomy (without therefore abandoning the ambition to retain a bilingual Flanders, while maintaining Wallonia as exclusively francophone). Although the anti-Belgian sentiments within it always remained marginal, Wallingant historians nevertheless strove for a correction of the allegedly

---

[52]See, for example, J. Stengers, 'De Belgische Revolutie', in Anne Morelli (ed.), *De grote mythen van België, Vlaanderen en Wallonië* (Brussel, 1996), pp. 127–35; J. Stengers, *Histoire du sentiment national en Belgique des origines à 1918*, 2 vols (Brussels, 2000–2). For a critique on Stengers, see Els Witte, 'Op zoek naar het natiegevoel in België: enkele kanttekeningen bij *Les Racines de la Belgique* van Jean Stengers', *Wetenschappelijke tijdingen* (2001), 176–87, and Beyen, 'Een onafwendbaar toeval'.

[53]A compilation of Stengers's contributions on colonial history can be found in J. Stengers, *Congo: mythes et réalités. 100 ans d'histoire* (Gembloux, 1989).

[54]This has become particularly visible in his curatorship of the exhibition 'Het geheugen van Congo: de koloniale tijd', which has been highly criticised (especially by Flemish critics) for being too sympathetic to Leopold. See J. Vellut (ed.), *Het geheugen van Congo: de koloniale tijd* (Tervuren, 2005).

[55]Most notably by D. Vangroenweghe, *Rood rubber: Leopold II en zijn Congo* (Brussel, 1985).

'unitarian' view of history as constructed by Pirenne.[56] The character of this cor-rection, however, was thoroughly different from the one attempted by their Flamingant colleagues. The latter tried, from the early decades of the twentieth century onwards, to perceive through the whole of the history of the Low Countries the traces of a Flemish nation (or at least a Flemish *folk*) – one that was older and therefore more authentic than the Belgian nation. Wallingant histori-ans tried to compensate for Pirenne's overemphasis on the history of Brabant and Flanders by focusing on the importance the eastern and southeastern provinces had had (especially until the thirteenth century) in the culture and economy of the Low Countries.[57] As the young Liège historian Léon-Ernest Halkin remarked in 1939, the aim of such a strategy was not to shed light on some pre-existing Walloon nation, but only on Walloon people in the past. Unlike his Flamingant colleagues, Halkin saw the task of writing the history of Wallonia as a complement to, rather than as a substitute for, Pirenne.[58]

The project of truly writing a national history of Wallonia – that is, of a region with distinct characteristics – only really started after the Second World War and resulted in works such as Lucien Marchal's *Histoire de Wallonie*, and above all in the multi-volume work *La Wallonie: le pays et les hommes* (1975–81). The acad-emic search for a Walloon national history thus flourished at a time when in Flanders this had become an 'academically incorrect' business. This difference was due to the fact that, on the one hand, Wallingantism never had received the same radically anti-Belgian overtones as Flamingantism, and, on the other hand, Walloon nationalism, unlike its Flemish counterpart, had not been discredited during the Second World War. On the contrary, a stereotypical – though factu-ally accurate – association between collaborationism and Flemish nationalism, on the one hand, and Resistance and Walloon 'regionalism', on the other, has come into being. This explains how, at the francophone University of Brussels, a course on the history of Wallonia and the Walloon movement could be run in 1979, and also why the political authorities of the Walloon region can overtly promote the search for a Walloon identity in the past.[59] One of the main instru-

[56]See the rather partisan and anti-Pirennist article by P. Carlier, 'Pirenne, historien de la Wallonie?', in F. Bierlaire and J-L. Kupper (eds), *Henri Pirenne: de la cité de Liège à la ville de Gand, Cahiers de Clio*, no. 86 (1986), 65–78; also see H. Hasquin, *Historiographie et pol-itique: essai sur l'histoire de Belgique et de Wallonie*, 2nd edn (Charleroi, 1982).
[57]Most elaborately in the work of the Pirenne admirer F. Rousseau, *La Meuse et le pays Mosan en Belgique: leur importance avant le 13e siècle* (Brussels, 1930).
[58]L-E. Halkin, 'L'enseignement de l'histoire nationale en Wallonie', *Histoire et critique: notes à l'usage des élèves du Cours de Critique*, unpublished syllabus, 1939; in a somewhat altered form, this text also appeared as *La Wallonie devant l'histoire* (Brussels, 1939).
[59]See, on these evolutions, C. Kesteloot, 'Ecrire l'histoire du Mouvement Wallon: une démarche historique et citoyenne?', *Bijdragen tot de Eigentijdse Geschiedenis*, nos. 13–14 (2004), 17–44.

ments of this quest was the *Encyclopédie du mouvement Wallon*, an obviously partisan undertaking which nevertheless managed to attract the collaboration of many important francophone historians. The difference from the aforementioned *Nieuwe Encyclopedie van de Vlaamse Beweging*, which appeared more or less at the same time, is striking. Whereas academic historians in Flanders seem to be mainly involved in the intellectual deconstruction of the Flemish nation (without denying its political existence), Walloon historians gladly participate in the construction of a Walloon nation.

Dutch national historiography, for its part, was largely unconcerned by the challenge of ethnicity. The main marker of ethnicity – language – appeared to be fairly unproblematic in the Dutch case. Certainly, some of the dialects spoken in the peripheral regions of the Netherlands differed from the standard language, which was mainly modelled on the Holland and Brabant idiom. Of these dialects, only Frisian managed to be recognised as a genuine language (and was officially accepted as such in the twentieth century). Together with the memory of a grand Frisian history, this Frisian tongue served as the basis for a separate Frisian identity, whose ethnic core had been underpinned since the early nineteenth century by archaeological and folkloric research.[60] However, the Frisian movement which tried to promote this identity never seriously threatened the construction of the Dutch national identity. Apart from the radically anti-Dutch and fascist tendencies that became manifest there during the interwar period, it largely remained a regionalist movement which tried to conserve a Frisian specificity *within* the Dutch nation.[61] Even the search for a Frisian national past was mainly framed within the overall Dutch master narrative.[62] Probably, there are two main reasons why the Frisian movement, unlike its Flemish counterpart, did not evolve into full-blown nationalism. On the one hand, there was the fact that Frisian-speakers never formed a majority or an economically crucial element within the Dutch population. Equally important, however, seems to have been the fact that the linguistic difference between Frisian and standard Dutch was much less than that between French and the Flemish dialects. Not only did this imply a mutual intelligibility between Dutch-speakers and Frisian-speakers (and, most often, the bilingualism of the latter), it also meant that the

---

[60]See, among others, A. van der Woud, *De Bataafse hut: verschuivingen in het beeld van de geschiedenis, 1750–1850* (Amsterdam, 1990).

[61]See G. Jensma, 'The Frisian situation: ethnolinguistic nationalism in the Netherlands', unpublished paper presented at the workshop 'Ethnolinguistic nationalism in Scandinavia and the Low Countries', Groningen, 19–20 May 2005. On the Frisian movement in the interwar period, see G. R. Zondergeld, *De Friese beweging in het tijdvak der twee wereldoorlogen* (Leeuwarden, 1978).

[62]See, for example, L. Brouwer, *De archeologie van een houding: Nederlandse identiteit in de Friesche Volksalmanak* (Groningen, 1998).

language border could hardly be turned into an ethnic border. Whereas the gap between Germanic and Romance languages was, until well into the twentieth century, generally considered to mark the difference between nearly incommensurable 'national characters', the differences between the Germanic tongues betrayed only slight variants of the same ethnic stock.

The insight that ethnicity never was a hotly debated topic within Dutch identity-building has led many commentators to the conclusion that no ethnic view on history, and therefore no ethnic nationalism, existed in the Netherlands. The origins of the Dutch nation would invariably have been sought in (peaceful) state-building and the development of a culture with proper features. In our view, ethnic explanations were not absent from the interpretations of national history, but they formed a background for them which was so obvious that they scarcely had to be made explicit.[63]

The idea that the Dutch originated from Germanic tribes (with a small Celtic substrate) has never been seriously put up for discussion, and has often formed the starting point for national histories (e.g. for Blok's *Geschiedenis van het Nederlandsche Volk*). Only the question of *which* Germanic tribes could be considered to be the true ancestors of the Dutch prompted some debate. During the nineteenth century, it appeared that the old Batavian myth, which had underpinned historical self-understanding during the republic, could no longer meet the academic standards of its time or the identification needs of the modern kingdom of the Netherlands. The Batavian myth fitted well the Hollandic, largely Protestant, and liberal elites of that state, but was ill-equipped to facilitate the integration of religious minorities and the peripheral regions (such as Frisia) into the Dutch nation.

As an answer to these new scientific and political needs, the origins of the Dutch nation were sought, from the last decades of the nineteenth century, in the lucky symbiosis of three Germanic tribes: the Franks dominating the west, the Frisians forming the ethnic core of the north and the Saxons, who constituted the majority of the eastern regions. This theme was dominant in both academic historiography and popular representations of the national past until the Second World War. Later, it retreated to the background because it had become scientifically obsolete, politically discredited and dysfunctional. Ethnic interpretations of the past were no longer acceptable because of the possible associations with racism and Nazism, *and* they were no longer needed because the Dutch national identity was solid enough without an ethnic background.

---

[63]See M. Beyen, 'Naties in gradaties: nationaal en historisch besef in België en Nederland', *Ons erfdeel* (2002), 233–41 which was a response to H. Roodenburg, 'A Self-effacing Nation: Religion, Ethnicity and the Nation-state in the Nineteenth- and Twentieth-century Netherlands', in R. Bendix and H. Roodenburg (eds), *Managing Ethnicity: Perspectives from Folklore Studies, History and Anthropology* (Amsterdam, 2000), pp. 143–54.

During its heyday, however, the theme of the Franks, the Frisians and the Saxons – unmistakably an ethnic explanation of the national past – had played an important role in consolidating Dutch national identity at a time in which it was imperilled by pillarisation and modernisation.[64] And even if the motif of the Franks, the Frisians and the Saxons was more or less marginalised after the Second World War, it still remains the case that no real alternative has been formulated. In other words, if in the Dutch master narrative an important role is played by tolerance and openness, there is little room for ethnic diversity.[65]

In Luxembourg the concept of ethnicity was always more riddled with ambiguities than in Belgium: although the population by and large spoke German dialects, it was dominated by Dutch monarchs and by French-speaking elites. The quest for an 'ethnic' reading of the Luxembourgian past seems to have been more successful. Therefore, ethnicity and language at first seemed resistant to producing 'sense' in the Luxembourgian context.

When the subject of ethnicity became relevant in the nation-building discourse of the second half of the nineteenth century, Luxembourgian historians were immediately confronted with a problem: had they tried to trace the ethnic origins of the Luxembourgers back to the local Celtic tribe of the Treveri, they would have created too close a connection to the neighbouring German city of Trier. Given the latter's frequent conflict with Luxembourg since medieval times and furthermore the hints at a possible 'Pan-German ancestry' for the Luxembourgers, the idea was not unproblematic. In addition Germany became more and more a synonym for 'the Other' in the nineteenth century, and as a result the Treveri were no longer a real option. At the beginning of the twentieth century the idea that Luxembourg was characterised by a mixture of different ethnicities emerged, thus giving birth to a new and better 'historic race'. In 1911 the very influential intellectual Nicolas Ries wrote: 'Owing to numerous and close relations between Gauls, Romans and Germans, three races and three religions, hostile to each other, clashed and merged on our soil, "in confinio babarorum", and gave birth to the Luxembourgian people.'[66] This idea of an ethnic

---

[64]See extensively on this topic: M. Beyen, 'A Tribal Trinity: The Rise and Fall of the Franks, the Frisians and the Saxons in the Historical Consciousness of the Netherlands since 1850', *European History Quarterly*, 30 (2000), 493–532; other references to the theme can be found in A. de Jong, *De dirigenten van de herinnering: musealisering en nationalisering van de volkscultuur, 1815–1940* (Nijmegen, 2001).

[65]See M. Beyen, 'The Netherlands: An Ethnic Nation in spite of Itself', in P. Broomans et al., *My Beloved Mothertongue. Ethnocultural Nationalism in Small Nations. Inventories and Reflections* (Louvain, forthcoming).

[66]'Par suite des relations nombreuses et intimes entre Gaulois, Romains et Germains, trois races et trois religions hostiles s'étaient heurtées et fusionnées sur notre sol, "in confinio barbarorum" et avaient donné naissance au peuple luxembourgeois': N. Ries, *Essai d'une psychologie du peuple luxembourgeois* (Diekirch, 1911), p. 19 and p. 35.

mixture bore a striking similarity to the concept of the Belgian 'soul', but turned out to be much more successful: it continues to play – less in an ethnic than a cultural sense – an important role in the self-definition of the Luxembourgers. In the context of the European Union, the metaphor of Luxembourg as an original Franco-German combination and/or a bridge between these two countries has proved to be powerful.

The success of this quest for an ethnic reading of the Luxembourgian past and present can be deduced from the growing importance of language in Luxembourg's national identity. Through a combined effort of the monarchs and the elites, *Letzebuergesch* became, from the late nineteenth century onwards, the main marker of Luxembourgian identity. Again, the difference with Belgium, where language became ever more the divisive factor, is striking. The main explanation probably has to be sought in the fact that in Luxembourg, the division between the two language communities does not coincide with the ideological division between left and right.

Accentuating the differences: gendered notions of national history

In none of the three countries was the nation as an organising concept of history seriously challenged by gender. And yet, here again, in the Belgian case gendered notions did contribute more than in the Netherlands and Luxembourg to the destabilisation of national history. More specifically, the dichotomy between a Catholic and a liberal view of history was doubled with a gender dichotomy. Whereas in the liberal narrative of struggle for freedom all the emphasis was on male virtues and male heroes, in the Catholic vision female monarchs appeared as the outstanding protectors of the Catholic faith, as those who created the peaceful circumstances in which the Belgian people could unfold their Catholic 'essence'. Among them, the most prominent places were taken by the Burgundian Duchess Mary,[67] the Archduchess Isabella[68] and the Austrian empress Maria Theresa.[69] This dichotomy is all the more striking because in the liberal 'pillar' women were respected more as intellectuals, and therefore also as historians. The national histories written by liberal women such as Isabelle Gatti de Gamond and Suzanne Tassier (the first female history professor), however, differed very little from the narratives of

---

[67]See, for example, P. Van Ussel, *Maria van Bourgondië* (Leuven, 1944).
[68]See, for example, C. Terlinden, *L'Archiduchesse Isabelle* (Brussels, 1943).
[69]See, for a relatively recent example, J. Gérard, *Marie Thérèse: impératrice des Belges* (Brussels, 1987).

their male colleagues.[70] The latter not only wrote her doctoral dissertation on one of the canonical moments of the secular Belgian struggle for freedom, the Brabant revolution of 1789,[71] but she also made efforts to construct the history of the 'thirty years' war' between 1914 and 1945 into one more episode of this struggle.[72]

In the Netherlands more conscious efforts have been made to construct a 'feminist' approach to history (efforts which resulted in the creation, by the 1930s, of the International Archive for Women's History, as a spin-off from Posthumus's International Institute for Social History).[73] Even if they also implied an ongoing interest in the history of *Dutch* feminism, these attempts seem not to have considerably changed the way of writing national historiography. Johanna Naber, for example, one of the most prominent feminist historians, remained well within the boundaries of the Orangeist and liberal master narrative that dominated national historiography in the first half of the twentieth century.[74] This symbiosis between Orangeist and feminist views was probably made easier by the fact that throughout the twentieth century the Netherlands was ruled by queens rather than kings. It is not surprising that it was Queen Wilhelmina, who considered herself to be more male than the members of her War Cabinet, who was the first of the Dutch monarchs of the nineteenth and twentieth centuries to be honoured with a full-scale, two-volume biography.[75]

Since the 1960s feminist historiography in the Netherlands has become more radical, and therefore it has left this Orangeist position. Its attacks on the male domination of the Dutch historical master narrative have at times been very outspoken.[76] Nonetheless, it is doubtful whether the national master narrative on

---

[70]On the traditional and surprisingly 'male' character of the *Histoire de Belgique* of the feminist Gatti de Gamond, see K. Wils, 'Science, an Ally of Feminism?', *Revue Belge de Philologie et d'Histoire*, 77 (1999), 416–39.

[71]S. Tassier, *Les Démocrates belges: étude sur le Vonckisme et la Révolution Brabançonne* (Brussels, 1930).

[72]S. Tassier, *Histoire de Guerre Mondiale: pour un musée de la Guerre Mondiale et un Office de Documentation contemporaine* (Brussels 1944). On her vain attempts to create this museum, see also Beyen, *Oorlog en Verleden*, pp. 251–4.

[73]See J. Tollebeek, 'Voor elke liefde een instituut', *De ziel van de fabriek: over de arbeid van de historicus* (Amsterdam, 1998), pp. 15–22.

[74]See M. Grever, *Strijd tegen de stilte: Johanna Naber (1859–1941) en de vrouwenstem in de geschiedenis* (Hilversum, 1994).

[75]See C. Fasseur, *Wilhelmina: de jonge koningin* (Amsterdam, 1998), and *Wilhelmina: krijgshaftig in een vormeloze jas* (Amsterdam, 2001); see on this topic also M. Grever, 'Van Landsvader tot moeder des vaderlands: Oranje, Gender en Nederland', *Groniek: Onafhankelijk Gronings Historisch Studentenblad*, 36 (2002), 131–50.

[76]Most notably so during a workshop in 2002 dedicated by feminist historians to the series 'Nederlandse beschaving in Europese context'. See M. Bosch, 'De IJkpunten geijkt …: Evaluatie van het NWO-onderzoeksprogramma "Nederlandse cultuur in Europese context" uit het perspectief van vrouwengeschiedenis en genderstudies', *Tijdschrift voor Sociale Geschiedenis*, 29 (2003), 1–20.

Dutch history has been seriously altered by this feminist historiography. By focusing on the early Dutch feminists of the late nineteenth and the early twentieth centuries, they might involuntarily have strengthened the classic trope of the Netherlands as an open, tolerant and progressive country.[77] The attention they paid in 1998 to the national exhibition of women's labour, held 100 years before in The Hague, contributed to this sense. In their analyses of this event, feminist historians remained far away from any nationalistic discourse, but nevertheless interpreted the exhibition – which was organised on the occasion of Wilhelmina's accession to the throne – as a glorious moment for both the international women's movement and the Dutch nation.[78]

In Luxembourg there has until now been no real development of a feminist historiography. Women historians are rare and failed to gain important institutional positions.[79] This is linked to the very late professionalisation of academic history writing. However, the way in which the national history of Luxembourg has been gendered does seem to confirm what has been written with regard to Belgium: within the traditional, mainly Catholic tales of the national past, women played an important role and are closely related to the dominant master narratives. Countess Ermesinde (1186–1247), as the creator of a Luxembourgian principality, and Charlotte (1896–1985), as the saviour of the nation, are representative of the two most important historical periods in the history of Luxembourg – the Middle Ages and the Second World War. The role that is ascribed to them resembles very much that of the good female monarchs within the Catholic Belgian narratives: they appear as good, caring mothers of the nation. Both figures are joined by the Virgin Mary, as the protector of the capital and the country, to form a central triptych in national historiography. In Belgium such an overt association with the Virgin Mary was much less evident, given the contested nature of Catholicism.

Conclusion

If there is one overall conclusion to be drawn, it should certainly be that the writing of national history was much more threatened by 'the Other' in Belgium than in the Netherlands and Luxembourg. A glance at the most recent attempts to write national histories in the three countries can only confirm this. In Luxembourg the most recent *Histoire du Luxembourg*[80] remains a classic narration

---

[77]Notably, the 'rediscovery' of the most famous feminist of this first-wave feminism, Aletta Jacobs, can be seen in this respect. See the recent biography on her: M. Bosch, *Een onwrikbaar geloof in rechtvaardigheid: Aletta Jacobs, 1854–1929* (Amsterdam, 2005).

[78] M. Grever and F. Dieteren (eds), *Een Vaderland voor vrouwen. A Fatherland for Women: The 1898 'Nationale Tentoonstelling van Vrouwenarbeid' in retrospect* (Amsterdam, 1998).

[79]Exceptionally, in every sense: G. Goetzinger, A. Lorang, and R. Wagner (eds), *'Wenn nun wir Frauen auch das Wort ergreifen ...': 1880–1950: Frauen in Luxemburg* (Luxembourg, 1997).

[80]G. Trausch (ed.), *Histoire du Luxembourg: le destin européen d'un 'petit pays'* (Toulouse, 2002).

of the national history without any hints that the writings of Benedict Anderson, Eric Hobsbawm or Pierre Nora had any influence. The importance granted to the Middle Ages, the very brief chapter dedicated to the early modern period, the 'European destiny' of the country are typical elements of a master narrative which has been relatively stable since the end of the Second World War.

In the Netherlands the prestigious five-volume series 'Nederlandse cultuur in Europese context' (the so-called *IJkpunten-reeks*) can be seen as a glorious return (though in a modernised guise) to a narrowly defined national history: that is to say, a national history starting with the birth of the republic at the end of the sixteenth century and, in spite of the title, largely denying the European context of Dutch history. Dutch historians, as we mentioned at the start, had never been very enthusiastic about the broadening of the perspective which had resulted in, among other things, the *Algemene Geschiedenis der Nederlanden*, and the recent deconstruction of nationalism ironically offered them the opportunity to return to a more narrow interpretation of the national past. Since it was pointless, as deconstructivists showed, to look for nations before the nation-states came into being, why would Dutch historians feel the need to look for national origins before the end of the fifteenth century?[81]

In Belgium a similar evolution of natural history writing can be observed: the last two decades have witnessed the return of the 'History of Belgium' as a (mostly non-academic) genre, a genre in which the origins of Belgium are situated in 1830, or, at the earliest, during the second half of the eighteenth century.[82] Unlike in the Netherlands, however, these new Belgian histories are deeply imbued with the postmodern, ironical stance that deconstructs the history of Belgium even while writing it. This stance was inherited from some essays dedicated in the 1980s to Belgian identity. In the most famous of these, *Het Belgisch Labyrinth* (1989), the journalist and poet Geert Van Istendael explicitly associates Belgian identity with the construction of the European Union. Because of its biculturalism, and therefore its resistance to ethnic nationalism, Belgian identity should, according to Van Istendael, be a model for European identity-building. He thus comes remarkably close to the Pirennist thesis of Belgium as a European microcosm. At the same time, it is made clear that Brussels' central position in the process of European integration does not endanger Belgian national identity and national history writing.

---

[81]See M. Beyen's review article on this series: 'Nederlands wonderjaren: beschouwingen bij de reeks "Nederlandse cultuur in Europese context"', *Ons Erfdeel: Algemeen-Nederlands Tweemaandelijks Cultureel tijdschrift*, 45 (2002), 522–35.

[82]For an academic variant of this tendency, see the multi-volume *Nieuwe Geschiedenis van Belgium/Nouvelle Histoire de Belgique*, an undertaking for which prominent Flemish and francophone historians took the initiative. It started to appear in 2005 and should be finished in 2007.

On the contrary, this central position can be interpreted as the fulfilment of a mission that in the patriotic discourse had always been assigned to Belgium.

Nonetheless, the revival of Belgian national history through this ironic and pro-European position might be very illusory. In *Een geschiedenis van België* Marc Reynebeau combines this postmodern deconstruction with a Marxist approach (which he has inherited from the Ghent school) in order to come to an inexorable *démasqué* of the Belgian state as a product of the nineteenth-century bourgeoisie.[83] The return to national historiography in Belgium thus seems to be everything but triumphant.

When looking for explanations for this striking difference between the Dutch and Luxembourgian national historiography, on the one hand, and their Belgian counterpart, on the other, we believe that the thesis of the 'belated' modernisation of the Netherlands and of Luxembourg can offer some help. In the Netherland and Luxembourg, in spite or maybe because of their modest beginnings, the nation-state had the time gradually to mature without seriously being threatened by the modern, democratic political forces engendered by the French and the industrial revo-lutions. These states were more or less outside the European history scene. Belgium, on the contrary, stood in the middle of these European evolutions, as the First World War would make painfully clear. Modernising forces were present from 1830 onwards, and contributed to a deep and broad politicisation of the whole of society before a genuine national consciousness had been able to take root. 'The Other', therefore, became a multi-headed monster devouring the Belgian nation (and its capacity to write its own history) from within. Only the future knows whether it will be the 'Other from without' (Europe) that saves it. It would, in any case, be a fine example of Belgian irony.

---

[83]M. Reynebeau, *Een geschiedenis van België* (Tielt, 2004).

12
National Historiography and National Identity: Switzerland in Comparative Perspective

Guy P. Marchal

This chapter aims to demonstrate how national histories are modelled and remodelled in line with contemporary political attitudes. The discussion focuses on texts that clearly present an interpretation of the historical process through which the status of the nation-state has been or is to be attained, seek to explain the character of the state through its history, and in so doing evolve models that are adopted by historians as well as by constitutional theorists and politicians and may play a significant role in public discourse: texts, that is to say, that may be treated as master narratives. Switzerland will be used as an example, for here, relative to elsewhere, such models were derived very straightforwardly from current political problems and experiences without any theoretical background. The purpose of the comparison with France that follows is to demonstrate that the findings reached in the Swiss analysis document a general phenomenon, namely the constructedness of national historiographies. This can be illustrated particularly clearly in cases where there have been major discontinuities in the evolution of a state, as was the case in Switzerland from 1798 and in France from 1789 until the middle of the nineteenth century. The main emphasis of the discussion rests on the nineteenth and early twentieth centuries, the period during which the master narratives emerged. This makes sense in the case of Switzerland, which is the only European country not to have suffered further radical breaks in its history at any time after 1848, and where consequently the master narratives have remained remarkably consistent and resilient to the present day. The issue of the relationship between religious denomination and national historiography is treated here mainly as an internal comparison. The relationship between race and nation in Switzerland is approached by way of external comparison with parallel examples of multilingual nations – here Belgium and Luxembourg[1] – while the issue of gender and national historiography is seen in relation to France and Germany.[2]

---

[1] See Beyen and Majerus, this volume (chapter 11).
[2] See Frey and Jordan, this volume (chapter 8).

Creating models: master narratives and the transition to the modern nation-state

Interpretative models in Switzerland: the relationship between 'Old Confederacy' and modern confederation

As Switzerland is one of the less well-known countries internationally, it may be useful to preface the discussion with an outline of the elements of Swiss history that provide the framework for the interpretative models.[3] The Swiss Confederation (*Schweizerischer Bundesstaat*) is in European terms a relatively late development, without ethnic or dynastic antecedents. In comprehensive Swiss histories it is therefore naturally the constitutional and public law issues that receive most attention. In this context Switzerland passed through two evolutionary phases with fundamental differences that outside observers, in particular, have tended to overlook.

First, the Old Confederacy (*Alte Eidgenossenschaft*): it consisted of a loose and complex system of alliances that had begun to form in the thirteenth century, and from the beginning of the sixteenth century it possessed a firm nucleus in the 13 'sovereign' *Orte* (city-states and rural communities, now known as cantons). This nucleus acquired a surrounding halo of varying numbers of independent, so-called 'adherent states' (*Zugewandte Orte*). From the beginning of the fifteenth century there were also subject lands (*Gemeine Herrschaften*), which might be under the control of all the *Orte* collectively or of a group of them. This whole complex structure was the 'Corpus Helveticum', as it came to be called in the course of the seventeenth century.[4] A central decision-making body was provided for in the so-called Assembly of the Confederates (*Eidgenössische Tagsatzung*), which functioned like a conference of ambassadors, and so remained ill defined. A significant event from the point of view of the present study was the Reformation, together with its aftermath, as the Corpus Helveticum now additionally split along confessional lines. Society generally and within individual *Orte* was not democratic in the modern sense. The ability to govern became limited to a ruling upper class which, in the sixteenth century, became more exclusive in character. Monarchical constitutions too were not entirely unknown in the Corpus Helveticum (the prince-bishopric of Basle, the prince-abbacy of St-Gall, the county of Neuchâtel, for instance). This older form of government

---

[3]*Handbuch der Schweizer Geschichte*, 2 vols (Zürich, 1972/7); *Geschichte der Schweiz und der Schweizer* (Basle, 1986; 1st edn: Basle, 1983); *Nouvelle histoire de la Suisse et des Suisses* (Lausanne, 1986; 1st edn: Lausanne, 1983); H. C. Peyer, *Verfassungsgeschichte der alten Schweiz* (Zürich, 1978).
[4]W. Oechsli, 'Die Benennungen der alten Eidgenossenschaft und ihrer Glieder', *Jahrbuch für schweizerische Geschichte*, 41 (1916), 51–230; 42 (1917), 87–258.

under the *ancien régime* came to an end in 1798 under the hammer blows of the French revolutionary armies.

The federal state that was founded in 1848 after 50 years of struggle, after the Helvetic Republic, mediation, restoration and finally a civil war, differed fundamentally from the old Corpus in that it completely reapportioned sovereignty between the *Bund* (Swiss Confederation) and the cantons, its essential aspects – sovereignty in external and internal affairs – being reserved to the *Bund*. The cantons retained only such autonomy as was explicitly accorded them in the federal constitution. The state's constitutional structures were simplified and unified: 22 cantons were brought together with equal rights in a federal constitution, and a Swiss national executive and legislature were formed. Switzerland was now a modern (nation-) state, utterly different from the Old Confederacy. The practical consequences of these developments were much more significant than is readily appreciated today. They may in broad terms be compared – provocatively, but by no means entirely fancifully – with the step involved in moving from the Europe of nation-states to a future European federal state. The Swiss constitution drew relatively recent centralist experience into an uneasy balance with the centuries-old federalist tradition. The balance has, ever since, tipped more and more towards the centralised confederation.

Any historical overview of Switzerland's path to nationhood thus has to take account of two constitutional forms of the Swiss state. And the particular manner in which an interpretation constructs the relationship between the two forms of constitution is one of the pivotal issues in the interpreting of Swiss history. If we wish to build up conceptual models, this is the place to start. At the same time it has to be borne in mind that contemporary political debate over Switzerland – which invariably resonates in the field of historical interpretation – has long been dominated by two dualisms. Confronting each other, as ever, are not simply two religious denominations, but also two constitutional concepts – traditional federalism and modern centralism. Over and above these dualities, there is the well-known fact that the Swiss population embraces four linguistic groups and cultures, demarcated along lines that follow neither the political nor the denominational boundaries.

For modern era historians, the historiographical starting point[5] has been the *Chronicon Helveticum* of Aegidius Tschudi (1505–72), which did not appear in

---

[5]For the following section – except where otherwise noted – all references are to be found in G. P. Marchal, *Schweizer Gebrauchsgeschichte: Geschichtsbilder, Mythenbildung und nationale Identität* (Basle, 2006), esp. pp. 203–30, 429–79 and passim (all further notes on secondary sources are also here). See also O. Zimmer, *A Contested Nation: History, Memory and Nationalism in Switzerland, 1761–1891* (Cambridge, 2003); idem, 'Competing Memories of the Nation: Liberal Historians and the Reconstruction of the Swiss Past, 1870–1900', *Past and Present*, 168 (1998), 194–226.

print until two centuries later (1734–6),[6] together with the *Geschichten schweiz-erischer Eidgenossenschaft* by Johannes von Müller, which came out between 1786 and 1805.[7] Borrowing much of his material wholesale from Tschudi, von Müller put forward a wide-ranging proto-national interpretation of the medieval confederacy from an eighteenth-century Enlightenment perspective. It was a consciously constructed vision of the confederacy as special among European states, free and distinctive since time immemorial: as a 'nation' that even in modern times could subsist only by maintaining its individual iden-tity within Europe. This vision was to have consequences. For our purposes, it must be borne in mind that Müller was still writing under the *ancien régime*. He thus had no mental reservations when he envisaged an unbroken histor-ical continuity stretching from first beginnings to his contemporary present.

The popular historical tradition, not in itself a topic to be pursued here, played a crucial role in the growth of national self-awareness after the total collapse of 1798. It adopted von Müller's historical vision lock, stock and barrel, crafting from it a presentation of Swiss identity that, with the added resonance of Friedrich Schiller's poetic vision, remained persuasive right into the twenty-first century. By contrast, the post-medieval centuries under the *ancien régime*, and the upheavals following the revolution, have to a remarkable extent faded from public memory.

However, the caesura of 1798 did produce a response in the first half of the nineteenth century from the then emerging discipline of academic historical studies in the modern sense. This may well be how we should understand the emergence in those years of the will, and indeed the opportunity, to initiate a critical review of the received historical tradition reaching back by way of von Müller and Tschudi to the contemporary sources. Under the immediate impact of the radically new post-1798 epoch, von Müller's unbroken vision, with its perception of the medieval confederacy as already manifesting the enduring character of the Swiss nation, was lost. Among those who subjected its ahis-torical quality to dispassionate analysis was Joseph Eutych Kopp, the pioneer of critical historiography.[8]

When a new generation of comprehensive histories of Switzerland appeared in the 1880s, it was not in fact simply the latest state of knowledge that shaped the new historical vision. Above all, it was contemporary experience of the new con-federation, of how it had proved itself on the foreign and domestic political scenes, having held its line in international disputes and successfully revised the

[6]A. Tschudi, *Chronicon Helveticum,* ed. B. Stettler, Quellen zur Schweizer Geschichte, Neue Folge, 1. Abt., *Chroniken* VII/1–13, H 1–3 (Basle, 1970–2001).
[7]J. von Müller, *Geschichten schweizerischer Eidgenossenschaft* (Leipzig, 1786–1805).
[8]J. E. Kopp, *Urkunden zur Geschichte der eidgenössischen Bünde,* vol. 1 (Lucerne, 1835), vol. 2 (Vienna, 1851) = Archiv für Kunde oesterreichischer Geschichtsquellen, 6.

constitution. The new histories were characterised by an optimistic faith in progress and by a liberal ideology from which the confederation itself was sprung. The massive histories written by Karl Dändliker or Johannes Dierauer, like the works of Wilhelm Oechsli, are clearly marked by this experience.[9] However, for all that the foundations they laid were to serve for much of the twentieth century, it is not to these works that we now address ourselves, but to Carl Hilty (1833–1909), who pioneered his generation's thinking on the philosophy of history.

It is symptomatic of the Swiss order of things that Hilty was not an historian but a professor of constitutional law, for the founding of the confederation presented historical scholarship with its precisely defined subject for investigation, and that led naturally to constitutional history. Hilty, however, offered more: he widened his compass to embrace what amounted in fact to a nationally focused philosophy of history. Nowhere else did he expound this philosophy of the state as directly or as coherently as in his *Vorlesungen über die Politik der Eidgenossen* ('Lectures on the Politics of the Confederates'), which appeared in 1875.[10]

Hilty's diaries reveal that his understanding of history was heavily influenced by Hegel's, which viewed historical epochs as 'unfoldings' of the World Spirit. Following in the footsteps of his other intellectual mentor, Carl Josias von Bunsen, Hilty found the yardstick for assessing development to be a matter of how closely the *spezieller Volksgeist* ('special national genius') at a given juncture approached the universal great ideas of humankind.[11] And it is a very Swiss trait in Hilty that for him this philosophical perspective on history – which he never formulates explicitly – should assume tangible form in a *Sittenlehre in nationalhistorischem Gewand* ('an ethic in the garb of a national history') and ultimately in *eine praktische Politik* ('a practical approach to politics'). The approach to politics was practical in the sense that not only was it well founded theoretically,

[9]S. Buchbinder, *Der Wille zur Geschichte: Schweizergeschichte um 1900 – die Werke von Wilhelm Oechsli, Johannes Dierauer und Karl Dändliker* (Zürich, 2002); K. Dändliker, *Geschichte der Schweiz mit besonderer Rücksicht auf die Entwicklung des Verfassungs- und Kulturlebens von den ältesten Zeiten bis zur Gegenwart*, 3 vols (Zürich, 1883–8); J. Dierauer, *Geschichte der schweizerischen Eidgenossenschaft*, Allgemeine Staatengeschichte, 1. Abt.: Geschichte der europäischen Staaten, 26, 5 vols (Gotha, 1887–1917); W. Oechsli, 'Orte und Zugewandte: eine Studie zur Geschichte des schweizerischen Bundesrechtes', *Jahrbuch für schweizerische Geschichte*, 13 (1888), 1–497; idem, *Die Anfänge der schweizerischen Eidgenossenschaft, zur 6. Säcularfeier des ersten ewigen Bundes vom 1. August 1291* (Berne, 1891); idem, *Geschichte der Schweiz im 19. Jh.*, Staatengeschichte der neuesten Zeit, 29/1 (Leipzig, 1903).
[10]C. Hilty, *Vorlesungen über die Politik der Eidgenossenschaft* (Berne, 1875).
[11]On Hilty's philosophy of history, see H. Mattmüller, *Carl Hilty, 1833–1909*, Basler Beiträge zur Geschichtswissenschaft, 100 (Basle, 1966), pp. 244–73.

it could be supported from historical experience. Historiography thus acquired an important function within the state.

In this connection Hilty wrote of great 'guiding ideas' that he saw as directing the life of a state and constituting its essential character. For Hilty, these political guiding ideas had been alive in the people at all times, and had been directed from the very beginning towards the 'true form of the confederation', which he believed had not as yet been realised. It was that settled form, he contended, that the 'national spirit' was ever striving to attain, because a robust national identity could continue to thrive only where the constitutional form and the national spirit were in harmony. Within this general aspiration Hilty identified a number of 'political guiding ideas' as active, having come into existence at the respective appropriate stages of national development. Initially sought 'unconsciously' and 'by instinct', they had gradually taken shape in the conscious domain, finally becoming maxims of the 'practical approach to politics'.

As his first guiding idea Hilty identified the preservation of 'the people's ancient traditional and natural freedom' from infringement by the absolute power of princes. This had been achieved by the assertion of freedom and of imperial immediacy, and that in turn had been made possible by giving the state *bündisch* ('confederate') structure. He held that this development was at first wholly conservative and defensive in nature. The realisation that the state needed an 'essential basis' in the form of 'a certain territorial area' had given rise to the second political guiding idea, that of the 'natural extent' of the 'circle of power'. This in turn, he went on to argue, had led to 'natural, necessary hostility' to Austria, the other power contending locally for territorial hegemony. This idea was linked to the martial spirit distinctive of Switzerland. At the same time, though, the very success of this idea had had certain negative consequences: the unequal membership status of the more recent adherents and the introduction of relationships of subjection had precluded the 'natural further development' of the federal state's earliest embryonic forms, which Hilty identified as having appeared in the first confederacies of 1291 and 1315. In his view Swiss foreign policy had lacked a whole-nation political principle because of the conflict of interests between the sovereign communities. Instead, the various mercenary treaties had drawn it into dependence on foreign powers.

Hilty wanted these political guiding ideas, gleaned from history, to direct 'the practical conduct of politics' in the present also. He considered that the confederation of free and equal 'confederate citizens' would not have been achieved as long as the cantonal restrictions remained in force; nor could the issue of the natural territorial limits be regarded as finally settled. In the status of neutrality guaranteed by the European powers Hilty saw no more than the modern institutionalised version of a dependence on foreign nations that precluded an autonomous Swiss foreign policy. The 'practical approach to politics', drawing on 'true historical spirit' rather than on 'historicism without the spirit', required that the spirit not be sacrificed to the form. The suppression of the spirit under the *ancien régime* in order to preserve the ossified form, Hilty felt, constituted the principal reason for the 'degenerate confederacy' and for the fact that 1798 eventually had to break what would not bend. The present-day 'ossified form', he declared, was the paralysing antagonism between 'federalism' and 'centralism'. The true political guiding idea of the contemporary present seemed to him to be national identity. In it he identified the latest unfolding of the 'world spirit', and in the call for a 'strong national identity' he saw the contemporary Swiss equivalent to the great 'world idea'.

Both Hilty's transparent interpretation of Swiss history and the great fact-laden overall accounts by the liberal historians thus are written from a common standpoint, a quite specific philosophically based idea of progress that envisages historical development from the very earliest times onwards as tending constantly, though not without retarding factors and caesurae, towards the ultimate goal prescribed by the progressively unfolding world spirit: the coming achievement of strong national identity embodied in the true confederation. In relation to this teleological understanding of national history, it was possible, so the thinking went, to clearly define and evaluate developments as positive (tending towards confederation) or negative (reflecting mere federalism, or contemporary internationalism).

That this reading of history was ideologically driven from the outset is best demonstrated by the relative ease with which the historiographical construct it proposes was applied to other, different ideas of progress. To illustrate the point, the sole, consistently Marxist comprehensive history of Switzerland – this too written by a non-historian – may be adduced here. Robert Grimm, the 1918 strike leader, using his six months of fortress imprisonment to compose his *Geschichte der Schweiz in ihren Klassenkämpfen* ('The History of Switzerland in its Class Struggles'),[12] relied in practice entirely on the account by Karl Dändliker. But this was more than enough for him to have the confederation originate from a progressive development in the Marxist sense, and to portray the latest workers' rising as a true successor movement to the 'class struggle of the "Markgenossen" [associates of primitive rural communities] and the citizens' against the aristocracy. The idea that he argued to be fundamental to Switzerland was that of class struggle – not the struggle for freedom. He saw evidence of the rightness of this view in the relationships of subjection introduced in the fifteenth century and regarded with disfavour by the liberal historians. It was these unequal relationships, Grimm argued, that demonstrated that the issue was not in fact freedom but, in the dialectical sense, the dominance of the class that is

---

[12]R. Grimm, *Geschichte der Schweiz in ihren Klassenkämpfen* (Berne, 1920), 2nd edn (Zürich, 1979).

victorious at a given time. This perspective, resting on one of the great liberal histories – not on fresh research – presents what might be termed a Marxist paraphrase on the liberal conceptual model. Although it rather oversimplifies the point, Grimm may be said to have replaced Hilty's guiding ideas for practical politics with the mechanisms of the Marxist dialectic – and it was what Dändliker had to say about the economy and about society that provided Grimm with the building-blocks for his argument. As with Hilty, development proceeded from the founding moment by way of the revolution to the present day, unidirectionally towards progress, even if there was a different understanding of the ultimate goal: for Hilty, a confederation characterised by strong national identity; here, the impending class supremacy of the proletariat. According to the particular end in sight, the respective development phases could be evaluated more or less in parallel in ideological terms: in Hilty, federalism, gradually ossifying, and its concomitant phenomena had been a retarding factor, whereas here they became a necessary and inevitable stage within the dialectical progress of history, a phase during which the current establishment class asserted its power *vis-à-vis* the progressive forces. It can thus be seen that the liberal, progress-oriented vision of history would lend itself to any ideology that relied on a progress model.

However, faith in progress had itself weakened, largely as a result of the shock of the First World War. The confederation and its parliamentarism now seemed inadequate to the circumstances of the times. Attempts to bring about constitutional change resulted in attention focusing temporarily on radical alternatives to the existing confederation. One context in which this happened was the historians' interpretation of the Swiss road to statehood.

In 1929 a Fribourg patrician named Gonzague de Reynold – Catholic, conservative and with a background in literary and cultural history – published *La Démocratie et la Suisse*, which confronted the liberal model itself with an unambiguous counter-position.[13] Like Hilty, who had contrasted 'theoretical' and 'practical' politics, de Reynold distinguished theoretical and historical conceptions of democracy. He too accorded primacy to the historical conception on the grounds that a people could be defined only in terms of its history. However, the historical construction was not begun from the current status quo, but rather on the basis of historical ground rules, as de Reynold perceived them: the *milieu naturel* in the first place, and the antecedents of the confederation. In his account, the political form comprising many autonomous communities and federalism grew out of the highly compartmentalised Alpine environment, and derives ultimately from the basic Roman imperial

---

[13]G. de Reynold, *La Démocratie et la Suisse: essai d'une philosophie de notre histoire nationale* (Berne, 1929).

concept of *Confoederatio Helvetica* – for de Reynold a brilliant accommodation to local conditions of which only Rome would have been capable – and from the particularist character of the medieval empire. Switzerland, then, had not sprung from the rebellion of freedom-loving shepherds seeking to found an independent democratic state, but was an outcome of the particularist principle. Constitutionally, it had not been a modern democracy but a mixed democracy as Thomas Aquinas would understand it: an aristo-democracy. The principal factor behind this had been the presence of stable, highly hierarchical families in the individual *Orte*. This system had reached its apogee in the fifteenth century. It had had additional support from the *esprit de corps*, a sense of corporate belonging that had no room for any concept of individual isolation in the crowd, and had precluded both *étatiste* centralism and monarchical absolutism. Family, corporation, community and federation: these had been the cornerstones of the historical democracy, and these had made the centralisation and egalitarianism of all theoretical democracy impossible. However, another thing that was prevented was the emergence of any great idea in the realm of foreign policy; this loss led eventually to neutrality, which was neither more nor less than an *'émasculation pour toute nation vivante'*.

In complete contrast to Hilty, de Reynold identifies the key constant of Swiss history as lying precisely in federalism, which here is seen in a favourable light, as a form appropriate not only to Swiss diversity but also to the 'doctrine of Empire, which in Switzerland has lived on'. Federalism, for de Reynold, brought with it an admirable measure of suppleness and resilience; it enabled Switzerland to endure inherent antinomies (*antinomies congénitales*) – including those existing on the level of *Weltanschauung*.

Thinking along these lines, de Reynold was bound to see the development of Switzerland since the Revolution, and particularly since the setting up of the confederation, as a breach with tradition, a development in the wrong direction. He held up his interpretation of 'historical democracy' in opposition to the 'theoretical' kind: in this reading, the Old Confederacy was in fact still alive, was the *pays vivant* subsisting among the Swiss people themselves. The confederation, by contrast, with its central institutions and programmeless parties, was merely the *pays légal*, separated by a deep chasm from the *pays vivant*, obsolete and spurious.

For our present purposes it is worth noting that de Reynold's text essayed an interpretation of Swiss history based on a fresh analysis and totally independent of the liberal historical construct, and aimed to expose the spuriousness of the liberal entelechy by reference to supposedly authentic medieval conditions and ideas. He was led by his decidedly individual notions of Roman history and a western empire of unbroken Christianity to fashion a view of history supported only by his own arbitrary collage of material and highly selective citation of earlier historians, to the extent of largely eluding serious academic comment. Yet it remains undeniable that his book was innovative, and consciously so. It was an attempt to counter the liberal conceptual model with a neoconservative one – which by its nature was, of course, bound to be ideologically determined. It was part of the stock-in-trade of the neoconservative and Frontist (far right) ideology of the 1930s – even across the linguistic and denominational divides – to hark back to the medieval confederacy and extol its corporative, indeed supposedly authoritarian, structures in contrast to the liberal understanding of democracy.[14] This nostalgic rhetoric reflected a perception, in the eyes of the Frontists, of growing general dissatisfaction with the Swiss democracy as a heritage from the liberal tradition.

While the historical accounts reviewed so far all seek to construct a narrative reaching from the beginnings to the present in line with this or that interpretation, there were also historians who chose to highlight what was new and radically different in the confederation of 1848. Eduard Fueter, for example, began his account – published in 1928 in the *Aufbau moderner Staaten* ('Structure of Modern States') series – with the lapidary statement: 'An account of modern Swiss history is entitled to begin its narration of events with the year 1848, omitting preliminaries.'[15] For at that date, he claimed, a wholly new era had begun, rendering the earlier points of contention obsolete 'at a stroke'. And William Rappard maintained in his *L'Individu et l'état* in 1936 that while Switzerland's history had begun with the first confederacies it was nonetheless the wholesale upheavals of 1798 and their principal consequences that must provide the basis for any understanding of modern Switzerland.[16] The paradox, he argued, was that after a century of free constitutional development, Switzerland was still living with a form of government much closer to the system imposed on it in 1798 (the *Helvétique*) than to that which had evolved during the many centuries of earlier history.

It is no accident that these two historians in particular, notably forthright in their judgement on the relationship between confederation and Old Confederacy, should both discard traditional political criteria. Fueter assigned a dominant role to economic and social history *vis-à-vis* the political variety, and presented an account which could have been attributed to the *Annales* school if that had not still been in its earliest infancy. Rappard, who did admittedly still

---

[14]A. Mattioli, *Intellektuelle von rechts: Ideologie und Politik in der Schweiz, 1918–1939* (Zürich, 1995); idem, *Zwischen Demokratie und totalitärer Diktatur: Gonzage de Reynold und die Tradition der autoritären Rechten in der Schweiz* (Zürich, 1994); P. Stadler, 'Zwischen Klassenkampf, Ständestaat und Genossenschaft: politische Ideologien im schweizerischen Geschichtsbild der Zwischenkriegszeit', *Historische Zeitschrift*, 219 (1974), 293–9.

[15]E. Fueter, *Die Schweiz seit 1848: Geschichte, Wirtschaft, Politik*, Aufbau moderner Staaten, 1 (Zürich and Leipzig, 1928).

[16]W. E. Rappard, *L'Individu et l'état dans l'évolution constitutive de la Suisse* (Zürich, 1936).

engage in the traditional type of debate, based his arguments on exogenous or at least non-party criteria in his diachronic study of certain structural givens – here the relationship between individual and state – as an approach to assessment of the historical development of the confederation.

This lucid discussion, emphasising the discontinuity between Old Confederacy and modern Switzerland, has to be seen alongside a diametrically opposed view which emerged in response to the spectacle of totalitarian regimes becoming established all around. This was the attempt to identify and describe the special character of the Swiss polity as a counterblast to the dictatorships, and also distinguishing it from the failing fledgling democracies. The key was found in the idea of *Genossenschaft* ('cooperative association'). An oration delivered in 1937 by Richard Feller as university principal, which attracted admiring comments at the time, addressed the significant topic of 'The Old Confederacy'.[17] He characterised *Genossenschaft* as the guiding idea particular to Switzerland. At that time there was wide acceptance, in the wake of Otto Gierke, that the term denoted corporations that dated back to the Middle Ages, were based on free association, and had a dialectical relationship to higher authority. Feller considered the *Genossenschaft* to be no mere jurists' construct but 'a living reality' embracing all the people, the expression of a degree of humanity persisting even in the modern state. Even if it had been the loser in the epochal struggle with the 'superhuman' state, it nevertheless continued to be active as a 'beneficent force'. The 'internal ethic' of the *Genossenschaft* with its self-regulating and equalising powers, Feller maintained, still constituted the essence of Switzerland's 'special path', irrespective of the forces of modernisation – and indeed all the more so at the present time, in confrontation with the totalitarian systems. Karl Meyer took a yet more decided view of the medieval confederacy as a force still affecting the present age. Contemporary Switzerland appeared to him as the 'still living memorial to a proud era of human life', specifically to 'the communal freedom movement of the Christian Middle Ages'.[18] Where Feller had still diagnosed the conflict between community and state as a step (which he deprecated) towards modernism, though seeing at the same time the ancient forces continuing to exert their 'beneficent' influence, Karl Meyer had the early confederacy, as he saw it, imposing itself as a presence from the past, like an erratic bloc, in the contemporary world of totalitarian states and unviable democracies, and this was how he explained its special-case character in the context of the present. The qualitative difference between Switzerland past and Switzerland present was simply ignored. It was this conceptual model that

---

[17]R. Feller, 'Von der Alten Eidgenossenschaft', in F. Strick (ed.), *Schweizerische Akademiereden* (Berne 1945), pp. 447–74.
[18]K. Meyer, *Aufsätze und Reden* (Zürich, 1952) p. 466.

later, during the Second World War, became an integral part of the so-called *Geistige Landesverteidigung* (Cultural Homeland Defence) – the emergency cultural policy with which the Swiss government sought to combat Nazi and fascist propaganda.

It can be noted only in passing here that there were, of course, other Swiss histories that by and large rejected such interpretations. In addition to Eduard Fueter, discussed above, mention should be made of the comparatively matter-of-fact 'Four-Man History', as it soon became known, of 1934,[19] and of the notable work by Emil Dürr, which appeared in 1933: it is extremely well informed, develops the history from the complex interplay of forces in the Swiss lands in the fourteenth and fifteenth centuries, and avoids subscribing to fashionable, teleological views.[20] It may be added that from the late 1960s onwards historical scholarship in Switzerland followed the international trend in addressing a broad range of issues that duly found their way into Swiss histories: at first only in a restrained manner, in the *Handbuch der Schweizer Geschichte* (1972–7), but then very markedly in the *Geschichte der Schweiz und der Schweizer* (1982–3). These latter works can scarcely be described as master narratives, however, as they can hardly be said to have had a reception sufficient to qualify them as such. There were two main factors involved here: on the one hand, the period since the 1960s in Switzerland has generally seen a decline in the importance attached to the 'national' question, and thus also of interest in 'Swiss history', while, on the other, the long-dominant, originally liberal master narrative has retained its currency among the conservative and traditionalist sectors of the population, along with an admixture of similarly tradition-laden threat perceptions and defensive reflexes, and Johannes von Müller's rousing vision of the founding of the state, often relayed via Schiller's *Wilhelm Tell*.[21]

Interpretative models in France: the relationship between the monarchy and the republican nation-state

The intention at this point is simply to use a further factually well-attested turning point in the development of a nation-state to show how explicatory models are developed by way of interpretative back-projection, with an eye to the current or still desired national political status. In France, this turning point is the revolution. The post-revolutionary French nation-state owed both its existence and its territorial extent to the activities of the kings of the past. Also, the young republic contained forces that were seeking to bring about a

---

[19]H. Nabholz, L. von Muralt, R. Feller and E. Bonjour, *Geschichte der Schweiz* (Zürich, 1932).
[20]E. Dürr, 'Von Morgarten bis Marignano', *Schweizer Kriegsgeschichte*, vol. 2, H. 4 (Berne, 1933), 713.
[21]For a recent instance, see P. Stadler, *Epochen der Schweizergeschichte* (Zürich, 2003).

reinstated monarchy. This is how the republican and the monarchist concepts of the state came to contend for an historical rationale for the nation-state.[22]

In 1828, at a time when an accommodation between the old and the new regimes was being sought, and indeed partly achieved during the July monarchy under the Orléans kings (1830–48) through the closeness of the monarchy to the liberal bourgeoisie, François-Pierre-Guillaume Guizot, an adherent of the liberal Orléans tradition, identified the birth of the modern French state as having occurred in the fifteenth century. It was then, during the conflict with England, that the national spirit (*esprit national*) first appeared. According to Guizot, a rationalised territory came into being at that time, expanded and underwent consolidation, and a state power arose capable of organising itself and enforcing its will. Under Charles VII the ruling power had attained an unprecedented degree of unity, regularity and consistency, and had definitively ended the feudal dominance of the aristocracy. But the rise of freedom of conscience and the release of the human spirit that Guizot believed he could see in the popular reform movement led by Jan Hus and in the early Renaissance paralleled the development of a profound incompatibility between the state as it grew ever more powerful and the individual who justifiably rebelled against this. Here one glimpses the future Guizot: as prime minister he was to pioneer a representative system of governance that would bridge the divide. However, he categorised the communal movements – those 'essays in republican organisation' – as running counter to the grand overall movement of a history which had its 'glorious goal' (*le but glorieux*) in attaining to a 'lofty and free unity'. In Guizot's reading, the force that moved with the general direction of the nation's history was in fact the fifteenth-century monarchy.

A different view, though agreeing on the direction, was taken by Augustin Thierry, another liberal historian, who had dedicated himself in particular to researching the role played by the *tiers état* in French history. For Thierry the earliest beginnings of the French state were to be found in the thirteenth century, in the early alliance of the monarchy and the bourgeoisie against the feudal aristocracy. Throughout French history, in his view, two things went hand in hand: the increasing numbers of free individuals under the aegis of the urban bourgeoisie, and the increasing tendency of the citizens collectively to place themselves

---

[22]On the following section, see C-O. Carbonell, 'Les Origines de l'état moderne: les traditions historiographiques françaises (1820–1990)', in W. Blockmans and J.-P. Genet (eds), *Visions sur le développement des états européens: théories et historiographies de l'état moderne*, Collection de l'Ecole française de Rome, 171 (Rome, 1993), pp. 297–312; E. Fauquet, 'La Place de l'histoire de France de Michelet', in Y.-M. Bercé and P. Contamine (eds), *Histoires de France, historiens de la France: actes du colloque international, Reims, 14–15 May 1993* (Paris, 1994), pp. 267–80; O. Dumoulin, 'Histoire et historiens de droite', in J.-F. Sirinelli (ed.), *Histoire des droites en France*, vol. 2 (Paris, 1992), pp. 327–98 (ch. 9).

directly under royal protection and royal jurisdiction. The jurists, bourgeois themselves, had destroyed the privileges and power of the feudal lords, benefiting both the king and the people, and had worked towards equality for the citizens and national administrative unity. The great movement for community autonomy, as expressed in the General Estates of the years 1355–7, had aspired to goals associated for Thierry with only the most recent of revolutions. And while Charles V did indeed fight against the citizens of Paris, Thierry concedes, he nevertheless adopted some of their political objectives. The victor had learnt a lesson from his defeated opponents. In that hour, truly, France was born. And for Thierry this same France still existed, regardless of the revolution, and now, so he hoped, under the July Monarchy of Louis Philippe, would attain its ultimate form; this would reflect the constitutional principle Thierry advocated, according to which the two mainstays of the eternal France and of the modern French nation-state were the royal power and the power of the bourgeoisie.

This vision of history was not universally shared. There were alternative constructions. In his *L'Ancien Régime et la révolution* (1856), the aristocratic liberal Alexis Clérel de Tocqueville set out to show how the centralisation of state power had grown gradually to start with, then from the seventeenth century onwards established itself inexorably, to the detriment of feudal and aristocratic freedoms. With the introduction of general taxation in the fifteenth century, he suggested, France had begun to drift towards a blatantly despotic centralism. The underlying reason for this, in de Tocqueville's argument, lay in the natural tendency of democratic peoples – or of the democratic sector of society – to centralise power for the sake of the equality of all. It was the same model that Thierry had propounded, but with negative replacing positive, for here aristocratic values were falling by the wayside.

A different view again was taken by advocates of the republican approach. Jules Michelet, in his great *Histoire de France*, sought to identify the spirit of the nation in the ordinary people as a whole, seen as shaping history. What, then, was the role of the monarchy? France's path to statehood, according to Michelet, began under Philippe le Bel. Michelet too identified the essential nature of this state as residing in its centralism, and in the despotism and exploitation of the people by a monarchy whose self-serving conduct he depicts in lurid detail. The historic moment, the dawning of salvation for France, was heralded for Michelet by the reign of the Sun King, Louis XIV, and was reaching fulfilment in the contemporary present, though in a strange inversion: 'Louis XIV completed the task of giving the country equality, that is to say, enabling the people to do without the monarchy.'[23] This cleared the road ahead, which was to lead by way of the revolution to the modern republic. Here, in contrast to Guizot, it was the

---

[23]Fauquet, 'Place de l'histoire'.

people that constituted the force driving with the flow of national history, while the monarchy was merely the factor that involuntarily helped the people to find self-expression.

A later advocate of the republican tradition, Tommy Perrens, published studies (in 1860 and 1872 respectively) of Etienne Marcel and of medieval democracy in France. By contrast again, Perrens here argued from the thesis of a dualism from which, in the fourteenth century, two rival states had been born. The first of these, brought into being by the General Estates of 1356 and 1357, had secured the great achievements of 1789 for the French nation; the other had crushed Etienne Marcel's Paris revolution and the Jacquerie, thereby diverting France over a period of five centuries from the path taken by England to parliamentary government. The Paris revolution, Perrens contended, had not been a premature, half-baked effort, but might in fact very well have succeeded. Historians were wrong to assume that everything that happens in history is a necessary stage in development, and that the progress made by French culture, and even liberty itself, could not have been achieved otherwise than at the price of centuries of despotism. For Perrens there was thus also a latent democratic tradition stretching back to the fourteenth century, one that had remained continuously alive and finally surfaced at the time of the revolution, while the monarchy represented a non-viable development and had been essentially dispensable.

To sum up what has been said here about French national historiography: all the master narratives during the period of constitutional struggles over monarchy and republic subscribed to the conceptual model of a bipolarity of throne and people developing at an early stage, assessed differently according to the authorial slant. In this way they constructed historical continuity either as legitimation for constitutional monarchy, or alternatively as legitimation for the republic, which would then likewise acquire roots reaching far back into pre-revolutionary history.

The master narrative as construction

It will no doubt have become clear that the various models described, whether relating to Switzerland or to France, were determined, broadly speaking, by considerations either extrinsic to the historical discipline or of a pre-scientific nature; that they have a background in contemporary constitutional issues; and that further relevant factors are immediate political context and the ideological stance of the author concerned. Only a process of back-projection, for instance, makes it possible for the relationship between federalism and centralism, or between individual and state, to become a continuous thread stretched far back into the earliest times and serving as a reference-line for the purposes of judging Swiss historical development. And depending on the political and ideological orientation of the writer, the guiding reference-line is always stretched back into the past in a new and different way, and the evaluative judgement is then also different. In

326 Guy P. Marchal

France, too, judgements like those that see the General Estates of the fourteenth century as direct antecedents of the revolution, and the monarchy as having paved the way for the republic, can only arise as a result of back-projection from one particular angle. For the Middle Ages and indeed the early modern period, even the conceptual framework used seems anachronistic. Thus, when it comes to the nation-state's history being written on the basis of this or that conceptual model, the result can fairly be described as a construction aimed at serving the particular teleology involved. This way of working is at its most transparent when applied to factually indisputable turning points in a nation's history as has been demonstrated and illustrated here, with reference first to the founding of the Swiss Confederation in 1848 with its antecedents, and then, for comparison, to the French Revolution and its aftermath.

National master narrative and religious denomination

A reading of the broad-scope alternative model that is de Reynold's riposte to the liberal master narrative prompts the question of whether further similar interpretative models may prove to have been used by professional historians of conservative, Catholic provenance. Here it is important to note at the outset that, in spite of the small population, Catholicism in Switzerland was characterised by plurality of background;[24] this in itself is sufficient reason to expect considerable diversity of standpoint. In contrast to the situation in Germany, where the mutual relations between historians were much more sharply aligned on confessional divisions,[25] the historians active in Roman Catholic central Switzerland enjoyed the wholehearted professional respect of their Protestant colleagues. The critical school had actually been launched in Catholic Lucerne, by Joseph Eutych Kopp, and historians from central Switzerland continued in later years to be particularly active in basic research. The most original mind among them was Robert Durrer (1863–1934), who had studied and taken his doctorate in Protestant Zurich, working under Wilhelm Oechsli, among others. It was Durrer, never visibly concerned to distance himself from the liberal

---

[24]M. Graetz and A. Mattioli (eds), *Krisenwahrnehmungen im Fin de siècle: jüdische und katholische Bildungseliten in Deutschland und der Schweiz, 1880–1914*, Clio Lucernensis, 4 (Zürich, 1997); U. Altermatt (ed.), *Katholische Denk- und Lebenswelten: Beiträge zur Kultur- und Sozialgeschichte des Schweizer Katholizismus im 20. Jahrhundert* (Fribourg, 2003); M. Grunewald and U. Puschner (eds), *Das katholische Intellektuellenmilieu in Deutschland, seine Presse und seine Netzwerke / Le Milieu intellectuel catholique en Allemagne, sa presse et ses réseaux (1871–1963)* (Berne, Brussels, Frankfurt/M, New York, Oxford and Vienna, 2006).
[25]On the following section – except where otherwise noted – see G. P. Marchal, 'Zwischen "Geschichtsbaumeistern" und "Römlingen": katholische Historiker und die Nationalgeschichtsschreibung in Deutschland und in der Schweiz', in Graetz and Mattioli, *Krisenwahrnehmungen*, pp. 177–210.

master narrative, who among other things produced the first complete edition of all the *Bundesbriefe* (federal charters) to be made accessible to the ordinary reader. This appeared in 1904.[26] Among the reasons for his relaxed stance was the fact that the liberal view of history had given currency to a kind of 'scientific myth' that told of early and future-conscious progress towards statehood; this approach had even generated imaginative re-creations of the very beginnings and assigned a central role in them to the Forest Cantons of central Switzerland. There were institutional factors involved too, foremost among them being the Allgemeine Geschichtsforschende Gesellschaft der Schweiz (Swiss Association for Historical Research), a grouping formed in 1841 which brought historians together with their subject colleagues, without regard to religious denomination, political affiliation or language group. Thus in 1850, even with the political wounds inflicted by the *Sonderbund* crisis still very raw, it was possible for a Catholic conservative, Philipp Anton von Segesser, of Lucerne, to be elected as the society's president. Yet it is undeniable that the Catholic cultural elite was numerically small, and in terms of employment prospects, relative to those of Reformed colleagues, it was institutionally disadvantaged. Indeed, the disadvantage this group suffered was of a positively structural character, if one stops to reflect that Catholicism was largely confined to rural areas, and the *Kulturkampf* only highlighted the point.

While the founding of the Catholic University of Fribourg in 1889 helped to reduce this disadvantage, there is no mistaking the language of perceived inferiority in such utterances as the address delivered by the Fribourg professor Albert Büchi to the Catholic Convention of 1903 under the title 'Die Aufgabe der Katholiken auf dem Gebiete der Geschichtsschreibung in der Schweiz' ('The Task Facing Catholics in the Field of Historiography in Switzerland'). The Department of History at Fribourg University was endowed, eventually, with five chairs, and at double the Swiss average ran Berlin and Vienna close in sheer size, while the descriptions of the scope of each chair reflected the latest state of the art in German university history departments. This made it clear that the Department of History at Fribourg was intended to render the charge of Catholic inferiority obsolete. That aim was duly realised at Fribourg as a result of notable achievements in various special fields, but in particular through basic research. In addition, efforts were made in the early stages to mount a challenge to Protestant historiography by way of research on Zwingli and the controversial figure of Cardinal Matthäus Schiner – and this shifted the focus to the fifteenth/sixteenth-century period. Revealingly, for our present enquiry, this shift of focus ruled out the possibility of any confrontation with the established liberal interpretation of the national history – which at the time, prompted by the anniversary

---

[26]R. Durrer, *Die Bundesbriefe der alten Eidgenossen, 1291–1513* (Zürich, 1904).

celebrations of 1886 (battle of Sempach, 1386) and 1891 (first Bundesbrief, 1291), was being concentrated mainly on the thirteenth and fourteenth centuries. In later times, too, the emphasis at Fribourg until the mid-1960s, where Swiss history was concerned, under Oskar Vasella (d. 1966), was the period of the Reformation and Counter-Reformation.[27] From the 1980s on, under Urs Altermatt, the limelight switched to contemporary history. The pronouncements from Fribourg were overtly Catholic in sentiment, but remained thoroughly scholarly in character.

Significantly, a *Fribourg History of Switzerland* was never contemplated. However, a number of histories of Switzerland had their source in and around Fribourg. One was Joseph Hürbin's two-volume *Handbuch der Schweizer Geschichte* (1900–6),[28] which relied for the period up to 1515 on the lecturing notes of Heinrich Reinhardt, a Lucerne scholar called to the Catholic University of Fribourg; another example was *Histoire de la Suisse* (1928) by the Fribourg professor Gaston Castella.[29] Neither of these amounted to a major overall interpretation of Swiss history, let alone an alternative reading. They are thoroughly pedestrian in style, relative to Dändliker or Dierauer, and seem to shy away from any attempt at a comprehensive interpretation. Their reporting of the factual issues broadly follows Dändliker and Dierauer. However, the polarisation discernible in those earlier accounts – centralism vs. federalism, federal state vs. federation of states – was typically avoided or glossed over. Hürbin, for instance, might report descriptively on the fact of the *Staatenbund* (federation of states), while omitting the value judgements that had been attached to it. What Hürbin gives his readers is in broad terms a factual history amplified by extra chapters on church history and on cultural, literary and art history. It is only in specific areas that a Roman Catholic standpoint becomes evident – in his negative view of late medieval state church tradition, the detailed analysis of the Reformation, and the points at which the Catholic side was accused of having thwarted the natural evolution towards a federal state. In this way any vigorous rival concept of the national historical development was rendered impossible. The great task of interpreting national history remained effectively the monopoly of liberal historiography.

Alps, not race

In an age of nascent great powers that drew their legitimation primarily from a common ethnic identity and language, Switzerland with its four languages

---

[27] See *Festschrift Oskar Vasella* (Fribourg, 1964); M. Jorio, 'Oskar Vasella (1904–1966): ein bedeutender Reformationshistoriker', *Zeitschrift für schweizerische Kirchengeschichte*, 90 (1996), 83–99.
[28] J. Hürbin, *Handbuch der Schweizer Geschichte*, 2 vols (Stans, 1900/6).
[29] G. Castella, *Histoire de la Suisse* (Einsiedeln, 1928).

found itself – like several other multilingual nation-states – in need of a rationale. Belgium had had its existence argued for on grounds of a geopolitical situation dating back to medieval times, as the crossroads of Latin and Germanic cultural influences, and was now assigned a role as crossroads of Europe. The tiny state of Luxembourg had had its existence within Europe justified on the grounds of its role as a bridge between the Germanic and Romance cultures. And in Switzerland too, a particular geopolitical location was used to build up the notion of a particular European mission.[30] From the heights of the St Gotthard pass – geographically perceived to be 'in the heart of Europe' and serving to link the peoples – Switzerland was to set the whole continent an example of different ethnic groups living peaceably together in a well-ordered state. This outwards-directed variant had its self-contained counterpart: that of Switzerland as the place of refuge in the central Alps for endangered or suppressed values such as freedom, human rights and the European ideals. These were to be safeguarded here for the sake of Europe's future, a vision expressed, for example, in the metaphor of Switzerland as 'guardian of Europe's mountain passes and pure water sources'. These ideas were recycled over and over again in varying formulations and seem to have become more firmly anchored in the national consciousness than the corresponding notions in Belgium and Luxembourg.

There was no race discourse in Switzerland in the national history context, whereas Belgium saw the emergence of a specifically Flemish national version, and later a Walloon national version, of Belgian national history, and in Luxembourg a 'historic race' was introduced, said to have been composed of Gauls, Romans and ancient Germans coming together to form the Luxembourg nation.

Carl Hilty (discussed above) declared in 1875 that it was neither language nor race that made Switzerland a nation, for 'all the influence that Nature, language, blood and tribal identity can muster' was tugging the Swiss apart, and towards their *Stammesgenossen* ('ethnic group'). The true foundation of the *Staat schweizerischer Eidgenossenschaft* ('nation state of the Swiss Confederation'), he maintained, was in fact an idea, 'a political way of thinking and political will, moving steadily towards ever greater clarity', and responsible for the successful bonding of the various ethnic groups into a single nation-state. Hilty here became the first exponent of the concept of the Swiss *Willensnation* ('nation shaped by the will of

---

[30]On the following section, see G. P. Marchal, 'La Naissance du mythe de Saint-Gothard ou la longue découverte de l'homo alpinus et de l'Helvetia mater fluviorum', in J.-F. Bergier and S. Guzzi (eds), *La Découverte des Alpes*, Itinera, 12 (Basle, 1992), pp. 35–53; Marchal, *Gebrauchsgeschichte*, pp. 463–79. See also O. Zimmer, 'In Search of Natural Identity: Alpine Landscape and the Reconstruction of the Swiss Nation', *Comparative Studies in Society and History*, 40 (1998), 637–65. For general treatment, see F. Walter, *Les Figures paysagères de la nation: territoire et paysage en Europe (16e–20e siècles)* (Paris, 2004), passim.

330 Guy P. Marchal

its people'): it represented a national identity that ranked 'high above mere blood ties and linguistic ties'. Johann Caspar Bluntschli, a Swiss constitutional historian, in a considered response to Hilty in 1875, preferred to see this in more factual terms. In his view, what held the Swiss together was quite simply the rule of law, and then above all their love of their homeland. He elaborated the idea of 'their homeland' in terms of its special landscape with its Alps, writing of a 'perfected and richly complex natural entity' that fostered a 'unique sense of shared homeland'. And so once again the Alps are brought forward, this time as the bedrock of national identity. It is of note that the function here attributed to the Alps of engendering unity and identity was an idea developed with input from all the linguistic groups. When the western Swiss scholar Ernest Bovet spoke out in 1909 against the 'aggressive racial theories', he saw the 'mysterious bond' that united the Swiss as lying in their history, in the 'common cult of independence' and, above all, in the Alps. Swiss national individuality derived in his view from the interaction of the natural world of the high mountains with the popular character. Bovet eventually summed this up in his vision of the spirit descending from the heights, of the genius of the Alps that had preserved Switzerland, had formed its democratic institutions and was now bringing the various languages together in a harmonious paean for the one common ideal. For the German- and Italian-speaking regions too there are similar affirmations. They certainly reflect what was a widespread self-image of the Swiss at the time. In the 1930s, in the context of 'Cultural Homeland Defence', such concepts became concentrated in what was first an Alpine and later specifically a St Gotthard myth which even left its mark on the publications of Swiss geographers.[31]

Different languages but a single ideal: this was the formula to convey succinctly the insight that although the assertion of Swiss national identity must rest in large part on the appeal to 'the Alps, link between peoples', there was more that could be done: an active policy on national history pursued concurrently would enable the French- and Italian-speaking sectors of the population to acknowledge the *urschweizerische* ('primitive Swiss') founding fathers of the confederacy as their own ancestors too.

It is true that in the 1930s racial discourse was taken up in Switzerland as in other countries: an anthropologist measured skulls[32] and an archaeologist

---

[31]M. Fahlbusch, M. Rössler and D. Siegrist, *Geographie und Nationalsozialismus: Drei Fallstudien zur Institution Geographie im Deutschen Reich und der Schweiz*, with appendix by P. Jüngst and O. Meder, Urbs et regio, 51 (Kassel, 1989).

[32]G. Kreis, 'Der "homo alpinus helveticus": zum schweizerischen Rassendiskurs der 30er Jahre', in G. P. Marchal and Aram Mattioli (eds), *Erfundene Schweiz: Konstruktionen nationaler Identität / La Suisse imaginée: bricolages d'une identité nationale*, Clio Lucernensis, 1 (Zürich, 1992), pp. 175–90 (with secondary reading); C. Keller, *Der Schädelvermesser: Otto Schlaginhaufen – Anthropologe und Rassenhygieniker: eine biographische Reportage* (Zürich, 1995).

traced the Swiss people back through an ancestry distinct from the Aryans to their own race of lake-dwellers.[33] Yet, considered in the round, all these things – except for the muscle-flexing by the loudmouthed racists of the pro-Nazi Frontist movement and their talk of 'healthy anti-Semitism in the Old Confederacy' – seem to amount in reality to nothing more than a marginal note to history, a note of mere academic or whimsical interest, and sometimes of both.

Gender and writing the nation

Switzerland was later in acquiring a representative female icon than the other republics (Venice, fourteenth century; the Netherlands, sixteenth century). In compensation, the chosen figure appears emancipated from the outset. Where other representative females were at first subjected to symbolic nuptials with their country's ruler – be it the doge, the line of the House of Orange or the French king – no such arrangements could be made for the Corpus Helveticum. And so, from first inception, 'Helvetia' has a self-reliant and virginal image. If one discounts the other female allegorical figures representing *Libertas* or *Abundantia* or *Fortitudo* and so on, the first explicit appearance of 'Helvetia' can be dated after the Peace of Westphalia to the 1670s. This figure met a need that could not be supplied by the earlier iconography featuring the Confederates' coat-of-arms: the need for a strong visual symbol, suitable for a republican context, of the unity that was the *idée maîtresse* of the age of sovereignty.[34] However, Helvetia was obliged to share the representative role with masculine identification figures such as Tell, the three original confederates of the Rütli Oath, or Winkelried. During the nineteenth century, in common with other countries, Switzerland decided to have an official state emblem, and, especially with circumstances in mind that required presentation of the single, overriding abstract concept of the state – for such settings as monuments, coins and medals, festivals and historical processions – Helvetia as a suitably appealing personification became a natural choice.[35] There is no evidence of any feminisation of hostile nations occurring in Switzerland. The characteristic threat discourse there is rather to invoke Tell or the

[33]K. Keller-Tarnuzzer, *Die Herkunft des Schweizervolkes* (Frauenfeld, 1936). Keller-Tarnuzzer was an archaeologist with interests in prehistory and ancient history.

[34]T. Maissen, 'Von wackeren alten Eidgenossen und souveränen Jungfrauen: zu Datierung und Deutung der frühesten "Helvetia"-Darstellungen', *Zeitschrift für Archäologie und Kulturgeschichte*, 56 (1999), 256–301; idem, *Die Geburt der Republic: Staatsverständnis und Repräsentation in der frühneuzeitlichen Eidgenossenschaft*, Historische Semantik, 4 (Göttingen, 2006), esp. pp. 253–77.

[35]G. Kreis, *Helvetia – im Wandel der Zeiten: die Geschichte einer nationalen Repräsentationsfigur* (Zürich, 1991); A. Stercken, *Enthüllung der Helvetia: die Sprache der Staatspersonifikation im 19. Jahrhundert*, Reihe historische Anthropologie, 29 (Berlin, 1998).

medieval battle victories, those key constants of Switzerland's historical self-image, as a signal of national readiness to take up arms against superior forces.

Swiss national historiography and historical culture appear to be – and are – a masculine product through and through, history during the nineteenth century being a field of almost exclusively masculine interest. Even so – and significantly enough, given the context – the year 1834 saw the appearance of a pamphlet entitled *Heroines of Switzerland*, written by a male philologist and a male historian and reproducing the conventional stereotypes of the age regarding women.[36] If we persist in seeking out a contribution by women to writing the nation, it cannot be a mere matter of analysing dissertation topics chosen by female authors, if only because many of the choices will have been influenced by the supervisor. It is much more to the point to ask whether women shared in creating the national master narrative, and, if so, how. Such an enquiry leaves us with no option but at least to outline the hard-won accession of women to the ranks of professional academic historians.[37] It is true that in 1887, at Zurich – and only after a long battle to be licensed at all – the first woman historian was able to conclude her studies with a doctorate,[38] and that subsequently further women were to gain doctorates – though they always remained substantially outnumbered by men. And yet, a few isolated special cases apart,[39] it was only after the educational offensive of the late 1960s that it became feasible for women to achieve professional status and carve out a career in the field of historical scholarship. If we compare this chronology with the development of historical scholarship as a system of knowledge that provides its own subject of investigation – albeit not independently of the social context – we find that at the period during which the history of nation-states and the writing of the nation in the

---

[36]J. J. Honegger and G. Meyer von Knonau, *Heldinnen des Schweizerlandes* (Zürich, 1834).

[37]I. Herrmann, 'Au croisement des impasses de la démocratie? Les femmes et l'écriture de l'histoire nationale Suisse', in I. Porciani and M. O'Dowd (eds), *History Women*, special issue of *Storia della Storiagrafia*, 46 (2004), 59–68; B. Ziegler, 'Historikerinnen an der Universität Zürich, 1900–1970', in C. Bosshart-Pfluger, D. Grisard and C. Späti (eds), *Geschlecht und Wissen/Genre et Savoir/Gender and Knowledge* (Zürich, 2004), pp. 237–48; B. Studer, '"Die Wissenschaft sei geschlechtslos und Gemeingut Aller": Frauen in der Genese und Tradition der historischen Disziplin', in Bosshart-Pfluger et al., *Geschlecht und Wissen*, pp. 361–78.

[38]M. von Salis, *Agnes von Poitou, Kaiserin von Deutschland: eine historisch-kritisch-psychologische Abhandlung* (Zürich, 1887) – hence earlier than the first female dissertation in Germany (Anna Gebser, Heidelberg, 1896/7: Porciani and O'Dowd, *History Women*, p. 22).

[39]Such as the exceptional case in Geneva, Marguerite Cramer, who lectured in 1914 on Genevan history in the capacity of a *professeur suppléant*. Others who should be mentioned are: Dr Jeanne Niquille (1894–1970), who entered the archive service in 1918 and later worked until 1957 as official archivist to the canton of Fribourg (see C. Bosshart-Pfluger, 'Jeanne Niquille (1894–1970): Staatsarchivarin ehrenhalber', *Freiburger Geschichtsblätter*, 75 (1998), 168–74); Berthe Widmer, from 1962 *Privatdozentin* (freelance university lecturer), then from 1972 personal chair, both at Basle.

context of nation-building positively dominated historical research, it was impossible for women to become career historians, and we find also that by the time this eventually did become possible, the topics mentioned had long since lost that dominant position. Historical research had moved on to new concepts and new problems. The Swiss women historians did more than simply benefit from this paradigm change: in the context of women's emancipation – for Swiss women did not achieve full and equal citizenship until granted active and passive voting rights in 1971 – they actually helped to bring it about. The issue cannot be pursued here;[40] however, this brief excursus was necessary because it shows why women historians intervening in the national history discourse were obliged to do so in fields other than that of historical scholarship. It also explains why, to hear their voices, we are obliged to follow them into these other fields, specifically those of literature and of political activism. Given the present research position, only three examples can be put forward here.

In other countries, in the nineteenth century, women interested in history would find a voice through such genres as historical novels, historical drama, belletristic historical studies, or juvenile literature, and by these means could certainly influence the writing of the nation.[41] Switzerland, at least on the occasion of the confederation jubilee in 1891, had one woman making her voice heard through an original historical novel entitled *Wilhelm Tell*. That she did so is noteworthy in view of the importance of the foundation tradition for the national historical discourse. A resident of Bergell, and writing under the pseudonym of Silvia Andrea, Johanna Gredig had since 1888 been publishing historical stories and novels in which wise women were regularly at the centre of the action. She also put the results of her own research into amplifying the story of the liberation with various female figures who would play an active part in political decisions and political action. But her attempt to retrieve the foundation narrative for women was to fail, because, as the author observed, already having 'their great Wilhelm Tell, provided by Schiller', the Swiss did not want to see 'a lesser Tell at his side' – nor, probably, to see the men they had made their heroes flanked by women playing an active role in events.[42]

The other two contributions to the national historical discourse were both made in 1934, by women who had completed doctorates in history. In 1901,

---

[40]See, for example, the relevant articles in *Geschichtsforschung in der Schweiz: Bilanz und Perspektiven, 1991 / L'Histoire en Suisse: Bilan et perspectives, 1991* (Basle, 1992).

[41]J. Tollebeek, 'Writing History in the Salon Vert', in Porciani and O'Dowd, *History Women*, pp. 35–40, esp. pp. 38ff.; M. Friedrich and M. Heidegger, 'Zwischen historischer "Dichtung" und akademischer "Wahrheit": zur Situierung von Frauen in der Verwissenschaftlichung', in C. Bosshart-Pfluger et al., *Geschlecht und Wissen*, pp. 278–85.

[42]S. Kubli and D. Stump (eds), *'Viel Köpfe, viel Sinn': Texte von Autorinnen aus der deutschsprachigen Schweiz, 1795–1945* (Zürich, Berne and Dortmund, 1994), pp. 109–19.

under the supervision of Professor Gustav Tobler at Berne, Maria Krebs had gained her PhD with a dissertation entitled *Die Politik von Bern, Solothurn, und Basel in den Jahren 1466–1468: Zeitgeschichtliches zum Mülhauser Krieg* ('The Politics of Berne, Solothurn, and Basle, 1466–1468: The Contemporary Background to the War of Mülhausen'). However, it was not as an historian but as a literary writer, and under the name of Maria Waser, that she was later to become a personality of real influence on the Swiss literary scene and the most celebrated Swiss woman writer of the first half of the twentieth century. It was in this role – paradoxically, because her own lifestyle followed traditional patterns – that she accepted a speaking invitation from the women's movement in 1928. In her address on 'The Mission of Women' she pressed for the political rights that women in any genuine democracy ought to possess. In 1934, the year after Hitler seized power in Germany, she reached out to the public at large with an essay, widely read and respected at the time, on *Lebendiges Schweizertum* ('Living Swissness'). It put forward a highly idiosyncratic – indeed visionary – interpretation of Swiss history, the course of which, she claimed, was determined by a masculine principle symbolised in Tell and a feminine one symbolised in Staufacher's wife. In her essay Waser interprets the course of Swiss history step by step, all the way to the present, as the resultant of the combined and equally valid action of these mutually complementary principles, with steps in development resulting from the preponderance of one or other principle on an alternating basis; and from this she inferred political lessons for contemporary Switzerland.[43]

The other female historian, four years younger, was Ida Somazzi, who took her doctorate only in 1919 after a long spell as a schoolteacher, initially as head of a private school in Argentina and later in Bolligen, near Berne. Her doctoral thesis was on the *Geschichte der obrigkeitlichen Lehrgotten im Alten Bern* ('History of the Officially Appointed Primary Schoolteachers in Berne').[44] Subsequently she became a committed protagonist of women's rights while discharging the duties of a series of other responsibilities: tutor at the college of education in Berne, member of the Executive Committee of the Swiss Union for the League of Nations, and later a member of the Swiss delegation at UNESCO and chair of the UN and UNESCO Study Commission on Women's

---

[43]M. Waser, 'Lebendiges Schweizertum: aus einem Vortrag', *Neue Schweizer Rundschau*, Neue Folge, 1 (1934), 709–22; idem, *Lebendiges Schweizertum*, Schriften für Schweizer Art und Kunst, 126/7 (Zürich, 1934); Marchal, *Gebrauchsgeschichte* (note 5), pp142s. On Waser (1878–1939): Kubli and Stump, *'Viel Köpfe'*, pp. 162–4; G. Küffer, *Maria Waser* (Berne, 1971).

[44]First published only in 1925, by the Central Committee of the Swiss Women Teachers' Association (Schweizerischer Lehrerinnen-Verein): I. Somazzi, *Geschichte der obrigkeitlichen Lehrgotte im Alten Bern: ein Beitrag zur Schulgeschichte und zur Geschichte der Frau im Dienste des öffentlichen Unterrichts* (Berne, 1925).

Issues. In 1933 she helped to set up the Arbeitsgemeinschaft Frau und Demo-kratie (Working Group on Women and Democracy), which was constituted from a number of women's pro-democracy groups of different political hues. In 1934, probably in the context of this working group, she delivered a lecture entitled *Der schweizerische Staatsgedanke im Sturm der Zeit* ('The Idea of the Swiss State amid the Storms of Our Age').[45] In response to the increasing ten-dency in Switzerland, as elsewhere, to question the value of democracy, the address called on women to equip themselves for mental and moral resistance to totalitarian ideas, and for the defence of the liberal and democratic state. To that end, Somazzi sought to draw 'principles and guiding ideas' from the past. She did this with a constitutional historian's perspective on the whole of Swiss history, and like Carl Hilty – but quite independently – she credited successive individual development phases with having respectively introduced the various constitutional solutions, new liberties and principles on which the contemporary, eminently democratic idea of the state reposed, and from which, in her view, the tasks ahead in turn derived. The lecture did not put forward an alternative vision of history from the female perspective. The gender issue was mentioned only in a bracketed aside. She told her audience that women were affected by all that was going on just as much as men, and should there-fore enjoy the same right to share in governing and regulating. 'The fact that this is not yet so has served German monarchists as an argument against democracy. To a Swiss woman, it is painful to see Switzerland providing this argument against itself.'[46] It may be added in conclusion that in Switzerland, as in other countries, the role women played in the state was subjected to con-sidered analysis. Here it is appropriate to single out the achievement of Martha Gostelis, who was a leading figure in the Swiss movement for votes for women. Though not an historian, she amassed a whole archive on the history of the women's movement, and in a blend of handbook and chronicle aptly entitled *Vergessene Geschichte* ('Forgotten History') she created a record of the situation and role of women in the Switzerland of 1914–63.[47]

Although for the moment only three Swiss examples can be introduced here, it is nonetheless remarkable that nothing comparable is to be found in France or Germany.[48] For Germany, mention should perhaps be made of the poet Ricarda

---

[45]On Ida Somazzi (1882–1963): M. Gosteli (ed.), *Vergessene Geschichte: illustrierte Chronik der Frauenbewegung, 1914–1963*, 2 vols (Berne, 2000), vol. 1, p. 584; *Im Gedenken an Dr. phil. Ida Somazzi* (Olten, 1963). Of her frequently cited political lectures, only the one discussed here ever appeared in print: I. Somazzi, *Der schweizerische Staatsgedanke im Sturm der Zeit* (Berne, 1934).

[46]Somazzi, *Der schweizerische Staatsgedanke*, p. 8.

[47]Gosteli, *Vergessene Geschichte*. See also B. Mesmer, *Staatsbürgerinnen ohne Stimmrecht: die Politik der schweizerischen Frauenverbände, 1914–1971* (Zürich, 2007).

[48]See Frey and Jordan, this volume (chapter 8).

Huch, who was encouraged by the publisher Atlantis in 1932 to write a large-scale *Deutsche Geschichte* (German History). Huch had gained her doctorate in 1892 at Zurich, as an historian, with a dissertation on the history of Swiss neutrality.[49] When she first came to public attention, it was in part through her historical writings, imaginative literature that treads a knife-edge between historical research and sensitively constructed fiction. However, she refused to lend herself to the national historical discourse of the time. In the three fat volumes of her history she presented an epic – indeed monumental – fresco of a vanished world, seen through a poet's vision and brought alive in perceptive descriptions and portraits of great individuals. It was the history of the Holy Roman Empire of the German nation, now vanished and gone, though its splendour still glinted from the rolling waters of Time that had submerged it, a remote realm different in every respect from the amoral modern *Machtstaat* (power state). Huch here placed great emphasis on the portrayal of women, and yet she presented such a conventional image of womanhood that this history never remotely became a 'gendered alternative' to the hoary masculine clichés.[50] Did Huch's *Deutsche Geschichte* make any impact? The first volume was published in Berlin in 1934; the second, though the date was still only 1937, in Zurich. Both these volumes did at least receive a short notice in the 'Comprehensive Histories' section of the *Jahresberichte für deutsche Geschichte* ('Annual Review of German Historical Studies').[51] Publication of the third volume, which Huch completed in 1941, was prevented by the National Socialist regime, and this volume did not finally appear until 1949.

If we are to reach a just verdict on these contributions to the writing of the nation, and on their reticence with regard to the gender issue, it is essential to bear in mind that from 1933 Switzerland came under mounting pressure from totalitarian political systems and their ideology. This confronted the women's movement, and the Arbeitsgemeinschaft Frau und Demokratie as well, with the ever-more acute dilemma of whether to continue the struggle against the limited democracy which excluded women, or to identify themselves with the campaign for Cultural Homeland Defence, and so defend the very principle of democracy that sustained the Swiss state.[52] They took the second course, and the contributions of Waser and Somazzi show how that might

---

[49]R. Huch, *Die Neutralität der Eidgenossenschaft, besonders der Orte Zürich und Bern, während des spanischen Erbfolgekrieges* (Zürich, 1892).

[50]R. Huch, *Deutsche Geschichte*, vol. 1, *Römisches Reich Deutscher Nation* (Berlin, 1934); vol. 2, *Das Zeitalter der Glaubensspaltung* (Zürich, 1937); vol. 3, *Untergang des Römischen Reiches Deutscher Nation* (Zürich, 1949).

[51]*Jahresbericht für deutsche Geschichte*, 9/10 (1934/5), 202; 13 (1937), 263.

[52]R. Stämpfli, 'Die Nationalisierung der Schweizer Frauen: Frauenbewegung und Geistige Landesverteidigung 1933–1939', *Schweizerische Zeitschrift für Geschichte*, 50 (2000), 155–80.

find expression: either the gender issue might be elevated to the level of myth or of abstract principle, and so ultimately lack any sense of urgency, or it might be played down, noted merely in passing. In the case of Ricarda Huch, however, who should likewise be counted among the resistance to the Nazi regime, we are looking at a purely personal development: ever since the 1910–20 period she had rapidly and increasingly radically distanced herself from the German women's movement and its objectives.[53] All these voices, speaking out in the midst of 'the storms of our age', may perhaps not be representative of the female writing of the nation. But they may possibly be cited as further examples of what Irène Herrmann describes as a fundamental paradox: that the female historians and the work they produced helped to consolidate the very same politico-social order that was ignoring them as women and as historians, and that it is precisely that neglect that confirms the quality of their work – because their work still found its place, unnoticed, in the institutional scholarly system, strengthening that system even as it excluded the authors.[54]

Concluding note

Switzerland is a small country characterised on the one hand by ethnic and religious diversity and on the other by the small-cell compartmentalisation of its politics, its cultural and psychological profile, and its economy and geography. In the approach to the problem of identifying what holds all this together, it was therefore constitutional rather than ethnic issues that presented a plausible background for the development of the master narratives. Given the intimacy and transparency of the Swiss public scene, the interdenominational differences of opinion could never reach the level of conflict that led to historians in the neighbouring large countries feuding passionately – from widely separated entrenched positions – over the true national history. In Switzerland, while violent social conflict did occur regionally, and on one occasion nationally, the disputes were never so fundamental in character as to trigger an alternative, class-based master narrative of any greater consequence than Grimm's paraphrase of liberal history. In neither case, one might say, did the potential for conflict reach critical mass. Instead, the transparency of small scale had the effect of bringing historians together in 1841 – ahead of comparable developments in other countries – in a national association that took no account of religious, linguistic or political provenance. It was probably for

---

[53]M. Frank, 'Ricarda Huch und die deutsche Frauenbewegung', *Studien der Ricarda-Huch-Gesellschaft*, 2 (Braunschweig, 1988), 65–74.
[54]Herrmann, 'Au croisement', p. 68.

the same reason that public statements at the national level by certain women commanded attention even while women were still denied political rights. Indeed, Edward Fueter may have been right in saying of Swiss historians that 'in this happy land, scholarly humanism and neohumanism [have achieved] a rare degree of fusion', and that this combined outlook has permeated 'the spirit of the historical organisations' and endowed them with 'security, depth and tolerance'.[55] In a small country, scholarship is under great pressure to justify itself. Where the people can vote for or against research projects, for or against the subsidising of education and the founding of universities and research institutes, it is incumbent on researchers to justify their activity to the public. This cost–benefit analysis, by now second nature to historians, may well explain why it is that the texts of the master narrative – texts that for a long time constituted the very backbone of Swiss historical scholarship – were directed at political doctrines with immediate practical application, and made little attempt to develop a body of scientific theory.[56] Its smallness notwithstanding, this 'Isle of the Blessed' was yet large enough for Swiss historical scholarship to build up a vigorous and relatively autonomous historical research tradition of its own, uninfluenced by contemporaneous developments on the international research scene. Karl Meyer could thus speak entirely aptly, in the 1930s, of *schweizergeschichtliche Wissenschaft* (literally, 'history-of-Switzerland scholarship'). And it was a first sign of a more open attitude when, in 1952, the Swiss specialist historical journal changed its name from *Zeitschrift für Schweizer Geschichte* ('Journal of Swiss History') to *Schweizerische Zeitschrift für Geschichte* ('Swiss Journal of History').

Translated by Michael Loughridge

---

[55]E. K. Fueter, 'Geschichte der gesamtschweizerischen Historischen Organisation: ein wissenschaftsgeschichtlicher Überblick', *Historische Zeitschrift*, 189 (1959), 449–505, 470.
[56]A particularly telling example of this is E. Gagliardi, *Geschichte der Schweiz von den Anfängen bis zur Gegenwart*, 2 vols (Zürich, 1920–27), 2nd edn (Zürich, 1934–7).

13
Portuguese and Spanish Historiographies: Distance and Proximity

Sérgio Campos Matos and David Mota Álvarez

Ever since the liberal revolutions of the nineteenth century, Iberian historiographies have been intimately connected to the consolidation of liberal states and their nation-building processes. In Spain, however, and contrary to what happened in Portugal where the issue was not relevant, alternative national projects emerged in the twentieth century, in Catalonia, the Basque country and Galicia. Such national projects included attempts to develop particular historiographies that claimed, rewrote or invented historical memories whose subject, at times, was no longer the Spain that had until then been the focus of historical discourse. Thus, in what follows we shall compare national historical experiences that are very diverse.

Historical unity and national identity were perceived differently in the two nations. Portugal achieved political and territorial unity (the latter in 1279) earlier than Spain (1492–1512). By the end of the fifteenth century, the territory that was to become Spain was split into several kingdoms – León, Castile, Aragón, Catalonia, Navarre. In Portugal a marked sense of national unity emerged around the monarchy, and the historiography linked to the royal house contributed significantly to its development until the first quarter of the nineteenth century. In Spain, which remained a politically divided territory until the end of the Middle Ages, a sense of national unity also emerged associated with the royal house, though accompanied by intense social and political resistance, as well as by an effort by a significant number of Spanish historians to explain Spain as a 'historical destiny', with a common geography and identity since time immemorial. The clash between different conceptions of state, nation and national identity is rather more obvious than in Portugal.

In Spain the question of the existence of a strong national identity is debatable, especially considering the emergence of peripheral nationalisms at the end of the nineteenth century and the feeble attempts to establish a national state undertaken by the central government – a topic that has been the object of extensive discussions in recent years. In Portugal, on the contrary, national identity is apparently not an issue,[1] although it has been the subject of considerable debate in recent decades.

At the end of the eighteenth century and early in the nineteenth, both states were already losing their relative power on the international scene,[2] and this fact was to have a deep influence on the historical culture of the two nations. The occupation of both territories by Napoleon's armies, followed by the British occupation of Portugal, as well as the consequences of the establishment of liberal regimes (1820–34) in societies that, from an economic and social viewpoint, shared many of the features of the Old Regime, helps explain a problem that affected both countries: the intrinsic weakness of the state, despite the adoption of a markedly centralised, French-inspired administrative model. The difficulties in and obstacles to the establishment of liberal states in both nations, with concurrent advances and retreats, must be seen against the backdrop of such structural features, the lack of social cohesion and lack of a strong spirit of citizenship among Peninsular national communities.[3] And although the constitutional monarchies showed little capacity to act on the cultural front, as witnessed by their inability to promote the symbols of national unity and identity, the non-state sector was to play a relevant role in the identification or popularisation of certain places of public memory, including historical celebrations that in some instances the authorities eventually endorsed. As happened in other European nations, the establishment of the state pre-dates the emergence of nationalism.

Several historians have stressed the close parallels between the contemporary history of both nations, from the establishment of liberal regimes in 1820 to the transition to democracy in the 1970s and the accession to the European Community (1986). The similarities between the contemporary histories of the two nations are also expressed in obvious links between their respective historiographies, although some national historical narratives in both countries were developed in almost complete ignorance of what was being done across the border. Portuguese historians most often ignored the work of their Spanish colleagues,

---

[1] P. Ruiz Torres, 'Les Usages politiques de l'histoire en Espagne formes, limites et contradictions', in F. Hartog and J. Revel (eds), *Les Usages politiques du passé* (Paris, 2001), p. 137; E. Lourenço, *O labirinto da saudade: psicanálise mítica do destino português* (Lisbon, 1978). We would like to express our gratitude to Stefan Berger, Mariano Esteban de Vega and Ana Luísa Paz for reading and commenting on this chapter and to Richard Correll for revising it.

[2] Telo and H. de La Torre Gómez, *Portugal e Espanha nos sistemas internacionais contemporâneos* (Lisbon, 2000), p. 318.

[3] J. Álvarez Junco, *Mater Dolorosa: la idea de España en el siglo XIX* (Madrid, 2001), p. 598, and B. de Riquer, 'El surgimiento de las nuevas identidades contemporáneas: propuestas para una discusión', in A.Mª. Garcia Rovira (ed.), *España, ¿nación de naciones?*, *Ayer*, 35 (1999), 29–35.

while Spain's historians were even less concerned with the historiography of their Peninsular neighbours.[4]

The following narrative strategies can be identified in Iberian historiographies. The first is a Catholic conservative model, which underlines the innate religiosity of the Spanish and the Portuguese as peoples chosen, from the very first settlers, by God. The Peninsular nations are thus shown to be the product of the Catholic religion, highlighting as foundational such mythical figures as Santiago, or mythical events such as the apparition of Christ to D. Afonso Henriques, the first king of Portugal, before the battle against the Muslims at Ourique (1139). However, they would only reach their golden age with the Catholic monarchs (Fernando and Isabella), the expulsion of the Jews, the introduction of the Inquisition and the Counter-Reformation. The Habsburg dynasty, and in Portugal the policies of D. Manuel I and D. João III, are given credit for the establishment of the empire and of religious unity, while the decisive role of the Church is given equal emphasis. The Peninsula is said to have gone into decline, in the case of Portugal with the loss of independence (1580–1640), and in the case of Spain with the reforms of a foreign dynasty, the Bourbons. In each case, the liberal revolutions are said to have prolonged the 'sickness' of the Iberian nations. Their redemption could come only through religious and political unity, and an imperial expansion motivated by an ideal of evangelisation overseas. From the 1930s onwards, this orthodox and providentialist concept of national history was inspired by the exclusivist-type nationalisms associated with the authoritarian regimes of Salazar and Franco.

The second model, opposed to the first, is putting liberalism and laicism at the heart of the national narrative. For liberal historians, the golden age was in the Middle Ages, where they celebrated the tradition of municipal charters and of the assemblies of the three estates that limited the power of the monarchy. The co-existence of different religious and ethnic groups – Christians, Jews and Moors – accentuated the internal diversity and distinguished the Iberian Peninsula from the other European nations. Absolutism, religious intolerance and 'errors' in imperial policies overseas are said to have led to decline in the sixteenth and seventeenth centuries with the Habsburgs, and in Portugal with the reign of D. João III (1521–57). Thus, social and political attempts to limit the central power of the monarchy aroused great interest. This model included historical narratives inspired by republican laicism and at times by Iberianism (which adopted a unitary or federalist viewpoint), claiming that national historical developments were determined by the struggle against political and religious despotism and for

---

[4] Alexandre Herculano (1810–77), Oliveira Martins (1845–94), Amador de los Rios (1818–78) and Sánchez Albornoz (1893–1984), among others, are exceptions.

decentralisation and regional autonomy.[5] Within this liberal and lay model, a 'popular front'-type variant emerged in the twentieth century inspired by revolutionary movements. It developed a materialist, class-centred and highly moral conception of history where the working-class movement was generally interpreted in national terms.[6] According to this variant, which has its roots in nineteenth-century socialism, but developed especially between the 1930s and the 1970s, the great force for progress is the working class, or the people in general. Within this historiography, of Marxist and internationalist inspiration, the dominant classes are identified with foreign interests at times of revolution – a key concept in these narratives.

This variant extends interpretations of the liberal, secular narrative strategy: a recognition of the importance of the Arab legacy in the Peninsula; a theory of decadence; a critical view of overseas expansion; and an indictment of foreign dependence (of Portugal on Britain, or Spain on France) as a factor in national decline. Within these liberal narratives we can also speak of Iberianist historical narratives (though they are never systematic) having the following features: 1) an underlining of geographical, religious, ethnic and linguistic unity at the Peninsular level; 2) an appreciation of the periods of apparent political unity under Carthaginian, Roman, Visigoth and Muslim rule; 3) the recognition of a single people and a single Peninsular nation up to the start of the Christian *Reconquista*; and 4) the granting by some authors that the independence of Portugal in the twelfth century may have been due to individual ambition and not to national or ethnic differences – in this respect, it could be considered an artificial nation. However, these arguments were not adopted by many Catalan or Portuguese Iberianists, who were more often federalist and emphasised the existence of a variety of Peninsular nations.[7]

The above distinction between the Catholic and the liberal strategies must, however, be nuanced, as there were distinct trends within Catholicism (namely regalism and ultramontanism): certain Catholic liberal historians emphasised the historical role of religious unity in state-building processes within liberal states; some liberal and republican historians made use of the concept of class and revolution (analogously to liberal French historians Augustin Thierry and Guizot); and, last but not least, there were socialist historians who nevertheless adopted the notions of organicism and race. Historicist ideas (in Karl Popper's sense) tended to predominate in all such narrative strategies until the last quarter of the twentieth century.

---

[5]Ruiz Torres, 'Les Usages', pp. 143–4; Álvarez Junco, *Mater Dolorosa*, p. 598.
[6]E. Ucelay da Cal, 'La historiografia dels anys 60 y 70: marxisme, nacionalisme i mercat cultural català', in J. Nadal et al., *La historiografia catalana balanç i perspectives* (Girona, 1990), pp. 78–9.
[7]See V. Martínez-Gil, *El naixement de l'iberisme catalanista* (Barcelona, 1997).

The development and diffusion of the contemporary historiographical trends discussed below occurred in both countries at the same time, namely from the beginning of the nineteenth century; we can argue that this was due to both countries' permeability to external influences – mainly French, German and English. Yet the distance between the two historical cultures increased from the seventeenth century, and after the restoration of the Portuguese state (1640) they turned their backs on one another. How can we explain the very common attitude of indifference and ignorance between neighbouring countries, which is apparent in their respective historiographies and even in the maps of the Iberian Peninsula until the 1980s? To compare the Peninsular historiographies, we shall distinguish the following broad historical periods:

1. From the beginning of the nineteenth century to about 1870 a new type of history emerged, whose subject was no longer the monarchy but the Spanish and Portuguese nations. A model of national historical narrative gradually developed that sought to convey legitimacy to the nation and the state through rationalist and political arguments, rather than providentialist and dynastic ones. At the debates in the Parliament of Cádiz (1812), and among intellectuals exiled in England and France from Portugal (e.g. Rocha Loureiro, José Liberato) and Spain (e.g. Alcalá Galiano, Martínez de la Rosa), new notions of nation emerged based on an historical pact of sovereignty. Spanish and Portuguese liberal exiles became acquainted with cultural and historiographical developments taking place in England and France, especially Guizot, Thierry and Thiers. From the 1840s onwards, the liberal historical narrative strategy emerged, focused on the Romantic definition of peoples' national character and identifying the broad trends of progress and decadence from an organicist perspective. The Inquisition and its relation with the absolutist state was another major topic for liberal historians. In Portugal the leading figure was Alexandre Herculano (1810–77), who was influenced by his readings of Thierry, Guizot and German historians such as Moeser, Humboldt, Niebuhr, Savigny, Heinrich Schaefer and Ranke.[8] His work complied with the new standards of scientific rigour, adopting an anti-absolutist and anticlerical slant. The focus on the municipalities and the medieval parliaments, which he considered to be at the origin of liberal institutions, was another feature of his national narrative and one that was passed on to later historians. In Spain, between 1850 and 1867, Modesto Lafuente (1806–66) published his *magnum opus* – a work in 30 volumes which emphasised the balance of powers between the monarchy, nobility, Church and the Cortes, and became the paradigm of a general history for a middle-class public. In Portugal, however, it

---

[8] F. Catroga, 'Alexandre Herculano e o historicismo romântico', in L. Reis Torgal et al., *História da história em Portugal, sécs. XIX e XX* (Lisbon, 1996), pp. 54–7.

was only with Pinheiro Chagas (1867–74)[9] that the public had access for the first time to a work covering the whole of the nation's history. These books would remain the most influential works until the 1920s.

With the proliferation of liberal histories, conservative Catholic narratives such as those of Victor Gebhardt (1864–67), Manuel Merry y Colón (1886–98) and Joaquim L. Carreira de Melo (1860) became a minority. Their dominant providentialism resisted the process of laicisation under way in both nations. Catholic historiography became more widespread in Spain than in Portugal, as happened with traditionalist and anti-liberal social and political movements that were socially more influential in regions such as Navarre or Aragón.

The victory of liberalism in the Peninsula, in its turn, precipitated the expulsion of those who did not share its ideas, such as the Miguelist Viscount of Santarém, historian of the Portuguese overseas expansion. This included those who sought to take matters further, such as the democratic republican Fernando Garrido: considered the father of Spanish labour history, he adopted a militant and 'idealistic' viewpoint, distinct from liberalism, which bore the stamp of Jacobinism and of authors such as Buckle.

2. During the last quarter of the nineteenth century and the first three decades of the twentieth century, positivism and a historicist approach dominated, and there was an emphasis on decadence and regeneration, while determinist theories of the origins of nation and state were disseminated. Various nationalist currents were present in historiographical discourse. Conservative nationalist works are dominated by a providentialist and ethnicist outlook that identifies race with nation. Cánovas del Castillo (1828–97), who edited an incomplete *Historia de España*, discussed the thesis of Renan. For him, history was a relevant factor in national construction, and the nation was the result of a constitution based on monarchy, parliaments and Catholicism. An example of the liberal strategy is the innovative and regenerationist project of Rafael Altamira (1866–1951), whose *Historia de España y de la civilización española* proposed the notion of a history of civilisation where the social subject became history's main actor.

In Portugal, Oliveira Martins (1845–94) renewed in critical terms the interpretations of the historical development of the Peninsular nations and included contributions from the emerging social sciences: history, geography, economics,

---

[9]M. Lafuente, *Historia general de España, desde sus tiempos más remotos hasta nuestros días*, 30 vols (Madrid, 1850–67); [M. Pinheiro Chagas], *História de Portugal desde os tempos mais remotos até à actualidade*, 8 vols (Lisbon, 1867–74). On Lafuente see M. Esteban de Vega, "Castilla y España en la 'Historia General' de Modesto Lafuente", in A. Morales y M. Esteban (eds), *Alma de España? Castilla en las interpretaciones del pasado español* (Madrid, 2005), pp. 96–101.

anthropology and social psychology. He was deeply influenced by Hegel's philosophy of history (the dialectical approach, history as revelation of the Idea) and by Michelet's and Renan's conceptions of writing history (indeed, anticipating the latter's notion of the conscience of a nation). But he was also influenced by German historiography (Niebuhr and Theodor Mommsen). Many other learned historical studies, often with a regional focus, were published up to the 1920s, but none contributed significantly to renew the debates or challenge the overall historical outlook.

3. The military dictatorship (1926–33) in Portugal and the civil war (1936–9) in Spain, followed by the establishment of Salazarism and Francoism, represented significant breaks with the liberal tradition. The civil war constituted the greatest rupture in history and historiography in twentieth-century Spain. During its first two decades (1939–59), the Franco regime presented itself in its propaganda as a crusade against separatism, communism and the enemies of religion.[10] In both countries, intellectuals and historians such as António Sérgio (1883–1969), Jaime Cortesão (1884–1960), Rafael Altamira, Sánchez Albornoz (1893–1984) and Américo Castro (1885–1972) were forced into exile, universities were subject to political control and lecturers who were sympathetic to the political opposition were dismissed. The break with the liberal tradition meant the triumph of the conservative Catholic currents that had been present throughout the nineteenth century. An image of two supposedly unproblematic countries with a glorious imperial tradition was henceforth conveyed. This historicist, conservative and exclusivist nationalism was allied to an integrist approach to Catholicism and a triumphalist conception of history, where only successes were worth remembering and defeats were forgotten. But the alternative to the dominant model of a nationalist conservative historiography remained alive in the liberal republican narrative strategy, which did not overlook ethnic minorities and considered Spain and its national identity as a problem worth discussing – see, for example, the debate between Sánchez Albornoz and Américo Castro (1956). These exiles advanced the thesis of two Spains – a liberal Spain, lay and progressive, and a traditionalist Spain, Catholic and imperialist – that had confronted one another over the centuries.

The civil war had a profound impact on Spain's sense of itself, leading many people, such as Ramos Oliveira (1907–73), to analyse critically the nation's past in order to explain the conditions that led to war. Many memoirs and papers were then published, written by eyewitnesses and participants in the war. Those in exile were very concerned with the 'Spanish problem' and the

---

[10]Anglo-Saxon historiography has contributed to the development of studies on this subject: e.g. Gerald Brenan, Raymond Carr, Hugh Thomas, Southworth, G. Jackson and Stanley Payne.

'Spanish self'. Examples of this are Américo Castro and Sánchez Albornoz; the essays of Carretero, defending a Castile within a plural, federal, and Iberianist Spain; the books by the former rector of the University of Barcelona, Bosch Gimpera, *Para la comprensión de España* (1943) and *El problema de España* (1963). In general, these debates in exile were not reflected in the Spanish historiography controlled by the Franco regime, with the exception of the polemic between Américo Castro and Sánchez Albornoz, which provoked some reactions from a minority of Francoist intellectuals, such as Laín Entralgo, who favoured a certain intellectual openness.[11]

In Portugal the debate around the formation of the state in the twelfth century continued, but there was no similar in-depth discussion of national history. Damião Peres's *História de Portugal* (1928–35) became a landmark in Portuguese historical culture from a nationalist perspective, albeit with nuanced contributions from different authors. One of them, Jaime Cortesão, would integrate the contributions of human geography, the economic and social history of Henri Pirenne and the sociology of Durkheim into his work *Democratic Factors in the Formation of Portugal* (1930). Between 1950 and 1975 several Portuguese and Spanish historians were influenced by the *Annales* – Magalhães Godinho (b. 1918) and Vicens Vives (1910–60), among others – and, particularly from the second half of the 1960s, by Marxist historiography,[12] which functioned as an ideological weapon against the Salazar and Franco regimes. We may take the case of the Portuguese António José Saraiva (1917–93), went into exile to France and the Netherlands. In the works of his early period, up to 1960, he emphasised social and economic factors for an understanding of cultural tendencies – although later he would revise this. For Spain we may note the influence of the works of the Frenchman Pierre Vilar, and the contribution of M. Tuñón de Lara (1915–97), who was exiled in France. Tuñón's principal intellectual points of reference were the *Annales*, but above all the work of Labrousse, Soboul and Vilar, and structuralism. Tuñón was also the organiser of the meetings of the Centre for Hispanic Studies in the University of Pau (1970–79).[13] These meetings were decisive for the renewal of methodology and theory in Spanish historiography, for the movement towards structuralist thought and the opening up of

---

[11]I. Cordero Olivero, *Los transterrados y España* (Huelva, 1997); J. Malagón, 'Los historiadores y la Historia en el exilio', in J. L. Abellán (ed.), *El exilio español de 1939*, vol. 5, *Arte y Ciencia* (Madrid, 1976), pp. 247–353.

[12]M. A. Cabrera, 'Developments in Contemporary Spanish Historiography: From Social History to the New Cultural History', *Journal of Modern History*, 77 (2005), 994–6.

[13]See M. Esteban de Vega, 'Ideological Organisations, Challenging the Paradigms of National History: The Pau Conferences (1970–1979) and Spanish Historiography', paper presented at the Workshop of the European Science Foundation, Institutions, Networks, and Communities of National Historiography: Comparative Approaches, Leuven, Belgium, November 2005.

new problems in national history, for the full incorporation of the contemporary period into academic historical studies and for the discussion of the bourgeois revolution and the history of the labour movement.

In Portugal, as in Spain, the gradual erosion of a nationalist historiography associated with Salazar's *Estado Novo* went hand in hand with a renewal of historical discourse from the 1940s. Magalhães Godinho developed a comprehensive interpretation of the past using concepts such as 'structure', 'conjuncture' and 'historical-geographic complex'. Noteworthy in his interpretation of Portuguese history are his Peninsula-wide approach, the stress on a universal humanism reflected in Portugal's historical experience and his argument about the failure of the Industrial Revolution and the establishment of a liberal-bourgeois society in nineteenth-century Portugal: this coincided with a similar thesis developed by J. M. Jover (1920–2006) for Spain.[14] In the wake of Magalhães Godinho, other historians[15] proposed new approaches to Portugal's historical development that were no longer influenced by the Catholic conservative model.

4. Since 1975 the influence of the *Annales* (especially of Lucien Febvre and Fernand Braudel) has been renewed and new themes have been incorporated into historical discourse. This is a period characterised by methodological relativism and by a multitude of different approaches. The restructuring of the Spanish state generated a lively interest in the history of the regions and, correspondingly, in national histories. However, general histories of Spain remain popular, and it would seem that the country is trying to come to terms with its national identity. In Portugal the demise of the *Estado Novo* created a new context for the social sciences, while historical research took many different directions. In the 1990s three new collective works on the history of Portugal were published, evincing a renewal of the discipline since the 1970s.[16] Historians now covered topics such as ethnic and religious minorities, marginalised groups, the places of collective memory and gender issues, as well as older topics which were reinterpreted with the help of new methodological perspectives. In both countries, particularly since the 1980s, historiography has tended to distance itself from ideologies. The disappearance of the Catholic nationalist narrative coincided with a more self-reflective approach among Catholic historians. The liberal model has also transformed itself, and the greater part of historiography

---

[14] V. Magalhães Godinho, *Estrutura da antiga sociedade portuguesa* (Lisbon, 1971), and J.M. Jover Zamora, *La civilización española a mediadados del s. XIX* (Madrid, 1991).

[15] J. Borges de Macedo, J. Serrão (editor of the influential *Dicionário de história de Portugal*, 1964–71), J. Barradas de Carvalho, and J. S. Silva Dias.

[16] J. Mattoso (ed.), *História de Portugal*, 8 vols (Lisbon, 1993); J. Medina (ed.), *História de Portugal dos tempos pré-históricos aos nossos dias*, 15 vols (Alfragide, 1993); and J. Serrão and A. H. de Oliveira Marques (eds), *Nova história de Portugal*, 10 vols (Lisbon, 1991–2004).

has abandoned teleological concepts of history and become more inclusive in its choice of topics and more problem-oriented. With it, a sense of the future was no longer teleological. With the transition to democracy and accession to the European Community (1986), theses of backwardness and the failure of the Industrial Revolution have been revised; Spain and Portugal have ceased to be seen as exceptions, and are more clearly integrated into the European context.

National character, *Reconquista*, overseas expansion

In both nations an old essentialist tradition dominated historical discourse until the mid-twentieth century. According to that tradition, nations possess a specific national spirit from primitive times. In the nineteenth century, it was clearly defined by German and French Romanticism (Herder, Thierry, Guizot, Michelet). Several Portuguese chroniclers and historians claimed to find the emergence of such a collective nature in the Middle Ages and made reference to a series of qualities – strength, courage, heroism, steadfastness, but also a love, passion and melancholy. The love of adventure, the 'maritime spirit', cosmopolitanism, 'religious enthusiasm' and 'personal heroism'[17] were not forgotten. According to Martins (and to Modesto Lafuente), successive generations of Spaniards shared a common character defined by the love of freedom and independence, and strong religious feelings, but also a tendency to be individualistic. Inspired by this notion, Martins developed a unitary view of the Peninsular nationalities, already present in Antero de Quental (1842–91), without, however, overlooking their differences. Had the national character remained unchanged over the centuries? Different authors provided different answers. For Oliveira Martins, overseas expansion, looting and interbreeding with other ethnic groups in the east (Gobineau's imprint is evident here) had weakened the Portuguese national character and caused degeneration, a widespread theme at the end of the nineteenth and the beginning of the twentieth centuries. But most historians dropped it in the 1940s. For other authors, the national character, the ancient qualities of the 'race' – the true and eternal essence of the nation – had remained unchanged despite the decline. Liberal narratives, in particular Herculano's and Lafuente's, considered Christianity the structuring element of such an essence, playing a central role in the establishment of political and territorial unity. Much later (1970), Caro Baroja would produce a critique of the myth of national character, while Vicens Vives would reject the rhetoric of a 'Spanish way'.

Two other themes were developed in parallel with the idealisation of the national character. Both were viewed as corresponding to historical missions and having a central place in the Iberian historiographies: the *Reconquista* and

---

[17]J. P. de Oliveira Martins, *História da civilização ibérica*, 8th edn (Lisboa, 1946 [1879]), p. 19.

the Discoveries (related to the expansion overseas). Such topics had a key role in the structuring of national identities in both countries. The process of recovery by the different Christian kingdoms of the territories taken by the Muslims in 711 extended over eight centuries in Spain and five centuries in Portugal, and was a powerful foundational myth in both cultures. For nineteenth-century historiography, it was the greatest collective enterprise of the Middle Ages in the Peninsula. In Portugal, Romantic and liberal intellectuals emphasised the efficacy of the Portuguese in that process and in an early definition of stable borders (the Treaty of Alcañices, 1297). In the struggle against the Arabs, the national qualities had soon become apparent, rooted in the spirit of the crusade and a medieval notion of honour.

In both liberal and conservative Catholic historical narratives the *Reconquista* was truly epic, the great national feat shared by all Spaniards. It also meant the triumph of European over Arab civilisation, and contributed to the consolidation of the nation from the point of view of its internal structure. And although Lafuente emphasised the role of the Asturian core (Pelayo and the victory of Covadonga), he did not overlook the role played by other territories, namely the Catalan and Aragonian regions. In Spain as well as in Portugal, the *Reconquista* was a struggle that nearly all nineteenth-century authors of general histories linked to religion, but most especially the Catholic historians.

Some twentieth-century authors stressed the importance of the *Reconquista* from a different perspective. It was the culmination of a process that produced the nation's spiritual character, not because it involved a struggle to defend Christianity, but because it meant 'the reconstruction of a national state and the forming of the Spanish soul'.[18] During Franco's and Salazar's regimes, the themes of the crusade and of Catholicism were once again used to explain the genesis of the Spanish and Portuguese nations. As time went by, and especially after the 1960s, the myth of the *Reconquista* began to lose its attractive power. Doubts were even raised regarding the very concept.

The other key theme in defining the Iberian nations' historical missions was that of the Discoveries and overseas expansion. In the mid-nineteenth century, several Portuguese historians engaged in an international debate on the claims of the Portuguese regarding voyages along the West African coast in the fifteenth century, opposing French claims to certain African territories that they felt belonged to Portugal by historical right. The link between nationalism and history became stronger in the works of the Viscount of Santarém (1791–1856), a historian who played a crucial role in the debate and who advanced Portuguese diplomacy in Africa.

---

[18] R. Altamira, *Los elementos de la civilización y el carácter de los españoles* (Buenos Aires, 1950), pp. 41–2.

The notion of a civilising mission among non-European peoples, identified with a maritime calling and the overseas expansion that had begun in the fifteenth century, became very common in Portuguese historical culture. To this theme (which is present in all national narratives) was added another, mainly by Catholic authors and by the conservative *Estado Novo* regime – the notion of an evangelising mission. According to them, Portugal was a bulwark of the West against the Ottoman threat, a nation that had been mobilised by a late and anachronistic ideal of crusade. As with Portuguese historiography, the Spanish historical discourse about Spanish America in the late nineteenth century also tended to emphasise the civilising pride and to praise discoverers (Colón, Cortés, Pizarro) using a nationalistic tone. This was common to most nineteenth-century historiographical currents, albeit with subtle differences. In liberal narratives the Discoveries were an important contribution by the Spanish to the geographical knowledge of the planet and to taking to the New World some 'civilising' elements, including their own language. In Catholic narratives, on the contrary, the important aspect was the dissemination of Catholicism. Furthermore, the Discoveries were seen as an extension of the *Reconquista* that had been completed in the Peninsula. Finally, liberal and republican historians oscillated between self-criticisms about the lootings and the killings carried out by the conquerors[19] and regret for the negative conse-quences that the discovery of the New World had for the Spanish economy and society – an attitude that could also be found in Portugal among authors such as Garrett, Herculano and Antero de Quental.

The way in which the Americas were perceived during the three first decades of the twentieth century[20] ranged from a liberal and progressive *hispano-americanismo* (Rafael Altamira, Rafael de Labra), which emphasised the impor-tance of the Americas to the regeneration of Spain and the need for cooperation based on a common cultural substratum, to a conservative *panhispanismo*, which resulted from the convergence of Catholicism and nationalism, thus combining the civilising and evangelising ideal. This latter trend produced the concept of *Hispanidad*.[21] According to its supporters, Spain had contributed enormously to world history by taking Christian civilisation to the Americas. Spain and the Americas thus shared a single moral ideal. This myth – like the one about Luso-Brazilian civilisation developed under Salazar's regime – was later to become a cornerstone of the Francoist regime and to influence its historiography, which

---

[19]See, for example, the biography of Las Casas by J. A. Llorente and R. García Cárcel, *La Leyenda Negra: historia y opinión* (Madrid, 1998), pp. 255–346.

[20]J. C. Mainer, 'Un capítulo regeneracionista: el hispanoamericanismo, 1892–1923', *La doma de la quimera* (Barcelona, 1988) and I. Muñoz Sepúlveda, *Comunidad cultural e hispano-americanismo, 1885–1936* (Madrid, 1994).

[21]Zacarías de Vizcarra and Ramiro de Maeztu.

turned into a eulogy of the conquest. In Portugal, historians' depictions of Brazil ranged from a patronising nationalism that sometimes expressed resentment at Brazil's independence (1822) to a fraternal outlook – the former colony that became a sister-nation, thus preserving the special relationship with Portugal. In any case, conservative Portuguese nationalists attempted to integrate Brazil into a supposedly single Lusiad civilisation. Until the mid-twentieth century, the colonial and imperial ideology strongly influenced the various narrative strategies, including the liberal republican one that represented the opposition to the *Estado Novo* regime. However, this republican tradition (Jaime Cortesão, António Sérgio, Magalhães Godinho) emphasised the humanism and universalism of the Portuguese in their diaspora and in their contacts with other peoples. The celebrations of the *5th Centenary of the Discovery of America* (1992) and of the Portuguese discoveries (1987–2000), with its criticisms directed at the conquest (influenced by *indigenismo*) and its celebrations of contacts and affinities between cultures, revealed the profound changes that had occurred not only in historiographical terms but also on the international scene over the last decades. The delusions of a conservative imperial nationalism had finally been overcome.

Theories of the nation: politics, ethnicity and class

The secularisation of historiography took decisive steps after the 1840s in both Portugal and Spain, generating heated debates among supporters of anticlericalism and ultramontanism. After the establishment of liberal regimes (1834) there were very few authors who embraced old myths such as Tubalism (concerning Tubal, Noah's grandson and supposed founder of the Peninsular kingdoms) or other providentialist myths about the origins of either nation, such as the miracle at Ourique or the myth of Santiago. The most influential national narratives (those of Herculano, Lafuente) still referred to Providence (albeit in an abstract sense) as a *ratio* underlying human actions. It should be noted that Lafuente, unlike Herculano, was not anticlerical and considered the Church and Catholicism a cornerstone of the Spanish nation. But what are truly noteworthy in such philosophies of history are the rational criteria that presided over actions and the element of free will involved.

According to Herculano and other Portuguese liberal writers of the nineteenth century, the nation was defined as a polity that had become separated from Spain in the twelfth century, not because of any ethnic, geographical or cultural factors but for political reasons, and as an act of will – the longing for independence by its elite. As for Lafuente, in Spain's case, the main element of historical continuity was the dynasty and, especially, the elites and the great men who embodied this desire for independence. The socialist Oliveira Martins agreed, and although he often referred to the Celtic soul he rejected the theory that some ethnic specificity of the Portuguese explained national independence.[22] Other authors, and in particular the republican Teófilo Braga (1843–1924),[23] who was influenced by French historians such as Thierry and Taine, stressed the ethnic factor (Mozarabs, Celts, Lusitanians). According to him, this ethnic factor – the predominance of Mozarabs (whom he identified with the popular strata) or the Celts – was the origin of the political separation between Portugal and Spain and explained their national differences.

Other historians developed these ethnic obsessions using supposedly scientific arguments, such as the dolichocephaly of the Portuguese, their different psychological profile and greater homogeneity.[24] Similar arguments can be found in the historiography influenced by Basque nationalism (Sabino Arana): the Basque race had supposedly preserved its racial purity, which dated back to a period before the invasions by Romans, Arabs and Jews.[25]

In Portuguese historical culture, the ethnicist identification of the Portuguese with the Lusitanians, and of Portugal with Lusitania, had become quite common from the fifteenth century onwards. In the nineteenth century it was still a powerful ethnic myth associated with the emergence of the mythical figure of Viriato, a shepherd and Lusitania's warlord, and the hero of the resistance against Rome. Herculano (1846) was the first historian to question the continuity that supposedly existed between the Portuguese and the Lusitanians: according to him, the Portuguese nothing in common with the Lusitanians from a linguistic, ethnic or religious viewpoint. But his radical arguments did not bear close examination and were later revised by the ethnologist Leite de Vasconcelos (1858–1941).

In all narrative strategies, many authors consider the pre-Roman peoples – the Celts and Iberians – as forming the ethnic origins of the Spanish people. Following in the steps of a long tradition in Spanish cultural history, Lafuente identified them as the first Spaniards: their merger (as Celtiberos) had produced the first Iberian nation. It is worth recalling that in 1821 Wilhelm von Humboldt had used linguistic arguments to link Hispanic populations to their Celtic and Iberian ancestry. Their ethnic origins (and not only in a biological, racial sense) lay with these peoples. Celticism became widespread in Galician historiography (Manuel Murguía, 1833–1923), and was used to build narratives of Galicia's national past based on this racial element. On the other hand, Gothicism, with remote origins in the fifteenth century, also had a significant

---

[22]S. Campos Matos, *Historiografia e memória nacional (1846–1899)* (Lisbon, 1998), pp. 315–39.

[23]T. Braga, *A pátria portuguesa: o território e a raça* (Porto, 1894).

[24]See, for example, A. A. Mendes Correia, *Raízes de Portugal* (Lisbon, 1938).

[25]F. Wulff, *Las essencias patrias: historiografía e historia Antigua en la construcción de la identidad española (siglos XVI–XX)* (Barcelona, 2003), pp. 156–7.

number of supporters.[26] Some authors (Lafuente, Cabanilles) described the Visigoths in almost mythical terms, because they were able to achieve political union under a single Crown, to forge a legislative union (*Fuero Juzgo*), and even adopt a single religion, following the conversion of Recaredo to Catholicism in 587.

At the end of the nineteenth and the beginning of the twentieth centuries, a theory of ethnic and geographical (sometimes also social and economic) opposition between the Iberian Peninsula's north and south emerged in both Spain and Portugal. In particular, its supporters emphasised the predominance of the Goths and a greater purity of the nobility in the north in its resistance to the Muslims, or they contrasted the predominance of Aryans in the north with that of Semitic peoples in the south (Arabs, Berbers). Aryanism and the theory of superior and inferior races were then very much in vogue, and Portuguese authors such as Oliveira Martins and Basílio Teles adhered to it. Supporters of *catalanismo* or *galeguismo* (M. Murguía) also disseminated this north/south opposition. In the case of Almirall, this was done by stressing the democratic spirit, federalism and virility of the north and by playing down the Semitic, unitary and feminine nature of the south.

In Spanish historiography, individual heroes such as the Ilergetes Indíbil and Mandonio (apart from Viriato, already adopted by Portuguese historians) or collective heroes (inhabitants of Sagunto and *numantinos*) symbolised the ethnic struggle against invaders (Carthaginians, Romans) – just like the Lusitanians in Portuguese historiography. This ethnic theory of the birth of the nation had many supporters among the nationalist conservatives of the first half of the twentieth century, including those who supported the Salazar and Franco regimes. According to them, a national Catholic, unitary and imperial essence had persisted throughout the ages, despite the denationalisation promoted by the forces of liberalism, Protestantism and democracy.

Rationalist authors such as Rafael Altamira (who stressed the plurality and complexity of the collective psyche) and António Sérgio (1883–1969) reacted against such ethnic theories. In the 1920s the latter put forward a Europeanist explanation for the origins of Portugal: at the roots of the independent state and nation was the presence in the territory of other European peoples, such as crusaders from northern Europe, Italian and Flemish merchants, religious orders such as that of Cluny. Sérgio thus related the independence of Portugal to the development of a European commercial bourgeoisie,[27] while an abstract concept of class was suggested as an alternative to the ethnic theory of the nation, which overemphasised the notion of race. It should be noted, however,

[26] J. N. Hillgarth, 'Spanish Historiography and Iberian Reality', *History and Theory*, 24 (1985), 23–43.
[27] A. Sérgio, *Breve interpretação da história de Portugal* (Lisboa, 1971 [1st edn 1928]).

that the latter theory was also associated with a popular and anti-monarchist interpretation of the nation's historical development (Teófilo Braga) and that a conservative version of it was used by traditionalist nationalism to revise historical discourse in the 1910s–1920s. There were, however, republicans who resisted ethnic determinism (Jaime Cortesão) and who emphasised geographical conditions and especially the role of the people as a whole. In Spanish historiography the notion of a unitary Peninsular geography and of natural borders – the Iberian Peninsula – had become much more common.[28]

From the point of view of nation-building, class was, all in all, a less significant element in Spanish and Portuguese historiographies, especially in the most influential historical works. Academic historiography had difficulties in integrating working-class and popular movements into its discourse. The national histories were written first and foremost for a middle-class public, while the concept of class was something that concerned outsiders.

There are, nevertheless, a few examples in the nineteenth century of works that show concern with social history[29] and with class issues: Lafuente believed that the *Germanías* (1519–22) were a social movement compared to the more political nature of the *Comunidades de Castilla* movement. The democratic-republican-federalist historians can be considered precursors of the historical literature focusing on social and class issues.[30] With these, social topics and the working classes became themes for historical investigation. The national Spanish context was not diluted but coexisted with pacifist and universalist ideals. Spain was seen as part of the Iberian Peninsula, of Europe and the world. However, works of 'working-class historiography' were few throughout the nineteenth century.[31] In such works an internationalist perspective was usually present. For anarchists and for the socialists associated with the First International (Francisco Mora), the nation represented a 'bourgeois category', and they were only interested in studying class exploitation. Class, and especially the working class, replaced the nation-state as the object of historical investigation (Farga Pellicer). Anselmo Lorenzo and Francisco Mora, on the other hand, kept a national perspective, though integrated in a wider context that

---

[28]For example, the Catalan author Bosch Gimpera, in 1937. There were some authors who argued for a special geographical nature of the Portuguese territory, different from that of Spain, which would explain the political separation (Elisée de Reclus, Silva Teles). Others argued that chance alone could explain the emergence and historical existence of the nation and independent state – according to this Iberianist theory the separation of Portugal was a historical accident.

[29]C. Forcadell, 'Sobre desiertos y secanos: los movimientos sociales en la historiografía española', *Historia Contemporánea*, 7 (1992), 101–16.

[30]For instance, F. Garrido, *Historia de las clases trabajadoras* (Madrid, 1870).

[31]We are grateful to F. de Luís for having made available to us his unpublished essay, 'La idea de España en la Historiografía obrera de fines del siglo XIX'.

they considered more relevant, that of the universal history of the working classes. Besides this internationalist approach adopted by most historians, there was a second trend that emerged especially among socialists (Juan José Morato) which was more interested in history and had Spain as its national reference. From this point of view, social classes were studied against the backdrop of the establishment of Spain as a nation.[32] From the end of the nineteenth century onwards, the national perspective gradually replaced the internationalist one (inspired by anarchism) among socialist authors. That approach was popularised in memoirs, essays and historical works written for a wider public.

In the historiographies allied to the authoritarian regimes, the masses and social classes disappeared. On the other hand, in a work by Ramos Oliveira, published in exile (Mexico), there was a clear intent to discuss the social roots of certain political movements (the bourgeois origins of Catalan nationalism) and historical events (the class interest in the politics of the *Restauración*). This attitude was consistent with the Marxist-Leninist ideology he professed.[33]

Vicens Vives wished to revitalise the Catalan industrial bourgeoisie so that it could once again play a relevant role in Catalonia and Spain. The history of the working-class movement emerged again in the 1950s, building on a tradition that had existed in the 1920s and 1930s (Reventós and others) and attempted to integrate national history. But it was dominated by a 'popular front' strategy that was inspired by the histories of Catalonia (e.g. that of F. Soldevila, 1934) and by the revolutionary ethos of the 1930s and the historians' commitment to the struggle of the oppressed classes: Catalonia oppressed by Madrid, and the working classes oppressed by the dominant class.[34] In the 1960s and 1970s there was a boom in these histories of the working-class movement. It included new works on economic history, debates on the transition from the Old Regime, the use by Artola of concepts from political sociology and the seminars at Universidade de Pau (Tuñón de Lara, P. Vilar).[35] In Spain and Portugal, the history of the social movements emerged as a critical alternative to the histories written by professional historians at the end of dictatorships of Franco and Salazar.

In Portugal, the reception of Marxism took place later than in Spain. Between the 1940s and the 1970s it had a powerful influence in both countries, which should be related to the political and social influence of communist parties in some social strata, including the intellectual elites. The historians that followed it

---

[32]J. J. Morato's *Notas para la historia de los modos de producción en España* (Madrid, 1897) was the first attempt at interpreting the history of Spain in Marxist terms.
[33]R. Oliveira, *Historia de España* (Mexico, 1953); G. Pasamar, 'Las "Historias de España" a lo largo del siglo XX', in R. García Cárcel (ed.), *La construcción de las historias de España* (Madrid, 2004), pp. 334–7.
[34]Ucelay Da Cal, 'La historiografía', pp. 61–4.
[35]See T. de Lara, *El movimiento obrero en la historia de España* (Madrid, 1972).

focused on themes that, in part, had already been addressed by liberal historiography: the revolution of 1383–85, the revolution of 1820 and liberalism, the development of capitalism. They emphasised the role of the popular classes and in particular that of the 'bourgeoisie' in the revolution of 1383 and in the liberal revolution of 1820. In their interpretation, the notion of class is always seen from a national perspective, and aristocratic antagonists are generally identified with foreign interests.[36] In the 1970s the liberal historian Silva Dias argued that the liberal revolution had not been a bourgeois revolution (where, as Marxist historians claimed, the bourgeoise had disempowered the aristocracy), but one that involved a 'a mix of social classes'. Portuguese Marxist historians made use of notions such as those of 'mode of production', 'social formations' and 'dependency relations' which were typical of historical materialism as conveyed by French authors (E. Labrousse, Pierre Vilar) and were later influenced also by British Marxist social history (Hobsbawm, Thompson). In contrast, German social history did not have a very significant impact on them.

The crisis in the history of the working-class movement, related to the 'disappearance of the working class as a historical subject' after the collapse of the Soviet Union, encouraged new approaches aimed at overcoming the 'old institutional history of the working class'. But such approaches (i.e. a history written 'from the bottom', a history of militants rather than political leaders) were adopted in the Iberian Peninsula only some time after they had become popular elsewhere.[37] Despite such new approaches, Iberian histories remained largely national ethnic in outlook, emphasising the values of national memory, a largely dominant religious faith (despite the reaction of secular republican authors who attempted to replace the Catholic religion with a civic one – the cult of the nation) and national languages.

Gender

Gender is mostly perceived as the role played by specific male and female characters in the Iberian national narratives, although the Iberian nations were themselves depicted as feminine figures. Thus, until the mid-twentieth century, as history was overwhelmingly written by men, we find a preponderance of the 'masculinisation of memory'. Not only were these characters quite often male, but the feminine stereotype was perceived in negative terms: in Spanish historiography, for example, Boabdil el Chico, the last Muslim king of Granada, was said to have 'wept like a woman for that which he was incapable of defending like a man' after being defeated by the *Reyes Católicos* (1492).

---

[36]A. Borges Coelho, *A Revolução de 1383* (Lisbon, 1965).
[37]À. Barrio Alonso, 'Historia obrera en los noventa: tradición y modernidad', *Historia Social*, 37 (2000), 143–60.

Spanish liberalism adopted as national symbols the feminine figure, or matron, and the lion (Queen Isabella II was also in a sense depicted as a matron). During the revolutionary period (1868–74) the images of the matron and the lion became institutionalised as images of Spain. On the one hand, these icons addressed the void left by the departure into exile of Isabella II, and on the other, they stressed the arrival of a new feminine figure, that of the republican matron (1873), a semi-naked woman draped in the national flag and wearing a Frigian cap. The influence of the French Marianne is quite obvious. Such influence was also strongly felt in Portugal during the First Republic (1910–26), and there is abundant iconography conveying the image of a maternal nation protecting its children – the citizens – who have to fulfil their duties to the nation.

Under the influence of gender studies, Iberian historians have begun to explore the role of women in national history, focusing in particular on the republican and revolutionary periods of the twentieth century. The attention of historians has been drawn to the presence of women in the Spanish Civil War, with the images of Dolores Ibarruri (*La Pasionaria*), the anarchist minister Federica Montseny or the women in arms, the *milicianas*. Overall, much more attention was now given to women in their diverse roles, as 'home front heroines'.[38] In Portugal, women were also represented as a political national force in the First Republic, with studies on the suffrage movement, but especially on the First World War effort of some republican writers. Historians have also begun to explore the diverse ways in which women contributed to nation-building in Portugal.

Naturally, several queens also became symbols of the monarchy. The image of Isabella I, *la Católica*, was especially brought to the fore by Spanish historiography in the nineteenth century. Isabella was considered a weightier figure than Fernando, possibly because she represented Castile, or because moderate historians wished to use her in order to legitimise their own queen, Isabella II (comparing the greatness of one to that of the other). During the Francoist period, Isabella *la Católica* was also used as a symbol of the Catholic woman and mother.

There is a mythical tradition concerning a woman who was considered responsible for one of the major ruptures in Spain's history, the Arab invasion in the eighth century. Florinda 'La Cava', having been raped by the last Visigoth king, Rodrigo, informed her priest of the outrage. The priest, Count Don Julián, was in charge of defending the border against the Arabs and, in revenge against his king, he opened the doors of the Peninsula to the Muslim invasion.

---

[38] M. Nash, *Rojas: las mujeres republicanas en la guerra civil* (Madrid, 1999).

Florinda's conduct was perceived as a dual treason – to the monarchy and to religion. The legend first emerged in the Middle Ages and there are echoes of it in the work of historians such as Menéndez Pidal.

Among the images of the nation as a woman in Iberian historiographies, one has to mention those instances where a masculinised heroine embodies the struggle for independence. One such case is the legend of the Portuguese baker-woman of Aljubarrota, who supposedly contributed to the victory of Portuguese troops over the Castilian forces that threatened the kingdom's independence at the battle of Aljubarrota (1385). Although the legend gradually lost its impact, by the nineteenth century it had become a national symbol whose influence reached well beyond the local setting where it had originally emerged. Herculano (1839) and Teófilo Braga (1885) were favourable to the dissemination of the legend, whereas Oliveira Martins considered it outdated. The legend of the baker-woman was used as an argument in the debates around Iberianism to strengthen Portuguese national sentiment and to promote an anti-Castilian attitude. In Spain, Agustina de Aragón – another woman-soldier – became a symbol of popular resistance in defending Zaragoza during the Napoleonic invasions.

The woman-martyr depicting the martyred nation is another type of gendered representation. An example is the myth surrounding Mariana Pineda promoted by liberal historiography. She was accused of conspiring against the government of Fernando VII, and executed in 1831. Mariana became a symbol of liberal Spain and of the struggle against absolutist Spain.

Alterity, continuities and discontinuities

Throughout its history, the Iberian Peninsula was invaded and colonised several times. Different peoples established themselves in its territory and left their mark. From a nationalist and essentialist viewpoint, the Other could be any of these conquering peoples (Carthaginians, Greeks, Romans, Visigoths, Arabs). Some were more easily assimilated than others, and authors easily admit the positive developments that came with the Roman invasion of the Peninsula and the unification achieved under the Visigoths.

Muslims, however, were generally considered by Iberian historiographies throughout the nineteenth century as an element foreign to the national character. Nevertheless, it was acknowledged that they had influenced, by a process of opposition as well as by one of inclusion, the formation of both nations. The Muslim conquest (711) was interpreted as a break with the historical development of Spain, since it interrupted the historical continuum represented by Spain's membership of Europe (Sánchez Albornoz). The identification of Spain with Christianity was a central theme in the Catholic conservative narratives (Menéndez Pelayo). Moderate liberal historians included the religious dimension in their depiction of national identity, contrary to lay historians. Altamira, for instance, stressed the ability of the inhabitants of the Peninsula throughout their history to assimilate other cultures, including Islam – all of which had contributed to the formation of the Spanish character. Spain was thus a territory of passage and meetings. A similar view had been defended by Teófilo Braga for Portugal and the Portuguese people.

The Muslim cultural and linguistic heritage was brought to the fore by certain liberal historians, such as the first great Spanish Arabist, José Antonio Conde (1766–1820), Pascual de Gayangos (1809–1897)[39] and, later, the Portuguese historian David Lopes (1867–1942). They all stressed the sophistication attained by Islamic culture in the Iberian Peninsula, in stark contrast with an uncultured Europe. With these historians emerged a new awareness of the need to give a historical meaning to the presence of Islam in Iberia, whose outcome would be Spanish Islam and its splendid culture. Furthermore, Muslim Spain had been characterised by its tolerance in comparison with the fanaticism of the invasions of the *almorávides* and the *almohades* from North Africa.

In the 1920s and 1930s the Arabist Ángel González Palencia (1889–1949) corrected the prevailing image of looting commonly associated with the Muslim invasion. Américo Castro, influenced by Palencia, criticised those theories that excluded Muslims from the definition of the Spanish nation and associated it with Catholicism. In 1948, in what became a well-known thesis, Castro argued that the fundamental fact that separated the history of Spain from that of other countries was the coming together of three medieval groups, Christians, Jews and Muslims, with the definitive (and all-excluding) triumph of the first group during the modern era. Since Américo Castro, the multicultural theme of the dialogue between Christians, Jews and Muslims has been addressed by liberal nationalists.[40]

Another debate in Spain's nineteenth-century historiography concerned the expulsion of the *Moriscos*[41] (Muslims who lived in Christian territories) in 1609. Catholic historians tended to view it as a positive development, since it prevented the emergence of a 'fifth column'. Liberal historians, on the other hand, criticised it from an economic perspective, as their expulsion meant the depopulation of the countryside and seriously affected Spanish agriculture. It also reflected to them the intolerance of the Catholic Church, which resulted in a massive intellectual loss. In conservative narratives, by contrast, it was perceived

---

[39]M. Manzanares, *Arabistas españoles del siglo XIX* (Madrid, 1972).

[40]Á. González Palencia, *Historia de la España musulmana* (Barcelona, 1925); A. Castro, *España en su historia: cristianos, moros y judíos* (Buenos Aires, 1948; rev. as *La realidad histórica de España*, México, 1954); E. Manzano Moreno, 'La interpretación utilitaria del pasado', in J. S. Pérez Garzón et al., *La gestión de la memoria: la historia de España al servicio del poder* (Barcelona, 2000), pp. 48–59.

[41]M. L. Candau Chacón, *Los moriscos en el espejo del tiempo* (Huelva, 1997).

as a positive step towards religious uniformity (Victor Gebhardt).[42] In the twentieth century, Caro Baroja (1914–95) and Domínguez Ortiz (1909–2003) viewed the Moors as a marginalised minority.

The depiction of Jews in Iberian historiographies in the nineteenth century is controversial. Their persecution was interpreted as a sign of religious fanaticism and a reaction against their economic influence (Herculano, Lafuente, Amador de los Ríos[43]). However, Lafuente glossed over the responsibility of the *Reyes Católicos*, and especially of Queen Isabella, in their expulsion (1492), while others asserted that they had merely acted in the spirit of the time (Gebhardt, Adolfo de Castro). Portuguese nineteenth-century historiography, on the other hand, tended to emphasise the pressure from the *Reyes Católicos* for the expulsion of Portuguese Jews, and the responsibility of D. Manuel I for that episode (1496). It also pointed to the role of D. João III in the establishment of the Inquisition in Portugal, with all of its negative consequences.

The statutes of blood cleansing and the initiatives of the Inquisition against those suspected of being Jewish fed the 'Dark Legend', which was then reinterpreted by Spanish liberals. They considered the expulsion of the Jews as a negative development, an economic and intellectual loss, but often balanced that against the religious unity of Spain that had henceforth been achieved.

Américo Castro also engaged in a rehabilitation of the memory of the Jews.[44] From the sixteenth century onwards, he argued, Spain lacked the intellectual and practical genius of Jewry and therefore did not participate in or contribute to the scientific and economic development of Europe. Sánchez Albornoz attacked this 'Semitic explanation' of Castro's.

Religion played a central role in defining the Other. Conservative authors considered religious heterodoxy (i.e. anything that did not follow the Catholic mainstream) as non-Spanish (Balmes, Menéndez Pelayo).[45] On the other hand, liberal historians such as Adolfo de Castro and the Portuguese António J. Saraiva denounced the barbarous behaviour of the Inquisition towards such groups, in line with the 'Dark Legend'. The study of attempts at spiritual renewal in the sixteenth century was particularly stimulated by French Hispanist Marcel Bataillon and the Portuguese Joaquim de Carvalho.[46]

---

[42]R. López-Vela, 'De Numancia a Zaragoza', in García Cárcel, *La construcción*, pp. 263–4.
[43]A. de los Ríos, *Historia social, política y religiosa de los judíos de España y Portugal* (1875–6). He adopted a Peninsular perspective in his study.
[44]Castro, *La realidad histórica de España*.
[45]M. Campomar Fornieles, *La cuestión religiosa en la restauración: historia de los heterodoxos españoles* (Santander, 1984).
[46]M. Bataillon, *Erasmo y España* (Paris, 1937; translated in Mexico in 1950); J.S. da Silva Dias, *Correntes de sentimento religioso em Portugal: século XVI a XVIII* (Coimbra, 1960) and *O Erasmismo e a Inquisição em Portugal: o processo de Fr. Valentim da Luz* (Coimbra, 1975); A. J. Saraiva, *Inquisição e cristãos novos* (Lisbon, 1969).

For Portuguese nineteenth-century historians, both liberal and Catholic, the Other was Spain, which they identified with Castile. This was a reductionist view of Spain but one that was most useful for Portuguese nationalism, which always perceived Castile as a dangerous neighbour. Although this was the dominant view among historians in the nineteenth century, there were two notable exceptions: Antero de Quental and Oliveira Martins. A Castile-centred perspective tended to predominate in Spain (Menéndez Pidal, Sánchez Albornoz). Castile would have been the soul and the centre of Peninsular unification. For Sánchez Albornoz, the independence of Portugal had been a 'historical accident'.

In Portuguese national memory, the kingdom's freedom had been threatened by Castile during the crisis of 1383–5, but following the victory at Aljubarrota (1385) and the emergence of the dynasty of Avis, the continuity of Portugal as an independent state had seemed assured. In the wake of the death of D. Sebastião, however, Portugal had been annexed to Felipe II's Spain (1580). For a significant number of Portuguese historians, the 'period of the Filipes' (1580–1640) was considered alien to the historical development of the country and as a period of decadence. There were nevertheless certain authors who argued that the union of the two dynasties and loss of independence were the consequence or endpoint of a process of decadence that had begun long before (José Liberato, Herculano, Rebelo da Silva). In 1640 the *restauração* took place, a movement that founded a new dynasty, that of Bragança, and restored Portugal's independence. This period was celebrated by the anti-Iberianist authors, but within Portuguese historiography there were authors who acknowledged that although political autonomy was recovered, the greatness of Portugal's golden age was forever lost. The dynasty of Bragança was thus linked to a long period of decadence.

This historiographical conceptualisation of a Spanish threat was a reaction against an Iberianist ideology which supported the political union of both states under a unitary or federalist model. This ideology became quite widespread from the mid-nineteenth century onwards, but in Portugal it declined after the 1880s. It nevertheless provoked intense debates which contributed to the development of Portuguese historiography from the mid-nineteenth century to the 1930s.

The supporters of a federal state based their arguments on history and a decentralising ideal, emphasising the role of the people, of municipalities and of the charters since the Middle Ages, while unitarians tended to reduce Portugal to an historical accident. The ideology of Iberianism had a different impact in Portugal and Spain, being more influential in the latter. Many Spanish historians contributed in one way or another to this Iberianist ideal.

The republic was proclaimed in Portugal in 1910. Spain remained the Other for republicans but more especially for conservative Catholics (a group that also included integralists). Two exceptions, however, are worth mentioning: the integralist author António Sardinha, who wrote about an *Aliança Peninsular*, based on a community of strategic and cultural interests rooted in the defence of

Catholicism, and Fidelino de Figueiredo and his cultural Hispanophilia. The historiography linked to Salazar's regime was characterised by an exclusivist type of nationalism and thus stressed the historical opposition between Portugal and Spain. In later decades, the tone became much less aggressive and a Peninsular perspective was sometimes present.

In Spanish historiography, Portugal was generally viewed as a friendly nation that belonged to the Hispanic 'family', but also as a satellite of England. Spain and Portugal had discovered the New World, and both countries were at the head of the same cultural community, the Ibero-American family. However, many historians in Spain regretted that the unification of the Peninsula had not been achieved under a single state and in accordance with natural geographic boundaries.

Liberal historians in Spain viewed France very differently. On the one hand, most authors dedicated significant efforts to describing the wars against Napoleonic France at the beginning of the nineteenth century. But such an anti-French consensus broke down when it came to interpreting the arrival of the French dynasty of the Bourbons on the Spanish throne in the wake of the War of Succession. According to Lafuente, it was a positive development for the nation, and he engaged in an effort to make Felipe V and his heirs look Spanish. His unifying policies were supported by liberal historians with a centralist slant but not by federalist authors (E. Chao, Pi y Margall). Carlos III's international policies and his *pactos de familia* became the most criticised topic in all national narratives, and were denounced as subjecting Spanish interests to those of France. Furthermore, Catholic conservative historians (Menéndez Pelayo) thought of the Bourbons as foreigners and as promoters of Gallican ideas that went against Spain's Catholic tradition. These historians always looked with suspicion to France, as they considered that it was the source of 'dangerous ideas' such as regalism and the Enlightenment. 'Revolutionary and atheistic France' became one of the demons of Francoist and Salazarist historiographies.

According to nineteenth-century historiography, the struggle against Napoleon's invasions was clear proof of what the Spanish nation was capable of doing to protect its independence – one of the major myths of Spanish nationalism. It was the people who saved the motherland,[47] a notion that should be seen against the backdrop of the emerging Romanticism and the concept of *Volksgeist*. Catholic conservative narratives emphasised the religious and monarchist dimensions of the struggle for independence. This nationalist tone when referring to the Napoleonic invasions was present throughout the greater part of the twentieth century, though in the works of Mercader and Artola there was an attempt to stress the role and importance of the *afrancesados*.

---

[47]P. Cirujano et al., *Historiografía y nacionalismo español (1834–1868)* (Madrid, 1985), pp. 190–4.

Despite the fact that Portugal also had its territory occupied by Napoleon's armies, the theme did not play the same role in Portuguese historiography as it did in Spain. A clear indication is the name given by Portuguese historians to the conflict –the Peninsular War – while the Spaniards called it the War of Independence.[48] But the same negative image of revolutionary France can be found among integralists and in Salazarist historiography.

How did Spanish historians view England and the English? England had been a dangerous enemy during the modern era, a country that opposed Catholicism and competed for colonial and maritime hegemony. Furthermore, in the wake of the War of Succession and the Treaty of Utrecht (1713), the British had taken over Gibraltar. In Portuguese historiography, only seldom are the English considered an enemy, though in some liberal and republican narratives (José Liberato, José de Arriaga) England is depicted as being responsible for the decadence of the country or for blocking its economic development – a theme that was later taken up by Marxist historians in the twentieth century (Armando Castro, M. Halpern Pereira).

Despite the period of Iberian union in Portugal (1580–1640) and the period of the so-called *Áustrias menores* in seventeenth-century Spain (*austracism*), as well as the French occupation (1808–14), the nineteenth century in general and the liberal civil wars in particular were seen as moments of discontinuity and of historical rupture as periods. There are common points between the two Peninsular liberal historiographies in defining those periods as periods of decline (from the seventeenth century to the first decades of the twentieth century; in the case of Portugal from the sixteenth century onwards) and of progress (the Middle Ages, the enlightened despotism of Pombal in Portugal, and the reign of Carlos III in Spain), and common points also in defining the 'causes' for decadence: the absolutism of some monarchs (the Habsburgs and the House of Bragança), the expulsion of the Jews, the Inquisition, the Counter-Reformation, the Jesuits and incompetent management of the wealth from overseas. The period during which there was an Iberian union was often depicted as one of imprisonment and disfranchisement, and the year 1580 was seen as truly catastrophic.

The sense of decadence had become entrenched in Portuguese and Spanish cultures since the overseas conquests of the sixteenth century. Such conquests had led to the accumulation of poorly managed riches and generated greed, looting, and a general moral decline. It was also associated with a lasting 'Dark Legend' about the Iberian nations that was conveyed in particular by the narratives of foreign travellers in the eighteenth century, and by the works of Montesquieu, Gibbon and Voltaire, becoming deeply rooted in Iberian polit-

---

[48]J. Álvarez Junco, 'La invención de la Guerra de la Independencia', *Studia Histórica: H.ª Contemporánea*, 12 (1994), 75–99.

ical and intellectual elites in the nineteenth century. The decline of the Portuguese and Spanish states on the international scene, which was aggravated in the 1890s (Britain's ultimatum to Portugal, 1890; Hispanic-American war, 1898), deepened the sense of crisis that would spill over into the twentieth century.

Until the mid-twentieth century the notions of progress and decadence were central to all narrative models, in both Portugal and Spain. In both historiographies the idea of a process of national development made up of alternating periods of autonomy and submission – but also of resistance to foreign rule, followed by the liberation from such rule – tended to dominate. So, we may say that the Iberian historiographies follow the three-phase *Christian-Hegelian scheme*. However, the times of foreign rule were not always viewed in purely negative terms (e.g. the Roman occupation).

Conclusion

Imported historical cultures had a widespread impact on Peninsular historiographies. This should be seen against the backdrop of the late professionalisation of the historians, the late establishment of liberal regimes (in the 1830s) and the persistence of authoritarian regimes in the Iberian Peninsula from the 1920s to the 1970s. Spain and Portugal being peripheral European nations which nevertheless kept their overseas colonies until very late (1974–5), it is easy to understand why nationalist historiographies (but especially Portuguese historiography, as Spain lost the most important parts of its empire in 1898) were obsessed with overseas expansion and empire. These played a key role in the structuring of prestige nationalisms (Anthony Smith), through imagined ethnic origins, a common historical destiny, religion and language. These obsessions did not decline until the 1950s and are visible, albeit in different terms, in the strategies of both the Catholic conservative and liberal historiographies.

Until the mid-twentieth century, Peninsular historiographies were dominated ideologically by essentialist and nationalist conceptions of nations. They were the outcome of an old cultural heritage that goes back to the medieval chroniclers and to classical historiography (*historia magistra vitae*) in its pragmatic approach. In both cases, these conceptions reflected historicist and defensive nationalisms at a time when the major centres for economic power and colonial enterprises were located in north-western Europe. The military actions of the Iberian states in the nineteenth century in Africa were mainly undertaken to preserve historical prestige and allegedly historical rights. The war against Napoleonic France, on the other hand, which was commonly considered a decisive moment in the founding of modern nationalism and of the notion of Spain itself, had had a defensive character. In any case, such wars contributed to strengthening the national consciousness of the invaded nations and were emphasised by those historians most influenced by nationalist ideologies, almost up to the present.

However, there were liberal and socialist historians both in Portugal and in Spain who were critical of the dominant nationalist rhetoric and who suggested alternative interpretations of their countries' historical development within a lay outlook. These were interpretations that took into account the different facets of national identity, considering not just the moments of national glory but also defeats and times of 'decadence' from which, it was felt, useful lessons could be drawn.

As with France and Belgium, the clerical vs. anticlerical debate deeply influenced nineteenth-century historical culture. The influence of Catholicism in defining national unity and in the structuring of historical narratives up to the mid-twentieth century is quite obvious, despite some differences between Portugal and Spain. In both historiographies, providential-type approaches of different kinds lasted until the 1960s. But in both countries, a vast and diversified range of national narratives and interpretations is to be found. Despite the longevity of the authoritarian regimes of the twentieth century, neither in Spain nor in Portugal is there an official canon. The conservative Catholic national narratives were more influential in Spain, while in Portugal liberal and republican lay narratives were more critical of absolutist kings and queens than their Spanish counterparts. In Portugal, one whole dynasty (Bragança) and part of another (Avis) were considered responsible for the country's decadence and backwardness, and identified with the Catholic Church, while the republican regime (1910–26) derived part of its legitimacy from a 'popular' conception of history (Teófilo Braga). In Spain, monarchs were not always criticised for the less positive policies of their reigns (such as the expulsion of Jews), and the first rather turbulent republican experiment (1873–4) failed to get as much sympathy from historians as did the first Portuguese republic (1910–26).

However, in both historiographies and in all narrative strategies, at least until the mid-twentieth century, theories of an historical drift of the Peninsular nations tended to dominate. These were historicist interpretations according to which Portugal and Spain had abandoned a general movement towards progress that could be or was being resumed. They were informed by organicist conceptions of decadence and progress and by an obsession with identifying (and exorcising) those responsible for the decline and for the abandonment of a predetermined historical destiny. The obsession with the theme of decadence is related to the gap between the consciousness of the current crisis and the memories of a glorious imperial past which played a central role in nationalisms and Peninsular historical cultures. After the 1960s this obsession was replaced by a more sober concern with understanding economic backwardness in a comparative perspective.

Despite the many commonalities between the two national historiographies, it remains a striking fact that, for much of the period under discussion here, Spanish and Portuguese historians have ignored each other and each other's histories. This has had much to do with the dominance of nationalist historiographies well into the 1960s and with the prevailing sense of the cultural distinctiveness of the two Peninsular nations. The border between the two nations (one of the oldest in Europe) became a powerful obstacle to the development of links between the Peninsular peoples and their elites. Among historians there was nevertheless a minority, who, from the mid-nineteenth century onwards, viewed the Iberian Peninsula as a whole, albeit bearing in mind national and regional differences. While Portugal was generally overlooked in the historiography of its larger neighbour, a few Spanish historians nevertheless emphasised the spirit of independence of the Portuguese and their national identity. Part of Portugal's intellectual elite felt attracted by Spain, but a feeling of looming threat and repulsion tended to predominate, especially in historical texts designed for a more popular audience. Generally speaking, an anti-Spanish sentiment tended to predominate among Portuguese elites. Such feelings were used to promote internal unity. In Spain, Portugal tended to be reduced to an 'artificial' nation. Since the 1980s, however, the situation has changed dramatically. There has been a significant increase in the mutual knowledge of the two peoples, and many scientific meetings have been organised on the relationship between the two nations in a whole range of areas, including history.

14
Habsburg's Difficult Legacy: Comparing and Relating Austrian, Czech, Magyar and Slovak National Historical Master Narratives

Gernot Heiss, Árpád v. Klimó, Pavel Kolář and Dušan Kováč

> Nevertheless, one should not imagine that the famous 'Kakanian' nationalism was an especially wild phenomenon. It was more historical than real.[1]

Introduction: the conceptual and periodic frame

Since Austria, Hungary, the Bohemian lands and Slovakia belonged to the Habsburg monarchy until 1918, the national master narratives that evolved and developed in connection with these areas and their populations were closely interrelated. Even though four independent national historical narratives can be identified, they form (because of their common reference to the Austro-Hungarian empire and their tight interactions) a close network of representations which must be examined in conjunction, with the application of methods of comparative history and attention drawn to historical transfer. Unlike Polish, Ukrainian, Slovene, Croatian, Bosnian, Serbian, Romanian and Italian national narratives, for example, Czech, Slovak and Hungarian narratives did not establish as many links with national movements outside the Habsburg state. Even German national historiography in Austria focused on the 'whole state' (*Gesamtstaat*), while emphasising at the same time its connections to the German or the Holy Roman Empire.

During the half-century prior to the First World War, a constitutional hierarchy developed within the Habsburg monarchy. The *Gesamtmonarchie*, the total united monarchy ruled by Austria, was ranked above the Kingdom of Hungary, which was ranked above the Kingdom of Bohemia, which, with its Czech majority, was nonetheless included politically in the 'kingdoms and countries represented in the Imperial Council' (i.e. the Cisleithanian,

---

[1] R. Musil, *Der Mann ohne Eigenschaften* (Reinbek, 2002), p. 529.

non-Hungarian or 'Austrian half of the empire'). In turn, Bohemia was ranked above the area containing a majority of Slovak people within the Kingdom of Hungary. This hierarchy, which had previously determined notions of nationhood on an informal level, influenced the selection of subjects of national master-narratives on which emphasis was placed (state, nation or *Volk*), as well as the selection of narrative models and specific images of friends and enemies.

This chapter shows how this complexity gave rise to numerous points of contact, parallels and overlaps, as well as contrasts among the four historical cultures. The master narratives relating the histories of the Austrians, Czechs, Magyars and Slovaks will be examined and compared according to their basic narrative structures as well as their concepts of themselves and strangers, their selection and understanding of Others and of 'internal enemies', and their representations of religion, class, ethnicity and gender. It should be stressed that these elements used for the construction of collective identities and their Others, respectively, are characterised only in comparison with the other national narratives. They can be understood only within the given context. They are therefore always related to a specific Other and would be used in a flexible, sometimes even contradictory way. 'Magyars' would be represented as an 'aristocratic, dominant nation' when confronted with the Slovaks as subjects of the King of Hungary, but as a 'suffering, suppressed people' in relation to the Austrian or 'German' imperial 'oppressors'. The various narrative models are just as closely interrelated and interdependent as those elements which serve to clarify differences or specificities between and within each of the national master narratives. Characterisations referring to religion or denomination, to social status or class, to ethnicity or gender, which tends to exclude others, generally occur in combination and rarely in isolation. Thus the figure of the Catholic priest who is defined as treacherous and feminine, and who practises a strange religion and belongs to a foreign people, is a figure of the Other which goes back to the Reformation and the French Revolution, and which can be found in numerous national master narratives and historical cultures. In the cases outlined below, the term 'Catholic' (papist) is identified, or at least associated, with the notion of being 'faithful to Habsburg'. Among non-Austrians, the same term is associated with things that are 'German', while among '*völkisch*-German' Austrians it is associated with being 'un-German'. This resulted in the ethnicisation of denominations, as can be observed elsewhere in Europe. This process affected in particular the perception of Jews, who were frequently associated with (the variously hated or admired) German culture in non-German narratives produced under the Habsburg monarchy from the nineteenth century onwards, whereas German nationalist anti-Semites defined them in terms of class, as foreign people (capitalists and leaders of the working classes) who exploited and seduced the German people.

In addition to this preliminary outline of concepts, one should take into account the historical periods during which these master narratives emerged. The nineteenth and twentieth centuries can be divided into five broad periods:

1 The time prior to the revolution of 1848/9, when particularly liberal concepts of national master narratives emerged out of France (the model of 1789, developed by Michelet and others) and notions of 'cultural nations' derived from Herder gained in influence, which thus challenged and in certain combinations even overrode dynastic and state-centred narratives.[2]

2 Between 1849 and 1918 – following Austria's elimination from the German Confederation, the Compromise of 1867 between Austria and Hungary and the failure of a Cisleithanian arrangement with the Czechs – the Habsburg monarchy was 'refounded' from within and national movements were reinforced and increasingly politicised.[3] The emergence and spread of ultramontanism in Catholic countries likewise gave succour to efforts made within Catholic circles to develop their own national master narratives,[4] while at the same time interpretations designed to undermine the influence of Rome also developed and had an ever-greater impact. From the turn of the century, existing ethnocentric tendencies became more radical and in some cases adopted popular *völkisch* tendencies.[5]

3 In the period between the two world wars, existing national master narratives were adjusted to the new legal and international situation. This

---

[2]J. Rak, *Bývali Čechové ... České historické mýty a stereotypy* (Jinočany, 1994), p. 4. Cf. E. Krekovič, E. Mannová and E. Krekovičová (eds), *Mýty naše slovenské* (Bratislava, 2005).

[3]Cf. O. Urban, *Die tschechische Gesellschaft, 1848–1918*, 2 vols (Vienna, 1994).

[4]Á. v. Klimó, *Nation, Konfession, Geschichte: zur nationalen Geschichtskultur Ungarns im europäischen Kontext (1860–1948)* (Munich, 2003).

[5]Peter Haslinger provides a more limited definition of the concept of 'folk history' (*Volksgeschichte*) in relation to Czech history. See P. Haslinger, 'Nationalgeschichte und volksgeschichtliches Denken in der tschechischen Geschichtswissenschaft, 1918–38', in M. Hettling (ed.), *Volksgeschichten im Europa der Zwischenkriegszeit* (Göttingen, 2003), pp. 272–300. Folk history in Hungary was marginal: see Á. v. Klimó, 'Volksgeschichte in Ungarn: Chancen, Schwierigkeiten, Folgen eines "deutschen" Projektes', in M. Middell and U. Sommer (eds), *Historische West- und Ostforschung in Zentraleuropa zwischen dem Ersten und dem Zweiten Weltkrieg: Verflechtung und Vergleich* (Leipzig, 2004), pp. 151–78. Slovak historiography was ethnocentric, though not *völkisch* in the same way as in German historiography. See D. Kováč, 'Die Slowakische Historiographie nach 1989: Aktiva, Probleme, Perspektiven', *Bohemia*, 37 (1996), 169–80. The case is different in Austria in the interwar period, where research into 'foreign Germanhood' (*Auslandsdeutschtum*) in relation to the 'pan-German conception of history' (*gesamtdeutsche Geschichtsauffassung*) plays a central role – for example, in the works of both Otto Brunner and Harold Steinacker, who were members of the National Socialist Party, as well as Hugo Hantsch, who was tried by the Nazis for his role in the Catholic authoritarian regime in power from 1934 to 1938: G. Heiss, 'Pan-Germans, Better Germans, Austrians: Austrian Historians on National Identity from the First to the Second Republic', *German Studies Review*, 16 (1993), 411–33.

trend won the approval of the Czechs and Slovaks, while the Hungarians and Austrians sought to affirm a revisionist position by disapproving of the Treaty of Trianon and the Treaty of Saint-Germain, respectively. Attempts were made to lend legitimacy to anti-liberal interpretations of the past when these four territories were temporarily incorporated into the sphere of influence of Nazi Germany between 1938 and 1945. The communists then developed national conceptions of history in relation to the strategies of the popular front from the mid-1930s onwards.[6]

4 After 1945 there followed a period of Sovietisation geared towards Stalinism, which later gave way to a less rigid state socialist political model in the former Habsburg territory, with the exception of Austria. Prior to the foundation of the German Democratic Republic (GDR), this process was generally expressed in the mode of earlier narratives of 'national liberation', which were initially mostly underpinned by anti-German sentiment. Although the history of the workers' movement subsequently superseded this narrative pattern, the basic thrust of the argument remained national.[7] In Austria, historians developed a new, non-German narrative of the nation-state which drew on the former model of a 'special development' within Babenbergian-Habsburg countries during the Middle Ages, or on the baroque and Josephinism as 'formative phases' of Austrian (political) culture.[8]

5 The changes that came about after 1989 had a considerable impact on the forms of national master narratives prevalent in the three post-communist countries. However, the 'renationalisation' of conceptions of history took place only on a limited scale, for historical narratives in the socialist states

---

[6]W. Pieck, G. Dimitrov and P. Togliatti, *Die Offensive des Faschismus und die Aufgaben der Kommunisten im Kampf für die Volksfront gegen Krieg und Faschismus* (Berlin, GDR, 1960), p. 161; L. Luks, *Entstehung der kommunistischen Faschismustheorie: die Auseinandersetzung der Komintern mit Faschismus und Nationalsozialismus, 1921–35* (Stuttgart, 1984). For Hungary, see M. Mevius, *Agents of Moscow: The Hungarian Communist Party and the Origins of Socialist Patriotism, 1941–53* (Oxford, 2005); Klimó, *Nation, Konfession, Geschichte*. For Austria it is worth mentioning the programmatic writings on the Austrian nation which Alfred Klahr published in 1937 on behalf of the KPÖ: A. Klahr [signed with the pseudonym Rudolf], 'Zur nationalen Frage in Österreich', *Weg und Ziel* (March/April 1937), republished in *Weg und Ziel*, 37 (1979), 23ff.
[7]L. Raphael, *Geschichtswissenschaft im Zeitalter der Extreme* (Munich, 2003), p. 58.
[8]E. Hanisch, *Der lange Schatten des Staates: Österreichische Gesellschaftsgeschichte im 20. Jahrhundert* (Vienna, 1994), p. 24. Cf. F. Heer, *Der Kampf um die österreichische Identität* (Vienna and Graz, 1981), pp. 86 and 113; E. Fischer, *Die Entstehung des österreichischen Volkscharakters* (Vienna, 1945).

had not abandoned the national thrust.[9] From the 1960s even the Habsburg monarchy had been gradually re-evaluated, in particular in the context of joint research carried out on the era of Francis Joseph.[10] In all countries, historical representations that addressed the themes of the state and its population increasingly adopted the approach of social and cultural history (often with relatively open conceptions of space).[11] On the margins of historical culture in post-communist countries, the 1990s witnessed a return of certain residual nationalist and sometimes also anti-Semitic tendencies from the interwar years, which often contained an element of anti-communism.[12]

Main subjects and reference frames of the master narratives

State vs. people

The four nations in the territory of the Habsburg monarchy gave rise to very different historical master narratives, each of which adopted a specific subject of the historical narrative. At one end of the spectrum are narratives of the *Gesamtstaat* characteristic of the mainstream in Austrian historiography. At the other end is the ethnocentric master narrative such as that of the Slovaks. In between we find narratives of Hungarian and Czech historiography, which are largely similar to each other. In these cases, the master narrative refers to medieval states with a Magyar (Árpáds) or Czech (Přemyslids) dynasty, respectively. These states provide a framework not only for the Middle Ages but also for modern history. In both cases, they have been perceived in historiographical writings in ethnic terms as 'nation-states'.

---

[9]Cf. A. Ivanišević, A. Kappeler, W. Lukan and A. Suppan (eds), *Klio ohne Fesseln? Historiographie im östlichen Europa nach dem Zusammenbruch des Kommunismus* (Vienna, Frankfurt/Main, Berlin, Bern, Brussels, New York and Oxford, 2002); Á. v. Klimó, 'Zeitgeschichte als Revolutionsgeschichte: "Gegenwartsgeschichte" in der ungarischen Historiographie des 20. Jahrhunderts', in A. Nützenadel and W. Schieder (eds), *Zeitgeschichte als Problem: Nationale Traditionen und Perspektiven der Forschung in Europa* (Göttingen, 2004), pp. 283–306.

[10]See the work and publications of the Commission for the History of the Habsburg Monarchy, 1848 until 1918, by the Austrian Academy of Sciences as conceived by Hugo Hantsch and continued by Adam Wandruszka and Helmut Rumpler.

[11]See, for example, the 12 volumes and three thematic volumes edited by Herwig Wolfram, *Österreichische Geschichte* (Wien, 1994–2006).

[12]In the case of Hungary, Éva Kovács and Gerhard Seewann speak of 'a flood of memories and images of history', which had previously been held back by a 'dam'. See É. Kovács and G. Seewann, 'Ungarn: der Kampf um das Gedächtnis', in M. Flacke (ed.), *Mythen der Nationen, 1945: Arena der Erinnerungen* (Mainz, 2004), vol. 1, pp. 817–46. For Slovakia, but also other countries, see D. Kováč, 'Paradoxa und Dillemata der postkommunistischen Geschichtsschreibung', in Ivanišević et al., *Klio ohne Fesseln?*, pp. 15–42.

In all cases, considerable continuity and sometimes even 'providential necessity'[13] were ascribed to these historical subjects, regardless of whether they were organised along ethnocentric or state lines or a mixture of the two. Various 'millennia' were celebrated in all four nations, and even specialist authors sometimes claimed that they had existed for over 1,000 years.[14] Master narratives geared towards the development of states are also inclined to place emphasis on imperial missions and historical 'tasks', whereas ethnocentric master narratives focus on myths of victimhood.

All national master narratives which emerged in relation to these four cases referred to the common state of the Habsburg monarchy since its formation in 1526. However, the relation to the state developed differently in each case. Austria was clearly identified with the *Gesamtstaat*. The Magyars focused their historical narrative on the Kingdom of Hungary, which played the role of a 'Magyar nation-state', whereby other peoples were referred to in passing as minorities, and generally in terms of objects rather than historical subjects. The Austrian history of the *Gesamtstaat* also contains 'ethnic' or even *völkisch* tendencies, which occur mainly in relation to what are called 'German historical tasks' and to the 'Holy Roman Empire of the German Nation'. Czech historiography focused on the 'historical' Bohemian state, in which the Czech nation was presented as an ethnic unity, while other ethnic groups, in particular the Germans, were represented merely as 'guests' or even as 'enemies'.[15] Although the *Gesamtstaat* of Austria was generally accepted by the population, and although the Czech historian František Palacký approved of it as a favourable frame for the Czech people, it was in principle considered to be a temporary phenomenon in comparison with Bohemia, which could boast a longer history.[16] As a result of German dominance during the nineteenth century, the main current of Czech national master narratives focused on the 'Czech people' rather than on countries bound to the Bohemian Crown, while Bohemian and Moravian Germans

---

[13]For example, J. A. Helfert, *Über Nationalgeschichte und den gegenwärtigen Stand ihrer Pflege in Österreich* (Prague, 1853), p. 54.

[14]Cf. F. Hadler, 'Meistererzählungen über die erste Jahrtausendwende in Ostmitteleuropa', *Comparativ*, 10/2 (2000), pp. 81–92; G. Heiss, 'Eine Kette von Begebenheiten 996/1996', in G. Heiss and K.P. Liessmann (eds), *Das Millennium: Essays zu tausend Jahren Österreich* (Vienna, 1996), pp. 9–27, 12–21.

[15]J. Štaif, 'The Image of the Other in the Nineteenth Century: Historical Scholarship in the Bohemian Lands', in N. M. Wingfield (ed.), *Creating the Other: Ethnic Conflict and Nationalism in the Habsburg Central Europe* (New York, 2003), pp. 81–102.

[16]Palacký's saying that 'We [Czechs] were there before Austria and will also be there after her' emphasises this point. On Palacký', see G. J. Morava, *Franz Palacký: eine frühe Version von Mitteleuropa* (Vienna, 1990); J.F. Zacek, *Palacký: The Historian as a Scholar and Nationalist* (The Hague, 1970); J. Kořalka, *Tschechen im Habsburgerreich und in Europa, 1815–1914* (Vienna, 1991).

responded by affirming their own histories. Finally, the Slovaks were deprived of any similar historical frame of reference. The Great Moravian Empire was the name given by historians to the state in which the ancestors of the Slovaks (together with the Moravians) lived, yet this state could by no means play a role comparable to that of the states of King Stephen or of Duke Wenceslaus.[17] This is why Slovak historiography uses the alternative term the 'state idea'. Slovak political programmes which developed from the mid-nineteenth century until 1993 can be understood in relation to this notion of 'statehood'.[18] Although the Habsburg monarchy, the Kingdom of Hungary and the Czechoslovak republic are presented as frames of national history, the subject of history is in fact the people of Slovakia, not the state.

Variety inherent in the master narratives

From the very beginning, all four historiographies were characterised by a number of internal variations. Slovak historiography was the most uniform; it developed under difficult institutional conditions and could establish itself less than in other countries. An ethnocentric current pervaded Slovak historiography. Parallel to the hegemonic narrative in Czech historiography, which focused on the people, there existed narratives well before 1918 which referred to the state (the Kingdom of Bohemia) or to the total monarchy, such as the conservative Catholic or the Bohemian local-patriotic narratives (Anton Gindely). In the case of Hungary, historiography before 1918 focused on the state or the nation while distinguishing between (generally Catholic) elites who were faithful to Habsburg and those (mainly Protestant) who were opposed.[19] It therefore distinguished between ideas characteristic of a multi-ethnic nation-state (St Stephen) on the one hand, and ideas characteristic of a mono-ethnic cultural nation (Árpád) on the other.[20] German-speaking historians in the Habsburg monarchy, like historians in the Austrian republic thereafter, had recourse to *Gesamtstaat*, German-*völkisch* and state-Austrian historiographical models, which they adopted in a variety of ways, while even combining contradictory elements from these concepts. The dynasty (or *Gesamtstaat*), and the three 'states' which were both legally and politically bound to it, remained a consistent topic well into the interwar years, even in 'pan-German' national historiography (*Gesamtdeutsche Geschichtsschreibung*).

---

[17]Myths about Great Moravia as former Great Slovakia, that is, as a Slovak state, are now rarely found in historiography. See Milan S. Ďurica, *Dejiny Slovenska a Slovákov* (Bratislava, 1996).
[18]See *Dokumenty slovenskej národnej identity a štátnosti*, vols 1 and 2 (Bratislava, 1998).
[19]Klimó, *Nation, Konfession, Geschichte*.
[20]J. Szűcs, *Nation und Geschichte* (Cologne and Vienna, 1981), p. 29.

New and old states after 1918

After the demise of the Habsburg monarchy, considerable differences among the four historiographies began to appear. The language used to describe this event is revealing. Hungarian and Austrian historians applied the notions of 'end', 'disintegration' and even 'catastrophe', whereas Czech and Slovak historical writings used the words 'beginning', 'liberation' and 'revolution'.

For the Austrians, 1918 marked the end of an historical task associated with the Habsburg empire, which was allied with Germany and in which the German Austrian were the lead ethnicity. However, this did not mean that Austrian historiography entirely renounced the former idea that Austria aimed to fulfil a mission, to be carried out within the context of the *Gesamtstaat* by the German-Austrian 'original people' (*Kernvolk*).[21] The basic idea according to which the Habsburg monarchy had developed out of the Babenbergian-Habsburg 'hereditary lands', in order to fulfil its 'historical duties' for the Christian Occident and/or the 'Holy Roman Empire of the German Nation', underpinned the basic concept of the history of Austria after 1918[22] and continued to exist even after 1945 in 'de-imperialised' versions of historical narratives. Consistent with the understanding of history in terms of the *Gesamtstaat*, which prevailed in the interwar years, this mission was interpreted as a form of German domination in Central Europe; the 'achievement' of the Habsburgs was thus measured against this 'task'.[23] Historiography written from the perspective of the Austrian state, which focused essentially on the history of the territory of the republic and its population, gained acceptance only after the Second World War.[24] The pioneering multi-volume work *Austrian History* adopted a pragmatic state perspective based on political conceptions of Austria in relation to specific historical eras. The sixteenth and seventeenth centuries, for example, are structured according to a 'history of state formation', to the

---

[21]For example, H. v. Srbik, *Österreich in der deutschen Geschichte* (Munich, 1936), p. 10.

[22]See J. Nadler and H. v. Srbik (eds), *Österreich: Erbe und Sendung im deutschen Raum* (Salzburg and Leipzig, 1937). Before 1918 the conservative Catholic philosopher and journalist Richard v. Kralik wrote his *Österreichische Geschichte* (Vienna, 1913), without including the history of Bohemia and Hungary during the Middle Ages.

[23]See O. Brunner, 'Die geschichtliche Funktion des alten Österreich', in F.G. Friedrich, *Kleinwächter*, and H. v. Paller (ed.), *Die Anschlussfrage in ihrer kulturellen, politischen und wirtschaftlichen Bedeutung* (Vienna and Leipzig, 1930), pp. 3, 6–11.

[24]For a programmatic commentary, see the preface to A. Lhotsky, *Geschichte Österreichs seit der Mitte des 13. Jahrhunderts (1281–1358)* (Vienna, 1967).

'conglomeration of countries' of the 'Habsburg Monarchy',[25] and, in the case of the twentieth century, to the 'territory of the Republic'.[26]

From 1918/20 onwards, in the wake of revisionist reactions to the Treaty of Trianon and the cession of territory belonging to the Kingdom of Hungary, state authority, in combination with a national *völkisch* ideology, was reinforced. For the Czechs and Slovaks, 1918 marked the emergence of a common state, which had not only to set up viable political institutions, but also to justify its place in the linear historical narrative of the region. The main points of reference for the new Czechoslovak master narrative consisted of ancient Slavs, Great Moravians, Hussites and the Bratriks in Slovakia, the Slavonic Congress and the barricades of 1848 in Prague, and the common cause fought during the First World War (in the Czechoslovak legions). Whereas Czech historians largely subscribed to this narrative, only a minority of Slovak historians supported this interpretation. Both the Catholic People's Party and the old guard of the Protestant Lutheran elites based in Turčiansky Sv. Martin continued to express support for Slovak national independence (that is, ethnic, linguistic and historical but not political independence), and thus asserted the independence of Slovak history.[27]

The historiography of the four Central European peoples was subjected to even more profound changes during the 1950s. Communist parties introduced a new conception of historiography for the Magyars, Slovaks and Czechs, which was to include an entirely new master narrative based on class distinctions. In Austria the gradual emergence of a new national identity in historiography was achieved at the expense of the German national perspective.

Gendering historical subjects

National stereotypes, whether ascribed from within or from outside an historical culture, harbour 'male' and 'female' attributes. This section examines cases which demonstrate the close correlation between such stereotypes and narratives contained in national historiographies. The degree to which they are associated with positive or negative values depends on each specific context. 'Masculinity' can be a sign of both 'state-forming powers' (as in the case of the Magyars) and brutal, aggressive behaviour (as in the case of the Austrian image of Prussia, or the Czech

---

[25]E. Hanisch, *Der lange Schatten des Staates. Österreichische Gesellschaftsgeschichte im 20. Jahrhundert. Österreichische Geschichte 1890-1990*, ed. T. Winkelbauer, *Ständefreiheit und Fürstenmacht: Länder und Untertanen des Hauses Habsburg im konfessionellen Zeitalter: Österreichische Geschichte, 1522–1699*, ed. H. Wolfram (Vienna, 2003), part 1, p. 9.
[26]Hanisch, *Der lange Schatten*, p. 15.
[27]The leader of this group, Jozef Škultéty, claimed that Czechs and Slovaks were divided not by language but the 'thousand-year-long dam' of history. See J. Škultéty, *Stodvadsa_ pät' rokov zo slovenského života, 1790–1914* (Turčiansky Sv. Martin, 1920).

image of the 'German'). 'Female' virtues such as the ability to resolve conflicts and to act as mediators (in particular in Austrian imperial discourse) are interpreted as qualities of leadership in the nation. Other 'female' concepts or narrative models such as the national Mariolatry (the veneration of the Virgin Mary as the queen of the Magyars or the Slovaks) correspond to myths of victimhood, and therefore place emphasis on moral superiority in the face of foreign aggressors or oppressors.

Characterisations of (German) Austrians as an integrative force within the multinational state served to legitimise the hegemony of German Austrians in the *Gesamtstaat*. After 1945 the definition of 'true Austrians'[28] as passive, gentle and soft,[29] in opposition to the stereotypical association of Germans with Prussian militarism and National Socialism,[30] drew on earlier characterisations and even maintained previous missionary claims. The 'effeminisation' of Austrians in contrast to the image of Germans coincided with the 'victim hypothesis', that is, the image of Austria as the first victim of Hitler's Germany, which was a convenient way of ascribing the responsibility for the crimes committed under the Nazi regime exclusively to Germany.

The purpose of discourse about Magyar masculinity was to justify claims to power within the Kingdom of Hungary. Female qualities were ascribed to Slovaks for the same reason. The Hungarian *Pallas* encyclopaedia writes that:

> The Slovak people loves its native country and is closely attached to its land, which it cultivates with unmatched diligence and steadfastness. Its people are typically gentle, have a melancholy disposition, and are patient and quick to learn. Their single main weakness is their tendency towards alcoholism and the pleasure they take in drinking schnapps. ... Slovak people believe in God, love their parish priests, teachers and squires; and the subversive activities of nationalities in recent times have proven clearly that their passions are not easily aroused.[31]

The similarities to descriptions of 'natives' by colonialists in this quotation are not a chance occurrence but a sign of the times, for they are an indication of asymmetrical political relations.

---

[28]Proclamation of the provisional Austrian government on 27 April 1945.
[29]'[W]hich are otherwise often characteristic of only children and women'. See F. Heer, 'Österreich?' *Die Furche: Kulturpolitische Wochenschrift*, Vienna, 26 October 1946, 1f. Cf. S. Mattl, 'Geschlecht und Volkscharakter: Austria Engendered', *Österreichische Zeitschrift für Geschichtswissenschaft*, 7 (1996), 499–516.
[30]See E. Fischer, *Die Entstehung des österreichischen Volkscharakters* (Vienna, 1945).
[31]See the article on 'Tótok', in *A Pallas Nagy Lexikona* (Budapest, 1897), vol. 16, p. 296. Unlike most articles in this encyclopaedia, no author was named for this entry.

Claims made in Czech discourses that gender relations were 'harmonious' were intended, by contrast, to underscore the 'barbarity' of German oppressors of women. In contrast to the imperial image of Austria, descriptions of Czechs and Slovaks in effeminate terms served to reinforce the myth of victimhood among these peoples in the face of rulers.[32]

When describing historical agents – nations, peoples and states – such gendered attributes were often used in connection with class attributes. Thus 'masculine' noble (Magyar) qualities were opposed to 'female' plebeian (Slovak) qualities.

Attributes of class in hegemonic master narratives

It is remarkable that Czech and Slovak historical narratives refer to their nations as 'plebeian', whereas the Austrians refrain from qualifying their nation in terms of class. One of the reasons for this may lie in the fact that independent journalists made a more significant contribution to Czech and Slovak historiography than elsewhere. With the exception of Austria, as noted above, social groups were generally described in terms of ethnicity, such as 'Jewish' bourgeoisie, 'German' aristocracy, that is, terms which were mostly used in connection with descriptions of the indigenous group, which celebrated a 'pure', 'genuine' national 'peasantry'.

In Austria, the German nationalist Austrian historians' thoroughly positive assessment of absolutism and centralism also influenced their assessment of the dynasty and nobility, which they praised for having played a leading role in furthering the cause of 'German' history.[33] The state-centred historiography assessed the noble estates (*Stände*) of the early modern age in a more ambivalent way. On the one hand, their role in preserving the unity of countries and in building a 'modern' regional government is described in positive terms. On the other hand, the noble estates are seen as the representatives of the particularist interests of its members, and as a political and denominational opponent of the princely rulers, who were the representatives of 'modern' tendencies (characteristic of central statehood). Ethnicised conceptions of 'class enemies' (of course, this is not the term used by the representatives of such ideologies) also find their way into Austrian historical culture, as well as into anti-liberal Catholic and conservative, and German nationalist or *völkisch*, secondary discourses prior to the Second World War, which portrayed Jews as leaders of workers and capitalists, as representatives of liberalism and Freemasonry, and of capitalism and 'industrialism'.

---

[32] J. Malečková, 'Nationalizing Women and Engendering the Nation: The Czech National Movement', in I. Blom, K. Hagemann, and C. Hall (eds), *Gendered Nations: Nationalism and Gender Order in the Long Nineteenth Century* (Oxford and New York, 2000), pp. 293–310.
[33] For example, the historians who uphold the pan-German conception of history. Cf. Nadler and Srbik, *Österreich*.

Before 1918 the most dominant master narrative to be found in Hungary was the national liberal narrative. This primarily represented the standpoint of the Magyar and Calvinist gentry, which was highly critical of the aristocracy and Habsburg monarchy. Anti-aristocratic, anti-bourgeois, anti-urban and anti-Semitic tendencies also arose from the late nineteenth century onwards, and were to grow stronger in the ethnocentric (though only marginally significant) historiography of the 1930s. After 1918, however, national conservative, Catholic and *völkisch* master narratives had a greater impact, which featured an 'alien' (*fremdvölkisch*) urban bourgeoisie as a common enemy (largely identified with Judaism), which 'corrupted' the 'pure' Magyar people (peasantry). For some Protestant intellectuals, the primary object of hatred was nevertheless the Catholic nobility. These intellectuals associated themselves with the glorified image of 'pure' peasantry, a motif that was later taken over by the communists in the context of the anti-fascist popular front (József Révai). In their bitter complaints about the 'Junker' after 1945, they consciously represented the class enemy (gentry and aristocracy) in ethnic terms, as 'German' aristocrats.[34]

Ethnically defined class enemies also operated within the hegemonic Czech historical narrative. The 'German' patriciate in the Bohemian towns and the 'German' nobility were represented as oppressors of the Czech people, which comprised various lower classes and was represented as democratic, egalitarian and averse to hierarchies (as in the early Middle Ages, and in particular under the Hussite democracy in the fifteenth century especially under the radical Taborites). The image of the nobility barely changed after 1918. A typical example of this is the pamphlet *The Bohemian Nobility*, written by the novelist Josef Holeček in 1918, in which the nobility is presented as pure German and treasonable, having betrayed the Czech people at the battle of the Marchfeld in 1278, for example. The negative image of the nobility and the emphasis placed on its German characteristics, which were perceived to be alien to the people, persisted after 1945. Zdeněk Nejedlý, the leading communist politician who concerned himself with cultural and educational policies, wrote a pamphlet in which he presented a radical image of Czech history as a battle of (Czech) lower classes against the (German) aristocracy, as a confrontation between 'popular classes' (*lidové vrstvy*) and the 'lords' (*panstvo*). This dualistic concept was also frequently used to distinguish within the nobility itself between peers (*páni*) and squires or yeomen (*zemani*), and assert that only the latter

---

[34]At that time, Protestant historians tried to identify Catholics with 'German culture' while identifying Calvinists and even Hungarian Lutherans with 'Western European' traditions (Geneva, Holland, Sweden, Finland). They claimed that 'Catholic Swabians', whom Maria Theresa had resettled during the eighteenth century in order to 'Germanise' Magyar regions, were responsible for having introduced 'fascist ideas'. See Á. v. Klimó, 'Die gespaltene Vergangenheit: die großen Kirchen im Kampf um die Nationalgeschichte Ungarns, 1920–48', *Zeitschrift für Geschichtswissenschaft*, 47 (1999), 874–91.

could be a true representative of the 'people', for the lower nobility was said to have led the Hussite movement while the upper nobility had been 'Germanised' as early as the Middle Ages. Narratives after 1945 suggest that the (equally German or 'Germanised') bourgeoisie, particularly in Prague, sided with the nobility after betraying the radical popular masses and made a pact with the patricians during the Hussite Wars. In 1620, after the demise of the old nobility, they claimed that only 'foreign adventurers, who had nothing in common with the people',[35] had come and that the bourgeoisie had been entirely Germanised. Towns were represented in a predominantly negative way, while the peasant class (especially smallholders) and the urban lower classes were seen as representatives, and often heroes, of national history.

From the nineteenth century onwards, Slovak historical narratives corresponded to Czech narratives insofar as they presented a 'plebeian' image of their own nation. Attempts to integrate the Slovak nobility into the national master narrative were criticised by the national politician Svetozár Hurban Vajansky, who, in the second half of the nineteenth century, defined members of the original ethnic Slovak nobility as a 'desiccated branch' of the nation. Instead, this narrative was dominated by members of the petty bourgeoisie, craftsmen and, above all, by the idealised 'peasantry'. The history of the Slovaks was therefore not presented as the history of rulers, battles and wars, but as the history of 'constructive', rather than 'destructive', middle and lower classes; this narrative was set against the image of the 'belligerent' noble Magyars, which loomed in the background.[36] After 1948 the communists derided the existing Slovak historiography as 'bourgeois', and attempted to promote Czechoslovak and Slovak 'proletarian' master narratives. However, representations of economic history and social history adhered to the national ethnic pattern, whereby emphasis was placed on 'revolutionary' traditions geared in particular towards an interpretation of history favoured by the Communist Party. In principle, however, an entirely new master narrative did not emerge.

Alternative subjects and reference frames

During the nineteenth and twentieth centuries, national historical master narratives developed and evolved in connection with changing social distinctions and political circumstances. 'Alternative' historical narratives emerged alongside national hegemonic narratives, and new interpretative paradigms – denomination, class or ethnic minorities – came to the fore.

---

[35]Z. Nejedlý, *Komunisté, dědici velikých tradic českého národa* (Prague, 1953), p. 20. See also E. Schmidt-Hartmann, 'Forty Years of Historiography under Socialism in Czechoslovakia: Continuity and Change of Patterns of Thought', *Bohemia*, 29 (1988), 300–24.
[36]See V. Mináč, *Dúchanie do pahrieb* (Bratislava, 1970).

Denominational narratives

The wide variety of denominations in Central Europe had a profound impact on the development of national historical master narratives. Only in Austria was the power of the Catholic Church unrivalled. In Slovakia, where the majority of people were also Catholic, the Protestant minority nonetheless had a greater influence on the development of the national historical culture. A similar situation was to be found in Hungary, where Calvinist and anti-Habsburgian institutions were dominant in spite of the Catholic majority in this country. Czech society was comparatively secular: the Hussite movement, alongside the anti-Habsburgian and therefore anti-Catholic bias, became solid pillars of the Czech national master narrative.

Catholicism played a key role in the national historiographies of the region. It had become the dominant religion in Central Europe, largely as a result of the denominational policy of the Habsburgs in the early modern period, and because the dynasty and the Catholic Church provided strong mutual support until 1918. In national liberal, as well as in Protestant, Marxist or *völkisch* constructions of national identities, the Catholic Church was perceived as an enemy figure, as a purveyor of 'a reactionary obstruction to progress', an 'ally' of the oppressors, a 'traitor' to the people and an agent of the Habsburg monarchy. Such narratives frequently distinguished between their 'own' lowly clergy 'close to the people', and an aristocratic, alien and high clergy. Anti-Catholicism was most strongly expressed by Czechs and Magyars, whereas Austrians and Slovaks adopted a more moderate stance, sometimes with predominantly trans-denominational narratives.

Austrian historical narratives consistently strove to adopt a detached approach to denominational contradictions. In general, even liberal and German nationalist historians expressed criticism only in relation to extreme cases of the Counter-Reformation (such cases were seen as a mistake even in Catholic Church history). In the time between the wars, and in Catholic Austrian nationalist historiography after 1945, Catholic historiographical discourse constructed an opposition between a Catholic universal integrative (Habsburg) Austrian way of being on the one hand, and a Protestant, divisive, militaristic, north German Prussian way of being on the other. Catholic denominational historiography thus presented a positive image of the dynasty and (German-Austrian) centralism, provided it did not touch on the subject of the Josephinian state church,[37] and was therefore in line with changes taking place in the historical master narrative of the *Gesamtstaat*. However, Protestant denominational historiography in Austria attempted to establish, step by step, a German federal narrative based on cultural history and the history of ideas.[38]

---

[37]E. Tomek, *Kirchengeschichte Österreichs*, 3 vols (Innsbruck and Wien, 1935, 1949, 1959).
[38]G. Loesche, *Geschichte des Protestantismus im vormaligen und im neuen Österreich* (Tübingen, 1902; 2nd edn: Wien–Leipzig, 1921).

In the case of Slovak historiography, one rarely finds anti-Habsburgian tendencies and even fewer expressions of anti-Catholicism, even though national
historical narratives were written by Protestants. If the national narrative were to
effectively provide orientation for a collective identity and national unity, it had
to take into consideration the Catholic majority. Since Slovak Lutherans used the
Czech language as a liturgical language and, until the mid-nineteenth century, a
literary language, Protestant historical narratives placed greater emphasis on the
common history of the Czechs and Slovaks than the Catholic narratives. However, this trend gradually declined in the second half of the nineteenth century.
It was within the fascist Slovak state (1939–45), set up and controlled by the
Catholic People's Party under the wing of Hitler's regime, which historians
attempted to rewrite Slovak history from the perspective of national conservative
Catholicism.[39] However, no new master narrative could be established in such a
short time. It was not until after 1945 that a specifically Catholic, anti-Czech
trend in Slovak national historiography made itself felt, albeit not in Slovakia but
among emigrant historians.

In response to the prevailing anti-Habsburgian and anti-Catholic sentiment in
Magyar and Czech historiography, an alternative Catholic conservative current
arose which was faithful to the Habsburg monarchy. This current prevailed
under Horthy, and held the Reformation and liberalism partially responsible for
the collapse of the Kingdom of Hungary (Gyula Szekfű). After 1945 communist
historical narratives played off the national Protestant tradition against the
national Catholic tradition.[40] The situation was similar in Czechoslovakia, where
the communist dictatorship fought a battle against the Catholic Church by challenging its role in national history. The Catholic Church constituted a stable
enemy in the Czech master narratives of all periods. It was considered to be the
main enemy of the glorified Hussite movement and, together with the Habsburgs, the main protagonist of the 'age of darkness' (*temno*) after 1620. In the
communist representation of Czech history, not only Jesuits but also the entire
baroque culture was incriminated.

However, a conservative discourse arose in reaction to this radical anti-
Catholic orientation in the first half of the twentieth century. In his work
The Errors and Dangers of Land Reform (1923), for example, Josef Pekař reassessed
the achievements of the baroque nobility in the seventeenth and eighteenth
centuries.[41] In the late 1930s, and in particular during the war, attempts were
made to develop a conservative Catholic historical narrative around the cult of

---

[39]This tendency reached its zenith in the work of F. Hrušovský, *Slovenské dejiny* (Martin,
1939).

[40]Klimó, 'Die gespaltene Vergangenheit'; Á. v. Klimó, '1848/49 in der politischen Kultur
Ungarns', in H. Fröhlich, M. Grandner, and M. Weinzierl (eds), *1848 im europäischen
Kontext* (Vienna, 1999), pp. 204–22.

[41]J. Pekař, *Irrtümer und Gefahren der Bodenreform* (Prague, 1923); on Pekař, see Z. Kalista,
Josef Pekař (Prague, 1994).

St Wenceslaus, which would lend legitimacy to the existence of the Protectorate of Bohemia and Moravia (1939–45) by accentuating the fact that the Bohemian lands once belonged to the Holy Roman Empire. After 1945 this narrative became discredited and disappeared entirely from official historical discourse. Only after 1989 did the Catholic conservative view of history resurface as an alternative to the hegemonic narrative when, for example, the works of Zdeněk Kalista were republished, and in articles published in the journal *Střední Evropa* ('Central Europe').[42]

Class-based master narratives

Marxism, with its model of a class-based historical narrative, provided a far-reaching challenge to traditional national historical cultures. In Austria, the Social Democratic movement gave rise to Marxist historical narratives very early on.[43] The Social Democrats Otto Bauer and Ludo Moritz Hartmann argued that the Austrian bourgeoisie had, by entering into an alliance with the dynasty, betrayed the liberal democratic principles of 1848, and that the workers' movement had therefore become the true representative of the German liberal democratic tradition of 1848. They saw the demise of the Habsburg empire as an opportunity for 'German Austrians' to push for closer political ties with democratic and industrialised Germany.[44] Even during the early years after the Second World War, a communist version of Marxism made its mark as a secondary alternative, with which Eva Priester wanted to free Austrian history 'from the jungle of the Pan-German representation', which had become 'the starting point and breeding-ground for anti-Austrian, Pan-German, anti-Slavic propaganda'. Instead, Priester aimed to present Austria (in 1949, in opposition to an 'Atlantic Combination') as 'something unique, something that had evolved organically'.[45] In the interwar years, in addition to communist historical journalism, even professional Czech historiography contained signs of a Marxist approach, as represented by the so-called 'historical group' in Prague.[46] This was not the case in Magyar and Slovak historiography.

---

[42]The most influential book was without doubt Kalista's *Tvář baroka* (Prague, 1992).

[43]See O. Bauer, *Geschichte Oesterreichs: eine Anleitung zum Studium der österreichischen Geschichte und Politik* (Vienna, 1911).

[44]See O. Bauer, *Die Nationalitätenfrage und die Sozialdemokratie*, Marx-Studien: Blätter zur Theorie und Politik des wissenschaftlichen Sozialismus, 2 (Wien, 1907), 524: 'If the capitalist class strives towards a big multinational state ruled by one nation, then the working class will take up the old bourgeois idea of the free nation-state.'

[45]E. Priester, *Kurze Geschichte Österreichs*, 1, *Entstehung eines Staates* (Vienna, 1946), p. 5, or E. Priester, *Kurze Geschichte Österreichs. 2. Aufstieg und Untergang des Habsburgerreiches* (Vienna, 1949), p. 6.

[46]See J. Petráň, ' Historická skupina', in *Studie z obecných dějin: sborník k sedmdesátým narozeninám Prof. Dr. Jaroslava Charváta* (Prague, 1975), pp. 11–47.

The situation changed in the 1950s. Whereas Marxist historiography in Austria was relegated to a marginal position, the communist parties of Czechoslovakia and Hungary declared Marxism to be the only possible and permissible method for writing history, and called for existing history to be rewritten. The emphasis on revolutionary traditions, uprisings, rebellions and strikes certainly paved the way for new research topics. However, the aim to fundamentally revise history proved to be a very complex undertaking.

The new vision of history made its most noticeable impact on the interpretation of twentieth-century history. Everything was subordinated to the argument that the Russian October Revolution heralded the beginning of a new age in world history, and that national histories must likewise be evaluated in terms of their particular relation to this event. Another element of this vision was the disapproval of the first ('bourgeois') Czechoslovak republic or the 'exposure' of the 'fascist' Horthy system.[47] While these attempts to re-evaluate history brought about certain changes to the political and ideological understanding of the new national history, they did not completely break with the existing hegemonic national historical narrative. In representations of the more distant past, continuity was still of the utmost importance: new definitions of historical phenomena were often used while the basic narrative structure remained the same. In Hungary, communist historical narratives referred back to the hegemonic liberal anti-Habsburg narrative, while Czech and Slovak Marxist-Leninist historiography enhanced the status of 'plebeian' traditions or of the 'heritage' of the revolutionary movements, above all that of Hussitism.[48] 'Class', as an historical subject, fused with the 'people', understood in terms of ethnicity. The class-based narrative thus lost its potential to challenge the hegemonic national master narrative. As a result, over time, the focus on class in the historical narratives of state socialist dictatorships proved to be of less importance than, for instance, in British, French or Italian historiography.

Alternative narratives based on ethnicity

In a multi-ethnic region such as Central Europe, varieties of historical narratives arose in which non-dominant ethnic communities or ethnic minorities

---

[47]In Slovakia, see L'. Holotík, *Štefánikovská legenda a vznik ČSR* (Bratislava, 1956).

[48]The first product of Czechoslovak Marxist-Leninist historical writing was a model of the future synthesis of Czechoslovak history. See *Přehled československých dějin*, vols 1, 2/1–2, 3 (Prague, 1958–61). Parallel to this, the two volumes of a history of Slovakia (*Dejiny Slovenska*, Bratislava, 1960, 1968) were published. On the syntheses of Czechoslovak history, see P. Kolář, 'Die nationalgeschichtlichen master narratives in der tschechischen Geschichtsschreibung der zweiten Hälfte des 20. Jahrhunderts: Entstehungskontexte, Kontinuität, Wandel', in C. Brenner et al. (eds), *Geschichtsschreibung zu den böhmischen Ländern im 20. Jahrhundert: Wissenschaftstraditionen – Institutionen – Diskurse* (Munich, 2006), pp. 209–41.

played a key role. In the ethnocentric master narrative of the Slovaks, other nations or ethnic groups were initially not mentioned. It is only since the rise of the ethnic territorial conception of Slovak history in recent years that initiatives have been taken to integrate other ethnic groups into the national master narrative.[49] The Czech historical master narrative was also 'ethnicised' at an early date: hence Palacký published his *History of Bohemia* first in German, then in Czech under the title *History of the Czech People*. The ethnocentric Czech representation of history consistently either refrains from mentioning the Germans or treats them as enemies.[50] On the other hand, the Germans living in the regions governed by 'the Bohemian Crown' created their own version of Bohemian history as a German alternative to the Czech version. This applies to the cases of Constantin Höfler, Adolf Bachmann and Bertold Bretholz, who wrote their histories in the second half of the nineteenth and early twentieth centuries. They represented the Germans in Bohemia and Moravia as either the descendants of the first proto-Germanic settlers or of the medieval 'bringers of culture'.[51]

Having been consistently focused on St Stephen's Crown, the Magyar master narrative dominant before 1918 simply turned the multinational state into a national Magyar state. Other nations and ethnic groups were only ever mentioned in passing. Movements calling for the autonomy of other peoples were rejected as 'hostile to the state', the Slovaks were simply deprived of their 'power to form a state', and Romanians and Serbs were regarded as 'spies' of other nation-states and therefore defined as enemies. Only Croats and Transylvanian Saxons enjoyed a greater degree of recognition on account of their 'historical' right to autonomy. And only in the late 1930s were attempts made, in the Pál-Teleki Institute, for example, to work out a narrative that approached a multiethnic version of Hungarian history. National minorities there are now too small in number to create their own alternative narratives. However, peoples from the former Kingdom of Hungary, such as the Slovaks, but also the Croats and Transylvanian Saxons, have written their own version of a common Hungarian history.

---

[49]Cf. E. Mannová (ed.), *A Concise History of Slovakia* (Bratislava, 2000); D. Kováč, *Dějiny Slovenska* (Prague, 1998).

[50]See J. Rak, 'Obraz Němce v české historiografii 19. století', in J. Křen and E. Broklová (eds), *Obraz Němců, Rakouska a Německá v české společnosti 19. a 20. století* (Prague, 1998), pp. 49–75, and J. Štaif, 'The Image of the Other in the Nineteenth Century: Historical Scholarship in the Bohemian Lands', in N. M. Wingfield (ed.), *Creating the Other: Ethnic Conflict and Nationalism in the Habsburg Central Europe* (New York, 2003), pp. 81–102.

[51]See M. Neumüller (ed.), *Die böhmischen Länder in der deutschen Geschichtsschreibung seit dem Jahre 1848*, 2 vols (Ústí nad Labem, 1996–7); P. Soukup and F. Šmahel (eds), *Německá medievistika v českých zemích do roku 1945* (Prague, 2004).

Only after 1945 was the Austrians' sense of belonging to the German people superseded by the idea of their belonging to an Austrian nation. In the modern age the history of Austria was consistently understood in terms of the history of a multinational state under German domination, and in relation to the history of Germany or to the 'Holy Roman Empire of the German Nation'. Only with this support in the 'empire' was Austria said to be able to fulfil its historical mission within the geographical territory of the monarchy and beyond. Traces of this idea that the Austrian people are destined to fulfil a historical mission can still be found after 1945, albeit without the imperialistic claim to power; this is often expressed in connection with the character of the Austrian nation, which – though occasionally defined biologically in terms of its 'blood combination' – is said to be particularly suited to play an integrative and peaceful role bringing together different peoples in Central Europe. From this perspective of an Austrian nation-state, it seems very difficult to outline an ethnically defined alternative to these master narratives. As a consequence, of the four national minorities (Slovenes, Czechs, Slovaks and Croats), only the Slovenes appear to be active subjects of history, and even this group is mentioned almost exclusively in regional histories, sometimes as a threat to state integrity.

Common to all these national master narratives was the fact that Jews, who made up a large minority in each of the four countries, were either excluded or represented as 'strangers' or 'enemies'. This applied to the Austrian, Czech and Hungarian Catholic conservative and radical nationalist historical narratives. Whereas historians in Austria gave greater attention to Jewish history after 1945, in particular in relation to the emancipation and to the Holocaust, it was not until after 1989 that Jews appeared in the historical narratives of the other three countries. However, anti-Semitic undertones have continued to appear in some school history manuals.[52] Even though these are generally the exception, there remains no doubt that Jewish history has been dealt with only in passing, even after 1989. This is especially apparent in writings about twentieth-century history, in which the Holocaust is either marginalised or treated in relation to the fate of 'national victims'. It is also clear that no narrative of Jewish history has emerged which could present an alternative to hegemonic master narratives. Initial attempts to undertake systematic research into Jewish history were made at the beginning of the twentieth century by Arthur Goldmann in Austria, Samuel Steinherz in Bohemia, and some historians in Hungary. However, these never developed into an independent narrative that could provide orientation for collective identities, for they were invariably integrated into the hegemonic master narrative. This marginalisation process is

---

[52]Czech Republic: P.K. Mráček, *Příručka církevních dějin* (Prague, 1995); Slovakia: Milan S. Ďurica, *Dejiny Slovenska a Slovákov* (Bratislava, 1996).

even more valid in the case of the Roma (Gypsies) for, even today, none of the four national historical narratives reserves a specific place for them. In Hungary, they are mentioned merely as a cultural fringe group in the context of folklore. Since 1989 efforts have been made to enhance the status of this significant ethnic minority in Hungary, the Czech Republic and Slovakia whereby memories of the Holocaust play a central role. These attempts to promote the integration process are nonetheless sluggish, and are often thwarted by the effective exclusionary mechanisms built into the hegemonic narratives.[53]

Myths of origin: where do we come from?

Origin myths, the continually contested ideas relating to a 'beginning' of state or national history, are not necessarily rooted in prehistory or in the Middle Ages. The ideas of a national 'rebirth' in the nineteenth and twentieth centuries can also be understood as origin myths, for they fulfil the same narrative function. They are evoked in relation to the main or alternative subjects of historical narratives and to their 'characters' or historical 'tasks' or 'missions', as outlined above. This is why they constitute moments to which subsequent narratives repeatedly refer throughout the course of history.

There are two basic types of origin myth: first, the myth of an 'original free community', which usually goes back to the pre- or early Middle Ages; second, the myth of state foundation during the Middle Ages. The myth of the state was most pronounced in Austria, in line with the constitutional hierarchy there; it was less pronounced in Magyar and Czech historiography, and even less so in Slovak historiography. The impact of the myth of freedom operated in reverse: it was most pronounced among the Slovaks, quite pronounced among Czechs and Magyars, and least of all among the Austrians.

The myths of freedom

The myth of an 'original' democracy in prehistoric times, which became known after the French Revolution and spread throughout Europe, attracted considerable support in three out of the four national historical cultures. This occurred as a result of the common sphere of communication among intellectuals and as a result of the competition between myths, which played a key role in the national movements within the Habsburg monarchy.[54]

---

[53]See also M. Steward, 'Remembering without Commemoration: The Devices and the Politics of Memory among East European Roma', in M. M. Kovács and P. Lom (eds), *Studies on Nationalism from CEU* (Budapest, 2004), pp. 115–28.
[54]On the spread of such myths in Europe, see the essays on numerous examples in M. Flacke (ed.), *Mythen der Nationen – ein europäisches Panorama: eine Ausstellung des Deutschen Historischen Museums* (Berlin, 1998).

A representative of the idea of the 'original freedom' of the Magyar people was the liberal Catholic priest Mihály Horváth (1809–1878), who was the most influential Hungarian historian during the period before 1867.[55] Horváth was considered to be the first Hungarian historian whose writings did not focus on the nobility as the *natio Hungariae*, but on a modern nation-in-the-making, which was distinguished from the Orthodox nations in the East on account of its cultural 'constitution'. In his main work he attempted to draw a line between the Christianised Magyars, who belonged to the 'West', and the Slavic nations.[56]

These myths of 'original' free communities, which were later to be enslaved by (German or Hungarian) feudal leaders and the Church, played a central role in the national movements of the Czechs and Slovaks in the *Vormärz* period prior to the revolutions of 1848. The specific narrative patterns with which these myths were conveyed reveal some interesting variations: the Slovaks were said to be descended from ancient Slavic tribes, which had settled in the area of present-day Slovakia as early as the fifth and sixth centuries. According to this narrative, the Slovak settlement thus preceded the Magyar settlement by 300 years. In some historical works produced during the eighteenth and nineteenth centuries, Skythes or Jazyges were defined as 'ancestors' of the Slovak people.

Linguistic arguments were applied to prove that Slovaks had preserved the ancient Slavic language better than other Slavs, and that their name was both more 'Slavic' and more original. These arguments were directed against the claim to power implicit in the myth of the 'acquisition of land' (*honfoglalás*) upheld under the leadership of Prince Árpád during the ninth century by seven Magyar tribes, which had migrated westwards from the Ural Mountains. Having been stripped of its earlier noble and class-based character, this myth played a key role in the Magyar national liberal master narrative from the mid-nineteenth century onwards, as well as in subsequent popular, democratic and socialist narratives.

For the state of Hungary the acquisition of land by the 'heathen tribes' was a prerequisite for the formation of the state. For the Magyar people, it signified the beginning of the process of 'becoming a people' and their claim to power over other peoples within the Kingdom of Hungary. The Slovaks, 'Prince Svätopluk's people', were thus said to have been defeated by the Magyar princes and had thus lost their right to equal rights. Other Magyar historical narratives also claimed that both the Slovaks and the Germans had settled in the Carpathian

[55]M. Horváth, *Polgárosodás, liberalizmus, függetlenségi harc*, selected and with an introduction by L. Pál (Budapest, 1986), pp. 5–16.
[56]Z. Tóth, 'Liberale Auffassung der Ethnizität in der "Ethnographie von Ungarn" von Pál Hunfalvy', in C. Kiss et al. (eds), *Nation und Nationalismus in wissenschaftlichen Standardwerken Österreich-Ungarns ca. 1867–1918* (Vienna, 1997), pp. 57–64.

Basin as late as the twelfth and thirteenth centuries. The Slovak historical narratives thus opposed the Magyar 'theory of subjugation' by suggesting that the Slavs had welcomed the Magyars in peaceful circumstances.

Since the publication of Palacký's major work, the main origin myth of the Czechs also made reference to the 'original democracy' of Slavic tribes. Palacký even claimed that such a democracy was also practised by other Slavic peoples, and argued that it had been destroyed by the authoritarian hierarchical feudalism of the German colonialists during the thirteenth century.[57] At the turn of the century, a heated controversy broke out about the ancient free tribal constitution (*zádruha*), the notion of which could be traced back to the handwritten forgeries of Königinhof and Grünberg at the beginning of the nineteenth century.[58] The narrative pattern that formed an integral part of the freedom myth, based on small communities defending themselves against larger ones in David and Goliath fashion, fused with Protestant myths of the Reformation and of Hussitism, especially in the Magyar and Czech contexts. Both national narratives likewise presented subsequent events – the revolution of 1848/9, the anti-fascist struggle for freedom against the Germans during the Second World War and finally the anti-Stalinist revolts in Hungary in 1956 – as a continuation of this chain of events.[59] In Austrian historiography this narrative of democracy and freedom was found only in secondary discourses, in relation to the revolution of 1848 in the writings of German national Social Democrats, for example, and sometimes in regional histories (of the free Slovene peasants during the investiture of the dukes of Carinthia, for example) and in relation to the notion of a social kingdom in Catholic legitimistic circles during the interwar years.[60]

State myths

The second basic type of origin myth arose in connection with a master narrative geared towards the state. It is somewhat conservative, often Catholic and frequently refers to (largely sacred) 'kingly founders of the state' such as St Stephen or St Wenceslaus. The narratives of the 'ruling' nations of the (German) Austrians and Magyars referred more explicitly to a state myth than did the narratives of

---

[57]J. Štaif, 'Konceptualizace českých dějin v díle Františka Palackého', *Český časopis historický*, 89 (1991), pp. 161–84, 166–7.
[58]See M. Nodl, 'Německá medievalistika v českých zemích a studium hospodářských a sociálních dějin', in P. Soukup and F. Šmahel (eds), *Německá medievistika v českých zemích do roku 1945* (Prague, 2004), pp. 21–65, 56–9.
[59]On the parallels between 1956 and 1848/9, see H. Nyyssönen, *The Presence of the Past in Politics: '1956' after 1956 in Hungary* (SoPhi, 1999).
[60]See August M. Knoll, Alfred Missong, Wilhelm Schmid, Ernst Karl Winter and H. K. Zeßner-Spitzenberg, *Die Österreichische Aktion: Programmatische Studien* (Wien, 1927).

the Czechs or Slovaks. For a long time, the myths of freedom and of state foundation were antagonistic elements within the Magyar narratives. This had a lot to do with the Protestant influence on the freedom myth, which was in turn counteracted by the Catholic appropriation of the myth of state foundation in connection with King Stephen, or rather St Stephen, who was said to have founded the Kingdom of Hungary in 1000, as well as the Christian Church in Hungary, an event symbolised by his coronation with the holy crown sent by the pope himself. One of the representatives of this Catholic dimension of the narrative was the very well and broadly educated priest Nepomuk János Danielik (1817–88).[61]

The idea of appealing to ancient Carolingian and Ottonian margraviates as the origins of Austria acquired central significance for the Austrian master narrative since they were perceived as the starting point of 'historical tasks' to which the Austrian dynasty had to respond throughout all periods of history. It presented Austria as a bulwark of the West or of the German empire,[62] and as a bridge to the peoples of the south-eastern part of Central Europe in order to Christianise and civilise them, and to organise peaceful coexistence for them. This task was fulfilled with the help of a 'German settlement' and a 'German law'. This foundation myth was reflected in the argument that Austria had benefited from a constitutional 'special development' (*Sonderentwicklung*) from the Middle Ages onwards which was valid for the imperial as well as for Austrian nationalist conceptions of history.[63] The pan-German conception, too, adopted the foundation myths, yet it rejected the idea of a 'special development', emphasising that the 'Austrian hereditary lands', which formed an integral part of the German empire, had to fulfil a 'German mission' in south-eastern Europe.

Czech historical culture gave rise to the myth of St Wenceslaus (Václav), which focused more explicitly on the state and on Catholic thought, and which simultaneously boasted the independence it had gained from the 'German' empire as well as its connection to the Christian West (in similar fashion to the myth of St Stephen in Hungary). This tradition continued to be embodied in the figure of Charles IV in his role as the King of Bohemia (in Czech: *český*

---

[61]A. Notter, *A Szent-István-Társulat története. A Szent-István-Társulat kiadása* (Budapest, 1904).

[62]Even Franz Martin Mayer, who otherwise adopted a neutral stance when it came to national questions, wrote, 'In similar fashion to Prussia, the origins of Austria thus go back to the border guards of the German Empire', in his *Geschichte Österreichs mit besonderer Rücksicht auf das Kulturleben*, 2 vols, 3rd edn (Vienna, 1909; [1st printing 1874, 2nd printing 1900/1]), I, p. 42.

[63]According to this argument, the Babenbergian Habsburgian countries developed considerable independence and a special status in relation to the 'empire' as early as the Middle Ages, in particular from 1156, when their status was raised to that of a dukedom and when the Babenberger Henry was granted the 'privilegium minus'.

král, that is, both the Bohemian and Czech king), especially in the writings of conservative and Catholic historians, for whom the era of Charles IV, rather than that of Hussitism, marked the climax of medieval Bohemian history.[64] In the hegemonic Czech historical narrative of the nineteenth century, the myths of freedom and of the state fused into one, for the founders of the state were increasingly perceived in terms of ethnicity.

The Slovaks also lay claim to a foundation myth focusing on the state, although this is less pronounced than in the Austrian, Hungarian and Czech examples. This myth refers mainly to the Great Moravian empire under Svätopluk, which is perceived as the original Slovak state, and to pre-state political units.[65] Slovak statehood goes back to the empire of the Franconian merchant Samo, who is said to have led an uprising of the Slavs against the Avars in the seventh century. The myth of Great Moravia can also be traced back to the myth of a common state for Czechs and Slovaks in the early Middle Ages.[66] This theory became a central component of official state doctrine from 1918 onwards, and persisted long enough to acquire a place in the professional historiography during the state socialist dictatorship.[67]

Temporal structures of the narratives

Three elements determine the fundamental temporal structure of the historical narratives: the speed at which historical events unfold, the rhythm of the rise and decline, and the periodisation, that is the organisation of the historical material in relation to time. These three elements are closely interrelated: periods in which many events take place appear to be more dynamic and 'faster' than quieter periods in which 'little' or 'insignificant' things take place. National historical narratives consist of 'narrated time', the apparent dynamism and speed of which are governed by the degree to which it approaches the *telos* of supra-historical developments – such as the national, social, or denominational emancipation (of the Czechs, Slovaks and in part the Magyars, for example) or the realisation of an 'historical task' (as in the case of the Austrians or Magyars). The relative dynamism or inertia of the historical development of a

---

[64]See, for example, Z. Kalista, *Karel IV: Jeho duchovní tvář* (Prague, 1971). On Kalista, see the collection of conference papers *Zdeněk Kalista a kulturní historie* (Semily, 2000).

[65]The Great Moravian myth is still to be found in Ďurica, *Dejiny Slovenska a Slovákov*.

[66]First traces of the Czechoslovakist' theory can be found as early as the mid-nineteenth century in the works of Slovak Protestant 'revivalists', then again in the early twentieth century in the work of Július Botto, *Slováci: vývin ich národného povedomia*, vols 1–2 (Martin, 1906, 1910).

[67]See the academic syntheses *Dejiny Slovenska*, vol. 1 (Bratislava, 1961), and *Přehled československých dějin*, vol. 1/1 (Prague, 1958), which, like *Přehled dějin Československa*, vol. 1 (Prague, 1982), were written jointly by Czech and Slovak historians.

nation (according to acceleration or delay, progress or decline, and backwardness) is thus determined by its 'supra-temporal' goal, which in turn determines
its periodisation.

Certain notions of the speed at which historical processes unfold are connected with attitudes to the past, present and future. Narratives of progress
geared towards the future are often combined with the idea of acceleration, in
contrast to narratives about what has already been achieved in history and
what should be preserved from the past. Finally, descriptions of the histories
of nations also refer to global processes in which, for example, the developments in nations which were undergoing a process of emancipation, in particular those of the Czechs or Magyars, were said to unfold 'faster' than those of
ruling nation-states or of the 'free' Slovaks. One example of a nation that
claimed to enjoy an 'accelerated' and therefore 'more progressive' development than other nations is named in Palacký's *History of Bohemia*,[68] which
defends the notion of the 'civilised nature' of the Bohemian Slavs prior to the
rise of Christianity. The temporal structure here presupposes a more general
progressive pattern (in terms of the 'acquisition of land', 'Christianisation',
the 'civilising process', 'modernisation' or 'European history') against which
specific national developments are measured. This tendency to interpret time
in the context of a universal historical framework gained support when historiography became more 'scientific' in the second half of the nineteenth century:
whereas Romantic historical narratives underscored the specificity of each
nation's historical development, professional historians increasingly strove to
couch national developments in the context of general (European) history.
Thus the conservative Czech historian Josef Pekař interpreted the defeat of the
Bohemian estates at the battle of White Mountain in 1620 not only as a
national catastrophe, but also as a battle between the absolute monarchy and
the nobility which characterised Europe at the time. In similar fashion, Gyula
Szekfű analysed the Magyar renewal of the eighteenth century in the context
of the European age of the baroque and the Enlightenment: as a development
that was evidently 'up-to-date'.[69]

The generally strong wish to assume that national historical understanding
is rooted in an eternally unchanging, timeless foundation and a clear objective is aptly expressed by the phrase 'historical' (and occasionally explicitly
'providential')[70] 'tasks'. The rate of acceleration or the degree of inertia of

[68]J. Štaif, *Historici, dějiny a společnost: historiografie v českých zemích od Palackého a jeho
předchůdců po Gollovu školu, 1790–1900* (Prague, 1997), vol. 1, p. 59.
[69]J. Pekař, *Bílá hora* (Prague, 1921). Szekfű and Bobrzynski take a similar approach: see
Maciej Janowski, 'Three Historians', *CEU History Department Yearbook* (2001–2), 199–232.
[70]See J. Chmel, 'Einleitung', in J. Chemel (ed.), *Monumenta Habsburgica*, Part 1: 'Akten zur
Geschichte Maximilians I.', parts I–III in 5 vols (Vienna, 1854–8), vol. 2, p. xiii; see ch. 1.

historical development is measured in terms of such attributions. In the case of Austria, the 'turbulent' times of rapid territorial expansion and the rise of central state power are described in no less positive terms than the 'standstill' in the 'meaningful' outcome of historical development – which aptly expresses how this multinational state is based on a system of laws and peace and acts as a bulwark at the same time.[71] The notion of stability that is typical of the Austrian narrative is expressed in terms of the superiority of the dynasty as, for example, in the image of Franz Joseph as the 'eternal emperor'.[72] Both 'fast' and 'slow' national historical paths can be evaluated either positively or negatively according to the circumstances – in similar fashion to patterns of behaviour determined by gender, where 'feminine' is associated with 'slow' (in the case of *Gesamtmonarchie* and Slovakia) and 'masculine' with 'fast' (Magyars, Czechs).

Whereas the dominant national liberal master narrative of the Magyars before 1918, like the Marxist-Leninist narrative later, was governed by a concept of progress directed towards the future within an accelerated timescale, the national conservative master narrative of the Horthy era focused on the Middle Ages in terms of decelerated narrated time with a shrinking future perspective.[73] The Czech historical narrative was consistently characterised by alternating 'faster' and 'slower' historical periods: the relatively slow and homogeneous early and high Middle Ages were followed by rapid acceleration in the fourteenth century, first as a result of the cultural development under Charles IV, and then in the run-up to the approaching changes brought about by the Hussite wars, characterised by a dynamic narrative of a rapid succession of events. This accelerated narrative projected a promising future which urged people to strive for national and denominational freedom (according to the Protestant liberal narrative) or for the social and national emancipation of the oppressed masses (according to the socialist narrative). The largely ambivalent period that followed was generally described as one of 'stabilisation' (of the class system, denominational relations or feudalism). Yet at the same time the narratives on this period were directed towards the decline of the Bohemian nobility in 1620, which constituted a further tragic turning point in Czech history and was followed by further deceleration. In Hungary likewise, after

---

[71]See O. Redlich, *Das Werden einer Großmacht: Österreich von 1700 bis 1740* (Brünn, 1938), p. vi.

[72]Such a narrative reached its peak in 1908 on the occasion of the 60th anniversary of the foundation of Francis Joseph's government, though its effects continued to be felt after 1918. On the popular images of the 'good old Emperor', see S. Beller, *Francis Joseph* (London and New York, 1996), pp. 1–3, which includes a large bibliography.

[73]This narrative focused on a 'calm' Middle Ages understood in static terms. See Klimó, 'Zeitgeschichte als Revolutionsgeschichte', pp. 283–306.

the heyday, there followed a phase of decline and thwarted development marked by catastrophe in the aftermath of the battle of Mohács in 1526.

For a long time, Slovak historiography perceived the Middle Ages to be a slow, 'empty time'. Only the history of the Great Moravian empire was described as a dynamic period. It was not until the onset of the national movement in the nineteenth century that history became more dynamic, when the advocates of a national 'awakening' arrived on the scene. Since historians considered that the intervening years were of no importance to national development, the historian Július Botto simply omitted the entire Middle Ages and early modern period from his work at the beginning of the twentieth century.[74]

Hungarian and Czech historiographies embarked on a radical revision of temporal structures when historians writing in the Stalinist vein attempted to create an overarching narrative in line with the concept of historical materialism: the prevailing model of historicity (in which the past operated as a model for the present and future) was to be replaced with radical futurity (in which the future would offer a model for the past and present), such that a utopian vision would dominate people's perception of history.[75] This led to a compression of the flow of time – and to 'leaps' or even 'explosions' in the Stalinist understanding of history. Descriptions of radical change occurring in revolutionary times regularly reduced the period of time in which events unfolded, that is, they confined the narrative flow to a very narrow range of action which underscored the impression that the development was unambiguous (or, in terms of Marxist historical determinism, 'correct') and irreversible.[76] From the 1960s onwards, the de-Stalinised or reformed Marxist-Leninist master narrative in Hungary and Czechoslovakia once again adhered more closely to a moderate model of progress. The widespread loss of utopia after the demise of reform communism during the 1970s finally put an end to any optimism based on the belief in progress. Subsequent socialist synthetic works such as the *History of Hungary* (1976–89) or the *Outline of Czechoslovak History* (1980–2) and the academic manual *Czechoslovak History* (published only in 1990), as well as the *History of Slovakia* (1st edn, 2 vols, 1961–8; 2nd edn, 6 vols, 1986–92), were written in a sober style and with a highly complex narrative.[77] In these works

---

[74]Botto, *Slováci*, p. X.

[75]M. Sabrow, 'Auf der Suche nach dem materialistischen Meisterton: Bauformen einer nationalen Gegenerzählung in der DDR', in K.H. Jarausch and M. Sabrow (eds), *Die historische Meistererzählung: Deutungslinien der deutschen Nationalgeschichte nach 1945* (Göttingen, 2002), pp. 33–77, 64.

[76]See K. Mehnert, *Weltrevolution durch Weltgeschichte: die Geschichtslehre des Stalinismus* (Stuttgart, 1953).

[77]Kolář, 'Die nationalgeschichtlichen master narratives'.

the pace of the revolutionary phases slowed down, for they were no longer recounted in terms of a rapid succession of actions taken by the 'people' and their 'enemies', but in terms of the 'more slowly' unfolding social structures and economic changes.

The temporal narrative principles of 'slowness' and 'speed' are closely connected to assessments of particular periods in terms of a 'rise' and 'decline'. They occur in conjunction with the elements of national historiography, as seen in the examples outlined above. In terms of gender, centralising master narratives of established nation-states tend to express 'male' discourses of rising and 'female' discourses of continuity, whereas narratives of 'oppressed' ethnic nations or national minorities give rise rather to 'female' narratives of victimhood and decadence as well as the idea of rebirth. The rise-and-decline pattern is determined by the way it relates to specific origins and goals. All narratives began with an origin myth, in which all dynamic forces that developed over the long term were already present. Each of the phases of rising and falling corresponded to the way in which the origin myths developed, that is, to the degree to which they approached the final goal of national development. The defeat of radical Hussites was therefore described as a particularly harsh setback, because they wanted to reinstate the 'original Slavic democracy' and, at the same time, were 'apostles' of the future national liberation and of a classless society.[78]

According to state-centred Austrian historical narratives, the term 'rise' referred to the development of Babenbergian Habsburg rule and its expansion in Central Europe as 'Austria's rise to great power status'. After 1945 historians saw the 'small state' conception in place as a form of 'stability' for the territory that had emerged at the end of the Middle Ages, which outlasted all the vicissitudes that characterised the relations in the south-eastern regions of Central Europe. They considered the Austro-Hungarian empire to have constituted a (tumultuous) interim period, such that 1918 and 1945 were significant dates after which Austria was able to regain the 'stability' of Habsburg rule characteristic of the late Middle Ages.[79]

The idea of decline in post-Habsburgian Central Europe arose in close connection with the upheavals experienced in 1918. Austrian historiography after 1918 interpreted the disintegration of the Austro-Hungarian empire in terms of historical decline which had been heralded by the gradual disintegration of the empire from the 1850s onwards. Austrian historians held national movements of other peoples to be responsible for the decline of the multinational state and singled out Czechs in particular, but also the 'false' policies of the Habsburgs in the nineteenth and twentieth centuries. Whereas the German

---

[78]This radical interpretation of Hussitism is most clearly expressed in Z. Nejedlý, *Komunisté*.
[79]See A. Lhotsky, *Ostarrîchi* (Vienna, 1947), pp. 27ff.

nationalist historians identified this 'wrong policy' with the separation of Austria from Germany and the Compromise of 1867, the liberal and Social Democrat minority, by contrast, considered the rejection of federalisation to be the main cause of the empire's collapse.[80]

A state-centred narrative of decline gained acceptance in Hungary after 1918, which was distinctly anti-liberal and partly also anti-Semitic and anti-socialist.[81] In the case of Czech historiography, earlier notions of decline from the early modern period continued to have an effect well after 1918: the 'age of darkness' (*temno*) that followed the battle of White Mountain in 1620 represented a *topos* which the entire range of narratives (even from the conservative Catholic perspective of Josef Pekař) referred to in terms of a catastrophe.[82] Even Marxist historiography adopted this image of decline in relation to the class struggle.[83] In this way, *temno* contained the germs of the future rebirth, and the Czech peasantry was presented as the sole guarantee of social and national continuity. The expression 'national rebirth' was later employed in the above-mentioned works of socialist historiography about Czechoslovak and Slovak history.

Spatial orientation

The spatialisation of state, nation and ethnos

The spatial orientation of national narratives refers, on the one hand, to inner space such as a state or a national territory and, on the other, to external space, to ethnic groups and peoples considered to share similar ethnic origins, to be like-minded or to have attained a similar level of political, religious or sociocultural development. Each of the four national master narratives contains a specific approach to state or national territory, based on given and

---

[80]A. Kernbauer, 'Konzeptionen der Österreich-Geschichtsschreibung 1848–1938', in H. Ebner, P.W. Roth, and I. Wiesflecker-Friedhuber (eds), *Forschungen zur Geschichte des Alpen-Adria-Raumes: Festgabe für Othmar Pickl zum 70. Geburtstag* (Graz, 1997), pp. 255–73.

[81]See above all the work by Gyula Szekfű, *Három nemzedék és ami utána következik*, 5th printing (Budapest, 1938); a modified version of this argument can be found in *A mai Széchenyi: Eredeti szövegek Széchenyi István munkáiból*, edited and with an introduction by G. Szekfű (Budapest, 1935).

[82]The White Mountain is dealt with by Palacký in the form of a tragedy. However, Palacký never produced a systematic presentation of this period. Conservative historiography in the nineteenth century describes the event as a 'tragic punishment' or a 'catharsis'. See, for example, W.W. Tomek, 'O nepokojích stavovských za Rudolfa II. a za Matyáše', *Časopis Musea Království českého*, 29 (1855). On the *topos* of the White Mountain, see J. Petráň and L. Petráňová, 'The White Mountain as Symbol in Modern Czech History', in M. Teich (ed.), *Bohemia in History* (Cambridge, 1998), pp. 143–63.

[83]Representative of this approach is A. Klíma, *Čechy v období temna* (Prague, 1958).

apparently naturally occurring ethnic and/or geographic criteria, and/or criteria that developed legally, culturally and historically over time. These contradictory aspects often occurred together and the differences between them appeared in more pronounced fashion when, for example, historical development was presented as something 'organic', or else 'naturalised' or 'eternalised' in relation to a national mission or to a national character.

Accounts of the history of the *Gesamtstaat*, which were mostly, but not exclusively, written by German-speaking historians, tended to explain and legitimise the development of the confederation of states primarily in terms of the dynastic policies of inheritance and marriage. The history of Habsburg rule formed the main thread of both types of representation: in those works in which the history of the three main sections of the monarchy prior to 1526 were presented separately and on an equal footing,[84] and clearly in those works which began with the history of the Babenbergian Habsburg countries in the Middle Ages and which included short retrospectives of the history of the new member countries within the chronology of expansions of Habsburg rule.[85] Josef Alexander Helfert argued against both representations in 1863, and in favour of a 'history of the Austrian *Gesamtstaat* and its entire people' as a 'total organism' (*Gesamtorganismus*) in which the historical events taking place within the territory of the subsequent Austrian empire should be presented 'in the form of a linear representation from the beginning until modernity, driven by an inner historical necessity', while revealing interconnections and the 'predestination' of the development of the Austrian empire.[86]

The contrast between an 'organic', ethnic principle of legitimacy and the artificial, 'mechanically' constructed dynastic multinational empire, which occurred only occasionally in polemic debates in Austria during the *Vormärz* period,[87] was evoked in the second half of the nineteenth century in order to

---

[84]J.F. Schneller, *Staatengeschichte des Kaiserthums Oesterreich von der Geburt Christi bis zum Sturze Napoleon Bonaparte's*, 4 vols (Graz, 1817–19); volumes 4 and 5 of this work conceived in 5 volumes appeared under the title *Oesterreichs Einfluß auf Deutschland und Europa seit der Reformation bis zu den Revolutionen unserer Tage*, 2 vols (Stuttgart, 1828).
[85]F. M. Reisser, *Geschichte der österreichischen Monarchie*, 4 vols (Wien, 1802); Jos[ef] C[alasanza] Arneth, *Geschichte des Kaiserthumes Oesterreich* (Wien, 1827). See W.W. Tomek, 'Ueber die Behandlung der österreichischen Gesamtgeschichte', *Zeitschrift für die österreichischen Gymnasien*, 4 (1853), 824–33, 833. Tomek criticizes this concept as a false attempt 'to create a special patriotism within all sections of the monarchy'.
[86]J. A. Frh. v. Helfert, *Oesterreichische Geschichte für das Volk* (Vienna, 1863), pp. 13f. See also Helfert, *Über Nationalgeschichte*, p. 59.
[87]See A. Lhotsky, *Österreichische Historiographie* (Vienna, 1962), p. 204. Lhotsky cites Joseph Frhr. v. Hormayr zu Hortenburg, who even then called Austria 'a state that had in reality merely been forged via marriage'.

reassess the history of the *Gesamtstaat*.[88] This was at a time when nationalism gave rise to the Romantic ideas of a natural development of peoples and states, and when the 'supranational' Habsburg monarchy was increasingly forced to legitimise its existence.

The argument that territory may be ascribed to a state as a result of historical development, the acquisition of rights and the emergence of social and cultural ties within its population is a significant element of the master narratives of three of the four nations. The exception to this pattern is Slovakia, where historical and legal arguments were combined with the notions of an 'organic, naturally arising' or ethnic and allegedly naturally evolving geographic development. In Slovak historiography, the administrative borders of Slovakia were defined only after the First World War, although the word 'Slovakia' was already in use during the eighteenth century when it referred to the area between the Tatra Mountains and the River Danube, that is, where the Slovaks live. Following international recognition of the Slovak borders in 1918, the Slovak master narrative increasingly relied on territorial principles, thus enabling the history of this country to reach back into pre-Slavic times.

Czech historiography in the tradition of Jaroslav Goll and Josef Pekař also drew on the legal and institutional development of state territory in order to bring into question an 'ahistorical', purely ethnocentric, pan-Slavic understanding of history. These historians defended the idea that the legal unity of the countries under the rule of the Bohemian Crown, which had evolved during the Middle Ages, should once again be recognised as a form of independent state law within the Habsburg monarchy; after 1918 the Czechoslovak state occupied what it saw as its 'historical borders' and considered the 'former Bohemian state' as the 'true historical centre of the present-day Czechoslovak Republic'.[89] Slovak historians refused to adopt this interpretation in which Slovak history could be understood as a mere appendage of Czech history, and defended instead an independent 'national history of the Slovak nation'.[90]

The ethnic standpoint, which found its way primarily into the Slovak and Hungarian master narratives, defined national territory on the basis of ancient

---

[88]On F. v. Krones and A. Huber see A. Kernbauer, 'Konzeptionen der Österreich-Geschichtsschreibung 1848–1938', pp. 269f. Cf. G. Heiss, 'Im "Reich der Unbegreiflichkeiten": Historiker als Konstrukteure Österreichs', *Österreichische Zeitschrift für Geschichtswissenschaft*, 7 (1996), 455–78, 455f.

[89]K. Krofta, *Die Deutschen in Böhmen* (Prague, 1924), p. 5, quoted in P. Haslinger, 'Nationalgeschichte und volksgeschichtliches Denken', pp. 272–99, p. 278. H. L. Agnew, 'New States, Old Identities? The Czech Republic, Slovakia, and Historical Understanding of Statehood', *Nationalities Papers*, 28 (2000), 619–50.

[90]D. Rapant, 'Československé dějiny: problémy a metody', *Od praveku k dnešku*, 2 (1930), 531–63.

laws acquired by early settlements and their long-established populations (the acquisition of land by adverse possession). Early settlers were often named in order to link legal claims to the national (state) territory with an ethnically defined community, such that, in historical representations since the Romantic age, the national territory often acquired the sacred qualities of a home, of a native soil of the people (*Volksboden*) or of a German cultivated land (*Kulturboden*), which is considered to be holy, or to have been sanctified by 'sacrifices'.[91]

At the same time, historians argued in geopolitical terms and wrote about spaces which were said to belong 'naturally' together and which had been 'naturally' united. In Austrian mainstream historiography the territory of the Austro-Hungarian empire, including the 'Bohemian fortress' and stretching as far as the Adriatic Sea, was, owing to a set of internal laws governing space from beyond the Carolingian Ottonian borderlands,[92] destined to form a single unit in order to assert its power and to protect the West.[93]

Each of the four master narratives refers very differently to the geographical foundations of the state. For Hungary and the German-Austrian countries, natural lines of communication were singled out as a way of fulfilling the national task of constructing bulwarks and bridges in Central Europe; the geographical opening of the four countries towards Vienna is seen as the basis for unity, while the mountain ranges are seen as natural borders and natural ramparts with which to defend the national territory against aggressive neighbours.

Orientation in relation to large areas

Spatial orientation in relation to something on the outside is a means of conveying values, a way of distinguishing the inside from 'barbarians' on the outside (Russians or the Balkans) or from 'aggressive' neighbours (the Germans). Similar values are conveyed by expansionist ventures pursued in the name of historical tasks understood to be inextricably linked to the fate of the nation but which go beyond state borders. The same applies to nations which lay claim to ethnic or even sociocultural bonds with other groups or nations that are considered to be 'related' to the insider group. Nations underpin such spatial orientations beyond state borders with reference to cultural and historical arguments or social

---

[91]Schneller, *Staatengeschichte des Kaiserthums Oesterreich*, vol. 1, *Ungarn's Schicksal und Thatkraft vor dem Verein mit Böhmen, Oesterreich und Steyermark. Zeitraum: von 1 bis 1526* (Graz, 1817), pp. xiiif.

[92]See A. Dopsch, 'Entstehung und Ausbildung des österreichischen Staates', in Dopsch, *Gesammelte Aufsätze*, vol. 2, *Beiträge zur Wirtschafts- und Sozialgeschichte* (Vienna, 1938; Aalen, 1968), pp. 205–23, p. 223.

[93]See O. Redlich, *Österreich-Ungarns Bestimmung*, Flugschriften für Österreich-Ungarns Erwachen, 12 (Warnsdorf i. B., 1916), p. 9.

traditions, such as a sense of cultural belonging to the 'Christian western world', to 'western civilisation' or to a specific civilisational tradition; or else they have recourse to cultural ethnic arguments with which to underpin their sense of belonging to 'Germanic Christian Central Europe' or to 'pan-Slavic cultural space', and even to ethnic arguments with which they claim to share an identity with Germanic, Slavic, Ural-Altaic or Turanian 'sister peoples'.

The 'ancient imperial alliance',[94] which formed a close historical bond between the Habsburg monarchy and the emperors of the Holy Roman Empire, was the mainstay of the outward orientation of German-language Austrian histories of the *Gesamtstaat*, which were legitimised on the basis of institutional and even German national historical narratives. At the height of their influence, German Austrian historians claimed that Austria had the task of establishing a major and peaceful power in Central Europe which could include all nations. Even after 1866, after the dissolution of the German Confederation, historians continued to recognise the need for the support of the Holy Roman Empire of the German nation (among the German people, or the Germanic Christian part of Central Europe) in history in order to guarantee the 'civilisational achievements' which the German Austrians were said to have achieved in East-Central Europe. Having acquired added legitimation as a result of the experience of 'comradeship in arms' during the First World War, this interpretation dominated the national master narrative characterising the 'pan-German conception of history' (*gesamtdeutsche Geschichtsauffassung*) during the interwar years, and which was further underpinned by revanchist and *völkisch* dimensions; the geopolitical ideas of the German people as the 'most supreme' people (*das führendste Volk*)[95] ultimately served the propaganda used to justify the aggressive expansionist policies of the National Socialist regime.

Until 1914 the Hungarian national master narrative drew inspiration primarily from western models, although there were notable differences between Anglophile (parliamentary), Francophile (democrats), Catholic (Hungary as a 'bulwark of Christianity') and Central European (Germano-centric) approaches; after the outbreak of the First World War, and in particular until 1945, there existed a growing bond with Germany and a notion of 'Central Europe' that was culturally superior to the West and strictly distinct from the 'Balkans' and from 'Slavic' Eastern Europe. From the 1960s onwards, and in contrast to the official bond between the People's Republic and the Soviet Union, dissidents in Hungary and in exile developed an idea of Central Europe which was understood to be distinct from the East, and which social historians such as Jenő Szűcs were able

---

[94] H. v. Srbik, *Geist und Geschichte vom deutschen Humanismus bis zur Gegenwart*, vol. 2 (Munich and Salzburg, 1951) p. 80.

[95] H. v. Srbik, *Mitteleuropa: das Problem und die Versuche seiner Lösung in der deutschen Geschichte* (Weimar, 1937), 38.

to adopt.[96] During the decade that preceded the upheavals of 1989, the Communist Party no longer took much interest in history prior to 1945, and therefore left the task of writing the history of this period increasingly to historians who drew on methods and ideas from the West. (A similar process took place in the Baltic countries and in Finland.)

Although pan-Slavic approaches dominated early Czech historiography, Palacký's work served to foster a notion of space in Central Europe in which the Kingdom of Bohemia was recognised as a stable part of the Austrian *Gesamtstaat*, which served to protect small nations located between Germany and Russia. After 1918 this protective function gave way to that of a 'bridge' or 'point of exchange' between West and East, which continued to prevail in socialist narratives. The *topos* of the 'interrelations' between Bohemia and German culture in relation to the cultural delimitation of space became central in the wake of Palacký's work. While conservative historiography (Pekař) defined this *topos* as a 'benefit',[97] radical national narratives refused to acknowledge any kind of positive German influence, and described the interactions rather as an unending battle, while emphasising endogenous or Slavic cultural roots. At the same time, they continued to believe in the integrity of the Bohemian countries while marginalising Germans, describing them as guests on 'ancient Czech land'.

In the first half of the nineteenth century, the Slovak master narrative adopted a 'pan-Slavic' perspective. Ján Kollár[98] 'discovered' traces of Slavic history not only in Prussia, Saxony, Brandenburg and Pomerania, but also in Italy. Even historians with a reputation of being more serious adhered to notions of all-Slavic culture. For example, Pavel Jozef Šafárik drew on a broad range of historical sources in order to prove that the ancient history of the Slovaks was identical to the history of the ancient Slavs, and that distinctions between Slavs were historically determined.[99] In the second half of the nineteenth century, and in particular during the era of dualism, the notion of Slavic reciprocity and Russian Messianism played a relatively prominent role in political concepts used by the Slovaks, although they were almost unheard of in historiography, which was devoted primarily to regional history. Professional historiography later accepted

---

[96]J. Szűcs, *Die drei historischen Regionen Europas* (Frankfurt/M, 1990).
[97]See Z. Kalista, *Josef Pekař* (Prague, 1994). See Z. Kalista, *Jesef Pekar* (Prague, 1994)
[98]J. Kollár, *Rozpravy o jmenách, počátkách i starožitnostech národu slavského a jeho kmeni* (Budín, 1830); Kollár, *Über die literarische Wechselseitigkeit zwischen den verschiedenen Stämmen und Mundarten der slawischen Nation* (Pest, 1837); Kollár, *Staroitalia slavjanská* (Vienna, 1853).
[99]P.J. Šafárik, *Slovanské starožitnosti* (Prague, 1837). Cf. Šafárik, *Geschichte der slawischen Sprache und Literatur nach allen Mundarten* (Pest, 1826); Šafárik, *Über die Abkunft der Slawen nach Lorenz Surowiecki* (Pest, 1828); *Munumenta Illyrica* (Prague, 1839); Šafárik and Konstantin A.C. von Höfler (eds), *Glagolitische Fragmente* (Prague, 1857).

Šafárik's theory about the Slavic origins of the Slovaks, but paid almost no attention to the Slavic conception of space. After 1918 Slovak historiography made no mention of Hungary as the scene of Slovak political history, and focused instead on the Czechoslovak 'conception of the state'.[100] However, the representation of the history of the Slovaks before 1918 in relation to its state affiliation to Hungary has increasingly made its mark since the 1960s.[101] This tendency to focus on the development of the state in the context of Slovak history (in relation to Hungary until 1918, and to Czechoslovakia after 1918) has become particularly apparent since 1989.[102]

From 1948 onwards, the communist parties attempted to impose a spatial interpretation on Slovak and Hungarian national narratives in accordance with 'proletarian internationalism': historiography was no longer meant to focus on national history, but on the '(real) socialist bloc'. According to plan, they began by researching bilateral relations with neighbouring countries. As a result of this propagandistic initiative, research focused increasingly on general history (not only in the 'socialist bloc') and thereby largely overcame the previous 'Slovako-centrism'. Thus the ground was prepared on which research in Slovakia after 1989 could turn to themes of European, and in particular Central European, history.

Conclusions

In contrast to the national master narratives of Spain, France or Italy, the interconnections between historical narratives of the former peoples of the Habsburg monarchy appear to have been far more intense. Instead of conflicts between the North and the South, divisions here ran between East and West. The divergent constitutional positions meant that, until 1918, the state played the main role in historical narratives in the cases of German Austrian and, to a lesser degree, Magyar historiography. In Czech and in particular Slovak historiography, emphasis was placed on an ethnic group, which was conceived to be just as permanent as the state in the Austrian and Magyar cases.

This perhaps explains the similarities with the narratives of countries whose constitutional systems are characterised by analogical asymmetrical relations, as in the cases of Norway, Denmark and Sweden, or Finland, Sweden and Russia,

[100]For narratives that do focus on Hungary, see F.V. Sasinek, *Dejiny kráľovstva uhorského*, vols 1–2 (Turčiansky Sv. Martin, 1869, 1871); J. Botto, *Krátka história Slovákov* (Turčiansky Sv. Martin, 1914).

[101]See the first academic synthesis, *Dejiny Slovenska*, I, II (Bratislava, 1961, 1968), and the second synthesis from the 1980s, *Dejiny Slovenska*, I, II, III, IV (Bratislava, 1986, 1987, 1992, 1986).

[102]Kováč, *Dějiny Slovenska*; Mannová, *Concise History*.

and also the various peoples living on the British Isles.[103] In these cases, the national master narratives were, for a long time, also marked by the contradictions between imperial elitist state-centred perspectives on the one hand, and ethnic plebeian democratic perspectives on the other. German Austrians and Magyars living wholly in the dualistic state from 1867 onwards adopted the perspective of a ruling nation-state, whereas the others saw themselves as 'oppressed' peoples; the former legitimised their supremacy by interpreting and constructing the past as they saw fit and by ascribing to themselves corresponding roles and tasks in the course of history, while the latter drew on history in order to lay claim to national emancipation and political participation within the Habsburg monarchy.

From the early nineteenth century onwards, earlier state, legal, social and political conflicts that went back to the Middle Ages and the early modern period were recounted in the new language of national history, which was clearly influenced by German and French historical narratives. By adhering to historicism of the kind advocated by Ranke, professional historians reinforced the focus on the state, such that even Czech historians writing from the end of the nineteenth century increasingly made reference to the notion of Bohemian statehood, while nonetheless maintaining the ethnic perspective. Only Slovak historians who remained independent from professional circles maintained the 'pre-professional' reference to ethnicity until 1918.

The main theme, as defined in the origin myth, focused on the goal to be fulfilled by the nation: either national emancipation (with respect to ethnicity) or the fulfilment of an historical task (with respect to statehood). Although this myth stood above the national historical narrative and also outside of historical time, it nevertheless defined the development of time by describing the historical process in terms of acceleration or slowing down on the path towards the goal, that is, towards the 'end of history'. The nature of the goal determined the degree to which various eras were interpreted as dynamic or calm.

The emphasis placed on alternatives to the hegemonic national historical narratives differed in each of the four national historiographies. The Slovak narrative appears to have been the most uniform, for it contained no relevant alternatives to the hegemonic national narrative. Magyar and Czech historiography had more evidence of contradictions within the political and social or religious life. For a long time, *Gesamtstaat* and *völkisch* German interpretations interacted and coexisted side by side in Austrian historiography. Alternatives to the main narratives of national historiographies were frequently determined

---

[103]On the problem of the development of national identities within monarchic unions in three different cases, see L. Eriksonas, *National Heroes and National Identities: Scotland, Norway, and Lithuania* (Brussels, 2004).

by religion, class and ethnicity. The significance and effect of ethnic factors then increased during the twentieth century in conjunction with *völkisch* ideology, and contributed to a further increase in the number of variations within the national master narrative during the interwar years. A Calvinist Magyar national narrative evolved in Hungary alongside and in opposition to the official Catholic nation-state narrative supported by the Horthy regime; in Austria, a Catholic universalist narrative evolved in opposition to the dominant German national 'pan-German conception of history'. Radical *völkisch* approaches common in German historiography during the interwar years nonetheless remained marginal in Hungarian and Austrian historiography. References to the people or *Volk* occurring in Czech, Slovak and partly also in Hungarian historical narratives drew explicitly on elements of social history insofar as they were geared to 'simple folk' or 'masses'. These were therefore adopted directly into socialist narratives after 1945.

The respective representations of one's own identity and that of strangers or foreigners, on which master narratives were based, also characterised the way in which nations were associated with gender and their Others: 'feminine' could be understood as an expression of imperial might, calmness and the ability to mediate, as in the case of the Austrian imperial dynasty; or else it could express passivity and a lack of qualities required for statehood, which Magyar historians occasionally ascribed to the Slovak people. Class differences or social conflicts between the nobility, peasants and workers also influenced the way in which themes were defined in Czech historiography, albeit less so in Austrian, and in Magyar and Slovak historiography.

In Austria, during the first decades after 1945, history was increasingly written from the perspective of the republic, and thereby served to underscore the independence of the state. By contrast, the regime change required the three other countries to offer a new interpretation of history. The legacy of the proletariat, revolution and the resistance of the 'masses' were to have a central place in the national master narrative, while the historiography adopted an 'international' perspective at the same time. The failure of this attempt to assert a new direction was evident from the fact that models that had evolved during the nineteenth century continued to operate after 1945, and have been preserved beyond the communist era in all three countries. The radical political changes led to re-evaluations of historical *topoi* which remained consistent over time: the German imperialist 'historical task' of Austria in southeastern Central Europe evolved into a task of mediation in a European context after 1945; during the same period, the Habsburg monarchy became a model for a new supranational Europe. In the communist period, historians ascribed an active rather than a passive role to the peasant nation of Slovaks, and represented the national and liberal emancipatory movements of the Czechs and Magyars as precursors of the radical changes brought about by socialism. These tendencies gradually weakened from the 1970s onwards, giving way to more pluralistic historical narratives: the increasing use of cultural, social and economic history caused the previously homogeneous yarn of 'national history' to split into several partial threads.

Translated by Peter Carrier

15

The Russian Empire and its Western Borderlands: National Historiographies and Their 'Others' in Russia, the Baltics and the Ukraine

Anna Veronika Wendland

The imperial centre and the 'peasant nations' of Russia's western borderlands

At first sight it may seem inappropriate to compare the historiographical narratives of non-dominant ethnic groups such as the Ukrainians, Lithuanians, Latvians and Estonians with Russian historiography, which represented the nominally dominant group within the Russian empire. However, there are good reasons for asymmetric comparison. Historians in all these cases were confronted with similar problems when attempting to define what national history was. In the last decade of the nineteenth century the large majority of the five ethnic groups to be discussed in this chapter were peasants. The rural population still lived in a world of its own, characterised by limited mobility, cyclic rhythms of work and leisure, and the predominance of oral culture.[1] What is more, there was a considerable cultural difference between the rural masses and the landowning elites and urban populations. The latter spoke languages other than the peasants' – Polish, Russian or German – though they used the vernacular for communication with the ordinary people. Multilingualism and multiple identities were the rule rather than the exception. Members of the gentry referred to themselves as *gente ruthenus (lituanus) natione polonus* ('a member of the Ruthenian/Lithuanian people and of the Polish nation'). The notion of the 'Polish nation' referred only to members of the

---

[1]According to the Russian imperial census of 1897, literacy rates differed considerably among Russians (29.3 per cent), Ukrainians (18.9 per cent), Lithuanians (48.4 per cent), Latvians (85 per cent) and Estonians (94.1 per cent), the latter profiting from a relatively well-developed village school system which had been established since the mid-nineteenth century: see A. Kappeler, *Russland als Vielvölkerreich: Entstehung–Geschichte–Zerfall* (München, 1992), p. 331 (table 9). However, oral culture played a major role in the cultural identity of literate peasants as well.

nobility, whereas the Polish-speaking peasant or burgher (the *lud* – people – in contrast to the *naród* – nation) was excluded from this definition of *natio*. Accordingly, a Polish noble could proudly refer to his East Slavic or Lithuanian ancestry, but define himself as a Pole. Similarly, the Ukrainian or German Baltic gentry combined local patriotism with tsarist loyalism and a commitment to Russian high culture.

In the nineteenth and even the twentieth centuries, every project purporting to write or rewrite the history of the 'awakening' nations of Ukraine and the Baltic countries or an innovative history of Russia on the basis of their quantitatively dominant social strata had therefore to confront a central problem: the narratives which had been perceived as 'national history' up to that point dealt with individuals, structures and events that had almost nothing in common with the historical and social experience of the masses, who were now declared to be the central factor in their own, new historiography. In the case of Ukrainians and Lithuanians, quasi-state traditions within the framework of the historical Polish-Lithuanian Commonwealth had been declining over a long period – from the late sixteenth century until the partitions of Poland. By 1800 early modern proto-national institutions and autonomous territories, such as the Grand Duchy of Lithuania and the Ukrainian Cossack hetmanate, had been abolished. Local gentry and urban elites had amalgamated with Polish and/or Russian imperial elites, albeit preserving a strong sense of local and regional patriotism. The Latvian and Estonian peasants and city dwellers on the territories of the former Teutonic Order (the historical regions of Estonia, Livonia and Curland) were subject to the domination of a German gentry and urban patricians. Even in the case of Russians, the languages spoken by the peasantry and the elite were very different. Moreover, a large section of the Russian nobility was of non-Russian descent. To complete this complex picture of socio-cultural-lingual interaction and coexistence in Russia's western borderlands, the Jews must be mentioned as an additional ethno-religious entity. They played a decisive role as an intermediate social stratum in rural areas and were an important factor in the big cities of the region.

As far as language and terminology are concerned, research on national narratives in this region has to deal with another specific problem. Historiographical studies of the nations on the western periphery of the Russian empire were initially published in the traditional languages of high culture which dominated in the region – Polish (for Lithuania and Ukraine), German (for the Baltics), Russian (for Ukraine) – and written for an educated public. In parallel, patriotic activists undertook the first attempts to write historiography in the vernacular, often borrowing abstract terms from a high-culture language or coining new ones. Though they had a clear idea of who belonged to the respective nation and who did not, there was almost no discussion about terminology or scholarly definitions of the 'national'. The term 'people'[2] was often used as equivalent to 'nation' and could mean an ethno-cultural entity, a collective of non-gentry social classes (the 'common people') or a political entity of citizens who had chosen to belong to the nation. Yet, there was one definition of 'people' which eventually clearly dominated within the historical discourses of Russia's western borderlands in the nineteenth and twentieth centuries. It was, by and large, identical to Grimm's and Meinecke's linguistic-cultural concepts of *Volk* and *Kulturnation*, respectively, and meant a community made up of individuals sharing a language, historical experience and culture (as opposed to *Staatsnation*, a political collective of citizens).[3] The cultural definition was the most adequate one in the case of non-dominant nations without historical statehood (the Latvians and Estonians), whereas Lithuanian and Ukrainian scholars would in parallel refer to the historical state traditions of a more (the medieval Grand Duchy of Lithuania, Kievan Rus) or less (the Ukrainian Hetmanate) distant past. However, in these cases, voluntarist *Staatsnation* concepts – which envisaged the nation as the collective of all those claiming to belong to it ('un plébiscite de tous les jours') – emerged only in the twentieth century. Thus as a rule, throughout the nineteenth century the abovementioned linguistic-cultural concept of the nation remained dominant.

The nineteenth century: traditional hegemonic historiographies vs. populist challenges

Dominant national historiographies in the Russian empire

After 1800 the traditionally dominant elite and statist historiographies largely ignored the indigenous peoples of the former Polish and now Russian borderlands, or mentioned them as a mere footnote to great events. Generally, historians dealing with recently partitioned Poland, the expanding Russian empire or the Baltics were still committed to the ideas and ideals of Enlightenment historiography.[4] Historians of Lithuania, for example, discussed questions of

---

[2] The terms referring to the 'people' were the following: *narod* (in Russian and Ukrainian), *tauta* (in Lithuanian and Latvian), *rahva* (in Estonian).

[3] F. Meinecke, *Weltbürgertum und Nationalstaat*, 6th edn (München, Berlin, 1922 [1907]), pp. 1–22, referring to Renan's 'L'Existence d'une nation est un plébiscite de tous les jours', in E. Renan, *Qu'est-ce qu'une nation?* (Paris, 1882), p. 27; on Jakob Grimm's position, see Leerssen, this volume (chapter 4).

[4] S. Berger, 'Geschichten von der Nation', in C. Conrad and S. Conrad (eds), *Die Nation schreiben: Geschichtswissenschaft im internationalen Vergleich* (Göttingen, 2002), pp. 49–77, p. 51. For a brief introduction to the meanings of English terms such as nation, nationalism, nationality, people, citizenship and so on when referring to Eastern Europe, see N. Davies, *God's Playground: A History of Poland*, vol. 2, *1795 to the Present* (New York, 1981), pp. 3–14.

scholarly objectivity, perspective or philological methodology in order to criticise pre-Enlightenment historical myths.[5] Astonishing theoretical erudition
could go in tandem with an almost complete lack of interest in the large
majority of the inhabitants of the respective region. The hegemonic narratives
were therefore 'master'-narratives in the literal sense of the term:[6] narratives
governed by the perspective of the rulers within the social hierarchy of
Eastern Europe, that is, the landed gentry and the imperial bureaucracy.

In German Baltic and Prussian surveys of Baltic history, the 'non-historic'
(*geschichtslose Völker*) Estonians and Latvians existed merely as an amorphous
ethnographic item or an object of colonisation. The Germans, however, were
depicted as an active element that had brought Christianity, progress, culture
and education to the savages. On the other hand, in spite of the dominating
Kulturträger paradigm, Baltic agrarian, urban and social history – both medieval
and modern – owes much to German Baltic authors who published extensively
on these matters, especially in the context of agrarian reform discourses in the
eighteenth and nineteenth centuries. However, even the reformist German perspective was predominantly a 'top-down' one, whereas the 'bottom-up' perspective of the Baltic peasantry was introduced into Baltic history writing only with
the emergence of Estonian and Latvian counter-narratives towards the end of the
nineteenth century.

Though the partitions had nominally transformed the Poles into a non-
dominant nation, Polish historiography on Lithuania and Ukraine continued
to be a hegemonic narrative. Polish authors saw the respective territories as
integral parts of the historical Commonwealth. Ethnic Lithuanians were given
less consideration because, as peasants, they did not belong to the Lithuanian
natio of mostly Polonised gentry within the Grand Duchy. From this perspective, Lithuania was an historical and judicial entity, encompassing not only
ethnic Lithuanian but also large East Slavic territories and their Orthodox
elites. The Polish position *vis-à-vis* the Ukrainians was somewhat more
complex: as Polish historiography from the end of the eighteenth century was
primarily concerned with the partition trauma, the Ukrainian crisis of the seventeenth century, which had been a major factor in the decline of the Commonwealth, played a prominent role in it. Thus, Ukrainians were described not as a
mere object of Polish eastward expansion and domination, but also as independent and active factors in Polish history. However, they were not perceived as an ethnically or linguistically defined entity, but rather described in
the terms of Polish estate society: peasant unrest was perceived as a destabilis-

---

[5]V. Krapauskas, *Nationalism and Historiography: The Case of Nineteenth-Century Lithuanian
Historicism* (New York, 2000), pp. 30–1.
[6]See Thijs, this volume (chapter 3).

ing factor within the old regime; the Ukrainian Orthodox clergy, the Cossacks or the petty Orthodox gentry were assessed as distinct participants in the conflict who were pursuing different estate interests. Disputes between different schools raged around the question of whether Polish policy concerning the Orthodox subjects of the kingdom (for example, the Union of Brest, Jesuit expansion to the East, Orthodox clergy and gentry loss of privilege) were mistaken or justified.[7]

In Russian historiography on Ukraine, an imperial narrative with an intrinsic national story-line already existed in the guise of enlightened and modern critical historiography. Thus, Russian statist and 'law school' historiography was centred on the *translatio* theory, defining Russia and its predecessor, the Moscow state, as the legitimate heir of the medieval Kievan Great Principality. Thus, integrating the history of Ukrainians and Belorussians into Russian state history was a matter of course. 'Russian'/'Rus' history was organised in a three-phase narrative: 1) the 'Russian' entity (Rus principalities); 2) decline (internal 'Russian' strife, Mongol invasion, Mongol/Lithuanian/Polish supremacy in Rus territories); and 3) the 'regathering' of 'Russian' territories as 'patrimonies' (*votchiny*) of Muscovite great princes and tsars. In the aftermath of the Polish November Rising (1830/1), the 'Western Russian' provinces became a popular object of research for Russian historiographers, ethnographers and sociologists. They were endorsed by state officials who realised that these regions were not simply identical to central Russia and needed closer scholarly investigation in order to control and contain political and social unrest there.[8] This officially subsidised scholarly interest arose at the same time as Romantic Slavophile interpreters of 'Western Russian' history declared Ukraine to be the 'real Russia', unspoilt by European high culture, scepticism and anti-religious propaganda. Later, Ukrainian history was instrumentalised to complete the Slavophile interpretation of Russian history as a history of struggle against foreign invaders from Europe and Asia. The historical social conflict between Ukrainian peasants and Polish magnates was idealised as a liberation struggle of Orthodox 'Russians'

---

[7]T. U. Raun, 'The Image of the Baltic German Elites in Twentieth-century Estonian Historiography: The 1930s vs. the 1970s', *Journal of Baltic Studies*, 30, 4 (1999), 338–51, 338; G. von Rauch (ed.), *Geschichte der deutschbaltischen Geschichtsschreibung* (Köln, 1986); H. von zur Mühlen, 'Die deutschbaltische Geschichtsschreibung 1918–1939/45 in Estland', in Rauch, *Deutschbaltische Geschichtsschreibung*, pp. 339–69; V. Krapauskas, *Nationalism and Historiography*, pp. 63, 69, 81; S. Velychenko, *National History as Cultural Process: A Survey of the Interpretations of Ukraine's Past in Polish, Russian, and Ukrainian Historical Writing from the Earliest Times to 1914* (Edmonton, 1992), pp. 19–39. For a closer survey on Polish positions concerning Poland's historical eastern borderlands, see Janowski, this volume (chapter 16).

[8]O. Subtelnyi, *Ukraiina: istoriia* [Ukraine: A History] (Kyiv, 1991), p. 251; A. Kappeler, *Kleine Geschichte der Ukraine* (München, 1994), p. 116.

against Western and Roman Catholic domination.[9] Even the positivist 'Moscow school' of structuralist social and economic history (Vasilii Kliuchevskii, Pavel Miljukov), which rejected state-centred political history, Slavophile inter-pretations and philological source-oriented approaches altogether, clung to the traditional centralist perspective on the western borderlands inhabited by Ukrainians and Belorussians. The Moscow school's preferred master narrative – Russian history as a history of expanding peasant colonisation beginning in the forest steppes on the Dnieper and subsequently moving to the Upper Volga region and eventually towards Siberia and Middle Asia – integrated the non-Russian Eastern Slavs into a continuum of 'Russian' history as statists and Slavo-philes had done before.[10]

The challenge from within

The challenge to traditional hegemonic narratives arose in the first decades of the nineteenth century. The Napoleonic campaign had brought the exper-ience of military violence, physical devastation and political disorientation to Russia's western borderlands. Among Russians, the war triggered proto-nationalist enthusiasm and generated consideration of Russia's special role in European history. Educated Poles, on the other hand, experienced the disaster of their attempts to restore independence in coalition with France. All over Eastern Europe, intellectuals with democratic and liberal aspirations who shared post-revolutionary disillusion embarked on a romantic quest for orien-tation, and encountered the humble 'people' as a potential source of political and cultural rebirth. Activists who were enthusiasts for the oral cultures in the countryside soon began to reject the traditional frameworks of statist, parti-cular territorial and estate history. Thus, national histories were redefined as histories of cultural-linguistic entities which, in the case of the Russian periphery, were identified in particular with one social class, the peasantry.

However, the first attempts to write populist histories of Ukraine and the Baltics were still far from being rectilinear and closed syntheses of the national history. They were a challenge from within: amateur and early professional

---

[9]Velychenko, *National History*, pp. 80–104; Kappeler, *Russland als Vielvölkerreich*, pp. 58–65; V. Tatishchev, *Istoriia rossiiskaia* [Russian [Imperial] History], vols 1–7 (1768; reprinted Moskva, 1962–3); T. M. Bohn, *Russische Geschichtswissenschaft von 1880–1905: Pavel N. Miljukov und die Moskauer Schule* (Köln, Weimar, Wien, 1998), pp. 257–60; D. Saunders, *The Ukrainian Impact on Russian Culture, 1750–1850* (Edmonton, 1985); P. Bushkovytch, 'The Ukraine in Russian Culture, 1790–1860: The Evidence of the Journals', *Jahrbücher für Geschichte Osteuropas*, 39 (1991), 339–63.
[10]V. O. Kliuchevskii, 'Kurs russkoi istorii' [A Course of Russian History], *Sochineniia v deviati tomach*, t. 1–5 (Moskva, 1987–9); Bohn, *Russische Geschichtswissenschaft*, pp. 93f., 177–85, 192, 200, 252–5.

historians still worked within the frameworks of their respective dominating high cultures (which meant that many of them spent most of their active lives in state service, often in St Petersburg), concentrating on selected epochs or on regional and particular history, and in parallel researching into problems of the hegemonic histories. All remained loyal subjects of the tsar and none pursued the writing of national histories with the explicit purpose of laying the theoretical foundations of a liberation movement or a future national state. There were early exceptions which had great impact on populist historiography, such as the attempts of Simonas Daukantas (1793–1864) and Teodor Narbutt (1784–1864) to write histories of Lithuania *ab ovo* (Daukantas in the vernacular, Narbutt in Polish). They combined a traditional approach (the Grand Duchy as reference frame) with the revolutionary element of ethnic Lithuanian history (the peasantry and the vernacular as the true heirs of Lithuanian-ness after the loss of statehood). However, in general, it was not until the end of the nineteenth century (as we will see below) – and often much later – that populists began to produce coherent surveys and works which encompassed all the historic regions of the respective territories.

This meant not only 'reconstructing' allegedly existing but forgotten histories, but, in the literal sense of the word, 'constructing' new national histories from former regional ones. In the case of Lithuania, the task was to unite the histories of 'Upper' and 'Lower' Lithuania (Samogitia). Estonian history was not identical to the past of the historical province of Estonia, but encompassed Livonia (partly inhabited by Latvians) as well – two regions which were rather different in their social, constitutional and economical structures. The Protestant Latvians had to integrate their Roman Catholic compatriots in Latgale into their project of *tauta* historiography. This proved to be a rather difficult venture because, in Latgale, local and confessional identities prevailed until the twentieth century (as they did in many other regions of Russia's western borderlands). Significant events in the history of the Baltic peasant nations – for example, the Livonian conversion movement to Orthodoxy as a form of peasant social protest in the 1840s – involved not just one ethnic group, rendering it complicated to treat such episodes as exclusively national history.[11] The Ukrainians faced a similar problem since 'Ukrainian' history in a national sense meant referring not only to Orthodox central Ukraine, but also to the Uniate western territories

---

[11]H. Kruus, *Grundriss der Geschichte des estnischen Volkes* (Tartu, 1932), pp. 79–87. Kruus's innovative interpretation of the conversion movement as the cultural expression of social unrest among Estonians (first presented in his 1930 doctoral dissertation) was of central significance for the formulation of a national view on nineteenth-century agrarian history, because it opposed German Baltic authors who argued that is was artificially created by Russian officials. The conversion movement was not exclusively Estonian, but encompassed Latvians as well. Cf. Raun, 'Image of the Baltic German Elites', pp. 342, 346.

which had been under Polish domination from the fourteenth century, belonged to another confession and never became parts of the Hetmanate.[12]

In Lithuania the relatively early attempts to establish a tradition of national history writing were brought to a standstill when the University of Wilno (Vilnius) was dissolved after the November Rising of 1830/1. Latvian and Estonian historiography still had not reached the stage of professionalisation and institutionalisation which was an important precondition for the production of comprehensive national histories. For this reason, until 1918, most works in Baltic national historiographies where popular-scientific and written by amateurs.[13] Within this context, Ukraine is an interesting exception. Regarding the state of primary research and institutionalisation of historiography, educated Ukrainians profited from the abovementioned governmental support which aimed at strengthening (or rediscovering) the 'Russian' identity of the East Slavs in the former Polish lands. Therefore, the founder of the critical scientific tradition in Ukrainian history, Mykola Kostomarov (1817–85), could refer to relatively well-researched source materials. Ukrainian history – labelled 'Southern Russian' history – was introduced in the curricula of higher learning, and the universities of Charkiv and Kiev, which had been established in order to replace the dissolved Polish colleges in Wilno and Kamianets-Podilsk, became centres of research where 'schools' of national Ukrainian historiography subsequently emerged.[14]

---

[12]Krapauskas, *Nationalism and Historiography*, pp. 63–83; on Polish-Lithuanian parallel research and publications (Joachim Lelewel, Ignacy Daniłowicz, Józef Jaroszewicz, Simonas Stanevičius, Motiejus Valančius) see Krapauskas, *Nationalism and Historiography*, pp. 25–43, 87–105. For Western European examples of parallelism of narratives cf. Berger, 'Geschichten von der Nation', p. 50; Krapauskas, *Nationalism and Historiography*, pp. 107–49; A. V. Wendland, 'Region ohne Nationalität, Kapitale ohne Volk: Das Wilna-Gebiet als Gegenstand polnischer und litauischer nationaler Integrationsprojekte (1900–1940)', *Comparativ*, 2 (2005), 77–100; A. Plakans, 'Looking Backward: The Eighteenth and Nineteenth Centuries in Inter-war Latvian Historiography', *Journal of Baltic Studies*, 30/4 (1999), 293–306, 300.

[13]Plakans, 'Looking Backward', pp. 293–4; Raun, 'Image of the Baltic German Elites', p. 338.

[14]Symptomatic for this constellation is that Kostomarov's historical biographies were published in Russia since 1873 as 'Russian History in Biographies of Her Most Important Representatives'; in Galicia, the same series came out in Ukrainian as 'The History of Ukraine in Biographies of Her Most Important Representatives'. N. I. Kostomarov, *Istoricheskie proizvedeniia: avtobiografiia* [Historical Works: Autobiography] (Kiev, 1989), p. 696; N. I. Kostomarov, *Russkaia istoriia v zhizneopisaniiakh ee glavnejshikh dejatelej* [Russian History in Biographies of Her Most Important Representatives](Sankt-Peterburg, 1873–1913); M. I. Kostomarov, *Istorija Ukraiiny v zhyttepysakh vyznachnykh iiii diiachiv* [The History of Ukraine in Biographies of Her Most Important Representatives] (L'viv, 1876; 2nd edn, 1913); Velychenko, *National History*, pp. 167–71, 189; A. Kappeler, 'Nationale Kommunikation unter erschwerten Bedingungen: Die Zeitschrift Kievskaja Starina (1882–1891/1906) als Organ der ukrainischen Bewegung im Zarenreich', *Der schwierige Weg zur Nation: Beiträge zur neueren Geschichte der Ukraine* (Wien, Köln, Weimar, 2003), pp. 136–50.

All the historiographies on Russia's western periphery in the first half of the nineteenth century had characteristics in common, in particular the pedagogical tone and rejection of the hegemonic (seen as elitist) gaze. History writing was to be a project addressed to both the masses and alienated elites in order to reveal to them the real 'spirit' of the people and its central role in history. All historians emphasised the historical role of the indigenous peasants as bearers of an eternal 'national character' and as guarantors of a primordial democracy which had allegedly persisted from prehistoric times until the Middle Ages, when foreign invaders established their alien and anti-democratic rule. In all five historiographies, including Slavophile Russian, medieval popular conventions (for example, the East Slavic *viche*) were hailed as the prototypes of modern democratic institutions. Ukrainians assumed that there was a line of continuity to the early modern Cossack assemblies (*kolo*); the Baltic nations emphasised the egalitarian constitution of their peasant communities, which was to be brutally trampled underfoot by German invaders.[15]

As far as the story-lines of the respective narratives are concerned, by and large the Ukrainian and Baltic gaze on national history were emplotted in a three-phase narrative similar to the abovementioned paradigm of Russian statist historiography. Yet they did not deal with state structures and elite politics as the Russians did, but with completely new types of agents in history. The structure may be described as follows: 1) a democratic and self-determined prehistory (Latvians, Estonians)/tribal prehistory and indigenous medieval principality (Lithuanians, Ukrainians) – all had in common an emphasis on an alleged social harmony; 2) decay/internal strife/loss of elites/foreign invasion and domination; and 3) early resistance movements, resulting in attempts at nation-building (Ukrainian peasant uprisings/ Cossacks) and modern national rebirth (the Baltics, Ukraine). Accordingly, medieval princes, Cossack leaders, rural social outlaws (such as the eighteenth-century Ukrainian *hajdamaks*) or other outstanding individuals (for example, the Livonian chronicler of Estonian descent Balthasar Rüssow), and, as far as phase 3 is concerned, heroic individuals of the national renaissance such as great poets and patriotic activists (Taras Ševčenko, Jonas Basanavičius) starred as heroes of national histories.[16] As 'villains' of the three epochs indigenous elites figured, seen as traitors to the national cause (because willingly acculturating to an alien dominant culture or concluding contracts with the enemy), or representatives of alien invasion/domination (for example,

---

[15]A. Kappeler, 'Die ukrainische und litauische Nationalbewegung im Vergleich', *Der schwierige Weg zur Nation*, pp. 88–98.

[16]L. Eriksonas, *National Heroes and National Identities: Scotland, Norway, and Lithuania* (Bruxelles and New York, 2004), pp. 4–24; M. Hellmann, *Grundzüge der Geschichte Litauens*, 4th edn (Darmstadt, 1990), pp. 35–52; Krapauskas, *Nationalism and Historiography*, pp. 63, 69, 81.

in the Ukrainian case, the Muscovite prince Andrej Bogoliubskij, the Mongol Baty-Khan, Polish magnates, Peter the Great and Catherine the Great, several pro-Polish or pro-Russian hetmans; in the Lithuanian case, allegedly pro-Polish Jogaila/Jagieło vs. pro-Lithuanian Vytautas). The friend/foe paradigm embodied in such hero vs. anti-hero stories arose from the historicist emphasis on the role of the individual in history and the widespread enthusiasm for biographies of 'great men'. It was rejected when professionalisation and the emergence of a positivist social historiography led to a more differentiated assessment of the social and economic motives of both heroes and villains.

The ambivalences of rediscovered tradition

In content, the populists carried out a negative transfer from neighbouring historiographies, referring to established hegemonic narratives *ex negativo*. As far as formal aspects are concerned, they all used the very narrative structures of dominant historiographies as a blueprint for the respective national counter-projects. They all attempted to establish a differing perspective on the very same historical individuals, structures and events. It was for this reason that new national histories in Russia's western borderlands had in common a specific ambivalence. On the one hand, they tried to represent the non-dominant populations as subjects, not as objects, of history – hence the emphasis on *making* history and on *activism*: democratism, underclass movements, dissent and resistance were the centre of attention. Yet, on the other, after overcoming a phase of enthusiasm with the collective of the 'people', almost all populist historians tried to find an answer to hegemonic elite histories by proving their ancient origins and by discovering/reinventing indigenous traditions, elites and heroic individuals in their own histories. At this stage, the new narratives emerged as full-fledged 'counter-narratives' in respect of previously dominant 'master narratives', thus developing their own potential to become 'master narratives'. It was no coincidence that these complete (since they included elites) narratives developed in parallel to the emergence of complementary social structures through social mobilisation within the respective national communities during the second half of the nineteenth century.[17]

Populist historiographical projects

In any case, the new narratives challenged the foundation myths and the self-perception of the dominant groups. Yet the Ukrainian narrative was the only one of the four non-dominant narratives which came into direct conflict with the Russian imperial narrative, whereas the others to a great extent referred to

---

[17]See Thijs's considerations on the 'metaphor of the master' in this volume (chapter 3). On 'complementary' national society, see K. W. Deutsch, *Nationalism and Social Communication: An Inquiry into the Foundations of Nationality*, 2nd edn (Cambridge, MA, 1966).

the hegemonic Polish and German Baltic narratives. Thus, Ukrainian researchers – like their Polish colleagues – had to manoeuvre carefully, or risked falling foul of censorship and sometimes even police action. Ukrainians rejected the Russian perspective on medieval Kiev as 'ancient Russia' and established their own *translatio* theory, drawing the line of continuity from Kiev to the western Ukrainian principality of Galicia-Volynia and the early modern Hetmanate with reference to linguistic and demographic arguments. In an embryonic stage, this challenge to Moscow was already formulated in the early nineteenth century, when Ukrainian elites hoped to be granted more autonomy in the course of reform politics under Tsar Alexander I (the anonymous 'Istorija Rusov', *c.*1805, published 1846).[18] The full-fledged and professionalised version of an independent Ukrainian narrative centred on the Cossacks and the social revolutionary movements as the bearers and guarantors of the 'native' Ukrainian democratic spirit was accomplished at the end of the nineteenth century and found expression in the 'Kiev school' founded by Volodymyr Antonovych (1834–1908), socialist-federalist interpretations in the works of Mykhailo Drahomanov (1841–95),[19] and eventually in the most outstanding work of populist Ukrainian historiography, the massive *Istorija Ukraïny-Rusy* of Mykhailo Hrushevskyi (1866–1934). This book established national history as a political and social history of Ukrainians, relying on established narrative source materials as well as on statistical data, and thus representing a synthesis of populist historicism and the innovative structural history of the 'Moscow school'. Like Henri Pirenne in the case of Belgium,[20] Hrushevskyi identified national history with the history of the 'people' (that is, the vast majority of the population) at a crossroads of cultures, the Latin West and the *Slavia orthodoxa*, the latter concept later being developed by the Ukrainian state school. Like Pirenne, Hrushevskyi became not only the founder of a canonical view of national history, but also a national symbol himself.

Hrushevskyi's work rejected the Russian narrative of Ukraine as a Russian province in its very title, conceiving the term 'Ukraiina-Rus' and thus claiming an historical continuity focused on the Ukrainian territories, leaving apart the history of Russia as one beginning only with the emergence of the Great Russian principalities on the northeastern flank of Kievan Rus. Accordingly, Russian

---

[18]Velychenko, *National History*, pp. 153–9.
[19]'Volodymyr Antonovych', in: *Entsyklopediia Ukraiinoznavstva*, t. 1 (L_viv, 1993), pp. 50f.; Velychenko, *National History*, pp. 176, 189, 199; A. Kappeler, 'Nationale Kommunikation', pp. 136–50; 'Mykhailo Drahomanov', in: *Entsyklopediia Ukraiinoznavstva*, t. 2 (L'viv, 1993), pp. 589–91; O. Subtelny, *The Mazepists: Ukrainian Separatism in the 18th Century* (New York, 1981); A. Kappeler, 'Die Kosaken-Ära als zentraler Baustein der Konstruktion einer national-ukrainischen Geschichte: Das Beispiel der Zeitschrift Kievskaja Starina 1882–1891', *Der schwierige Weg zur Nation*, pp. 123–35.
[20]See Deneckere and Welskopp, this volume (chapter 6) and Leerssen, this volume (chapter 4).

versions of the 'reunification' of Ukraine with Russia in the course of the seventeenth and eighteenth centuries were contrasted with a Ukrainian version describing this as breach of treaties and annexation.[21]

As for the Baltic countries, Lithuanians claimed to be a nation as 'historical' as the Poles, referring to the heroic history of the Grand Duchy of Lithuania as a medieval East European great power. Latvians sought to prove the existence of a Latvian early medieval kingdom.[22] On the other hand, the majority of publications on Latvian history dealt with the peasantry and consequently concentrated on a perspective highlighting estate relationships and social conflict 'from below'.

Estonian historiography strictly avoided the ambivalence of referring to the people and reinvented elitism in the same narrative, perhaps because it was taken for granted that, for serious research, there was no forgotten Estonian historical state organisation to be rediscovered. The Estonian narrative therefore was the most consistently populist: it resolutely focused on underclass history, revealing the narrative of Baltic Germans as *Kulturträger* as misleading. It contrasted the violence of invasion, the successive enslavement of free peasants and the social tensions within the estate society with the picture of a functioning democratic, self-sufficient, harmonious and egalitarian Estonian society which allegedly had existed before the invasion. However, Estonian historians deplored the weakness of native egalitarian peasant society in the face of foreign military and bureaucratic assaults, thus citing the 'lack of state structures' as the reason for a century-long subjugation. Accordingly, modern nation-building was depicted as a structural prerequisite for the eventual 're-emergence' of the Estonians as historical subjects.[23]

As far as Russian historiography is concerned, there were many directions of historical research which, in principle, had the potential to challenge traditional state-centred and centralist narratives. Enlightenment historiography in and on Russia had produced several works which referred to the empire as a multinational state. The Slavophile interest in peasant communities and

---

[21]M. Hrushevskyi, *Istoriia Ukraiiny-Rusy* [History of Ukraine-Rus], t. I–XI (Kyïv, 1913–36; repr. Kyïv, 1991–8); Mikhail Grushevskii, *Ocherk istorii ukrainskago naroda* [Outline of the history of the Ukrainian people] (1904; 2nd edn, repr. Kiev, 1991); F. P. Shevchenko, V. A. Smolii, 'M. S. Grushevskii: Kratkii ocherk zhizni i nauchnoi deiatelnosti' [M. S. Hrushevskyi: A Short Outline of his Life and Scholarly Work], in Grushevskii, *Ocherk*, pp. 345–64; Velychenko, *National History*, p. 178; M. S. Hrushevskyi, 'Zvychaina skhema "ruskoii" istorii i sprava racionalnoho ukladu istorii skhidnoho slovianstva' ['The Conventional Scheme of "Rus" History and the Project of a Rational Approach to the History of the East Slavs'], in V. Lamanskii (ed.), *Stati po slavianovedeniiu*, t. 1 (Sankt-Peterburg, 1904), pp. 298–304; T. Kuzio, 'Historiography and National Identity among the Eastern Slavs: Towards a New Framework', *National Identities*, 3/2 (2001), 109–32.

[22]Krapauskas, *Nationalism and Historiography*, pp. 107–49.

[23]Kruus, *Grundriss*, pp. 14–15.

popular culture was in stark contrast to statist views, as were interpretations that regarded regional historic developments (for example, the constitution of city republics such as Novgorod or Pskov, or regions with distinct, partly non-Russian historical traditions, such as Kazan) as potential alternative models to Muscovite autocracy and centralism.[24] But these approaches were gradually replaced by the imperial-as-national paradigm of a teleological development of 'Russian' (*russkaia*) history from Kiev via Muscovy to Petersburg's 'Russian' (*rossiiskaia*) Empire. The Slavophiles turned to a reactionary affirmation of autocratic governance (plus communitarianism and Orthodoxy) as an allegedly typical Russian characteristic, and regional history was implicitly seen as an integral part of Russian general history (as was Ukrainian history).

However, the 'Moscow school' of historical sociology – by the end of the nineteenth century the leading historiographical school in Russia – challenged the very theoretical and methodological premises of statist historicism and interpretations that confirmed the status quo. Driven by emancipatory motives, Kliuchevskii and his pupils sought to draw conclusions for actual social and political reform from historical research. Accordingly, they were concerned with the ambivalences of Russian history, characterised by the weakness of civil society in comparison to the omnipotent state bureaucracy on the one hand, and by evident regional under-governance and failure of the state on the other. Thus, the main interest of research was focused on social and institutional history, on the geographic, climatic and economic factors in Russian history, and on comparative approaches which placed Russia in a European and worldwide historical context. Elite history never vanished from the scope of investigation, being redefined as a social history of elites, whereas in the case of the peasant nations, the very elites had to be rediscovered. After all, research was based on the positivist assumption that history was an exact science, enabling the historian to draw general conclusions about 'laws' from a set of (often cliometric) source data, and thus providing information and orientation for future social reform.[25]

---

[24]Such as Johann Gottlieb Georgi, *Opisanie vsekh v rossiiskom gosudarstve obitajushchikh narodov, takzhe ikh zhiteiskikh obriadov, ver, obyknovenii, zhilishch, odezhd i prochikh dostopamiatnostei* [Description of all Peoples Living in the Russian State, of their Customs, Believes, Dwellings, Garments and Other Noteworthy Features], 3 vols (St Petersburg, 1776–7); Kappeler, *Russland als Vielvölkerreich*, p. 15; P. Bushkovitch, 'The Formation of a National Consciousness in Early Modern Russia', *Harvard Ukrainian Studies*, no. 10 (1986), 355–76; M. von Hagen, 'Writing the History of Russia as Empire: The Perspective of Federalism', in C. Evtuhov, B. Gasparov, A. Ospovat, and M. v. Hagen (eds), *Kazan, Moscow, St. Petersburg: Multiple Faces of the Russian Empire* (Moscow, 1997).
[25]V. O. Kliuchevskii, 'Kurs russkoi istorii I, Lekciia 1' [A Course of Russian History, Lecture 1], *Sochineniia*, t. 1, pp. 33–48; Velychenko, *National History*, p. 103; Bohn, *Russische Geschichtswissenschaft*, pp. 198–203; V. O. Kliuchevskii, 'Proiskhozhdenie krepostnogo prava v Rossii' [The Origins of Serfdom in Russia], in *Sochineniia*, t. 8, pp. 120–93.

Were Others really Others?

All that has been said so far on the complex interaction of established and new narratives, of underclass, state and elite histories in Russia and its western borderlands, leads us to the question of the extent to which *class* can be addressed as an Other of the national master narrative in our case. First, we have seen that in the cases on the Russian periphery, national history was conceived largely as popular history, though a growing interest in rediscovering elite history can be observed in parallel with the social mobilisation of the non-dominant nations. At any rate, in contrast to hegemonic historiographies of the region and to other European historiographies, writing national history in these cases and in Russia was considerably more concerned with the question of class. Non-dominant historiographies and innovative Russian historiography concentrated on the historiography of a specific social class, the peasantry (and urban underclasses emerging from it), and when reasoning about elite social history, they addressed the problem of 'lacking' or alienated classes.

Non-dominant histories merged the notion of 'the people' (the subject of history 'from below') rising to nationhood as we encounter it in republican and democratic narratives, with ethnic connotations. Therefore, speaking in terms of the terminology proposed by Gita Deneckere and Thomas Welskopp in this volume, they represent an early type of historiography which tended to ethnicise (and subsequently nationalise) class concepts, combining elements of histories of *le peuple* (France, Belgium), *the common people* (Britain) and *das Volk* (Germany).[26] Consequently, in the twentieth century, the non-dominant narratives were open to both (Soviet) socialist and non-Marxist ethnocentric interpretations. This fact may explain why, though class history was such a central point in these historiographies, they never developed towards counter-national internationalist social histories.

In the case of Ukraine, the focus was on the peasantry plus Cossackdom as a frontier-society phenomenon encompassing, but not identical with, the peasantry, banditry and Orthodox petty gentry. Besides, when historiography received new impulses from positivist social science, narrating national history always coincided with the narration of changing social formations: 1) tribal society/ societies with indigenous elites and/or egalitarian self-administration; 2) foreign rule and transformation of indigenous into alienated elites; and 3) national awakening founded on the quantitatively dominant social class or on new elites emerging from the peasantry. Thus, we can observe that populist national historiographies of the 'peasant nations' were very familiar with a concept of class as an agency in feudal social conflict, hence it should be considered rather as a complementary element than as a competing concept.

---

[26]See Deneckere and Welskopp, this volume (chapter 6).

Yet class had, and has still, the potential to become a competing concept. Thus, by the 1870s Mychajlo Drahomanov was criticising neo-elitist aspects in Galician Ukrainian historiography and disapproving of the tendency to conceal class antagonisms within Ukrainian history for the sake of nation-building.[27] In the twentieth century, socialist interpretations concentrated on the economic constitution of societies and on class struggle (and on the industrial proletariat) as the driving force in history. Accordingly, socialist historians highlighted 'real' underclass history (for example, the agrarian proletariat or the Cossack rank and file in contrast to the estate interests of Cossack officers) and began to challenge the established populist historiography as old-fashioned historicism. However, in the Ukrainian narrative, a central aspect of class history in Ukraine remained almost unconsidered. The history of the industrial proletariat in the Donbass–Dnepr region does not fit into ethnic Ukrainian conceptions which ignore the working classes outside the agrarian world. Thus, the historical experience of the Russian-speaking industrial city, which consisted not only of Ukrainian but in large parts of Russian and, to a lesser extent, Jewish migrants, even today constitutes an Other to the Ukrainian national narrative (as does the city as a whole): a world of different historical, cultural and social experience which has been traditionally researched within the narrative of 'Russian' industrialisation and 'Russian' class struggle, though there was plenty of interaction between rural and urban Ukraine, especially where history after the Second World War is concerned. This blind-spot in Ukrainian historiography continues to be problematic, when attempts to integrate the industrial southeast into a new narrative of modern Ukrainian nation-building meet a certain reluctance within the Donbass population, whose collective memory is still imbued with Soviet proletarian pride.

Religion is another implicit Other of the national narrative, but to an extremely differing extent as far as the different historiographies are concerned. Though the ideas of direct interference of divine or satanic forces that had been present in pre-Enlightenment Eastern European historiography were now rejected in the name of rationalism and objectivity, the very structure of populist story-lines was based on religious patterns of narration. The societies of phase 1 were depicted as a lost paradise from which strife and foreign intervention had driven

---

[27]M. P. Drahomanov, *Literaturno-publitsyystychni pratsi u dvokh tomakh* [Essays on literature and journalistic works in two volumes], t. 1–2 (Kyiv, 1970); M. P. Drahomanov, *Vybrane: Mii zadum slozhyty ocherk istoriii tsyvilizaciii na Ukraiini* [Selected Works: My Project of a Survey on the History of Civilization in Ukraine] (Kyiv, 1991); M. P. Drahomanov, *Propashchyj chas: ukraiintsi pid moskovskym tsarstvom (1654–1876)* [Lost Time: The Ukrainians Under Muscovite Tsardom, 1654–1876] (Lviv, 1901), in idem, *Literaturno-publitsysty-chni pratsi*, pp. 559–74; I. Lysiak-Rudnytskyi, 'Mykhailo Drahomanov' and 'Drahomanov iak politychnyi teoretyk' [Drahomanov as Political Theorist], *Istorychni ese*, t. 1 (Kyiv, 1994), pp. 281–8 and 299–348, respectively.

out the nation. Later, national master narratives paralleled patterns known from Christian salvation history: the triple structure of the narrative and the structuring of national history in quasi-metaphoric epochs of foreign invasion (in parallel with passion and death), ruin (descent into the realm of the dead) and resurrection. This was no coincidence, but due to the fact that many nineteenth-century historians were well acquainted with both theology – many of them were members of the clergy – and the clerical chronicles of the pre-Enlightenment period. Thus, they did not even reflect on *how* they arranged and organised the factual material drawn from the sources – it seemed almost natural to do it in this way. Even anticlerical historians did not pay attention to this intrinsic religious aspect of their works. As far as the reading public in Eastern Europe is concerned, not only the educated classes but literate peasants or educated people of peasant origin were equally well acquainted with the Christian paradigm, since the New Testament, accounts of the lives of saints and popular religious tracts often were the only literature read at school and in church. In the case of Lithuanians and Ukrainians, historians were familiar with and inspired by the quasi-religious Polish narrative of Poland as the 'Christ of nations', a term that introduced the metaphors of passion, death and anticipated resurrection into East-Central European history.

As for historicist references to national culture and customs as an individual result of divine will and planning, perspectives differed within the national historiographies. Many authors, in particular those belonging to the Ukrainian Greek Catholic, Lithuanian Roman Catholic or (in the case of Latvians and Estonians) Protestant clergy, took this Rankean assumption for granted. Yet an explicitly clerical or confessional perspective was developed only in the case of Galician Ukrainian and Lithuanian historiography. Generally speaking, in the Baltics and in Russian Ukraine, the confession of the non-dominant nations and of those representing traditionally hegemonic narratives was identical (Roman Catholic Poles and Lithuanians; Protestant Estonians, Latvians and Germans; Orthodox Ukrainians and Russians), so that national narratives could scarcely draw inspiration from confessional conflict. In Lithuania, towards the end of the nineteenth century a new conflict line emerged in that secular liberal interpretations contrasted with clerical Catholic ones, the latter emphasising the civilising role of the Church in Lithuanian history and its contribution to the struggle against Russian intervention in educational and religious affairs. In Austrian Galicia, confessional differences coincided with social, economic and political ones, since the dominant Poles were Roman Catholic and the rural Ukrainian underclasses were Uniate. Though this confession was established by the union of the Orthodox Church in the Commonwealth with Rome in 1596 and therefore was a product of early modern Polish compulsory integration politics, it developed into a Ukrainian national church in Galicia, especially after the Theresian and Josephian reforms had granted it equal rights with the Roman Church and introduced the new official term of 'Greek' Catholicism.

In the nineteenth century, the first generation of intellectuals who discovered popular culture and investigated national history emerged largely from the Greek Catholic clergy, which was the only educated class within Galician Ukrainian (Ruthenian) society. In the revolution of 1848, many of them opposed Polish claims on eastern Galicia, and afterwards discovered Russophilism as a counter-programme to Polish domination. Until the ascent of a younger generation of secular populist historians from the 1860s, these Russophiles dominated Galician Ukrainian politics and the educational sphere. Ecclesiastic history was their favourite discipline, and they emphasised the role of the Orthodox Church and of religious lay brotherhoods as the natural historical leaders in the Ruthenian struggle against Polish Roman Catholic eastward expansion. Yet as conservatives, they were not enthusiastic about the democratic, anarchic and revolutionary aspects of peasant revolts and Cossack campaigns against Poland, which were hailed as national heroism by the populists. However, the Russophiles, often accused of being traitors to the national Ukrainian cause in populist historiography of the nineteenth century, were the first to (re)discover the role of elites in Ukrainian history. Even overtly laicist Ukrainian authors who used to criticise clerical politics and the inclination of the Russophiles towards reactionary and pan-Slavist Russian positions such as Pogodin's recognised the historical role of the Ukrainian clergy – whether Orthodox or Uniate – as a national 'gentry substitute' after the assimilation of the East Slavic aristocracy into Polish culture.[28]

Whereas Estonians and Latvians did not formulate explicitly confessionalised story-lines in their historical narratives, religious issues played a role in the Lithuanian case. Lithuanian liberals, following the pattern established by Daukantas, used to couple the narrative of indigenous democratism with the emphasis on pagan culture, which was positively contrasted with brutal colonisation and compulsory baptism.[29] This was innovative and distinguished the Baltic perspective within European historiography insofar as the positive assessment of 'the baptism' of pagan populations used to be a pivotal point in most European national narratives, marking the 'entry into history' of a community and the beginning of histories of national civilisation.

Thus, the Baptism of Rus as a rule used to be positively referred to in the Ukrainian narrative, no matter whether populist or Russophile. In Ukrainian and Russian historiography, the question of whether Scandinavian traders and pirates were to be addressed as the founders of medieval Kievan statehood (the 'Normannic theory') caused controversy. Hence baptism and the integration into a

---

[28]A. V. Wendland, *Die Russophilen in Galizien: Ukrainische Konservative zwischen Österreich und Russland, 1848–1915* (Wien, 2002).
[29]Krapauskas, *Nationalism and Historiography*, pp. 50, 78–9.

Slavo-Byzantine cultural context, symbolised by pre-modern Church Slavonic high culture and the Cyrillic alphabet, were seen as a major precondition for indigenous Slavic nation-building in both the Russian and Ukrainian perspectives.

In the Russian case, belonging to the Orthodox faith was seen as a, if not the, precondition for belonging to the Russian people, thus excluding non-Orthodox *inovercy* from the national narrative, but including Orthodox Ukrainians (and Uniate Ukrainians, who were seen as forcedly converted Orthodox). In contrast, populist Ukrainian ecclesiastic history challenged treating Russianness and Orthodoxy as synonyms. It referred to the transnational context and to the cosmopolitan character of Ukrainian Orthodoxy in the Middle Ages and the early modern epoch (symbolised, for example, by Kievan sacral architecture and by institutions such as the Kievan Mohyla academy) in order to reject Russian claims to the exclusive religious representation of Ukraine. Ukrainian historians criticised the contemporary Russian Orthodoxy in the Ukrainian lands as an impoverished version of the brilliant Orthodox culture that had existed in Ukraine for centuries before tsarist rule.[30] Russophile Ukrainian historians, on the other hand, always brought Orthodoxy to the fore as the central point uniting Ukrainians (Ruthenians), Russians and Belorussians within an 'all-Russian' culture. In the case of Russia, the Orthodox Church, and first of all monastic colonisation, was of central importance for the national narrative of virtually unlimited Russian expansion and for a project aiming at the (allegedly re-) unification of all East Slavs within a 'Great Russian nation'.[31]

Though, from the Russian perspective, Russianness was almost identical with belonging to the Orthodox Church, there was a great populist interest in doing research into heretic movements, as the Old Believers who, after being expelled from the Russian core regions, themselves became colonisers of Siberia and were supposed to have conserved ancient Russian customs and the patriarchal ethics of Old Russia longer than the rest of the populace.

There was yet another religious or rather socio-ethno-religious phenomenon all five national narratives were confronted with: Jewry was, so to say, an absent or hidden Other in the historiographies of Russia's western periphery. The former eastern provinces of the Polish Commonwealth now constituted the

---

[30] R. Vulpius, *Nationalisierung der Religion: Russifizierungspolitik und ukrainische Nationsbildung 1860–1920* (Wiesbaden, 2005), pp. 242–6.

[31] For *bolshaia russkaia natsiia* (in contrast to the ethnonymic adjective *velikorusskaia*, which is also 'Great Russian' in English translation, and to *rossiiskaia [imperiia]*, which stresses the transnational character of post-Petrine imperial Russia) as the national 'project' of the Russian state and society since 1863, see A. Miller, *'Ukrainskii vopros' v politike vlastej i russkom obshchestvennom mnenii (vtoraja polovina XIX v.)* [The 'Ukrainian Question' in the Policy of the Authorities and in Russian Public Opinion (Second Half of the 19th century)] (Sankt-Peterburg, 2000), pp. 31–45; Vulpius, *Nationalisierung der Religion*, pp. 68–70.

territorial base of the Pale of Settlement to which Jewish residence in Russia was restricted. Jews had been of central importance in the medieval international trade of this historical region, and they represented the majority or significant percentages of its urban population. From an historical perspective, as an intermediate and urban social element they had been not only in confessional but also in social antagonism with the peasantry. As a result, Jews were involuntarily involved in social conflicts between Poles on the one side and Ukrainians or Lithuanians on the other. In the case of Ukraine, the early modern social-revolutionary movements, perceived as a first national resurrection by populist historians, meant a catastrophe of inconceivable scale to Jews, as tens of thousands were murdered in pogroms staged by Cossack armies and peasant rebels in the seventeenth century. In the Ukrainian narrative, Jews were implicitly presented as an alien Other in the social conflict with the Poles because of their functions as the magnates' tax collectors, innkeepers and estate administrators. On the other hand, they were an absent or at least marginalised Other, as their significance for the territorial history of Ukraine was practically ignored. A similar marginalisation of the Jewish element in the historical narrative we can observe in the case of Lithuania.

Yet ignorance or marginalisation of Jewish history did not mean that populist history writing was equivalent to a specific, allegedly primeval native anti-Semitism. Modern anti-Semitic interpretations of the Jew as a racial Other who was responsible for all the negative consequences of modernisation diffused into Russia's peripheries along the paths of modernisation and with the assistance of Great Russian reactionary circles. Russian state officials, the clergy, the military and parts of the Russian urban underclasses constituted the main clientele of anti-Semite societies which were as ardently anti-Ukrainian and anti-Polish as they were anti-Jewish. Nevertheless, it was only at the end of the twentieth century that the absent-Other paradigm in Baltic and Ukrainian historiography (Jewish history is 'not our history') was generally questioned. Since Western European and North American research on Russia's western borderlands began to discuss multi-perspective approaches, there have been new attempts to write territorial rather than national histories of the respective countries, including the Jewish element.[32]

Gender, or rather the phenomenon of gendering dominant vs. non-dominant narratives, is another implicit Other to be taken into account. This part of the survey poses questions rather than commenting on already researched facts. At any rate, gender, like religion was a matter of emplotment and

[32]Kappeler, *Russland als Vielvölkerreich*, pp. 220–4; Heinz-Dietrich Löwe, *Antisemitismus und reaktionäre Utopie: russischer Konservatismus im Kampf gegen den Wandel von Staat und Gesellschaft 1890–1917* (Hamburg, 1978).

metaphorology[33] rather than an explicitly mentioned issue in the respective national historiographies. However, Hrushevskyi may serve as an example of the fact that the discovery of women in history *as a group* (and as a legitimate research field in historiography) emerged with the historical-sociological interest in non-dominant social groups. He highlighted questions of female roles and gender status in Ukrainian history in the respective socio-historical sections of his survey.[34] There were also discussions about the role of great women in the national awakening (for example, the poets Lesia Ukrainka in Ukraine or Lydia Koidula in Estonia) before 1900. But only at the end of the twentieth century did research in and into Eastern Europe, influenced by gender studies in the West, begin to touch on the history of women as an independent subject and to introduce gender-based perspective in historical writing. In the case of the historiographies discussed here, nevertheless, gender never became an alternative narrative in contrast to nation, but rather a complementary one which aims to provide additional analytical instruments for the study of nation-building and the emergence of civil society.

In Eastern Europe's national perspective, gender represented a minor problem with respect to social and ethnic conflict. The human rights of women were regarded as secured through the struggle for the emancipation of the non-dominant national collective. Since the last third of the twentieth century, researchers in gender and (post-)colonial studies have referred to this fact as the most significant characteristic of feminist movements in non-dominant Eastern European nations and in 'Third World' societies. As Marta Bohachevsky-Chomiak points out in her pioneering work on women in Ukrainian community life,[35] there were (and are) several aspects typical of the mobilisation of women in non-dominant agrarian societies. First of all are the prevalence of pragmatic feminism, reservations about feminist theory ('feminists despite themselves') and scepticism towards ideologies and political parties. Whereas central aspects of community life that female activists were interested in – education, health, child care, female work at home and outside the home – have been traditionally belittled as so-called 'women's affairs', gender hisstorians regard them as the basic precondition for the building of civil society and hence of nation-building in non-dominant nations.

A second point which is under revision is the role of women in traditional, 'economically backward' communities in comparison to western industrial

---

[33]M. Vollmann, 'Bauten, Organismen, Väter: Eine Dresdner Tagung zur Metaphorologie', *Frankfurter Allgemeine Zeitung*, nr. 178, 3. August 2005, S. N3.
[34]Hrushevskyi, *Istoriia Ukraiiny-Rusy*, t. 1, *Do pochatku XI vika* [Till the Beginning of the 11th century], pp. 337–53.
[35]M. Bohachevsky-Chomiak, *Feminists Despite Themselves: Women in Ukrainian Community Life, 1884–1939* (Edmonton, 1988).

societies. Studies of Russian and Ukrainian peasant women, of female Russian rulers, of female university students and physicians or of autobiographical sources have shown that tsarist Russia offered much more space – and alternative spaces – for female economical and cultural autonomy than did contemporary western societies.[36] This fact has instigated discussions on the pitfalls of the global narrative of 'backwardness' and 'progress', which can be read as a narrative from a male perspective which claims to be a universal pattern.

This brings us to the question: to what extent was the category of gender a determining factor in the interaction of non-dominant and dominant narratives? It is obvious that gendered and body metaphors played an important role in the emplotment of national histories. The myth of Baltic egalitarian peasant societies implied an egalitarian relationship of genders, similar to trends in Scandinavian historiographies. In Russian and Ukrainian historiography, pre-Christian tribal society was described as a patriarchal, archaic world characterised by elite polygamy, promiscuity and a weak social position held by women. The emergence of a church-controlled national 'civilisation' was declared to be the precondition for the emergence of 'morals' ruling gender relationships and for the improvement of women's status. Hrushevskyi presents a modernised version of the gender/civilisation paradigm, discussing the question of 'prehistoric matriarchate' and 'tribal/medieval patriarchate', the forms of families and the female judicial status before Christianisation, critically referring to the abovementioned myths on the basis of a thoroughly researched cross-disciplinary source corpus (travellers' reports, Indo-European linguistics and ethnographics).[37]

The very notion of the popular masses as the bearers of a supposedly 'untouched' or 'unspoilt' national culture and the patriotic cults centred on the territory and the native soil implicitly relied on gendered thinking: non-dominant populations which had to be made nationally conscious through 'awakening' and education were imagined as a feminine element (unspoilt/ elementary/uncultivated/emotional/vulnerable/subject to repression/not represented in public affairs), whereas the reconstructed, nationally conscious collective was seen as a masculine body (trained/educated/rational/organised/

---

[36] J. Herzberg and C. Schmidt (eds), *Vom Wir zum Ich: Individuum und Autobiographik im Zarenreich* (Köln, 2007); B. E. Clements, B. A. Engel and C. D. Worobec (eds), *Russia's Women: Accommodation, Resistance, Transformation* (Berkeley, CA, 1991); B. A. Engel, *Between the Fields and the City: Women, Work and Family in Russia, 1861–1914* (Cambridge, 1994); D. Neumann, *Studentinnen aus dem Russischen Reich in der Schweiz 1867–1914* (Zürich, 1987). For a general survey on feminist approaches to Ukraianian culture and history, see Solomiia Parlychko, *Feminizm* [Feminism] (Kyiiv, 2002).

[37] See Malečková, this volume (chapter 7), with reference to Swedish, Russian state schools, and Slavophile historiography; Hrushevskyi, *Istoriia Ukraiiny-Rusy*, t. 1, 337–53.

participating in public affairs/ready for defence/ready to attack). Needless to say, not only in historiography but also in politics this collective was imagined as a collective of men as far as 'universal' suffrage and eligibility were concerned.

In this context, it would be worth researching whether periods of foreign rule and social suppression were described by metaphors of sexual harassment and rape. Supposedly they were, but it is to be questioned whether in historiography or in political rhetoric, literature or the press. As far as Ukraine is concerned, a well-known sexualised narrative representing the fate of the nation does exist: in Ševčenko's poem 'Kateryna', a Muscovite soldier seduces the heroine, symbolising Ukraine, and jilts her after she becomes pregnant. However, the historical narrative Ševčenko alludes to (the history of the annexation and integration of Ukrainian lands into Russia since 1654) refers to judicial and military categories (breach of treaties, interference, introduction of Russian serfdom), not to gendered or sexualised ones.

As far as national heroes are concerned, the national narratives of Russia, Ukraine and the Baltics mostly refer to men: Vladimir the Saint (Olga and Catherine the Great, the latter a contested hero, representing exceptions rather than the rule), Aleksandr Nevskij, Peter the Great, Vytautas, hetman Ivan Mazepa, the national awakeners of the nineteenth century. Heroic collectives (rebel or colonising peasants, Cossacks) of social history are conceived as male collectives as well. Though in memorials, architecture and iconography the allegory of the awakening nation used to be a woman, men dominated the narratives.

Another question concerns the nation embodied in symbols and metaphors evoking family and/or maternity. Perhaps it would be worth discussing whether terms such as the 'birth' or 'rebirth' of nations assume that there are mothers (the 'motherland'?) who give birth. In the case of East Slavs, there is a possible parallel between the popular maternity cults associated with the soil (*mat' syraja zemlja*), the conception of the mother of God (in popular culture, the Christian variant of *mat' syraja zemlja*) as patron saint of the country and the conception of the fatherland as a 'motherland' (*nen'ka Ukraina, matuška Rossija, rodina-mat'*, the latter being emphasised during the Second World War). Family conceptions are present in the Russian and Ukrainian references to Kiev as a 'mother': in the Russian narrative, the claim on Kiev is often justified with the hint at the chronicler's description of Kiev as 'the *mother* of Russian cities', whereas Ukrainians refer to the exact translation – 'of the cities of Rus' – which allows the integration of the mother-city into the Ukrainian continuity narrative. In Russia, paternalism and metaphors referring to the tsar or to a lord as 'father' (*batjuška*) were common in displays of autocracy and tsardom; conflicts with the Ukrainians were described as a 'family quarrel' in which foreigners, especially Poles, had better not to interfere. But in all these cases, the extent to which this type of gendering made inroads into professional historiography must be subjected to closer scrutiny.[38]

The twentieth century: ethnocentrism, socialism, Eurasianism, new statism and the quest for new national histories

By the end of the nineteenth century, alternative interpretations challenged the eventually established populist national narratives of the type analysed above. They became an important factor in modifying and/or modernising national master narratives in almost all directions, ranging from socialist to biologist and racist reinterpretations of national histories. However, the national narrative did not disappear from historiography. State-endorsed innovations – Marxism, or official ethnocentric interpretations of history which were favoured by the regimes of the interwar Baltic states – coexisted with traditions of populist national history writing in Eastern Europe.

As has been emphasised, both socialist and ethnocentric approaches were immanent in early variants of populist historiography. A specific research interest into the history of underprivileged classes was a core characteristic, and historiographers having clear conceptions about who had to be included or excluded from the national collective, paved the way to ethnocentrism. Thus, the Estonian historian Hans Kruus (1891–1976), professor of Estonian and Nordic history at Tartu University, rejected an integrated territorial history of Estonians and German Balts in the introduction to the German version of his survey on Estonian history: 'This book does not intend to provide a systematic and general history of the territory inhabited by Estonians. Its central object is the historical development of the Estonian people.'[39] As we have seen, populist ethnocentrism was based on a cultural-linguistic notion; thus, theoretically, an individual could become a member of the national collective not only by birth, but by acculturation. Yet there were exceptions based on ethno-confessional markers. Jews, even when familiar with and positively inclined towards the national cultures, were still being perceived as a distinct Other, not as Russians,

---

[38]Berger, 'Geschichten von der Nation', p. 66. Concerning gendered metaphorology and the gendering of the nation and of distinct historical experiences, cf. K. Theweleit, *Männerphantasien*, Bd. 1, *Frauen, Fluten, Körper, Geschichte*, 3rd edn (München, Zürich, 2000), pp. 311–76; A. Sinjawskij, *Ivan der Dumme: Vom russischen Volksglauben* (Frankfurt/M., 1990), pp. 198–207.

[39]'Inhaltlich hat das vorliegende Buch es sich keineswegs zur Aufgabe gestellt, eine allgemeine, systematische Geschichte des von den Esten bewohnten Gebietes zu bringen. Zentrales Objekt der Darstellung ist vielmehr der historische Werdegang des estnischen Volkes': H. Kruus, 'Geleitwort', in *Grundriss*, pp. 5–6; on similar positions of other Estonian historians see Raun, 'Image of the Baltic German Elites', p. 341.

Ukrainians or Lithuanians of the Jewish faith. This was partly due to the fact that a confessionalisation process as it had developed after legal emancipation of Jews in France, Britain or Germany never took place in Eastern Europe. Even in the twentieth century Jews remained a distinct ethno-religious group in the perception of both Jews and non-Jews, and thus were excluded from the national narratives of the latter.

Nevertheless, the markers of distinction remained the traditional ones until new ones emerged at the end of the nineteenth century with the arrival of Darwinism, biological determinism and eugenics. In Eastern Europe, attempts to introduce biologist definitions of the 'people' emerged predominantly after the First World War. With the foundation of new states and in the wake of controversies about borderlines, historiography began to refer to arguments based on archaeological and biometric data. Now the phenomenon once called the 'popular spirit' was redefined as rooted in biological facts. Lithuanian historiographers attempted to legitimise claims on multicultural areas such as Vilnius and its hinterland as 'primeval Lithuanian' with the argument that archaeological and ethnographic data had proved that the local, nationally indifferent population was in fact Lithuanian.[40]

However, these attempts never achieved the stage of synthesis (and the specific combination of innovation in methodology and anti-modern content) of Nazi *Volksgeschichte*, even in Latvia and Estonia, where the acceptance of German historiography was traditionally intensive. First, as the Balts, by and large, had been successful in state- and nation-building after 1918, there was no urgency to conceive a biologist counter-history to both liberal historicism and Marxism in order to compensate for the experience of national failure, as was the case in Germany.

Second, especially as far as Latvia and Estonia are concerned, professional historians in the interwar period adopted a more moderate tone with respect to their former antagonists' research. When Baltic historians reached a high level of professionalisation, they produced many innovative works in agrarian social history, including new approaches inspired by ethnology, historical

---

[40]C. Mick, 'Die Ukrainermacher und ihre Konkurrenten', *Comparativ*, 2 (2005), 60–76, 60; Wendland, 'Region ohne Nationalität', pp. 93–100; I. Lysiak-Rudnytskyi, 'Franciszek Duchiński i ioho vplyv na ukraiinsku politychnu dumku' [Franciszek Duchiński and his Influence on Ukrainian Political Thought], in *Istorychni ese*, t. 1 (Kyïv, 1994), pp. 265–80; A. V. Wendland, 'Volksgeschichte im Baltikum? Historiographien zwischen nationaler Mobilisierung und wissenschaftlicher Innovation in Estland, Lettland und Litauen (1919– 1939)', in M. Hettling (ed.), *Volksgeschichten im Europa der Zwischenkriegszeit* (Göttingen, 2003), pp. 205–38; A. Motyl, *The Turn to the Right: The Ideological Origins and the Development of Ukrainian Nationalism, 1919–1929* (Boulder, CO, 1980); J. A. Armstrong, *Ukrainian Nationalism*, 3rd edn (Englewood Cliffs, NJ, 1990).

demographics and archaeology. As a rule, Baltic authors now referred to the works of their German Baltic predecessors without polemics. They partly revised their perspective on the German elites (for example, elite initiatives in favour of agrarian reform and popular education) in native nation-building. This was especially the case in Estonia, where German Baltic scholars were relatively well integrated into the historical discourse. Blatant nationalist polemics on history migrated to the genre of popular history and symbolic politics.[41]

Lithuanian authors referred to medieval elites with classic arguments of *Volksgeschichte*, since the 'statehood' of the Grand Duchy stood for the ideal of the shared ethnicity of rulers and ruled (the 'native' elite) as the precondition for social harmony.[42] However, in historical Lithuania, the majority of the ruled were Orthodox East Slavs, and the rulers, albeit nominally Lithuanian, were committed to a specific transnational high culture with Lithuanian, East Slavic and (after the unions with Poland) Polish-Latin elements. In producing such ambivalences, the Lithuanian approach was typical for the creative inter-war ventures of Baltic historians to create new official state histories for instruction in schools and universities. Even if the historical statehood which was supposed to corroborate the grand narrative of progress towards the national state did not fit into the ethnocentric narrative, it was pragmatically integrated into the narrative.

The Balts were much more inclined towards a positive assessment of modernisation processes as the central precondition for modern nation- (and society) building. Thus, whereas German *Volk* historians denounced the nine-teenth century as the epoch of disintegration of traditional social orders, the Balts declared it an heroic epoch. Moreover, in the case of Estonian and Ukrainian historiography, ethnos-centred history was not an equivalent of narrow isolationism. The nation at the crossroads of European cultures was a leitmotiv of the Ukrainian narrative, and Tartu historians researched

---

[41]Plakans, 'Looking Backward', pp. 296–9, 301–2; von zur Mühlen, 'Deutschbaltische Geschichtsschreibung', pp. 340, 350–1; Raun, 'Image of the Baltic German Elites', pp. 344–5; A. Fülberth, 'Stadtplanung als Gegenstand öffentlichen Diskurses in den Hauptstädten des Baltikums während der Zwischenkriegszeit', in A. Hofmann and A. V. Wendland (eds), *Stadt und Öffentlichkeit in Ostmitteleuropa: Beiträge zur Entstehung moderner Urbanität zwischen Berlin, Charkiv, Tallinn und Triest* (Stuttgart, 2002), pp. 73–80.

[42]A. Šapoka, *Lietuvos istorija* [A History of Lithuania](Kaunas, 1936); F. Balodis and A. Tentelis (eds), *Latviešu vēsture* [A History of the Latvians], vol. 1 (Riga, 1938); A. Švābe, *Latvijas vēsture 1800–1914* [A History of Latvia, 1800-1914] (Uppsala, 1958); J. von Hehn, 'Lettische Geschichtsschreibung: Zu A. Švabes "Geschichte Lettlands 1800–1914"', *Jahrbücher für Geschichte Osteuropas*, 8 (1960), 365–77.

'Estonian and Nordic' history, placing Estonia in the context of Baltic Sea and Scandinavian history.[43]

The Ukrainians shared the fate of failure with the Germans, since the Ukrainian state founded in 1918 did not survive because of Allied lack of interest in Ukrainian independence and Soviet/Polish annexation of Ukrainian lands. But new racist or biologist interpretations of Ukrainian history, though enjoying considerable popularity in the western Ukrainian nationalism of the interwar era, never became established in professional historiography. Yet there was another historiographical reaction to the failure of state-building: the Ukrainian 'statist' school – Viacheslav Lypynskyi (1882–1931) and Dmytro Doroshenko (1882–1951) – rejected the traditional enthusiasm of populist history writing for social revolution as 'destructive'. The statists contrasted it with their own innovative approach, putting the emphasis on the role of Ukraine 'between East and West' and on constructive, state-building elements in Ukrainian history. Thus, statists could include elites that were perceived as non-Ukrainian by the populists (for example, Poles and Russians on Ukrainian territory). Besides, the state school aimed at the construction of a counter-narrative of elite-based Ukrainian continuity (from medieval feudal elites to Orthodox gentry and Cossack elites, and to modern aristocratic elites in Ukraine) which had to serve as legitimation of a modern nation-building project of the future.[44]

---

[43]Kruus, *Grundriss*; H. Kruus, H. Moora, E. Laid and J. Mägiste (eds), *Eesti ajalugu* [A History of Estonia], 3 vols (Tartu, 1935–40); J. Liebe, A. Oinas, H. Sepp and J. Vasar (eds), *Eesti rahva ajalugu* [A history of the Estonian people], 3 vols (Tartu, 1932–7); Wendland, 'Volksgeschichte im Baltikum', pp. 217–34; J. Hackmann, 'Ethnos oder Region? Probleme der baltischen Historiographie im 20. Jahrhundert', *Zeitschrift für Ostmitteleuropa-Forschung*, 50 (2001), 531–6. 'Estonian and Nordic history' was the name of one of the history chairs in Tartu: see Hain Rebas, 'Zur Wiederbelebung der Ostseeidentität: neue übergreifende Möglichkeiten der Ostseehistoriker', in E. Kuparinen (ed.), *Am Rande der Ostsee: Aufsätze vom IV. Symposium deutscher und finnischer Historiker in Turku, 4.–7. September 1996* (Turku, 1998), pp. 29–55, p. 34.

[44]N. Iakovenko, 'Ukraiina mizh Skhodom i Zakhodom: proektsiia odniieii ideii' [Ukraine Between East and West: Projections of One Idea], in Natalia Iakovenko, *Paralelnyi svit. Doslidzhennia z istoriii uiavlen ta idej v Ukraiini XVI–XVII st.* (Kyïv, 2002), pp. 333–65; Velychenko, *National History*, pp. 188f., 193; I. Lysiak-Rudnytskyi, 'Viacheslav Lypynskyi' and 'Politychni ideii Viacheslava Lypynskoho z perspektyvy nashoho chasu' [The Political Ideas of Viacheslav Lypynskyi from Modern Perspective], *Istoryčni ese*, t. 2 (Kyïv, 1994), pp. 125–42 and 153–66, respectively; V. Lypynskyi, 'Uchast shliakhty u velykomu ukraiinskomu povstanni pid provodom hetmana Bohdana Khmelnytskoho' [The Participation of the Gentry in the Great Ukrainian Rising under Hetman Bohdan Khmelnytskyi], *Tvory*, t. 2 (Philadelphia, 1980); V. Lypynskyi, 'Ukraiina na perelomi 1657–1659' [Ukraine's Upheaval 1657–1659] in *Tvory*, t. 3 (Philadelphia, 1991); 'Dmytro Doroshenko', in *Entsyklopediia Ukraiinoznavstva*, t. 2, pp. 583f.; D. Doroshenko, *Narys Istoriii Ukraiiny* [An Outline of the History of Ukraine], t. 1–2 (Warszawa, 1932; repr. Kyiv, 1991).

However, Ukrainian statism was, above all, a phenomenon of émigré historiography. The mainstream of Ukrainian historiography after 1918 was anchored in Soviet Ukraine; Marxist interpretations were no longer marginalised, but endorsed by the new regime. During the relatively 'liberal' and internationalist epoch of the 1920s, historians who had not emigrated or been expelled as supporters of the Whites worked within the newly established Soviet research networks and tried to rescue pre-revolutionary traditions of research. Pre-Stalinist Marxist historians emphasised elements of the populist narrative which matched Marxist approaches (such as the role of social antagonism in the 'struggle for liberation' and peasant uprisings as early forms of class struggle). Thus, a number of fine works in agrarian and social history were published, and, as was the case in Baltic historiography, innovative methodologies were introduced and findings of neighbouring disciplines discussed. Matvii Iavorskyi's survey on the history of Ukraine (1929)[45] referred to findings of Soviet Orientalists and Judaists when describing Ukraine as a contact zone of many cultures.

However, after Stalin came to power and in the aftermath of the physical and institutional liquidation of Ukrainian humanities, Marxist visions of a Ukrainian history 'between East and West' had to give way to xenophobic 'ethnic histories composed of class language'.[46] Most pre-revolutionary achievements of populist historiography were now declared to be bourgeois nationalism and alternative aspects immanent in socialist historiography that might have been a source of innovation, for example, a new comparativism rooted in internationalism, never developed. The opposite was the case, as the historiography of the Soviet republics revolved around a reinterpreted paradigm of national history. Stalinist Ukrainian history marginalised or denounced as oppressors virtually all non-Ukrainians and non-Russians, above all the Poles. Additionally, from the end of the 1930s to the 1950s, Stalinist Russo-centrism became a new compulsive narrative in all Soviet republics. From then on, Ukrainian and – after 1940/45 – Baltic historiography had to display their respective histories of annexation to Russia as teleological histories of progress.

This was the mainstream of official historiography in the non-Russian Soviet republics until 1985, with the exception of the thaw in the 1960s, when a partial re-autonomisation of national narratives occurred and previously prohibited populist classical works were again accessible – if not to the rank and file, at least to researchers. Disciplines of historiography which were not as heavily exposed to regime interference, such as agrarian history and historical demography, were another exception. Studies in this field avoided the equation of progress with Russianisation. Additionally, as far as the history of the Baltic provinces of the

---

[45]M. Iavorskyj, *Istoriia Ukraiiny v styslomu narysi* [The History of Ukraine in a Short Outline], 3rd edn (Kyïv, 1929).
[46]To quote Chapter 5 (Deneckere and Welskopp); Iakovenko, 'Ukraiina', pp. 345–7.

seventeenth to the nineteenth centuries is concerned, the 'progress' paradigm was less contested, because during this period Russian (and Swedish) imperial interference in the autonomous rule of German *Ritterschaften* certainly had a modernising effect by reforming the inherited corporate structure, urging the landed gentry to social reform and improving the social status of the peasantry. It was for this reason that, in principle, the populist national narrative which envisaged national history as a process of gradual emancipation from German overlordship survived within a new framework that was only nominally Marxist. Complementary non-Marxist initiatives emerged from Baltic émigré historiography which, inspired by modernisation theories, saw urbanisation, the emergence of agrarian capitalism, communication and inner stratification processes as the main factors in Estonian and Latvian nation-building.[47]

The same has to be said as far as Russian history is concerned. On the one hand, post-1917 Marxist historiography tended to amalgamate Russian ethnic, underclass and socialist movement history in order to explain that the revolution was the teleological culmination in Russian history that transformed backward (in Marxist terms) Russia into the avant-garde of world revolution. But the agents of the *ancien régime* who were officially denied a positive role in Russian history returned by the back door, since the central narrative of Russian expansion and imperial grandeur was subsequently affirmed by Stalinist Russian historiography.

Beyond its function in historiography proper, the Stalinist Russocentric narrative served as a compulsory civilian religion which had to tie together Soviet society during the enormous social upheavals caused by forced collectivisation, industrialisation and the Second World War. Its ethnocentric – in late Stalinism, overtly racist and anti-Semitic – gaze made it a perfect mobilising

---

[47]Cf. Hans Kruus on the role of Swedish and Russian imperial politics in Estonia and Livonia in the seventeenth and eighteenth centuries, *Grundriss*, pp. 22–69. Kruus's career under Soviet rule is symptomatic of his position at the crossroads of ethnocentrist and socialist historiography. He became the rector of Tartu University and deputy prime minister under Soviet rule (1940/1) and stayed in Soviet Estonia after the Second World War. In 1950–3 he was in prison for 'bourgeois nationalism': see Raun, 'Image of the Baltic German Elites', p. 345. G. von Pistohlkors, 'Regionalismus als Konzept der baltischen Geschichte: Überlegungen zum Stand der Geschichtsforschung über die baltischen Provinzen Russlands im 19. Jahrhundert' and '"Russifizierung" und die Grundlagen der deutschbaltischen Russophobie', *Vom Geist der Autonomie: Aufsätze zur baltischen Geschichte* (Köln, 1995), pp. 21–41 (here pp. 30–5) and 55–68, respectively; J. Kahk, *Peasant and Lord in the Process of Transition from Feudalism to Capitalism in the Baltics: An Attempt of Interdisciplinary History* (Tallinn, 1982); Heldur Palli, 'Estonian Households in the 17th and 18th centuries', in Richard Wall (ed.), *Family Forms in Historic Europe* (Cambridge, 1983), pp. 207–16; E. C. Thaden (ed.), *Russification in the Baltic Provinces and Finland 1855–1919* (Princeton, NJ, 1981) – see especially the contributions of Andrejs Plakans and Toivo Raun; Raun, 'Image of the Baltic German Elites', p. 346.

ideology against imagined internal and real foreign enemies. As Deneckere and Welskopp point out, in Stalinist historiography the concept of 'class' as a socio-economic category of analysis was 'deflated' to mere class rhetoric and eventually replaced by the concept of the loyal 'Soviet people'. It was allegedly transnational, but in fact a revived version of earlier Russophile conceptions of the 'Great Russian People': rather nationalist, but socialist 'in content'.[48]

Thus, it was Russian émigré historiography that produced the only serious challenge to both nationalised communist and traditional imperial Russian narratives. Trotskyist interpretations, though sharing the teleological perspective on the prehistory of the revolution, attacked Stalinist Soviet historiography as disguised neo-imperialism. However, they did not principally do away with leftist ethnocentrism when referring to the histories of the 'suppressed' nations.

The so-called 'Eurasian' approach – of George Vernadsky (1887–1973), N. S. Trubetskoi (1890–1938) and P. N. Savitskii (1895–1968) – revived the discussion on the Russian 'separate path' development. The Eurasians rejected Eurocentrism in Russian history, arguing for an appropriate and unbiased perception of the Asian element in it. They reinterpreted Russian imperial history as a history of East Slavic-Asian (peasant–nomad society) interaction, first on the medieval steppe frontiers, then under Mongol rule and eventually during East Slav expansion to the Tatar regions on the lower Volga, to Siberia and middle Asia. As for the theoretical and methodological arsenal, this approach was based largely on geo- and social history. In the Soviet Union the ethnographer Lev Gumilev (1912–92) developed Eurasianism towards a comprehensive history of civilisations in Eastern Europe, the northern Pontic and northern Caspian steppes and western Asia, thus laying the foundations for a (potentially) entirely new narrative of Russian history embedded in universal history. This approach was innovative in rejecting traditional conceptions of ethnicity and conceiving the notion of a Eurasian 'super-ethnos' comprising East Slavs and non-Slavic ethnic groups in Russian Asia. On the other hand, it was rather traditionalist in declaring Great Russian culture to be the unifying element within the super-ethnos.

However, none of those interesting approaches was able to replace the traditional Russocentric (and intrinsically anti-Asian) Russian narrative. Only in the 1990s, when Gumilev's works were eventually published, can we observe a renaissance of Eurasianism in Russia, but devoid of its transnational and

---

[48]The original Leninist term to conceptualise Soviet politics concerning (and Soviet historiography about) the non-Russian Soviet republics in the 1920s was 'national in form, socialist in content'. See Deneckere and Welskopp, this volume (chapter 6); M. Hildermeier, *Geschichte der Sowjetunion 1917–1991* (München, 1998), pp. 554–60; Kappeler, *Russland als Vielvölkerreich*, pp. 305–8.

interactional aspects, and therefore narrowed to a mere geopolitical substitute ideology in order to legitimate Russian neo-imperial politics.[49]

After 1990: rediscovering and rethinking the national narratives

As has been mentioned, under post-Second World War Soviet rule, compulsory Marxism was only an apparent alternative to pre-war or pre-1917 narratives. Leszek Kołakowski's statement about Poland refers to the Soviet republics as well: he observes a 'nationalisation of communism in its Leninist form' and argues that the internationalist and comparative potential of Marxist analysis was never realised in the historiographies of the Socialist Bloc.[50] Thus, phenomena of transculturalism, social mobilisation (as a variant of class formation), acculturation, transfer of values and social practices between classes and cultural groups, as well as comparative approaches formulated in other socialist countries (Hroch, Szűcs), were largely ignored,[51] whereas the traditional tendency to perceive social conflicts as national ones persisted.[52] When Russians, Ukrainians and Balts embarked on a quest for new national historiographies after the disintegration of the Soviet Union and the achievement of independence, many of them found the old ones – using a re-exploration of outstanding 'bourgeois' classical studies on the one hand, and a tendency towards uncritical adoption of revived national myths on the other. As a result, a cyclic development was accomplished: if nineteenth-century populist historiography with its specific parallel concern for class and ethnicity was open to nationalised class conceptions and, eventually, to doctrinaire Soviet ethnocentrism, the (re)turn to overt nationalism was already

---

[49]L. Trotzkij, *Geschichte der russischen Revolution*, 3rd edn (Frankfurt/M., 1983); G. Vernadsky, *A History of Russia* (New Haven, 1929); L. N. Gumilev, *Etnosfera: istoriia liudei i istoriia prirody* [Ethnosphere: A History of People and a History of Nature] (Moskva, 1993); L. N. Gumilev, *Drevniaia Rus i Velikaia step* [Ancient Rus and the Great Steppe] (Moskva, 1993); L. N. Gumilev, *Ritmy Evrazii* [Eurasia's Rythms](Moskva, 1993); S. B. Lavrov, 'L. N. Gumilev i evraziistvo' [L. N. Gumilev and Eurasianism], in Gumilev, *Ritmy Evrazii*, pp. 7–19; Bohn, *Russische Geschichtswissenschaft*, pp. 323–30; 'Evraziistvo' [Eurasianism], in *Noveishii filosofskii slovar*, 3rd edn (Minsk, 2003), pp. 351–3; L. Luks, 'Die Ideologie der Eurasier im zeitgeschichtlichen Zusammenhang', *Jahrbücher für Geschichte Osteuropas*, 34 (1986), 374–95; C. J. Halperin, 'Russia and the Steppe: George Vernadsky and Eurasianism', in *Forschungen zur Osteuropäischen Geschichte*, 36 (1985), 55–94.
[50]L. Kołakowski, 'Marxistische Philosophie und nationale Wirklichkeit', *Der revolutionäre Geist*, 2nd edn (Stuttgart, 1977), p. 39.
[51]M. Hroch, *Social Preconditions of National Revival in Europe: A Comparative Analysis of the Social Composition of Patriotic Groups among the Smaller European Nations* (Cambridge, 1985); J. Szűcs, *Die drei historischen Regionen Europas* (Frankfurt/M., 1990 [1983]).
[52]Concerning similar cases in Poland, Czechoslovakia and Hungary, see F. Hadler, 'Drachen und Drachentöter: Das Problem der nationalgeschichtlichen Fixierung in den Historiographien Ostmitteleuropas nach dem Zweiten Weltkrieg', in Conrad and Conrad, *Die Nation schreiben*, pp. 137–64, esp. pp. 147–61.

inherent in Soviet historiography. Especially those historians who had quickly turned from 'Histomat' to national consciousness were convinced that historiography had to provide the new states with an integrative ideology, a conviction that was warmly welcomed by the new (or old-new) rulers.

In the five historiographies, the post-Soviet reassertion of older narratives was accompanied by research into former taboos – for example pre-Soviet independence/pre-revolutionary Russia, post-Second World War partisan warfare against Sovietisation, compulsory collectivisation, the Ukrainian famine of 1932/3, the Stalinist purges which resulted in the physical extinction of virtually all Ukrainian and considerable parts of Russian elites. In general, the reconstruction of national 'victim histories' led to a certain reluctance to confront the native taboos which did not match the victim narrative, such as the fascist and authoritarian elements in interwar western Ukrainian and Baltic nationalism, the anti-Polish massacres committed by Ukrainian partisans in Volhynia during the war or the collaboration of Ukrainians and Balts in the mass murder of the East European Jews. There were even attempts to contrast 'our Holocaust' (the Ukrainian famine, the Soviet mass deportations of Balts) with 'not ours' (the Shoa),[53] based on the assumption that the fates of Jewish citizens were not part of one's own 'national' history.

However, in none of these cases can we speak of a mere reintroduction of stale ethnocentrist or imperial Russocentric narratives. These narratives, accomplishing a cyclic development which had begun in the mid-nineteenth century, diffused from scholarly spheres back to popular history, and to public opinion. After the liberalisation of society and the opening of the archives, epochal innovations occurred which led to a new pluralism of approaches and methods.

Mark von Hagen's observations on Russia may serve as an analytical tool with respect to historiographies of the Baltic states and Ukraine. Von Hagen discerns four trends: 1) 'internationalisation' (of the scholarly discourse which furthers communication of native and foreign researchers and transfers of knowledge and methods); 2) 'repatriation' (of émigré and outcast pre-revolutionary historiographies, and of neglected branches such as ecclesiastic history); 3) 'decentring' of research foci (from the metropolises to regions, peripheries, provinces); and 4) 'pluralisation'.[54] The latter concerns subjects (micro-history, gender history, histories of victims of state repression of indigenous populations, or of marginalised social groups, and histories of under-researched epochs such as late Stalinism), narratives (ethnocentric and neo-imperial narratives coexist with liberal

---

[53]S. Troebst, 'Holodomor oder Holocaust?', *Frankfurter Allgemeine Zeitung*, nr. 152, 4. July 2005, 8.

[54]M. von Hagen, 'From Russia to Soviet Union to Eurasia: A View From New York Ten Years after the End of the Soviet Union', in A. Ivanišević, A. Kappeler, W. Lukan and A. Suppan (eds), *Klio ohne Fesseln? Historiographie im östlichen Europa nach dem Zusammenbruch des Kommunismus* (Wien et al., 2002 [= *Österreichische Osthefte*, 44 (2002), H. 1–2]), pp. 43–60.

deconstructivist and 'revisionist' ones) and institutions: innovative historical research often migrates from established to recently founded institutes, or to related sciences such as sociology, archival sciences and ethnology.[55]

In spite of the refreshing pluralism of perspectives on the national histories which I would call the fundamental innovation of the 1990s, we have to question whether the national or, in the case of Russia, the imperial-as-national paradigm has really been discarded and replaced by Others, for example the regional/territorial paradigm which is of increasing importance, or transnationalism, which is a recent research trend. The answer is no. This refers both to public opinion, where thinking on one's own history is rarely congruent with the discussions within inter-culturally informed scholarly spheres, and to the scholarly discourses under scrutiny in this chapter.

Within all the countries discussed, the new plurality of perspectives and subjects, especially the attempts to write revisionist histories, are not always welcomed, but in contrast often rejected as anti-patriotic. In Russia, government control of public discourse is increasing, and state institutions directly interfere where historical consciousness is assumed to be easily shaped, for example the

---

[55]E. Zubkova: '"Goldene Zeit' der Geschichtsforschung? Tendenzen der postsowjetischen Historiographie in Russland', in Ivanišević et al., *Klio ohne Fesseln*, pp. 80–91; J. Hrycak, 'Ukrainian Historiography, 1991–2001: The Decade of Transformation', in Ivanišević et al., *Klio ohne Fesseln*, pp. 107–26; S. Kivimäe and J. Kivimäe, 'Geschichtsschreibung und Geschichtsforschung in Estland 1988–2001', in Ivanišević et al., *Klio ohne Fesseln*, pp. 159–68; K. Maier, 'Geschichtsschreibung und Geschichtsforschung in Estland: Zwischenbilanz von 1988–2001', in Ivanišević et al., *Klio ohne Fesseln*, pp. 171–8; U. von Hirschhausen, 'Die Nationalisierung der Geschichte und ihre Grenzen: Vier Thesen zur postkommunistischen Historiographie Lettlands 1991–2001', in Ivanišević et al., *Klio ohne Fesseln*, pp. 195–200; A. Nikžentaitis, 'Die Geschichtsschreibung in Litauen: Zehn Jahre nach der Wende', in Ivanišević et al., *Klio ohne Fesseln*, pp. 201–18; J. Scherrer, '"Sehnsucht nach Geschichte": der Umgang mit der Vergangenheit im postsowjetischen Russland', in Conrad and Conrad, *Die Nation schreiben*, pp. 165–206. An example of competing historiographies on Ukraine, O. Subtelny, *Ukraine: A History* (Toronto, 1988), represents a modernised populist approach to Ukraine's history as a history centred on the ethnic Ukrainians. The work became a textbook in Ukrainian schools and universities – O. Subtelny, *Ukraiina: istoriia* (Kyïv, 1991) – the English original (Toronto, 1988) reads *Ukraine: A History*, but the Ukrainian translation may be read not as 'a' but as 'the' history of Ukraine. The works of the outstanding American Ukrainian statist historian Ivan Lysiak-Rudnytsky, who stressed the European role of Ukraine as a cultural borderland *sui generis* 'between East and West', have been published in Ukraine since the mid-1990s: I. Lysiak-Rudnytskyi, *Istorychni ese*, t. 1–2 (Kyïv, 1994); I. Lysiak-Rudnytsky, *Essays in Modern Ukrainian History* (Edmonton, 1986). For revisionist surveys and critique of the populist and statist continuity scheme see I. Hrytsak, *Narys istoriï Ukraïiny: formuvannia modernoii ukraïinskoii naciii XIX–XX stolittja* [Outline of the History of Ukraine: The Formation of the Modern Ukrainian Nation in the 19th and 20th century] (Kyïv, 1996); N. Iakovenko, *Narys istoriï Ukraïiny* [Outline of the History of Ukraine](Kyïv, 1997). An innovative territorial approach to Ukrainian history is P. R. Magocsi, *A History of Ukraine* (Toronto, 1996).

production of school textbooks. Moreover, a majority of ethnic Russians still agree to a greater or lesser extent with the pre-1990 heroic-passionate master narrative of contemporary Soviet history. This narrative is the success story of the Soviet Union, conceived once again in three phases (industrialisation, overcoming of fascist aggression in the 'Great Patriotic War', rise to great power status). Everything challenging this narrative – native deconstructivism or concurring narratives of non-Russian ethnic groups – is perceived as a potential threat to Russia's integrity. In Ukraine we observe a hybrid case, because divided histories have produced divided memories. On the one hand, the abovementioned Soviet great power narrative, centred on the experience of Nazi occupation and its overthrow, is broadly present within the older generations and the Russian-speaking industrial regions. On the other, in western Ukraine, the national populist narrative has completely replaced the Soviet one, as is the case in the Baltic countries.

However, even the very challenges to both neo-imperialist Russo-centric regime-affirming discourses (in Russia) and narrow nationalist histories (in the Baltics and Ukraine) cannot exist without the imperial/national framework. Thus, Baltic and Ukrainian revisionists want to write *other* histories, but naturally enough histories of their nations. Most Russian professional historians of the modern period continue to write *rossijskaja* (Russian imperial) and not *russkaja* (Russian ethnic) history, because it is almost impossible to conceive of Russian history after the sixteenth century without regarding the interaction of Russians with the non-Russians they ruled. Thus, the Kazan quarterly *Ab imperio* (no mere coincidence that it is periphery-based) has tried to establish a 'new imperial history' of Russia in Russia. Developing Andreas Kappeler's approach of a *Russland als Vielvölkerreich* (Russia as a Multinational Empire), the editors call for a comparativist decentring of research into the Russian empire. In trying to overcome the divide between particularist bottom-up 'minority' perspectives and the top-down gaze of Russian historical agents, new imperialism envisages Russian history as a multi-focal history which highlights the *interaction* of dominant and non-dominant nations. Mark von Hagen depicts the 'new imperial' narrative as an innovative, pluralistic form of Eura-sianism which has nothing to do with recent pseudo-scientific attempts to re-establish Russocentric *Sonderweg* ideologies under the label of Eurasianism. Nevertheless, *Ab imperio* remains within a Russian tradition in paying tribute to the imperial framework as the dominant spatial and structural paradigm.[56]

---

[56]A. Semyonov, 'From the Editors: A Window on the Dilemmas of History Writing on Empire and Nation', *Ab imperio. Studies of New Imperial History and Nationalism in Post Soviet Space*, 2 (2003), 387–94; I. V. Gerasimov, S. V. Glebov, A. P. Kaplunovskii, M. B. Mogilner and A. M. Semenov (eds), *Novaia imperskaia istoriia postsovetskogo prostranstva: sbornik statei* [The New Imperial History of the Post-Soviet Space: A Collection of Essays], (Kazan, 2004); von Hagen, 'From Russia to Soviet Union to Eurasia', pp. 49–60.

Some considerations on historiographical transfer vectors and the lives of master narratives

The Eastern European historiographies discussed here developed within continental European post-Enlightenment trends. They all share, to a greater or lesser extent, elements of Central European historicism (or 'historicist nationalism'),[57] but also of projects opposed to historicism. The former's influence is evident in the epochal historicisation of communities that before had been declared to have no history at all, and in the attempts to determine a 'national' character in historical institutions, developments or behaviours and to reveal historical continuity which had been concealed by foreign narratives. Another element that has been described as typical for German historicism – professionalised, methodologically standardised historiography playing the role of a leading science and 'civil religion' within an emancipating social stratum – can be observed on Russia's periphery too. Yet whereas the Prussian-educated bourgeoisie (the social base of the 'Little German' school) eventually conceived of national history as state history, East-Central European populists formulated it as a history of ethnic groups. On the other hand, the rejection of historicist idealism and state-centred histories in the name of positivist historical sociology and the self-ascribed role of the historian in social reform discourses is also of central importance to the historiographies discussed here.[58] However, it would be a simplification to assume a rectilinear west-to-east transfer. In our case, positive and negative references to knowledge and the scientific approaches of European neighbours occurred in almost all directions.

1 *Intra-periphery and intra-regional transfer between (historically) dominant and non-dominant historiographies (German Baltic/Baltic; Polish/Russian/Lithuanian/Ukrainian historiography).* Dominant historiographies were not only direct sources of knowledge or points of (positive or negative) reference, but also functioned as transfer nodes between Western and Eastern European historiographical traditions. Non-Russian historiographers who, as intellectuals, were multilingual and participated in the scholarly discourses of the Russian empire rapidly received ideas coming from outside. Thus, the specific parallel concern of the non-dominant nation historiographies for *demos* and *ethnos* may be interpreted as partly influenced by ideological transfers from the German sphere (Herderian Romantic ethnocentrism, *Volksgeschichte*). On the

---

[57]Cf. Leerssen's conceptualisation, this volume (chapter 4).

[58]F. Jaeger and J. Rüsen, *Geschichte des Historismus: eine Einführung* (München, 1992), pp. 1–10, 41–72. For historicism in Russia see T. M. Bohn, 'Paradigmawechsel in der russischen Historiographie? Sechs Thesen und drei Prognosen', in Ivanišević et al., *Klio ohne Fesseln*, pp. 93–105, 97–8.

other hand, we find examples of limited or blocked western-to-eastern transfer vectors, because language skills and traditional communication channels prefigured knowledge transfers. Thus, there was virtually no reception of the *Annales* school in the Baltics and Ukraine, though, as far as agrarian history of the 1920s and 1930s is concerned, Baltic, Ukrainian and French authors adopted parallel approaches. Presumably, it was the less important role of French as a scholarly lingua franca in Eastern Europe and the unwillingness of German *Landesgeschichte* to refer positively to the republican *Annales* which inhibited the further export of its ideas to the East. In Russia, the native tradition of historical sociology eventually facilitated the reception of the *Annales* and the translation of its major works. However, even access to Russian translations did not lead to enthusiastic reception of the *Annales* in the Baltics and Ukraine.[59]

2 *Centre and peripheries.* In the case of Ukraine, transfers between imperial centre (Russian historiography), imperial periphery (Ukraine), and external peripheries (Ukrainian Galicia under Austrian rule; émigré historiography) occurred in both directions. Galician Ukrainian historians were inspired at an early stage by Russian research on Ukraine; at the end of the nineteenth century impulses ran from Galicia to the Russian empire and vice versa; publishing in Galicia was an opportunity for Russian Ukrainians to get round censorship.

3 *Transnational transfers.* A still under-researched phenomenon of transfer which deserves closer attention is the intra-Russian transfer of knowledge through transnational networks of scholars. These networks – such as learned societies in the Baltics or the Russian Imperial Geographic Society – were of importance for professionalisation within the non-dominant historiographies. Moreover, they played a leading role in the emergence of civil society on Russia's periphery. The new national historiographies owed to them the discovery and editing of large amounts of source materials, as well as the technical prerequisites of scientific communication and publication. The regional ('northwestern', 'southwestern') sections of the Imperial Geographic Society served as a substitute for national institutions during periods of political persecution of Lithuanian, Ukrainian and Polish scholarship. Moreover, there was a lively intra-Russian knowledge transfer between different historical schools (Kievan historians and the Moscow school; St Petersburg as a centre for populist literature). It is no accident that it was a scholar from Finland, Arno Rafael Cederberg (1885–1948), who held the first chair of Estonian and Nordic history in Tartu after 1919. He played a leading role in training the first post-imperial

---

[59] Kivimäe and Kivimäe, 'Geschichtsschreibung', p. 168; Hrycak, 'Ukrainian Historiography', p. 120.

generation of Estonian scholars and in encouraging a non-nationalist approach which embedded Estonian history in a broader Baltic and Scandinavian context.[60]

4 *Limits of transfer*. The example of Tartu, however, illustrates the limits of intra-imperial transfers. Thus, acknowledgement of the achievements of the 'Moscow-Tartu' semiotic school (Jurii Lotman) could have been of great methodological value for the investigation of peasant and elite cultures, their symbolic worlds and communication. However, during Soviet rule, even in its very homeland, Tartu, historians tended to stress social antagonism rather than ask questions of the semiotic systems of communication between the antagonists and their impact on processes of social mobilisation and the emergence of new national high cultures. Only in the post-Soviet period did historians realise the modernising potential of the semiotic school.[61] Thanks to the emergence of political and methodological pluralism and the gradual reception of Western cultural studies, research of myths, symbols and communication systems within both emancipatory movements and ruling elites is now rapidly developing. In this context, findings close to home may be increasingly influential in post-Soviet historiographies.[62]

To give a summary in the terms of 'hegemony' and 'challenge' which constitute the central idea of our East European case studies, we can observe three paradigms of transformation processes in historiography and consequently three types of master narrative formation in Russia and its western borderlands. In fact, both ruptures and continuities within 'outside' contemporary history have directly influenced the rise and decline of historical national narratives.

1 *Persistence/continuity*. In Russia, the 'imperial narrative as national' master narrative persists, though subject to major modifications under different regimes and perspectives. Transnational or national alternatives (Eurasianism, conceptions of Russian history based exclusively on the Great Russian regions) are marginalised, or never seriously pursued. In recent public discourses under increasing state control, the Soviet master narrative is purged of its Marxist implications and re-established as a Russian integrative ideology.

[60]J. Hackmann, *Voluntary Associations and Region Building: A Post-national Perspective on Baltic History*, Center for European Studies, Working Paper Series, 105 (Harvard, 2002), pp. 1–18; Krapauskas, *Nationalism and Historiography*, pp. 36f. Rebas, 'Zur Wiederbelebung der Ostsee-identität', p. 34.
[61]This is discussed by Jaroslav Hrytsak in the 'Historiographic forum' in *Ab imperio*, no. 1 (2002), 470–544.
[62]J. A. Lotman, *Russlands Adel: Eine Kulturgeschichte* (Köln, 1997); Kivimäe and Kivimäe, 'Geschichtsschreibung, p. 169; von Hagen, 'From Russia to Soviet Union to Eurasia', pp. 55–6.

2 *Sequence/discontinuity*.[63] In the Baltics, hegemonic master narratives have changed in the wake of political system transformation, the German Baltic perspective being replaced by the national narratives during the interwar era, and the Soviet imperial narratives replacing the national ones during Soviet occupation or expatriating them to émigré historiography. After 1991 the Soviet narrative is entirely banished from Baltic historiographies as foreign, whereas national counter-narratives are re-established as dominant narratives, enriched by modernising impulses from West German and Northern American émigré history. 'Baltic history' as a transnational and territorial alternative approach to the history of Latvia and Estonia remains marginalised as a former German Baltic project, whereas attempts to envisage national history in the maritime context of a Baltic-Scandinavian 'Baltic Sea' history so far are restricted to the circles of a few specialists in transnational history.[64]

3 *Coexistence*. In Ukraine, the populist national narrative does not become hegemonic until the 1990s. However, it is never extinguished but rather coexists with the dominant Russian one as a Soviet Ukrainian variant of populist narratives. Particularist national, modern state school and new territorial approaches survive/emerge in émigré historiography. After 1991 we can observe the coexistence of master and counter-narratives with changing roles: the former Soviet Ukrainian master narrative becomes a counter-narrative since a faction of society remains committed to it, whereas the formerly marginalised 'servant' is on course to become the new 'master'.

At the end of the twentieth century, the 'nation' (or the 'nation' conceived as an empire) seems to have outplayed all the Others in the narratives under consideration. However, since younger generations of historians have begun to tackle the problem of the 'national' from other perspectives which have been under-researched before, things are in motion again. Under the influence of constructivist theories of nationalism, territorial approaches and comparative history, the ethnocentric paradigm with its teleological narratives and Manichaean friend-or-foe perspective is being questioned. Moreover, modern cultural studies and new approaches to imperial history accentuate transnational, situational or multiple identities, internal differentiation within allegedly monolithic groups and transfer processes between different groups inhabiting the same territory.[65] Thus, the emergence of a new understanding of national history is to be expected.

---

[63]Andrejs Plakans and Toivo Raun propose the terms of 'replacement', 'discontinuity', or 'fragmentation': Plakans, 'Looking Backward', p. 293; Raun, 'Image of the Baltic German Elites', p. 338.
[64]Rebas, 'Zur Wiederbelebung der Ostseeidentität', pp. 29–31, 33, 35.
[65]Raun, 'Image of the Baltic German Elites', p. 349.

16
Mirrors for the Nation: Imagining the National Past among the Poles and Czechs in the Nineteenth and Twentieth Centuries

Maciej Janowski

To be a respectable nation, accepted as such by its neighbours and the powers of this world, can mean various things in modern Europe. We can be reasonably sure, however, that one of the main criteria is having a national history. Lack of it (or failing to display it appropriately) threatens the nation with relegation to the limbo of 'non-historical nationalities', ethnographic items (*Völkerruinen*, as Friedrich Engels called the Czechs in 1849[1]) doomed to make way for the 'cultural' nations, more vital and blessed with a more glorious past. The present chapter aims to show how two national elites on the European periphery tried to build a modern vision of their national histories (and thus avoid the degradation). If Poland is given priority (with the Czech case mainly a 'non-symmetrical' comparison) this is not due to the author's patriotic bias, but only to his lamentable ignorance that precludes him from treating both cases on an equal basis.

Contrary to appearances, we should not suppose that nation-building was the only, or even central, aim of nineteenth-century historians. A legion of epigones, popularisers, authors of patriotic booklets, school handbooks, and so on never concealed their political or socio-pedagogical aims of 'edifying', 'awakening' or 'developing' the 'people', the 'nation' or the 'masses'. Those who considered themselves 'serious' historians, however, in Poland or Bohemia as well as elsewhere, considered the objective truth their loftiest aim[2] (although at least some of them saw the impossibility of attaining it no less clearly than their postmodernist twenty-first-century colleagues). František Palacký, romantically known as 'father of the nation', the archetypical historian–nation-builder, wanted to

---

[1]F. Engels, 'Der magyarische Kampf', in Karl Marx and Friedrich Engels, *Werke*, vol. 6 (Berlin, DDR, 1959 [1849]), pp. 165–73, p. 172; available online at: http://www.mlwerke.de/me/ me06/ me06_165.htm.
[2]A. Wierzbicki, *Historiografia polska doby romantyzmu* (Wrocław, 1999), p. 100.

provide his 'beloved nation with a true picture of its past, a picture that could serve as a mirror for the nation to get to know itself and to reflect its needs'.[3] In a private letter he declared his resolution to write the truth, warts and all, for this or that nation ('*padni komu padni*', in a neat Czech phrase).[4]

There is no reason to doubt the subjective sincerity of such declarations. Most nineteenth-century historians did not see a contradiction between their 'national' and 'professional' obligations. Many of them managed to convince themselves that their professional skills would protect them from gross misinterpretation, and intuitively cherished the hope that national apology and historical truth were neither contradictory nor mutually exclusive. The more sophisticated sometimes seemed to advocate a sort of duplicity (writing freely to intellectual colleagues, and providing material for patriotic education when acting as popularisers), while those of a more bellicose temperament believed that a critical stance towards national history is a patriotic requirement if history is to have an educational value and considered telling unpopular truths a part of an historian's social duty. All historians tried to balance their patriotic zeal with their desire for professional respectability. In the work of various authors the scales are tipped in favour of one side or another, but the desire to find an equilibrium seems general and sincere. A few notorious falsifications (such as that of allegedly ancient Czech manuscripts) do not change the fact that it is unconscious bias rather than conscious lies that characterises the national historical narratives.

*

In Poland the story begins with the Enlightenment. In the 1760s a generation of reformers came on the scene, striving to modernise economics and culture. The former Jesuit Adam Naruszewicz, member of the reforming circle, was commissioned by King Stanislaus Augustus to write a new synthesis of Polish history.

The use of considerable primary source material, his stress on 'criticism' of the old medieval 'tales' and the rational secular structure of the narrative make Naruszewicz a representation of Enlightenment historiography. Centring on political and partially economic history, in his *Memoir on Writing National History* (1775) Naruszewicz stressed, in Voltairean vein, the necessity to study 'the customs of the country, the characters of peoples and ages', including even the

---

[3]F. Palacký, *Dějiny národu českého v Čechách a v Moravě* (Prague, 1998), p. 8 [facsimile of edition published Prague, 1907].
[4]Palacký to Jan Kollár, 24 November 1830, quoted in J. Kořalka, *František Palacký (1798–1876): životopis* (Prague, 1998), p. 147.
[5]A. Naruszewicz, *Memoriał względem pisania historii narodowej* (1775), in: M. H. Serejski (ed.), *Historycy o historii*, vol. 1 (Warsaw, 1963), pp. 34–5.

evolution of fashion.⁵ As often happens, the execution was much more traditional, with Naruszewicz keeping closely to the chronological order and leaving
everything outside pure political history to his lengthy footnotes.

Naruszewicz believed the anarchy of the nobility to be the cause of every evil,
to be cured only by strong central power. This idea has remained ever since an
important tenet of Polish historical thought, but it was also the cause of many
disputes. It was refined in the second half of the nineteenth century by the so-
called Cracow historical school. Eminent historians such as Józef Szujski and
Michał Bobrzyński endowed the Naruszewicz thesis with all the necessary features of full-fledged historical theory, notably through its setting in the intellectual context of the European (mainly German, partly also British) historiography
of the time. The Cracow school saw Poland as a deviation from the 'normal'
Western (that is, universal) pattern of development. Unable to build the modern
structures of centralised government and to overcome the ever more anachronistic estate system, Poland easily fell prey to its more modern neighbours.

In the meantime, between Naruszewicz and the Cracovians, the potent school
of Romantic historiography, with Joachim Lelewel as its prophet, claimed the
hearts and minds of educated Poles. In contrast to the Occidentalist belief in the
universal validity of 'proper' Western development, Lelewel's school advanced
the vision of indigenous Polish evolution. Where the 'pessimists' saw hopeless
anarchy and backwardness (the term did not yet exist in the nineteenth century,
but the idea is clearly there), Lelewel and his epigones perceived the glorious tradition of democracy and freedom. They contrasted it with Western absolutism
and treated it as a source of pride rather than embarrassment. In the second half
of the nineteenth century this 'optimistic' attitude of Romantic historiography
was reworked, modernised and included in respectable positivist historical theories
by the so-called Warsaw historical school (Tadeusz Korzon, Władysław Smoleński).

Here it is appropriate to turn to the Czech case. The Czech Enlightenment,
for all its importance, did not create a counterpart to Naruszewicz. The only
historical debate of note was around the biography of St John Nepomucene.⁶
Although the question was potentially explosive (being dangerously close to
the delicate problem of the role of Roman Catholicism in Czech history), this
potential was only revealed a few generations later.

Thus, it was only Romanticism, with František Palacký's great opus, that created
a coherent interpretation of Czech history. His story is very similar to (and probably influenced by) the Lelewelian one. Both start with the vision of the old
Slavonic primitive democracy that had, regrettably, to give way to Western (that

---

⁶For a very good account of the role of the legend of St John Nepomucene in Czech historiography and national culture, see V. Vlnas, *Jan Nepomucký česká legenda* (Prague,
1993).

is, German) feudalism in the High Middle Ages. The Slavonic love of liberty, however, survived Western influence and returned in the early modern epoch as the Hussite movement in Bohemia (or, in Lelewel, as the gentry democracy in Poland-Lithuania). This golden age of Czech (or Polish) history was followed by the decline of Slavonic liberty in the seventeenth century (with the Jesuits as a conventional scapegoat in both cases). It was newly revived with the Czech national awakening (and in Poland with the democratic movements after the partitions).

The historiographical reaction to Romanticism came some half a generation later than in the Polish case, with the appearance of the so-called Jaroslav Goll school in the 1880s. Its forerunners were Václav Vladivoj Tomek and Antonín Rezek, pro-Habsburg conservatives sympathetic to the idea of the strong state. Goll and his followers (especially Josef Pekař) questioned Palacký's vision of early Slavonic harmony and acknowledged the German influences in the Middle Ages. Pekař attempted sacrilege: an historical contextualisation of the Hussite movement, perceived as a 'normal' medieval heresy rather than the forerunner of modern liberal democracy. Neither Goll nor Pekař concentrated on the problems of state power as much as the Cracow school (here Rezek would provide a better analogy). Still, they were much more interested in the evolution of the state than Palacký, who, in Romantic vein, spoke first of all about the nation.

The early twentieth century witnessed a wave of new polemics in both countries, questioning the 'sober' tenets of the Cracow school and Goll and his followers. In Bohemia the main protagonist of the 'neo-Palackian' heroisation of Hussitism and the Slavonic idea of freedom was Thomas Masaryk, whose famous book *The Czech Question* (1895) triggered a great national debate that was to last for generations (and, in certain respects, even to the present day).[7] In Poland no polemicist of the stature of Masaryk challenged the dominant view, but a new generation of historians, with Szymon Askenazy to the fore, glorified the nineteenth-century insurrections and defended the institutions of the old Commonwealth. In both countries it seemed that independence in 1918 vindicated the Romantic-heroic vision of the past against its more sceptical antagonists.

Thus, in both Poland and Bohemia we encounter a certain dualism of historical thinking.[8] In Poland, one can speak about Romantic vs. positivist historiography, optimists vs. pessimists, democrats vs. conservatives, republicans vs. monarchists, and so on. In Bohemia, we have the 'Palacký school' and 'Goll

---

[7] The early phase of the debate is covered by M. Havelka (ed.), *Spor o smysl českých dějin 1895–1938* (Prague, 1995).

[8] See M. H. Serejski, *Naród a państwo w polskiej myśli historycznej* (Warsaw, 1975), passim.

school', but most of the above typologies could be, with some reservations, used in the Czech case too. This dual perception of national history survived beyond 1918, in some respects even to the present day. Needless to say, this division should not be considered absolute: it is only one of numerous possible schemes of arranging an immense amount of material, one that seems to fit well the purposes of the present chapter.

Reading the works of Palacký, Lelewel, Bobrzyński, Pekař, and so on today we may well ask: whose history do they write? Who are the 'we' whose history they purport to present? In the Polish case Naruszewicz understood the problem clearly: 'It is not an easy task to write a history of a great, ancient nation, unified from numerous provinces often inimical to one another, a nation with no clearly organised government, and infinitely complicated by thousands of private intrigues and factions,' he complained. A historian's task is 'collecting, that is the composing of this awkward, shapeless and unorganised mould.'[9] Naruszewicz had a ready solution: he wrote a history of a still existing state, and the nation for him was equivalent to the Polish-Lithuanian polity.

Soon, however, the final partition of the old Commonwealth (1795), followed by the growth of the modern nation idea in its various manifestations, opened up the question of the scope of Polish history. It cannot be reduced to the history of the Polish state, as it no longer exists: where, then, lies the region whose history we profess to write? Is it defined by the borders of the whole old Polish-Lithuanian Commonwealth before the first partition? Or do we find any other determinants of 'Polishness': ethnic, historical, legal, religious, cultural?

By and large, nineteenth- and twentieth-century historians, whatever their theoretical allegiance, limited their interest to the Polish ethnic group. They usually did not define it, but tended to delimit it roughly by language or by real or alleged cultural proximity to Poland. Usually its existence was implicitly assumed as an axiom without discussion. In the nineteenth century, and until 1945, this 'ethnic' attitude was accompanied by the memory of the old Commonwealth that still dominated the geographical imagery of Polish historians. Therefore, they were rarely interested in the ethnic Polish minority beyond the western frontier of the pre-partition Commonwealth. This minority gradually made an appearance on the pages of their books from the late nineteenth century, but on the whole remained marginal until 1945. The subject known under its German name *Volksgeschichte*, popular throughout Europe in the inter-war period, was most successful in those nations that suffered territorial losses during and after the First World War and had to leave part of their ethnic group

---

[9]Naruszewicz, *Memoriał*, p. 31.

beyond their frontiers. Thus, Poland and Bohemia 'missed the boat', so to speak: they achieved statehood embracing most of the Polish- or Czech-speaking population before *Volksgeschichte* had developed in Germany as a research programme. Some works on the ethnic Poles in Silesia and East Prussia displayed certain analogies with the *Volksgeschichte* attitude: the Polish peasant, defending his land against the German influx, became a symbol of Polishness on the western borderlands. Certain elements were resurrected after 1945: communist propaganda in Poland, backed by surviving pre-war nationalists, upgraded the ethnic Poles in Germany to an almost central place in Polish history. The Poles east of the post-Second World War Polish–Soviet frontier underwent the opposite fate, and mention of their existence became almost taboo (with the exception of the limited circulation of strictly professional publications). After 1989 in turn, the renewal of interest in the Poles in the 'eastern borderlands' was accompanied by a quick decline in research into the history of the Polish 'western' minorities.

The official historiography after 1945, backed by communist propaganda, made another attempt to redefine the concept of Polish national territory: it started to treat the contemporary Polish state as a geographical framework for Polish history. Maps of 'Polish lands under the partitions' usually covered the territory of present-day Poland and took care not to include the Lithuanian or Ruthenian lands. (By the same token, historical maps in Czechoslovakia covered the post-1945 territory even if dealing with, say, medieval trade routes.) The claim made by some popularisers that the first railway on Polish soil connected Breslau (Wrocław) and Ohlau (Oława) in Silesia (territory that was incorporated into the Polish state only in 1945) provides a *reductio ad absurdum* of the retrospective use of the territory of the 'Polish People's Republic' by official historiography after 1945.

This began to change in the 1980s, with the weakening of the communist regime. Thus, for example, the maps supplementing the outline of Polish history by Władysław Czapliński cover the vast territory between the Baltic and the Black Sea (irrespective of the dimensions of the Polish state at any given epoch).[10] Since the 1980s, and especially after 1989, historical cartographers were free to cover any territories they wanted.

And yet even now synthetic works on Polish history still concentrate on the Polish ethnic group. Why? The reason cannot be reduced to the pressure of nationalist ideology or (before 1989) political limitations. The core problem is intellectual: Polish historiographers still do not seem to be decided on what sort of Polish history to write. What are the alternatives to the dominant history of 'ethnic' Poles? Should we aim to include all ethnic groups in the predominantly Polish ethnic territory (such as Jews and Germans) as equal

[10]W. Czapliński, *Zarys dziejów Polski do roku 1864* (Cracow, 1985).

factors in Polish history? Should we, perhaps, write the history of the territories of the old Commonwealth, giving equal treatment to all peoples living there, thus seeing the Polish nation as just one of the successor nations of a defunct polity whose history should be told in parallel with those of the Lithuanians, Belorussians and Ukrainians? Is it technically possible to organise such centrifugal processes of national diversification into one coherent narrative? Some historians have tried to analyse the pre-partition Commonwealth as a multi-ethnic state. Thus, Henryk Litwin wrote about the nationalities of the seventeenth-century Commonwealth, treating the Poles as just one ethnic group among many, and Andrzej Kamiński some years later presented a 'history of the Commonwealth of many nations' as a 'civil society', preferring to write about the 'Commonwealth' rather than about 'Poland'.[11] As regards the history of the nineteenth century, without clear-cut political frontiers, the case seems much more difficult. Piotr Wandycz attempted to write the history of the 'lands of partitioned Poland, 1795–1918', with 'emphasis on the state territory of the [former] commonwealth';[12] perhaps inevitably, however, his narration centres on the Polish ethnic group. Thus, Wandycz's attempt still remains an unfulfilled postulate.

Unlike Poland, until the mid-nineteenth century the Bohemian Crown retained vestiges of statehood (such as a separate coronation) within the conglomerate of the Habsburg lands. Even later the Kingdom of Bohemia, Margravate of Moravia and tiny principality of Silesia (not to be confused with the much larger Prussian Silesia) were still commonly referred to as the 'Bohemian lands'. Thus, while the separate statehood of the Bohemian Crown had become weaker since the sixteenth century, it was never eradicated, as was the case with the Polish-Lithuanian Commonwealth in 1795 when even the name 'Poland' was erased (to be temporarily restored by the Congress of Vienna in 1815).

At the same time, however, it seems that the 'core' Polish area in the Vistula basin was less contested through history than the Czech 'core' in central Bohemia. Notwithstanding the huge, and extremely important, presence of Germans, Jews, Ruthenians, Lithuanians, and so on, the 'Polishness' of the territories around Warsaw or Cracow remained largely undisputed. Czech intellectuals, including historians, had to deal with the fact of the strong presence of German ethnicity and culture very close to the heart of what was perceived as Czech national territory, whereas in the Polish case the problem in relation to other ethnicities was usually a problem of the borderlands. In this limited

---

[11]H. Litwin, *Narody Pierwszej Rzeczypospolitej*, in A. Sucheni-Grabowska and A. Dybkowska (eds), *Tradycje polityczne dawnej Polski* (Warsaw, no date), pp. 168–218; A. Sulima Kamiński, *Historia Rzeczypospolitej wielu narodów, 1505–1795* (Lublin, 2000).
[12]P. S. Wandycz, *The Lands of Partitioned Poland, 1795–1918* (Seattle and London, 1974), p. xi.

sense we can say that the Bohemian lands through most of their history were bilingual and bi-ethnic in a way the Polish lands never were. The problem of how to include (if at all) other ethnicities in the historical narrative, while important in both cases, was more acute (because more central to the definition of identity) with the Czechs than with the Poles.

Czech historians did not concern themselves particularly with such former Bohemian territories as Lusatia, lost after the Thirty Years War, or the greater part of Silesia, lost to Prussia in the mid-eighteenth century. They were always somehow marginal to the inner development of Bohemia proper. Much more serious was the problem of Moravia, a land with its own political institutions, clearly separate from the Kingdom of Bohemia in the narrow sense. When Palacký started his brilliant career, he was entrusted by the Bohemian estates with writing the history of the land. As an official 'historiographer of the Kingdom of Bohemia', he was to provide the (mainly German-speaking) Bohemian nobility with legal arguments to defend the estate privileges against the Viennese bureaucracy. There was no place for Moravia in this estate-oriented ideology of *Landespatriotismus*. The Moravian estates had their own 'historiographers' to write their own history and to defend their own privileges. Thus, it was a real novelty when Palacký proclaimed (in the introduction to the first volume of the Czech version of his *magnum opus*, in 1848) his intention to deal with both Bohemia and Moravia. This remained a standard practice in the Czech historiography: Moravia became a subject of regional history within the history of Bohemia. It is only in recent years that 'Moravianism' as a regional phenomenon and identity has become an object of research.[13]

Another question was the place of Czech (and Moravian) history within the broader political entities. In the nineteenth century many Czech historians wanted to show that Habsburg history, contrary to German claims, cannot be reduced to the history of its German-speaking population. At the time of the most concerted centralisation attempts from Vienna, in the 1850s, an eminent conservative historian, Vaclav Vladivoj Tomek, published an inspiring essay, 'On the Synchronic Method in Habsburg Historiography'.[14] He argued that the Habsburg monarchy was comprised of three main building-blocks: the Bohemian Crown, the Hungarian Crown and the German-Austrian 'hereditary lands'. Consequently, a historian of the monarchy should confer equal attention on all three entities. While the 'tactical' political context of the 1850s is obvious, the essay demonstrates the nature of its author's geographic imagery.

---

[13]See J. Malíř and R. Vlček (eds), *Morava a české národní vědomí od středověku po dnešek* (Brno, 2001).
[14]V. V. Tomek, 'O sinchronické methodě při dějepise rakouském', *Časopis Českého Musea* (1854), 375–406.

The interwar Czechoslovakia presented historians with a new problem: is it legitimate to project the 'Czechoslovak' idea backwards? Most Czech historians would say yes, and indeed find it relatively easy to do so: Slovak history became a sort of appendix to the works which retained their focus on Bohemia. Just before 1914 Josef Pekař published a 'history of our monarchy', which he reworked after 1918 and published as a 'short history of Czechoslovakia'. (He considered it one of his most important works and regretted that the public largely ignored it, put off by its textbook style.) Whether in its 'Habsburg' or 'Czechoslovak' version this is, however, a synthesis of *Czech*, not Czechoslovak or Austro-Hungarian, history. The non-Czeck regions were dealt with as well, but far less detail was provided for them. This 'method' was applied by legions of historians of much lesser ability than Pekař, and thus the 'Czechoslovakisation' of Czech history could be deemed complete. What the Slovaks thought about it is not hard to guess. After 1989 Czechoslovak history turned Czech history again (and the most important Czech historical periodical, the *Czechoslovak Historical Review*, returned to its pre-communist name of the *Czech Historical Review*).

The Bohemian Germans used to be excluded from the Czech narratives. Not only those historians noted for their strong national sentiment, but those like Pekař, with some sympathy for German cultural influences and with no radical anti-German views, treated the German ethnic group as marginal. Almost half a century after Pekař's death, a brilliant synthesis of Czech nineteenth-century history appeared, Otto Urban's *Czech Society, 1848–1918* (1982). This book, an example of the highest professional standards rarely attained in the years of post-1968 communist 'normalisation', with no anti-German bias discernible, is again the history of *Czech* not *Bohemian* society. On the other hand, František Kutnar and Jaroslav Marek in their *History of Czech and Slovak Historiography* (another instance of a brilliant book appearing, as if by mistake on the part of the censor, in the midst of the re-communisation of the 1970s)[15] attempt to do full justice to the German historiography of Bohemia. As a result we obtain three separate narratives of what is essentially three separate historiographies (Czech, Bohemian German and Slovak). The problem, as in the Polish case, is intellectual rather than ideological. The unification of Bohemian Czech and Bohemian German history into a common narrative has proved extremely difficult, although there is no doubt that the Germans are more and more 'in' the modern Czech historiography (like the non-Polish ethnicities in the Polish

---

[15]F. Kutnar, *Přehledné dějiny českého a slovenského dějepisectví*, 2 vols (Prague, 1973, 1977); Marek's name was not allowed to appear on the title-page for political reasons. For an orthodox 'Marxist-Leninist' criticism of this book, denouncing it as 'unbelievably belated epilogue of Pekař-like falsifications of our national history', see J. Haubelt, 'O výkladu dějin českého a slovenského dějepisectví Františka Kutnara', *Československý Časopis Historický*, 27/6 (1979), 907–15 (quotation p. 915).

case). A popular textbook of the 1990s is entitled characteristically *History of the Lands of the Bohemian Crown*: while concentrating on the standard Czech history, it stresses the existence of other allegiances besides the modern national idea in the nineteenth century.[16]

These allegiances have been analysed in depth by Jiři Kořalka, who presented five possible means of growth for collective identities among the inhabitants of nineteenth-century Bohemia (Austrianness, Germanism, Slavism, historical *Bohemismus*, and the ethnic Czech national identity). The importance of his essay lies not only in showing interesting research perspectives but in questioning the widespread belief in the inevitability of 'one's own' nation-building process.[17]

Both historiographies have traditionally excluded the Jews from their focus. Assimilated individuals could enter the national history only by overachieving, usually paying with their own blood. The most popular Jew in the Polish patriotic vision was Colonel Berek Joselewicz, who took part in the 1794 Kościuszko uprising and in the Napoleonic Wars, and was killed in action in 1809. The Jewish assimilation was among the few aspects of Jewish history that were researched. Both Polish and Czech historiographers became aware of the wider dimensions of the Jewish problem only in the last decades of the twentieth century. The problem was much more important for Polish historiography than for Czech, on account of the much more important role of the Jews in the country's history (not to mention the Holocaust and all the associated controversies). The road to a new understanding of Polish Jewish history began with an influential book by an eminent émigré sociologist, Aleksander Hertz, *Jews in Polish Culture* (published in Polish in Paris in 1961; English translation, 1988). As with other non-Polish ethnicities, the younger generation of researchers has started to work more and more on Jewish history, revealing to historians of other specialisms the multi-layered world of Polish Jewish culture that was hitherto unknown to many. Whether and how this knowledge will be integrated into the general synthesis of Poland's past remains to be seen.

The social composition of a nation presents a problem as important as its ethnic and territorial setting. For many nineteenth-century Polish historians the nation was basically the nobility and peasantry. Lelewel wrote on the 'lost citizenship of the peasant estate in Poland', deploring the allegedly declining position of the peasantry during the Middle Ages. His competitors and conservative critics Karol Boromeusz Hoffman and later Michał Bobrzyński considered peasant oppression one of the dominant threads of Polish history, and responsibility for it was one of the gravest accusations made against the old Commonwealth. This

---

[16]*Dějiny zemí Koruny České*: vol. 1, ed. P. Čornej; vol. 2, ed. P. Bělina and J. Pokorný, 3rd edn (Praha, 1995).

[17]J. Kořalka, 'Pět tendencí moderního národního vývoje v Čechach', in idem, *Češi v Habsburské Říší a v Evropě* (Prague, 1996), pp. 16–82.

was one of the few points where both schools of thought converged. The peasantry was usually depicted in Polish history as a passive object rather than an active subject. Its redemption was described as a condition of future independence, but its history was covered rather sketchily,[18] not only on ideological but also methodological grounds (as a 'silent' stratum producing few sources, peasants were difficult to deal with before the inclusion of new types of sources by world historiography in the late nineteenth/early twentieth centuries).

Czech peasants, by contrast, better educated and therefore producing more sources, were easier to deal with: thus, in 1907 Josef Pekař could analyse the memoirs of the eighteenth-century peasant František Jan Vavák as an important source for studying the growth of Czech national consciousness. The growing interest in economic history since the late nineteenth century, including the problem of the genesis of serfdom, opened new perspectives for studying the role of the peasantry in both countries.

The case of the urban population was more difficult, as the bigger cities happened to be mostly German – in Poland at least until the sixteenth century, in Bohemia well into the nineteenth. For the Polish Enlightenment reformers (as for most nineteenth- and twentieth-century modernisers) the strong 'middle estate' was a necessary element of a 'normal' society, but the Enlightenment historiography mainly neglected the problem. It was only in the Napoleonic period that an amateur historian and economist, Wawrzyniec Surowiecki, created an enthusiastic eulogy of middle-class virtues. Somehow surprisingly, Joachim Lelewel did not like cities: his democratism was more of a rural, gentry–peasant character, and the German character of the medieval city in Poland made him uneasy. The later Polish historiography subscribed rather to the vision of Surowiecki, enriched by more and more detailed empirical findings. The idea that the weakness of the towns was among the causes of collapse of the old Polish state was accepted as a commonplace. As a result, historians tended to downplay rather than stress (as Lelewel did) the German element in Poland's medieval towns. The reader of synthetic works could easily suppose that almost the only thing the Germans did in Polish cities was 'polonise themselves rapidly'.

The synthetic vision of Czech history traditionally marginalised urban history (with the obvious exception of Prague) when dealing with the periods before the nineteenth century. After the National Revival the cities entered the mainstream of the narrative, as it is the urban population that became the most important agent of the nation-building process.

The Palacký generation of Czech national awakeners, democratic as they were, considered the nobility an indispensable element of national culture. With the patriotic Polish and Hungarian gentry as an example, they tried to attract the

---

[18]Which is strongly stressed by Elżbieta Cesarz, *Chłopi w polskiej myśli historycznej doby porozbiorowej 1795–1864* (Rzeszów, 1999), pp. 303–4 and passim.

German-speaking Bohemian nobility to the Czech national movement. Later, however, a strong native nobility was perceived as a handicap. Instead of being courted, it was rejected, and the peasant, 'democratic' character of the nation became a source of pride rather than embarrassment. Again, the Goll school developed a revisionist picture, stressing the role of the nobility in the Czech National Revival. This however did not change the dominant view.

The Marxist historiographies in both countries had much to draw on, although, it seems, more in the Czech case[19] than in the Polish one. Working-class history had to be developed from almost nothing, but the old images of the progressive but suppressed peasantry and the treacherous nobility, as well as (in the Polish case) the underdeveloped third estate, could easily be used. The Marxists in Poland, however, did much more than adorn the old clichés with the new 'class struggle' phraseology. They presented the oppressed classes not only as a legitimate element of the historical narrative (this had mostly been done), but as a central agent of national development. The social struggle of the peasantry and workers had, it was claimed, an 'objectively' patriotic character. This was a revolutionary change: hitherto most critics of the Polish nobility had not disputed the latter's central place in the Polish nation-building process. Now, the Marxist historiography denied this very fact. Thus, one may add, Polish opinions on the role of the nobility became very close to the dominant Czech ones. (A certain rivalry between the 'brotherly' communist parties played a role: no party wanted to have a less 'progressive' pedigree than its neighbours.) In inverse proportion to the weakening of communism, interest in the history of the upper classes was gradually growing. In Poland they were treated positively (sometimes exceedingly so), and in Bohemia at least were readmitted to the nation.

Well into the twentieth century women were another marginalised group.[20] Lelewel clearly did not like them. His women, at least in his most popular work, the *Polish Past Simply Told*,[21] are almost exclusively the foreign wives of the Polish kings and princes – most of them *schwarzcharakters*, introducing pernicious foreign customs and intriguing against the Polish tradition. Of course, nobody doubted that the Polish women belonged to the Polish nation, in the same way that since the Enlightenment nobody doubted the Polishness of the peasantry. They were, however, instinctively considered 'passive' members, represented by their fathers and husbands (as was the case in the political and civil sphere, according to many legal theories of the age). One could expect, perhaps, those

---

[19]See M. Górny, *Między Marksem a Palackým: historiografia w komunistycznej Czechosłowacji* (Warsaw, 2001).

[20]Cf. M. Hoszowska, *Siła tradycji, presja życia: kobiety w dawnych podręcznikach dziejów Polski (1795–1918)* (Rzeszów, 2005), passim.

[21]J. Lelewel, *Dzieje Polski potocznym sposobem opowiedziane*, in idem, *Dzie_a*, vol. 7, ed. J. Bieniarzówna (Warsaw, 1961 [1829]).

women who did find their place in nineteenth-century history books to be paragons of feminine virtue, maternity and self-sacrifice. And indeed, the readiness of women to sacrifice themselves and to see their sons suffer was lauded, especially in popular works. At least equal space, however, is occupied by quite another species: women patriots who displayed military valour, for example Emilia Plater, who fought and died in the 1831 uprising. Some women writers are included, for example Elżbieta Drużbacka, a mid-eighteenth-century late baroque poetess, or notably Princess Izabela Czartoryska, an aristocrat of the late eighteenth/early nineteenth century, author of a patriotic play and of a popular history textbook for the lower classes. Their role, however, is less important than that of the 'fighters'. Women, like the Jews in this respect, had to 'overachieve' in order to find a place in the national pantheon. The Czech feminine ideal seems to be more pacific and culture-oriented, with women such as the mid-nineteenth-century novelist Božena Němcová to the fore.

Women's history started to be treated more seriously in the interwar period (which coincides with the first generation of female professional historians), but only more recently has it begun to occupy an important place. Studies on the social and cultural history of Polish women abound (notably those initiated by Anna Žarnowska at Warsaw University) and feminist interpretations of history have begun to appear. These two threads have only recently begun a cautious convergence. Women's history, like Jewish history, has received a strong impulse from abroad in the work of foreign researchers, which stimulates the 'locals' to react.

Among new interpretations of the nation-building process let us mention the literary historian Vladimir Macŭra. He shows how incomplete and in a sense artificial the edifice of Czech national culture was in the mid-nineteenth century: the national awakeners had constructed a culture for a society that did not yet exist. A similar thesis is advocated by Tomasz Kizwalter, who has argued that the Polish national idea as we know it is a creation of the early twentieth century.[22] His argument is close to a Gellnerian one, connecting the growth of national consciousness with modernisation and capitalist economics (although he seems to put more stress than Gellner on intellectual history). Books such as these may either (hopefully!) augur the transformation of the paradigm or remain a minority tradition.

Both the Polish and the Czech historiography in the early nineteenth century were wavering between the concepts of the political and the ethnic nation, the latter slowly gaining priority. Contrary to popular opinion, this does not by itself foster ethnic conflict: the idea of an ethnic nation excluded the

---

[22]V. Macura, *Znamení zrodu: české obrození jako kulturní typ* (Praha, 1983); T. Kizwalter, *O nowoczesności narodu: przypadek polski* (Warsaw, 1999).

neighbouring ethnicities from the national community, but this ethnic exclusivity did not necessarily mean ethnic intolerance. Sometimes it implied acknowledgement of the right of ethnic minorities to exist, and thus could open the door to acceptance of multi-ethnicity which was blocked by the Jacobinist idea of the unitary political nation.

The prevailing interpretation of the national community in both cases tended to be socially inclusive (usually with the exception of the Bohemian nobility) and ethnically exclusive. Somewhat oversimplifying, we may say that the job of historians was to nationalise the pre-nationalist past. The Polish-Lithuanian Commonwealth, a late medieval/early modern supra-ethnic conglomerate not unlike the Holy Roman Empire, the Habsburg lands or the (Hungarian) Crown of St Stephen, were all made to look on the pages of Polish history books like a Polish state. The same happened with the lands of the Bohemian crown at the hands of the Czech historians.

*

Turning to the origins of the nation, the Slavs, according to Lelewel, were not migrants: '2000 years ago, and even earlier, between those rivers [the Oder, Vistula, Danube, Diester, Dniepr] the same nation was living that lives here now, which is called the Slavs. This numerous nation has had various names, such as the Getes, Dacians, and plenty of others.'[23] Besides, they were freedom lovers: they have had an electoral system since time immemorial, and the Poles were 'the first nation on the earth' to develop parliamentary institutions. Finally, they enjoyed social justice: the peasants were free and lost this freedom only after the introduction of feudal inequalities on the Western model, following the introduction of Christianity.

The Romantic vision of the Slavonic past, freedom-loving, simple and unspoiled, is, by and large, Tacitus' *Germania* rendered Slavonic, and as such belongs to the wide and respectable family of myths of origins, developed by many cultures. František Palacký puts forward a similar view, with a slightly different emphasis. In a Herderian vein he depicts a tension between the peace-loving Slavs and warrior-like Germans. This tension serves as one of the organising principles of his story. Palacký offers a theoretical justification of the study of origins: 'We should not neglect anything that could help us to gain detailed knowledge of the early Czech institutions and customs.' Through them one can see 'the real spirit and original character of every nation'. From this spirit and character a 'nation's history is born, as a flower

---

[23]J. Lelewel, 'Dzieje Polski, potocznym sposobem opowiedziane', in idem, *Dzieła*, vol. 7 (Warsaw, 1961), p. 48. My insertion.

from a seed and a fruit from a flower. This [knowledge] is a key that opens for us the understanding of what has happened, where and why.'[24]

A major controversy over the history of Polish origins was sparked by Lelewel's contemporary Wacław Aleksander Maciejowski, who claimed to have found traces of the Eastern Christian rite in the earliest Polish history. The political implications in Russian Poland were obvious and most Polish historians criticised him, although his professional acumen as a pioneer of Polish legal history were never questioned. Maciejowski was one of the rare Polish supporters of the idea of Slavonic unity and he tried to identify common features of various Slavonic legislative systems. The problem of the Eastern Slavonic rite in tenth-century Poland lost its ideological importance in the twentieth century – or so it seemed until late 2006, when the eminent literary historian Maria Janion, author of excellent studies on Polish Romanticism, published a lengthy essay dealing with an allegedly suppressed Slavonic substratum of Polish history. The unfulfilled promise for Eastern rite Christianity to develop in medieval Poland is seen by her as a lost chance for an 'alternative' creation of the Polish identity, opposed to the dominant stream – Catholic, pro-Western, male, intolerant, exclusivist towards Russia and the whole 'Eastern' heritage, and thus 'Orientalist' in Edward Said's sense. Janion attempts to 'rescue' the Slavonic myth from the radical right (in whose possession it remained from the late nineteenth century) and reformulate it in terms close to feminist and leftist ideas, so that it may become a weapon against radical nationalism.[25]

There were Czechs also looking for the Eastern rite, trying to connect the Hussite movement with the allegedly continuous tradition of St Cyril and Methodius. This idea was rejected by most professional historians and especially (no wonder!) by the Catholic, Occidentalist and conservative Jaroslav Goll, who deplored this 'sort of historical Romanticism' and stressed that it is supported mainly by Russian historians.[26]

The origins of Poland were also discussed in connection with the conquest theory of state-building. Conquest could explain the social conflict between nobility and peasantry by stressing their different ethnic origins. The theory

---

[24]Palacký, *Dějiny národu českého*, pp. 44–5.

[25]See M. Janion, *Niesamowita słowiańszczyzna: fantazmaty literatury* (Cracow, 2006), as well as a polemical review article: J. Tazbir and J. Tazbir, 'Cienie zapomnianych przodków', *Tygodnik Powszechny*, no. 3, 21 January 2007, with Janion's reply: 'Opowiadać o ludzkim cierpieniu: z Marią Janion rozmawia Andrzej Franaszek', *Tygodnik Powszechny*, no. 5, 11 February 2007. See also M. Janion, 'Polen in Europa', in C. Kraft and K. Steffen (eds), *Europas Platz in Polen: Polnische Europa-Konzeptionen vom Mittelalter bis zum EU-Beitritt* (Osnabrück, 2007), pp. 31–66.

[26]J. Goll's review of recent Czech historical literature in *Revue Historique*, 9 (1879), 430–8, reprinted (in Czech translation) in J. Goll, *Posledních padesát let české práce dějepisné* (Prague, 1926), p. 19.

was more popular among the democratic left than among conservatives (as it endowed the oppressed with the honour of being the descendants of an ancient, if conquered, race). In the twentieth century, conquest theories declined in importance and popularity, but a new debate opened on the alleged Slavonic autochthonism. This idea became a political issue because of the Polish-German conflict: thus, in the 1930s the remains of the prehistoric settlement close to the village of Biskupin in the Poznań region were declared a monument of the old Slavonic culture. The thesis was accepted by communist propaganda after the Second World War and more or less buried only in recent decades.

The quest for identity was closely connected to the debate about the place of the Poles and Czechs in relation to East and West.[27] Almost everybody stressed the Western allegiance, which, however, could appear in various forms. Polish historians either stressed the positive role of (allegedly) peaceful, benign and tolerant Polish cultural expansion to the East (a milder version of the *Drang nach Osten* mythology, often referred to as 'Jagellonian idea', from the name of the dynasty ruling in the fifteenth and sixteenth centuries), or the importance of the western borderlands and struggle against German expansion (the so-called 'Piast' idea, from the name of the medieval ruling dynasty that waged numerous wars with the Germans). Only a few Polish historians (such as Oskar Halecki) stressed the role of Eastern influences on Polish culture. With the growing interest in seventeenth-century and baroque culture, these influences, both Muslim and Orthodox/Eastern Slavonic, are being more acknowledged, if not always appreciated. Andrzej Walicki has coined the term 'Easternisation' of Polish culture and applied it to the seventeenth century.[28]

Czech historians have asked a different question about foreign influences: is it Catholicism or Protestantism that has determined the Czech identity? The 'mainstream' answer (Palacký and Masaryk) was of course Protestantism, the forerunner of which was the Hussite movement. The revisionist answer, as usual, came from Josef Pekař and later from his disciple Zdenek Kalista. A brilliant and elegant analyst and interpreter of baroque culture, Kalista was imprisoned by the communists between 1951 and 1961, and was rarely allowed to publish in communist Czechoslovakia; most of his works became available to a broader reading public only after 1989.

An analogous debate concerning the role of Roman Catholicism in Polish culture was much weaker – among professional historians the most important debating point was the case of St Stanislaus, bishop of Cracow, killed under mysterious circumstances on the order of King Boleslaus the Bold (or, according

---

[27]A. Wierzbicki, *Wschód-Zachód w koncepcjach dziejów Polski: z dziejów polskiej myśli historycznej w dobie porozbiorowej* (Warsaw, 1984), pp. 21–2 and passim.
[28]A. Walicki, *Poland between East and West: The Controversies over Self-Definition and Modernization in Partitioned Poland* (Cambridge, MA, 1994), p. 9.

to other chronicles, by the king himself) in 1079. It gave a pretext for broad generalisations about the relation of secular and sacerdotal power in Polish history.

Another important stream of thought can be mentioned only in passing: since the nineteenth century numerous historians, in Poland and Bohemia, tried to put the history of their countries into a regional context – Central, Eastern, or East-Central European. Ideological and territorial content varied from Slavonic (Maciejowski) or Habsburg (Tomek) in the nineteenth century, to Marxist or anti-Marxist in the twentieth. All these ideological differences notwithstanding, this area of inquiry produced numerous interesting works; the school of Marceli Handelsman in interwar Poland especially deserves to be mentioned, which undertook wide-ranging research on national movements in East-Central and southeastern Europe. This direction of research continued after the Second World War and produced, in the works of Henryk Wereszycki and Józef Chlebowczyk, some of the most interesting achievements of the Polish historiography.

A question often asked of Poles is: what is 'our' contribution to European culture? What did we 'give' to the rest of the world? The popular answer is simple. The Poles built a parliamentary system before other nations did, contributed to American independence (Pułaski and Kościuszko), saved the French Revolution by the uprising of 1794 (engaging Prussian troops) and were the first to face Hitler in 1939. Through the Solidarity movement and Pope John Paul II they were the most important factor in destroying communism too. As regards the Czechs, they gave birth to the modern idea of religious tolerance and paved the way to the Reformation and thus to the collapse of the medieval (that is, repressive) world. They gave to the world the humanitarian ideal (*humanita*, as Masaryk used to say).

At the same time, Polish culture developed a parallel self-critical picture. An ironic jester, exposing a long sequence of self-inflicted misfortunes, is almost as venerable a person in Polish modern culture as the arch-priest of past national greatness. (Members of the Cracow historical school called themselves 'the Stańczyks' after the sixteenth-century court jester Stańczyk, renowned for his courage in telling unpopular truths.) Polish culture, according to its critics, was both belated and inferior in comparison with European cultural centres. Having only a few people and institutions at its disposal, it never could digest the Western ideas it borrowed, so it remained superficial. The Lithuanian union weakened Polish state by giving it immense territories it was unable to administer. The gentry lifestyle, rural, agricultural, parasitic, only strengthened the superficial, passive and receptive character of Polish culture. The partitions in the late eighteenth century were the consequence of these shortcomings.

Even Lelewel, otherwise optimistic, could state, for example, that Poland belonged to the northeastern part of the continent which, as opposed to the southwest, was characterised by passivity and relative poverty.[29] A century later Władysław Konopczyński, by no means a friend of the Cracow historical school, stressed the political passivity and social egoism of the Polish gentry, as well as the internal sources of the political crisis in pre-partition Poland.[30] Much more radical was the leading 'iconoclast' among interwar historians, Olgierd Górka, who attacked the historical novels of Henryk Sienkiewicz, reproaching them with idealising the old Commonwealth and nationalist (anti-Ukrainian) bias. His book launched a wide public debate, engaging most of the leading Polish historians.[31]

In the mid-twentieth century, theories of economic backwardness reinforced the 'critical' picture in Poland (such as excellent works by Witold Kula and Marian Małowist).[32] In recent decades much-debated essays by Jan Józef Lipski on two traditions of Polish patriotism, Jerzy Jedlicki on collective responsibility for the nation's past, Jan Błoński on Polish attitudes towards the Holocaust and Jan Tomasz Gross's book *Neighbours* can be seen as belonging to the same self-critical tradition.[33] This eternal debate reached a new turn in the early twenty-first century, as a new generation of (mainly right-wing) historians and historical essayists revived the apologetic view and proclaimed the need for state sponsored history policy' that would support a positive image of Polish history.

An analogous critical stream of Czech culture is to be found in *belles-lettres* rather than in historical works; it is epitomised (obviously) by the Good Soldier Švejk. One should, however, mention (apart from Goll, Pekař or, later, Macůra) three important essays. Just after the First World War Emanuel Rádl, professor of biology in Prague, published a passionate appeal for a Czech–German compromise. Most of his book deals with the Czech–German past, criticising Czech

[29]J. Lelewel, *Statystyka, czyli teoria, czyli zasady*, in idem, *Dzieła*, vol. 2, *Pisma metodologiczne* (Warsaw, 1964), p. 356.
[30]Cf. W. Konopczyński, *Dzieje Polski nowożytnej*, vols 1–2 (Warsaw, 1936), e.g. vol. 1, pp. 424–6.
[31]O. Górka, *'Ogniem i Mieczem' a rrzeczywistość historycznaa*, 2nd edn (Warsaw, 1986; 1st edn, 1934). Cf. Z. Romek, *Olgierd Górka: historyk w służbie myśli propaństwowej 1908–1955* (Warsaw, 1997), pp. 68–78.
[32]W. Kula, *An Economic Theory of the Feudal System: Towards a Model of the Polish Economy, 1500–1800* (London, 1976); M. Małowist, *Wschód a zachód Europy w XIII–XVI wieku*, 2nd edn (Warsaw, 2006).
[33]J. J. Lipski, 'Two Fatherlands, Two Patriotisms', *Survey* (autumn 1982), reprinted in R. Kostrzewa (ed.), *Between East and West: Writings from Kultura* (New York, 1990), pp. 52–71. J. Jedlicki, 'Heritage and Collective Responsibility', in I. Maclean, A. Montefiore, and P. Winch (eds), *The Political Responsibility of Intellectuals* (Cambridge, 1990). J. Błoński, 'The Poor Poles Look at the Ghetto', in A. Polonsky (ed.), *My Brother's Keeper? Recent Polish Debates on the Holocaust* (London, 1990), pp. 34–52. J. T. Gross, *Neighbours: The Destruction of the Jewish Community in Jedwabne* (Princeton, NJ, 2001).

historians' tendency to treat ethnic conflict as the central point of the whole of Czech history. Rádl, an admirer of Masaryk, took absolutely seriously the latter's concept of the ethical character of the Czech national movement, and derived from it the moral need for the just treatment of all ethnicities in the new state.[34] Some 60 years later Pavel Tigrid, an émigré intellectual, published a book entitled, after the manner of Bernard Shaw, *The Intelligent Woman's Pocket Guide to Her Own Fate.* Tigrid writes contemptuously about 'typical Czech realism', often tantamount to opportunism and subservience to the Nazis and the communists.[35] Once we remember that 'realism' was the name Masaryk gave to his political philosophy, we see the sting of Tigrid's criticism.

Finally, a lengthy essay on Czechs in modern history by 'Podiven'[36] provoked lively discussion in the early 1990s. It tried to reformulate the history of Bohemia to include some of the minorities discarded by the 'official' Palacký–Masaryk stream of thinking – especially the Catholics and the nobility, as well as in part the Germans. It seems, however, that Czech professional historiography was on the whole more optimistic about the nation's past than was the Polish.[37]

Polish and Czech 'self-critical' interpretations, though similar in tone, differ in content. The Poles often reproach their compatriots for a romantic addiction to insurrections. The Czechs, on the contrary, were (self-)criticised for their lack of resistance and combat spirit.[38] Do these contradictory self-stereotypes reflect real differences between national cultures (due, perhaps, to different social structures)? Without trying to answer this, let us stress the importance of the 'self-critical' themes. After all, the consciousness of common vices may also serve nation-building, helping to homogenise that great, amorphous imaginary 'we' which forms the subject of national history.

*

Let us turn to a wider comparative perspective. Like Palacký or Lelewel, part of the Hungarian historiography praised the native democratic tradition, especially in the form of the early modern principality of Transylvania. On the eve of the First World War the representative of Hungarian *Geistesgeschichte*, Gyula

---

[34]E. Rádl, *Válka Čechů s Němci* (Prague, 1993; 1st edn, 1928).
[35]P. Tigrid, *Kapesní průvodce inteligentní ženy po vlastním osudu* (Prague, 1990), p. 113.
[36]Podiven [Milan Otáhal, Petr Přihoda, Petr Pithart], *Češi v dějinách nové doby* (Prague, 1991); for the sharp criticism of this and other 'revisionist' interpretations see *Spory o dějiny: sborník kritických textů* (Prague, 1999), passim.
[37]See Górny, *Między Marksem a Palackym*, pp. 191ff.
[38]See, for example, Podiven, *Češi*, p. 641.

Szekfű, attacked the myth of Transylvania, giving rise to a debate not unlike that over Bobrzyński's views or Pekař's polemics with Masaryk.[39]

Ukrainian historical thought of the late nineteenth and early twentieth centuries is usually seen as competition between the 'populist' and 'etatist' school. The populists (such as Mykhailo Hhrushevskyi) were not too far from the Romantic Polish and Czech views, extolling ancient Cossack liberties. The leading 'etatist', Viyaceslav Lypynskyi, stressed the role of the nobility in Ukrainian history (which makes him close to Pekař and Szekfű), as well as the importance of state institutions (which brings him close to Bobrzyński).

Is it not tempting to borrow the Ukrainian classification and divide all the East-Central European nineteenth-century historiographies into 'populist' and 'etatist' categories? Alternatively, we could borrow from the Hungarian historiography the division between the pro-Habsburg loyalists (*labanc*) and anti-Habsburg insurrectionists (*kuruc*), or from the Romanian historiography a useful notion of 'Protochronism', meaning the belief that 'our' country has reached a certain level of development before the West. The 'anti-Protochronists' could be conveniently labelled 'historists' (meaning those who judge past epochs according to their own standards, not according to the standards of the present day). Thus, could we conclude with stating that the dualism observed earlier in the Polish and Czech historiography is a regional, East-Central European feature? Or, perhaps, simply European? After all, most nations believe they have had an ancient (native) liberty that later gave way to (imported) slavery. Palacký, Lelewel, and so on, with their vision of the 'organic' growth of liberty, can be seen as part of a version of what Herbert Butterfield called the 'Whig interpretation of history'. Their critics, in turn, can be related to the conservative criticism of the Whig interpretation that can be traced in Britain at least to David Hume.[40] Debate about the inclusion of the non-dominant ethnicities and various social strata in the national narrative is also a general phenomenon.

There exists, however, a regional specificity. Through most of the nineteenth century the East-Central European nations were oscillating between various forms of foreign dominance. To fight or accommodate? What are the limits of morally and politically acceptable compromise? These are the themes debated, sometimes openly, more often allusively, by the nineteenth- and twentieth-century Poles, Hungarians, Czechs, and so on. It is no surprise then that historians addressed these problems too. The case was different in the German and

---

[39]For the Bobrzyński–Pekař–Szekfű comparison, see my essay 'Three Historians', *CEU History Department Yearbook* (2001–2), 199–232.

[40]See E. F. Miller, 'Hume on Liberty in the Successive English Constitutions', in N. Capaldi and D. Livingston (eds), *Liberty in Hume's History of England* (Dordrecht, 1990), pp. 53–104.

Russian historiographies. They did not seem to develop under the threat of foreign domination (with the exception, perhaps, of Napoleonic domination in Germany in the early nineteenth century). They both stressed the state rather than the ethnic nation as the main subject of their studies. Indeed, the legal-constitutional German historiography had a great influence on the anti-Romantic turn of the East-Central European historiographies.

*

The differing views of national history do not make it easy to reach a conclusion. The mirror that historians held up to their compatriots all too often reflected a flattering image. However, in many instances it did try to be honest and to balance vices with virtues, or even – as did the Cracow historical school – to stress the first rather than the second. It is because of these criticisms that the Polish and Czech historiographies of the nineteenth and twentieth centuries remain alive: a passion for understanding, Aristotelian curiosity, is dominant and redeems their numerous imperfections.

17

National Historiographies in the Balkans, 1830–1989

Marius Turda[1]

Introduction

The use of historiography in nation-building processes in the Balkans began in the nineteenth century.[2] Undoubtedly, this process was encouraged by significant geopolitical developments in the region, namely the Serbian uprisings (1804–13 and 1815) and the Greek War of Independence (1821–32). Collectively, these countries among the host of Ottoman or Habsburg provinces aspiring to become autonomous or independent (such as the Danubian principalities, Croatia or the Bulgarian lands), witnessed how a new generation of intellectuals struggled to conceptualise the physical and spiritual boundaries of the political entities they hoped to establish in the immediate future. It was widely agreed that two preconditions needed to be fulfilled in order for strong and independent states to emerge: the internal consolidation of society by way of social and economic reforms, and the creation of a national culture. If the former was assumed to be under way in light of the revolutions and political reforms that characterised the Balkans at the time, the latter was considered to be still in its infancy.

Under the spell of Romantic nationalism, historians in the Balkans began to look to their native traditions for intellectual inspiration. Some, for example, assumed that their religious confessions (Orthodoxy, Catholicism), in tandem

---

[1]I want to thank Chris Lorenz, Stefan Berger and Tudor Georgescu for their useful comments and suggestions.
[2]G. Iggers, *The German Conception of History: The National Tradition of Historical Thought from Herder to the Present*, rev. edn (Middleton, CT, 1969); S. Berger, M. Donovan and K. Passmore (eds), *Writing National Histories: Western Europe since 1800* (London, 1999); M. Todorova (ed.), *Balkan Identities: Nation and Memory* (London, 2003); I. Z. Dénes (ed.), *Liberty and the Search for Identity: Liberal Nationalisms and the Legacy of Empires* (Budapest, 2006); and B. Trencsényi and M. Kopeček (eds), *Discourses of Collective Identity and Central and Southeast Europe (1770–1945): Texts and Commentaries*, vol. 1 (Budapest, 2006).

with the predominantly agricultural traditions, could serve as the necessary foundation on which to construct a new national culture. Within this transformation, which Miroslav Hroch aptly described as 'the search for a new collective spirit',[3] history was portrayed as a truly universal science, the repository of mankind's values, as well as shaping national consciousness and culture. No nation could claim individual existence without an understanding of its past. As elsewhere in Europe, it was this axiom that animated historiographical literature produced in the Balkans during the nineteenth and twentieth centuries.[4]

In the Balkans, historical narratives were produced not only by professional historians, but also by professionals from other disciplines (such as literature or ethnography) as well as by politicians. It was, in fact, at the confluence between historiography and politics that national master narratives interacted with narratives of ethnicity, class, religion and gender. In the first section of this chapter I discuss historiographical constructions such as 'historical rights' and 'historical continuity', which stand out in Balkan mythopoeia (although certainly not restricted to the Balkans),[5] and how they influenced the development of national historiographies in Romania, Bulgaria, Serbia and Croatia. But the sense of historical continuity was not solely related to historiography. It also spurred politicians to new actions. The revolutionary period between 1830 and 1850, in the Balkans as elsewhere, awakened not only interest in national history, but also a belief in the right and capacity of nations to determine their own fate. To revolutionaries and conservatives alike, the glories of the past formed an inextricable part of the nation's present and future destiny. The expectation of a national palingenesis was shared by all. There were, of course, differences about the means to be employed in order to reach this regenerated nation. The conservatives' vision of gradual transformation of the traditional society which preserved rather than challenged centuries of social relations was opposed by the emerging liberal nationalism of the revolutionaries, and their faith in the democratic republics which were to emerge from the collapse of the old, absolutist regimes. In this context, history played an important role: a nation's past was both testimony to

[3]M. Hroch, 'National Romanticism', in B. Trencsényi and M. Kopeček (eds), *Discourses of Collective Identity in Central and Southeast Europe (1770–1945): Texts and Commentaries,* vol. 2 (Budapest, 2006), p. 6.
[4]C. Norton (ed.), *Nationalism, Historiography and the (Re)Construction of the Past* (Washington, 2007).
[5]For the general relationship between the notions of origin, continuity, and rights in historical writing see C. Lorenz, 'Towards a Theoretical Framework for Comparing Historiographies: Some Preliminary Considerations', in P. Seixas (ed.), *Theorizing Historical Consciousness* (Toronto, 2004), pp. 25–48.

its inevitable progress and a way of inspiring an ever-expanding consciousness within the nation.

Such were the new ideas about nationalism and liberalism which circulated in the Balkans before and especially after the revolutions of 1848. The generic term 'Balkan' is taken here to mean an area of geographical divisions between Eastern and Western Europe, and religious interactions between Christianity and Islam. It is thus a geographical and religious 'signifier', which (following Maria Todorova) covers 'Albanians, Bulgarians, Greeks, Romanians, and most of the former Yugoslavs', including the Croats, considering that 'parts of Croat-populated territories were under Ottoman rule for considerable lengths of time'.[6] Such a broad geographical coverage should not obfuscate the specificity of each country included in this survey. I subsequently turn, in the second section, to one of the most pressing conceptual issues pertaining to any national historiography in the Balkans: the concept of national uniqueness, in connection with which I address how social and biological categories such as class and gender shaped historical narratives of national belonging.

The repeated return of the motif of national uniqueness influenced debates not only on the nation's past but, equally importantly, on its future. I show in the third section that as a result of specific historical circumstances (a lengthy modernisation of society, for example), this discussion of the future not only was more intense but also a constant feature of national historiographies in the Balkans. It characterised both the racial utopia of the fascists and the socialist utopia of the communists. The last section provides an overview of the main themes that the communist regimes used in national histories throughout the Balkans. Here the focus is on long-term narratives of national identity which formed the main ingredients of national historiographies before the Second World War, and which, after the transformation of the Balkan countries into People's Democracies, reflected the new socialist revolution. By examining this fusion between nationalism and communism I hope to show how historiography gradually shifted its emphasis from an internationalised, Soviet-oriented history to national variants of autochthonous communism.

The general argument is that the emergence of national historiographies in the Balkans should be seen as part of a larger process of cultural and political transformation that these countries experienced during critical stages in their

---

[6]M. Todorova, *Imagining the Balkans* (Oxford, 1997), p. 31. See also D. I. Bjelić and O. Savić (eds), *Balkan as Metaphor, between Globalization and Fragmentation* (Cambridge, MA, 2002); and K. E. Fleming, 'Orientalism, the Balkans, and Balkan Historiography', *American Historical Review*, 105/4 (2000), 1218–33.

consolidation as national states.[7] Once national historiographies in Romania, Bulgaria, Serbia and Croatia are viewed in a comparative framework, one can question their representation of national specificity and suggest a more integrative conceptual apparatus, one that is equally attentive to historical idiosyncrasy and similarity. Like other attempts at reassessing 'the standard concept of the unity of national history', this chapter 'questions the metaphysical boundaries that underlie every nationalist project'.[8] In broader terms, looking at the specific historiographical terrain on which Balkan intellectuals and politicians have evolved since the beginning of the nineteenth century will enable us to resist teleological interpretations of the nation which have dominated the intellectual discourse in the Balkans.

Historical rights and historical continuity

Modern Serbia, Romania and Bulgaria were all established in the nineteenth century, while no independent Croatian state existed before 1941. Such historical circumstances favoured the emergence of a particular form of historical writing, based on the idea of an incomplete state and a failed nationalist mission.[9] In this context, historiography was considered the most appropriate tool in assisting the state and accomplishing the nation's perceived destiny. Moreover, it was hoped that historiography would assist intellectuals in their attempts to define a specific national identity for their communities.

First and foremost, national historiography in the Balkans brought about the historical knowledge needed to substantiate theories on the nation and state. Within this process, two principles were elevated to the status of scientific dogmas: the concept of historical and/or natural rights and the idea of historical continuity. Taken together or separately these two principles shaped

[7]C. Jelavich and B. Jelavich, *The Establishment of the Balkan National States, 1804–1920* (Seattle and London, 1977), though slightly outdated in its interpretation is still one of the best overviews of the topic. See also M. Glenny, *The Balkans, 1804–1999: Nationalism, War and the Great Powers* (New York, 1999); S. K. Pavlowitch, *A History of the Balkans, 1804–1945* (London, 1999). For individual cases, see R. J. Crampton, *A History of Bulgaria, 1878–1918* (New York, 1983); K. Hitchins, *Rumania, 1866–1947* (Oxford, 1994); V. Roudometof, 'The Social Origins of Balkan Politics: Nationalism, Underdevelopment, and the Nation-State in Greece, Serbia and Bulgaria, 1880–1920', *Mediterranean Quarterly*, 11/3 (2000), 144–63; and M. Mazower, *The Balkans: From the End of Byzantium to the Present Day* (London, 2000).
[8]See 'Inter-texts of Identity', introduction to Trencsényi and Kopeček, *Discourses*, vol. 1, pp. 1–32.
[9]See F. Kellogg, *A History of Romanian Historical Writing* (Bakersfield, CA, 1990); L. Boia, *History and Myth in Romanian Consciousness* (Budapest, 2001); M. Biondich, '"We Were Defending the State": Nationalism, Myth, and Memory in Twentieth-Century Croatia', in J. R. Lampe and M. Mazower (eds), *Ideologies and National Identities: The Case of Twentieth-Century Southeastern Europe* (Budapest, 2004), pp. 54–81.

both the formation of national, social and biological identities, and the production of historiographical arguments that accompanied it. As elsewhere in Europe, it was during the 1830s and 1840s that these two processes intersected in the Balkans for the first time. Yet this fusion of ideas functioned in parallel with other projects of identity-building, such as the idea of a federation of the peoples of the Balkans.[10] To give one oft-quoted example, the Illyrian ideal of Slavic harmony and brotherhood was supported by both Serb and Croat national ideologues. When the Ban of Croatia, Josip Jelačić (1801–59), addressed the Croatian parliament (Sabor) in 1848 and claimed that 'We are all one nation, putting aside differentiation between the Serbs and the Croats', he was consciously putting forward the idea of trans-ethnic identity and shared regional history.[11]

The Croat writer and politician Janko Drašković (1770–1856) had earlier proposed these ideas in his 'Dissertation, or Treatise' (1832), combining them with an emphasis on vernacularism, namely the introduction of the Croatian language in the political sphere in place of Latin or German. From the 1820s onwards, distinctions between the nation and the state became one of the tenets of the new nationalism developing in Croatia.[12] With the development of Hungarian nationalism, Croatian cultural leaders were divided between two sources of symbolic legitimisation. The first centred on the state (Hungary), while the second embraced the nation (Croat-Illyrian).[13] That the latter form of political loyalty was slowly gaining ground became clear in 1832 when the Croatian neo-Štokavian language was accepted as the official language of the Royal Academy of Science in Zagreb.

While the Croats advocated the use of their language, Serb writers too began to argue for the use of vernacular Serbian instead of the Slaveno-Serbian literary language created in the eighteenth century. Works such as the *Serbian Dictionary* by the language reformer Vuk Stefanović Karadžić (1787–1864) are

---

[10]C. Jelavich, *South Slav Nationalisms: Textbooks and Yugoslav Union before 1914* (Columbus, OH, 1990); M-L. Murgescu, *Între 'bunul creştin' şi 'bravul român': rolul şcolii primare în construirea identităţii naţionale româneşti (1831–1878)* (Bucreşti, 2004); and R. Pârâianu, 'The History Textbooks Controversy in Romania: Five Years On', in *Magyar Lettre International*, 58 (2005) (available at http://www.eurozine.com/articles/2005-11-11-paraianu-en.html; accessed 10 January 2007).

[11]Quoted in D. Rihtman-Auguštin, 'The Monument in the City Square: Constructing and Erasing Memory in Contemporary Croatia', in Todorova, *Balkan Identities*, p. 181. See also D. Rihtman-Auguštin and J. Capo Žmegač, *Ethnology, Myth and Politics: Anthropologizing Croatian Ethnology* (Aldershot, 2004).

[12]M. Turda, 'Nation States and Irredentism in the Balkans, 1890–1920', in L. Eriksonas and L. Müller (eds), *Statehood beyond Ethnicity: Trans-national Perspectives onto Smaller States in Europe, c. 1600–2000* (Brussels, 2005), pp. 275–301.

[13]S. B. Kimball, *The Austro-Slav Revival: A Study of Nineteenth Century Literary Foundations* (Philadelphia, 1973).

important in this context. Yet Karadžić was adamant in equating nationality with language rather than religion, thus rejecting the identification of Serbian national identity with Orthodoxy. To him, Serbs, most Croats and Muslims spoke the same language (neo-Štokavian).

Karadžić and Drašković were concerned not only with linguistic rights. The recognition of the right to use the national language was based on a larger agenda which, as in Romania and Serbia, fused the concepts of historical and natural rights. Drašković thus proposed the creation of 'Great Illyria': a political entity consisting of Dalmatia, Bosnia and Croatia which was territorially, culturally and linguistically distinct from the Hungarian state while being part of it economically.[14]

Gradually, however, these literary efforts turned towards supporting the idea of national individuality. The Montenegrin prince-bishop Petar II Petrović Njegoš (1813–51) used the historical battle of Kosovo (1389) to describe the revival of the nation in a period of revolutionary change.[15] Similarly, the Romanian historian Mihail Kogălniceanu (1817–91) combined the political and social agendas of the French Revolution with the Romantic ideals of cultural distinctiveness. Methodologically, Kogălniceanu was influenced by the German historians Alexander von Humboldt (1769–1859) and Leopold von Ranke (1795–1886), as well as the Russian historian Nikolai Karamzin (1766–1826).[16] The latter's *History of the Russian State* (1816–29) provided a model of national history that Kogălniceanu found particularly attractive. Impervious to contemporary critical tendencies in historiography, such as those voiced by Barthold G. Niebuhr (1776–1831) or August L. Schlözer (1735–1809), Karamzin had produced an historical narrative centred on great heroes and popular wisdom as reflected in the medieval Russian chronicles. Similarly, Kogălniceanu believed that national history should glorify the heroic past of the Romanians, which could teach them how to build a prosperous future. He was, however, more critical of historical sources than was Karamzin. The importance of historical origins notwithstanding, the historian should, Kogălniceanu believed, be as interested in finding a balance between respecting 'historical truths' (based on Ranke's call for *wie es eigentlich gewesen*) and his nationalist commitments (favouring one historical narrative over others).[17]

[14]E. M. Despalatović, *Ljudevit Gaj and the Illyrian Movement* (New York, 1975).
[15]A. B. Wachtel, 'How to Use a Classic: Petar Petrović Djegoš in the Twentieth Century', in Lampe and Mazower, *Ideologies and National Identities*, pp. 131–53. See also his *Making a Nation, Breaking a Nation: Literature and Cultural Politics in Yugoslavia* (Stanford, CA, 1998).
[16]J. L. Black, *Nicholas Karamzin and Russian Society in the Nineteenth Century: A Study in Russian Political and Historical Thought* (Toronto, 1975).
[17]B. Jelavich, 'Mihail Kogălniceanu: Historian as Foreign Minister, 1876–8', in D. Deletant and H. Hanak (eds), *Historians as Nation-Builders: Central and South-East Europe* (London, 1988), pp. 87–105.

Prior to Kogălniceanu's call for objectivity in historiography, two perspectives on the origins of the Romanians vied for acceptance. The predominant view of the Romanians' historical origins was represented by the Transylvanian school in Habsburg Transylvania, whose members insisted on the 'pure' Latin origin of the Romanians.[18] A rival perspective emerged in Wallachia and Moldavia at the beginning of the nineteenth century and came to stress the Dacian ancestry of the Romanians. The clerical historian Naum Râmniceanu (1764–1839), for example, argued that, apart from the Romans, the Dacians too played an important part in the Romanian ethnogenesis. He also resurrected the themes of medieval glory described by the Moldavian chronicles of the seventeenth and eighteenth centuries. Situated at the intersection of these directions, Kogălniceanu embraced both, but offered a new approach to understanding them.[19] He contended that the debate about historical origins was not simply about historical sources, but also denoted the basis of social order and the source of national character.

Kogălniceanu was reluctant to credit either the excessive Latinism of some of his contemporaries or the obsessive longing for the medieval glory of the Moldavian and Wallachian ruling princes as advocated by traditionalist epigones such as Râmniceanu. Instead, he offered a third option, based largely on liberal rather than traditionalist nationalism. Kogălniceanu believed in constitutional government and civil liberties, not in autocratic rulers, and posited that the 'people', and not individuals, should be the centre of national history. The 'people' (by which he meant the peasantry and the educated elite representing it) he deemed the source of national consciousness and independence. In this context, the role of the historian was paramount. More than politicians, poets and philosophers, historians could unite the past, present and future of the nation in a totalising narrative: they were, Kogălniceanu continued, those who shaped the destiny of the nation.

Kogălniceanu brought these ideas together in his 'Speech for the Opening of the Course on National History, delivered at the Mihăileanu Academy' in Iaşi in 1840. He aimed to familiarise the Romanian public with contemporary developments in Western European historiography while, at the same time, signalling the necessity of a Romanian contribution to the general developments in European historiography. One major principle guided Kogălniceanu's lecture: if the task of history was to offer guidance for the present and models to emulate in the future, then the study of the past should not be based on nationalist passions but strive to reveal the Rankean quest for 'historical truth'. It was a programmatic

---

[18]A. Armbruster, *Românitatea românilor: istoria unei ideei* (Bucureşti, 1972).
[19]'Naum Râmniceanu: Important Treatise', in Trencsényi and Kopeček, *Discourses*, vol. 1, pp. 324–31.

declaration but difficult to maintain in a century of intense nationalist movements.[20]

The programme of national revival initiated by Kogălniceanu, Karadžić and others conflated several cultural traditions; these authors insisted on the necessity of historical continuity, but also argued for the importance of exploring and adopting new intellectual models. The Romanian historian Nicolae Bălcescu (1819–52) insisted in *The Course of Revolution in the History of the Romanians* (1850) that his fellow Romanians should look to the past as a source of models of civic enlightenment. Like many historians in the Balkans at the time, Bălcescu was a revolutionary and an ideologue, actively involved in politics and contemplating solutions for a nation caught between the high ambitions of its elite and a disillusioned political environment.[21]

In *The Course of Revolution* Bălcescu hoped to offer a critical interpretation of the Romanian revolution of 1848 by creating a genealogy of the idea of the revolution – one whose origins were to be found in the Romanians' heroic past. He was critical of the view that described the revolution in the Danubian principalities and Transylvania as a mere reflection of the revolutions in Paris or Vienna. Instead, Bălcescu argued that the history of the Romanians testified to their revolutionary spirit and love of liberty. By viewing the revolutions in Moldavia, Wallachia and Transylvania as parts of the same European phenomenon he also depicted the history of the Romanians from these different territories as belonging to the same national tradition. The revolution nurtured the national spirit and determined, Bălcescu believed, the special mission the Romanians had to accomplish in the world.[22]

Like Karadžić and Kogălniceanu, Bălcescu's discussion of Romanian national identity was based on the argument that the Romanians had enjoyed sovereignty in the past and had defended it heroically. The medieval princes of Wallachia and Moldavia, especially Michael the Brave (r. 1593–1601), were depicted as glorious defenders of the Romanian revolutionary tradition. According to Bălcescu, the Romanians had passed through various stages of revolutionary activity that corresponded to the internal evolution of Romanian society. He thus termed Tudor Vladimirescu's revolt of 1821 a 'democratic' revolution, as it called for equality and freedom for the Romanians. In 1848 the Romanians revolted over social rights and in favour of economic independence: it was a

---

[20]A. Zub, *Mihail Kogălniceanu istoric* (Iași, 1974).

[21]For the Romanian context, see A. Duțu, *Romanian Humanists and European Culture: A Contribution to Comparative Cultural History* (Bucharest, 1977); and S. Fischer-Galati et al. (eds), *Romania between East and West* (Boulder, CO, 1982).

[22]'N. Bălcescu: The Course of Revolution in the History of the Romanians', in A. Ersoy, M. Górny and V. Kechriotis, *Discourses of Collective Identity in Central and Southeast Europe (1770–1945): Texts and Commentaries*, vol. 3 (Budapest, in press).

'social' revolution. It was only after social and economic rights were achieved that the Romanians could prepare their 'national' revolution. Echoing Kogǎlniceanu's idea of social solidarity, Bǎlcescu urged the Romanians to repeat what history had already shown was possible: the realisation of national unity and a Romanian nation conscious of its identity. Revolution was thus portrayed as both a progressive force and a repository of traditions. It was thus the historical subject that defined the particular conditions of the Romanians – their glorious history, their constant struggle against the foreign oppressor and their love of freedom – along with the universal aspiration for liberty and fraternity among nations.[23]

Yet this message of revolutionary 'brotherly love' did not suppress the expression of ethnic and religious individuality, according to which each nation construed its own history. Liberal historians and politicians in Romania, Bulgaria or Serbia advocated the creation of modern forms of national allegiances based on patriotism and loyalty to the state, while simultaneously accentuating the role of ethnicity and language in shaping national character. Bulgarian nationalists, for instance, used this strategy to counteract Greek territorial ambitions legitimised on religious grounds. Even the idea of a 'pure and sacred republic' advocated by the Bulgarian national hero Vassil Levski (1837–73) promoted the spread of both 'democracy' and nationalist irredentism, that is, the unification of all territories where 'the Bulgarians live – Bulgaria, Thrace and Macedonia'.[24]

Couched in a revolutionary rhetoric, a similar irredentist agenda was proposed by the Serbian politician Svetozar Miletić (1826–1901) in his 'The Eastern Question' (1863). By rising against the Ottoman empire, the Balkan nations (he referred in particular to the Serbs, the Bulgarians, the Romanians and the Greeks) would not only bring Turkish rule to an end, but also create the conditions for a 'Balkan confederation' comprising independent nation-states.[25] However, considering the predominantly rural character of their societies, political elites in the Balkans were caught in a dual discourse (social emancipation for the peasantry and political development). This is what Diana Mishkova described as the 'anomaly of Balkan liberalism' in Serbia, Bulgaria and Romania: 'In each of these countries the apparent challenge to any modernising elite would have been its ability to devise means to energise an immobile, largely traditional rural

---

[23]B. Werner, *Nicolae Bǎlcescu (1819–1852): ein rumänischer revolutionärer Demokrat im Kampf für soziale und nationale Befreiung* (Berlin, 1970).

[24]A. Izvorska, 'Varying Concepts of Bulgarianhood and Their Reflection on the Perception of Ethnic Minorities in Bulgaria', in S. G. Markovich et al. (eds), *Problems of Identity in the Balkans* (Belgrade, 2006), p. 143. See also N. Genchev, *The Bulgarian National Revival Period* (Sofia, 1977); C. Riis, *Religion, Politics, and Historiography in Bulgaria* (Boulder, CO, 2002); and E. Gellner, 'Ethnicity and Faith in Eastern Europe', in S. R. Graubard (ed.), *Eastern Europe … Central Europe … Europe* (Boulder, CO, 1991), pp. 267–82.

[25]'S. Miletić: The Eastern Question', in Ersoy et al., *Discourses*, vol. 3.

society that almost totally lacked the ferments of modern capitalism and democracy.'[26] In addition to ideas of historical continuity and pre-eminence, historiography was now harnessed to a social mission: to awaken the majority of the population, the peasantry, from the 'slumber of centuries of oppression' and transform it into an active force.[27]

The speech that the Serbian politician Pera Todorović (1852–1907) delivered to the Assembly of the People's Radical Party in Kragujevac in 1870 depicted the peasantry as an active social class and political force, and not merely the repository of national traditions. This strategy became even more explicit in the writings of the Bulgarian revolutionary poet Hristo Botev (1848–76), who envisaged in his 'The People (Yesterday, Today and Tomorrow)' (1871) the national revolution in both national and social terms. The Bulgarian *chorbadzhiis* and clergy were encouraged to work with the 'noble peasant' – seen as innocent, moral by nature and uncorrupted by civilisation. Like Bălcescu, Botev opted for the organicity of the nation: its spirit was not assimilated during the 'Ottoman period' because of the peasants' inherent resistance to imposed foreign institutions.[28]

Paralleling the emergence of the peasantry as a category of social analysis was the debate on 'natural and artificial paths of development', a conceptual dispute characterising all historiographical narratives in the Balkans. Not surprisingly, these concerted reflections on cultural, political, social and economic backwardness provided a particular environment for competing political and cultural theories.[29] The idea that the nation resides within the peasantry enabled historians in the Balkans to attempt to integrate the traditional rural civilisation in the long-term project of their countries' institutional and political modernisation. Ultimately, the peasantry's transformation from an element surviving at the margins of national narratives to a central historiographical trope served as a principle not only for the nascent political liberalism, but also for the formulation of nationalist and populist doctrines.[30]

In his 'Nationality' (1853) the Romanian liberal politician Ion C. Brătianu (1821–91) insisted that the two principles of nationalism and liberalism are complementary. Indeed, such a view was common among revolutionaries throughout Europe. It was Giuseppe Mazzini (1805–72), a leading figure of European

[26]D. Mishkova, 'The Interesting Anomaly of Balkan Liberalism', in I. Z. Dénes (ed.), *Liberty and the Search for Identity: Liberal Nationalisms and the Legacy of Empires* (Budapest, 2006), p. 401.
[27]Glenny, *Balkans*, pp. 1–69.
[28]S. Dimitrov, *La Vie et l'œuvre de Hristo Botev* (Grenoble, 1941).
[29]More recently this has been analysed by M. Todorova, 'The Trap of Backwardness: Modernity, Temporality, and the Study of Eastern European Nationalism', *Slavic Review*, 61/1 (2005), 140–64.
[30]M. Bucur (ed.), *Jules Michelet și revoluționarii români în documente și scrisori de epocă* (1846–1974), (Cluj-Napoca, 1982).

liberal nationalism, who in his 'On Nationality' (1852) described the principle
of nationality as one of the formative forces of the modern world, composed of
natural elements such as language and ethnic origin, and moulded into the consciousness of the people by education. This theory of the nation was based on
the assumption that ethnic groups were intrinsic parts of nature and hence combined two traditions: the Romantic idea of national individuality and the liberal
notions of individual equality and universal unity.[31]

The liberal theory of the nation in the Balkans derived from French and Italian
nationalism.[32] Brătianu and others combined Michelet's and Mazzini's views on
the natural tendency of individuals to associate in larger groups (family, tribe
and nation) according to their interests and physical needs, with Romantic ideas
about immutable ethnic characteristics.[33] The rights of the nation derived,
Brătianu claimed, from the rights of men which were by definition individual
and universal. But these rights were also the creation of nature, and as such
were governed by natural laws, including the need for territory or expansion.

One could find such definitions of the nation in other Balkan countries as
well. In 1844 the Serbian minister of the interior, Ilija Garašanin (1812–74),
outlined the territorial ambitions of the Serbian state in 'Načertanije' ('The
Draft').[34] Influenced by ideas of Slavic unity as advocated by Polish and Czech
revolutionaries in exile (some of whom found hospitality in Serbia), Garašanin
envisaged the construction of a 'Greater Serbia' to serve as a catalyst for the
unification of the Slavs in the Balkans:

> If Serbia considers thoroughly what she is at the moment, what her pos-
> ition is and what the nature of the nation surrounding her is, she will
> invariably arrive at the conclusion that she is still very small, and that she
> cannot remain thus. Only in alliance with her neighbouring nations can
> she ensure a future for herself; and this must be her sole task.[35]

When Garašanin expanded the symbolic boundaries of the Serb nation to
include other Slavs he was glorifying the idea of a common past and initiated
a programme of national rejuvenation based on historical continuity.[36]

Restoring medieval empires excited the imagination of a range of Balkan
politicians. Others went further and claimed a direct territorial continuity

---

[31]B. Valota, 'Giuseppe Mazzini's "Geopolitics of Liberty" and Italian Foreign Policy
toward "Slavic Europe"', *East European Quarterly*, 37/2 (2003), 151–6. See also P. Alter,
Nationalism (London, 1994).
[32]*I. I. Brătianu (1821–1891): A Biographical Sketch* (București, 1893).
[33]M. Viroli, *For Love of Country: An Essay on Patriotism and Nationalism* (Oxford, 1995).
[34]D. MacKenzie, *Ilija Garašanin: Balkan Bismarck* (Boulder, CO, 1985).
[35]'Ilija Garašanin: The Draft', in Trencsényi and Kopeček, *Discourses*, vol. 2, p. 239.
[36]I. Banac, *The National Question in Yugoslavia: Origins, History, Politics* (Ithaca, NY, 1984).

between ancient empires and modern nation-states. The period 1870–1920 is particularly illustrative. In Romania, for example, the theory of historical continuity was paramount in the articulation of a Romanian national consciousness common to all Romanians – both from within and outside Romania. In the early 1870s the historian Bogdan P. Haşdeu (1838–1907) published *The Critical History of the Romanians*,[37] a book heavily criticised by the historian Gheorghe Panu (1848–1910) for its lack of respect for historical sources.[38] According to Lucian Boia, Haşdeu was 'an autodidact with an immense body of knowledge', but 'with fantastic inclinations and a tendency towards the most unexpected intellectual constructions'.[39] Despite his distortion of historical sources, Haşdeu was nevertheless an active supporter of the idea of a Romanian political and historical continuity from ancient to modern times. Even the most important representative of the 'critical school of historiography' in late nineteenth-century Romania, A. D. Xenopol (1847–1920), was equally preoccupied with the idea of historical continuity, as is illustrated by his six-volume *The History of Romanians from Trajan Dacia*.[40]

Reflecting on historiography's development during this period, Boia noted: 'Nationalism was now expressed in more reasonable and subtle historiographical forms, and with varying intensity from one historian to another and from one phase to another.'[41] In Romania it was the historian Nicolae Iorga (1871–1940) who most successfully provided Romanian nationalism with the essential notions of historical continuity and cultural unity. This iconic figure of Romanian national historiography created and cultivated narratives of origins from which Romanian 'imagined communities' extracted their sentiment of national belonging and affiliation.[42]

The period between 1914 and 1918 was an important phase in the development of new historiographical narratives in the Balkans. In his *Histoire des Roumains de Transylvanie et de Hongrie* (1915) Iorga, for example, constructed a direct lineage between the Roman colonists of Dacia and modern Romanians,

---

[37]B.B. Haşdeu, *Istoria critică a românilor* (Bucureşti, 1984).

[38] See G. Panu, 'Studiul istoriei la romani', in E. Lovinescu (ed.), *Antologia ideologiei junimiste* (Bucureşti, 1943), pp. 283–398.

[39]Boia, *History and Myth*, p. 52.

[40]A.D. Xenopol, *Istoria românilor din Dacia Traiană* (originally published between 1888 and 1893). See also P. A. Hiemstra, *Alexandru D. Xenopol and the Development of Romanian Historiography* (New York, 1987).

[41]Boia, *History and Myth*, p. 64.

[42]B. Anderson, *Imagined Communities: Reflections on the Origin and Spread of Nationalism*, rev. edn (London, 2006). See also T. Baycroft and M. Hewitson (eds), *What Is a Nation? Europe 1789–1914* (Oxford, 2006).

from both the Kingdom of Romania and Transylvania.[43] These attempts to prove historical continuity produced a new ethno-political and historical legitimacy. Transylvania was Romanian, Iorga argued, not only because the majority of the population was Romanian, but also because its soul and spirit were Romanian.[44] Like many historians in the Balkans, Iorga was also actively involved in politics. Indeed, he considered the political arena the ideal place to test historical concepts. As Maurice Pearton observed, '[Iorga's] involvement in Romanian politics stemmed directly from his view of history – and that in two related senses: history offers lessons and authorises action; action was imperative, in the Romanian case, to unify and free Romanian culture by giving it political expression, and to maintain the identity achieved.'[45]

A similar position was enjoyed in Serbia by Stojan Novaković (1842–1915), the 'patriarch of modern Serbian historiography'.[46] Like Iorga, Novaković excelled in numerous historical disciplines, including historical geography, heraldics and numismatics. He was particularly interested in the history of the Middle Ages and the nineteenth century. Both periods were seen as paradigmatic for the evolution of Serbian history: the first witnessed the collapse of the Serbian state and its incorporation in the Ottoman empire; the second, its modern revival. Notwithstanding the glorification of the past, Novaković insisted, the ambition of the new Serbian state should be to strengthen its vision of the future. 'The need for our century', he remarked, 'is not to revive what was left from [the Middle Ages]. We have to look today at the past only to learn from our own mistakes and not to repeat them.'[47]

Such dispassionate statements were, however, not meant to sever the connections with the past. In a diverse ethnic, religious and linguistic environment such as the Balkans, the theory of historical rights and historical continuity became a dominant historiographical narrative, which demonstrated the continuity of the nation and its intimate relationship with the territory it occupied (or should have occupied).[48] As scholars of nationalism argue, national identities are

---

[43]See W. Oldson, *The Historical and Nationalistic Thought of Nicolae Iorga* (Boulder, CO, 1973); N. M. Nagy-Talavera, *Nicolae Iorga: A Biography* (Iaşi, 1998); and A. Miskolczy, 'Nicolae Iorga's Conception of Transylvanian Romanian History in 1915', in L. Péter (ed.), *Historians and the History of Transylvania* (Boulder, CO, 1992), pp. 129–65.

[44]N. Iorga, *Desvoltarea ideii unităţii politice a Românilor* (Bucureşti, 1915).

[45]M. Pearton, 'Nicolae Iorga as Historian and Politician', in Deletant and Hanak, *Historians as Nation-Builders*, p. 170.

[46]D. Djordjević, 'Stojan Novaković: Historian, Politician, Diplomat', in D. Deletant and H. Hanak (eds), *Historians as Nation-Builders: Central and South-East Europe* (London, 1988), p. 51.

[47]Quoted in Djordjević, 'Stojan Novaković', p. 66.

[48]N. Iorga, *Histoire des Roumains des Balcans* (Bucarest, 1919).

construed to distinguish a collective identity from that which resides outside.[49] Likewise, Romanian, Bulgarian, Serbian and Croat national identities were defined against Others, a defensive strategy that was vigorously promoted as a unifying national principle.[50]

In his 1918 *Book for the Bulgarians*, Anton Strashimirov (1872–1937) aimed to devise a more encompassing theory of national character in order to integrate different historical traditions. He thus established an inclusive relationship between an ideal-type Bulgarian nation and the regional specificity of the Bulgarians.[51] In fact, it was this relationship which enabled the theory of historical continuity to integrate additional features such as irredentism, and thus create an auspicious environment for competing territorial claims to emerge. And historiography was a discipline engaged in this process. In addition to ethnography and *Völkerpsychologie*, historiography provided Bulgarian nationalism with sufficient arguments to lay nationalist claims on territories outside Bulgaria, such as Macedonia.[52] Bulgarian nationalists argued that all Slav-speakers in Macedonia were 'Bulgarians'.[53] While definitions of nationality proposed by Greek nationalists combined religion with the influence the ecumenical Orthodox patriarchate had over the Christian population in Macedonia for centuries, Bulgarian writers have stressed language as the visible marker on which Bulgarian national and ecclesiastical autonomy from the ecumenical patriarchate was based in 1870.[54]

Ultimately the theory of historical rights and historical continuity morphed into narratives of exclusion and historical destiny, as explored by the Serbian historian Ilarion Ruvarac (1832–1905) in his 1888 *On Prince Lazar*. Like other conceptualisations of heroism and martyrdom, Ruvarac assigned a prominent discursive role to the tropes of bravery, betrayal and sacrifice.[55] Although oral poetry and folk legends were still considered crucial historical sources in Serbia,[56] Ruvarac insisted on a rigorous inventory of historical

---

[49]For the classical discussion of this aspect, see F. Barth (ed.), *Ethnic Groups and Boundaries: The Social Organization of Culture Difference* (Oslo and London, 1969), pp. 9–38.

[50] H. Michael, *Ours Once More: Folklore, Ideology and the Making of Modern Greece* (Austin, 1982); and S. Mitu, *National Identity of Romanians in Transylvania* (Budapest, 2001).

[51]S. Popov, *Anton Strashimirov* (Sofia, 1987).

[52]M. Todorova, 'Self-Image and Ethnic Stereotypes in Bulgaria', *Modern Greek Studies Yearbook*, 8 (1992), 139–63.

[53]R.J. Crampton, *Bulgaria, 1878–1918: A History* (New York, 1983).

[54]R. von Mach, *The Bulgarian Exarchate: Its History and the Extent of its Authority in Turkey* (London, 1907).

[55]See H. White, *Metahistory: The Historical Imagination in Nineteenth-Century Europe* (Baltimore, MD and London, 1974).

[56]M. A. Mügge, *Serbian Folk Songs: Fairy Tales and Proverbs* (London, 1916).

sources. Like Kogălniceanu, Ruvarac argued that the historian's ultimate goal must be the formulation of 'historical truth'. He consequently challenged the romantic glorification of a distant medieval past and insisted on objective knowledge and the use of proper historical sources.[57]

Ideas of 'historical rights' and 'historical continuity' became the defining conditions of all forms of historiographical narratives in the Balkans. Their canonisation over two centuries has tended to render them ubiquitous: they have come to encapsulate the very essence of each national tradition, rather than the outcome of constructed traditions of historiographical representation. Not surprisingly, it has become difficult to distinguish between historical concepts and the idea of national history in the Balkans.

Gender, class and historical representation

During the nineteenth and twentieth centuries, historiographies in the Balkans heavily employed notions of national peculiarity to highlight the cultural and political differences between their national traditions and those underlying Western European patterns.[58] However, such claims of separate historical development were rarely endorsed by historiography in their entirety.[59] One example worth considering is the relationship between gender and nationalism, as gendered historiographical narratives provide a good illustration of the emergence of a new historical genre defined by its struggle with master narratives of the nation.[60] The preference for feminine representations of the nation was, at one level, a matter of narrative technique; at another, its purpose was to incorporate emotional and ideological dimensions.

Nations are frequently conceived of as female entities, as Benedict Anderson's widely accepted idea of the nation as an imagined community indicates. Thus, national communities often rely on the gender recognition of identity and the interchange of power between men and women.[61] Starting with the mid-nineteenth century, women were transformed historiographically, evidenced in processes such as the feminisation of the land and the nation.

---

[57]'Ilarion Ruvarac: On Prince Lazar', in Ersoy et al., *Discourses*, vol. 3.
[58]D. Chirot (ed.), *The Origins of Backwardness in Eastern Europe: Economics and Politics from the Middle Ages until the Early Twentieth Century* (Berkeley, CA, 1991).
[59]D. Mishkova, 'The Uses of Tradition and National Identity in the Balkans', in Todorova, *Balkan Identities*, pp. 269–93.
[60]G. Mosse, *The Image of Man: The Creation of Modern Masculinity* (New York, 1996).
[61]J. Edmunds, 'Redefining Britannia: The Role of "Marginal" Generations in Reshaping British National Consciousness', in H. Brocklehurst and R. Philips (eds), *History, Nationhood and the Question of Britannia* (Basingstoke, 2004), pp. 73–84.

According to Nira Yuval-Davis and Floya Anthias, women have participated in nationalist processes:

> (a) as biological reproducers of members of ethnic collectivities; (b) as reproducers of the boundaries of ethnic/national groups; (c) as participating centrally in the ideological reproduction of the collectivity and as transmitters of its culture; (d) as signifiers of ethnic/national difference – as a focus and symbol in ideological discourses used in the construction, reproduction, and transformation of ethnic/national categories; (e) as participants in national, economic, political and military struggles [62]

Gendering national historiographies in the Balkans encapsulated all these categories of nationalist identification.

The various revolutions and wars of independence fought in the nineteenth century fused feminine symbols with Romantic conceptions of the nation. Women were seen as mothers and educators, fulfilling both a biological and a patriotic obligation. Needless to say, the majority of those authors portraying the nation in feminine terms were men. Thus the historian Nicolae Bălcescu devoted considerable attention to women in his programmes for the social and moral revival of the Romanians. As long as women, whether in the confined space of their homes or in public spaces, were aware of their national mission, their role was deemed paramount in the revolutionary imaginary of the period.[63] The poet Alecu Russo (1819–59), for example, depicted Romania as an ancient goddess. Since the revolution of 1789, female revolutionary symbols stood for numerous qualities and virtues. It was the French historian Jules Michelet (1798–1874) who, in his 1854 *Les Légendes démocratiques du nord* (an account of Russia, the Polish lands and the Danubian principalities), portrayed 'Romania' as a delicate yet determined woman escaping the despotic oppression of the Turks. At the same time, 'Romania' was described as a country peopled by a sturdy peasantry embodying the democratic virtues of the land. Michelet had never visited Romania, but he provided his disciples such as Alecu Russo with an intellectual and political model for constructing a gendered version of Romanian identity, which the latter developed fully in 'The Song of Romania' (1850).[64]

---

[62] In N. Yuval-Davis and F. Anthias, 'Introduction' to idem (eds), *Woman–Nation–State* (New York, 1989), p. 7.

[63] R. M. Popa, 'Dimensiuni ale patriarhatului în gândirea liberală *românească* între 1848 și al Doilea Război Mondial', in M. Bucur and M. Miroiu (eds), *Patriarhat și emancipare în istoria gândirii politice românești* (Iași, 2002), pp. 25–71.

[64] T. Vârcolici, *Alecu Russo* (București, 1964). See also A. Ciupală (ed.), *Despre femei și istoria lor în România* (București, 2004).

Similarly, Draga Dejanović's 'To Serbian Mothers' (1871) demonstrates the significance of locating gender in the definition of the national community. An actress and politician, Dejanović (1840–71) argued that the duty of Serbian mothers was to foster a deep allegiance to the nation and instil it in future generations. The text thus revealed the ways in which gender was inherent to national identity, delineating how nationalism often relied on the subordination of women to men and the gendered division between public and private spheres. Illustrating historical events through the eyes of women, Dejanović did not simply include women in the Serbian national narrative, but rather, by demonstrating how gender roles shaped constructions of national community, she articulated the ways in which the definitions of the nation should be widened to include both men and women.[65]

During the nineteenth century these gendered narratives of the nation were, however, atypical. The predominant view remained the traditionalist, 'patriarchal' one: women were considered objects of adoration, completely subject to their 'irrational nature'; hence their presence in politics and public affairs was not welcome. Even the liberal Mihail Kogălniceanu agreed, and he was not the only progressive Romanian intellectual to deny women intellectual abilities.[66] The most celebrated literary critic of the period, Titu Maiorescu (1840–1917), also questioned women's role in culture and politics.[67] It was this stereotypical characterisation of women that nationalist activists, such as the Serbian Draga Dejanović or the Croat Dragojla Jarnević (1812–75), sought to repudiate through involving women in the national movement and domestic politics.[68]

It was as a consequence of dramatic historical events – the First World War – that this representation of women was challenged. With regard to Romania, Maria Bucur argues that:

gendered images of heroism and virtue played a more public role between 1914 and 1918 than during any previous crisis, rendering women's position in society an issue of broad public concern for the first time. In this process, notions of patriotism, heroism, and virtue came to reinforce and encode gender divisions in a more well-defined public debate than ever

[65]'Draga Dejanović, 'To Serbian Mothers', in Ersoy et al., *Discourses*, vol. 3.
[66]Popa, 'Dimensiuni ale patriarhatului', pp. 55–60.
[67]Ş. Mihăilescu, 'Xenopol, Adela', in F. de Haan, K. Daskalova, and A. Loufti (eds), *A Biographical Dictionary of Women's Movements and Feminisms: Central, Eastern, and South Eastern Europe, 19th and 20th Centuries* (Budapest, 2006), p. 613. See also Ş. Mihăilescu, *Din istoria feminismului românesc: antologie de texte (1838–1929)* (Iaşi, 2002).
[68]I. Pantelić, 'Dejanović, Draga', and S. Prlenda, 'Jarnević, Dragojla', in de Haan et al., *Biographical Dictionary*, pp. 106–7 and 185–8, respectively.

before, as both policy makers and publicists sought to construct agency as a male prerogative.[69]

The two heroines analysed by Bucur – Queen Marie of Romania (1875–1938) and Ecaterina Teodoroiu (1894–1917) – occupied (albeit briefly) the domain of historiographical representation, a field hitherto populated by male heroes. Unfortunately, the social and political conditions of women did not improve just because the revolutionary imaginary needed them. Other conditions were required, and Romanian women, as elsewhere in the Balkans, would have to wait until after the First World War for their political emancipation.[70]

In addition to gender, another concept that challenged the master narratives on the nation in the Balkans was class. In his 1872 *Serbia in the East*, Svetozar Marković (1846–75), the founder of the socialist movement in Serbia, offered a vision of a radically changed social and political organisation for Serbia in the context of the liberated Balkan countries, and in accordance with the principles of *narodnik* (populist) socialism.[71] The Romanian social theorists Constantin Dobrogeanu-Gherea (1855–1920) and Constantin Stere (1865–1936) supported a similar programme. Moreover, in 1907 Romania was torn apart by a violent peasant revolt. Its origins, how it manifested itself and, most importantly, its brutal crushing by the government called into question the content and direction of Romania's political and cultural development.[72] One of the first cultural responses to this new situation was a political current known as 'poporanism' (from *popor*, people). Although it was a derivation of the Russian *narodnichestvo*, its adherents (particularly Constantin Stere) refused to identify with Russian populism, claiming that poporanism was the result of Romanian conditions alone.[73]

---

[69]M. Bucur, 'Between the Mother of the Wounded and the Virgin of Jiu: Romanian Women and the Gender of Heroism during the Great War', *Journal of Women's History*, 12/2 (2000), 31. See also N. M. Wingfield and M. Bucur (eds), *Gender and War in Twentieth-Century Eastern Europe* (Bloomington, IN, 2006).

[70]A. Gr. Cantacuzino, *Rostul femeii în viața politică* (București, 1924).

[71]W. D. McClellan, *Svetozar Markovic and the Origin of Balkan Socialism* (Princeton, 1964); G. Ionescu and E. Gellner (eds), *Populism: Its Meaning and National Characteristics* (London, 1969); J. Schmidt, *Populismus oder Marxismus: zur Ideengeschichte der radikalen Intelligenz Rumäniens, 1875–1915* (Tübingen, 1992); and V. Pinto, 'The Civic and Aesthetic Ideals of the Bulgarian *Narodnik* Writers', *Slavonic and East European Review*, 32/74 (1954), 344–66.

[72]P. G. Eidelberg, *The Great Rumanian Peasant Revolt of 1907: Origins of a Modern Jaquerie* (Leiden, 1974).

[73]M. Kitch, 'Constantin Stere and Romanian Populism', *Slavonic and East European Review*, 53/131 (1975), 248–71; Z. Ornea, *Poporanismul* (București, 1972); and V. Ciobanu, *Poporanismul: geneză, evoluție, ideologie* (București, 1946).

Romanian poporanism had basic assumptions about the character of Romanian society in common with similar movements in the Balkans. These included the praise of rural communities, organicism and limited state intervention. Furthermore, the populists argued that the rural character of the Balkans should be preserved, and modernisation should reflect, first and foremost, the peasantry's economic and social progress.[74] These authors did not necessarily advocate the transformation of the peasantry in general, but specifically supported the improvement of small and medium-sized peasant property. In other words, their main concern was the creation of a middle class between the peasantry and urban bourgeoisie; for Gherea, moreover, it was just as important to establish a specific economic 'path', which he fully explored in *Neo-Serfdom* (1910).[75]

Symbolic geography and patterns of development

Many of these social and intellectual debates about gender and class surfaced after the territorial changes following the end of the First World War, when historians in the Balkans realised that the new political context required corresponding cultural and social projects. Take Romania. With the incorporation of Transylvania, Bukovina and Bessarabia, Romania acquired a significant number of ethnic minorities (28 per cent of the total population in 1921), which not only changed Romanians' self-perception as the majority, but also challenged their social and economic status. In Transylvania, furthermore, one finds that Hungarians and Germans not only were largely urbanised, but at least until 1920, they occupied central positions in the administrative and economic sectors. Successive Romanian governments during the interwar period attempted to redress this situation and create a strong Romanian urban class. The brand of nationalisation involved elites and cultural institutions from Bucharest, united in their attempts to offer new cultural and national identity projects to all Romanians.[76]

These projects did not go unchallenged. Many traditionalist authors viewed urbanisation as a social mechanism aimed at destroying the peasantry. In opposition to the poporanists, traditionalists viewed the peasantry as a fixed constant whose function was to provide national history with a sense of continuity. The

---

[74]R. Daskalov, 'Ideas about, and Reactions to Modernization in the Balkans', *East European Quarterly*, 31/2 (1997), 141–80, and his *The Making of a Nation in the Balkans: Historiography of the Bulgarian Revival* (Budapest, 2004).
[75]C. D. Gherea, 'Neoiobăgia', in *Opere complete*, vol. 4 (Bucureşti, 1977); and M. Schafir, '"Romania's Marx" and the National Question: Constantin Dobrogeanu-Gherea', *History of Political Thought*, 5/2 (1984), 295–314.
[76]J. Rothschild, *East Central Europe between the Two World Wars* (Seattle, 1974); I. Livezeanu, *Cultural Politics in Greater Romania: Regionalism, Nation Building and Ethnic Struggle, 1918–1930* (Ithaca, NY, 1995).

nation's ongoing existence was not guaranteed by a democratic society with a politically active peasantry, but by an ethnic state dominated by national elites. This historiographical mythopoeia consisted of two complementary models, one in which the peasantry was the soul of the nation and another in which a cultural and religious elite fused universalism with nationalist projects. Interestingly, the conflation of these models was attempted in a return to historical tropes associated with medieval glory, especially the Byzantine legacy; for it was assumed that it was in the Byzantine autocracy that ruling elites were connected to the core of European civilisation and lived in perfect harmony with their subject peasantry.

In Romania, Nicolae Iorga was particularly interested in reviving the continuities between the Byzantine empire and the Romanian principalities of the Middle Ages, which he considered to be the defenders of Orthodoxy after the fall of Constantinople in 1453. Iorga deliberately constructed an image of Byzantium that served Romanian national interests: a strategy devised to distinguish the Romanian principalities from other Orthodox contenders in the Balkans which were under direct Ottoman occupation, such as the Bulgarians, the Greeks and the Serbs.[77]

A more nuanced interpretation was provided by two of the most influential Bulgarian historians of the interwar period, Nayden Sheytanov (1890–1970) and Petar Mutafchiev (1883–1943). According to them, Bulgarian culture faced an ontological crisis due to the corrosive effects of modernity and westernisation. Mutafchiev, for instance, argued that the causes for this crisis should be found in the 'spirit of Byzantium', which profoundly marked the evolution of Bulgarian culture from early medieval times and which, more than any other factor, created the existing cultural and social cleavages in Bulgarian society.[78]

This glorification of medieval Byzantium in Romania and Bulgaria served several purposes. Projecting the nation into the past provided a refutation of Eurocentric representations of Balkan modernity as 'backward'. Iorga did not subscribe to the view that cultural values moved from the (western) centre of modernity to its 'developing' (eastern) margins, but argued that Romanians, in particular, were the bastion of European civilisation in the East. This historiographical strategy, in fact, masked the cultural difficulties facing intellectuals

---

[77]N. Iorga, *Byzance après Byzance* (Bucarest, 1935). See also S. Antohi, 'Romania and the Balkans: From Geocultural Bovarism to Ethnic Ontology', *Tr@nsit Online*, 21 (2002) (accessed 16 November 2006); and A. Pippidi, 'Changes of Emphasis: Greek Christendom, Westernization, South-Eastern Europe, and Neo-Mitteleuropa', *Balkanologie*, 3/2 (1999), 93–106.

[78]'Nayden Sheytanov: Bulgarian Worldview' and 'Petar Mutafchiev: Towards the Philosophy of Bulgarian History. Byzantinism in Medieval Bulgaria', in M. Turda and D. Mishova (eds), *Discourses of Collective Identity in Central and Southeast Europe (1770–1945)*, vol. 4 (Budapest, in press).

in the Balkans when they related to Europe's symbolic geography.[79] A radical alternative was offered in Yugoslavia by the poet and essayist Ljubomir Micić (1895–1971), who argued for a 'rejuvenation of old Europe by Barbarian young forces', in an attempt to 'Balkanise Europe, that is, to reverse European cultural domination and to infuse the West with Balkan spirit'.[80]

Other theoretical conceptualisations aspired to grasp the historical interdependence between the Balkans and the West 'without either collapsing particular differences into a dubious universalism or celebrating particularisms for their own sake'.[81] In Romania the literary critic Eugen Lovinescu (1881–1943) outlined in *The History of Modern Romanian Civilization* (1924–5) a 'third way' between the 'Europeanists' and the 'traditionalists'. If the former considered Romanian culture as part of a larger European context, the latter suggested that Romania was a peasant country, whose model of development should be based on its unique rural cultural heritage. Like other 'modernists', Lovinescu also considered that modern Romanian civilisation began in the first half of the nineteenth century, with the 1848 generation. This generation undertook the enormous task of importing Western institutions and creating a modern Romanian state. Nevertheless, imitation was not pursued uncritically, but generated a new attitude towards modernisation, a condition Lovinescu named 'synchronism' – a fusion between Western ideas and Romanian conditions.

Lovinescu based his synchronic model on seven laws (or phases). At first, Romanian elites considered total imitation as the main means of introducing Western ideas into Romanian culture. This imitation occurred without Romanians questioning the nature of what they were adopting. The imitation, according to the second law, was integral. However, in the third phase, as imitation continued, a critical spirit emerged. This critical attitude did not oppose imitation as – according to Lovinescu's fourth law – a nation's originality was based not only on autochthonous resourcefulness, but also on the adaptation of imported ideas. Ultimately, any imitation took a synchronic, national form, as the fifth law stipulated.

But since cultural values could not be uniformly reduced to a set of observable principles, they could not be copied directly, but only highlighted indirectly through examples of intellectual achievements. It follows that representations of European values could not be reduced to mere imitation and that the superficial modernisation of Romania did not suffice to create a European country. It was at

---

[80]E. Levinger, 'Ljubomir Micić and the Zenitist Utopia', in T. O. Benson (ed.), *Central European Avant-Gardes: Exchange and Transformation, 1910–1930* (Cambridge, MA, 2002), p. 260. See also T. Miller, 'Incomplete Modernities: Historicizing Yugoslav Avant-Gardes', *Modernism/Modernity*, 12, 4 (2005), 713–22.

[81]M. Ahiska, 'Occidentalism: The Historical Phantasy of the Modern', *South Atlantic Quarterly*, 102, 2–3 (2003), 364.

this point that Lovinescu offered the most important detail of his theory, the sixth law: imitation was not confined to the present; it must be projected into the past as well. By doing so, Lovinescu denied both the aura of cultural superiority attached to Romanian medieval history by Iorga and other traditionalists, and the idea of an eternal peasant culture advocated by the poporanists. For him, traditional ideas were 'sociologically impossible'. Interestingly, the point of formulating such a devastating critique of Romanian cultural discourses was not to reject the idea of historical change. On the contrary, according to the seventh law, it was precisely this lack of a 'glorious cultural past' that made possible the creation of a modern Romanian civilisation.[82]

Lovinescu's ideas about the necessity of a new national narrative also influenced historiography. Gheorghe I. Brătianu (1898–1953), author of *La Mer Noire* (1949),[83] Petre P. Panaitescu (1900–67) and Constantin C. Giurescu (1901–77) were three prominent historians advocating a return to objectivity and comparative history. As early as 1931 they founded a new historical periodical, the *Romanian Historical Journal*, in which they argued for the primacy of historical methodology over political and nationalist allegiances: 'History should not be shifted onto the level of political and social struggles.' And further, 'Between patriotism and objectivity there is no antinomy.'[84] By rejecting previous historiographical narratives and the artificial disjuncture between synchronic (European culture) and diachronic (Romanian past) approaches, this new trend in Romanian historiography treated history as a perpetually evolving entity. National history was thus in need of a new epistemological paradigm, and some historians in the Balkans (Brătianu, for example), recognised it in the totalising historical framework advocated by the French historians Lucien Febvre (1878–1956) and Marc Bloch (1886–1944).

However, this was an interpretation which existed at the margins of the mainstream historiographical field. With the emergence of authoritarian regimes in Romania and Bulgaria, as well as the success of fascist movements, especially the Iron Guard and the Ustaša in Romania and Croatia respectively, various nationalist and racist interpretations of the past became widespread in the late 1930s. Fascists throughout the Balkans claimed to represent the 'true' nation and the authority of the state; they were anti-liberal, anti-democratic and anti-Semitic. The Legionary and the Ustaša movements portrayed their coming into existence

---

[82]E. Lovinescu, *Istoria civilizației române moderne* (București, 1924–5); and V. Nemoianu, 'Variable Sociopolitical Functions of Aesthetic Doctrine: Lovinescu vs. Western Aestheticism', in K. Jowith (ed.), *Social Change in Romania: A Debate on Development in a European Nation* (Berkeley, 1978), pp. 174–207.

[83]Gh. I. Brătianu, *La Mer Noire: des origines à la conquête ottomane* (Monachi, 1969).

[84]Quoted in Boia, *History and Myth*, p. 67. See also Al. Zub, *Istorie și istorici în România interbelică* (Iași, 1989).

as the culmination and vindication of Romanian and Croatian history: they signified the renewal of Romania's and Croatia's primacy in the world as creative nations.[85] Because both movements claimed to represent the nation, it was important to prove its descent from glorious historical moments in the Romanian and Croatian past. Moreover, as its propagandists proclaimed self-consciously, Legionary and Ustaša nationalisms would regenerate Romanian and Croat nations and based them on two new principles, one ethnic, the other religious. According to the first, a new definition of the nation was proposed, one that placed emphasis on racial characteristics and their connection to specific mechanisms of national identification.[86]

The equation of Romanian-ness with Orthodoxy and of Croat-ness with Catholicism was another central facet of the fascist regenerative project for the nation.[87] As Mark Biondich pointed out in his study of the Catholic Church in the Independent State of Croatia (1941–5):

> Many Catholic intellectuals in Croatia claimed that the Orthodox of Croatia and Bosnia-Herzegovina were not Serbs at all. Rather, they were for the most part regarded as 'Croats' who had adopted a Serb consciousness in the nineteenth century because of their religious affiliation and the 'nationalising' work of the Serbian Orthodox Church.[88]

Yet the fusion of fascism and religion in Croatia and Romania was not unique in the Balkans, and indeed in Europe, at the time. For during the 1940s Serbia and Bulgaria also exhibited numerous features that endorsed ultra-nationalism and fascism.[89]

Post-1945 historiography: continuities and discontinuities

With the establishment of communist regimes in the Balkans this historiographical conversion came to an end but not forgotten. In Yugoslavia, for

---

[85]On Romania see R. Ioanid, *The Sword of the Archangel: Fascist Ideology in Romania* (Boulder, CO, 1990); on Croatia see S. Ramet (ed.), *The Independent State of Croatia (NDH), 1941–45*, special issue of *Totalitarian Movements and Political Religions*, 7/4 (2006).

[86]M. Turda, 'The Nation as Object: Race, Blood and Biopolitics in Interwar Romania', *Slavic Review* 66, 3 (2007), 413–41.

[87]M. Feldman and M. Turda (eds),'*Clerical Fascism' in Interwar Europe*, special issue of *Totalitarian Movements and Political Religions* (Oxford, 2008).

[88]M. Biondich, 'Controversies Surrounding the Catholic Church in Wartime Croatia, 1941–45', *Totalitarian Movements and Political Religions*, 7, 4 (2006), 429–57, 435.

[89]M. Falina, 'Between "Clerical Fascism" and Political Orthodoxy: Orthodox Christianity and Nationalism in Interwar Serbia', *Totalitarian Movements and Political Religions*, 8/2 (2007), 247–58.

instance, Serbian historiography (which claimed democratic, anti-fascist credentials) would always counteract Croat claims for greater autonomy by invoking the experience of 1941–5. In Romania, on the other hand, where prominent Romanian historians were imprisoned after 1947, Legionary fascism was catalogued as 'alien' to Romanian traditions; an ideology imposed by 'imperialist' Nazi Germany.[90]

Not surprisingly, in Romania, where there was no solid anti-fascist tradition, the ideological changes brought about by communism were radical.[91] Between 1948 and 1958 (the 'official' period of Romania's transformation into a socialist republic) official historiography stressed the Slavs and their role in the formation of the Romanian people. Thus Mihail Roller's *The History of R.P.R* (the Romanian Popular Republic) – published in successive editions between 1947 and 1965 – interpreted the main historical events in terms of class struggle, eliminating any 'national pride' from Romanian history, which was now seen as an appendix to the great historical saga of the Soviet Union.[92]

A similar historiographical transformation took place in Bulgaria.[93] According to Ana Izvorska, 'The Communist idea of Bulgarianhood strongly emphasised the Slavic descent of Bulgarians, while it tried to push Bulgar roots under the carpet, because in this way Bulgarians came closer to the Russians.'[94] It was thus assumed that the native population in both Bulgaria and Romania was Slavic. Somehow it seemed easier to argue this in the case of Bulgaria as the Bulgarian language was of Slavic extraction.[95] This historiographical transformation proved more testing in the case of Romania. As Dennis Deletant observed: 'In a campaign unique in the satellite states of the Soviet Union, efforts were made to obscure the Latin origin of Romanian with emphasis placed on the phonological, morphological and lexical influence of the Slavonic languages upon Romanian.'[96]

---

[90]M. Fătu and I. Spălățelu, *Garda de Fier: Organizație teroristă de tip fascist* (București, 1971).
[91]K. Hitchins, 'Rumania', *American Historical Review*, 97/4 (1992), 1064–83, and idem, *Mit și realitate în istoriografia românească* (București, 1997).
[92]M. Roller (ed.), *Istoria R.P.R.: manual pentru învățămîntul mediu* (București, 1952).
[93]A. Hranova, 'Historical Myths: The Bulgarian Case of Pride and Prejudice', in P. Kolstø, *Myths and Boundaries in South-Eastern Europe* (London, 2005), pp. 297–323.
[94]Izvorska, 'Varying Concepts of Bulgarianhood', p. 146.
[95]M. Pundeff, 'Bulgarian Historiography, 1942–1958', *American Historical Review*, 66/3 (1961), 682–93.
[96]D. Deletant, 'The Past in Contemporary Romania: Some Reflections on Recent Romanian Historiography', in L. Péter (ed.), *Historians and the History of Transylvania* (Boulder, CO, 1992), p. 135.

Nevertheless, the new ideologues were not deterred in their attempts to make national narratives accord with Marxist-Leninist principles. As Katherine Verdery remarked:

> While literature and art, for Marxist-Leninist leaders, are merely means for expressing new social values to raise the consciousness of the 'masses', history, for them, undergirds the very foundations of rule. Marxism-Leninism everywhere has justified itself within a theory of history – dialectical or historical materialism – for which it claims the status of science.[97]

A further change in Romanian historiography occurred when Nicolae Ceauşescu (1918–89) came to power in 1965. After he delivered his 'July theses' in 1971, the 'cultural revolution' commenced: nationalism became the norm and autochthonism was revived. Not surprisingly, then, the 1974 *Programme of the Romanian Communist Party* (issued for the Eleventh Party Congress) contained a detailed summary of Romanian history.[98] Official historiography became subordinate to political ideology: 'Historiography became, therefore, inevitably political.'[99] In neighbouring Yugoslavia, it was Tito's report to the Fifth Congress of the Communist Party of Yugoslavia in 1948 that fulfilled the corresponding mission, at least until the 1980s, namely to offer a 'pragmatic consensus of Communist historical interpretation' of disparate national histories.[100] It was a form of ideological appropriation tailored to the needs of communism, which now became the omnipotent factor shaping the content of historiographical discourse and determining the domination of one historiographical narrative over others.

New syntheses of national history were published throughout the Balkans, but the main themes (including historical continuity, the struggle for independence, the role of the nation in defending European civilisation and the victimisation complex) were similar to those of the pre-1945 period.[101] Some topics, such as the Dacian–Roman continuity in Romanian historiography, became ubiquitous in the official discourse, generating a veritable 'Dacomania' among historians and party officials alike.

---

[97]K. Verdery, *National Ideology under Socialism: Identity and Cultural Politics in Ceauşescu's Romania* (Berkeley, CA, 1991), p. 215.
[98]*Programul Partidului Comunist Român de făurire a societaţii socialiste multilateral dezvoltate şi înaintare a României spre comunism* (Bucureşti, 1975).
[99]Verdery, *National Ideology under Socialism*, p. 216.
[100]I. Banac, 'Yugoslavia', *American Historical Review*, 97/4 (1992), 1085. See also W. S. Vucinich, 'Postwar Yugoslav Historiography', *Journal of Modern History*, 23, 1 (1951), 41–57.
[101]For the Romanian case, see Ş. Pascu, *Formarea naţiunii române* (Bucureşti, 1967). For a critical analysis of the period see K. Jowitt, *Revolutionary Breakthroughs and National Development: The Case of Romania, 1944–1965* (Berkeley, CA, 1971).

This excessive politicisation of historiography was, however, not uniform. While in Romania and Bulgaria the fusion between official dogmatism and history continued throughout the 1970s and 1980s, Yugoslavia witnessed the emergence of a 'reformist' narrative that attempted to counteract centralist discourses advocated by the federal government. In Croatia, for instance, emphasis was placed on moments in the national history which were marginalised by the official Yugoslav historiography.[102] According to one contemporary, 'Croatian historiography, especially in the postwar period, suffers from minimising, ignoring, and even consciously falsifying historical truth concerning the Croatian people.'[103] It was in many respects a reaction against meta-narratives of brotherly unity imposed by the League of Communists of Yugoslavia during the Tito period.[104] Verdery's remarks about Romania apply to Croatia as well: 'One important aspect of the history to which the political apparatus aspired was the new subject being constructed: the *entire* Romanian people. Class struggle was gradually fading out along with the separation between the Party and Romanians' other history.'[105]

Yugoslav communist historiography certainly vied with national narratives maintained by the countries composing the federation, especially after the emergence of concerted reformist tendencies among Yugoslav leaders during the 1960s. As Ivo Banac argued, 'The tense early 1970s can only be understood as a conflict over the future of Yugoslavia.'[106] Not surprisingly, repeated disagreements emerged between Croat and Serbian historiographical traditions, which after the death of Tito in 1980 eventually degenerated into straightforward ideological and methodological conflicts, culminating in the historical revisionism orchestrated by the Serbian Academy of Sciences and Arts.[107] It became clear that even in the only communist country in Eastern Europe that allowed for alternative national narratives to coexist, a uniform communist historiography failed to construct a sense of belonging and togetherness after almost half a century of domination.

Concluding remarks

In 1992 Maria Todorova commented that, since its inception, 'Bulgarian historiography has evolved almost exclusively according to the precepts of what

---

[102]A. Cuvalo, *The Croatian National Movement, 1966–1972* (Boulder, CO, 1990), pp. 115–25.
[103]Quoted in Cuvalo, *The Croatian National Movement*, p. 116.
[104]I. Banac, *The National Question in Yugoslavia: Origins, History, Politics* (New York, 1984).
[105]Verdery, *National Ideology under Socialism*, p. 248. See also L. Boia (ed.), *Miturile comunismului românesc* (Bucureşti, 1998).
[106]Banac, 'Yugoslavia', p. 1088.
[107]Ibid., pp. 1099–1103.

was considered to be its duty to shape the national consciousness and thus fulfil an important social function.'[108] Yet all historiographies in the Balkans have experienced a similar trajectory. Since their emergence as modern states, Romania, Bulgaria, Serbia and Croatia have been defined in opposition, either to something external (Europe, the Balkans, the Slavic world) or internal (the Hungarians, the Jews, the Greeks, the Serbs, and so on).

After 1989, debates on the role of history in the newly 'liberated' societies in the Balkans vividly re-emerged.[109] Above and beyond illustrating the fate of post-communist societies seized by national radicalism, the Balkan example also illustrates something that few would have imagined before 1989: despite successive programmes of social homogenisation engineered by nationalism and communism, Romanians, Bulgarians, Serbs and Croats are extremely polarised and divided. There is, as many have observed, an intense conflict for their loyalty and identity. They vacillate between glorifying their *'eternal'* nation-state and Europe (or the European Union), unable to reach a comfortable compromise.

Some of the reasons for this situation have been described above and can be summarised as follows. First, interpretations of national history were based on theories of historical rights and continuities that favoured one ethnic group over others, and did not allow for complementary visions of peaceful coexistence to materialise. Second, national historiographies in the Balkans were subjected to many of the social and political changes the region experienced in the nineteenth and twentieth centuries. After 1947, for example, the vectors of authority were directed from academic institutes and universities to the headquarters of the Communist Party, thus curbing even those fragile claims to objectivity that historians had harboured before the Second World War.

Finally, questions concerning the content of national history constitute some of the most crucial problems confronting modern historiography in the Balkans. They also highlight the need for a common theoretical denominator in studying these phenomena. In nationalist historiographies, a plurality of interpretations never implies a plurality of histories, let alone a plurality of pasts. Thus, multiple reflections on the nation, the state and individuals are inconceivable according to nationalist narratives. It is this continuous, reciprocal influence of politics, nationalism and history that arguably was more intense in national historiographies in Romania, Bulgaria, Serbia and Croatia than anywhere else in Europe.

---

[108]M. Todorova, 'Bulgaria', *American Historical Review*, 97/4 (1992), 1117.
[109]M. Bakić-Hayden and R. M. Hayden, 'Orientalist Variations on the Theme "Balkans": Symbolic Geography in Recent Yugoslav Cultural Politics', *Slavic Review*, 51/1 (1992), 1–15.

18
History Writing among the Greeks and Turks: Imagining the Self and the Other

Hercules Millas

Introduction

The dynamics of nation-building in Greece and Turkey were different. The Greeks first developed a national identity, then went through a fierce nine-year war of independence (1821–9) against the Ottoman empire, and finally established their national state. Meanwhile the political leaders of the Ottoman empire, which was threatened with disintegration, tried to create a citizenship identity ('Ottomanism') that would secure the loyalty of all its subjects, Muslims and Christians alike. As the Greeks, Serbians and Bulgarians rejected this option and established their own nation-states, the Ottomans next tried 'Islamism' as a reference of unity. But an alliance of all the Muslim populations could not be secured either, and the Albanians and later the Arabs seceded. 'Turkism', that is, a national identity, was initiated as a political project, promoted by the state, starting with the Young Turks (1908). Finally, decisive battles in Anatolia won against the Greek irredentist forces were the highlight of a successful war of independence (1922) that gave a new impetus in creating 'the nation' and its state: the modern Turkish republic.[1]

There are other differences too. Greece is a small country in terms of its population and its area with respect to its neighbour. Turkey has a heritage of a sophisticated state apparatus, whereas the Greek state is relatively new. The Turks believe that they have an uninterrupted presence in history, having established various states at various times and places, whereas the Greeks believe that they have an uninterrupted presence in history in *one place*, in spite of the 'loss' of their state and independence for four centuries, succumbing to the 'invasion' of the Other. The Greeks were the first in the Balkans to

---

[1]For these typical models in creating nation-states (first the state or first the nation), see Hugh Seaton-Watson, 'On Trying to be a Historian of Eastern Europe', in D. Delatant and H. Hanak (eds), *Historians as Nation Builders* (London, 1988).

establish a 'national consciousness' and a national state, whereas the Turks were among the last. The Greeks have a sense that in the last 200 years they have extended their borders, 'liberating' traditional Greek lands (but not all), whereas the Turks have the grievance that they have lost 'lands' that were originally Ottoman, in other words, theirs. The Greeks are mostly Christians, the Turks mostly Muslims, and for some, this religious difference is of significance: many (Greeks, Turks and third parties) identify Christians with the West and Muslims with the East.

There are similarities too. Each side fought its 'war of liberation' against the other in order to establish its nation-state (in 1829 and 1922). Because of this unique coincidence both communities perceive the other as the historical enemy, and the other operates as a constituent of a modern national identity. Grievances and insecurity with respect to sovereignty (or historical) rights are expressed mostly between the lines in both national historiographies. Greeks claim the heritage of the ancient Greeks and of the Byzantines, whereas the Turks insist that there is no connection between modern Greeks and ancient civilisations. A perception of being 'autochthons' on the Greek side and 'newcomers' on the Turkish side is felt in the respective historical narratives. Some Turks still call Central Asia their home (*ana yurt*), whereas others propose historical theses to promote the idea of a homeland within the borders of present-day Turkey. The controversies on claims and 'legitimacy' are still alive (expressed as phobias *vis-à-vis* the Other), but both sides declare that they do not experience any insecurity on issues of sovereignty.

Greek historiography and the perception of the nation (*ethnos*)

During the age of revolutions and on the eve of the Greek war of independence, that is, in the years 1780–1830, some Grecophone intellectuals of the Diaspora who lived in various cities of Western Europe and who were influenced by the French Revolution and the ideological controversies of the time spread republican ideas within their ethnic communities and proposed radical actions against 'the tyrant', the Ottoman ruler. Others, such as those close to the conservative patriarchate of Constantinople, who lived within the Ottoman state, anathematised them as 'atheists' and advised prudence and adherence to 'paternal ideals'. For the latter, Ottoman rule was God's will, probably a punishment for not being pious enough. It was during this period that questions related to national/ethnic identity were posed for the first time: are we *Romeoi* (Romans, in the sense of Byzantines), *Grekoi* (Greeks, 'as westerners call us'), Hellenes (as the 'Ancients') or Orthodox Christians? There were serious political, ideological and identity disagreements among the Grecophone intellectuals of that time, but all shared a sense of belonging to a common *genos* (in the sense of a community/race).

The Grecophone Orthodox Christian community living in the Ottoman empire under the official status of a millet (religious community), and which in modern times could be identified as an 'ethnic group', perceived itself as a *genos*. *Genos* is a Greek word etymologically originating from Sanskrit, meaning a group of the same origin (*genus* in Latin, *gen/gene* in English). During the years of nation-building the word *genos* was gradually replaced by *ethnos*, and the latter was and is still used in Greek in the sense of 'nation'. There is no other word for 'nation' and the ethnic/national distinction does not exist among the Greeks in general, but only among a small group of historians who are aware of the latest trends in historiography.[2] 'Ethnic' (*ethnikos*) is used for 'national'. In other words, in Greek historiography 'Greekness' and Greek nationhood are heavily loaded with a sense of 'ethnicity' and not with citizenship and/or loyalty to a state. This may be due to the historical fact that the Grecophones did not directly associate 'identity' and 'state', since a communal identity (as *genos*, characterised by a consciousness of a religious difference *vis-à-vis* the Muslim Ottoman state) was widespread and established among them long before the existence of a state with which the community identified itself.

Therefore those who do not possess the basic 'national' prerequisite of Greekness, namely Greek Orthodox belief, were almost completely absent from Greek historiography. Groups that ethnically would have been defined as minority groups were perceived to belong to another nation/*ethnos*. As a popular belief that is encountered in historiography too, 'Greekness' is associated with a common language, a common origin and a common religion, in other words with an ethnicity. The notion of 'citizenship' (or loyalty to a state) is not fashionable in the Greek discourse. On the other hand, Orthodox Christian Grecophones are seen as 'Greeks' irrespective of their citizenship and self-identification.

The forerunner of republicanism among the Grecophones was the Jacobin-type intellectual Rigas Velestinlis (1757–97), who planned a revolution against the Ottoman monarchs. His sense of history was one of class controversy, the people being on one side and the dominating aristocrats on the other. For Velestinlis all ethnic groups, irrespective of religion, origin and language, ought to unite against the tyrants. He foresaw a state where all ('Greeks, Bulgarians, Albanians, Wallachians, Armenians, Turks and all other kinds of peoples', as Article 7 in his 'constitution' stated) would be equal and sovereign. Religion is not even mentioned in his writings. Apparently he was – if his vision is expressed in modern terminology – in favour of a strictly secular state where

---

[2]The prestigious Babiniotis dictionary (G. Babiniotis, *Lexiko tis neas ellinikis glossas [Dictionary of the Modern Greek Language]*, Athens, 1998) defines 'ethnic/*ethnos*' the same way as one would define 'nation'; it adds that 'foreigners' use the Greek word 'ethnic' to denote national groups and minorities.

class privileges would not exist. He was executed by the Ottomans in 1797 and his ideals were soon silenced. He was reclaimed twice much later and 'appropriated': first, at the beginning of the nineteenth century, by nationalists who presented him as a national hero fighting for a Greek state and 'the nation', and, a century later, by socialists as an 'internationalist'. Actually he can be envisaged as a proto-nationalist republican, who had not yet aligned himself wholly with the Greek nationalist/ethnic movement.[3]

The ideals of Greek intellectuals who were for an ethnically/nationally independent state can be traced in the political pamphlets of Adamantios Korais (1748–1833), who lived in Paris, as well as in the historical analysis entitled *Hellenic Nomarchy* (in the sense of 'reign of law') which was published anonymously in 1806. These texts were clearly anticlerical, even sceptical, on issues of religion, and they were attacked by the Greek Orthodox patriarchate of Istanbul as anti-religious. Their discourse was ethnic/national in the sense of an identity that was defined as a historical continuum based on language and culture. A class controversy was indirectly voiced in these texts, since it was pointed out that some (e.g. religious dignitaries and wealthy farmers) lived in luxury, whereas the laymen suffered. In fact, during this pre-revolutionary period a contention prevailed between middle-class/secular intellectuals on the one hand and the religious/conservative groups on the other, even though both sides tried to prove that their visions were not in opposition to communal traditions and values.

The Greek state and Helleno-Christianity

The republican discourse was silenced before the termination of the uprising for independence and even forgotten after the founding of the new Greek nation-state. The founding of the Holy Alliance (of throne and altar) in 1815 and Metternich's determination to discourage popular class and anti-royalist revolutions should have played a decisive role in this. Instead, a simple national myth dominated historiography during the nineteenth century: the Greeks, the descendants of the glorious ancient Greeks, after many centuries under the tyrannical 'Turkish yoke' staged a national revolt and won their independence anew.[4] Greek Orthodox Christianity, which constituted the basic belief of

---

[3]See A. B. Daskalakis, *To politeuma tou Riga Belestinli* [*The Polity of Rigas Velestinlis*] (Athens, 1976).

[4]See, for example, S. Trikoupis (1788–1873), *I istoria tis Ellinikis epanastaseos* [*The History of the Greek Revolution*], vols 1–4 (London, 1853–1957); I. Philimon (1798–1873), *Dokimion istorikon peri tis Ellinikis epanastaseos* [*Historical Essay on the Greek Revolution*], vols 1–4 (Athens, 1859–61); A. Frantzis (1778–1851), *Istoria tis anagenithisis Ellados* [*The History of Greek Rebirth*], vols 1–4 (Athens, 1839–41).

most of the Grecophones, was dextrously integrated into the ancient heritage. According to this ideological construction, the ancient Greeks were somehow the heralds of the new 'light', of Christianity. The term 'Helleno-Christianity' was invented (by S. Zambelios in the mid-nineteenth century) to express this national harmony, and religion was thus 'ethnicised' during this nation-building phase.[5] Greekness was closely associated with a religion, and even with a part of it: with the Greek Orthodox Church and its legacy. The class dimension of the Greek revolution was completely silenced in the nineteenth century.

The sense of 'being the offspring of a glorious past' was initiated and encouraged to a great extent by European republican intellectuals. The Romantic movement also gave momentum to this (modern) Greek revival. The Greeks themselves, on the other hand, promoted the idea of their resurrection because it was to their political advantage to appear as a nation that was heir to a glorious past but which had suffered and had been unfairly treated by the (Muslim) Other. In fact, the national enterprise was presented basically as 'religious liberation'. In the Greek national iconography Greece was represented as a suffering woman mostly dressed in a torn ancient Greek robe. This image accorded with the grammatically feminine definite article that defines in Greek the word 'Greece' (η Ελλάς).

It was during the nineteenth century that the Other – the Ottoman Turk – was constructed in Greek historiography as the absolute negative Other: despotic, barbaric, backward, uncivilised, cruel, corrupt, perverted, exploitative, and so on. This image in general was not different from the one prevalent in the West. The more the Other was negative, the more the Greek revolution and the new state were justified and legitimised. The Ottoman period was described in almost all historical texts of the nineteenth century as a period of darkness, of the death of the nation; on the other hand, the successful Greek revolution was named – and it is still known as – the 'Resurrection of the Nation'. The story of the nation is narrated in terms of the familiar story of Jesus Christ: death, resurrection and eternal life thereafter. The fighters of the revolution and of the subsequent wars are called 'ethno-martyrs'. The losses in this war are 'sacrifices made on the altar of the homeland'. Even the patriarch of Constantinople, who opposed and condemned the Greek revolutionaries of 1821 – but who was still hanged by the Sultan for his inability to control his 'flock' – is metamorphosed into a 'martyr of the Greek nation'. This grand narrative presents all Greeks, the nation, being united and in harmony, and consistently against the Other. Class differences and skirmishes are redundant in this narrative, as the Orthodox affiliation was considered the pillar of the nation.

---

[5] S. Zambelios, *Asmata dimotika tis Ellados* [*Folk Poems of Greece*] (Athens, 1852).

A major 'addition' to this historical narrative was initiated after an unexpected challenge. In the 1830s the German historian Jakob Philipp Fallmerayer (1790–1861) made public his views: modern Greeks could not be the descendants of ancient people because there was a great gap between the ancient and modern Greeks. According to him, modern Greeks are 'Hellenised' Slavs and Albanians who moved to Greece during the eighth century. Racially, the modern Greeks were not the continuation of the old civilisations. The glorious ancient civilisation had perished without leaving any heirs.[6]

This thesis was perceived as a direct threat to the modern Greek identity based on the belief in the revival of the ancient nation. The confusion and agony were overcome by the discovery (for some, by the invention) of the Byzantine empire. The immediate reaction culminated in the publication in 1852–3 of the studies of the best-known Greek historian, K. Paparrigopoulos (1815–91).[7] With his *History of the Hellenic Nation* he cut the Gordian knot by demonstrating that the Byzantine empire was 'Greek', thus securing the 'uninterrupted continuation' of the Greek nation from antiquity to the present. Paparrigopoulos is still very popular among Greeks: his thesis, which is the most official interpretation of the national historiography, is welcomed as common sense, and his general approach is followed by many Greek historians. His work is the closest to what could be called a master narrative.

Today we are in a position to suspect that there were also political considerations behind this thesis of 'Greek Byzantium': it legitimised the Greek claims to Ottoman lands. The decades 1850–1920 became the years of a national ideal known as the *Megali Idea* ('Great Idea'), according to which the Greeks could and should 'liberate' all of their lost and enslaved lands and populations. Greek historiography was marked for a few decades by this irredentist historical interpretation. This idea, which was first voiced in the Greek parliament in 1844, proved unrealistic and was finally abandoned when the Greek armies were decisively defeated in Anatolia in 1922.

In the second half of the nineteenth century and the first quarter of the twentieth Greek historiography turned to the study of the Greeks of Byzantium, as well as of the Greeks living outside the national borders of Greece and especially in Anatolia (Asia Minor). The prominent historian Pavlos Karolidis (1849–1930) is remembered mainly for this enterprise.[8] The general tendency was to portray

---

[6]See, for example, J. P. Fallmerayer, *Geschichte der Halbinsel Morea wahrend des Mittelalters*, vol. 1 (Stuttgart, 1830). Also G. Valoudis, 'J. Ph. Fallmerayer und die Entstehung des neugriechischen Historismus', *Südostforschungen*, 29 (1970).

[7]K. Paparrigopoulos, *Istoria tou Ellinikou ethnous* [*The History of the Hellenic Nation*], vols 1–5 (Athens, 1865–74).

[8]P. Karolidis, *Sygkhronos istoria ton Ellinon kai lipon laon tis Anatolis apo to 1821 mehri to 1921* [*Modern History of Greeks and Other Nations of Anatolia from 1821 to 1921*], vols 1–7 (Athens, 1922–6).

the Greeks as a great nation that created superior civilisations but had to face the menace of the Turks, who dominated 'our' lands and who retained them, enslaving part of 'our nation'. The 'Greek lands' were perceived to extend beyond the borders of the new state. What legitimised the unity of the nation (the *ethnos*) was not the state but an historical 'essence' or 'Greek culture', defined by an enduring language and a religious affiliation expressed as Christian Orthodoxy.

Alternative approaches: class analysis and religion

Greek national/nationalistic historiography was challenged from the first quarter of the twentieth century. Following the Russian Revolution of 1917, the Marxist movement in Greece developed relatively rapidly as an alternative worldview. The Greek Communist Party of the time opposed the expedition against the Ottoman state that was defeated in the First World War, not only because it was in general against irredentism but also because it was against British policy and in favour of the Turkish Kemalist resistance which had friendly relations with the Bolshevik regime.

Yanis Kordatos (1891–1961), the former secretary of the Greek Communist Party, a young lawyer who dedicated his life to history writing, in 1924 challenged the taboo of the Greek revolution, claiming that it was not a national uprising against the Turks, but a class struggle of the oppressed masses against the oppressors who happened to be both Turkish and Greek dignitaries and landlords.[9] Starting with his first book, he showed that not only the Sublime Porte but also the patriarchate of Istanbul was against the revolution. He published his studies in a hostile social environment, facing fierce opposition and threats, but insisted on claiming that modern Greeks were a new nation and not the 'continuation' of ancient people. He was the first to use the term *ethnotita* ('ethnic group') to describe the Grecophone communities of the Middle Ages, distinguishing them qualitatively from the modern Greek nation.

The approach of Yanis Kordatos, who was apparently influenced by Marxist historiography, was a negation of the traditional national paradigm. He published studies on ancient Greece, the Byzantine period and modern Greece, as well as works on such topics as the life of Christ, Greek philosophy and Greek literature. It is interesting to note that, even though he negated the 'diachronic' existence of a Greek nation, all his work covers the cultures and people that the traditional Greek national historiography considered as 'Greek'. A more careful analysis of this work may show that his approach is a combination of class analysis not completely disconnected with the national paradigm.

---

[9]See, for example, Y. Kordatos, *Istoria tis neoteris Elladas*, vols 1–4 (Athens, 1957–8).

This blending of the two paradigms becomes apparent when the portrait of the Other *vis-à-vis* 'us' is examined. The Turks, even though they were not presented with permanently negative racial characteristics, still appeared as backward and generally negative, for 'historical' reasons. This controversial approach is also found in subsequent Marxist historians who followed Kordatos. Nikos Svoronos (1911–90), for example, who stated in the 1970s that the modern Greek national consciousness appeared for the first time in the thirteenth century (and not in ancient Greece), did not express a very different opinion about the Other either. In fact, Greek Marxist historiography did not revise the traditional image and 'role' of the Turks, even though these historians did not reproduce extreme nationalist stereotypes.[10]

A number of religious researchers constituted a small group of historians that were relatively distant from the national paradigm and seemed closer to the Marxist approach. Trying to negate the ethnic/national understanding that set barriers between groups of people based on ethnic characteristics – language, race, colour, and so on – and appropriating a more universal approach (a more 'ecumenical' approach, as they would say), they developed an all-inclusive discourse. They voiced, mostly in encyclopaedias financed and published by the Greek Orthodox Church and in personal publications, a comprehensively different historiography, distant from the nationalist one, evaluating correctly both the contingent character of the 'nation' but also its limitation in envisaging a reconciliation of the 'human race of the Creator'.[11]

However, in their enthusiasm to stress the importance and the contribution of the Greek Orthodox Church they seemed to reproduce the old demarcation lines that were set between East and West, between believers and unbelievers, or between the Greek Orthodox communities and the Others. At times when they criticised the intellectuals of the 'Greek Enlightenment' – of the period when the Greek intelligentsia was under the spell of the developments in Western Europe – they sounded like the Marxists who opposed some Western ideals (capitalism, exploitation, imperialism); when they expressed their reservations about the Other opposing Catholicism, Protestantism, and so on, they were reminiscent of the Manichaeism of the nationalists and the barriers set between nations.

In recent decades a considerable number of Greek liberal historians, following the professionalisation of historians and having come into contact with the latest trends, have produced texts that are distanced from the nationalist paradigm. This modern approach, which typically presents its methodology

---

[10]N. Svoronos, *Histoire de la Grèce moderne* (Paris, 1972).
[11]See, for example, *Thriskeftiki kai ithiki egkiklopedia [Encyclopaedia of Religion and Ethics]*, vol. 5 (Athens, 1964); G. Metallinos, *Tourkokratia [Turkish Rule]* (Nea Smyrni, 1988).

and interpretation as 'academic', uses a language special to a field of interest and voices a new paradigm, but it is not readily deciphered and understood by the public. This anti-nationalist historiography manages to coexist with the popular understanding of (national) history without creating serious conflicts and clashes, exactly because of its specialised covert discourse. In practice it neither publicly challenges national taboos nor blatantly contradicts traditional interpretations. It operates protected against probable attacks within a specialised group of academics.

This school of thought has gained momentum. A series of studies that question nationalistic and semi-nationalistic interpretations related to Greek history have been published in book form or in specialist periodicals.[12] The historians concerned are inclined to investigate ignored fields, such as the Greek case of nation-building and the history of marginalised ethnic groups, such as the Jews, the Albanians and the Turks of Greece. Various ethnographic studies and local histories by professional historians and historically minded intellectuals have also been published in recent years. However, the phenomenon of Rigas Velestinlis of the 1790s, the 'Greek national hero' as he is characterised by Greek historiography, has still to be redefined, and his ideals in favour of a republic in which 'all will be sovereign' irrespective of ethnicity, religion, and language, still awaits its historian.

The political conjuncture and the rise of Turkish ethnic nationalism

During the last decades of the Ottoman empire the authorities initiated various desperate efforts to save the state. Parallel to economic and administrative reforms, the 'identity' of the citizens also became a major issue. As happened with the Greeks, discussions took place as to what this 'identity' ought to be. The agents during these debates, however, were different on the two sides: in the Greek case the state was still nonexistent and intellectuals initiated the discussion, whereas in the Turkish case the state itself and its dignitaries played a major role in trying to determine under what umbrella the loyalty of subjects of the empire could be secured.

The crisis of successive 'secessions' in the Ottoman empire started with the Greek revolution of 1821. Up to that time the empire had lost lands as a result of attack by foreign countries (Russia, Austria, France), but not because of its subjects wanting their own state. With the Tanzimat reforms in 1839, nine years after the establishment of the modern Greek state, the state policy known as

---

[12]For examples of history journals published in Athens, see *Ta Istorika*, *Istor*, and *Historein*, which is published in English.

'Ottomanism', intended to secure equality and peace among all citizens, was introduced. However, Bulgarians seceded and Armenians were next in line. Islamism was supposed to secure at least the loyalty of the Muslim populations of the empire. But there was unrest among the Arabs, and the Muslim Albanians seceded too. 'Turkishness' seemed an alternative to accomplish a unitary state by combining citizenship and ethnicity.

In the Ottoman period history writing in the modern sense developed during these turbulent years. The traditional Ottoman historians, who exceeded 500 in number[13] and were known as *vakanüvisler* ('recorders of incidents'), had been mostly concerned with the political affairs of the empire. The 'modern' historians differed mostly in being much better informed about developments in the West and about the kind of history that was produced there, but most importantly in being the bearers of a new identity, Turkishness, that was in the ascendant. Ahmet Cevdet Pasha (1822–95), with his 12-volume *History of Cevdet*, was a high-ranking civil servant.[14] He was influenced by the Arab historian and philosopher Ibn-Khaldun (1332–1406), who believed in the eventual demise of any state. Cevdet's influence on subsequent generations looking for rather more optimistic worldviews, however, was limited.

Two historians of the Western world inspired Turkish 'consciousness' and Turkish historiography. The French historian David Léon Cahun (1841–1900) and the Hungarian philologist Ármin Vámbéry (1832–1913) were both renowned among Ottoman intellectuals, the first for his book *Introduction à l'histoire de l'Asie, les Turks et les Mongoles* (1896), and the second for his studies on the Turkish language which he started publishing from 1858.[15] These western sources gave an impetus to Turkish nationalism, to 'Turkishness', then known as Pan-Turkism and/or Turanism/Pan-Turanism, and which among the Young Turks was conceived as an ideal which would unite all Turkic people, of the Balkans as well as of Asia. This unity was understood as an ethnic and cultural unity, which found expression above all in a common language. Interestingly Vámbéry tried to develop a Hungarian national historical interpretation of an 'Asiatic past', but in practice he inspired the Turkish nationalists and an 'Asian' ideal in a distant country.

The Ottoman/Turkish historians of this period did not develop systematic contact with historians of other countries; their sources were rather erratic and few historians produced prominent works during this period. Ziya Gökalp (1876–1924), who was influenced by the teachings of Emile Durkheim, and Yusuf Akçura (1876–1935), a Turk from Russia who was influenced by the

---

[13]See F. Babinger (1891–1967), *Geschichtsschreiber der Osmanen und Ihre Werke* (Leipzig, 1927).

[14]A. Cevdet Pasha, *Tarih-i Cevdet [History of Cevdet]*, 12 vols (Istanbul, 1853–91).

[15]See M. Jacob Landau, *Pan-Turkism in Turkey: A Study of Irredentism* (London, 1981).

nationalist movements of the Tatars, were the most influential historians of the period prior to the founding of the modern Turkish democratic state.[16] The Romantic understanding of the 'people' and the views of Herder, the original, 'very old' cultural past of the nation, the positivism of Comte, social Darwinism and the teachings of Gobineau were some of the main ideas that dominated the understanding of their texts.

Islam, the religion of the nation-to-be, was mentioned and even stressed by these historians, not so much as a characteristic of the nation but as a reference in demarcating the Self and the Other, the enemy of the state and of the country. The idea that was highlighted was nationalism (*milliyetçilik*), which was not very clearly defined, but understood as union on a cultural/ethnic/racist basis. The main concern was to demonstrate the historical importance of the Turkish nation. Issues of the Turkish language were widely discussed, and literary texts played an important role in spreading the idea of the nation. During this initial period of nation-building the nation was understood as the union of the Turks, where the Turks were perceived as a group with certain ethnic characteristics: a common language, culture, religion, history and ideals. As in Greece, during this period there was no clear distinction between nationhood and ethnicity. Turkish nationalists perceived the citizens of the country that were not Muslims and spoke a language different from Turkish as members of another nation, though they also preserved the notion of citizenship and loyalty to the state as a means of legitimising membership of the nation.

The modern Turkish state and secular nationalism

With the defeat of the Ottomans in the First World War the country was occupied by the Allies. The Greek army occupied western Anatolia, the ancient Ionian lands, taking a step towards the 'Great Idea', that is, in the direction of establishing the 'Greek' Byzantine state anew. The Turkish liberation war followed and was won – and this is the self-image of many Turks – against the biggest powers of the world (the United Kingdom, Italy and France). But it was only the Greeks who had come to stay, and the critical battles and the associated military victories were won in practice against the Greeks (1922).[17]

Turkish nation-building gained new momentum with the systematic fostering of national identity in the newly established modern Turkish state, the

---

[16]See, for example, Z. Gökalp, *Turkish Nationalism and Western Civilization: Selected Essays of Z. Gökalp* (London, 1959), and Y. Akçura, *Türkçülüğün Tarihi* [The History of Turkishness] (Istanbul, 1998).

[17]For a detailed account of the role of the 'Greek' in the formation of Turkish nationalism, see H. Millas, 'Milli Türk Kimliği ve Öteki (Yunan)' ('The National Turkish Identity and the Other/the Greek'), in *Modern Türkiye'de Siyasi Düşünce*, vol. 4, *Milliyetçilik* (İstanbul, 2002).

Republic of Turkey (1923). The bases of Turkish national ideology and national narratives were founded by intellectuals who were mostly literary authors and poets. In many cases the historians followed. Even prominent Turkish historians and spokesmen of Turkish national ideology, such as Ziya Gökalp (1876–1924) and Fuat Köprülü (1890–1966), started their political activities in literary journals together with the nationally influential short-story writer Ömer Seyfettin (1884–1920). In the Turkish case there has not been an historian who attained the social recognition of, say, the Greek Paparrigopoulos, nor a corresponding *oeuvre* of indisputable validity to be considered a master narrative. The historiography is more diversified, probably because society has not yet attained a consensus on some issues.

As was the case with the Greeks, there is no clear distinction in the Turkish language between the meanings of the words 'national' and 'ethnic'. Millet, an old Arabic word that once had various meanings, was eventually used to denote the nation. *Milli* and *milliyetçilik* mean 'national' and 'nationalist', and both have a very positive meaning since they denote the 'modern' ideology that is distanced from the refuted 'Ottoman understanding' characterised as conservative and backward, basically because it lacked the Turkish 'national consciousness', that is, nationalism. Many Turks identify themselves as nationalists, but this is not understood in the Western sense. In fact, 'Atatürk nationalism' is a constitutional requirement. The word 'ethnic' (*etnik*) has recently been used by the new generation of academics mostly in connection with existing local minority and ethnic (Kurdish) issues that Turkey faces. However, unlike Greece, where the concept of a common origin of the nation is very strong, and probably the legacy of an empire, the notion of 'citizenship' (*vatandaşlık*, being a subject of a state) is also encountered.

The main issue of concern to history writing during the first years of the Turkish republic was the legitimisation of initiatives taken by the new republic. Notions such as 'modernisation', 'westernisation', 'equality of the genders' and 'positivism' (actually the word 'science' was used) were presented as positive axioms, and the past evaluated anew accordingly. The ancient regime of the Ottomans was criticised as backward and conservative, even though it was not rejected in its totality. Great effort was exerted to demonstrate that the Turks had been a great nation throughout history, having established many states and founded an important civilisation.

In the 1930s a great historical project was initiated with the encouragement of Mustafa Kemal Atatürk, the leading figure of the modern Turkish nation-state. The project was called the 'Turkish History Thesis' (THT) and its main purpose was to create a grand national narrative that would assist Turkish nation-building. According to this thesis, the Turks were the oldest people on earth and originally lived in Central Asia; they then migrated and founded almost all the major civilisations (Mesopotamian, Ionian, ancient Greek, and

so on). They had come 'very early' to Anatolia. All ancient people were actually Turks – even Homer was presented as a Turk whose real name was Omer.
Related to this, a second thesis, the 'Sun Language Theory', propagated the
idea that all languages were derived from Turkish.

These extreme views were popularised mostly through textbooks published
by the state apparatus, and it is in these books that one can find their most
systematic presentation. Almost all professional historians in the country were
mobilised to find the historical 'facts' that would prove the above ethnocentric understanding. This thesis was the main 'history' that was read and taught
in Turkey for about two decades. The thesis approached racism at the end of
the 1930s as Dr Afet Inan (1908–85), a protégé of Atatürk, investigated the
origin of the Turkish people by taking measurements of their skulls.[18] Eventually the Western view that the Turks belong to the 'yellow race' was refuted.
During the Second World War some of the Turkish intelligentsia briefly flirted
with racist ideals that were popular in many countries in Europe, and this was
indirectly reflected in historiography, too. At this time neither class analysis
nor religious historical interpretations were welcomed by the authoritarian
Turkish regime, which censored all views that did not endorse the dominant
secular and nationalist interpretations of history.

Legitimising identities and sovereignty rights

During the first decades of the modern Turkish nation-state, Turkish historiography was marked by two concerns: 1) deciding on and establishing a national
identity, and 2) founding a basis for legitimising the modern state, in other
words, the newly secured sovereignty rights. Both concerns were directly connected with the main political and cultural issues that shook the Balkans and
caused a series of wars and suffering related to ethnic cleansing.

The identity issue was expressed as a question of the kind 'Who are we that
want to create a nation? Who is included and who excluded in our enterprise?' The answer had to satisfy the citizens that were supposed to form a
social union with considerable cohesion. Sovereignty, on the other hand, was
threatened by the real or imaginary enemies that had claims on the lands of
this new country. Both issues were directly connected to 'history' and had to
be dealt with by this discipline. A third concern, which was only indirectly
connected with 'history', was the legitimacy of the leading cadre of the new

---

[18]See, for example, A. Inan, *Türkiye Halkının Antropolojik Karakterleri ve Türkiye Tarihi:
Türk Irkının Vatanı Anadolu [The Anthropological Characteristics of the Turkish People and
the History of Turkey: Anatolia, the Fatherland of the Turkish Race]* (Ankara, 1947).

state and more precisely with the governing Kemalist elite. This was mostly done by denigrating the Ottoman past (and its leaders) and presenting the present (and its leaders) as the hope for the future.

Most of the Turkish historiography of the twentieth century developed around these parameters. The Turkish history thesis proposed a Turkish identity that had its sources in Central Asia, and mostly for that reason it incorporated serious shortcomings in legitimising the historical rights of existing borders. It tried to solve the dilemma by constructing a 'history' where all autochthonous nations in the area were 'Turkish'.

The highly secular THT did not prove very effective. It satisfied neither the masses who felt themselves in alliance with traditional Islam – which was pushed aside by the positivist leading elite, together with the Ottoman legacy, in favour of an imagined 'pagan' Central Asia – nor the intellectuals and people of common sense who could not tolerate the idea that all neighbouring communities and countries throughout history were actually Turks (in which case why all these wars?). The THT was never officially refuted, but gradually, and especially after 1970, it was abandoned, even though its spirit is still felt in some textbooks. Two other grand theories were proposed in the 1950s/1960s and 1970s/1980s that dealt with the above-mentioned national concerns. The first was initiated by an historian who spread his ideas publishing mostly literary texts such as novels and 'narrations', Cevat Şakir (1886–1973), and by Kemal Tahir (1910–73), an author who published historical novels and influenced a number of historians that mostly propagated the idea that the Turkish historical case can be best explained by the Marxist model of the 'Asian mode of production'. Turkish historians who developed related theories to define the history of Anatolia are İdris Küçükömer (1925–1987) and Sencer Divitçioğlu (b. 1927). According to these historians, the class and religious conflicts that shaped the Western world did not take place in Anatolia.[19] This school, which I will call 'Anatolianism', did not appear as an organised movement but rather as an understanding that is still popular among intellectuals sympathetic to the Western way of life and having 'leftist' tendencies. The second grand narrative, known as the Turkish-Islamic Synthesis (TIS), was initiated by intellectuals of more conservative tendencies.

Anatolianism and the Turkish-Islamic Synthesis

Anatolianism, as expressed in a series of publications by various intellectuals, has been a major theme in Turkish historiography. It is an unofficial and non-systematic historical thesis that proposes an 'identity' and a scheme to

---

[19]See, for example, İ. Küçükömer, *Düzenin Yabancılaşması* [*The Alienation of the Social Order*] (Istanbul, 1989; 1st edn, 1969); S. Divitçioğlu, *Asya Üretim Tarzı ve Osmanlı Toplumu* [*Asian Mode of Production and Ottoman Society*] (Istanbul, 2003; 1st edn, 1967).

legitimise the new Turkish state. Contrary to the THT, which locates Turkishness in Central Asia, this new theory presented all the people who once lived in Anatolia (mainland Turkey) as 'our' ancestors and the present Turks as their descendants. As a consequence, the present Turks were not seen as the people that once came from the East but were considered 'autochthons'. The history of Anatolia was mostly perceived as a unique case, justified as an outcome of a different course of development, and rather superior to the Western model where class prevailed, definitely more just and humane, often theoretically legitimised as the 'Asian mode of production'.

Accordingly, the ancient Greeks were no longer presented as Turks, but the Greeks and especially the Ionians who once lived in Anatolia were presented as the ancestors of the Turks. This theory, like the THT, is also basically secular, downgrading the Islamic tradition. However, it propagated the idea that the Turkish state (the Ottoman and the present) was a special case in history. It was presented as benevolent, just and caring for its subjects. Therefore all subjects were very happy and loyal to this (Turkish) state. The subsequent revolts of the various ethnic populations are either ignored or explained as 'foreign intrigues'. Deconstructing this understanding, one concludes that in Ottoman society there was no class struggle, but the state operated for the benefit of all. It was the West and its imported feudalism and capitalism that caused the economic and social problems in the Ottoman empire and consequently in modern Turkey. In the 1960s and 1970s mostly young historians published studies along these lines.[20]

This theory, which has many variations and is popular still among Turkish intellectuals even today, had the advantage of being capable of endorsing the Turks as an autochthonous people and at the same time legitimising the existing state: it is legitimate because it has been lawful, benevolent and 'accepted' by all. The question of identity, however, still presented difficulties because it posed a dilemma. Islam was not considered a necessary constituent of the Turkish identity because in such a case the previous pagan and Christian people who lived in Anatolia had to be considered the Other. Religion, language and even culture and civilisation were therefore silenced in this theory, and the 'geographical' aspect of identity, as well as biological continuity, was predominant: the subordination of all to Anatolian geography thus secured 'an ethnic/national unity'. This approach, however, was not in harmony with the religious sentiments of the majority of Turks.

The role of the Other (the Greek) is unique in the texts of the 'Anatolianists'. He appears as an historical witness testifying to the righteousness, moral superiority, magnanimity, and so on of the Turkish state. This Other is developed as an

---

[20]The prime minister of Turkey used this theory in his book addressed to European readers when he tried to advance the idea that Turkey should be accepted as a member of the European Community. See T. Özal, *La Turquie en Europe* (Paris, 1988).

antithesis to Greek accusations that the historical Turk is all-negative. This Turkish myth perceived the Greeks as being happy with the political dominance of the Turks. The Other in the case of the Anatolianists is one who is not from the local area, but the West in general. This Western world is invariably portrayed as imperialistic and/or nationalist, with strong prejudices against the Turks and the East. The self-image of the Anatolianists is quite comforting: they conceive of themselves as 'humanitarians', anti-nationalists, modern, progressive and secular. Closer analysis reveals a special 'class' relationship: within the 'community' (the state and/or nation) there is no class strife, but the relationship with the West is marked by class conflicts, expressed in terms of 'exploitation' and 'imperialism'.

The Turkish-Islamic Synthesis (TIS) is one of the most recent national historical interpretations. According to this theory, which reached maturity in the 1980s, the present-day Turks are people who came to Anatolia from the East in the twelfth century having accepted Islam. Thus, Islam is considered part of the national identity as well as the Asian heritage. The followers of the TIS accord importance also to the Ottoman heritage, which they consider significant and superior. The legitimacy of the 'state' is based rather on historical victories and the balance of power in the geographical environment. This theory is popular among political groups that see themselves as nationalists, a word that means in this context 'loving their country and the Turks', whereas others identify them as the 'extreme right'.[21] İbrahim Kafesoğlu is one of the most esteemed historians of this school, which propagates its ideas through extensive publications, numerous journals and newspapers.[22]

The Other in the case of the TIS is almost everyone who differs from the 'Turks', both ethnically and religiously. The tendency to perceive minorities or ethnic groups of non-Turkic origin as foreign is typical. The non-Muslim minorities are very often perceived on a class basis and are described as wealthy communities involved in trade and industrial production (avoiding the word 'capitalists' to distance themselves from Marxism), in close cultural and/or economic contact with the West, and taking advantage of the Turks economically.[23] The Other in this case encompasses different religion, ethnicity and class (he is from the upper class and exploitative).

---

[21]It is interesting that the TIS is reminiscent of the Greek understanding of 'Helleno-Christianity'. They both search for national identity and their national historical origin in two components: ethnicity and religion.
[22]See: İ. Kafesoğlu, *Türk İslam Sentezi [Turkish-Islamic Synthesis]* (Istanbul, 1999).
[23]The title of a book by Salahi Sonyel is typical of how non-Muslim minorities are perceived: *Minorities and the Destruction of the Ottoman Empire* (Ankara, 1993).

Alternative Turkish historiographies

The various historical theses mentioned above form the main trends in the
Turkish historiography developed after the founding of the Turkish nation-
state. Hence a Turkish national master narrative is deeply contested both
among professional historians and among the various political groups that
espouse one of these interpretations. History became a weapon of diverse
ideological camps in Turkey all struggling to mobilise their supporters and
defeat their opponents. In the process of all this contestation Turkish nation-
building (ethnogenesis) took place.

A radical challenge to the above historical interpretations came, as happened with the case of Greece, first from the Marxist intellectuals and later
liberal academics who followed the trends of a more international, and sometimes even anti-national profession. The Marxists, who operated more as intellectuals than as historians, challenged the ethnic, 'black and white' approach
whereby the Turkish side always appeared in a good light and the Other the
reverse. This tendency was expressed mostly in literary texts such as novels or
newspapers, and in many cases seriously challenged old and established historical 'truths'. Kemal Tahir, a novelist who introduced the Marxist 'Asiatic
mode of production' to the Turkish historiography in order to stress the peculiarity of his national history, was mentioned above. Of the earliest Turkish
Marxist historians, Mete Tuncay (b. 1936) has played a major role in questioning national narratives, such as the THT and later the TIS.

After 1980 in particular, a group of historians appeared, conscious of a Marxist
tradition and organised around the Economic and Social History Foundation of
Turkey and the publishing house İletişim, which published a series of journals
and books in line with modern developments in historiography. They dealt with
local history and with taboo issues, such as the past and present of the ethnic
and minority groups of Turkey and the population exchange of 1923 (see below).
They also reviewed the Turkish historiography critically. This group keeps a
deliberate distance from nationalist discourse, and is highly critical of ethnocentric approaches. They have been aware of new developments in the field of
historiography, and ready to study and discuss new approaches in history. Zafer
Toprak and Şevket Pamuk, who mostly deal with the economic history of
Turkey, and Çağlar Keyder, who shows an interest in Ottoman history, can be
mentioned as examples of this trend.[24]

---

[24]See, for example, Z. Toprak, *Türkiye'de Milli İktisat [National Economy in Turkey]* (Istanbul,
1982); Ş. Pamuk, *Osmanlı-Türk İktisadi Tarihi, 1500–1914 [Economic History of Ottoman State-
Turkey, 1500–1914]* (Istanbul, 1988); Ç. Keyder, *State and Class in Turkey: A Study in
Capitalist Development* (London, 1987).

Class and economic analysis predominate in their works. For some (Keyder, for example), Christian minority groups are not seen as 'foreign' bodies within the Ottoman state but an economically productive (positive) power. Societal events such as ethnic cleansing are explained on the basis of economic turmoil. When the relationship of states is on the agenda the model becomes rather Leninist where imperialist motifs are used to explain the intentions of the Western powers.

This group of historians, who are politically mostly uncommitted, is also characterised by its zeal in cooperating with the Other. Probably what is new and most important in Greek and Turkish historiography is what has been initiated by the historians of the two countries since 1995, and especially since 2000. Both sides have shown a willingness to study issues that are of interest to both and have jointly produced historical texts. There are a few projects of this kind running at present.

This is not only an indication of the widening of the spectrum of research in history writing but also of a change of philosophy and state of mind, surpassing ethnocentric approaches. These historians seem to believe that one-sided national interpretation may not be enough to produce historical narratives that bear international validity. Definitely they are more 'cosmopolitan' in their understandings as well as more relaxed in their communication with the Other and in being exposed to contact with the views of the Other.

An assessment

Both the modern Greek and Turkish states were founded through a proclaimed process of negating the Ottoman empire and traditional social formations: Greece by rejecting the Ottoman legacy altogether, Turkey by transforming it and by re-evaluating it. Irrespective of the degree of success of this rejection and transformation, the national founding myths of the two countries, which were used to legitimise their new political formations, differ and in some respects are almost opposed to each other. The national myths are so deeply rooted that it is difficult to use a lexicon that is not nationally biased. The term 'the two societies', the Greeks and the Turks, is a modern invention. In the Ottoman milieu there were not clear-cut distinct communities with established 'ethnic' characteristics. For example, there were Turkophone Orthodox Christian and Grecophone Muslim communities which in 1923 were forcefully exchanged as Greeks and as Turks respectively. The criterion for nationality/ethnicity was in practice their religious beliefs. The exchange included about two million people.

Even though the religious bias was quite distinctive in both the Greek and the Turkish cases, the legitimacy of the new identity was based mostly on a discourse of 'nation', with an imagined ethnic uniformity. In other words, declarations of secularism and ethnic/national approaches should be considered with caution, since religious background and identity seem to have influenced perceptions and behaviour, both of the individuals and of the states. In other words, religion either played a direct role within the said states, for example as expressed with Helleno-Christianity and TIS, or was used indirectly to describe the 'national' aspect of the citizens – mostly the Self and the Other as well as the minorities in each state.

Political confrontations between Greeks and Turks (or Greek Orthodox and Muslim populations) were often the result of coincidence. The conflicting parties then chose different constructed identities (Greekness vs. Turkishness) in order to legitimise and explain the struggles with each other. Class analysis and/or Marxist explanations were developed to highlight economic power relationships; 'exploitation' and 'imperialism' were developed to justify historical enmities and/or current personal or communal interests. In this case, too, a distinction should be made between 'genuine' class analysis that transcends nationalism and sets the basis for a new paradigm, and a class analysis that in fact explains and consequently legitimises national histories. In some of the cases mentioned above, analytical tools such as 'imperialism', 'capitalists' and 'exploitation', mostly directly borrowed from Marxist literature, are utilised to 'explain' nationalistic behaviour.

The historiography that was developed in Greece and Turkey following the establishment of the two nation-states can be seen as a kind of a Greek–Turkish dialogue (or quarrel) on history where the Greeks first posed their arguments and then the Turks developed their counter-arguments.[25] The main concerns seem to be the 'identity of the nation' and the sovereignty rights of the countries, something that is understandable taking into consideration the political strife of recent decades. Anderson defines a nation as a 'political community imagined as both inherently limited and sovereign'.[26] By 'limited' it is meant that beyond national boundaries lie other nations. By 'sovereignty', but also by other sacred principles voiced by all nation states such as 'liberty' and 'independence', is meant the subduing of the imaginable rivals, the enemies, the Other. The Other, as the one beyond our living space, is a *sine qua non* of every nation.

---

[25]Consider, for example, the following Greek-Turkish 'historical' grand narratives and arguments/counter-arguments: 1) We the Greeks are the descendants of the glorious ancients. No, you are not, Greeks are actutally Turks. 2) The Ottomans were barbarians. No, they were magnanimous and tolerant. 3) The Ancient Greek and Byzantine lands are ours. No, modern Greeks are a different race from the ancient Greeks and Byzantines. 4) You as a nation behaved as invaders in recent centuries. No, you had the *Megali Idea* and you were the invaders in recent decades. And so on.

[26]B. Anderson, *Imagined Communities* (London and New York, 1990), p. 15.

A premise not clearly stated but always insinuated in both Greek and Turkish historiography is that the Other had been harmful and/or a threat since it caused, among other ills, economic difficulties and 'our exploitation'. This negative aspect of the Other has, in other words, a class dimension in the consciousness of each nation. The Other is sketched as the appropriator of the nation's means of survival. The Greek historiography described the dominating Ottomans as a kind of upper class that exploited the Greeks; conversely, the Turkish one described the Greeks and the Greek minorities as exploiters and 'rich', too. The religious difference is suggested directly or indirectly every time the Other is described as negative or different. Among the ills of the Other the destruction of 'our sacred places' is quite often called to mind. Interestingly, the national flags of both countries each carry a different religious symbol that had been in a contention for many centuries in Europe: a cross and a crescent. Religion and class analysis are in most cases subordinated to and mostly used to legitimise an ethnic/national narrative.

Even if there are a number of historians who do not agree with this view, the dominant narrative in both countries presents the 'West' as siding with the nation's Other. The West in this case is shown as 'imperialistic', 'biased owing to religious differences' (the West is 'Christian' for the Turkish side, 'Catholic' and/or 'Protestant' for the Greek side), or simply as the aggressive Other. The cases where Greece and Turkey had been favoured and/or assisted by the West are also 'forgotten' in the respective nationalist historiographies. This approach *vis-à-vis* the role of the West shows how historical religious controversies are used in modern times. It should be added that both historiographies infer that 'their country' is located between the East and the West, in other words, in the centre of the world.

Gender, in fact 'women', plays a supplementary role in both historiographies. The national issue seems to bear a masculine importance. In both cases 'our' women (and to a lesser degree children and old people) are presented as the part of the population that must be protected from the ill intentions of the Other. The Other is shown threatening the honour of 'our' women – a metaphor that is often used, especially in literary texts. There is a renowned story in Greek history where Greek women (the Souliots) jumped to their death from a high cliff, dancing a national dance, rather than be captured by the Ottomans. There are many women heroines fighting against the Other, participating in a 'men's war'. These women do not symbolise any particularities of 'women' but live and fight like men. This participation operates as an indication that the people act as a whole.

In the Turkish historiography women are also portrayed as assisting the men: psychologically supporting their husbands who are fighting at the front; carrying ammunition; being involved in the fighting themselves and tending the wounded. Turkish women, contrary to Greek heroines, rarely participate in actual fighting. In the republican national discourse the Turkish woman is the main criterion for the 'modernisation' of the country: her dress, her role in the society, her legal status, and so on are of special importance.

In general the Greek historiography seems to be characterised by a greater uniformity in describing both the past of the nation as well as the Other. The Turkish historiography presents greater diversity. This should be related to the rela-tively late formation of nation-building in the Turkish case, as well as to the multi-ethnic/national heritage of the Ottoman Empire (the millet system) and to its legacy.

19
Narratives of Jewish Historiography in Europe

Ulrich Wyrwa

In 1846 an essay on the philosophy of history and the history of religion entitled 'The Construction of Jewish History'[1] appeared in the *Journal for the Religious Interests of Judaism* (*Zeitschrift für die religiösen Interessen des Judenthums*). The author was Heinrich Graetz,[2] a historian whose work at that time was still under the influence of the speculative historicism of one of Hegel's pupils, Christlieb Julius Braniß.[3] One of Graetz's early essays on the philosophy of history had set out to explain the 'totality of Judaism' in such a way that 'its very essence, the sum total of its powers, must be explicated in terms of history'. Graetz wanted to explore and expose 'the very origins of the idea of Judaism that was to prove to be so fertile', and thereby attempt to 'construct Jewish history on the basis of its conceptual foundations'.[4] What he perceived to be an ongoing threat to the very existence of Jewish religious tradition should, he claimed, be countered by remembering the Jewish past. His goal was to seek orientation in the present on the basis of history.

---

[1] H. Graetz, *Die Konstruktion der jüdischen Geschichte: eine Skizze* (1846; Berlin, 1936 [with footnotes and a postface by Ludwig Feuchtwanger]).

[2] On Graetz, see the biography by Philipp Bloch, published in H. Graetz, *Geschichte der Juden von den ältesten Zeiten bis auf die Gegenwart*, 11 vols (Berlin, Leipzig and Magdeburg, 1853–76), vol. 1, final rev. edn (Leipzig, 1908; [reprint Berlin, 1998]), pp. 1–72; see also the biographical entry by Nils Römer, in A. Herzig (ed.), *Schlesische Lebensbilder*, vol. 8 (Neustadt an der Aisch, 2004), pp. 190–5 (commissioned by the Historical Commission for Silesia); M. Brann (ed.), *Heinrich Graetz: Abhandlungen zu seinem 100. Geburtstag* (Vienna and Berlin, 1917); S. W. Baron, 'Heinrich Graetz, 1817–1891: A Biographical Sketch', in idem, *History and Jewish Historians*, (Philadelphia, 1946), pp. 263–69; idem, 'Graetzens Geschichtsschreibung: eine methodologische Untersuchung', *Monatsschrift für Geschichte und Wissenschaft des Judentums*, 62 (1918), 5–15.

[3] On Braniß, see G. Scholtz, *Historismus als spekulative Geschichtsphilosophie: Christlieb Julius Braniß (1792–1873)* (Frankfurt/M, 1973).

[4] Graetz, *Die Konstruktion*, pp. 8f.

Following his essay 'The Construction of Jewish History', Graetz published a major 11-volume work on the history of the Jews, covering all periods of history until the present,[5] in which he went beyond the speculations on the philosophy of history contained in his early writings. This work was translated into several European languages and became one of the most influential narratives of Jewish historiography. However, it was by no means the only narrative work of Jewish historiography to appear in Europe during the nineteenth and twentieth centuries.[6] There were four different types of narratives which succeeded each other in time and overlapped in many ways: a narrative of universal history, of regional or local history, of liberal civil history and of Zionist history.[7] While these various narrative patterns reflected similar attitudes and basic convictions, the meanings underlying the notions of Jewish religion and the Jewish people were repeatedly defined anew. Even when focusing on particular regions or nations in their work on Jewish history, Jewish historians generally remained faithful to the universal values of the Jewish religious past. Following an outline of the four overlapping narratives in Jewish historiography, this chapter will enquire to what extent the concepts of class and gender were incorporated into Jewish historiography. The final remarks will address the transnational and European dimensions of Jewish historiography.

---

[5]Graetz, *Geschichte der Juden*.

[6]On the emergence and development of Jewish historiography, see esp. A. Herzig, 'Juden und Judentum in der sozialgeschichtlichen Forschung', in W. Schieder and V. Sellin (eds), *Sozialgeschichte in Deutschland: Entwicklungen und Perspektiven im internationalen Zusammenhang*, vol. 4, *Soziale Gruppen in der Geschichte* (Göttingen, 1987), pp. 108–32; M. A. Meyer, 'The Emergence of Jewish Historiography: Motives and Motifs', *History and Theory*, 27 (1988), 160–75; Y. H. Yerushalmi, *Zakhor: Jewish History and Jewish Memory* (New York, 1989); A. Funkenstein, *Perceptions of Jewish History* (Berkeley, 1992); I. Schorsch, *From Text to Context: The Turn to History in Modern Judaism* (Hanover, NH and London, 1994); E. Schulin, '"Das geschichtlichste Volk": die Historisierung des Judentums in der deutschen Geschichtswissenschaft des 19. Jahrhunderts', in Schulin, *Arbeit an der Geschichte: Etappen der Historisierung auf dem Weg zur Moderne* (Frankfurt/M and New York, 1997); S. Feiner, *Haskalah and History: The Emergence of a Modern Jewish Historical Consciousness* (Oxford, 2002); M. Brenner, *Propheten des Vergangenen: Jüdische Geschichtsschreibung im 19. und 20. Jahrhundert* (München, 2006).

[7]Ongoing debates about Jewish historiography are dealt with in M. Brenner and D. N. Myers (eds), *Jüdische Geschichtsschreibung heute: Themen, Positionen, Kontroversen* (Munich, 2002); a reader with essays on the history of Jewish historiography is M. Brenner, A. Kauders, G. Reuveni and N. Römer (eds), *Jüdische Geschichte lesen: Texte der jüdischen Geschichtsschreibung im 19. und 20. Jahrhundert* (Munich, 2003); for a treatment of the European dimensions of Jewish historiography, see U. Wyrwa, 'Die europäischen Seiten der jüdischen Geschichtsschreibung: eine Einführung', in idem (ed.), *Judentum und Historismus: zur Entstehung der jüdischen Geschichtswissenschaft in Europa* (Frankfurt/M and New York, 2003), pp. 9–36.

I

The first narrative of Jewish historiography, one formulated in terms of a universal history, emerged during the nineteenth century at a moment when history established itself as one of the main academic disciplines and also became a central authority within Judaism. The starting point of this new conception of the Jewish past was the Association for the Culture and Science of the Jews (Verein für die Cultur und Wissenschaft der Juden), founded in 1820 in Berlin.[8] The members of this association wanted to preserve Jewish culture and to emphasise the relevance of Judaism in the present day by reinterpreting its past and encouraging academic debate about history. The historian Isaak Markus Jost developed this universal narrative systematically within the context of the science of Judaism, the *Wissenschaft des Judentums*.[9]

Jost's aim was to disseminate the ideas of the European Enlightenment within Judaism and to understand the essence of Judaism by means of historical study,[10] for only 'in history can we truly understand the Israelites'.[11] In contrast to the 'collector of anecdotes', the historian faces the task of representing the 'labyrinth' of the past in all its complexity, and of educating the Jews by enquiring into their history in relation to the Enlightenment and European civilisation.[12] Jost's universal narrative of Enlightenment history encompassed the Jewish past not only in Europe, but also in Asia, Africa and America.[13]

When Jost wrote about the 'Jewish people', he was referring primarily to cultural tradition and historical experience rather than to the heritage of Halacha, Jewish religious law. Jost therefore gave primacy to cultural over ethnic criteria when determining whether someone belonged to Judaism. He was a proponent of the universalist heritage of European Enlightenment insofar as he defended the idea of progress and adhered to the aim of improving humanity on the basis of civilisatory standards. According to Jost, historical development would guide

---

[8]On the association and its founders Leopold Zunz and Eduard Gans, see N. N. Glatzer (ed.), *Leopold Zunz: Jude – Deutscher – Europäer. Ein jüdisches Gelehrtenschicksal des 19. Jahrhunderts in Briefen an Freunde* (Tübingen, 1964); R. Blänkner, G. Göhler and N. Waszek (eds), *Eduard Gans (1797–1839): politischer Professor zwischen Restauration und Vormärz* (Leipzig, 2001).

[9]On Jost, see M. Reuwen, 'I. M. Jost und sein Werk', *Boulettin des Leo Baeck Instituts*, 3 (1960), 239–58.

[10]I. M. Jost, *Geschichte der Israeliten seit der Zeit der Maccabäer bis auf unsre Tage, nach den Quellen bearbeitet von I. M. Jost, Lehrer und Erzieher in Berlin*, 9 vols (Berlin, 1820–28), vol. 1, pp. viiif.

[11]I. M. Jost, *Allgemeine Geschichte des Israelitischen Volkes*. The preface to this work has been reprinted in Brenner et al., *Jüdische Geschichte lesen*, pp. 24–34.

[12]I.M. Jost, *Geschichte der Israeliten*, vol. 5 (Berlin 1825), p. v.

[13]Jost, *Geschichte der Israeliten*, vol. 5 passim.

humanity towards humaneness and provide the Jews with freedom and equal rights.

Heinrich Graetz, the second historian whose works adhered to a universalist narrative of Jewish historiography, did not agree with this version of Jewish history founded on an optimistic belief in progress. Graetz accused Jost of having presented a one-sided version of Jewish history and of having remained faithful to the Enlightenment 'even when it had become antiquated'. Graetz claimed that Jost's 'essential mistake' had been to lend 'heroic Jewish history a dry and philistine character', and to 'tear to shreds the heroic drama which had lasted several thousands of years'.[14]

Following early speculation on the philosophy of history in his work on the 'construction of Jewish history', Graetz spent the years 1853–76 working on a history of the Jews, which focused on the continuity of Jewish history from its beginnings until the present. This work draws on abundant evidence to present a compassionate universal history of the Jews in the form of a 'history of suffering and scholarship'. In the wake of this 11-volume universal history, there followed a popular three-volume summary, which enjoyed an extremely broad circulation among the Jewish population.[15] Even though Graetz was severely criticised by a large number of contemporary reviewers in Germany,[16] this work established itself as one of the most influential narratives of Jewish historiography. In celebration of his hundredth birthday, Graetz was consequently praised as a 'backward-looking prophet'.[17]

Martin Philippson's *Modern History of the Jewish People* likewise adopts a universalist narrative.[18] Although this work was conceived as the continuation of 'the Graetz', bringing it up to the present day, it did not adopt its predecessor's narrative of Jewish history as a history of suffering and scholarship.[19] In Philippson's eyes, recent Jewish history, the age of emancipation, was a success story. And although this story was threatened by modern anti-Semitism, it had not been refuted. Moreover, whereas Graetz's narrative was written primarily from a Jewish perspective, Philippson's narrative could be characterised as a history of relations. According to the preface of the first volume, the history of the Jewish people reflects 'the destinies of the whole world'.[20] As a German patriot and a

---

[14]Graetz, *Geschichte der Juden* (1908), vol. 11, pp. 425f.

[15]H. Graetz, *Volkstümlich Geschichte der Juden von den ältesten Zeiten bis zur Gegenwart*, 3 vols (Leipzig, 1888); A. Schulin, 'Das geschichtlichste Volk', 147.

[16]J. Meisl, *Heinrich Graetz: eine Würdigung des Historikers und Juden zu seinem 100. Geburtstag* (Berlin, 1917), pp. 59f.

[17]Meisl, *Heinrich Graetz* , p. 61.

[18]I. Schmidt, 'Martin Philippson: biographische Studien zur deutsch-jüdischen Geschichte des 19. und frühen 20. Jahrhunderts', MA thesis, Technical University of Berlin, 1988.

[19]M. Philippson, *Neueste Geschichte des jüdischen Volkes*, 3 vols (Berlin, 1907–11).

[20]Philippson, *Neueste Geschichte des jüdischen Volkes*,vol. 1, p. i.

European, Philippson defended the emancipation of the Jews. He was convinced that 'the situation of the Jews in all civilised countries around the mid-seventies' of the nineteenth century 'was a cause for satisfaction and raised high hopes for the future', until anti-Semitism cast a cloud over these hopes.[21] However, Philippson's central category was not the notion of the Jewish people, as the title of his work suggested, but the concept of a 'tribal and religious community'. Like his predecessors, Philippson consequently did not define belonging to Judaism in terms of ethnicity.

Although the concept of the 'Jewish people' appears in the title of Philippson's work, he did not use it as a category for exploring and representing Jewish history. This concept however is central to Simon Dubnow's work. Like the works of his predecessors, Dubnow's ten-volume *World History of the Jewish People* also adopts a universalist narrative of Jewish historiography.[22] In his memoirs he noted that he had started out with cosmopolitan and humanistic ideas and subsequently went through a process of 'nationalisation'.[23] In his 'Essay on the Philosophy of History' of 1893, Dubnow wrote, 'if there are "historical" and "unhistorical" peoples on earth', then the Jewish people 'must indisputably be categorised as "the most historical"'.[24] Dubnow therefore defined 'Jewish national existence' less as an ethical category and more as the result of 'historical consciousness'. Dubnow saw historical knowledge as the 'cornerstone of national unity'.[25] His historiographical work was based, as he claimed in the introduction to the first volume, on the 'idea of the intrinsic cultural value' of the Jewish people.[26] The object of Dubnow's writings was, in short, the Jewish people, 'national individuality, and the origins and growth of this individuality'.[27] And his narrative was universalist insofar as he conceived of Jewish history specifically in terms of a 'world history', which encompassed the entire 'cultural world' and 'the historical being of humanity throughout its entire duration'.[28]

The historical conceptions of the universalist narrative outlined above presented Jewish history primarily as a tale of suffering and, as Heinrich Graetz

---

[21]Philippson, *Neueste Geschichte des jüdischen Volkes*, p. 391.

[22]S. Dubnow, *Weltgeschichte des jüdischen Volkes: von seinen Uranfängen bis zur Gegenwart*, 10 vols (Berlin, 1925–9). On Dubnow see also the new edition of his autobiography: S. Dubnow, *Buch des Lebens: Erinnerungen und Gedanken. Materialien zur Geschichte meiner Zeit*, ed. V. Dohrn, trans. Barbara Conrad and Vera Bischitzky, vol. 1 (1860–1903), vol. 2 (1903–1922), vol. 3 (1922–1933) (Göttingen, 2004, 2005).

[23]S. Dubnow, *Mein Leben*, translated from the Russian (Berlin, 1937), p. 58.

[24]S. Dubnow, *Die Jüdische Geschichte. Ein geschichtsphilosophischer Versuch* (1893: Berlin, 1898), p. 6; cf. E. Schulin, 'Das geschichtlichste Volk', 114.

[25]Dubnow, *Die Jüdische Geschichte*, p. 7.

[26]Dubnow, *Weltgeschichte*, vol. 1, p. xxi.

[27]Dubnow, *Weltgeschichte*, p. xvi.

[28]Dubnow, *Weltgeschichte* , p. viii.

noted in his diary, a 'tearful history of religion',[29] which developed in a more progressive way only with the onset of the emancipation. Salo W. Baron, the last historian who worked on a universal history of the Jews, adopted an entirely different approach. Having been born in Galicia, grown up in Vienna, and emigrated to the US in 1927, Baron was appointed to the first chair of Jewish history in a secular university. In a programmatic essay published in 1928, he claimed 'that we may have to revaluate radically our notions of Jewish progress under Western liberty'.[30] The situation of Jews in Europe during the Middle Ages, argued Baron, was not at all as miserable and pitiful as it had often been represented, which is why he placed special emphasis on the fact that 'the Jewish community enjoyed full internal autonomy'.[31] Moreover, he claimed that the ghettos had originally been set up by Jews acting in their own interest to protect their communities and that, in legal terms, the status of Jews was by no means worse than that of other social groups. 'Surely it is time', he concluded, 'to break with the lachrymose theory of pre-Revolutionary woe.'[32] Baron applied this approach in his monumental work *A Social and Religious History of the Jews* which, in spite of its eight published volumes, remained unfinished.[33] 'Common origins, a common destiny and a common culture' of the Jews had guaranteed the continuity and unity of Jewish history.[34] Despite obvious discrepancies between Baron's conceptions of history and those of Jost, Graetz, Philippson and Dubnow, Baron's lecture on 'World Dimensions of Jewish History' demonstrates to what extent he also adhered to a universalist narrative of Jewish historiography. In this piece he explains that there has always been a 'profound correlation ... between the Jewish and general historical development' and that the Jewish people have always taken 'a direct interest in international developments on account of their territorial dispersal'.[35]

What Baron had in common with Jost, Graetz, Philippson and Dubnow, in spite of his criticism of the tearful image of the Jewish past, was his universal historical approach to Jewish history and his conviction that Judaism should

---

[29]H. Graetz, *Tagebuch und Briefe*, ed. Reuwen Michael (Tübingen, 1977), p. 133.
[30]S. W. Baron, 'Ghetto and Emancipation: Shall We Revise the Traditional View?', *Menorah Journal*, 14 (1928), 515–26, 516. On Baron, see the biography by R. Liberles, *Salo Wittmayer Baron: Architect of Jewish History* (New York, 1995), and Brenner, *Propheten des Vergangenen*, pp. 165–75.
[31]Baron, 'Ghetto and Emancipation', p. 519.
[32]Baron, 'Ghetto and Emancipation', p. 526.
[33]S. W. Baron, *A Social and Religious History of the Jews*, 18 vols, 2nd edn (New York, 1952–83).
[34]Quoted in S. W. Baron, 'Sozial- und Religionsgeschichte der Juden' (1952), in Brenner et al., *Jüdische Geschichte lesen*, p. 74.
[35]This quotation is a translation of the German translation: S. W. Baron, 'Weltdimensionen der jüdischen Geschichte' (1962), in Brenner et al., *Jüdische Geschichte lesen*, p. 152.

be conceived of primarily on the basis of common historical experience rather than as an ethnic unit.

II

The confidence with which authors of the universal historical narrative (with the exception of Baron) looked to the future was shared by authors who worked on local and regional narratives of Jewish history. Jewish historians working 'on the spot', who collected traces of the Jewish past in their communities, also devoted themselves to recording the history and memories of this past. They adopted the same universalist narrative pattern, albeit less in order to construct Jewish historical consciousness than to secure the social integration of Jewish citizens and to encourage a specifically Jewish patriotism. Nevertheless, the local and regional approaches to history adopted a narrative technique of their own.

Representations of the history of Jewish communities in Cologne[36] and Frankfurt am Main[37] show to what extent local historical studies adopted the 'tearful' approach. Even local historical studies written by students within the framework of their academic studies followed this pattern, which is evident in the successive dissertations about the Jewish communities of Mainz, Speyer and Worms, which are the oldest Jewish settlements in Germany.[38]

However, historical treatises on the history of Jewish communities during the modern era place emphasis on the successful commitment of Jews to their emancipation and on the motif of progress.[39] The logic of the local historical narrative consisted in reminding the Jewish population of both their persecution and the suffering inflicted on them, and in fostering awareness of their social advancement and successful integration.[40]

---

[36]E. Weyden, *Geschichte der Juden in Köln am Rhein von der Römerzeit bis auf die Gegenwart: nebst Noten und Urkunden* (Cologne, 1867); C. Brisch, *Geschichte der Juden in Cöln und Umgebung aus ältester Zeit bis auf die Gegenwart: nach handschriftlichen und gedruckten Quellen bearbeitet*, 2 vols (Mühlheim an der Rhein, 1879/82).

[37]E. Schwarzschild, *Die Gründung der israelitischen Religionsgesellschaft zu Frankfurt am Main und ihre Weiterentwicklung bis zum Jahre 1876* (Frankfurt/M, 1896).

[38]L. Rothschild, 'Die Judengemeinden zu Mainz, Speyer und Worms von 1349–1438: ein Beitrag zur Geschichte des Mittelalters', dissertation, Marburg, 1904; E. Carlebach, 'Die rechtlichen und sozialen Verhältnisse der jüdischen Gemeinden: Speyer, Worms und Mainz von ihren Anfängen bis zur Mitte des 14. Jahrhunderts', dissertation, Rostock, 1900.

[39]J. Ehrenfreund, 'Erinnerungspolitik und historisches Gedächtnis: zur Entstehung einer deutsch-jüdischen Wissenschaft im Kaiserreich (1870–1914)', in Wyrwa, *Judentum und Historismus*, pp. 39–61.

[40]See, for example, L. Geiger, *Geschichte der Juden in Berlin: Festschrift zur zweiten Säkular-Feier* (Berlin, 1871); the same narrative pattern is followed by H. Jolowicz, *Geschichte der Juden in Königsberg in Preussen: ein Beitrag zur Sittengeschichte der preussischen Staaten* (Posen, 1867).

The most significant work which adopted this local historical narrative in Germany was *Germania Judaica,* a monumental work first proposed in 1903 by the Society for the Promotion of the Science of Judaism (Gesellschaft zur Förderung der Wissenschaft des Judentums), which was designed to present, in alphabetical order, the history of all sites in Germany in which Jews had lived or were living.[41] This narrative, which emphasised the integration of the Jewish population into middle-class society, was characteristic of works in the fields of both urban and regional history,[42] and could be found not only in Germany but also other countries and regions of Europe.

On the occasion of the demolition of the Bevis Marks Synagogue in London in 1886, for example, which had been built in the early eighteenth century, a historical exhibition was staged[43] which stimulated the development of Anglo-Jewish historiography and gave cause for the publication of a collection of essays about the regional histories of Jewish communities in Great Britain.[44] In France, historians likewise began to take an interest in the history of the regional peculiarities of Alsatian Jews[45] as well as in the Sephardic community in Bordeaux.[46]

A history of the Jewish community of Poznan was published as early as 1865,[47] followed by studies on Warsaw and Lvov.[48] Meanwhile, the city of Cracow acquired a special significance for the historical memory of Polish Jews because it was home to one of the oldest and most highly populated Jewish communities in the Polish-speaking area.[49] Even small and remote Jewish commun-

---

[41]*Germania Judaica*, vol. 1, *Von den Ältesten Zeiten bis 1238: nach dem Tode von Marcus Brann*, ed. I. Elbogen, A. Freimann and H. Tykocinski, part 1, A–L. (Frankfurt/M, 1917); part 2, M–Z (Frankfurt/M, 1934); later volumes published since 1968 by Mohr Siebeck, Tübingen, and completed in 2003 with volume 3.3.

[42]See, for example, L. Donath, *Geschichte der Juden in Mecklenburg von den ältesten Zeiten (1266) bis auf die Gegenwart (1874): auch ein Beitrag zur Kulturgeschichte Mecklenburgs* (Leipzig, 1874).

[43]M. B. Hart, 'Jüdische Geschichtsschreibung in England', in Wyrwa, *Judentum und Historismus*, p. 65.

[44]See the article by J. Jacobs, 'London Jewry 1290', in *Papers Read at the Anglo-Jewish Historical Exhibition* (London, 1887). Quoted in M. Hart, 'Jüdische Geschichtsschreibung in England', p. 74.

[45]E. Scheid, *Histoire des juifs d'Alsace* (Paris, 1887); A. Glaser, *Geschichte der Juden in Straßburg von der Zeit Karls des Großen bis auf die Gegenwart* (Strasbourg, 1894).

[46]T. Malvezin, *Histoire des juifs à Bordeaux* (Bordeaux, 1875).

[47]J. Perles, *Geschichte der Juden in Posen* (Breslau, 1865).

[48]H. Nusbaum, *Szkice historyczne z zycia Zydow w Warszawie* (Warsaw, 1881); J. Caro, *Geschichte der Juden in Lemberg von den ältesten Zeiten bis zur Theilung Polens im Jahre 1792 aus Chroniken und archivalischen Quellen* (Cracow, 1894).

[49]See F. Guesnet, 'Krakau und die Anfänge der Historiographie der polnischen Juden', in M. Graetz (ed.), *Schöpferische Momente des europäischen Judentums in der frühen Neuzeit* (Heidelberg, 2000), pp. 351–64, 361f.

ities, like the one on Corfu. were the object of historical studies which adopted a regional historical narrative.[50]

In Italy, the Jewish population also turned its attention to regional and local history in line with the tradition of *campanilisimo*, the Italian form of local patriotism. Several essays on urban history consequently appeared in Jewish journals such as *Educatore Israelita, Il Vessillo Israelitico, Corriere Israelitico* and *Rivista Israelitica*.[51] What particularly interested Jewish intellectuals in Italy during the nineteenth century was the exceptional wealth of the history of the Jews in Sicily before their expulsion.[52] The Jewish history of Italy aroused interest among people in Italy and in other European countries. The Jewish community of Venice, for example, was the focus of essays published in *Educatore Israelita*, in the French language journal *Revue des Etudes Juives* and in the British journal *Jewish Quarterly Review*.[53] However, the history of the Jewish community of Rome was presented mainly by Jewish historians from Germany, who pursued the 'tearful' image of medieval history and to a progressive image of modern history. Abraham Berliner, for example, concluded the introduction to his work on the history of the Jews of Rome thus: 'There are eclipses of the sun in history like those in nature. The history of the Jews of Rome will provide us with a wealth of learning and experience, such that darkness will finally give way to light, allowing the sun of justice to rise in all its glory.'[54] Paul Rieger concluded the second volume of his work on the history of the Jewish community of Rome (written with Hermann Vogelstein) in the same vein, claiming that, 'Like the whole of Jewish history, the history of the Jews in Rome is a journey through darkness to radiant light!'[55]

III

In addition to the universalist historical narrative and the regional or local historical narrative, the third type of narrative about the Jewish past that con-

---

[50] J. A. Romanos, 'Histoire de la Communauté israélite de Corfou', and D. Kaufmann, 'Contributions à l'histoire des juifs de Corfou', *Revue des Etudes Juives*, 23 (1891).

[51] See G. L. Voghera, 'Die jüdische Geschichtsschreibung in Italien im 19. Jahrhundert', in Wyrwa, *Judentum und Historismus*, pp. 119, 127.

[52] I. La Lumia, 'Gli ebrei siciliani', *Nuova Antologia*, 4 (1867); see also B. Lagumina and G. Lagumina (eds), *Codice diplomatico dei giudei di Sicilia*, 3 vols (Palermo, 1884–95).

[53] J. Ravà, 'Gli ebrei in Venezia', *Educatore Israelita*, 19 (1871), 20 (1872); D. Kaufmann, 'Notes sur l'histoire des juifs de Venise', *Revue des Etudes Juives*, 21 (1890); D. Kaufmann, 'A Contribution to the History of the Venetian Jews', *Jewish Quarterly Review*, 2 (1890).

[54] A. Berliner, *Geschichte der Juden in Rom von der ältesten Zeit bis zur Gegenwart*, 2 vols (Frankfurt/M, 1893), vol. 1, p. viii.

[55] H. Vogelstein and P. Rieger, *Geschichte der Juden in Rom*, 2 vols (Berlin, 1896), vol. 2, p. 410.

cerns us here is the liberal civil narrative, which consisted in focusing on the relations between Jews and non-Jews in the various nation-states and areas in Europe where people shared a common language. In the age of historicism, when nations in Europe defined their self-understanding in relation to the past and legitimised their respective traditions on the basis of history,[56] Jewish intellectuals strove to devise an historical narrative that would do justice both to their claims to be integrated into the middle-class societies of the various nation-states and to their own experiences and self-perception as Jews, that is, as a distinct group with its own religious traditions.[57]

The liberal narrative was in keeping with the need to integrate and preserve religious and cultural traditions. It focused on aspects of relational history, the role of Jews as citizens, and the reciprocal influence and mutual effects resulting from encounters between Jews and non-Jews in the various nation-states of Europe. Ideally, texts which adhered to the liberal civil narrative were conceived as part of a process of mutually contingent, interlocking cultural relations, and consistently exposed the faults and obstacles which were used to hinder the recognition of Jews as equal partners. Yet these representations of Jewish history reveal not only the resistance, on the part of non-Jewish representatives, to encounters between the religions, but also the vitality and dynamic nature of Jewish religious tradition, which enabled it to renew and 'reinvent' itself.[58]

Just as representations of national histories in Europe during the age of nation-states differed from one another, allowing particular national narratives to emerge in relation to their specific historical contexts, Jewish populations also developed similarly distinct narrative strategies representing their relations to and within the various nation-states and areas sharing a common language in Europe. In France, for example, the relational historical narrative of Jewish historiography was characterised by the same event, the French Revolution, which had had a greater impact than any other event on French national historiography.[59] In his historical treatise on Mosaic institutions, for example, Joseph Salvador pinpointed analogies between Mosaic law and the constitution of 1791 and the Declaration of the Rights of Man, and treated the legislative work accomplished by Moses as equivalent to the work of the French National Assembly.[60] Jewish intellectuals in France developed a 'pugnacious

---

[56]On historicism as a European phenomenon, see F. Jaeger and J. Rüsen, *Geschichte des Historismus: eine Einführung* (Munich, 1992), pp. 75–81.
[57]See Ehrenfreund, 'Erinnerungspolitik und historisches Gedächtnis', especially the section 'Die Dialektik von innerer und äußerer Geschichte', pp. 50–2.
[58]See S. Volkov, 'Die Erfindung einer Tradition: zur Entstehung des modernen Judentums in Deutschland', *Historische Zeitschrift*, 253 (1991), 603–28.
[59]See P. Simon-Nahum, 'Jüdische Historiographie im Frankreich des 19. Jahrhunderts', in Wyrwa, *Judentum und Historismus*, pp. 91–116.
[60]J. Salvador, *Histoire des institutions de Moïse et du peuple hébreu*, 3 vols (Paris, 1828), vol. 1.

history',[61] and French Jewish historians who were concerned about political issues became actively involved in the historical and political debates that were taking place in the public sphere at that time, especially the Dreyfus affair.[62]

In Great Britain, the relational historical narratives of Jewish historiography and non-Jewish historiography were essentially subject to the same development, that is, the rapid socioeconomic change in the country brought about by the Industrial Revolution. British Jewish historians did not fail to point out the high proportion of Jewish people involved in business and in the emergence of British capitalism.[63]

Jewish historiography in Polish-speaking areas focused on the same historical and political experience which was at the centre of non-Jewish Polish historiography: the division of the Polish state between Russia, Prussia and Austria.[64] The Jewish population associated memories of the former Polish Republic of the Gentry with those of the specific situation and the freedoms it granted to Jews. The Jewish historians Aleksander Kraushar and Hermann Sternberg, for example, presented Polish Jewish history as an integral part of general Polish history and defended Poland's status as a nation-state, as well as the rights of Polish Jews to civil equalities.[65]

In the Hungarian part of the Habsburg monarchy, history as a discipline enjoyed an equally good reputation within both Jewish and non-Jewish circles, and Jewish intellectuals considered themselves to be an integral part of Hungarian political and public life.[66] The myth of the first Hungarian king, St Stephen, played an equally prominent role in their historical memory as the battle of the Hungarian state against the Ottoman empire and the revolution of 1848–9. The primary task of Hungarian Jewish historiography was considered to be to support the quest of Hungarian Jews to obtain emancipation and social integration by equipping them with sound historical arguments.[67] Their main aim was to provide Hungary with a 'useful past'.[68]

---

[61]Simon-Nahum, 'Jüdische Historiographie in Frankreich', p. 108.

[62]Simon-Nahum, 'Jüdische Historiographie in Frankreich', pp. 115f.

[63]Hart, 'Jüdische Geschichtsschreibung in England', p. 73.

[64]See F. Guesnet, 'Geschichte im Kontext: Entwicklungsbedingungen der jüdischen Historiographie im polnischen Sprachraum im 19. Jahrhundert', in Wyrwa, *Judentum und Historismus*, pp. 131–46.

[65]A. Kraushar, *Historya Zydow w Polsce*, 2 vols (Warsaw, 1865–6); H. Sternberg, *Versuch einer Geschichte der Juden in Polen* (Warsaw, 1860); H. Sternberg, *Geschichte der Juden in Polen unter den Piasten und den Jagiellonen: nach polnischen und russischen Quellen* (Leipzig, 1878).

[66]G. Miron, 'History, Remembrance, and a "Useful Past" in the Public Thought of Hungarian Jewry (1938–1939)', *Yad Vashem Studies*, 32 (2004), 131–70, esp. 131–4.

[67]L. Löw, *Zur neueren Geschichte der Juden in Ungarn: Beitrag zur allgemeinen Rechts-, Religions- und Kulturgeschichte* (Budapest, 1874); J. Bergl, *Geschichte der ungarischen Juden: nach den besten Quellen* (Leipzig, 1879).

[68]Miron, 'History, Remembrance, and a "Useful Past"', p. 133.

There were few countries in Europe in which the Jewish population, along-side Russian settlers, had so little cause to look back on successful integration into society as in Romania. Nevertheless, even in this young nation-state, Jewish historiography adopted a relational historical narrative, albeit with four significant points of criticism. The stubborn disdain with which Romanian Jews were confronted and the vehement anti-Semitic social climate in the newly created state of Romania were therefore central topics in Romanian Jewish historiography.[69] A major contribution to Romanian Jewish historio-graphy was made by the brothers Moses, Elias and Wilhelm Schwarzfeld.[70] They were active supporters of the Societatea Istorică Juliu Barasch, a society for research into the Jewish history of Romania founded in 1866 in Bucharest.[71] From 1874, Elias Schwarzfeld was the editor of the journal *Revista Izraelită*, in which numerous articles about Romanian Jewish history were published, and Moses was the editor of the yearbook *Anuarul Pentru Izraeliți* from 1877, which was firmly devoted to the Jewish history of Romania. Elias severely criticised anti-Semitic policies in Romania in his writings, and was consequently expelled from the country in 1885. He then settled in Paris, where he worked on a contemporary historical work about the conditions in which Jews lived in Romania from the Berlin Congress of 1878 until the turn of the century.[72]

Whereas historical circumstances forced Romanian Jewish historiography to concentrate on the social problems and conflicts between the Jewish and non-Jewish population, Italian Jewish historiography could not only look back on an exceptional success story but also ground its self-understanding on the fact that Jews had been living on the Italian peninsula for a very long time. In this context, Giuseppe Levi Gattinara wrote a series of articles about Italian Jewish history for the journal *Educatore Israelita*, in which he began by emphasising that Italy was the oldest native country of the Jews since the downfall of the ancient Jewish state.[73]

---

[69]I. Loeb, *La Situation des israélites en Turquie, en Serbie et en Roumanie* (Paris, 1877).

[70]I. Singer, 'Schwarzfeld', in *The Jewish Encyclopedia: A Descriptive Record of the History, Religion, Literature, and Customs of the Jewish People from the Earliest Times to the Present Day*, vol. 11 (New York, 1905), pp. 119–21.

[71]'Historiographie', in *Enzyclopädia Judaica: das Judentum in Geschichte und Gegenwart*, vol. 8 (Berlin, 1931), pp. 139–40.

[72]E. Sincerus (pseud.) [Elias Schwarzfeld], *Les Juifs en Roumanie depuis le traité de Berlin (1878) jusqu'à ce jour: les lois et leurs conséquences* (London, 1901).

[73]G. L. Gattinara, 'Degli ebrei in Italia e della loro condizione politico civile antica e moderna: sunto storico', *Educatore Israelita*, 1 (1853), 246–51; 2 (1854), 203–8, 235, 263, 306, 335.

By contrast, German Jewish historiography was dominated by a combination of universal, regional and local historical studies. One work dealing with German Jewish history in Germany in a relational historical narrative mode was typical insofar as it was published at a time when Jews in Germany were being denied their status as members of the German nation. The German Jewish historian Ismar Elbogen published a history of the Jews as late as 1919, which adopted a classical universal historical narrative from antiquity to the present.[74] In 1935 Elbogen then published a history of the Jews in Germany devoted exclusively to communities within the 1871 borders of imperial Germany and which may be classified as the first work on German Jewish history written in a liberal narrative mode.[75]

On 9 November 1938 the increasingly limited niches in which Jews had the opportunity to carry out historical research in Germany were suspended altogether. After 1945 every analysis of Jewish history was overshadowed by the Holocaust. Nevertheless, the memory of the German Jewish past had not been extinguished.[76]

IV

The *Aliyah*, the migration of Jews to Palestine, and the foundation of the state of Israel gave rise to a fourth type of narrative in Jewish historiography, a Zionist narrative whose origins lay in the reaction of sections of a young generation of Jewish intellectuals to the rise of anti-Semitic movements and violence in Europe towards the end of the nineteenth century. Jewish intellectuals adopted the concepts of *Volk* and nation in order to create a new conception of the Jewish past – concepts which emerged at a time when the idea of integral nationalism had become the guiding principle of a youth movement opposed to the liberal political persuasion of the previous generation. Whereas Heinrich Graetz fostered a culturalist notion of the Jewish people and Simon Dubnow argued in favour of autonomy for Jewish people in the Diaspora, the Zionist narrative turned the concept of the Jewish people into an ethnic category. Zionist historians no longer defined the Jewish people in terms of common historical experience, but in terms

---

[74]I. Elbogen, *Geschichte der Juden seit dem Untergang des jüdischen Staates* (Leipzig, 1919).

[75]I. Elbogen, *Die Geschichte der Juden in Deutschland: eine Einführung* (Berlin, 1935). After the Holocaust, Eleonore Sterling revised and completed this work, and this new version has since been reprinted several times: I. Elbogen and E. Sterling, *Die Geschichte der Juden in Deutschland* (Frankfurt am Main, 1966); further editions have been published in Wiesbaden (1982), Frankfurt am Main (1988), and Hamburg (1993).

[76]The Leo Baeck Institute, founded in 1955, became a centre of German Jewish historiography. See C. Hoffmann (ed.), *Preserving the Legacy of German Jewry: A History of the Leo Baeck Institute 1955–2005* (Tübingen, 2005); R. Nattermann, *Deutsch-jüdische Geschichtsschreibung nach der Shoah: die Gründungs- und Frühgeschichte des Leo Baeck Institute* (Essen, 2004).

of common descent. The Jewish people became an active historical agent, based on a Romantic vision of *Volk* and national life.[77] Inspired by historicism, Zionist intellectuals conceived of the Jewish people as an historical entity, and the notion of the Jewish nation underpinned the historical legitimisation of Zionism as a political movement. Moreover, the Zionist narrative differed from both the universal historical and the relational historical narratives insofar as it was based on the negation of exile. Life in the Diaspora was interpreted as merely a phase of the Jewish past on the path to redemption, and Zionism as the culmination of an historical process.[78]

One of the most influential initiators of the Zionist narrative was the historian Ben-Zion Dinaburg (alias Dinur), who settled in Palestine in 1921 and defined six essential factors underpinning the 'uniqueness of Jewish history'. According to Dinur, the people of Israel has from their very beginnings been characterised by 'ethnic uniqueness' in terms of religion, community (*kahal*) and common sacred language. Moreover, he argued, *Eretz Israel* is the Promised Land, and the Jewish people have distinguished themselves in their quest for state sovereignty.[79]

Another initiator of the Zionist narrative was Yitzhak Fritz Baer, who, prior to emigrating in 1930, had worked at the Academy for the Science of Judaism. In his work on exile and the historical treatment of exile since the Hellenistic Diaspora, which was published in Berlin in 1936, Baer wrote, 'Political slavery, dispersion, longing for liberation and reunification' are the major themes characteristic of exile.[80] 'Having been enslaved, scorned, and outcast throughout the world, the Jewish people hopes to achieve political reunification on its native soil and a complete resettlement of its population.' The Jewish people, he claimed, had lost their belief 'in a national future' and in the 'traditional powers of religion', which had led to the 'denationalisation of belief'. Baer expressed his opposition to the relational historical narrative of Jewish history, saying, 'The special national political constitution of the Diaspora and the common consciousness of the Jewish nation have been destroyed.' The historical consciousness of modern Judaism, he said, was suffering from the effects of a 'wrongly understood religious and political heritage'.[81]

---

[77]A. Raz-Krakotzkin, 'Geschichte, Nationalismus, Eingedenken', in Brenner and Myers, *Jüdische Geschichtsschreibung heute*, pp. 181–206, 182f.

[78]M. Zimmermann, 'Volk und Land: Volksgeschichte im deutschen Zionismus', in M. Hettling (ed.), *Volksgeschichten im Europa der Zwischenkriegszeit* (Göttingen, 2003), pp. 96–119.

[79]B.-Z. Dinur, 'Die Einzigartigkeit der jüdischen Geschichte' (1968), in Brenner et al., *Jüdische Geschichte lesen*, pp. 127–31; M. Zimmermann, 'Volk und Land', p. 108.

[80]Y. F. Baer, *Galut* (Berlin, 1936), p. 6; see also the excerpt printed in Brenner et al., *Jüdische Geschichte lesen*, pp. 179–88.

[81]Baer, *Galut*, pp. 98–100.

In the programmatically entitled preface to the first issue of the Zionist journal *Zion*, called 'Our Way' (in Hebrew, 1936), Dinur and Baer presented Jewish history as national history.[82] These authors, who were both based at the newly founded Hebrew University in Jerusalem, were among the founders of what soon became known as the 'Jerusalem school' of Jewish historiography.[83] Historians who were considered to belong to this school had all acquired their education in Germany and Europe, but at the same time distanced themselves from the idea of the 'science of Judaism'. However, historians of the Jerusalem school did not form a closed group, nor did they defend any coherent methods or common conceptual precepts, but rather made up what David Myers calls a 'loose intellectual team'.[84]

Gershom Scholem, the historian of Jewish mysticism, was a member of this circle. However, although he was also a staunch critic of the 'science of Judaism' and one of the first activists in the Zionist movement, he had no intention of writing a heroic history of Judaism or of devising a monolithic historiography.[85] His primary concern was the 'question of the status of Judaism and its tradition in a secularised and mechanised world'.[86] Scholem sought an answer to this question in the mystical aspects of Jewish tradition. As David Biale has pointed out, Scholem's history of the Kabbalah represented more than just a 'counter-history' of Judaism, for 'his historiography and political reflection represented from within Zionism' a 'kind of "counter nationalism"'.[87] Scholem's conception of the Jewish past can therefore be characterised as an anarchistic Zionist narrative which did not focus on a Jewish state, but on 'founding a new community of the Jews'.[88]

The focal point of the Zionist narrative was nevertheless the state of Israel. And criticism of the Zionist narrative from within the Jewish world, and the ongoing historians' debate in Israel, was clearly rooted in the relationship between Zionism and the Arab population in Palestine. This criticism focuses on the fact that this Arab population has traditionally been excluded from Jewish historiography.[89]

---

[82]According to Zimmermann, 'Volk und Land', p. 108.

[83]D. N. Myers, 'Was there a Jerusalem School? An Inquiry into the First Generation of Historical Researchers at the Hebrew University', *Studies in Contemporary Jewry*, 10 (1994), 66–92.

[84]D. N. Myers, *Re-inventing the Jewish Past: European Jewish Intellectuals and the Zionist Return to History* (New York, 1995), p. 76.

[85]D. Biale, 'Scholem und der moderne Nationalismus', in G. Smith and P. Schäfer (eds), *Gershom Scholem: zwischen den Disziplinen* (Frankfurt/M, 1995), pp. 257–74.

[86]G. Scholem, 'Reflections on Jewish Theology', in Scholem, *On Jews and Judaism in Crisis: Selected Essays* (New York, 1976), quoted in the preface by Gary Smith in Smith and Schäfer, *Gershom Scholem*, p. 10.

[87]Biale, 'Scholem und der moderne Nationalismus', p. 258f.

[88]Biale, 'Scholem und der moderne Nationalismus', p. 263.

[89]B. Schäfer, 'Einführung', in Schäfer (ed.), *Historikerstreit in Israel* (Frankfurt/M, 2000), pp. 7–14.

V

In universal and regional as well as in liberal and Zionist historical narratives, Jewish history has generally featured as a history of suffering and scholarship, albeit with a variety of thematic foci and intentions. However, very little attention was paid to social discrepancies within Jewish communities or to the social status of Jews in relation to the Christian population. The British historian B. Lionel Abrahams therefore appealed to colleagues to include analyses of living conditions and everyday life in their studies of Jewish history, and consequently he wrote about class relations within Jewish communities.[90] Yet Abrahams' approach was an exception which proved the rule, for his proposal was not taken up and developed in Jewish historiography. Martin Philippson's work was characterised as a 'breakthrough towards an integrative social history',[91] for example, yet the notion of class was of as little use to him as an analytical category as it was to Simon Dubnow or Salo Baron. Even Jacob Katz and Jacob Toury, the founders of a social history of the Jews, made no use of the concept of class in their works on Jewish history.[92]

The first historian to make use of class as an analytical historical category was the socialist Zionist Raphael Mahler, originally from Galicia.[93] In his treatise on Jewish history during the modern era, published in 1961, Mahler bemoaned the fact that the term 'working class' had never previously been used in Jewish historiography.[94] In *A History of Modern Jewry (1780–1815)*, published in 1971, he reproached Jewish historians for having overlooked the role of social dynamics as well as class conflict and social conflict more generally within Jewish communities. Mahler considered that class had played a fundamental role in the development of the Jewish people and in historical research more generally.[95] Nevertheless, his approach to Jewish historiography has not been pursued.

Whenever Jewish history has been narrated in terms of a history of suffering and scholarship, it has been primarily a history of suffering and scholarly men. The specifically masculine character of this narrative is particularly evident in the

---

[90]B. L. Abrahams, 'The Condition of the Jews of England at the Time of Their Expulsion in 1290', *Transactions*, 2 (1894–5, 1896), pp. 77–8; see also Hart, 'Jüdische Geschichtsschreibung in England', p. 75.

[91]So Herzig, 'Juden und Judentum in der sozialgeschichtlichen Forschung', p. 113.

[92]Shulamit Volkov and Frank Stern (eds), *Sozialgeschichte der Juden in Deutschland: Festschrift zum 75. Geburtstag von Jacob Toury*, Tel Aviver Jahrbuch für deutsche Geschichte, 20 (Gerlingen, 1991); J. Katz, 'Zur jüdischen Sozialgeschichte', in J. Katz, *Messianismus und Zionismus: zur jüdischen Sozialgeschichte* (Frankfurt/M, 1993), pp. 9–20.

[93]R. Mahler, *A History of Modern Jewry (1780–1815)* (London, 1971).

[94]R. Mahler, 'Geschichte Israels in der neuesten Zeit' (1961), in Brenner et al., *Jüdische Geschichte lesen*, pp. 80–90, 83.

[95]Brenner et al., *Jüdische Geschichte lesen* , p. xi.

works of Heinrich Graetz. Although women certainly play a role in his *History of the Jews*, men are presented as the key agents of Jewish history. Graetz describes one rabbi in medieval Spain as a 'man of principle'.[96] At the head of a small Jewish community near Montpellier was, as Graetz puts it, a man who excelled 'in all questions of science and law'.[97] And he describes another rabbi in medieval Barcelona as a 'man with a keen and lucid power of judgement, sound moral fibre and a strong character'.[98] He was also full of praise 'if a man remained sober in the midst of indescribable rapture'.[99] A Jewish doctor expelled from Portugal appeared to him to be a 'sensible and wise man', an 'important scholar' and a 'conscientious and kind man'.[100] Graetz describes one rabbi in the seventeenth century as 'a man living in an age of weaklings',[101] and another rabbi from Strasbourg in the eighteenth century as a 'man with an almost patriarchal stature, sound moral fibre, and gentle manners'.[102] He extolled one emancipated Jew in the nineteenth century as 'the embodiment of Jewish refinement', emphatically qualifying him as 'a complete man'.[103] Another committed to the political emancipation of the Jews at that time is described as a 'noble-minded man', 'a man through and through'.[104] A Jewish scholar living in Italy during the early modern period had, according to Graetz, 'buried himself in books so much that his body bore traces of profound suffering. Weak, yellow, and dehydrated, and afflicted with fever, he crept around like a dying man.'[105]

In contrast to the narrative of suffering and scholarly men, the Zionist narrative presented an image of a powerful and resistant, and even physically well-trained, Jewish man, for which the writer and early Zionist activist Max Nordau (1849–1923) coined the term 'muscular Judaism'.[106] Although narratives of Jewish historiography were geared chiefly to men as the carriers of Jewish culture,

---

[96]Graetz, *Geschichte der Juden* (1908), vol. 6, p. 108.

[97]Graetz, *Geschichte der Juden* vol. 6, p. 204.

[98]Graetz, *Geschichte der Juden*, vol. 7, pp. 144f.

[99]Graetz, *Geschichte der Juden*, vol. 7, p. 222. Graetz refers here to the behaviour of advocates of the mystical movement in the fourteenth century.

[100]Graetz, *Geschichte der Juden*, vol. 9, pp. 327f.

[101]Graetz, *Geschichte der Juden*, vol. 10, p. 421.

[102]Graetz, *Geschichte der Juden*, vol. 11, p. 261.

[103]Graetz, *Geschichte der Juden*, vol. 11, p. 405.

[104]Graetz, *Geschichte der Juden*, vol. 11, p. 440.

[105]Graetz, *Geschichte der Juden*, vol. 9, p. 386.

[106]M. Nordau, 'Muskeljudentum', *Jüdische Turnzeitung*, 1 (1900), 1, 10–11; see also, on the relation between the history of the body and German Jewish history, D. Wildmann, 'Der Körper im Körper: jüdische Turner und Turnvereine im deutschen Kaiserreich, 1898–1914', in P. Haber, E. Petry and D. Wildmann, *Jüdische Identität und Nation: Fallbeispiele aus Mitteleuropa* (Cologne, 2006), pp. 50–86 and 130–39, and D. Wildmann, 'Jewish Gymnasts and Their Corporeal Utopias in Imperial Germany', in M. Brenner and G. Reuveni (eds), *Emancipation through Muscles: Jews in European Sport* (Lincoln, 2006).

certain historians in the nineteenth century, such as Meyer Kayserling, occasionally turned their attention to the status of women in Jewish history.[107] This broadening of topics to include questions of gender history had been prompted by attacks made by anti-Semitic authors who alleged that in Judaism, unlike Christianity, women were discriminated against.[108] The first edition of the memoirs of Glückel von Hameln in 1896, a businesswoman from Hamburg whose writings provided an impressive picture of everyday Jewish history in the early modern period, was another response to such attacks.[109] Italian Jewish historiography of this period also drew attention to the role of women,[110] and the journal *Il Vessillo Israelitico* published a bibliographical article on the subject as early as 1875.[111]

Although Selma Stern, the first academically qualified woman historian to work on Jewish history, wrote numerous articles about women as historical protagonists, she ceased exploring the role of women in Jewish history when she was appointed to a post at the University for the Science of Judaism (Hochschule für die Wissenschaft des Judentums) and began working on Jewish history.[112]

The first book to be published by the Leo Baeck Institute was Hannah Arendt's biography of Rahel Varnhagen.[113] Nevertheless, as Ruth Nattermann shows in her study of the history of this institution, women's history was a severely neglected topic there.[114] Even in the 1950s the concept of gender had not become a central category of historical research. The first work to appear on the subject of women's and gender history was Marion Kaplan's investigation of the origins of the Jewish middle class and of the changes in family life, in which she

[107]M. Kayserling, *Die jüdischen Frauen in der Geschichte, Literatur und Kunst* (Leipzig, 1879).

[108]See S. Heschel, 'Nicht nur Opfer und Heldinnen', in Brenner and Myers, *Jüdische Geschichtsschreibung heute*, pp. 139–62, 140; Brenner, *Propheten des Vergangenen*, pp. 184–93.

[109]In 1896 David Kaufmann published an edition of these memoirs in Yiddish. In 1913 there followed a German edition: *Denkwürdigkeiten der Glückel von Hameln*, edited and translated from the Jewish-German, with commentaries, by Alfred Feilchenfeld, a reprint of the 4th edn of 1923 (Frankfurt/M, 1987). On the state of research in this field, see M. Richarz (ed.), *Die Hamburger Kauffrau Glikl: jüdische Existenz in der Frühen Neuzeit* (Hamburg, 2001); E. Grözinger, *Glückel von Hameln: Kauffrau, Mutter und erste jüdisch-deutsche Autorin* (Teetz, 2004).

[110]L. D. Torre, *Nuovi studi sulla donna israelita* (Padova, 1864); F. Servi, *La Donna israelita nella società* (Casale, 1896); U. Passigli, *La Donna ebrea* (Mortara, 1899).

[111]Oscar Greco, 'Bibliografia femminile israelitica italiana del XIX secolo', *Il Vessillo Israelitico*, 23 (1875).

[112]M. Sassenberg, *Selma Stern (1890–1981): das Eigene in der Geschichte. Selbstentwürfe und Geschichtsentwürfe einer Historikerin* (Tübingen, 2004), pp. 164–74.

[113]H. Arendt, *Rahel Varnhagen: The Life of a Jewess* (London, 1957).

[114]Nattermann, *Deutsch-jüdische Geschichtsschreibung*, pp. 263–7.

focused on the importance of women as custodians of and passing on religious traditions.[115]

VI

The binational or transnational aspects of the Jewish past and the criticism of essentialist approaches to Jewish identity, as well as of nationalist perspectives within relational historical narratives, offer an opportunity to take a closer look at the European dimensions of Jewish historiography and to reappraise the Jewish past in Europe. The European dimensions of Jewish history acquired special significance in particular within universal historical narratives, in which the notion of Europe became a central category with which to structure the past. In Simon Dubnow's *World History*, for example, the Jewish past is divided into Oriental and European phases.[116] In his *History of the Jews*, Heinrich Graetz repeatedly placed emphasis on the exceptional features of European Jewish history and in particular criticised 'boundary-post patriotism', according to which German Jews had to be entirely German and French Jews entirely French, an attitude 'prevalent throughout Europe'.[117] Isaak Markus Jost likewise considered it essential that Judaism should recognise its affinities with 'European civilisation'.[118]

What enabled Jewish historiography in Europe to become a European historiography of the Jews was, after all, the transnational exchange of Jewish historians and European cultural transfer. The emergence and development of Jewish historiography was a part of this process. Evidence for this can be found not only in the essays about the history of the Jews of Venice, which appeared in the British and French journals quoted above, or in the studies about the history of the Jewish community of Rome, which had been prompted by a Jewish foundation in Vienna and written by German Jewish historians, but also in the biographies of Jewish historians in Europe. Many of these lived in very different worlds, but were members of European Jewish networks concerned with historical research, and experienced life in a number of different European countries during the course of their careers; they therefore can be described as the pioneers of European Jewish historiography.[119]

A European narrative of Jewish historiography could also draw inspiration from a study written by the Italian Rabbi Flaminio Servi about the role of Jews

---

[115]M. Kaplan, *The Making of the Jewish Middle Class. Women, Family, and Identity in Imperial Germany* (New York and Oxford, 1991).
[116]Dubnow, *Weltgeschichte*, vol. 1, p. xxiv.
[117]Graetz, *Geschichte der Juden*, vol. 11, p. 428.
[118]Jost, *Allgemeine Geschichte*, vol. 2, p. 544.
[119]See U. Wyrwa, 'Jewish Historiography in Europe: Transnational Biographies, Cultural Transfer and European Intellectual Exchange' (forthcoming).

in Europe in the development of civilisation,[120] and from the British Jewish historian Lucien Wolf. In his entry for the *Encyclopaedia Britannica*, Wolf writes that 'Jews have been Europeans for over a thousand years' and that 'the emancipated Jews were Europeans in virtue of the antiquity of their western settlements, and of the character impressed upon them by the circumstances of their European history'.[121]

The complete works of the British Jewish historian Cecil Roth, which include studies of British Jewish and Italian Jewish history,[122] a history of the Jews of Venice and a comprehensive study of the history of the Jews from 'the beginnings until the new state of Israel', represent a synthesis of all the narratives.[123] In addition, Roth has considerably furthered our understanding of the European dimension of Jewish history. His extensive study of the contribution made by Jews to European civilisation appeared in 1938,[124] the year in which he gave a speech at the Jewish Historical Society of England with the programmatic title 'The Jew as a European'.[125] Roth can thus be described as the initiator of a specifically European Jewish narrative.

Moreover, the narratives of Jewish history in Europe, which convey the cumulative experience of dealing with cultural diversity and heterogeneous worlds, can serve as a stimulus when developing the framework for an integrated narrative of the history of Europe,[126] which thrives above all on the recognition of the Other and on the capacity to sustain cultural difference. The transnational and relational as well as global dimensions of Jewish history testify to an approach to the historiography of Europe which does not fall into the pitfall of essentialist narratives, and which avoids resorting to a conception of Europe as a self-contained bloc.

Translated by Peter Carrier

---

[120]F. Servi, *Gli israeliti d'Europa nella civiltà: memorie storiche, biografiche e statistiche dal 1789 al 1870* (Turin, 1871).

[121]L. Wolf, 'Anti-Semitism', in *The Encyclopaedia Britannica: A Dictionary of Arts, Sciences, Literature, and General Information*, 11th edn, vol. 2 (New York, 1910), pp. 134–46.

[122]On Roth, see D. B. Ruderman, 'Cecil Roth, Historian of Italian Jewry: A Reassessment', in D. N. Myers and D. B. Ruderman (eds), *The Jewish Past Revisited: Reflections on Modern Jewish Historians* (New Haven and London, 1998), pp. 128–42; Brenner, *Propheten des Vergangenen*, pp. 175–83. See also C. Roth, *A History of the Jews in England* (Oxford, 1941); C. Roth, *The History of the Jews of Italy* (Philadelphia, 1946).

[123]C. Roth, *History of Jews in Venice* (Philadelphia, 1930); Roth, *Geschichte der Juden: von den Anfängen bis zum Neuen Staate Israel* (Stuttgart, 1954).

[124]C. Roth, *The Jewish Contribution to Civilisation* (London, 1938).

[125]C. Roth, *The Jew as a European*, presidential address delivered before the Jewish Historical Society of England on 2 January 1938 (London, 1938).

[126]Cf. D. Diner, 'Geschichte der Juden: Paradigma einer europäischen Historie', in G. Stourzh (ed.), *Annäherungen an eine europäische Geschichtsschreibung* (Vienna, 2002), pp. 85–103.

20
Conclusion: Picking up the Threads

Stefan Berger and Chris Lorenz

Reviewing the chapters in this volume leaves little doubt that national master narratives in historical writing in Europe have been extraordinarily successful in subsuming its potential Others over the last two centuries. Only rarely did those others develop into genuine alternatives to national history writing. However, as was to be expected on the basis of their conceptual history as codes of difference, the nation and its Others in Europe have produced blends of a bewildering variety, overlapping, submerging and intermingling with one another.

Ethnicity/race and nation

Cultural constructions of ethnicity were often at the heart of nineteenth-century constructions of national master narratives. Ethnic narratives were crucial in challenging multinational and imperial states, supporting secessionist nationalisms and carving out a space for independent statehood. Where the national story could be hung on the continued existence of a *state* and its institutions, ethnicity was often far less important than in places where such an institutional backbone was missing. Thus, for example, British statehood and the framing of the national history around the development of the constitution overwrote the stories of potential ethnic conflict between the English and the people on the Celtic fringes of Britain for much of the nineteenth and twentieth centuries, with Ireland being the obvious exception. By contrast, in much of Eastern Europe the absence of continuous state histories produced a multitude of ethnic narratives often sharing the same geographical spaces.

Apart from the state, the *dynasty* could be another symbol of integration and unity and a possible focus for the narration of nation. As successful dynasties tended to identify themselves and were identified with 'their' nation-states, usually no firm line can be drawn between dynastic and nation-state loyalties. National stories were often stories about monarchs and the expansion of dynastic power. In empires, such as the Habsburg, the emperor and the dynastic principle often sought to replace and overwrite national loyalties and identities. However, as the nineteenth century progressed, this proved to be increasingly difficult. Similarly, in weak multinational states, such as Spain, the monarchy struggled to keep together the different nationalities and cope with stirrings of separate national narratives in Catalonia and the Basque country. Only in strong multinational states, such as Britain, where the national story-lines merged with imperial story-lines which emphatically included the Welsh and the Scots, did the power of national history not pose a serious threat to the existence of the composite national state. However, the failure to bind Catholic Ireland into the Union produced separate national story-lines which eventually led to the formation of an independent Irish nation-state in 1922.

Within empires and multinational states, diverse national narratives often had a *different status*. In the Russian empire, for example, German narratives were frequently identified with Christianity, progress and culture, whereas Lithuanian and Ukrainian narratives enjoyed far less positive imaging. Establishing one's own national narrative and rejecting the hegemonic claims of other narratives became an important task of nation-builders within empires. The first step was to move out of the 'history-less' status and give one's own nation subject status – if need be by constructing and inventing a history. Empires, on the other hand, were keen to disallow such subject-formation at the periphery, even if many empires nationalised their cores in the course of the long nineteenth century. Contiguous empires also toyed with various ideas of autonomy at their peripheries (Hungary in the Habsburg empire; Finland in the Romanov empire), whilst overseas empires, especially the British, explored ways of accommodating the colonial nationalisms of its white settler colonies.[1] Yet, nationalising the cores of empires often meant ethnicising them. The core of the British empire was routinely perceived as English, whereas the Russian empire before 1917 and the Soviet empire after the mid-1920s were Russocentric, often attempting to repress parallel or different storylines emerging in history books.

In the period between 1918 and 1945, ethnic *definitions of the nation* led to civil war, border conflicts, total war and genocide. Many nations attempted to extend the boundaries of their existing nation-state by claiming that large ethnic minorities belonging to the nation found themselves outside the nation-state and needed to be regained. German *Ostforschung* after 1918 and the Greek *Megali* idea were two examples. For the Greek national history, the Byzantine lands were really Greek and therefore had to be liberated from the

---

[1]S. Berger and A. Miller, 'Nation-Building and Regional Integration, c. 1800–1914: the Role of Empires', *European Review of History*, 15, 3 (forthcoming 2008).

Turks. For the dominant German national narrative, the 'lost territories' in East Central Europe were really German and therefore the Versailles Treaty had to be repealed and the territories had to be re-incorporated into the German Reich.

The parallel construction of different ethnic narratives on the same territorial space made the principle of ethnicity so explosive, as it immediately raised the question what to do with the 'ethnic Other'. Even in more established nation-states, ethnic minorities within the borders of the nation were frequently ignored. The Samis in Norway, Sweden and Finland, the Inuit in Denmark, the Sinti and Roma in Hungary, Romania and Slovakia – as ethnic minorities they all were silenced by the national histories of the states they lived in. Multi-ethnic national narratives are only a development of the more recent past. They sadly emerged at a time when the rich tapestry of ethnic identities in Europe had been cleansed through two world wars and several genocides and when the state boundaries coincided with the ethnic boundaries as never before. Postmodern critiques of the national principle championed and celebrated multiple ethnic narratives and compared the nation to a fractured mirror in which all sorts of different constructions found its place. One might ask whether a postmodern national history can actually exist that is more than a self-reflexive essay on the many historiographical constructions of national identity.[2] Yet such limitation seems eminently preferable to the return of fixed and exclusive ethnic narratives. For even in the 1990s, as Yugoslavia demonstrates, ethnicity lost none of its deadly and genocidal force when it came to the construction of a unified national history which meant eradicating multiple forms of ethnic constructions on the same territory.[3]

With the racialisation of ethnic understandings of the nation through the reception of Social Darwinist thought in the late nineteenth century, race began to take on meanings which transcend the national paradigm; for example, in the concept of a Nordic race among *völkisch* historians in Germany. However, these developments need to be set alongside the far more prominent trends which nationalised racial thought and developed an historical understanding of race within national frameworks. To continue with the German example, whilst the Nazi historians could make use of race if they wanted to emphasise the solidarities of members of other Aryan nations with Nazi Germany, they still

---

[2] For examples of such a self-reflexive postmodern national history, see the work of Konrad Jarausch and Michael Geyer, in particular *Shattered Past. Reconstructing German Histories* (Princeton, NJ, 2003), and *ÖZG* Themenheft 7/1996/4, 'Welches Österreich soll es sein?'.
[3] On Yugoslavia, see H. Sundhausen, 'Jugoslawien und seine Nachfolgestaaten', in: M. Flacke, *Mythen der Nationen: 1945: Arena der Erinnerungen*, vol. 1 (Berlin, 2004), pp. 373–426.

focused on racialising the historical consciousness of Germans and applying racial categories to the history of the nation.

In the late twentieth century, national narratives in various parts of Europe keep emphasising ethnicity as a marker of identity as a result of a perceived threat to the national principle from the European Union. Nowhere in Europe have European narratives replaced the national narratives. In fact, it has turned out to be extremely difficult to construct European histories based on the history of a continent that has been made and remade out of war and conflict. Hence, history is a poisoned chalice for European identity, characterised by fundamental ambivalences, whereas national narratives continue to thrive on various concoctions of an alleged national past. Characteristically, although most individual national histories in Europe follow 'progressive' story-lines, it would not be hard to argue that Europe's nations collectively produced Europe's 'fall' in the first half of the twentieth century.

What remains striking when one looks at the power of ethnic narratives to challenge existing multinational states and empires is how much more successful those multinational states in Western Europe have been in surviving the onslaught of ethnic national narratives. Whether one considers Spain, Britain or Belgium, they still exist as national entities (albeit in all three cases challenged by regional nationalisms), whereas the Soviet Union, Yugoslavia and Czechoslovakia have all disintegrated when faced with the power of ethnic story-lines. Comparing Belgium and Czechoslovakia one might, of course, wonder whether the happy and peaceful parting of the ways between Czechs and Slovaks is not preferable to the ongoing pain and misery involved in the unhappy marriage of the Flemish and the Walloon parts of Belgium. Although we must look at each case on its own merits, and while each case will reveal an individual set of explanations for why the ethnic narratives developed different energies and results, one cannot help wondering whether the European Union and its institutional framework has had a part in stabilising national frameworks in Eastern Europe after the collapse of communism.

Religion and nation

Considering religion, church history continued to be a prominent strand of historiography in many national historiographies throughout the nineteenth and early twentieth centuries. However, it developed almost in a parallel universe with national history and rarely, if ever, set itself up as a conscious alternative to national history. Instead, religion as a rule was written into the national narratives. This took the form of Protestant historians identifying Protestantism as a central ingredient of their nations' national character. The Finnish historian Renvall, for example, wrote about Catholicism being alien to the Nordic soul, and many a Protestant historian in Germany reflected openly about Catholic historians as a monstrosity and a blemish on the integrity of the profession. In Hungary, Protestant Hungarian nobles had formed the backbone of national resistance against the Catholic Habsburgs. Narratives which came to regard Protestantism as central ingredient of national identity often linked Protestantism to the evolution of the political nation. Constructions of British and German constitutionalism, as well as Swiss republicanism, all heavily depended on understandings of Protestantism. Catholic narratives were consciously excluded, although individual Catholics, such as Lord Acton in Britain and Franz Schnabel in Germany, could become respected members of the historical professions. Yet most of their colleagues remained resolutely Protestant or at the very least 'culturally Protestant'.

In religiously mixed countries, such as Germany, Switzerland, the Netherlands or indeed Slovakia, it tended to be the Protestant story-lines which dominated the profession. In mono-confessional countries, such as Norway, it was easy to regard religion as unimportant, as there was no tension between nation and religion. Thus when religion and nation 'overlap', religion as a 'code of difference' remains what we could call 'submerged'. Hence religion is taken for granted in those national histories rather than problematised.

This is usually different in multi-confessional nations or nations with a strong liberal-secular tradition. In countries, such as France and Spain, a strongly liberal and secular national historiography wrote national history in a way that laid the blame for almost everything that was wrong about French and Spanish history at the door of the Catholic Church. This was particularly visible in their writings about the Inquisition in Spain. In those secular-liberal strands of historiography, which were by no means restricted to the Catholic countries of Europe, national identity took on forms of secular millenarianism in which liberal politics was replacing religion as the key to salvation.[4]

However, as more recent writings on the role of religion in nineteenth century Europe have pointed out, earlier assumptions about the decline of its importance and the extent of secularisation during this period may have been somewhat premature.[5] All over Europe, the confessionalisation of societies had a lasting impact on conceptions of national history. Religion provided key symbols, rituals and collective practices underpinning national master narratives. Patron saints and religious festivals could provide expressions of national sentiment and ambition. Religious identity was also closely linked to linguistic identity, as the Latin script came to be identified with Roman Catholicism and the Cyrillic script with Orthodoxy. Especially where the ruler of the state was at the same time the

---

[4]E. Kedourie, *Nationalism* (Oxford, 1993); H-G. Haupt and D. Langewiesche (eds), *Nation und Religion in der deutschen Geschichte* (Frankfurt/M, 2001).
[5]O. Blaschke, 'Das 19. Jahrhundert: ein zweites konfessionelles Zeitalter?', *Geschichte und Gesellschaft,* 26 (2000), 38–75.

ex officio head of the Church, as in Russia and in Prussia, a dynastic historiography could merge with a religious one to produce powerful national narratives.

Religion also served as a tool for national historians to demonstrate key differences *vis-à-vis* dominant groups in empires. In the Habsburg empire, for example, Catholicism was widely identified with German pro-empire sentiments, whereas Protestantism in its Hussite (Czech), Calvinist (Magyar) and Lutheran (Slovak) versions was connected to the allegedly repressed nations within the empire. Confessional differences became markers of ethnic divisions 'overlapping' each other. However, some empires, notably the Ottoman, found it easier than nation-states to live with several separate religions co-existing with various degrees of autonomy.

Within multi-confessional nation-states, diverse confessional communities (Protestants, Catholics, Orthodox Christians, Jews) shaped separate national narratives which underpinned distinct religious milieus. In Switzerland, Germany and the Netherlands national narratives became pillarised along confessional lines. In France and Belgium by contrast, the major dividing line was between secular narratives and their Catholic alternatives. This was similar in countries which were confessionally homogeneous. In Lutheran Sweden and Catholic Spain, the dividing line also ran between secular and religious national narratives. In Cold War Italy, Catholic national historiography portrayed Catholicism as the last bulwark against evil, atheist communism. In nineteenth-century Eastern Europe, religion served as an important marker of difference in multi-confessional border areas, for example, between Orthodox Russians, Uniate Ukrainians and Roman Catholic Poles.[6]

Religion and nationalism usually formed strong alliances, but there could also be considerable tensions. In some national narratives, particular confessions were externalised as 'foreign'. Hence, British nineteenth-century narratives depicted Catholicism as a foreign, continental European and French influence which stood against the indigenous Protestant British empire.[7] In the Dutch national narratives – focused on the war of independence against the Spanish Catholic 'oppression' – being Dutch also meant being Protestant well into the nineteenth century. Confessional aspects only became important in national rivalries, where hostile nations claimed allegiance to different confessions. Where nations adhered to the same confession, as with Catholicism

---

[6]On the strong impact of religion on nationalising tendencies in Central and Eastern Europe, see J. Bahlke and A. Strohmeyer (eds), *Konfessionalisierung in Ostmitteleuropa. Wirkungen des religiösen Wandels im 16. Und 17. Jahrhundert in Staat, Gesellschaft und Kultur* (Stuttgart, 1999); H-C. Maner and M. Schulze Wessel (eds), *Kirche und Staat, Religion und Gesellschaft in Ostmitteleuropa in der Zwischenkriegszeit* (Stuttgart, 2002).

[7]See, for example, K. Robbins, *History, Religion and Identity in Modern Britain* (London, 1993).

in Poland and Lithuania or with Protestantism in Germany, Estonia and Latvia, national rivalries had to be linked to other differences.

If religious narratives became a central ingredient in many national histories across Europe, it was perhaps not by chance that in nineteenth-century Italy, the neo-Guelphs failed to build the Italian nation-state around the papacy. It is certainly rare for a nation to define itself exclusively by religion. Unsurprisingly it was a Frenchman, Ernest Renan, in his classic attempt to define a nation, who argued that religion is not a sufficient basis for the establishment of modern nationality.[8] Yet religion undoubtedly belonged to one of the most powerful bonds within many national communities and those which aspire to become one.

If nineteenth-century European liberals tended to be hostile to organised religion, they often found it easier to accommodate their liberal values with Protestantism. Hence many historiographies were characterised by a 'cultural Protestantism', in which religion mattered. Religious beliefs had a lasting influence on both French (Thierry, Guizot) and German (Ranke, Droysen, Sybel) nineteenth-century historiography. Not infrequently, historians understood their own work as tracing and documenting God's actions in the past, 'scientific' methods notwithstanding. Great personalities in history were presented as agents of a higher will.

Many nineteenth-century German historians had studied theology and had come from families of vicars and pastors. In their writings, religious discourses became nationalised and national discourses became sacralised. Religion not only served the nation, but also became a crucial element of understanding it. For many the nation became the new religion. It was no accident that the structure of national narratives often paralleled the structure of the New Testament, thus creating a strong narratological 'overlap' between the nation and religion as codes of difference. The suffering, death and resurrection of Jesus equalled the destruction, ruin and eventual resurrection of the nation.

To name just three examples of this general pattern, in Polish and Spanish national narratives, Poland and Spain were referred to as 'Christ of nations', whilst the Hungarian national narrative described Hungary as the 'holy nation' in which comparisons with the passion of Christ were easily made. So the Christian-Hegelian three-stage narrative model, which depicts history as a process of transformation beginning with an original state of purity, unity and salvation, followed by a stage of impurity, disunity and corruption, and ending with a stage of regained purity, unity and – now conscious – salvation, seems to form the basis for many national histories in Europe. In this sense, many or even

---

[8]E. Renan, 'What is a Nation?' [1882], reprinted in V. P. Pekora (ed.), *Nations and Identities* (Oxford, 2001), pp. 172f.

most national master narratives in Europe are 'prefigured' by the religious master narrative of Christianity (Hayden White's thesis of a narrative 'prefiguration' of history is surely right).[9]

In many nations, the relationship between religious and national identity was symbiotic and the 'overlap' between the respective codes of difference complete, leading to the phenomenon of 'submersion' of both types of collective identity. Hence, Orthodoxy and Romanianness became virtually synonymous, as did Catholicism and Polishness. The Swedish nation was constructed as a Lutheran bulwark against Russian (and by implication also Orthodox) expansion. Sweden had defended European Protestantism against the Catholic Counter-Reformation in the Thirty Years' War. Denmark was often identified with a rather inward-looking Lutheranism in the nineteenth century. In Palacky's narration of the Czech nation, fifteenth-century Hussitism was the central ingredient of Czech national identity.

As a consequence of this complete 'overlap', religious figures often became national heroes: Jan Hus in the Czech lands, Martin Luther in Germany, Zwingli and Calvin in Switzerland. Kings, such as St. Stephan and St. Wenzel, who had been declared saints by the Catholic Church, were equally important in the national pantheon. In Poland and Lithuania, the Catholic Church as an institution was constructed as guarantor of the survival of the nation during prolonged periods of statelessness. Catholicism was crucial to the national narratives produced under Franco and Salazar. Both Spain and Portugal, it was argued, achieved national greatness only by fusing Church and Crown. Greek national narratives presented the Orthodox Church as a bridge to the classical heritage of Greece. 'Helleno-Christianity' became the cradle of European civilisation and culture and therefore established a superior position of the modern Greek state over all its rivals.

Arguably, religion played the greatest role in the construction of national narratives where *national missions* were defined in religious terms – the future orientation of historical narratives being the charactertistic of the 'modern' regime of historicity (as defined by Hartog). Spanish and Portuguese national narratives stressed how both nations brought Catholicism to half the globe and how they drove the Muslims and Jews out of the Iberian Peninsula. Poland, Russia, Greece and the nationalities of the Habsburg empire also presented their national histories in terms of shielding Christian Europe from the infidels. The battle of Mohacs against the Ottomans in 1526 was presented as national cata-

[9]H. White, *Metahistory: The Historical Imagination in Nineteenth Century Europe*, (Baltimore, 1974). For a more detailed analysis of the nation and religion, see A. D. Smith, 'Religion: Nationalism and Identity', in Smelser and Baltus (eds), *International Encyclopedia of the Social & Behavioral Sciences*, pp. 13085–90.

strophe for Hungary where the Hungarians sacrificed themselves for the sake of Christian Europe. The Greek struggle for independence was presented as a model for other Christian nations in the Balkans to establish their national narratives against the foremost Islamic power in Europe. The *Reconquista* in Spain was an epic of national recovery in which European triumphed over Arab culture. So, in many national histories in Europe, Islam represents the negative Other of Christianity. Also in the domain of religion, antagonism and conflict have been the rule in European history and the idea of 'peaceful coexistence' was a late invention.

Class and nation

As the discourse of class emerged in the nineteenth century, its propagators almost invariably attempted to link it to the national discourse by claiming that the social, cultural and political exclusion of the working class from the nation was unjust. The workers formed the 'true nation' and therefore needed to reassert themselves by struggling against their exclusion from the nation by other classes. It was those enjoying 'privilege' at the cost of others who were branded parasitical and standing in the way of unity.

This central concern with unity linked class and national narratives. Like national narratives, class narratives were obsessed with finding the origins of national class struggles and creating a continuous history from the dim and distant past to the present. Both narratives were concerned with eradicating sectional, 'selfish' interests. But where was that selfishness located? In many countries, it was the aristocracy, but increasingly the bourgeoisie and the middle classes formed the key adversary of unity. This kind of discourse raised the question which social class should be regarded as the main carrier of the national idea.

The answer was remarkably diverse in different parts of Europe. In Poland, it was the gentry and many historians, such as Lelewel, stressed the importance of the struggle of the gentry against absolutism in the fifteenth and sixteenth centuries for nation formation. In more industrialised countries, notably Britain, constructions of the nation were predominantly middle-class and framed the national story-lines around issues of continuing industrial, political and cultural progress. In Scandinavia, Finland and the Ukraine, where free peasants formed an important section of the population, the nation was constructed around ideas of peasant liberties which had to be defended against encroachments by an indigenous or, more often, 'foreign' elite.

Where the class enemy was foreign, class conflict easily became ethnicised, thus creating an overlap between the ethnic and class codes of difference. Hence, in the Habsburg empire, the German-speaking elite was frequently perceived in national narratives of non-Germans as major national and class enemy.

Some smaller nations, such as the Czechs and Slovaks self-consciously tended to depict themselves as plebeian nations who stood against 'foreign' elites and aristocratic privilege. However, to complicate matters further, all European nations witnessed contested and competing constructions of national identity around particular social classes.

In many places, class conflict became a major source of disruption for narratives of national unity. The hegemonic elites usually came to perceive class as a threat, and indeed, class belonged firmly to the language of revolutionary socialism in the nineteenth century. Hence 'professional' historians, who were often close to the state elites, tended to ignore class conflict. However, there were also some spectacularly prominent multi-volume examples of class histories in the second half of the nineteenth century.[10] Economic and social history journals were founded in many nation-states around the turn of the century and reflected a growing interest in class. But denial and repression from the 'professional' and 'scientific' historians could not prevent the appearance of class histories, which frequently emerged in the surroundings of the organised labour movement. Labour activists made class a topic and mostly chose the nation-state as framework for their class histories. Such a choice already indicated the desire on behalf of many socialists not to transcend the national story-lines but to reframe them into stories which would be able to incorporate class. Eduard Bernstein's histories in Germany, Jean Jaures' in France, Filippo Turati's in Italy and Robert Grimm's in Switzerland are examples of such inclusive class histories. Their class narratives were alternative national narratives including different visions of national identity rather than attempts to overcome national identity.

In different European nation-states, these efforts met with diverse levels of resistance from 'scientific' historiography. Beatrice and Sidney Webb and the London School of Economics were vital in paving the way for social and class history in interwar Britain. Historians not associated with the labour movement often used narrative constructions of 'the people' to defuse the disruptive potential of class and to unify the national narrative. Writing national history in the framework of 'the people' allowed historians as diverse as G. M. Trevelyan and Arthur Bryant to merge class and nation and write an inclusive national history.[11] In Germany the inclusion of class into national narratives had to

---

[10]See, for example, E. Levasseur, *Histoires des classes ouvrières en France depuis la conquête de Jules César jusqu'à la Révolution*, 2 vols. (Paris, 1859); idem, *Histoires des classes ouvrières en France depuis 1789 jusqu'à nos jours*, 2 vols. (Paris, 1867); F. Garido, *Historia de las clases trabajadores*, 4 vols (Madrid, 1870).

[11]On Trevelyan, see D. Cannadine, *G. M. Trevelyan: a Life in History* (London, 1992); on Bryant, see J. Stapleton, *Sir Arthur Bryan and National History in Twentieth-Century Britain* (Lanham, MD, 2005). Stapleton is also interesting on the relationship between Trevelyan and Bryant.

wait until the 1960s and 1970s. The German history profession was one of the most rigorous in attempting to prevent the emergence of class narratives well into the twentieth century. Gerhard Ritter's description of Eckart Kehr as '*Edelbolschewist*' and Hans Rothfels' successful attempt to prevent Gustav Mayer access to archival material in the 1920s are just two prominent examples of such attempts at exclusion.

Class narratives were often centrally grouped around revolutions and revolutionary events. Revolutions were represented as the foundational moments, or origins, of nations, such as France (1789) or Russia (1917), but they were also moments in which class and nation came into conflict. Revolution was frequently an absent Other even in those national story-lines that did not have a successful revolution of their own. Some national stories, such as the British and the German, were preoccupied with demonstrating that revolution was *not* necessary – presenting their own particular histories as the 'normal' way. Here revolution and class were frequently depicted as standing outside the national tradition, being alien and foreign imports with no roots in the indigenous national tradition.

Narratives of revolution were invariably narratives of the extension of democratic rights and liberties. As such, they highlighted existing disunities and exclusion. Where they failed, questions surrounding the lack of unity lingered. Where they succeeded, claims of refound unity laid the foundation of revolutionary myths of origins, of nations reborn, rejuvenated and unified by the revolutionary experience. Yet everywhere we also find counter-revolutionary narratives which present a quite different picture of the revolution as dividing the nation and usurping and destroying national traditions, confirming Rigney's thesis of the 'agonistic dimension' of (revisionist) historical narratives. Hence, the republican French narratives viewed 1789 as a source of unity and strength, whereas the Catholic French narratives lamented the revolution as the decline of traditional French values and norms.

Even within the pro-revolutionary narratives, class variants could put a very different gloss on how the narrative was framed. As long as the Greek revolution was represented as a national rising against Turkish oppression, it was a story of national unity. Nevertheless, when Yanis Kordatos interpreted the revolution primarily as a social rather than a national rising directed against both Turkish and indigenous Greek oppressors of the people, class reframed the national history in important ways. However, class was thoroughly nationalised everywhere and the historians of class tended to adopt national frameworks. There were some exceptions to the rule, such as Artur Rosenberg, whose *Democracy and Socialism* of 1938 was a conscious attempt to replace the national framework with comparative perspectives. Institutions such as the International Institute of Social History in Amsterdam, founded in 1935, also explicitly encouraged the writing of a transnational and comparative history of class.

Since 1945 there have been attempts to privilege 'class' over 'nation' as the basic framework of analysis and narrative, for example, in the work of Eric Hobsbawm and, in a very different way, Jürgen Kuczynski. Yet, at best, this should be seen only as a distinct minority tradition among the strong stream of national class histories. Class became an important part of national history from the 1960s onwards and challenged the older, almost exclusively political constructions of the nation. Yet social histories by no means signalled the abandonment of earlier national commitments. The hyper-nationalism of German *Volksgeschichte*,[12] the intense patriotism of leading figures of the Annales school, the much commented on Englishness of the Webbs or the Dutchness of the self-proclaimed Marxist Jan Romein indicate that class and national perspectives could coexist rather than be opposites. National institutes, dedicated to the study of class and labour history, were founded after the Second World War and often took the nation as framework for a class perspective on history (e.g. the Italian Istituto Gramsci, the French Institut français d'histoire sociale or the German Friedrich-Ebert-Stiftung).

Social history, often informed by a class perspective, had its heyday in the 1960s and the 1970s. With the onset of a new, post-industrial era from the late 1970s and the vanishing of left-wing hopes for a working-class reform or revolution, the class master narratives declined and found themselves in serious crisis. Political history bounced back and a new cultural history also challenged the social historical approaches from the 1980s onwards.[13] Only in communist states did class master narratives claim predominance, largely because of the tied nature of communist historiographies.

Between 1917 and 1992, communist Eastern Europe witnessed the most significant and sustained efforts to merge class and national narratives, thus overcoming the tensions between these two narrative constructions of identity. Communist historiography celebrated the Russian Revolution of 1917 as key event of the twentieth century. The Soviet Union became the fatherland of the international proletariat, which had to be protected against international capital.

Yet internationalism rarely replaced the national orientation in communist historiographies. Across communist Eastern Europe after 1945, existing national paradigms were simply painted red. In many countries, such as Hungary, Slovakia and Poland, the lack of an indigenous Marxist historiography was a

---

[12]On *Volksgeschichte*, see P. Schöttler (ed.), *Geschichtsschreibung als Legitimationswissenschaft 1918–1945* (Frankfurt/M, 1997); M. Hettling (ed.), *Volksgeschichten im Europa der Zwischenkriegszeit*, (Göttingen, 2003); W. Oberkrome, *Volksgeschichte. Methodische Innovation und völkische Ideologisierung in der deutschen Geschichtswissenschaft 1918–1945* (Göttingen, 1993).
[13] For an excellent summary of the development of class and labour history in Western Europe, see M. van der Linden and L. Heerma van Voss, 'Introduction', in idem (eds), *Class and other Identities. Entries to West European Labour Historiography* (Amsterdam, 2001); D. Dworkin, *Class Struggles* (Harlow, 2007).

crucial problem. Here the merger between class and national paradigms had to be created from nothing. Elsewhere, such as in the Czech historiography, they could rely on antecedents in the interwar period. After all, the united front strategies of the 1930s had already witnessed communist attempts to nationalise its historical narratives. The strong nationalisation of class narratives through-out Eastern Europe also helps to explain why many Eastern European coun-tries witnessed a relatively smooth transition from communist to nationalist narratives in the post-Cold War period.

Gender and nation

The gendering of national histories has long been an important characteristic of national narratives throughout Europe. The history profession was, until recently, a predominantly male enterprise. The male identities of historians produced highly gendered fantasies which influenced their views on national history. While research on gender and nationalism has become a major area of research over the past decade,[14] we still know relatively little about the way that national histories were gendered in many parts of Europe. The studies of Bonnie Smith on France, Ilaria Porciani on Italy and Mary O'Dowd on the British Isles need to be complemented by similar studies in other countries.[15] The rediscovery of historical texts produced by women put women back on the map of historical writing from where they had been largely excluded by a male-dominated profession. Women played an important role in nineteenth-century scholars' families and in popular non-scientific forms of historical writing. It therefore requires an expansion of the genre of history writing, if we want to recover fully the contribution that women made to historical writing.

In many national histories, the enemies of the nation were depicted in fem-inised forms. At the same time, in periods of decline and facing successful attacks from abroad, national historians talked about 'the rape of their nation',

---

[14]Specifically on historiography, see J. Scott, *Gender and the Politics of History*, (New York, 1988); B. Smith, *The Gender of History: Men, Women and Historical Practice* (Cambridge, MA, 1998); K. Canning, *Gender History in Practice: Historical Perspectives on Bodies, Class, and Citizenship* (Ithaca, NY, 2006). See also more generally, I. Blom, K. Hagemann and C. Hall (eds), *Gendered Nations. Nationalisms and Gender Order in the Long Nineteenth Century* (Oxford, 2000).

[15]Smith, *The Gender of History*; I. Porciani, 'Les historiennes et le Risorgimento', *Mélanges de l'école française de Rome – Italie et Méditerranée* 112 (2000), 317–57; M. O'Dowd, 'Women', in Ilaria Porciani and Jo Tollebeek (eds), *Writing the Nation*, vol. 2: *Setting the Standards: Institutions, Networks and Communities of National Historiography* (Basingstoke, 2009); M. O'Dowd and I. Porciani (eds), *Women Historians*, special issue of *Storia della Storiografia*, 46 (2004); A. Epple, *Empfindsame Geschichtsschreibung: Eine Geschlechtergeschichte der Historio-graphie zwischen Aufklärung und Historismus* (Cologne, 2003).

identifying the enemy nation as male rapist. National saints were male and female (such as Brother Klaus in Switzerland or Jeanne d'Arc in France). In the tradition of the High Middle Ages, the allegorical representations of the state were often female, yet active representatives of the states were mostly male (the exception being Marianne in France). In many national histories, the awakening of national consciousness was identified with masculine strength and virility. In countries which relied heavily on natural metaphors to describe national character, such as Switzerland and Austria, those scenarios of nature were also heavily gendered.[16]

Male historians often started out to construct national histories as manly histories. As Thomas Babington Macauley stated categorically, his English history was not for ladies, coffee tables or for girls' boarding schools; it was for men who were engaged in affairs of the state.[17] Indeed, many national heroes that we find in national histories are men. Founders of nations, such as Bismarck, Garibaldi or William of Orange, stand alongside national saviours such as Winston Churchill or William Wallace, reformers of the nation, such as Peter the Great or the Freiherr vom Stein, generals and military leaders, such as von Moltke, de Gaulle or Gustav Wasa, cultural icons, such as Shakespeare, Dante, Cervantes, Goethe or Molière, and great religious leaders, such as Jan Hus or Martin Luther.[18] Women occasionally make an appearance as anti-heroes. Thus, for example, Lelewel depicts the foreign-born wives of Polish kings as importers of distasteful foreign customs weakening the good, indigenous Polish traditions. In addition, some Spanish national narratives make a woman, Florinda 'La Cava', the main culprit in the story of the Arab invasions of the peninsula in the eighth century.

Where national historians ascribed attributes to national collectives, they often took care to give them male connotations. Thus, nations were invariably described as organised, educated, rational and virile. The history of state formation and the history of war (both histories are deeply interconnected) were manly themes celebrating the virtues of warriors and statesmen. The close relation between war, the military and nation-state formation excluded women.[19] And yet the maleness of national story-lines was rarely straightforward. Wars in

---

[16]ÖZG Themenheft, 7/1996/4, 'Welches Oesterreich soll es sein?'; for Switzerland, see G. P. Marchal, *Schweizer Gebrauchsgeschichte. Geschichtsbilder, Mythenbildung und nationale Identität* (Basel, 2006) and G. P. Marchal and A. Mattioli (eds), *Erfundene Schweiz. Konstruktionen nationaler Identität* (Zurich, 1992).

[17]Cited in B. Stuchtey, 'Literature, Liberty and Life of the Nation: British Historiography from Macauley to Trevelyan', in S. Berger, M. Donovan and K. Passmore (eds), *Writing National Histories. Western Europe since 1800* (London, 1999), p. 31.

[18]On national heroes, see L. Eriksonas, *National Heroes and National Identities: Scotland, Norway and Lithuania* (Brussels, 2004).

[19]U. Frevert, *A Nation in Barracks: Modern Germany, Military Conscription and Civil Society* (Oxford, 2004).

particular were often connected to brutalities, atrocities and aggression more generally, which were turned against their male perpetrators. Thus, for example, national histories across Europe dealing with Germany as a major Other, routinely deplored the militarism and aggressiveness of a male-dominated paradigm conceptualised in the term 'Prussianism'. The Austrian empress Maria Theresa, portrayed as the good 'mother' of all Austrians, was juxtaposed in Austrian national narratives against the evil and brutal Frederick II of Prussia who treated the nations around Prussia with as much contempt as he did his own subjects. Czech historians contrasted the alleged harmony between the sexes in the Czech lands with the situation in Germany, where women were repressed by men. The pacific feminine nature of the nation was at times stressed positively against the aggressive and brutal posturing of its enemies.

However, to complicate matters even further, women were not only glorified as pacifiers but also as warriors. German 'sword virgins' fighting against the French occupation in the wars of liberation at the beginning of the nineteenth century, Polish women taking up arms in the 1831 uprising against Tsarist Russia, Boadicea fighting the Roman occupiers of Britain, or the bakeress of Aljubarrota, contributing to the victory of Portugal over Castillian forces in the battle of Aljubarrota in 1385, are prominent examples of warrior women whose courage and fighting spirit set an example to future generations of nationalists. Some national narratives did their best to edit out these episodes of traditional gender inversion and omit them from their national story-lines. In some cases, knowledge of the existence of such female combatants in national struggles had to be recovered (often by women and gender historians) in the second half of the twentieth century.[20] Nevertheless, warrior-like female figures, the most famous being, of course, Jeanne d'Arc, were not unknown to many national narratives in Europe.

Most national narratives were not so much one-sidedly male as they were concerned with depicting the nation as a family in which male and female virtues were combined to produce perfect national harmony and unity. Hence, male and female images often appeared next to each other. References to the tsar as a father figure in Russian national narratives coincided with invocations of 'mother Russia'. Frederick II of Prussia appeared next to Queen Luise of Prussia. The figure of Britannia was put alongside that of John Bull in British national narratives. Allegories of the nation tended to be female, and the portrayals of an 'awakened' people were often littered with female attributes; they were unspoilt, untouched, pure, emotional and vulnerable. In every national story then, we find women, and representations of women, who matter in

---

[20]K. Hagemann, *'Männlicher Muth und teutsche Ehre': Nation, Krieg und Geschlecht in der Zeit der antinapoleonischen Kriege Preussens* (Paderborn, 2002).

national histories. But when and where did women matter at particular junctures in a nation's history? They matter as queens and rulers, such as Elizabeth I in England, as saints, as mythical founding mothers, such as Libuše in the Czech lands, as those who sacrificed themselves for the nation, such as Wanda in Poland and Princess Olga in Russia. There is no shortage of ancient and not-so-ancient female heroines in national narratives and they often served as a model mother and a role model for contemporary women of the nation-state. Fascist Spanish national narratives thus often depicted Isabel the Catholic as a model to be emulated by the nationally minded women of Spain. Collectively, national histories tended to stress how virtuous the women of the nation were. Female virtue demonstrated the superior moral character of their nation over that of others. Women were the integrative, bridge-building, friendly, protective and homely face of the nation; the counterpart to the warriors and statesmen who guided the nation through peril and helped it into being.

The positive portrayal of women and feminine virtues was often linked to the introduction and defence of Christianity. Just as the Christian religion was represented as softening the barbarian, pagan cultures of Europe and introducing more femininity into national characters, so in representations of nations like Hungary, Slovakia or Poland, cults of Mary were integrated, As such, the sacrifice of the mother of God and of Jesus himself were often likened to the suffering of the nation. Furthermore, just as suffering and death in the New Testament were followed by resurrection, so would the nation one day rise like the phoenix from its ashes. Thus the narratological structure of many national histories was based on the fundamental text of Christian religion. In this sense, those who argue that Turkey does not share 'the historical traditions of Europe' have a point – although the conclusion that therefore Turkey should not become a member-state of the EU is of course a *non sequitur*.

However this may be, it was not only in the context of the sacralisation of the nation that women became prominent players in national narratives. Women also were secular martyrs in liberal, anti-absolutist national histories. Thus, for example, Marianna Pineda, executed by the Spanish monarchical government of Fernando VII in 1831, became a symbol of liberal Spain in many national narratives. If women played an important part in the national narratives of most European nations throughout the nineteenth and twentieth centuries, the entire stories no doubt remained male-dominated. A continuous and persistent self-feminisation of the national narrative, as in Austria, remained the exception rather than the rule.

With some notable exceptions, such as the Swiss case, women's history in its heyday in the late nineteenth and the last third of the twentieth centuries set itself up consciously ignoring the grand national narratives and writing a history in which women figured more prominently. Women's history was to a large extent about making women visible in history. While this was done so successfully that many women historians eventually moved on to gender history, they rarely sought to contribute to the rewriting of national histories from a woman's or gender perspective despite the fact that their spatial framework was also often national. Instead they concentrated on forms of social or cultural history writing which bypassed the nation. Following the emergence of second-wave feminism in the 1960s and 1970s, many women historians took up the challenge of recovering the lives of ordinary working-class women. During the 1980s and 1990s, the activities of women on behalf of the nation moved centre-stage, but within the debates surrounding history and national identity, women tended to be underrepresented.

Of course, some of the more sensitive historians in the nineteenth and twentieth centuries had clear suspicions about the national, religious or class biases hidden in most national history writing – notwithstanding the traditional emphasis on 'scientific' methods.[21] The most well-known arguments to overcome these biases by using the comparative method have been formulated by Marc Bloch (1886-1944) and Henri Pirenne (1862-1935). For both men, comparison served an epistemological and a political function at the same time. First, comparison was the only means to break out of the national framework usually taken for granted in history, thus anticipating many recent arguments in favour of transnational approaches. Only the comparative method allowed for grounded statements about the specificity and generality of historical phenomena, and for an empirical justification of the attribution of causes. Therefore, from an epistemological point of view, comparison is the only methodological 'reality check' available to historians – the broader this 'check' the stronger is the empirical support of the knowledge claims involved.[22]

Next to this epistemological function, Bloch and Pirenne saw the comparative method as the only way to 'neutralise' the political and cultural biases of historians. Political bias was recognised as a problem of scientific history after the First World War had shown how easily 'scientific' historians could evolve into overtly nationalist historians without any professional alarm bells ringing, critical method notwithstanding. Pirenne and Bloch regarded comparative history as the only means to 'correct' the national biases and the nationalist myopia of 'scientific' historians. As Pirenne notes, 'the comparative method alone can diminish racial, political, and national prejudices among historians' meaning 'the comparative method permits history in its true perspective'.[23]

---

[21]See C. Lorenz, 'Scientific/Critical History', in A. Tucker (ed.), *The Blackwell Companion to Historiography and Philosophies of History* (Cambridge, 2008), pp. 393–403.

[22]For comparative method, see Lorenz, *Konstruktion der Vergangenheit*, ch. 10 and 11.

[23]H. Pirenne cited in H. Meyerhoff (ed.), *The Philosophy of History in Our Time* (New York, 1959), pp. 98–9. Bloch shared this belief. See, M. Bloch, *Aus der Werkstatt des Historikers. Zur Theorie und Praxis der Geschichtswissenschaft*, ed. P. Schöttler (Frankfurt and New York, 2000).

Cultural transfer and national historiographies

What also emerges very clearly from any comparison of national historiographies is the importance of histories of cultural transfer. Towering intellectual figures, such as Herder, Hegel, Mill, Marx and Lamprecht, had a profound
impact in almost all European countries on the ways in which national historians devised and structured their histories. However, there is an equally
important but often neglected form of more limited regional transfer, where
neighbouring countries, belonging to what Stefan Troebst has called *Geschichtsregionen* (historical regions), have mutually influenced each other.[24] Yet geographical proximity did not always lead to processes of cultural transfer, as the
case of Spain and Portugal demonstrates.

   However, overall it is striking how easily ideas crossed national borders. The
linguistic abilities of historians facilitated such reception of 'foreign' ideas and
their adaptation in diverse national surroundings. On balance, ideas from
Germany, France and Britain were particularly prominently received in the
smaller countries of Europe. Only very occasionally was this process reversed
and in almost all cases such reception processes needed translations in order
to be effective – the Belgian Henri Pirenne being a good example. However,
even among bigger countries, we can find intense interest. Thus, for example,
one third of all references in the *Introduction aux études historiques,* published
by Charles-Victor Langlois and Charles Seignobos in 1898, were to German
books and the whole foundational history of the Annales school in the interwar period is an impressive chapter in the story of Franco-German processes of
cultural transfer.[25] The reception of German historical thought also stood at
the beginning of the professionalisation of English historical writing in the
second half of the nineteenth century and exchanges between British and
German historiographies have remained intense ever since.[26]

   Sometimes, very personal connections could encourage transfers, as was the
case with relations, marriages or friendships. Thus, for example, the marriage
of Leopold von Ranke to Clara Graves in 1843 brought Ranke into direct contact with many Anglo-Irish and English relatives and friends of his wife.[27] At

---

[24]S. Troebst (ed.), 'Geschichtsregionen: Concept and Critique', special issue of the *European Review of History,* 10, 2 (2003).

[25]G. Chaix, 'De la fascination allemande à l'ouverture européenne. Die französische Geschichtsschreibung im 20. Jahrhundert', in H. Duchhardt (ed.), *Nationale Geschicht-skulturen – Bilanz, Ausstrahlung, Europabezogenheit,* (Mainz, 2006), p. 113.

[26]B. Stuchtey and P. Wende (eds), *British and German Historiography 1750–1950. Traditions, Perceptions and Transfers* (Oxford, 2000); S. Berger, P. Lambert and P. Schumann (eds), *Historikerdialoge. Geschichte, Mythos und Gedächtnis im deutsch-britischen kulturellen Austausch 1750–2000* (Göttingen, 2003).

[27]A. Boldt, *Leopold von Ranke and Ireland* (Lampeter, 2007).

other times, professional relations were to the fore, as was the case with reviews of academic works in historical journals or meetings at conferences, such as the world history congresses.[28]

Political exile often proved immensely fruitful for the transfer of ideas from one country to another.[29] Such transfer did not always have to be in the direction of the exiles to their host countries; it was equally possible for the exiles to take with them ideas from their host countries once they were able to return to their own country. Thus, for example, it has been debated to what degree Hans Rothfels underwent an intellectual transformation in his American exile which allowed him to play a positive role in the reconstruction of the German history profession after 1945.[30] Similarly, many of the leading GDR historians, such as Jürgen Kuczynski and Alfred Meusel, had important experiences in their years of exile which arguably influenced their work in the early GDR, even if here their freedom was more tightly circumscribed by the SED.[31]

Arguably, a particularly important role in the transfer of ideas was and is played by those historians who specialise in histories of nations other than their own. David Blackbourn's and Geoff Eley's fundamental critique of the German *Sonderweg* in the mid-1980s, for example, had its origins in their awareness of the British critiques of the Whig interpretation of English national history. More recently, the transnationalisation of academic labour markets has arguably furthered the cultural transfer of ideas and practices in historical writing. The proliferation of academic exchange programmes has worked in the same direction.

The chapters in this volume only begin to explore the ways in which all such transnational intellectual crossings were at work in the writing of national histories in Europe and much more needs to be done in this area of historiographical connections, perceptions and transfers. At the beginning of the twenty-first century, an extensive range of fields of history, such as gender, migration, diaspora, welfare or police history, have recognised the importance of transnational approaches and have developed sophisticated tools to take into account both comparative perspectives and the history of cultural transfers. In all of these areas (and many others) we have seen a marked trend away from national history. For

---

[28]K. D. Erdmann, *Toward a Global Community of Historians. The International Historical Congresses and the International Committee of Historical Sciences 1898–2000* (Oxford, 2005).

[29]See, for example, in the context of the Third Reich, P. Alter, *Out of the Third Reich: Refugee Historians in Post-War Britain* (London, 1998).

[30]P. Th. Walther, 'Hans Rothfels im amerikanischen Exil', in J. Hürter and H. Woller (eds), *Hans Rothfels und die deutsche Zeitgeschichte* (Munich, 2005), pp. 83–96.

[31]M. Keßler, *Exilerfahrung in Wissenschaft und Politik. Remigrierte Historiker in der frühen DDR* (Cologne, 2001).

the history of historiography, this volume and the series of which it is part also seek to denationalise the perspective on history writing. In its European focus, however, it is part and parcel of what Wolfgang Schmale has described as *Europäistik*.[32] And yet, despite such signs of a contemporary denationalisation of professional history writing, we only have to look at appointment practices, curricula and the broader historical cultures in most nation-states in Europe to realise that national history is far from beleaguered or embattled and that only few national historians are actually waving the white flag.

National histories and non-spatial identities

As the chapters above amply demonstrate, national histories have often underpinned exclusive, xenophobic and intolerant national identities which were quick to exclude, isolate, persecute and even eradicate those who were represented as not belonging to the (typically homogeneous) national community. Attempts in some of the literature on nationalism to delineate a benign and positive patriotism from a cancerous and negative nationalism are futile, as they overlook how both patriotism and nationalism rely on homogenised and exclusive images of national history. In practice, therefore, there is no neat distinction between where patriotism ends and nationalism begins.

Independent of this view there are strong arguments for the thesis that the practical function of history is located in the critical analysis and in the deconstruction of (national) traditions instead of trying to underpin (national) identity constructions with 'history' – although this is exactly what the recent calls for a new 'canon of history' amount to in European nations confronting 'unintegrated' (mostly Muslim) immigrant communities. As the present volume indicates, the conception of a homogeneous nation has a bad 'integrative' historical record in Europe, to say the least. Therefore, from an historical point of view, the idea that more instruction in national history would stimulate 'integration' lacks a factual foundation. Although political communities need solidarities in order to function, there is much to be said for trying to locate these at levels other than those of identities based on traditional notions of 'shared histories'.[33]

If we take this view and just look at academic history writing at the beginning of the twenty-first century, we could end this volume on an optimistic

[32]W. Schmale, 'Europäische Geschichte als historische Disziplin. Überlegungen zu einer "Europäistik"', *Zeitschrift für Geschichtswissenschaft*, 46 (1998), 389–405.
[33]A. Megill, 'Historical Representation, Identity, Allegiance', in S. Berger, L. Eriksonas and A. Mycock (eds), *Narrating the Nation. The Writing of National Histories in Different Genres* (Oxford, 2008), pp. 29–54; for the practical functions of history and the problem of history and identity, see Lorenz, *Konstruktion der Vergangenheit*, ch. 14.

note, for it would appear that in many national historiographies in Europe today, there is a prominent move towards transnational and comparative perspectives which seek to overcome the traditional national orientations and frames of history writing by building in some form of reflexivity. The warning of Michel Werner, Bénédicte Zimmermann and Ute Frevert that transnational history too is in danger of reifying the nation (because it still takes the nation as its frame of reference) can only be countered in practice by systematically confronting the national framework with its alternatives, as Arif Dirlik and Francois Hartog both have proposed.[34] The same goes for Dominic Sachsenmaier's argument that 'Europe' cannot be taken as a self-contained unit because it has been interacting with the 'rest of the world' for at least some 500 years. Since the sixteenth century, in this interaction Europe not only changed the larger part of 'the rest of the world' fundamentally, but the reverse also holds true – a fact denied if 'Europe' is represented as a self-contained unit of historical analysis. In this respect postcolonial studies represent a 'point of no return' for national historiography too. Going 'beyond the nation-state' in 'Europe' therefore inevitably points in the direction of and the discussions on global history.[35]

Transnational history as entangled European, imperial and global history has overwhelmingly been written as the history of transfers and adaptations, making the borders between nations more fuzzy or dissolving them altogether and thereby questioning, and not endorsing, nations as units of investigation. Today, many historians no longer see their prime task in underpinning national identities, but in critically reflecting on the practices of past nationalisms and their consequences. However, as we have seen, simultaneously many other historians still see 'their' nation as their prime cause. Moreover, it can sometimes also be observed that where 'scientific' historians withdraw from the national story-lines, others emerge, all too willing to fill the gap. TV history and popular histories are still overwhelmingly *national* history. Sometimes, as in Britain, professional historians, such as David Starkey, Simon Schama and Niall Ferguson, provide the popular national TV master narratives. whereas in Germany, it is specific TV historians, such as Guido Knopp, who are catapulted to national celebrity status by their series on national historical topics.

---

[34]See Werner and Zimmermann, 'Beyond Comparison', 32; U. Frevert, 'Europeanising German History', *Bulletin of the German Historical Institute Washington,* 36 (2005), 9–24; A. Dirlik, 'Performing the World: Reality and Representation in the Making of World History(ies)', *Bulletin of the German Historical Institute, Washington D.C,* 37 (2005), 9–27; Hartog, 'Time, History and the Writing of History', 111.

[35]See D. Sachsenmaier, 'Recent Trends in European History: The World Beyond', *Journal of Modern European History* (forthcoming 2008); J. Osterhammel and N. Petersson, *Die Geschichte der Globalisierung* (Munich, 2003).

And, writing in 2007, it is still the case that even if we just look at academic history, in most European countries one must specialise in its national history in order to make a career as a university historian. Hence, on balance, we need not fear for the persistence and longevity of national historical narratives in Europe.

Selected Bibliographies

1 Introduction: National History Writing in Europe in a Global Age

Ankersmit, F., *History and Tropology: The Rise and Fall of Metaphor* (Berkeley, CA, 1994)

Ankersmit, F., 'The Sublime Dissociation of the Past: Or How to Be(come) What One is No Longer', *History and Theory*, 40, 3 (2001), 295–323

Applegate, C., 'A Europe of Regions: Reflections on the Historiography of Sub-National Spaces in Modern Times', *American Historical Review* 104, 4 (1999), 1157–82

Assmann, A., 'History and Memory', in Smelser, N., Baltus, P. (eds), *International Encyclopedia of the Social & Behavioral Sciences,* vol. 10 (Oxford 2001), pp. 6822–9

Baker, T. N., 'National History in the Age of Michelet, Macauly, and Bancroft', in Kramer, L., Mah, S. (eds), *A Companion to Western Historical Thought* (Oxford, 2002), pp. 185–201

Bentley, M., *Modernizing England's Past. English Historiography in the Age of Modernism 1870–1970* (Cambridge, 2005)

Berger, S., H. Feldner and K. Passmore (eds), *Writing History. Theory and Practice* (London, 2003)

Berger, S., 'A Return to the National Paradigm? National History Writing in Germany, Italy, France, and Britain from 1945 to the Present', *Journal of Modern History*, 77 (2005), 629–78

Berger, S. (ed.), *Writing the Nation: Towards Global Perspectives* (Basingstoke, 2007)

Berger, S., Eriksonas, L., Mycock, A. (eds), *Narrating the Nation: The Representation of National Narratives in Different Genres* (Oxford, 2008)

Billig, M., *Banal Nationalism* (London, 1995)

Boer, P. den, *History as a Profession: The Study of History in France, 1818–1914* (Princeton, NJ, 1998)

Bouchard, G., *The Making of the Nations and Cultures of the New World: An Essay in Comparative History* (Montreal, 2008)

Bues, A., Rexheuser, R. (eds), *Mittelalterliche nationes – neuzeitliche Nationen. Probleme der Nationenbildung in Europa* (Wiesbaden, 2003)

Cohen, D., O'Connor, M. (eds), *Comparison and History: Europe in Cross-National Perspective* (London, 2004)

Dirlik, A., 'Performing the World: Reality and Representation in the Making of World History(ies)', *Bulletin of the German Historical Institute, Washington D.C,* 37 (2005), 9–27

Frevert, U., Blackbourn, D., 'Europeanizing German History', *Bulletin of the German Historical Institute, Washington D.C.,* 36 (2005)

Gillingham, J., 'Civilizing the English? The English Histories of William of Malmesbury and David Hume', *Historical Research*, 124 (2001), 17–43

Hartog, F., *Régimes d'historicité. Presentisme et expériences du temps* (Paris, 2003)

Hartog, F., 'Time and Heritage', *Museum International*, 57, 227 (2005), 7–18

Helmrath, J., Muhlack, U., Walther, G. (eds), *Diffusion des Humanismus: Studien zur nationalen Geschichtsschreibung europäischer Humanisten* (Göttingen, 2002)

Hirschli, C., 'Das humanistische Nationskonstrukt vor dem Hintergrund modernistischer Nationalismustheorien', *Historisches Jahrbuch*, 122 (2002), 355–96

Hutton, P., 'Recent Scholarship on Memory and History', *The History Teacher,* 33, 4 (2000), 533–48

Iggers, G., *The German Conception of History: The National Tradition of Historical Thought from Herder to the Present*, 2nd rev. edn (Middletown, CT, 1983)

Lingelbach, G., *Klio macht Karriere. Die Institutionalisierung der Geschichtswissenschaft in Frankreich und in den USA in der zweiten Hälfte des 19. Jahrhunderts* (Göttingen, 2003)

Lorenz, C., *Konstruktion der Vergangenheit* (Vienna and Cologne, 1997)

Lorenz, C., 'Comparative Historiography: Problems and Perspectives', *History and Theory,* 38, 1 (1999), 25–39

Lorenz, C., 'La linea di confine. La Storia "scientifica" fra costruzione e decostruzione del mito', *Quaderni Storici,* 121,1 (2006), 289–311

Lorenz, C., 'Towards a Theoretical Framework of Comparing Historiographies: Some Preliminary Considerations', in Seixas, P. (ed.), *Theorizing Historical Consciousness* (Toronto, 2004), pp. 25–48

Lorenz, C., 'Scientific/Critical History', in A. Tucker (ed.), *Blackwell Companion to Historiography and Philosophies of History* (Cambridge, 2008)

Maier, C. S., 'Transformations of Territoriality 1600–2000', in Budde, G., Conrad, S., Jansz, O. (eds), *Transnationale Geschichte. Themen, Tendenzen und Theorien* (Göttingen, 2006), pp. 32–56

Megill, A., 'Fragmentation and the Future of Historiography', *American Historical Review,* 96, 3 (1991), 693–8

Megill, A., '"Grand Narrative" and the Discipline of History', in Ankersmit, F., Kellner, H. (eds), *A New Philosophy of History* (London, 1995), pp. 151–74

Melman, B., *The Culture of History. English Uses of the Past* (Oxford, 2006)

Nora, P., 'Between Memory and History: *les Lieux de Memoire*', *Representations,* 26 (1989), 7–25

O'Brien, P., 'Historiographical Traditions and Modern Imperatives for the Restoration of Global History', *Journal of Global History,* 1 (2006), 3–39

Osterhammel, J., Petersson, N., *Die Geschichte der Globalisierung* (Munich, 2003)

Paul, H., *Masks of Meaning. Existentialist Humanism in Hayden Whites Philosophy of History* (Groningen, 2006)

Phillips, M., 'Distance and Historical Representation', *History Workshop Journal,* 57 (2004), 123–41

Phillips, M., 'History, Memory and Historical Distance', in Seixas, P. (ed.), *Theorizing Historical Consciousness* (Toronto, 2004), pp. 86–109

Rigney, A., 'Narrativity and Historical Representation', *Poetics Today,* 12, 3 (1991), 591–605

Rigney, A., 'Time for Visions and Revisions: Interpretative Conflict from a Communicative Perspective', *Storia della Storiografia,* 22 (1992), 86–91

Sachsenmaier, D., 'Recent Trends in European History: The World Beyond', *Journal of Modern European History* (forthcoming 2008).

Samuels, M., *The Spectacular Past. Popular History and the Novel in Nineteenth-Century France* (New York, 2004)

Schilling, H., 'Nationale Identität und Konfession in der europäischen Neuzeit', in Giesen, B. (ed.), *Nationale und kulturelle Identität: Studien zur Entwicklung des kollektiven Bewußtseins in der Neuzeit* (Frankfurt/M, 1991), pp. 192–252

Scholz, G., *Zwischen Wissenschaftsanspruch und Orientierungsbedürfnis, Zu Grundlage und Wandel der Geisteswissenschaften* (Frankfurt/M, 1991)

Smith, B., *The Gender of History: Men, Women, and Historical Practice* (Cambridge, MA, 1998)

Stauber, R., 'Nationalismus vor dem Nationalismus? Eine Bestandsaufnahme der Forschung zu "Nation" und "Nationalismus" in der frühen Neuzeit', *Geschichte in Wissenschaft und Unterricht,* 47 (1996), 139–65

Taylor, B., 'Introduction: How Far, How Near: Distance and Proximity in the Historical Imagination', *History Workshop Journal*, 57 (2004), 117–22

Thorstendahl, R., Veit-Brause, I. (eds), *History-Making. The Intellectual and Social Formation of a Discipline* (Stockholm, 1996)

Weber, W., *Priester der Klio: historisch-sozialwissenschaftliche Studien zu Herkunft und Karriere deutscher Historiker und. zur Geschichte der Geschichtswissenschaft 1800–1970* (Frankfurt/M, 1987)

Till, K. E., *The New Berlin. Memory, Politics, Place* (Minnesota, 2005)

Werner, M., Zimmermann, B., 'Beyond Comparison: *Histoire croisée* and the Challenge of Reflexivity', *History and Theory*, 45, 1(2006), 30–50

Winter, J., 'The Generation of Memory: Reflections on the "Memory Boom" in Contemporary Historical Studies', *Bulletin of the German Historical Institute Washington D.C.*, 27 (2006), 69–92

Woolf, D., 'Of Nations, Nationalism, and National Identity: Reflections on the Historiographic Organization of the Past', in Wang, Q. E., Fillafer, F. L. (eds), *The Many Faces of Clio: Cross-cultural Approaches to Historiography* (Oxford, 2007), pp. 71–104

2 Representations of Identity: Ethnicity, Race, Class, Gender and Religion. An Introduction to Conceptual History

Adhikari, M., *Not White Enough, Not Black Enough: Racial Identity in the South African Colored Community* (Athens, OH, 2005)

Angehrn, E., *Geschichte und Identität* (Berlin and New York, 1985)

Assmann, J., 'The Mosaic Distinction: Israel, Egypt, and the Invention of Paganism', *Representations* 56 (1996), 48–67

Balibar, E., 'Fictive Ethnicity and Ideal Nations', in Hutchinson, J., Smith, A. D. (eds), *Ethnicity* (Oxford 1996), pp. 162–8

Berger, P. L., Luckmann, T., *The Social Construction of Reality* (New York 1966)

Bolaffi, G., et al. (eds), *Dictionary of Race, Ethnicity and Culture* (London 2003)

Bos, J., *Reading the Soul. The Transformation of the Classical Discourse on Character, 1550–1750* (Leiden, 2003)

Bruce, S., *God is Dead: Secularization in the West* (Oxford, 2002)

Bruce, S., *Choice and Religion: A Critique of Rational Choice Theory* (Oxford, 1999)

Brunner, O., Conze, W., Koselleck, R. (eds), *Geschichtliche Grundbegriffe. Historisches Lexikon zur politisch-sozialen Sprache in Deutschland*, vol. 6 (Stuttgart, 1990)

Butler, J., *Gender Trouble. Feminism and the Subversion of Identity* (New York and London, 1999)

Canning, K., *Gender History in Practice: Historical Perspectives on Bodies, Class, and Citizenship* (Ithaca, NY, 2006)

Castells, M., *The Power of Identity. The Information Age: Economy, Society and Culture. Volume II* (Oxford, 1997)

Crowell, S. G., 'There *is* no Other. Notes on the Logical Place of a Concept', *Paideuma* 44 (1998), 13–29

Dijksterhuis, E. J., *Mechanization of the World Picture* (Oxford, 1961)

Dworkin, D., *Class Struggles* (Series History: Concepts, Theories and Practice) (Harlow, 2007)

Eley, G., 'Historicizing the Global, Politicizing Capital: Giving the Present a Name', *History Workshop Journal*, 1 (2007) 154–88

Feichtinger, J. (ed.), *Habsburg Postcolonial: Machtstrukturen und kollektives Gedächtnis* (Innsbruck, 2003)

Finley, M., 'Myth, Memory and History', *History and Theory*, 4, 3 (1965), 281–302

Flynn, T., 'Foucault's Mapping of History', in Gutting, G. (ed.), *The Cambridge Companion to Foucault* (Cambridge, 2005), pp. 29–48

Habermas, J., *Eine Art Schadensentwicklung. Kleine Politische Essays VI* (Frankfurt/M, 1987)

Israel, J., *The Radical Enlightenment : Philosophy and the Making of Modernity* (Oxford, 2001)

Kastoryano, R. et al. (ed.), *Les Codes de Différence. Race – Origine – Religion. France – Allemagne – Čtats Unis* (Paris, 2005)

Kippenberg, H. G., *Die Entdeckung der Religionsgeschichte. Religionswissenschaft und Moderne* (Munich, 1997)

Knapp, G-A., 'Traveling Theories: Anmerkungen zur neueren Diskussion über "Race, Class, and Gender"', *Österreichische Zeitschrift für Geschichtswissenschaften* 16, 1 (2005), 88–111

Koller, C., *Fremdherrschaft. Ein politischer Kampbegriff im Zeitalter des Nationalismus* (Frankfurt/M, 2005)

Koselleck, R., *Futures Past: On the Semantics of Historical Time* (Cambridge, MA, 1985)

Kramer, L., Maza, S. (eds) *A Companion to Western Historical Thought* (Oxford, 2002)

Leerssen, J., 'The Politics of National Identity', in idem, *National Thought in Europe. A Cultural History* (Amsterdam, 2006), pp. 105–73

Levy, D., Sznaider, N., *The Holocaust and Memory in a Global Age* (Philadelphia, 2005)

Lorenz, C., 'Won't you tell me where have all the good times gone?' On the Advantages and Disadvantages of Modernization Theory for History', in Wang, Q. E., Fillafer, F. L. (eds), *The Many Faces of Clio: Cross-cultural Approaches to Historiography* (New York and Oxford, 2007), pp. 104–27

Marquard, O., *Apologie des Zufälligen* (Stuttgart, 1986)

McLellan, D., *The Thought of Karl Marx: An Introduction* (New York, 1971)

McLeod, H., Ustorf, W. (eds), *The Decline of Christendom in Western Europe: 1750–2000* (Cambridge, 2002)

Naimark, N., *Fires of Hatred. Ethnic Cleansing in Twentieth-Century Europe* (Harvard, MA, 2001)

Niethammer, L., *Kollektive Identität. Heimliche Quellen einer unheimlichen Konjunktur* (Reinbek, 2000)

Norris, P., Inglehart, R., *Sacred and Secular: Religion and Politics Worldwide* (Cambridge, 2004)

O'Brien, P.,'Historiographical Traditions and Modern Imperatives for the Restoration of Global History', *Journal of Global History*, 1 (2006), 3–39

Osterhammel, J., *Europe, the 'West', and the Civilizing Mission* (London, 2006)

Runia, E., 'Presence', *History and Theory*, 45, 1 (2006), 1–30

Sachsenmaier, D., 'Recent Trends in European History: The World Beyond', *Journal of Modern European History* (forthcoming 2008).

Scott, J., *Gender and the Politics of History* (New York, 1988)

Skinner, Q., *Visions of Politics, Vol. 1: Regarding Method* (Cambridge, 2002)

Smelser, N., Baltus, P. (eds), *International Encyclopedia of the Social & Behavioral Sciences*, vol. 10 (Oxford, 2001)

Taylor, C., *Multiculturalism and the Politics of Recognition* (Princeton, NJ, 1992)

Yamane, D., 'Secularization on Trial: In Defense of a Neosecularization Paradigm', *Journal for the Scientific Study of Religion*, 36, 1 (1997), 109–22

Young, L. (ed.), *Rational Choice Theory and Religion: Summary and Assessment* (New York, 1997)

3   The Metaphor of the Master 'Narrative Hierarchy' in National Historical Cultures of Europe

Appleby, J., Hunt, L., Jacob, M., *Telling the Truth about History* (New York, 1994)

Bender, T., 'Wholes and Parts: The Need for Synthesis in American History', *Journal of American History*, 73 (1986), 120–36

Bender, T., 'Strategies of Narrative Synthesis in American History', *American Historical Review*, 107 (2002), 129–53

Berkhofer, R. F., *Beyond the Great Story: History as Text and Discourse* (Cambridge, MA, 1995)

Conrad, C., Conrad, S. (eds), *Die Nation schreiben: Geschichtswissenschaft im internationalen Bereich* (Göttingen, 2002)

Cox, J. (ed.), *Contesting the Master Narrative* (Iowa, 1998)

Hausen, K., 'Die Nicht-Einheit der Geschichte als historiographische Herausforderung: zur historischen Relevanz und Anstößigkeit der Geschlechtergeschichte', in H. Medick and A-C. Trepp (eds), *Geschlechtergeschichte und Allgemeine Geschichte: Herausforderungen und Perspektiven* (Göttingen, 1998), pp. 17–55

Jarausch, K. H., Geyer, M., *Shattered Past: Reconstructing German Histories* (Princeton, NJ, 2003)

Klein, K. L., 'In Search of Narrative Mastery: Postmodernism and the People without History', *History and Theory*, 34 (1995), 275–98, p. 276

Lévi-Strauss, C., *Tristes tropiques* (Paris, 1955)

Lyotard, J-F., *La Condition postmoderne: rapport sur le savoir* (Paris, 1979)

Megill, A., '"Grand Narrative" and the Discipline of History', in Ankersmit, F.R., Kellner, H. (eds), *A New Philosophy of History* (London, 1995), pp. 151–73

Middell, M., 'Europäische Geschichte oder *Global History – Master Narratives* oder Fragmentierung?', in Jarausch, K., Sabrow, M. (eds), *Die historische Meistererzählung: Deutungslinien der deutschen Nationalgeschichte* (Göttingen, 2002), pp. 214–52

Novick, P., *That Noble Dream: The 'Objectivity Quest' and the American Historical Profession* (Cambridge, 1988)

Painter, N. I., 'Bias and Synthesis in History', *Journal of American History*, 74 (1987), 109–12, 111

Rigney, A., *The Rhetoric of Historical Representation: Three Narrative Histories of the French Revolution* (Cambridge, 1990), pp. 36–7

Rosenzweig, R., 'What *Is* the Matter with History?', *Journal of American History*, 74 (1987), 117–22

Ross, D., 'Grand Narrative in American Historical Writing: From Romance to Uncertainty', *American Historical Review*, 100 (1995), 651–77

Sperber, J., 'Master Narratives of Nineteenth-Century German History', *Central European History*, 24 (1991), 69–91

Stone, L., 'The Revival of Narrative', *Past and Present*, 85 (1979), 3–24

Wertsch, J. V., *Voices of Collective Remembering* (Cambridge, 2002)

Winkler, M., Kliems, A. (eds), *Sinnstiftung und Narration in Ost-Mittel-Europa* (Leipzig, 2006)

4   Nation and Ethnicity

Berger, S. et al. (eds), *Writing National Histories: Western Europe since 1800* (London, 1999)

Berlin, I., *Three Critics of the Enlightenment: Vico, Hamann, Herder*, ed. Henry Hardy (London, 2000)

Beyen, M., 'A Tribal Trinity: The Rise and Fall of the Franks, the Frisians and the Saxons in the Historical Consciousness of the Netherlands since 1850', *European History Quarterly*, 40, 4 (2000), 493–532

Boer, P. den, *Geschiedenis als beroep: De professionalisering van de geschiedbeoefening in Frankrijk (1818–1914)* (Nijmegen, 1987)

Blokker, J. et al., *Het voorouder-gevoel: De vaderlandse geschiedenis met schoolplaten van J. H. Isings* (Amsterdam, 2005)

Boia, L., *History and Myth in Romanian Consciousness* (Budapest, 2001)

Borchardt, F. L., *German Antiquity in Renaissance Myth* (Baltimore, MD, 1971)

Borst, A., *Der Turmbau von Babel: Geschichte der Meinungen über Ursprung und Vielfalt der Sprachen und Völker*, 4 vols in 6 (München, 1995)

Branch, M. (ed.), *National History and Identity: Approaches to the Writing of National History in the North-East Baltic Region, Nineteenth and Twentieth Centuries* (Helsinki, 1999)

Brown, K. S., Hamilakis, Y. (eds), *The Usable Past: Greek Metahistories* (Lanham, MD, 2003)

Carbonell, C-O., 'Guizot, homme d'état, et le mouvement historiographique français du XIXe siècle', in *Actes du colloque François Guizot (Paris, 22–25 octobre 1974)* (Paris, 1976), pp. 219–37

Clogg, R., 'The Greeks and Their Past', in Deletant and Hanak, *Historians as nation-builders*, pp. 15–31

Deletant, D., Hanak, H., *Historians as Nation-Builders: Central and South-East Europe* (London, 1988)

Denneler, I., *Friedrich Karl von Savigny* (Berlin, 1985)

Derks, H., *Deutsche Westforschung: Ideologie und Praxis im 20. Jahrhundert* (Leipzig, 2001)

Ditt, K., 'Die Kulturraumforschung zwischen Wissenschaft und Politik: Das Beispiel Franz Petri (1903–1993)', *Westfälische Forschungen*, 46 (1996), 73–176

Driel, L. van, Noordegraaf, J., *De Vries en Te Winkel: Een duografie* (Den Haag, 1998)

Ebeling, F., *Geopolitik: Karl Haushofer und seine Raumwissenschaft, 1919–1945* (Berlin, 1994)

Flacke, M. (ed.), *Mythen der Nationen: Ein europäisches Panorama* (München and Berlin, 1998)

Frantzen, A. J., Niles, J. D. (eds), *Anglo-Saxonism and the Construction of Social Identity* (Florida, 1997)

Fürbeth, F. et al. (eds), *Zur Geschichte und Problematik der Nationalphilologien in Europa: 150 Jahre Erste Germanistenversammlung in Frankfurt am Main (1846–1996)* (Tübingen, 1999)

Gazi, E., *Scientific National History: The Greek Case in Comparative Perspective (1850–1920)* (Frankfurt, 2000)

Hayman, J. G., 'Notions of National Characters in the Eighteenth Century', *Huntington Library Quarterly*, 35 (1971), 1–17

Henkes, B., Knotter, A. (eds) *De Westforschung en Nederland, Tijdschrift voor geschiedenis*, 118, 2 (2005)

Hettling, M. (ed.), *Volksgeschichten im Europa der Zwischenkriegszeit* (Göttingen, 2003)

Hobsbawm, E. J., Ranger, T. (eds), *The Invention of Tradition* (Cambridge, 1983)

Hroch, M., *Die Vorkämpfer der nationalen Bewegung bei den kleinen Völkern Europas: Eine vergleichende Analyse zur gesellschaftlichen Schichtung der patriotischen Gruppen* (Praha, 1968)

Jourdan, A., 'The Image of Gaul during the French Revolution: Between Charlemagne and Ossian', in Brown, T. (ed.), *Celticism* (Amsterdam, 1996), pp. 183–206

Juaristi, J., *El bosque originario: Genealogías míticas de los pueblos de Europa* (Madrid, 2000)

Juaristi, J., *El linaje de Aitor* (Madrid, 2000)

Kalmar, I., 'The *Völkerpsychologie* of Lazarus and Steinthal and the Modern Concept of Culture', *Journal of the History of Ideas*, 48 (1987), 671–90

Kemiläinen, A., 'Fiction and Reality in Writing of National History in Finland from the 19th Century on', in M. Řezník and I. Sleváková (eds), *Nations, Identities, Historical Consciousness: Volume Dedicated to Prof. Miroslav Hroch* (Prague, 1997), pp. 29–52

Kemiläinen, A., *Finns in the Shadow of the 'Aryans': Race Theories and Racism* (Helsinki, 1998)

Kliger, S., *The Goths in England: A Study in Seventeenth and Eighteenth Century Thought* (Cambridge, MA, 1952)

Kohler, D., 'Naissance de l'historiographie grecque moderne: Autour de l'*Histoire du peuple grec* (1861–1875) de Constantin Paparrigopoulos (1815–1891)', in Espagne, M., Werner, M. (eds), *Philologiques, I: Contribution à l'histoire des disciplines littéraires en France et en Allemagne au XIXe siècle* (Paris, 1990), 279–309

Klimó, Á. von, 'Volksgeschichte in Ungarn (1939–1945): Chancen Schwierigkeiten und Folgen eines "deutschen" Projekts', in Middell, M., Sommer, U. (eds), *Historische West- und Ostforschung in Zentraleuropa zwischen dem Ersten und dem Zweiten Weltkrieg: Verflechtung und Vergleich* (Leipzig, 2004), pp. 151–78

Kohn, H., *Pan-Slavism, Its History and Ideology* (New York, 1960)

Krapauskas, V., *Nationalism and Historiography: The Case of Nineteenth-Century Lithuanian Historicism* (New York, 2000)

Kuehnemund, R, *Arminius, or The Rise of a National Symbol in Literature* (Chapel Hill, NC, 1953)

Lamarcq, D., Rogge, M., *De taalgrens: Van de oude tot de nieuwe Belgen* (Leuven, 1996)

Leerssen, J., 'Outer and Inner Others: The Auto-image of French Identity from Mme de Staël to Eugène Sue', *Yearbook of European Studies*, 2 (1989), 35–52

Leerssen, J., *Remembrance and Imagination: Patterns in the Historical and Literary Representation of Ireland in the Nineteenth Century* (Cork, 1996)

Leerssen, J., 'A la recherche d'une littérature perdue: Literary history, Irish identity and Douglas Hyde', *Yearbook of European Studies*, 12 (1998), 95–108

Leerssen, J., 'The Rhetoric of National Character: A Programmatic Survey', *Poetics today*, 21, 2 (2000), 267–92

Leerssen, J., Rigney, A. (eds), *Historians and Social Values* (Amsterdam, 2001)

Leerssen, J., 'Literary Historicism: Romanticism, Philologists, and the Presence of the Past', *Modern Language Quarterly*, 65, 2 (2004), 221–43

Leerssen, J., *National Thought in Europe: A Cultural History* (Amsterdam, 2006)

Lindheim, R., Luckyj, G. S. N. (eds), *Towards an Intellectual History of Ukraine: An Anthology of Ukrainian Thought from 1710 to 1995* (Toronto, 1996)

Luckyj, G. S. N., *Panteleimon Kulish: A Sketch of His Life and Times* (New York, 1983)

MacDougall, H. A., *Racial Myth in English History: Trojans, Teutons, and Anglo-Saxons* (Hanover, NH, 1982)

Mörke, O., 'Bataver, Eidgenossen und Goten: Gründungs- und Begründungsmythen in den Niederlanden, der Schweiz, und Schweden in der frühen Neuzeit', in Berding, H. (ed.), *Mythos und Nation: Studien zur Entwicklung des kollektiven Bewußtseins in der Neuzeit*, 3 (Frankfurt, 1996), pp. 104–32

Mout, M. E. H. N., '"Vader van de natie": František Palacký (1798–1872)', in Bossenbroek, M. P., Mout, M. E. H. N. Musterd, C. (eds), *Historici in de politiek* (Leiden, 1996), pp. 55–76

Murphy, D. T., *The Heroic Earth: Geopolitical Thought in Weimar Germany, 1918–1933* (Kent, OH, 1997)

Oberkrone, W., *Volksgeschichte: Methodische Innovation und völkische Ideologisierung in der deutschen Geschichtswissenschaft, 1918–1945* (Göttingen, 1993).

Poliakov, L., *Le Mythe aryen: Essai sur les sources du racisme et des nationalismes*, new edn (Bruxelles, 1987)

Pomian, K., 'Francs et Gaulois', in Nora, P. (ed.), *Les Lieux de mémoire*, 2 (Paris, 1997), pp. 2245–2300

Prymak, T. M., *Mykola Kostomarov: A Biography* (Toronto, 1996)

Raphael, L., *Von der Volksgeschichte zur Strukturgeschichte: Die Anfänge der westdeutschen Sozialgeschichte, 1945–1968* (Leipzig, 2002)

Rigney, A., *The Rhetoric of Historical Representation: Three Narrative Histories of the French Revolution* (Cambridge, 1990)

Rigney, A., 'Mixed Metaphors and the Writing of History', *Storia della Storiografia*, 24 (1993), pp. 149–59

Schöffer, I., 'The Batavian Myth during the Sixteenth and Seventeenth Centuries', in Bromley, J. S., Kossmann, E. H. (eds), *Britain and The Netherlands*, 5 (The Hague, 1975), pp. 78–101

See, K. von, *Barbar Germane Arier: Die Suche nach der Identität der Deutschen* (Heidelberg, 1994)

Senn, A. E., *Jonas Basanavicius: The Patriarch of the Lithuanian National Renaissance* (Newtonville, MA, 1980)

Senn, A. E., 'The Lithuanian Intelligentsia of the Nineteenth Century', in Loit, A. (ed.), *National Movements in the Baltic Countries during the Nineteenth Century* (Uppsala, 1985), pp. 311–15

Skurnowicz, J. S., *Romantic Nationalism and Liberalism: Joachim Lelewel and the Polish National Idea* (Boulder, CO, 1981)

Smiles, S., *The Image of Antiquity: Ancient Britain and the Romantic Imagination* (New Haven, CT, 1994)

Sperber, D., 'The Epidemiology of Beliefs', *Explaining Culture* (Oxford, 1996), ch. 4

Sperber, D., *La Contagion des idées* (Paris, 1996)

Spiering, M. (ed.), *Nation Building and Writing Literary History* (Amsterdam, 1999)

Štaif, J., 'František Palacký a česká historická pamet' (jublieum r. 1898)', in Řezník, M., Sleváková, I. (eds), *Nations, Identities, Historical Consciousness: Volume Dedicated to Prof. Miroslav Hroch* (Prague, 1997), pp. 229–50

Stan, V., *Nicolae Bălcescu, 1819–1852* (Bucureşti, 1977)

Stanzel, F. K., 'Das Nationalitätenschema in der Literatur und seine Entstehung zu Beginn der Neuzeit', in Blaicher, G. (ed.), *Erstarrtes Denken: Studien zu Klischee, Stereotyp und Vorurteil in englischsprachiger Literatur* (Tübingen, 1987), 84–96

Stanzel, F. K. et al. (eds), *Europäischer Völkerspiegel: Imagologischethnographische Studien zu den Völkertafeln des frühen 18. Jahrhunderts* (Heidelberg, 1999)

Stepan, N., *The Idea of Race in Science: Great Britain, 1800–1860* (London and Oxford, 1982)

Suny, R. Grigor, Kennedy, M. D. (eds), *Intellectuals and the Articulation of the Nation* (Ann Arbor, MI, 1999)

Theis, L., 'Guizot et les institutions de mémoire: un historien au pouvoir', in Nora, P. (ed.), *Les Lieux de mémoire*, 3 vols (Paris, 1997), vol. 1, pp. 1575–97

Thierry, A., *Histoire des Gaulois depuis les temps les plus reculés jusqu'à l'entière soumission de la Gaule à la domination romaine* (Paris, 1828)

Van Delft, L., *Littérature et anthropologie: Caractère et nature humaine à l'âge classique* (Paris, 1993)

Viallaneix, P., Ehrard, J. (eds), *Nos ancêtres les Gaulois: Actes du colloque international de Clermont-Ferrand* (Clermont-Ferrand, 1982)

Walicki, A., *Philosophy and Romantic Nationalism: The Case of Poland*, new edn (Notre Dame, IN, 1994)

Welz, G., 'Die soziale Organisation kultureller Differenz: zur Kritik des Ethnosbegriffs in der anglo-amerikanischen Kulturanthropologie', in Berding, H. (ed.), *Nationales Bewußtsein und kollektive Identität: Studien zur Entwicklung des kollektiven Bewußtseins in der Neuzeit*, 2 (Frankfurt, 1994), 66–81

Wirtz, M., *Josef Dobrovský und die Literatur: Frühe bohemistische Forschung zwischen Wissenschaft und nationalem Auftrag* (Dresden, 1999)

Woud, A. van der, *De Bataafse hut: Verschuivingen in het beeld van de geschiedenis (1750–1850)* (Amsterdam, 1990)

Zacek, J. F., *Palacký: The Historian as Scholar and Nationalist* (The Hague, 1970)

5   Religion, Nation and European Representations of the Past

Altermatt, U., *Katholizismus und Moderne: zur Sozial- und Mentaltätsgeschichte der Schweizer Katholiken im 19. und 20. Jahrhundert* (Zurich, 1989)

Amerongen, M. Van, Cornelissen, I., *Tegen de revolutie: het evangelie! Het kerkvolk in de Nederlandse politiek of: het einde van een christelijke natie* (Amsterdam, 1972)

Asad, T., *Formations of the Secular: Christianity, Islam, Modernity* (Stanford, CA, 2003)

Banac, I., 'Historiography of the Countries of Eastern Europe: Yugoslavia', *American Historical Review* (October 1992), 1090–1

Bellah, R. N., Hammond, P. E., *Varieties of Civil Religion* (San Francisco, 1980)

Bentley, M., *Modern Historiography: An Introduction* (London, 1999)

Berger, S., Donovan, M., Passmore, K. (eds), *Writing National Histories* (London, 1999)

Blaschke, O., 'Das 19. Jahrhundert: Ein Zweites Konfessionelles Zeitalter?', *Geschichte und Gesellschaft*, 26 (2000)

Blom, J.C.H., Talsma, J., *De verzuiling voorbij: godsdienst, stand en natie in de lange negentiende eeuw* (Amsterdam, 2000)

Breisach, E., *Historiography, Ancient, Medieval and Modern* (Chicago, 1983)

Brown, C. G., *The Death of Christian Britain* (London, 2000)

Burleigh, M., *Earthly Powers: The Clash of Religion and Politics in Europe, from the French Revolution to the Great War* (New York, 2006)

Burrin, P., 'Political Religion', *History and Memory*, 9 (1997), 321–49

Chadwick, O., *The Secularization of the European Mind in the Nineteenth Century* (Cambridge, 1976)

Clark, C., Kaiser, W. (eds), *Culture Wars: Secular-Catholic Conflict in Nineteenth-Century Europe* (Cambridge, 2003)

Deák, I., 'Historiography of the Countries of Eastern Europe: Hungary', *American Historical Review* (October 1992), 1046

Döllinger, I., *European Intellectual History* (Englewood Cliffs, 1986)

Gentile, E., *The Sacralization of Politics in Fascist Italy* (Cambridge, MA, 1996)

Gentile, E., *Politics as Religion* (Princeton, NJ, 2001)

Flacke, M. (ed.), *Mythen der Nationen: ein Europäisches Panorama* (2000)

Friedrich, C. J. (ed.), *The Philosophy of Hegel* (New York, 1954)

Gerber, M., Walkowitz, R. L. (eds), *One Nation under God? Religion and American Culture* (Cambridge, MA, 1999)

Geurts, P.A.M., Janssen, A.E.M., *Geschiedschrijving in Nederland*, vol. 1 (The Hague, 1981)

Geyer, M., Lehmann, H. (eds), *Religion und Nation: Beiträge zu einer unbewältigten Geschichte / Nation and Religion: An Unfinished History* (Göttingen, 2003)

Haan, I. de, *Het beginsel van leven en wasdom: de constitutie van de Nederlandse politiek in de negentiende eeuw* (Amsterdam, 2003)

Haupt, H-G., Langewiesche, D. (eds), *Nation und Religion in der Deutschen Nation* (Frankfurt, 2001)

Haupt, H-G., Langewiesche, D. (eds), *Nation und Religion in Europa: Mehrkonfessionelle Gesellschaften im 19. und 20. Jahrhundert* (Frankfurt, 2004)

Hill, R., *Lord Acton* (New Haven, CT, 2000)

Hitchins, K., 'Historiography of the Countries of Eastern Europe: Romania', *American Historical Review* (October 1992), 1071–5

Howard, T. A., *Religion and the Rise of Historicism: W.M.L. de Wette, Jacob Burckhardt and the Theological Origins of Nineteenth-Century Historical Consciousness* (Cambridge, 2000)

Jacobetti, E. E., *Revolutionary Humanism and Historicism in Modern Italy* (New Haven, CT and London, 1981)

Kaupisch, K., 'The "Luther Renaissance"', *Journal of Contemporary History*, 2, 4 (1967), 29–49

Klimó, Á. von, 'Das Ende der Nationalismusforschung? Bemerkungen zu einigen Neuerscheinungen zu "Politische Religion", "Fest" und "Erinnerung"', *Neue Politische Literatur*, 48 (2003), 271–91

Laqueur, W. and G. L. Mosse, *Historians in Politics* (London and Beverly Hills, CA, 1974)

Lefebvre, G., *La Naissance de l'historiographie moderne* (Paris, 1971)

Lehmann, H., *Protestantisches Christentum im Prozeß der Säkularisierung* (Göttingen, 2001)

Loesdau, A., Meier, H. (eds), *Zur Geschichte der Historiographie nach 1945. Beiträge eines Kolloquiums zum 75. Geburtstag von Gerhard Lozek* (Berlin, 2001)

Mews, S. (ed.), *Religion and National Identity* (Oxford, 1982)

Meyer, F., Myhre, J. E. (eds), *Nordic Historiography in the 20th Century* (Oslo, 2000)

Nora, P. et al., *Realms of Memory: The Construction of the French Past*, vol. 1, *Conflicts and Divisions* (New York, 1996)

Nord, P., *The Republican Moment: Struggles for Democracy in Nineteenth-Century France* (Cambridge, MA, 1995)

O'Brien, C. C., *God Land: Reflections on Religion and Nationalism* (Cambridge, MA, and London, 1988)

Oegema, J., *Een vreemd geluk: de publieke religie rond Auschwitz* (Amsterdam, 2003)

Paxton, R. O., *The Anatomy of Fascism* (New York, 2004)

Putelis, A., 'Folklore and Identity: The Situation in Latvia', *Novo Religion*, 3, 1 (1999), 119–36

Rémond, R., *L'Anticléricalisme en France de 1815 à nos jours* (Paris, 1976)

Robbins, K., *History, Religion and Identity in Modern Britain* (London and Rio Grande, 1993)

Rooden, P. van, *Religieuze regimes: over godsdienst en maatschappij in Nederland, 1570–1990* (Amsterdam, 1996)

Rooden, P. van, 'History, the Nation and Religion: The Transformations of the Dutch Religious Past', http://www.xs4all.nl/~pvrooden/Peter/publicaties/1999a.htm.

Safranski, R., *Das Böse oder Das Drama der Freiheit* (München, 1997)

Stowers, S., 'The Concepts of "Religion", "Political Religion" and the Study of Nazism', *Journal of Contemporary History*, 42, 1 (2007), 9–24

Veer, P. van der, *Islam en het 'beschaafde Westen'* (Amsterdam, 2002)

Walinski-Kiehl, R., 'Reformation History and Political Mythology in the German Democratic Republic', *European History Quarterly*, 34 (2004), 43–67

Welch, C., *Protestant Thought in the Nineteenth Century*, vol. 1, *1799–1870* (New Haven, CT, 1972), pp. 121–3.

Young, A., *Religion and Society in Present-Day Albania*, Working Paper, 97.3, Institute for European Studies (April 1997)

Zimmer, O., A Contested Nation: History, Memory and Nationalism in Switzerland, 1761–1891 (Cambridge, 2003)

6   The 'Nation' and 'Class': European National Master Narratives and Their Social 'Other'

Alexopoulos, G., *Stalin's Outcasts: Aliens, Citizens, and the Soviet State, 1926–1936* (New York, 2003)

Baberowski, J., *Der Sinn der Geschichte: Geschichtstheorien von Hegel bis Foucault* (Munich, 2005)

Berger, S., Feldner, H., Passmore, K. (eds), *Writing History: Theory and Practice* (London, 2003)

Berger, S., Donovan, M, Passmore, K. (eds), *Writing National Histories: Western Europe since 1800* (London and New York, 1999)

Blaas, P. M. B., *Continuity and Anachronism: Parliamentary and Constitutional Development in Whig Historiography and the Anti-Whig Reaction between 1890 and 1930* (The Hague, 1978)

Blockmans, W., Philippe Genet, J. (eds), *Visions sur le développement des états européens: théories et historiographies de l'état moderne* (Rome, 1993)

Boer, P. den, *Geschiedenis als beroep: de professionalisering van de geschiedbeoefening in Frankrijk 1818–1914* (Nijmegen, 1987)

Braverman, H., *Labor and Monopoly Capitalism: The Degradation of Work in the Twentieth Century* (New York and London, 1974)

Brockhaus, E., *Zusammensetzung und Neustrukturierung der Arbeiterklasse vor dem Ersten Weltkrieg: zur Krise der professionellen Arbeiterbewegung* (Munich, 1975)

Butterfield, H., *The Whig Interpretation of History* (London, 1965 [1931])

Buchbinder, S., *Der Wille zur Geschichte. Schweizergeschichte um 1900: die Werke von Wilhelm Oechsli, Johannes Dierauer und Karl Dändliker* (Zurich, 2002)

Calvert, P., *The Concept of Class: An Historical Introduction* (London, 1982)

Cannadine, D., *G.M. Trevelyan: A Life in History* (London, 1993)

Clive, J., *Macaulay: The Shaping of the Historian* (Cambridge, 1987)

Cobban, A., *Historians and the Causes of the French Revolution* (s.l., 1970)

Comité pour une Nouvelle Histoire de la Suisse (ed.), *Geschichte der Schweiz und der Schweizer*, 3rd edn (Basel, 2004)

Conrad, C., Conrad, S. (eds), *Die Nation schreiben: Geschichtswissenschaft im internationalen Vergleich* (Göttingen, 2002)

Conze, W., *Die Strukturgeschichte des technisch-industriellen Zeitalters als Aufgabe für Forschung und Unterricht* (Cologne and Opladen, 1957)

Crew, D. F., *Town in the Ruhr: A Social History of Bochum, 1860–1914* (New York, 1979)

Dawley, A., *Class and Community: The Industrial Revolution in Lynn* (Cambridge, MA, 1976)

Defuisseaux, L., *Les hontes du suffrage universel* (Brussels, s.d.)

Deneckere, G., *Sire, het volk mort: social protest in België 1831–1918* (Antwerp, 1997)

Edwards, R. C., *Contested Terrain: The Transformation of the Workplace in the Twentieth Century* (New York, 1979)

Foner, E., 'Why Is There No Socialism in the U.S.?', *History Workshop*, 17 (1984), 57–80

Furet, F., *Penser la Révolution française* (Paris, 1978)

Furet, F., *La Révolution en débat* (Paris, 1999).

Furet, F., *Edgar Quinet et la question du jacobinisme 1865–1870* (Paris, 1986).

Furet, F., *Marx and the French Revolution* (Chicago and London, 1988) [first published in French in 1986].

Gotthardt, C., *Industrialisierung, bürgerliche Politik und proletarische Autonomie: Voraussetzungen und Varianten sozialistischer Klassenorganisationen in Nordwestdeutschland 1863 bis 1875* (Bonn, 1992)

Ginneken, J. van, *Crowds, Psychology and Politics, 1871–1899* (Cambridge, 1992)

Gautschi, W., *Der Landesstreik 1918* (Zurich 1968)

Gordon, D. M., Edwards, R. C., Reich, M., *Segmented Work, Divided Workers: The Historical Transformation of Labor in the United States* (Cambridge, MA, 1982)

Gutman, H. G., *Work, Culture, and Society in Industrializing America: Essays in American Working-Class and Social History* (New York, 1976)

Gutman, H. G., *Power & Culture: Essays on the American Working Class*, ed. Ira Berlin (New York, 1987)

Hamburger, J., *Macaulay and the Whig Tradition* (Chicago, 1976)

Hasquin, H., *Historiographie et politique: Essai sur l'histoire de Belgique et la Wallonie* (Charleroi, 1981)

Hettling, M. (ed.), *Volksgeschichten im Europa der Zwischenkriegszeit* (Göttingen 2003)

Hettling, M. et al., *Eine kleine Geschichte der Schweiz: der Bundesstaat und seine Traditionen* (Frankfurt/M, 1998)

Hildermeier, M., *Geschichte der Sowjetunion 1917–1991* (Munich, 1998)

Hobsbawm, E. J., *Nations and Nationalism since 1780: Programme, Myth, Reality* (Cambridge, 1991 [1990])

Katznelson, I., Zolberg, A. R. (eds), *Working-Class Formation: Nineteenth-Century Patterns in Western Europe and the United States* (Princeton, NJ, 1986)

Kenyon, J., *The History Men: The Historical Profession in England since the Renaissance* (London, 1983)

Klimó, Á. von, *Nation, Konfession, Geschichte: zur nationalen Geschichtskultur Ungarns im europäischen Kontext (1860–1948)* (Munich, 2003)

Kraditor, A., *The Radical Persuasion* (Baton Rouge, 1981)

Lidtke, V. L., *The Outlawed Party: Social Democracy in Germany, 1878–1890* (Princeton, NJ, 1966)

Lucas, E., *Zwei Formen des Radikalismus in der deutschen Arbeiterbewegung* (Frankfurt/M, 1976)

McKibbin, R., 'Why Was There No Marxism in Great Britain?', *English Historical Review*, 99 (1984), 297–331

Montgomery, D., *The Fall of the House of Labor: The Workplace, the State, and American Labor Activism, 1865–1925* (Cambridge, 1987)

Montgomery, D., *Workers' Control in America: Studies in the History of Work, Technology, and Labor Struggles*, 2nd edn (Cambridge, 1981)

Oberländer, E., *Sowjetpatriotismus und Geschichte: Dokumentation* (Cologne, 1967)

Pieck, W., Dimitroff, G., Togliatti, P., *Die Offensive des Faschismus und die Aufgaben der Kommunisten im Kampf für die Volksfront gegen Krieg und Faschismus* (Berlin, GDR, 1960)

Prothero, I., *Artisans and Politics in Early Nineteenth-Century London: John Gast and His Times* (London, 1981)

Rosenzweig, R., 'Sources of Stability and Seeds of Subversion: David Brody and the Making of the "New" Labor History', *Labor History*, 34 (1993), 503–9

Roth, K. H., Behrens, E., *Die 'andere' Arbeiterbewegung und die Entwicklung der kapitalistischen Repression von 1880 bis zur Gegenwart: ein Beitrag zum Neuverständnis der Klassengeschichte in Deutschland* (Munich, 1974)

Studer, B., Vallotton, F. (eds), *Histoire sociale et mouvement ouvrier: un bilan historiographique 1848–1998/Sozialgeschichte und Arbeiterbewegung: eine historiographische Bilanz 1848–1998* (Zurich 1997)

Tacke, C. (ed.), *1848: Memory and Oblivion in Europe* (Brussels, 2000)

Tenfelde, K. (ed.), *Arbeiter im 20 Jahrhundert* (Stuttgart, 1991)

Thompson, E. P., *The Making of the English Working Class* (Harmondsworth, 1963)

Tollebeek, J., Verbeeck, G., Verschaffel, T., *De lectuur van het verleden* (Leuven, 1998)

Tollebeek, J., *De ekster en de kooi: Nieuwe opstellen over de geschiedschrijving* (Amsterdam, 1996)

Trevelyan, G. M., *Illustrated English Social History* (London, 1942)

Trotskij, L., *Geschichte der russischen Revolution*, 3rd edn (Frankfurt/M, 1982)

Vanschoenbeek, G., 'Socialisten: gezellen zonder vaderland? De Belgische Werkliedenpartij en haar verhouding tot het "vaderland België", 1885–1940', *Bijdragen tot de Eigentijdse Geschiedenis / Cahiers d'Histoire du Temps Présent*, 3 (1997), 240–5

Wehler, H-U. (ed.), *Moderne deutsche Sozialgeschichte*, 5th edn (Cologne, 1976)
Wehler, H-U. (ed.), *Klassen in der europäischen Sozialgeschichte* (Göttingen, 1979)
Wilson, A. and T. G. Ashplant, 'Whig History and Present-Centered History', *Historical Journal*, 31 (1988), 1–16
Winkler, H. August, *Der lange Weg nach Westen*, vol. 1, *Deutsche Geschichte vom Ende des Alten Reiches bis zum Untergang der Weimarer Republik*; vol. 2, *Deutsche Geschichte vom 'Dritten Reich' bis zur Wiedervereinigung*, 4th edn (Munich, 2002)
Zwahr, H., *Zur Konstituierung des Proletariats als Klasse: Strukturuntersuchung des Leipziger Proletariats während der industriellen Revolution* (Berlin, GDR, 1978)

7   Where Are the Women in National Histories?

Anderson, B., *Imagined Communities: Reflections on the Origins and Spread of Nationalism* (London, 1983)
Arlt, F., *Die Frauen der altisländischen Bauernsagen und die Frauen der vorexilischen Bücher des Alten Testaments, verglichen nach ihren Handlungswerten, ihrer Bewertung, ihrer Erscheinungsweise, ihrer Behandlung: Ein Beitrag zur Rassenpsychologie* (Leipzig, 1936)
Bachofen, J. J., *Myth, Religion, and Mother Right*, trans. Ralph Manheim (New Jersey, 1967)
Bäumer, G., *Adelheid, Mutter der Königreiche* (Tübingen, 1936)
Bednaříková-Turnwaldová, R., Birnbaumová, A., Tumlířová, M., Veselá, B. (eds), *Česká žena v dějinách národa* (Praha, 1940)
Bleuel, H. P., *Sex and Society in Nazi Germany* (Philadelphia and New York, 1973)
Blom, I., 'Women in Norwegian and Danish Historiography, c.1900–c.1960', in Porciani, I, O'Dowd, M. (eds), *History Women*, 130–51
Blom, I., Hagemann, K., Hall, C. (eds), *Gendered Nations: Nationalisms and Gender Order in the Long Nineteenth Century* (Oxford and New York, 2000)
Breuilly, J., *Nationalism and the State* (Manchester, 1982)
Bridenthal, R., Grossmann, A., Kaplan, M. (eds), *When Biology Became Destiny: Women in Weimar and Nazi Germany* (New York, 1984)
Buschan, G., *Leben und Treiben der deutschen Frau in der Urzeit* (Hamburg, 1893)
Calo, J., *La Création de la femme chez Michelet* (Paris, 1975)
Canning, K., *Languages of Labor and Gender: Female Factory Work in Germany, 1850–1914* (Ithaca, NY and London, 1996)
Canning, K., *Gender History in Practice: Historical Perspectives on Bodies, Class, and Citizenship* (Ithaca, NY and London, 2006)
Casalena, M. P., 'La Participation cachée des femmes à la construction del l'histoire nationale en Italie et en France (1800–1848)', in Porciani, I., and O'Dowd, M. (eds), *History Women*, 41–58
Červenák, B. P., *Zrcadlo Slovenska* (Pešt', 1844)
Colley, L., *Britons: Forging the Nation, 1707–1837* (New Haven, 1992)
Davis, N. Z., '"Women's History" in Transition: The European Case', *Feminist Studies*, 3 (spring/summer, 1976), 83–103
Die Ura Linda Chronik: Übersetzt und mit einer einführenden geschichtlichen Untersuchung herausgegeben von Herman Wirth (Leipzig, 1933)
Doran, Dr., *Lives of the Queens of England of the House of Hanover*, 1 (London, 1855)
Duby, G., *The Knight, the Lady and the Priest: The Making of Modern Marriage in Medieval France*, trans. Barbara Bray (New York, 1983)
Duby, G., *Love and Marriage in the Middle Ages*, trans. Jane Dunnett (Chicago, 1994)
Dvorský, F., *Staré písemné památky žen a dcer českých* (Praha, 1869)

Eley, G., 'Playing it Safe. Or: How is Social History Represented? The New *Cambridge Social History of Britain*', *History Workshop*, 35 (1993), 206–20

Enciclopedia italiana di scienze, lettere ed arti, 10 (Roma, 1932)

Epple, A., *Empfindsame Geschichtsschreibung: eine Geschlechtergeschichte der Historiographie zwischen Aufklärung und Historismus* (Köln, Weimar, Wien, 2003)

Franz, L., *Die Muttergöttin im Vorderen Orient und in Europa* (Leipzig, 1937)

Gazi, E., 'Engendering the Writing and Teaching of History in Mid-War Greece', in Porciani, I., O'Dowd, M., *History Women*, 119–29

Gellner, E., *Nations and Nationalism* (Ithaca and London, 1983)

Gentile, G., *Genesis and Structure of Society* (Urbana, IL and London, 1966) [written in 1944]

Grossmann, A., 'Feminist Debates about Women and National Socialism', *Gender and History*, 3 (1991), 350–58

Hagemann, K., Schüler-Springorum, S. (eds), *Home/Front: The Military, War and Gender in Twentieth-Century Germany* (New York and Oxford, 2002)

Haigh, C. (ed.), *The Cambridge Historical Encyclopedia of Great Britain and Ireland* (Cambridge, 1985)

Hall, C., *Civilising Subjects: Colony and Metropole in the English Imagination, 1830–1867* (Chicago and London, 2002)

Hall, C., *White, Male and Middle-Class: Explorations in Feminism and History* (Cambridge, 1992)

Hall, C., McClelland, K., Rendall, J. (eds), *Defining the Victorian Nation: Class, Race, Gender and the British Reform Act of 1867* (Cambridge, 2000)

Hall, P., *The Social Construction of Nationalism: Sweden as an Example* (Lund, 1998)

Haller, J., *Der Eintritt der Germanen in die Geschichte* (Berlin, 1939)

Hanawalt, B.,'Golden Ages for the History of Medieval English Women', in Stuard, S. M. (ed.), *Women in Medieval History and Historiography* (Philadelphia, 1987), 1–24

Hull, I., 'Feminist and Gender History through the Literary Looking Glass: German Historiography in Postmodern Times', *Central European History*, 22 (1989), 279–300

Jacobeit, W., Lixfeld, H., Bockhorn, O. (eds), *Völkische Wissenschaft: Gestalten und Tendenzen der deutschen und österreichischen Volkskunde in der ersten Hälfte des 20. Jahrhunderts* (Wien, Köln and Weimar, 1994)

Jonáš, K., *Žena ve společnosti lidské, zvláště v Anglii a v Americe* (Praha, 1872)

Kaarninen, M., Tiina Kinnunen, T, '"Hardly Any Women at All": Finnish Historiography Revisited', in Porciani, I., O'Dowd, M. (eds), *History Women*, 152–70

Karamzin, N. M., *Istoriya gosudarstva rossiiskago*, 1, 5th edn (Sanktpeterburg, 1842)

Kocka, J., *Klassengesellschaft im Krieg: Deutsche Sozialgeschichte, 1914–1918* (Göttingen, 1973)

Konopczyński, W., *Kiedy nami rządziły kobiety* (London, 1960)

Koonz, C. *Mothers in the Fatherland: Women, the Family, and Nazi Politics* (New York, 1987)

Krásnohorská, E., *Ženská otázka česká* (Praha, 1881)

Lamprecht, K., *Deutsche Geschichte: Zur jüngsten deutschen Vergangenheit*, 2, 1 (Freiburg im Breisgau, 1903)

Lelewel, J., *Dzieje Polski potocznym sposobem opowiedziane* (Warszawa, [1829] 1961)

Lenderová, M., *K hříchu i k modlitbě: žena v minulém století* (Praha, 1999)

Lepetit, B., 'Histoire des femmes, histoire sociale: présentation', *Annales*, 48 (1993), 997–98

Macaulay, C., *The History of England from the Accession of James I to the Elevation of the House of Hanover*, 1–5 (London, 1769–72)

Maitzen, R. A., *Gender, Genre, and Victorian Historical Writing* (New York and London, 1998)

Malečková, J., 'Gender, Nation and Scholarship: Reflections on Gender/Women's Studies in the Czech Republic', in Maynard, M., Purvis, J. (eds), *New Frontiers in Women's Studies: Knowledge, Identity and Nationalism* (London, 1996), 96–112

Martineau, H., *The History of England during the Thirty Years' Peace, 1816–1846*, 1 (London, 1849)

Maulde La Clavière, R. de, *The Women of the Renaissance: A Study of Feminism*, trans. George Herbert Ely (London, 1900)

Mayer, T. (ed.), *Gender Ironies of Nationalism: Sexing the Nation* (London and New York, 2000)

Melman, B., 'Gender, History and Memory: The Invention of Women's Past in the Nineteenth and Early Twentieth Centuries', *History and Memory*, 5 (1993), 5–41

Meyer, H., *Ehe und Eheauffassung der Germanen* (Weimar, 1940)

Meyer, H., 'Die Eheschließung im *Ruodlieb* und das Eheschwert', *Zeitschrift der Savigny-Stiftung für Rechtsgeschichte*, 52 (1932), 276–93

Michelet, J., *Histoire de France au Moyen Age*, 6 (Paris, n.d.)

Michelet, J., *La Femme* (Paris, 1860)

Michelet, J., *Les Femmes de la révolution*, in Michelet, J., *Œuvres complètes*, 39 (Paris, n.d.)

Mironov, B. N. (with Ben Eklof), *The Social History of Imperial Russia, 1700–1917*, 1–2 (Boulder, CO, 1999–2000)

Mongellas, F., *De l'influence des femmes sur les moeurs et les destinées des nations; sur leurs familles et la société, et de l'influence des moeurs sur le bonheur de la vie*, 1 (Paris, 1828)

Mosher, S. (ed.), *Women in Medieval History and Historiography* (Philadelphia, 1987)

Neckel, G., *Liebe und Ehe bei den vorchristlichen Germanen* (Leipzig and Berlin, 1932)

Neumann, S. K., *Dějiny ženy: populární kapitoly sociologické, etnologické a kulturně historické*, 1–4 (Praha, 1931–2)

Novák, A., *Podobizny žen* (Praha, Brno, [1918] 1940)

Nováková, T., *Slavín žen českých*, 1, *Od nejstarších dob do znovuzrození národa českého* (Praha, 1894)

O'Dowd, M., 'Interpreting the Past: Women's History and Women Historians, 1840–1945', in Angela Bourke et al. (eds), *The Field Day Anthology of Irish Writing*, 5 (New York, 2002), 1102–5

Offen, K., '"Woman Has to Set her Stamp on Science, Philosophy, Justice, and Politics": A Look at Gender Politics in the "Knowledge Wars" of the European Past', in Bosshart-Pfluger, C., Grisard, D., Späti, C. (eds), *Geschlecht und Wissen/Genre et Savoir – Gender and Knowledge: Beiträge der 10. Schweizerischen Historikerinnentagung 2002* (Zürich, 2004), 379–93

Offen, K., Roach Pierson, R., Rendall, J. (eds), *Writing Women's History: International Perspectives* (Bloomington, 1991)

Ozouf, M., *Les Mots des femmes: essai sur la singularité française* (Paris, 1995)

Ozouf, M., 'Liberty, Equality, Fraternity', in Nora, P. (ed.), *Realms of Memory: The Construction of the French Past*, 3, *Symbols* (New York, 1998), 77–114

Palacký, F., *Dějiny národu českého v Čechách a v Moravě*, 1, 1 (Praha, 1848)

Partenheimer, D., *An English Translation of Bachofen's Mutterrecht (Mother Right) (1861): A Study of the Religious and Juridical Aspects of Gynecocracy in the Ancient World* (Lewiston, Queenston and Lampeter, 2003)

Pelcel, F. M., *Nová kronika česká*, 1 (Praha, 1791)

Perrot, M., *Les Femmes ou les silences de l'histoire* (Paris, 1998)

Pickering-Iazzi, R. (ed.), *Mothers of Invention: Women, Italian Fascism, and Culture* (Minneapolis and London, 1995)

Pogodin, M. M., *Drevnyaya russkaya istoriya do mongol'skago iga* (Moskva, 1871)

Pois, R. (ed.), *Race and Race History and Other Essays by Alfred Rosenberg* (New York, Evanston, San Francisco and London, 1970)

Pomata, G., 'Rejoinder to Pygmalion: The Origins of Women's History at the London School of Economics', in Porciani, I., O'Dowd, M. (eds), *History Women*, 79–104

Porciani, I., 'Les Historiennes et le Risorgimento', *Mélanges de l'École française de Rome: Italie et Méditerranée*, 112 (2000), 317–57

Porciani, I., O'Dowd, M. (eds), History Women, *Storia della storiografia*, 46 (2004)

Rauch, A., *L'Identité masculine à l'ombre des femmes: de la Grande Guerre à la Gay Pride* (Paris, 2004)

Re, L., 'Fascist Theories of "Woman" and the Construction of Gender', in Pickering-Iazzi, R. (ed.), *Mothers of Invention: Women, Italian Fascism, and Culture* (Minneapolis and London, 1995), 76–99

Rendall, J., 'Tacitus Engendered: "Gothic Feminism" and British Histories, c. 1750–1800', in Cubitt, G. (ed.), *Imagining Nations* (Manchester and New York, 1998), 57–74

Riot-Sarcey, M., 'The Difficulties of Gender in France: Reflections on a Concept', *Gender and History*, 11 (1999), 489–98

Rosenberg, A., *The Myth of the Twentieth Century: An Evaluation of the Spiritual-Intellectual Confrontations of Our Age* (Newport Beach, 1982)

Roynette, O., 'La Construction du masculin de la fin du XIXe siècle aux années 1930', *Vingtième siècle: revue d'histoire*, 75 (2002), pp. 85–96

Sasinek, F. V., *Dejiny drievnych národov na území terajšieho Uhorska*, 2nd edn (Turč. Sv. Martin, 1878)

Scott, J. W., *Gender and the Politics of History* (New York, 1999)

Shashkov, S. S., *Istoriya russkoi zhenshchiny*, 2nd edn (S. Peterburg, 1879)

Shul'gin, V., *O sostoyanii zhenshchin v Rossii do Petra Velikago: istoricheskoe issledovanie* (Kiev, 1850)

Smith, A., *The Ethnic Origins of Nations* (Oxford, 1986)

Smith, B., *The Gender of History: Men, Women, and Historical Practice* (Cambridge, MA and London, 1998)

Smith, N. C., *Irish Women Historians, 1900–1950*, in Porciani, I., and O'Dowd, M., *History Women* (eds), 69–78

Solov'ev, S. M., *Istoriya Rossii s drevneishikh vremen*, 1 (Moskva, [1851] 1959)

Staël, Baronne de, *Considérations sur les principaux événemens de la Révolution française*, 1–3 (Paris, 1818)

Stloukal, K. (ed.), *Královny, kněžny a velké ženy české* (Praha, 1940)

Strickland, A., *The Life of Queen Elizabeth* (London, 1906 [1910])

Stuard, S. M., 'Fashion's Captives: Medieval Women in French Historiography', in Stuard, S. M. (ed.), *Women in Medieval History*, 59–80

Szarmach, P. E., Tavormina, M. T., Rosenthal, J. T. (eds), *Medieval England: An Encyclopedia* (New York and London, 1998)

Thébaud, F., *Écrire l'histoire des femmes* (Fontenay-aux-Roses, 1998)

Treitschke, H. von, *Politics*, 1, trans. Arthur James Balfour (New York, 1916)

Trevelyan, G. M., *English Social History: A Survey of Six Centuries. Chaucer to Queen Victoria* (London, New York, Toronto, [1942] 1946)

Vannucci, A., *Storia dell'Italia antica*, 3rd edn (Milano, 1873)

Villari, P., *L'Italia e la civiltà* (Milano, 1925)

Vocel, J. E., *Pravěk země české* (Praha, 1868)

Wasylewski, S., *Portret kobiecy w Polsce XVIII wieku* (Warszawa, 1926)

Wenz-Hartmann, G., *Lebensbilder germanischer Frauen* (Leipzig, 1940)

Winock, M., 'Joan of Arc', in Nora, P. (ed.), *Realms of Memory: The Construction of the French Past*, 3, *Symbols*, 433–80

Wirth, H., *Was heißt deutsch? Ein urgeistesgeschichtlicher Rückblick zur Selbstbesinnung und Selbstbestimmung*, 2nd edn (Jena, 1934)

Zabelin, I. E., *Domashnii byt russkikh tsarits v XVI i XVII stoletiyakh* (Novosibirsk, [1901] 1992)

Żarnowska, A., Szwarc, A. (eds), *Kobieta i społeczeństwo na zemiach polskich w XIX wieku* (Warszawa, 1995)

Żarnowska, A., Szwarc, A. (eds), *Kobieta i edukacja na zemiach polskich w XIX i XX wieku*, 1–2 (Warszawa, 1995)

Žena v českém umění dramatickém (Praha, 1940)

8   National Historians and the Discourse of the 'Other': France and Germany

Arendt, H.,'Race Thinking before Racism', *Review of Politics*, 6 (1944)

Aron, R., Elegy, G., *Histoire de Vichy* (Paris, 1954)

Ayçoberry, P., *The Nazi Question: An Essay on the Interpretations of National Socialism* (London, 1981)

Bardèche, M., *Nuremberg ou la terre promise* (Paris, 1947)

Barnes, I., 'Fascism and Technocratic Elitism: The Case of Maurice Bardèche', *Wiener Library Bulletin*, NS, 34, 53–4 (1981), 36–40

Berger, S., Donovan, M., Passmore, K. (eds), *Writing National Histories* (London, 1999)

Besier, G., *Religion, Nation, Kultur* (Neukirchen-Vluyn, 1992)

Biddiss, M., *Father of Racist Ideology: The Social and Political Thought of Count Gobineau* (London, 1970)

Birnbaum, P., *'La France aux Français': Histoire des haines nationalistes* (Paris, 1993)

Burleigh, M., 'The Knights, Nationalists and the Historians: Images of Medieval Prussia from the Enlightenment to 1945', *European History Quarterly*, 17 (1987), 35–55

Chamberlain, H. S., *Die Grundlagen des Neunzehnten Jahrhunderts* [1899], 2 vols (Munich, 1938)

Cohn, N., *Warrant for Genocide* (London, 1996)

Conrad, C., Conrad, S. (eds), *Die Nation schreiben* (Göttingen, 2002)

Crossley, C., *French Historians and Romanticism* (London, 1993)

Delacroix, C., Dosse, F., Garcia, P. (eds), *Les Courants historiques en France 19e–20e siècle* (Paris, 2005)

Downs, L. L., *Writing Gender History* (London, 2004)

Duby, G., Perrot, M., *Histoire des femmes en Occident*, 5 vols (Paris, 1988–92; repr. 2002)

Duby, G., Perrot, M. (eds), *Femmes et histoire* (Paris, 1993)

Dumoulin, O., *Marc Bloch* (Paris, 2000)

Epple, A., *Empfindsame Geschichtsschreibung* (Köln, 2003)

Flood, C., 'The Politics of Counter-Memory on the French Extreme Right', *Journal of European Studies*, 35 (2005), 221–36

Frevert, U., *Militär und Gesellschaft im 19. Jahrhundert* (Stuttgart, 1997)

Frey, H., 'Dominique Venner: Arms and the Man', *Modern and Contemporary France*, NS, 4, 4 (1996), pp. 509–12

Friedländer, S., *Nazi Germany and the Jews*, vol. 1, *The Years of Persecution, 1933–39* (London, 1998), pp. 49–55

Gildea, R., *The Past in French History* (New Haven and London, 1996)

Gossman, L., *Between History and Literature* (Cambridge, MA, 1990)

Griffiths, R., *The Reactionary Revolution: The Catholic Revival in French Literature, 1870/1914* (London, 1966)

Hagemann, K., 'Nation, Krieg und Geschlechterordnung', *Geschichte und Gesellschaft*, 22 (1996), 562–91

Hampson, N., 'The Idea of Nation in Revolutionary France', in Forrest, A., Jones, P. (eds), *Reshaping France: Town, Country and Region during the French Revolution* (Manchester, 1991), pp. 13–25

Hardtwig, W., Schütz, E. (eds), *Geschichte für Leser: Populäre Geschichtsschreibung in Deutschland im 20. Jahrhundert* (Stuttgart, 2005)

Hettling, M., Nolte P. (eds), *Nation und Gesellschaft in Deutschland* (Munich, 1996)

Jordan, S. (ed.), *Lexikon Geschichtswissenschaft: Hundert Grundbegriffe* (Stuttgart, 2002)

Jordan, S., 'Literaturbericht: Theorie und Geschichte der Geschichtswissenschaft', *Geschichte in Wissenschaft und Unterricht*, 56 (2005), pp. 426–38

Kelly, A. (ed.), *The German Worker: Working Class Autobiography from the Age of Industrialization* (Berkeley, CA and London, 1988)

Kemlein, S. (ed.), *Geschlecht und Nationalismus in Mittel- und Osteuropa, 1848–1918* (Osnabrück, 2000)

Lacoste, C., 'Les Gaulois d'Amédée Thierry', in Viallaneix, P. and Éhard, J. (eds), *Nos ancêtres les Gaulois* (Clermont Ferrand, 1982), pp. 203–9

Lavabre, M-C, 'Histoire, mémoire, et politique: le cas du PCF', thèse de doctorat d'Etat, Institut d'études politique (Paris, 1992)

Lavau, G., *A quoi sert le Parti communiste français* (Paris, 1981)

Lebovics, H., *True France: The Wars over Cultural Identity, 1900–1945* (Ithaca, NY, 1992)

Lenoble, J., Dewandre, N. (eds), *L'Europe au soir du siècle* (Paris, 1992)

Maurras, C., *Devant l'Allemagne éternelle* (Paris, 1937)

McClelland, J.S., *The Crowd and the Mob* (London, 1989)

Mellon, S., *The Political Uses of History* (Stanford, CA, 1958)

Morgan, S. (ed.), *The Feminist History Reader* (London, 2006)

Nora, P. (ed.), *Les Lieux de mémoire*, vol. 3, *Les Frances*, 3, *De l'archive à l'emblème* (Paris, 1992)

Nora, P. (ed.), *Essais d'ego-histoire* (Paris, 1987), pp. 270–300

Ozouf, M., *Les Mots des femmes: Essai sur la singularité française* (Paris, 1995)

Planert, U. (ed.), *Nation, Politik und Geschlecht* (Frankfurt, 2000)

Mosse, G. L., *Nationalismus und Sexualität* (Munich and Vienna, 1985)

Poliakov, L., *Histoire de l'antisémitisme*, vol. 2 (Seuil, 1981)

Reboul, J., *M. Bainville contre l'histoire de France* (Paris, 1925)

Remond, R., *La Droite en France, de 1815 à nos jours* (Paris, 1954)

Ritter, G., *Europa und die Deutsche Frage* (Munich, 1948)

Ritter, J., Gründer, K. (eds), *Historisches Wörterbuch der Philosophie*, vol. 8 (Basel, 1992)

Sandkühler, H. J. (ed.), *Europäische Enzyklopädie zu Philosophie und Wissenschaften*, vol. 4 (Hamburg, 1990)

Schnabel, F., 'Der Ursprung der vaterländischen Studien', *Blätter für deutsche Landesgeschichte*, 88 (1951), 4–27

Schönwälder, K., 'The Fascination of Power: Historical Scholarship in Nazi Germany', *History Workshop Journal*, 43 (1997), pp. 133–55

Schulze, W., Oexle, O. G. (eds), *Deutsche Historiker im Nationalsozialismus* (Frankfurt/M, 1999)

Seliger, M., 'Race Thinking during the Restoration', *Journal of the History of Ideas*, 19 (1958), pp. 273–82

Sieburg, H-O, *Deutschland und Frankreich in der Geschichtsschreibung des 19. Jahrhunderts (1848–1871)* (Wiesbaden, 1958)

Smith, A. D., *Chosen Peoples: Sacred Sources of National Identity* (Oxford, 2003), pp. 106–14

Soubol, A., *Précis d'histoire de la Révolution Française* (Paris, 1962)

Taine, H. A., *The Origins of Contemporary France* (Chicago, 1974)

Thébaud, F., *Écrire l'histoire des femmes* (Fontenay-aux-Roses, 1998)

Thierry, A., *Histoire de la conquête de l'Angleterre par les Normands*, 3 vols (Paris, 1825)

Verdès-Leroux, J., *Au service du parti* (Paris, 1983)

Viallaneix, P., *La Voie Royale* (Paris, 1959)

Virgili, F., 'L'Histoire des femmes et l'histoire des genres aujourd'hui', *Vingtième siècle*, 75 (2002), 5–14

Vossler, O., *Der Nationalgedanke von Rousseau bis Ranke* (Munich and Berlin, 1937)

Weber, M., *Wirtschaft und Gesellschaft* (Tübingen, 1922)

Wilson, S., 'A View of the Past: Action Française Historiography and its Socio-Political Function', *Historical Journal*, 19 (1976), 145, 149–50

Winock, M., 'Qu'est qu'une nation?', *L'Histoire*, 201 (1996), 8

Wolf, B., *Sprache in der DDR* (Berlin and New York, 2000)

Zantop, S., *Colonial Fantasies: Conquest, Family, and Nation in Precolonial Germany 1770–1870* (Durham, NC and London, 1997)

9 Ethnicity, Religion, Class and Gender and the 'Island Story/ies': Great Britain and Ireland

Alter, P. (ed.), *Out of the Third Reich: Refugee Historians in Post-War Britain* (London, 1998)

Arnstein, W. L., *Protestant versus Catholic in Victorian England* (London, 1982)

Arx, J. P. von, *Progress and Pessimism: Religion, Politics and History in Late Nineteenth-Century Britain* (Cambridge, MA, 1985)

Aston, N. (ed.), *Religious Change in Europe, 1650–1914* (Oxford, 1997)

Bauman, M., Klauber, M. I., *Historians of the Christian Tradition: Their Methodology and Influence on Western Thought* (Nashville, TN, 1995)

Beckett, I. F. W., 'Women and Patronage in the Late Victorian Army', *History* 85, 279 (July 2000) pp. 463–80

Ben-Israel, H., *English Historians on the French Revolution* (Cambridge, 1968)

Bentley, M., *Modernizing England's Past: English Historiography in the Age of Modernism 1870–1970* (Cambridge, 2005)

Berg, M., *A Woman in History: Eileen Power 1889–1940* (Cambridge, 1996)

Berger, S., Donovan, M., Passmore, K. (eds), *Writing National Histories: Western Europe since 1800* (London, 1999)

Briggs, A., *Collected Essays: Volume One: Words, Numbers, Places, People* (Brighton, 1985)

Brocklehurst, H., Phillips, R. (eds), *History, Nationhood and the Question of Britain* (Basingstoke, 2004)

Brockliss, L., Eastwood, D. (eds), *A Union of Multiple Identities: The British Isles c.175–c.1850* (Manchester, 1997)

Brown, C., *The Death of Christian Britain* (London, 2001)

Burke, P. (ed.), *History and Historians in the Twentieth Century* (Oxford, 2002)

Burrow, J., *A Liberal Descent: Victorian Historians and the English Past* (Cambridge, 1981)

Butterfield, H., *The Englishman and His History* (Cambridge, 1944)

Caldecott, G., Morrill, J. (eds), *Eternity in Time: Chrisopher Dawson and the Catholic Idea of History* (Edinburgh, 1997)

Cannadine, D., *G. M. Trevelyan: A Life in History* (London, 1992)

Cannadine, D., *Class in Britain* (London, 1998)

Chadwick, O., *Acton and History* (Cambridge, 1998)

Chapman, M., *The Celts: The Construction of a Myth* (London, 1992)

Clark, J.C.D., 'Protestantism, Nationalism and National Identity, 1660–1832', *The Historical Journal* 43, 1 (2000)

Clive, J., *Thomas Babington Macaulay: The Shaping of the Historian* (London, 1973)

Cole, G.D.H., *A Short History of the British Working Class Movement 1789–1927* (London, 1932)

Colley, L., *Britons: Forging the Nation, 1707–1837* (London, 1994)

Colls, R., *The Identity of England* (Oxford, 2002)

Comerford, R.V., Cullen, M., Hill, J., Lennon, C. (eds), *Religion, Conflict and Co-Existence in Ireland* (Dublin, 1990)

Comerford, R.V., *Ireland* (London, 2003)

Cowling, M., *Religion and Public Doctrine in Modern England: Volume III Accommodations* (Cambridge, 2001)

Curtis, L.P. Jr, *Anglo-Saxons and Celts: A Study of Anglo-Irish Prejudices in Victorian England* (Bridgeport, 1968)

Dawson, C., *Christianity & The New Age* (London, 1931)

Davidoff, L., Hall, C., *Family Fortunes: Men and Women of the English Middle Class 1780–1850* (London, 1987)

Dunn, W.H., *James Anthony Froude: A Biography* (Oxford, 1961, 1963)

Eastwood, D., 'History, Politics and Reputation: E. P. Thompson Reconsidered', *History* 85, 280 (October 2000) pp. 634–54

Feske, V., *From Belloc to Churchill: Private Scholars, Public Culture and the Crisis of British Liberalism, 1900–1939* (Chapel Hill, NC and London, 1996)

Foster, R.F., *Paddy and Mr Punch: Connections in Irish and English History* (London, 1993)

Forbes, D., *Hume's Philosophical Politics* (Cambridge, 1975)

Foster, J., *Class Struggle and the Industrial Revolution* (London, 1974)

Froude, J.A., 'The Condition and Prospects of Protestantism' in *Short Studies of Great Subjects* Second Series (London, 1871)

Garrard, J., Jary, D., Goldsmith, M., Oldfield, A. (eds), *The Middle Class in Politics* (Farnborough, 1978)

Geyer, M. H., Paulmann, J. (eds), *The Mechanics of Internationalism* (Oxford, 2001)

Gooch, G. P., *Under Six Reigns* (London, 1985)

Gooch, G.P., *A Study in History and Politics* (London, 1982)

Griffiths, T., *The Lancashire Working Classes c.1880–1930* (Oxford, 2001)

Hale, J. (ed.), *The Evolution of British Historiography: From Bacon to Namier* (London, 1967)

Hamburger, J., *Macaulay and the Whig Tradition* (Chicago, 1976)

Harrison, B., *Separate Spheres: The Opposition to Women's Suffrage in Britain* (London, 1978)

Harrison, B., *Prudent Revolutionaries: Portraits of British Feminists between the Wars* (Oxford, 1987)

Hastings, A., *The Construction of Nationhood: Ethnicity, Religion and Nationalism* (Cambridge, 1997)

Heeney, B., *The Women's Movement in the Church of England 1850–1930* (Oxford, 1988)

Hill, R., *Lord Acton* (New Haven, CT and London, 2000)

Holmes, C., *Immigration & British Society, 1871–1971* (London, 1988)

Homans, M., Munich, A. (eds), *Remaking Queen Victoria* (Cambridge, 1997)

Hooker, R., Sargent, J. (eds), *Belonging to Britain: Christian Perspectives on Religion and Identity in a Plural Society* (London, 1991)

Johnson, R., McLennan, G., Schwarz, B., Sutton, D. (eds), *Making Histories: Studies in History-writing and Politics* (London, 1982)

Johnson, P., *Saving and Spending: The Working-class Economy in England 1870–1939* (Oxford, 1985)

Jones, G. S., *Languages of Class* (Cambridge, 1985)

Jones, E., *The English Nation: The Great Myth* (Stroud, 2003)

Joyce, P., *Visions of the People: Industrial England and the Question of Class, 1848–1914* (Cambridge, 1991)

Kaye, H., *The British Marxist historians: An Introductory Analysis* (Cambridge, 1984)

Kidd, C., *British Identities before Nationalism* (Cambridge, 1999)

Kidd, A., Nicholls, D., *The Making of the British Middle Class* (Stroud, 1998)

Kent, S.K., *Gender and Power in Britain, 1640–1990* (London and New York, 1999)

Kenyon, J. P., *The History Men: The Historical Profession in England since the Renaissance* (London, 1983)

Kramnick, I. (ed.), *Lord Bolingbroke: Historical Writings* (Chicago, 1972)

Kuhn, W. H., *Democratic Royalism: The Transformation of the British Monarchy, 1861–1914* (Basingstoke, 1996)

Llywelyn, D., *Sacred Place, Chosen People: Land and Identity in Welsh Spirituality* (Cardiff, 1999)

MacDougall, H., *Racial Myth in English History* (Montreal and Hanover, NH, 1982)

Macfarlane, A., *The Origins of English Individualism* (Oxford, 1978)

Malmgreen, G. (ed.), *Religion in the Lives of English Women* (Beckenham, 1986)

Matthew, D., *Britain and the Continent, 1000–1300: The Impact of the Norman Conquest* (London, 2005)

McDowell, R.B., *Alice Stopford Green: A Passionate Historian* (Dublin, 1967)

McIntire, C.T., *Herbert Butterfield: Historian as Dissenter* (New Haven, CT and London, 2004)

McKibbin, R., *Classes and Cultures: England 1918–1951* (Oxford, 1998)

McLean, Iain, McMillan, A., *State of the Union: Unionism and the Alternatives in the United Kingdom since 1707* (Oxford, 2005)

Meacham, S., *A Life Apart: The English Working Class 1890–1914* (London, 1977)

Mitchell, L. (ed.), *The Writings and Speeches of Edmund Burke* vii *The French Revolution 1790–1794* (Oxford, 1989)

Mitchel, P., *Evangelicalism and National Identity in Ulster 1921–1998* (Oxford, 2003)

Namier, J., *Lewis Namier: A Biography* (London, 1971)

Namier, L.B., *Vanished Supremacies* (London, 1962)

Newton, D. J., *British Labour, European Socialism and the Struggle for Peace, 1889–1914* (Oxford, 1985)

Norman, E. R., *Anti-Catholicism in Victorian England* (London, 1968)

Norman, E.R., *The English Catholic Church in the Nineteenth Century* (Oxford, 1984)

Panayi, P., *Immigration, Ethnicity and Racism in Britain 1815–1945* (London, 1994)

Paz, D. G., *Popular anti-Catholicism in mid-Victorian England* (Stanford, CA, 1992)

Pocock, J.G.A., *The Discovery of Islands: Essays in British History* (Cambridge, 2005)

Rendall, J., *The Origins of Modern Feminism: Women in Britain, France and the United States, 1780–1860* (London, 1985)

Rendall, J. (ed.), *Equal or Different: Women's Politics, 1800–1914* (Oxford, 1987)

Reynolds, K. D., *Aristocratic Women and Political Society in Victorian Britain* (Oxford, 1998)

Robbins, K., 'Lord Bryce and the First World War', *Historical Journal* 10: 2 (1967), pp. 255–77

Robbins, K., *Nineteenth-Century Britain: Integration and Diversity* (Oxford, 1988)

Robbins, K., 'History, the Historical Association and the "National Past"', reprinted in his *History, Religion and Identity in Modern Britain* (London, 1993)

Robbins, K., 'An Imperial and Multinational Polity: The "Scene from the Centre", 1832–1922' in Grant, A., Stringer, K. (eds), *Uniting the Kingdom? The Making of British History* (London and New York, 1995)

Robbins, K., 'Labouring the Point', *Historical Journal*, 47, 3 (2004), 775–84

Savage, M., Miles, A. (eds), *The Remaking of the British Working Class 1840–1940* (London, 1994)

Scott, C., *Christopher Dawson: A Historian and His World* (London, 1982)

Sims-Williams, P., 'Celtomania and Celtoscepticism', *Cambrian Medieval Celtic Studies* 36 (1998), pp. 1–36

Smith, B., *The Gender of History: Men, Women, and Historical Practice* (Cambridge, MA and London, 1998)

Spencer, I. R.G., *British Immigration Policy: The Making of Multi-Racial Britain* (London, 1977)

Stuchtey, B., Wende, P. (eds), *British and German Historiography, 1750–1950* (Oxford, 2000)

Tanner, D., Williams, C., Hopkin, D. (eds), *The Labour Party in Wales, 1900–2000* (Cardiff, 2000)

Taylor, M., 'John Bull and the Iconography of Public Opinion in England c.1712–1929', *Past & Present* 134 (February 1992), pp. 93–128

Thompson, D., *Queen Victoria: Gender and Power* (London, 1990)

Thompson, D. (ed.), *Outsiders: Class, Gender and Power* (London, 1993)

Trevelyan, G.M., *John Bright* (London, 1913)

Tulloch, H., *James Bryce's 'The American Commonwealth': The Anglo-American background* (Woodbridge, 1988)

Turville-Petre, T., *England the Nation: Language, Literature and National Identity, 1290–1340* (Oxford, 1996)

Ward, P., *Red Flag and Union Jack: Englishness, Patriotism and the British Left, 1881–1924* (Woodbridge, 1998)

Ward, P., *Britishness since 1870* (London, 2004)

Wormell, D., *Sir John Seeley and the Uses of History* (Cambridge, 1980)

10   Nordic National Histories

Ahtiainen, P., *Kulttuuri, yhteisö, yksilö. Gunnar Suolahti historiantutkijana* [Culture, Community, Individual. Gunnar Suolahti as a Historian] (Helsinki, 1991)

Arup, E., *Danmarks historie*, Bd. I–II (København, 1925–32)

Auer, V., Jutikkala, E., *Finnlands Lebensraum* (Berlin, 1941)

Blom, I., Sogner, S. (eds), *Med kjønnsperspektiv på norsk historie: fra vikingtid til 2000-årsskiftet* (Oslo, 1999/2005)

Carlsson, S. et al., *Den svenska historien*, Bd. I–X (Stockholm, 1966–8)

Childs, M. W., *Sweden: The Middle Way* (New Haven, CT, 1936)

Dahl, O., *Historisk materialisme: historieoppfatningen hos Edvard Bull og Ottar Dahl* (Oslo, 1974)

Dahl, O., *Norsk historieforskning i det 19. og 20. århundre* (Oslo, 1990)

Engman, M., Kirby, D. (eds), *Finland: People, Nation, State* (London, 1989)

Fulsås, N., *Historie og nasjon: Ernst Sars og striden om norsk kultur* (Oslo, 1999)

Haapala, P., 'Väinö Linnan historiasota' ['Väinö Linna's War on Historians'], *Historiallinen Aikakauskirja* (2001), no. 1, 25–34

K. Helle et al. (eds), *Aschehougs norgeshistorie*, 12 vols (Oslo, 1994–8)

Hubbard, W. H., *Making a Historical Culture: Historiography in Norway* (Oslo, 1995)

Jaakkola, J., *Suomen historian ääriviivat* ['An Outline of Finnish History'] (Helsinki, 1940)

Jensen, B. E. et al., Danmarkshistorie: en erindringspolitisk slagmark (Copenhagen, 1997)

Jensen, B. E., 'Writing European History – the Danish Way', in Pók, Á. et al. (eds), *European History: Challenge for a Common Future* (= Shaping European History, vol. 3), edition Körper-Stiftung (Hamburg, 2002)

Jensen, B. E., *Historie – livsverden og fag, Gyldendal* [History – Life-world and Academic Discipline] (Copenhagen, 2003)

Jussila, O., *Maakunnasta valtioksi: Suomen valtion synty* [The Making of the Finnish State] (Porvoo, 1987)

Jussila, O., *Suomen suuriruhtinaskunta, 1809–1919* [The Grand Duchy of Finland] (Helsinki, 2004)

Jutikkala, E., *Pohjoismaisen yhteiskunnan historiallisia juuria* [Historical Roots of the Nordic Society] (Helsinki, 1965)

Kaarninen, M., Kinnunen, T., '"Hardly women at all"': Finnish Historiography Revisited', *Storia della Storiorafia*, 46 (2004), 152–70

Kaelble, H. (ed.), *The European Way: European Societies during the Nineteenth and Twentieth Centuries* (Oxford and New York, 2004)

Katainen, E. et al. (eds), *Oma pöytä: naiset historiankirjoittajina Suomessa* ['Women Writing History in Finland'] (Helsinki, 2005)

Kirby, D.G. (ed.), *Finland and Russia, 1808–1920: A Selection of Documents* (London, 1975)

Kjeldstadli, K. (ed.), *Norsk innvandringshistorie*, 3 vols (Oslo, 2003)

Klinge, M., *Keisarin Suomi* [Finland – Emperor's Land] (Helsinki, 1997)

Klinge, M., *Idylli ja uhka: Topeliuksen aatteita ja politiikkaa* [Ideas and Politics of Z. Topelius] (Helsinki, 1998)

Liikanen, I.,'Kansa'['People'], in *Käsitteet liikkeessä* [History of Concepts] (Tampere, 2003), pp. 357–408

Ljungh, A., *Sedd, eller osedd? Kvinnoskildringar i svensk historieforskning, mellan åren 1890 till 1995* (Lund, 1999)

Lönnroth, E.K., Björk, R. (eds), *Conceptions of National History: Proceedings of Nobel Symposium 78* (Berlin and New York, 1994)

Meyer, F., Myhre, J. E. (eds), *Nordic Historiography in the 20th Century* (Oslo, 2000)

Moberg, V., *A History of the Swedish People* (New York, 1972)

Munch, P. A., *Det norske Folks Historie*. 6 vols (Christiania [Oslo], 1852–59)

Mykland, K. (ed.), *Norges historie*, 15 vols (Oslo, 1976–80)

Ohlander, A-S., Strömberg, U-B., *Tusen svenska kvinnoår: svensk kvinnohistoria från vikingatid till nutid* (Stockholm, 1996)

Sars, J. E., *Udsigt orer den norske Historie*. 4 vols (Kristiania [Oslo]. 1873–91)

Schybergson, M.G., *Finlands historia* (Helsingfors, 1887, 1889)

Seip, J. A., *Utsikt over Norges historie*, vol. 1 (Oslo, 1974)

Setälä, P., Manninen, M. (eds), *The Lady with the Bow: The Story of Finnish Women* (Helsinki, 1990)

Steen, S., *Det frie Norge*, 8 vols (Oslo, 1951–73)

Stormbom, N.-B., *Väinö Linna: kirjailijan tie* (Helsinki, 1963)

Stråth, B., Sørensen, Ø. (eds), *The Cultural Construction of Norden* (Oslo, 1997)

Sulkunen, I., *Suomalaisen Kirjallisuuden Seura, 1831–1892* [History of the Finnish Literary Society] (Helsinki, 2004)

Svanberg, I. and M. Tydén, *Tusen år av invandring: en svensk kulturhistoria* (Stockholm, 1998)

Torstendahl, R. (ed.), *An Assessment of Twentieth-Century Historiography: Professionalism, Methodologies, Writings* (Stockholm, 2000)

Valenius, J., *Undressing the Maid: Gender, Sexuality and the Body in the Construction of the Finnish Nation*, Bibliotheca Historica, 85 (Helsinki, 2004)

Vind, O., *Grundtvigs historiefilosofi*, Skrifter/udgivet af Grundtvig-Selskabet, 32 (København, 1999)

Wallette, A., *Sagans svenskar: synen på vikingatiden och de isländska sagorna under 300 år* (Malmö, 2004)

11   Weak and Strong Nations in the Low Countries: National Historiography and its 'Others' in Belgium, Luxembourg and the Netherlands in the Nineteenth and Twentieth Centuries

Aerts, R., Liagre Böhl, H. de, Rooy, P. de, Velde, H. te, *Land van kleine gebaren: een politieke geschiedenis van Nederland, 1780–1990* (Nijmegen, 1999)

Baudet, H., Meulen, H. van der (eds), *Kernproblemen der economische geschiedenis* (Groningen, 1978)

Bendix, R., Roodenburg, H. (eds), *Managing Ethnicity: Perspectives from Folklore Studies, History and Anthropology* (Amsterdam, 2000)

Beyen, M., *Held voor alle werk: de vele gedaanten van Tijl Uilenspiegel* (Antwerpen and Baarn, 1998)

Beyen, M., '"Een werk waarop ieder Vlaming fier kan zijn?" Het boek *100 Groote Vlamingen* als praalfaçade van het Vlaams-nationale geschiedenisbouwwerk', in Tollebeek, J., Verbeeck, G., Verschaffel, T. (eds), *De lectuur van het verleden: opstellen over de geschiedenis aangeboden aan Reginald de Schryver* (Leuven, 1998), pp. 411–40

Beyen, M., 'Natural-born Nations? National historiography in Belgium and the Netherlands between a "Tribal" and a Social-Cultural Paradigm', *Storia della Storiografia*, 38 (2000), 17–22

Beyen, M., 'A Tribal Trinity: The Rise and Fall of the Franks, the Frisians and the Saxons in the Historical Consciousness of the Netherlands since 1850', *European History Quarterly*, 30 (2000), 493–532

Beyen, M., *Oorlog en Verleden: nationale geschiedenis in België en Nederland, 1938–1947* (Amsterdam, 2002)

Beyen, M., 'Naties in gradaties: nationaal en historisch besef in België en Nederland', *Ons erfdeel* (2002)

Beyen, M., 'Belgium: A Nation that Failed to Become Ethnic', in Eriksonas, L., Müller, L. (eds), *Statehood before and beyond Ethnicity: Minor States in Northern and Eastern Europe* (Brussels, 2005), pp. 341–52

Beyen, M., 'Een onafwendbaar toeval: de Belgisch-patriottische geschiedschrijving over de Belgische Revolutie', in Rietbergen, P., Verschaffel, T. (eds), *De erfenis van 1830* (Louvain, 2006), pp. 75–89

Beyens, N., 'Van nieuwe Belgen en vaderlandsloze beeldenstormers', in *Nieuwste Tijd: Kwartaalschrift voor eigentijdse geschiedenis*, 1 (2002), 71–86

Beyen, M., 'Nederlands wonderjaren: beschouwingen bij de reeks "Nederlandse cultuur in Europese context"', *Ons Erfdeel: Algemeen-Nederlands Tweemaandelijks Cultureel tijdschrift*, 45 (2002), 522–35

Bierlaire, F., Kupper, J-L. (eds), *Henri Pirenne: de la cite de Liège à la ville de Gand, Cahiers de Clio*, no. 86 (1986)

Blaas, P. B. M., 'De prikkelbaarheid van een kleine natie met een groot verleden: Fruins en Bloks nationale geschiedschrijving', *Theoretische Geschiedenis*, 9 (1982), 271–303

Blaas, P. B. M., 'De visie van de Groot-Nederlandse historiografen: aanleiding tot een nieuwe historiografie?', in Craeybeckx, J., Daeleman, F., Scheelings, F.G. (eds), '*1585: Op gescheiden wegen ...*': handelingen van het colloquium over de scheiding der Nederlanden, gehouden op 22–23 november 1985, te Brussel (Leuven, 1988), pp. 197–218

Blaas, P. B. M., *De burgerlijke eeuw: over eeuwwenden, liberale burgerij en geschiedschrijving* (Hilversum, 2000)

Bologne, M., *La Révolution prolétarienne de 1830* (Brussels, 1930)

Bosch, M., 'De IJkpunten geijkt ... : Evaluatie van het NWO-onderzoeksprogramma "Nederlandse cultuur in Europese context" uit het perspectief van vrouwengeschiedenis en genderstudies', *Tijdschrift voor Sociale Geschiedenis*, 29 (2003), 1–20

Bosch, M., *Een onwrikbaar geloof in rechtvaardigheid: Aletta Jacobs, 1854–1929* (Amsterdam, 2005)

Broomans, P. et al., *My Beloved Mothertongue. Ethnocultural Nationalism in Small Nations. Inventories and Reflections* (Louvain, forthcoming)

Brouwer, L., *De archeologie van een houding: Nederlandse identiteit in de Friesche Volksamanak* (Groningen, 1998)

Cornelissen, J.D.M., *Rembrandt: de eendracht van het land. Een historische studie* (Nijmegen, 1941)

Cornelissen, J. D. M., *Johan de Witt en de vrijheid: rede uitgesproken op den 22sten dies natalis der R.K. universiteit te Nijmegen op 17 Oct. 1945* (Nijmegen, 1945)

Fasseur, C., *Wilhelmina: de jonge koningin* (Amsterdam, 1998), and *Wilhelmina: krijgshaftig in een vormeloze jas* (Amsterdam, 2001)

François, L., *De Boerenkrijg: twee eeuwen feit en fictie* (Leuven, 1998)

Gérard, J., *Marie Thérèse: impératrice des Belges* (Brussels, 1987)

Ginderachter, M. Van, *Het rode vaderland: de vergeten geschiedenis van de communautaire spanningen in het Belgische socialisme voor WOI* (Tielt, 2005), pp. 275–81

Goetzinger, G., Lorang, A., Wagner, R. (eds), '*Wenn nun wir Frauen auch das Wort ergreifen ...*': 1880–1950: Frauen in Luxemburg (Luxembourg, 1997)

Grever, M., *Strijd tegen de stilte: Johanna Naber (1859–1941) en de vrouwenstem in de geschiedenis* (Hilversum, 1994)

Grever, M., Dieteren, F. (eds), *Een Vaderland voor vrouwen. A Fatherland for Women: The 1898 'Nationale Tentoonstelling van Vrouwenarbeid' in retrospect* (Amsterdam, 1998)

Grever, M., 'Van Landsvader tot moeder des vaderlands: Oranje, Gender en Nederland', *Groniek: Onafhankelijk Gronings Historisch Studentenblad*, 36 (2002), 131–50

Haitsma Mulier, E. O. G., Janssen, A. E. M. (eds), *Willem van Oranje in de historie: vier eeuwen beeldvorming en geschiedschrijving* (Utrecht, 1984)

Hasquin, H., *Historiographie et politique: essai sur l'histoire de Belgique et de la Wallonie*, 2nd edn (Charleroi, 1982)

Hunink, M., *De papieren van de revolutie: het Internationaal Instituut voor Sociale Geschiedenis, 1935–1947* (Amsterdam, 1986)

Israel, J., *The Dutch Republic: Its Rise, Greatness and Fall, 1477–1806* (Oxford, 1995)

Jong, A. De, *De dirigenten van de herinnering: musealisering en nationalisering van de volkscultuur, 1815–1940* (Nijmegen, 2001)

Kesteloot, C., 'Ecrire l'histoire du Mouvement Wallon: une démarche historique et citoyenne?', *Bijdragen tot de Eigentijdse Geschiedenis*, nos. 13–14 (2004), 17–44

Kill, J., *1000 jähriges Luxemburg: woher? – wohin? Ein Beitrag zum besseren Verständnis der Geschichte des Luxemburger Landes* (Luxembourg, 1963)

Leuker, M-T., *Künstler als Helden und Heilige: nationale und konfessionelle Mythologie im Werk J.A. Alberdingk Thijms (1820–1889) und seiner Zeitgenossen* (Münster, 2001)

Mijnhardt, W. W. (ed.), *Kantelend geschiedbeeld: Nederlandse historiografie sinds 1945* (Utrecht and Amsterdam, 1983)

Morelli, A. (ed.), *De grote mythen van België, Wallonië en Vlaanderen* (Brussels, 1996)

Noordegraaf, L., 'Nicolaas Wilhelmus Posthumus (1880–1960): van gloeiend marxist tot entrepreneur', in Blom, J. C. H. (ed.), *Een brandpunt van geleerdheid in de hoofdstad: de Universiteit van Amsterdam rond 1900 in 15 portretten* (Hilversum/Amsterdam, 1992), pp. 287–312

Otto, A. *Het Ruisen van de Tijd: over de Theoretische Geschiedenis van Jan Romein* (Amsterdam, 1998)

Peeters, E. *Het labyrint van het verleden: natie, vrijheid en geweld in de Belgische geschiedschrijving, 1787–1850* (Leuven, 2003)

Prevenier, W., 'L'Ecole des "Annales" et l'historiographie néerlandaise', *Septentrion*, 7 (1978), 47–54

Raedts, P., 'Katholieken op zoek naar een Nederlandse identiteit, 1814–1898', *Bijdragen en de Mededelingen betreffende de geschiedenis van de Nederlanden*, 107 (1992), 713–25

Reynebeau, M., *Een geschiedenis van België* (Tielt, 2004)

Schelven, A. A. van, *Willem van Oranje: een boek ter nagedachtenis van idealen en teleurstellingen* (Amsterdam, 1933)

Scuto, D., *Sous le signe de la grande grève de mars 1921* (Esch-sur-Alzette, 1990)

Stengers, J., 'Le Mythe des dominations étrangères dans l'historiographie belge', *Revue Belge de Philologie et d'Histoire*, 59 (1981), 382–401

Stengers, J., *Congo: mythes et réalités. 100 ans d'histoire* (Gembloux, 1989)

Stengers, J., 'Avant Pirenne: les preuves de l'ancienneté de la nation belge', *Bulletin de la Classe des Lettres et des Sciences Morales et Politiques de Belgique*, 6th ser., vol. 7 (1996), 551–72

Stengers, J., 'De Belgische Revolutie', in Morelli, A. (ed.), *De grote mythen van België, Vlaanderen en Wallonië* (Brussel, 1996)

Stengers, J., *Histoire du sentiment national en Belgique des origines à 1918*, 2 vols (Brussels, 2000–2)

Terlinden, C., *L'Archiduchesse Isabelle* (Brussels, 1943)

Tollebeek, J., 'Geyl en Van der Essen', *Ex officina*, 3 (1986) 139–51

Tollebeek, J., *De toga van Fruin: denken over geschiedenis in Nederland sinds 1860* (Amsterdam, 1990)

Tollebeek, J., *De ijkmeesters: opstellen over de geschiedschrijving in Nederland en België* (Amsterdam, 1994)

Tollebeek, J., 'De Guldensporenslag: de cultus van 1302 en de Vlaamse strijd', in Morelli, A. (ed.), *De grote mythen uit de geschiedenis van België, Vlaanderen en Wallonië* (Berchem, 1996), pp. 191–202

Tollebeek, J., 'Historical Representation and the Nation-state in Belgium, 1830–1850', *Journal of the History of Ideas*, 59 (1998), 329–53

Tollebeek, J., 'Voor elke liefde een instituut', *De ziel van de fabriek: over de arbeid van de historicus* (Amsterdam, 1998)

Trausch, G. (ed.), *Histoire du Luxembourg: le destin européen d'un 'petit pays'* (Toulouse, 2002)

Ussel, P. Van, *Maria van Bourgondië* (Leuven, 1944)

Valk, H. de, 'Nationale of pauselijke helden? De heiligverklaring van de martelaren van Gorcum in 1867', *Trajecta*, 6 (1997), 139–55

Vangroenweghe, D., *Rood rubber: Leopold II en zijn Congo* (Brussel, 1985)

Velde, H. te, Verhage, F. (eds), *De eenheid en de delen: zuilvorming, onderwijs en natievorming in Nederland 1850–1900* (Amsterdam, 1996)

Vellut, J. (ed.), *Het geheugen van Congo: de koloniale tijd* (Tervuren, 2005)

Vermeulen, U., 'Katholieken en liberalen tegenover de Gentse Pacificatiefeesten (1876)', *Handelingen der Maatschappij voor Geschiedenis en Oudheidkunde te Gent*, nieuwe reeks, 20 (1966), 167–85

Verschaffel, H., 'Marnix van Sint-Aldegonde, een symbool in de clerico-liberale strijd', *Spiegel Historiael*, 20 (1985), 190–5

Vos, L., 'Reconstructions of the Past in Belgium and Flanders', in Coppieters, B., Huysseune, M. (eds), *Secession, History and the Social Sciences* (Brussels, 2002), pp. 179–206

Wey, C., 'Le Centenaire de l'Indépendance et sa commémoration en 1939', *Hémecht*, 41 (1989), pp. 29–53

Wils, K., 'Tussen metafysica en antropometrie: het rasbegrip bij Léon Vanderkindere', in Beyen, M., Vanpaemel, G. (eds), *Rasechte wetenschap? Het rasbegrip tussen wetenschap en politiek vóór de Tweede Wereldoorlog* (Leuven/Apeldoorn, 1998), pp. 81–99

Wils, L., *Vlaanderen, België, Groot-Nederland: historische opstellen, gebundeld en aangeboden aan de schrijver bij het bereiken van zijn emeritaat aan de K.U. Leuven* (Leuven, 1994)

Wils, K., 'Science, an Ally of Feminism?', *Revue Belge de Philologie et d'Histoire*, 77 (1999), 416–39

Witte, E., 'Op zoek naar het natiegevoel in België: enkele kanttekeningen bij *Les Racines de la Belgique* van Jean Stengers', *Wetenschappelijke tijdingen* (2001), 176–87

Woud, A. van der, *De Bataafse hut: verschuivingen in het beeld van de geschiedenis, 1750–1850* (Amsterdam, 1990)

Zeijden, A. van der, *Katholieke identiteit en historisch bewustzijn: W.F.J. Nuyens (1823–1894) en zijn 'nationale' geschiedschrijving* (Hilversum, 2002)

Zondergeld, G.R., *De Friese beweging in het tijdvak der twee wereldoorlogen* (Leeuwarden, 1978)

12 National Historiography and National Identity: Switzerland in Comparative Perspective

Altermatt, U. (ed.), *Katholische Denk- und Lebenswelten: Beiträge zur Kultur- und Sozialgeschichte des Schweizer Katholizismus im 20. Jahrhundert* (Fribourg, 2003)

Bercé, Y.-M., Contamine, P. (eds), *Histoires de France, historiens de la France: actes du colloque international, Reims, 14–15 May 1993* (Paris, 1994)

Blockmans, W., Genet, J.-P. (eds), *Visions sur le développement des états européens: théories et historiographies de l'état moderne*, Collection de l'Ecole française de Rome, 171 (Rome, 1993)

Bosshart-Pfluger, C., 'Jeanne Niquille (1894–1970). Staatsarchivarin ehrenhalber', *Freiburger Geschichtsblätter* 75 (1998) 168–74

Buchbinder, S., *Der Wille zur Geschichte: Schweizergeschichte um 1900 – die Werke von Wilhelm Oechsli, Johannes Dierauer und Karl Dändliker* (Zürich, 2002)

Carbonell, C.-O., 'Les origines de l'Etat moderne: Les traditions historiographiques françaises (1820–1990)', in Blockmans, W., J.-P. Genet (eds), *Visions sur le développement des états Européens. Théories et Historiographies de l'Etat moderne* (*Collection de l'Ecole Française de Rome* 171) (Rom, 1993), pp. 297–312

Castella, G., *Histoire de la Suisse* (Einsiedeln, 1928)

Dändliker, K., *Geschichte der Schweiz mit besonderer Rücksicht auf die Entwicklung des Verfassungs- und Kulturlebens von den ältesten Zeiten bis zur Gegenwart*, 3 vols (Zürich, 1883–8)

Dierauer, J., *Geschichte der schweizerischen Eidgenossenschaft*, Allgemeine Staatengeschichte, 1. Abt.: Geschichte der europäischen Staaten, 26, 5 vols (Gotha, 1887–1917)

Dumoulin, O., 'Histoire et historiens de droite', in Sirinelli, J.-F. (ed.), *Histoire des droites en France*, vol. 2 (Paris, 1992), pp. 327–98

Dürr, E., 'Von Morgarten bis Marignano', *Schweizer Kriegsgeschichte*, vol. 2, H. 4 (Berne, 1933)

Durrer, R., *Die Bundesbriefe der alten Eidgenossen, 1291–1513* (Zürich, 1904)

Fahlbusch, M., Rössler, M., Siegrist, D., *Geographie und Nationalsozialismus: Drei Fallstudien zur Institution Geographie im Deutschen Reich und der Schweiz*, with appendix by P. Jüngst and O. Meder, Urbs et regio, 51 (Kassel, 1989)

Fauquet, E., La Place de l'Histoire de France de Michelet', in Bercé, Y.-M., Contamine, P. (eds), *Histoires de France, Historiens de la France* (Actes du colloques international, Reims, 14 et 15 mai 1993) (Paris, 1994), pp. 267–80

Feller, R. 'Von der Alten Eidgenossenschaft', in Strick, F. (ed.), *Schweizerische Akademiereden* (Bern 1945), pp. 447–74

Frank, M., 'Ricarda Huch und die deutsche Frauenbewegung', *Studien der Ricarda-Huch-Gesellschaft*, 2 (Braunschweig, 1988), 65–74

Friedrich, M., Heidegger, M., '"Zwischen historischer Dichtung und akademischer Wahrheit". Zur Situierung von Frauen in der Verwissenschaftlichung', in Bosshart-Pfluger, C., Grisard, D., Späti, C. (ed.), *Geschlecht und Wissen – Genre et Savoir – Gender and Knowledge* (Zürich, 2004), pp. 278–85

Fueter, E., *Die Schweiz seit 1848: Geschichte, Wirtschaft, Politik*, Aufbau moderner Staaten, 1 (Zürich and Leipzig, 1928)

Fueter, E. K., 'Geschichte der gesamtschweizerischen Historischen Organisation: ein wissenschaftsgeschichtlicher Überblick', *Historische Zeitschrift*, 189 (1959), 449–505

Gagliardi, E., *Geschichte der Schweiz von den Anfängen bis zur Gegenwart*, 2 vols (Zürich, 1920–27), 2nd edn (Zürich, 1934–7)

Gosteli, M. (ed.), *Vergessene Geschichte: illustrierte Chronik der Frauenbewegung, 1914–1963*, 2 vols (Berne, 2000), vol. 1

Graetz, M., Mattioli, A. (eds), *Krisenwahrnehmungen im Fin de siècle: jüdische und katholische Bildungseliten in Deutschland und der Schweiz, 1880–1914*, Clio Lucernensis, 4 (Zürich, 1997)

Grimm, R., *Geschichte der Schweiz in ihren Klassenkämpfen* (Berne, 1920), 2nd edn (Zürich, 1979)

Grunewald, M., Puschner, U. (eds), *Das katholische Intellektuellenmilieu in Deutschland, seine Presse und seine Netzwerke / Le Milieu intellectuel catholique en Allemagne, sa presse et ses réseaux (1871–1963)* (Berne, Brussels, Frankfurt/M, New York, Oxford and Vienna, 2006)

Handbuch der Schweizer Geschichte, 2 vols (Zürich, 1972/7)

Herrmann, I., 'Au croisement des impasses de la démocratie? Les femmes et l'écriture de l'histoire nationale Suisse', in Porciani, I., O'Dowd, M. (eds), *History Women*, special issue of *Storia della Storiagrafia*, 46 (2004), 59–68

Hilty, C., *Vorlesungen über die Politik der Eidgenossenschaft* (Berne, 1875)

Honegger, J.J., Meyer von Knonau, G., *Heldinnen des Schweizerlandes* (Zürich, 1834)

Huch, R., *Die Neutralität der Eidgenossenschaft, besonders der Orte Zürich und Bern, während des spanischen Erbfolgekrieges* (Zürich, 1892)

Huch, R., *Deutsche Geschichte*, vol. 1, *Römisches Reich Deutscher Nation* (Berlin, 1934)

Huch, R., *Deutsche Geschichte*, vol. 2, *Das Zeitalter der Glaubensspaltung* (Zürich, 1937)

Huch, R., *Deutsche Geschichte*, vol. 3, *Untergang des Römischen Reiches Deutscher Nation* (Zürich, 1949)

Hürbin, J., *Handbuch der Schweizer Geschichte*, 2 vols (Stans, 1900/1906)

Jorio, M., 'Oskar Vasella (1904–1966): ein bedeutender Reformationshistoriker', *Zeitschrift für schweizerische Kirchengeschichte*, 90 (1996), 83–99

Keller-Tarnuzzer, K., *Die Herkunft des Schweizervolkes* (Frauenfeld, 1936)

Keller, C., *Der Schädelvermesser: Otto Schlaginhaufen – Anthropologe und Rassenhygieniker: eine biographische Reportage* (Zürich, 1995)

Kopp, J. E., *Urkunden zur Geschichte der eidgenössischen Bünde*, vol. 1 (Lucerne, 1835), vol. 2 (Vienna, 1851) = Archiv für Kunde oesterreichischer Geschichtsquellen, 6

Kreis, G., *Helvetia – im Wandel der Zeiten: die Geschichte einer nationalen Repräsentationsfigur* (Zürich, 1991)

Kubli, S., Stump, D. (eds), *'Viel Köpfe, viel Sinn': Texte von Autorinnen aus der deutschsprachigen Schweiz, 1795–1945* (Zürich, Berne, Dortmund, 1994)

Küffer, G., *Maria Waser* (Berne, 1971).

Maissen, T., 'Von wackeren alten Eidgenossen und souveränen Jungfrauen: zu Datierung und Deutung der frühesten "Helvetia"-Darstellungen', *Zeitschrift für Archäologie und Kulturgeschichte*, 56 (1999), 256–301

Maissen, T., *Die Geburt der Republic: Staatsverständnis und Repräsentation in der frühneuzeitlichen Eidgenossenschaft*, Historische Semantik, 4 (Göttingen, 2006)

Marchal, G.P., *Schweizer Gebrauchsgeschichte: Geschichtsbilder, Mythenbildung und nationale Identität* (Basle, 2006)

Marchal, G. P., 'La Naissance du mythe de Saint-Gothard ou la longue découverte de l'homo alpinus et de l'Helvetia mater fluviorum', in Bergier, J.-F., Guzzi, S. (eds), *La Découverte des Alpes*, Itinera, 12 (Basle, 1992), pp. 35–53

Marchal, G.P., Mattioli, Aram (eds), *Erfundene Schweiz: Konstruktionen nationaler Identität/La Suisse imaginée: bricolages d'une identité nationale*, Clio Lucernensis, 1 (Zürich, 1992)

Marchal, G. P.,'Zwischen Geschichtsbaumeistern und Römlingen. Katholische Historiker und die Nationalgeschichtsschreibung in Deutschland und in der Schweiz', in Graetz, M., Mattioli, A. (eds), *Krisenwahrnehmungen im Fin de Siècle. Jüdische und Katholische Bildungseliten in Deutschland und der Schweiz (1880–1914)* (Clio Lucernensis 4) (Zürich, 1997), pp. 177–210

Mattioli, A., *Intellektuelle von rechts: Ideologie und Politik in der Schweiz, 1918–1939* (Zürich, 1995)

Mattioli, A., *Zwischen Demokratie und totalitärer Diktatur: Gonzage de Reynold und die Tradition der autoritären Rechten in der Schweiz* (Zürich, 1994)

Mattioli, A., Graetz, M. (eds), *Krisenwahrnehmungen im Fin de Siècle. Jüdische und Katholische Bildungseliten in Deutschland und der Schweiz, 1880–1914* (Clio Lucernensis 4) (Zürich, 1997)

Mattmüller, H., *Carl Hilty, 1833–1909*, Basler Beiträge zur Geschichtswissenschaft, 100 (Basle, 1966), pp. 244–73

Mesmer, B., *Staatsbürgerinnen ohne Stimmrecht: die Politik der schweizerischen Frauenverbände, 1914–1971* (Zürich, 2007)

Meyer, K., *Aufsätze und Reden* (Zürich, 1952)

Müller, J. von, *Geschichten schweizerischer Eidgenossenschaft* (Leipzig, 1786–1805)

Nabholz, H., von Muralt, L., Feller, R., Bonjour, E., *Geschichte der Schweiz* (Zürich, 1932)

Nouvelle histoire de la Suisse et des Suisses (Lausanne, 1986; 1st edn: Lausanne, 1983)

Oechsli, W., 'Orte und Zugewandte: eine Studie zur Geschichte des schweizerischen Bundesrechtes', *Jahrbuch für schweizerische Geschichte*, 13 (1888), 1–497

Oechsli, W., *Die Anfänge der schweizerischen Eidgenossenschaft, zur 6. Säcularfeier des ersten ewigen Bundes vom 1. August 1291* (Berne, 1891)

Oechsli, W., *Geschichte der Schweiz im 19. Jh.*, Staatengeschichte der neuesten Zeit, 29, 1 (Leipzig, 1903)

Oechsli, W., 'Die Benennungen der alten Eidgenossenschaft und ihrer Glieder', *Jahrbuch für schweizerische Geschichte*, 41 (1916), 51–230; 42 (1917), 87–258

Peyer, H.C., *Verfassungsgeschichte der alten Schweiz* (Zürich, 1978)

Porciani, I., O'Dowd, M., *History Women* (= *Storia della Storiagrafia* 46 (2004))

Rappard, W.E., *L'Individu et l'état dans l'évolution constitutive de la Suisse* (Zürich, 1936)

Reynold, G. de, *La Démocratie et la Suisse: essai d'une philosophie de notre histoire nationale* (Berne, 1929)

Salis, M. von, *Agnes von Poitou, Kaiserin von Deutschland: eine historisch-kritisch-psychologische Abhandlung* (Zürich, 1887)

Somazzi, I., *Geschichte der obrigkeitlichen Lehrgotte im Alten Bern: ein Beitrag zur Schulgeschichte und zur Geschichte der Frau im Dienste des öffentlichen Unterrichts* (Berne, 1925)

Somazzi, I., *Der schweizerische Staatsgedanke im Sturm der Zeit* (Berne, 1934)

Schweizer Geschichte, Neue Folge, 1. Abt., *Chroniken* VII, 1–13, H 1–3 (Basle, 1970–2001)

Stadler, P., 'Zwischen Klassenkampf, Ständestaat und Genossenschaft: politische Ideologien im schweizerischen Geschichtsbild der Zwischenkriegszeit', *Historische Zeitschrift*, 219 (1974), 293–9

Stadler, P., *Epochen der Schweizergeschichte* (Zürich, 2003)

Stämpfli, R., 'Die Nationalisierung der Schweizer Frauen: Frauenbewegung und Geistige Landesverteidigung 1933–1939', *Schweizerische Zeitschrift für Geschichte*, 50 (2000), 155–80

Stercken, A., *Enthüllung der Helvetia: die Sprache der Staatspersonifikation im 19. Jahrhundert*, Reihe historische Anthropologie, 29 (Berlin, 1998)

Strick, F. (ed.), *Schweizerische Akademiereden* (Berne 1945), pp. 447–74

Studer, B., 'Die Wissenschaft sei geschlechtslos und Gemeingut Aller. Frauen in der Genese und Tradition der historischen Disziplin', in Bosshart-Pfluger, C., Grisard, D., Späti, C. (eds), *Geschlecht und Wissen – Genre et Savoir – Gender and Knowledge* (Zürich, 2004), pp. 361–78

Tollebeek, J., "Writing History in the *Salon Vert*', *Storia della Storiagrafia* 46 (2004) (=O'Dowd, M., Porciani, I. (eds), *History Women*) 35–40

Tschudi, A., *Chronicon Helveticum*, ed. B. Stettler (*Quellen zur Schweizer Geschichte* Neue Folge 1. Abt: *Chroniken* VII, 1–13, H 1–3) (Basel, 1970–2001)

Walter, F., *Les Figures paysagères de la nation: territoire et paysage en Europe (16e–20e siècles)* (Paris, 2004)

Waser, M., 'Lebendiges Schweizertum: aus einem Vortrag', *Neue Schweizer Rundschau*, Neue Folge, 1 (1934)

Ziegler, B., 'Historikerinnen an der Universität Zürich, 1900–1970', in Bosshart-Pfluger, C., Grisard, D., Späti, C. (eds), *Geschlecht und Wissen/Genre et Savoir/Gender and Knowledge* (Zürich, 2004), pp. 237–48

Zimmer, O., *A Contested Nation: History, Memory and Nationalism in Switzerland, 1761–1891* (Cambridge, 2003);

Zimmer, O., 'Competing Memories of the Nation: Liberal Historians and the Reconstruction of the Swiss Past, 1870–1900', *Past and Present*, 168 (1998), 194–226

Zimmer, O., 'In Search of Natural Identity: Alpine Landscape and the Reconstruction of the Swiss Nation', *Comparative Studies in Society and History*, 40 (1998), 637–65

13   Portuguese and Spanish Historiographies: Distance and Proximity

Altamira, R., *Los elementos de la civilización y el carácter de los españoles* (Buenos Aires, 1950)

Álvarez Junco, J., 'La invención de la Guerra de la Independencia', *Studia Histórica: H.ᵂ Contemporánea*, vol. 12 (1994), 75–99

Álvarez Junco, J., *Mater Dolorosa: la idea de España en el siglo XIX* (Madrid, 2001)

Barrio Alonso, À., 'Historia obrera en los noventa: tradición y modernidad', *Historia Social*, 37 (2000), 143–60

Bataillon, M., *Erasmo y España* (Paris, 1937; translated in Mexico in 1950)

Braga, T., *A pátria portuguesa: o território e a raça* (Porto, 1894)

Cabrera, M. A., 'Developments in Contemporary Spanish Historiography: From Social History to the New Cultural History', *Journal of Modern History*, 77 (2005), 994–6

Campomar Fornieles, M., *La cuestión religiosa en la restauración: historia de los heterodoxos españoles* (Santander, 1984)

Candau Chacón, M. L., *Los moriscos en el espejo del tiempo* (Huelva, 1997)

Castro, A., *España en su historia: cristianos, moros y judíos* (Buenos Aires, 1948; rev. as *La realidad histórica de España*, México, 1954)

Catroga, F., 'Alexandre Herculano e o historicismo romântico', in Reis Torgal, L. et al., *História da história em Portugal, sécs. XIX e XX* (Lisbon, 1996), pp. 54–7

Chagas, M. Pinheiro, *História de Portugal desde os tempos mais remotos até à actualidade ...*, 8 vols. (Lisbon, 1867–74)

Cirujano, P. et al., *Historiografía y nacionalismo español (1834–1868)* (Madrid, 1985), pp. 190–4

Coelho, A. Borges, *A Revolução de 1383* (Lisbon, 1965)

Cordero Olivero, I., *Los transterrados y España* (Huelva, 1997)

Correia, A.A. Mendes, *Raízes de Portugal* (Lisbon, 1938)

Dias, J. S. da Silva, *Correntes de sentimento religioso em Portugal: século XVI a XVIII* (Coimbra, 1960)

Dias, J.S. da Silva *O Erasmismo e a Inquisição em Portugal: o processo de Fr. Valentim da Luz* (Coimbra, 1975)

Figueiredo, Fidelino, 'Historiografia portuguesa do século XX', *Revista de História*, São Paulo, 20 (1954)

Forcadell, C., 'Sobre desiertos y secanos: los movimientos sociales en la historiografía española', *Historia Contemporánea*, 7 (1992), 101–16

García Cárcel, R., *La Leyenda Negra: historia y opinión* (Madrid, 1998)

Garrido, F., *Historia de las clases trabajadoras* (Madrid, 1870)

Godinho, V. Magalhães, *Estrutura da antiga sociedade portuguesa* (Lisbon, 1971)

Godinho, V. Magalhães, *Ensaios III. Sobre teoria da história e historiografia* (Lisbon, 1971)

González Palencia, Á., *Historia de la España musulmana* (Barcelona, 1925)

Hartog, F., Revel, J. (ed.), *Les Usages politiques du passé* (Paris, 2001)

Hillgarth, J. N., 'Spanish Historiography and Iberian Reality', *History and Theory*, 24 (1985), 23–43

Israel, J. I., 'The Decline of Spain: A Historical Myth?', *Past and Present*, 91 (May 1981), 170–80

Jover Zamora, J. M., *La civilización española a mediadados del s. XIX* (Madrid, 1991)

Kagan, R. L., 'Prescott's Paradigm: American Historical Scholarship and the Decline of Spain', *The American Historical Review*, 101, 2 (April 1996), 423–46

Lafuente, M., *Historia General de España, desde sus tiempos más remotos hasta nuestros días*, 30 vols. (Madrid, 1850–67)

López Vela, R , 'De Numancia a Zaragoza: la construcción del pasado nacional en las historias de España del ochocientos', García Cárcel, R. (ed.), *La construcción de las historias de España* (Madrid, 2004), 195–298

Lourenço, E., *O labirinto da saudade: psicanálise mítica do destino português* (Lisbon, 1978)

Macedo, Jorge B. de, *Da história ao documento.Do documento à história* (Lisbon, 1995)

Mainer, J. C., *La doma de la quimera* (Barcelona, 1988)

Malagón, J., 'Los historiadores y la Historia en el exilio', in Abellán, J. L. (ed.), *El exilio español de 1939*, vol. 5, *Arte y Ciencia* (Madrid, 1976), pp. 247–353

Manzanares, M., *Arabistas españoles del siglo XIX* (Madrid, 1972)

Manzano Moreno, E., 'La interpretación utilitaria del pasado', in Pérez Garzón, J. S. et al., *La gestión de la memoria: la historia de España al servicio del poder* (Barcelona, 2000), pp. 48–59

Marques, A. H. Oliveira, *Antologia da historiografia portuguesa,* 2nd edn, 2 vols. (Lisbon, 1974–75)

Martínez-Gil, V., *El naixement de l'iberisme catalanista* (Barcelona, 1997)

Martins, J. P. de Oliveira, *História da civilização ibérica*, 8th edn (Lisbon, 1946 [1879])

Matos, S. Campos, *Historiografia e memória nacional no Portugal do século XIX (1846–1899)* (Lisbon, 1998)

Mattoso, J. (ed.), *História de Portugal*, 8 vols (Lisbon, 1993)

Medina, J. (ed.), *História de Portugal dos tempos pré-históricos aos nossos dias*, 15 vols (Alfragide, 1993)

Morales Moya, A. y Esteban de Vega, M. (eds), *¿Alma de España? Castilla en las interpretaciones del pasado español* (Madrid, 2005)

Morato, J. J., *Notas para la historia de los modos de producción en España* (Madrid, 1897)

Muñoz Sepúlveda, I., *Comunidad cultural e hispano-americanismo, 1885–1936* (Madrid, 1994)

Nash, M., *Rojas: las mujeres republicanas en la guerra civil* (Madrid, 1999)

Neves, J., 'A imaginação da nação na historiografia comunista portuguesa', *Ler História*, 46 (2004), 59–84

Oliveira, R., *Historia de España* (Mexico, 1953)

Pasamar, G., 'Las "Historias de España" a lo largo del siglo XX', in García Cárcel, R. (ed.), *La construcción de las historias de España* (Madrid, 2004), pp. 334–7

Riquer, B. de, 'El surgimiento de las nuevas identidades contemporáneas: propuestas para una discusión', in Garcia Rovira, A. M. (ed.), *España, ¿nación de naciones?*, Ayer, 35 (1999), 29–35

Saraiva, A. J., *Inquisição e cristãos novos* (Lisbon, 1969)

Sérgio, A., *Breve interpretação da história de Portugal* (Lisboa, 1971 [1st edn 1928])

Serrão, J., Oliveira Marques, A. H. de (eds), *Nova história de Portugal*, 12 vols (Lisbon, 1991–2004)

Sobral, J.M., 'O Norte, o Sul, a raça, a nação – representações da identidade nacional portugue sa (séculos XIX-XX)', *Análise Social*, vol.XXXIX, 171 (2004), 255–84

Torgal, Luís R., *História e ideologia* (Coimbra, 1989)

Torre Gómez, H. de La and Telo, A., *Portugal e Espanha nos sistemas internacionais contemporâneos* (Lisbon, 2000)

Tunon de Lara, M., *El movimiento obrero en la historia de España* (Madrid, 1972)

Ucelay da Cal, E., 'La historiografia dels anys 60 y 70: marxisme, nacionalisme i mercat cultural català', in Nadal, J. et al., *La historiografia catalana balanç i perspectives* (Girona, 1990), pp. 78–9

Vakil, AbdoolKarim, 'Quesotes inacabadas: colonialismo, Islão e Portugalidade', Margarida C. Ribeiro and A.P. Ferreira (eds), *Fantasmas e fanatasias imperiais no imaginário português contemporâneo* (Oporto, 2003), 255–94

Wulff, F., *Las essencias patrias: historiografía e historia Antigua en la construcción de la identidad española (siglos XVI-XX)* (Barcelona, 2003), 3

14   Habsburg's Difficult Legacy: Comparing and Relating Austrian, Czech, Magyar and Slovak National Historical Master Narratives

Agnew, H. L., 'New States, Old Identities? The Czech Republic, Slovakia, and Historical Understanding of Statehood', *Nationalities Papers*, 28 (2000), 619–50

Beller, S., *Francis Joseph* (London and New York, 1996)

Blom, I., Hagemann, K., Hall, C. (eds), *Gendered Nations: Nationalism and Gender Order in the Long Nineteenth Century* (Oxford and New York, 2000)

Botto, J., *Slováci: vývin ich národného povedomia*, vols 1 and 2 (Martin, 1906, 1910)

Dopsch, A., *Gesammelte Aufsätze*, vol. 2, *Beiträge zur Wirtschafts- und Sozialgeschichte* (Vienna, 1938; Aalen, 1968)

Ďurica, M. S., *Dejiny Slovenska*, vols 1–6 (Bratislava 1986–91)

Eriksonas, L., *National Heroes and National Identities: Scotland, Norway, and Lithuania* (Brussels, 2004)

Fellner, F., *Geschichtsschreibung und nationale Identität Probleme und Leistungen der österreichischen Geschichtswissenschaft* (Vienna, etc., 2002)

Fischer, E., *Die Entstehung des österreichischen Volkscharakters* (Vienna, 1945)

Flacke, M. (ed.), *Mythen der Nationen – ein europäisches Panorama: eine Ausstellung des Deutschen Historischen Museums* (Berlin, 1998)

Hadler, F., 'Meistererzählungen über die erste Jahrtausendwende in Ostmitteleuropa', *Comparativ*, 10, 2 (2000), pp. 81–92

Hanisch, E., *Der lange Schatten des Staates: Österreichische Gesellschaftsgeschichte im 20. Jahrhundert* (Vienna, 1994)

Haslinger, P., 'Nationalgeschichte und volksgeschichtliches Denken in der tschechischen Geschichtswissenschaft, 1918–38', in Hettling, M. (ed.), *Volksgeschichten im Europa der Zwischenkriegszeit* (Göttingen, 2003), pp. 272–300

Heer, F., *Der Kampf um die österreichische Identität* (Vienna and Graz, 1981)

Heiss, G., 'Pan-Germans, Better Germans, Austrians: Austrian Historians on National Identity from the First to the Second Republic', *German Studies Review*, 16 (1993), 411–33

Heiss, G., Liessmann, K. P. (eds), *Das Millennium: Essays zu tausend Jahren Österreich* (Vienna, 1996)

Heiss, G., 'Im "Reich der Unbegreiflichkeiten": Historiker als Konstrukteure Österreichs', *Österreichische Zeitschrift für Geschichtswissenschaft*, 7 (1996), 455–78

Helfert, J. A., *Über Nationalgeschichte und den gegenwärtigen Stand ihrer Pflege in Österreich* (Prague, 1853)

Holotík, Ľ., *Štefánikovská legenda a vznik ČSR* (Bratislava, 1956)

Horváth, M., *Polgárosodás, liberalizmus, függetlenségi harc* (Budapest, 1986)

Ivanišević, A., Kappeler, A., Lukan, W., Suppan, A. (eds), *Klio ohne Fesseln? Historiographie im östlichen Europa nach dem Zusammenbruch des Kommunismus* (Vienna, Frankfurt/M, Berlin, Bern, Brussels, New York and Oxford, 2002)

Janowski, M., 'Three Historians', *CEU History Department Yearbook* (2001–2), 199–232

Kalista, Z., *Karel IV: Jeho duchovní tvář* (Prague, 1971)

Kalista, Z., *Josef Pekař* (Prague, 1994)

Kernbauer, A., 'Konzeptionen der Österreich-Geschichtsschreibung 1848–1938', in H. Ebner, P. W. Roth and I. Wiesflecker-Friedhuber (eds.), *Forschungen zur Geschichte des Alpen-Adria-Raumes: Festgabe für Othmar Pickl zum 70. Geburtstag* (Graz, 1997), pp. 255–73.

Klimó, Á. v., 'Die gespaltene Vergangenheit: die großen Kirchen im Kampf um die National-geschichte Ungarns, 1920–48', *Zeitschrift für Geschichtswissenschaft*, 47 (1999), 874–91

Klimó, Á. v., '1848/49 in der politischen Kultur Ungarns', in Fröhlich, H., Grandner, M., Weinzierl, M. (eds), *1848 im europäischen Kontext* (Vienna, 1999), pp. 204–22

Klimó, Á. v., *Nation, Konfession, Geschichte: zur nationalen Geschichtskultur Ungarns im europäischen Kontext (1860–1948)* (Munich, 2003)

Klimó, Á. v., 'Volksgeschichte in Ungarn: Chancen, Schwierigkeiten, Folgen eines "deutschen" Projektes', in Middell, M., Sommer, U. (eds), *Historische West- und Ostfors-chung in Zentraleuropa zwischen dem Ersten und dem Zweiten Weltkrieg: Verflechtung und Vergleich* (Leipzig, 2004), pp. 151–78

Klimó, Á. v., 'Zeitgeschichte als Revolutionsgeschichte: "Gegenwartsgeschichte" in der ungarischen Historiographie des 20. Jahrhunderts', in Nützenadel, A., Schieder, W. (eds), *Zeitgeschichte als Problem: Nationale Traditionen und Perspektiven der Forschung in Europa* (Göttingen, 2004), pp. 283–306

Kolář, P., 'Die nationalgeschichtlichen master narratives in der tschechischen Geschichts-schreibung der zweiten Hälfte des 20. Jahrhunderts: Entstehungskontexte, Kontinuität, Wandel', in Brenner, C. et al. (eds), *Geschichtsschreibung zu den böhmischen Ländern im 20. Jahrhundert: Wissenschaftstraditionen – Institutionen – Diskurse* (Munich, 2006), pp. 209–41

Kollár, J., *Rozpravy o jmenách, počátkách i starožitnostech národu slavského a jeho kmenů* (Budín, 1830)

Kollár, J., *Staroitalia slavjanská* (Vienna, 1853)

Kollár, J., *Über die literarische Wechselseitigkeit zwischen den verschiedenen Stämmen und Mundarten der slawischen Nation* (Pest, 1837)

Kováč, D., *Dějiny Slovenska* (Prague, 1998)

Kováč, D., 'Die Slowakische Historiographie nach 1989: Aktiva, Probleme, Perspektiven', *Bohemia*, 37 (1996), 169–80

Kovács, É., Seewann, G., 'Ungarn: der Kampf um das Gedächtnis', in Flacke, M. (ed.), *Mythen der Nationen, 1945: Arena der Erinnerungen* (Mainz, 2004), vol. 1, pp. 817–46

Kořalka, J., *Tschechen im Habsburgerreich und in Europa, 1815–1914* (Vienna, 1991)

Krekovič, E., Mannová, E., Krekovičová, E. (eds), *Mýty naše slovenské* (Bratislava, 2005)

Lhotsky, A., *Österreichische Historiographie* (Vienna, 1962)

Luks, L., *Entstehung der kommunistischen Faschismustheorie: die Auseinandersetzung der Komintern mit Faschismus und Nationalsozialismus, 1921–35* (Stuttgart, 1984)

Mannová, E. (ed.), *A Concise History of Slovakia* (Bratislava, 2000)

Mattl, S., 'Geschlecht und Volkscharakter: Austria Engendered', *Österreichische Zeitschrift für Geschichtswissenschaft*, 7 (1996), 499–516

Mayer, F. M., *Geschichte Österreichs mit besonderer Rücksicht auf das Kulturleben*, 2 vols, 3rd edn (Vienna, 1909 [1st edn 1874]), I

Mehnert, K., *Weltrevolution durch Weltgeschichte: die Geschichtslehre des Stalinismus* (Stuttgart, 1953)

Mevius, M., *Agents of Moscow: The Hungarian Communist Party and the Origins of Socialist Patriotism, 1941–53* (Oxford, 2005)

Morava, G.J., *Franz Palacký: eine frühe Version von Mitteleuropa* (Vienna, 1990)

Mináč, V., *Dúchanie do pahrieb* (Bratislava, 1970)

Nadler, J., Srbik, H. v. (eds), *Österreich: Erbe und Sendung im deutschen Raum* (Salzburg and Leipzig, 1937)

Neumüller, M. (ed.), *Die böhmischen Länder in der deutschen Geschichtsschreibung seit dem Jahre 1848*, 2 vols (Ústí nad Labem, 1996–7)

Nodl, M., 'Německá medievalistika v českých zemích a studium hospodářských a sociál-ních dějin', in Soukup, P., Šmahel, F. (eds), *Německá medievistika v českých zemích do roku 1945* (Prague, 2004), pp. 21–65

Notter, A., *A Szent-István-Társulat története. A Szent-István-Társulat kiadása* (Budapest, 1904)

Nyyssönen, H., *The Presence of the Past in Politics: '1956' after 1956 in Hungary* (SoPhi, 1999)

Paller, H. v. (ed.), *Die Anschlussfrage in ihrer kulturellen, politischen und wirtschaftlichen Bedeutung* (Vienna and Leipzig, 1930)

Petráň, J., ' Historická skupina', in *Studie z obecných dějin: sborník k sedmdesátým narozeninám Prof. Dr. Jaroslava Charváta* (Prague, 1975)

Petráň, J., Petráňová, L., 'The White Mountain as Symbol in Modern Czech History', in Teich, M. (ed.), *Bohemia in History* (Cambridge, 1998), pp. 143–63

Pieck, W., Dimitrov, G., Togliatti, P., *Die Offensive des Faschismus und die Aufgaben der Kommunisten im Kampf für die Volksfront gegen Krieg und Faschismus* (East Berlin, 1960)

Rak, J., *Bývali Čechové ... České historické mýty a stereotypy* (Jinočany, 1994)

Rak, J., 'Obraz Němce v české historiografii 19. století', in Křen, J. and Broklová, E. (eds), *Obraz Němců, Rakouska a Německá v české společnosti 19. a 20. století* (Prague, 1998), pp. 49–75

Raphael, L., *Geschichtswissenschaft im Zeitalter der Extreme* (Munich, 2003)

Rapant, D., 'Československé dějiny: problémy a metody', *Od praveku k dnešku*, 2 (1930), 531–63

Redlich, O., *Das Werden einer Großmacht: Österreich von 1700 bis 1740* (Brünn, 1938)

Sabrow, M., 'Auf der Suche nach dem materialistischen Meisterton: Bauformen einer nationalen Gegenerzählung in der DDR', in Jarausch, K.H., Sabrow, M. (eds), *Die historische Meistererzählung: Deutungslinien der deutschen Nationalgeschichte nach 1945* (Göttingen, 2002), pp. 33–77

Schmidt-Hartmann, E., 'Forty Years of Historiography under Socialism in Czechoslovakia: Continuity and Change of Patterns of Thought', *Bohemia*, 29 (1988), 300–24

Schneller, J.F., *Staatengeschichte des Kaiserthums Oesterreich von der Geburt Christi bis zum Sturze Napoleon Bonaparte's*, 4 vols (Graz, 1817–19)

Škultéty, J., *Stodvadsať' päť' rokov zo slovenského života, 1790–1914* (Turčiansky Sv. Martin, 1920)

Soukup, P., Šmahel, F. (eds), *Německá medievistika v českých zemích do roku 1945* (Prague, 2004)

Srbik, H. v., *Österreich in der deutschen Geschichte* (Munich, 1936)

Srbik, H. v., *Mitteleuropa: das Problem und die Versuche seiner Lösung in der deutschen Geschichte* (Weimar, 1937)

Srbik, H. v., *Geist und Geschichte vom deutschen Humanismus bis zur Gegenwart*, vol. 2 (Munich and Salzburg, 1951)

Štaif, J., 'Konceptualizace českých dějin v díle Františka Palackého', *Český časopis historický*, 89 (1991), pp. 161–84

Štaif, J., *Historici, dějiny a společnost: historiografie v českých zemích od Palackého a jeho předchůdců po Gollovu školu, 1790–1900* (Prague, 1997), vol. 1

Štaif, J., 'The Image of the Other in the Nineteenth Century: Historical Scholarship in the Bohemian Lands', in Wingfield, N. M. (ed.), *Creating the Other: Ethnic Conflict and Nationalism in the Habsburg Central Europe* (New York, 2003), pp. 81–102

Steward, M., 'Remembering without Commemoration: The Devices and The Politics of Memory among East European Roma', in Kovács, M. M., Lom, P. (eds), *Studies on Nationalism from CEU* (Budapest, 2004), pp. 115–28

Szekfű, G., *Három nemzedék és ami utána következik*, 5th printing (Budapest, 1938)

Szűcs, J., *Nation und Geschichte* (Cologne and Vienna, 1981)

Szűcs, J., *Die drei historischen Regionen Europas* (Frankfurt/M, 1990)

Tomek, E., *Kirchengeschichte Österreichs*, 3 vols (Innsbruck and Wien, 1935, 1949, 1959)

Tóth, Z., 'Liberale Auffassung der Ethnizität in der "Ethnographie von Ungarn" von Pál Hunfalvy', in Kiss, C. et al. (eds), *Nation und Nationalismus in wissenschaftlichen Standardwerken Österreich-Ungarns ca. 1867–1918* (Vienna, 1997), pp. 57–64

Urban, O., *Die tschechische Gesellschaft, 1848–1918*, 2 vols (Vienna, 1994)

Wolfram, H. (ed.), *Österreichische Geschichte* (Wien, 1994–2006)

Zacek, J. F., *Palacký: The Historian as a Scholar and Nationalist* (The Hague, 1970)

Zöllner, E., 'Bemerkungen zu den Gesamtdarstellungen der Geschichte Österreichs. Leistungun – Aufgaben – Probleme', in E. Zöllner, *Probleme und Aufgaben der Österreichischen/Geschichtsforschung, Ausgewählte Aufsätze* (Vienna, 1984)

15   The Russian Empire and its Western Borderlands: National Historiographies and Their 'Others' in Russia, the Baltics and the Ukraine

Armstrong, J. A., *Ukrainian Nationalism*, 3rd edn (Englewood Cliffs, NJ, 1990)

Balodis, F., Tentelis, A. (eds), *Latviešu vēsture* [A History of the Latvians], vol. 1 (Riga, 1938)

Bohachevsky-Chomiak, M., *Feminists despite Themselves: Women in Ukrainian Community Life, 1884–1939* (Edmonton, 1988)

Bohn, T. M., *Russische Geschichtswissenschaft von 1880–1905: Pavel N. Miljukov und die Moskauer Schule* (Köln, Weimar and Wien, 1998)

Bushkovitch, P., 'The Formation of a National Consciousness in Early Modern Russia', *Harvard Ukrainian Studies*, no. 10 (1986), 355–76

Bushkovitch, P., 'The Ukraine in Russian Culture, 1790–1860: The Evidence of the Journals', *Jahrbücher für Geschichte Osteuropas*, 39 (1991), 339–63

Clements, B. E., Engel, B. A., Worobec, C. D. (eds), *Russia's Women: Accommodation, Resistance, Transformation* (Berkeley, CA, 1991)

Conrad, C., Conrad, S. (eds), *Die Nation schreiben: Geschichtswissenschaft im internationalen Vergleich* (Göttingen, 2002)

Davies, N., *God's Playground: A History of Poland*, vol. 2, *1795 to the Present* (New York, 1981)

Deutsch, K. W., *Nationalism and Social Communication: An Inquiry into the Foundations of Nationality*, 2nd edn (Cambridge, MA, 1966)

Doroshenko, D., *Narys Istoriii Ukraiiny* [An Outline of the History of Ukraine], t. 1–2 (Warszawa, 1932; repr. Kyiv, 1991)

Drahomanov, M. P., *Literaturno-publitsyystychni pratsi u dvokh tomakh* [Essays on literature and journalistic works in two volumes], t. 1–2 (Kyiv, 1970)

Drahomanov, M. P., *Vybrane: Mii zadum slozhyty ocherk istoriii tsyvilizaciii na Ukraiini* [Selected Works: My Project of a Survey on the History of Civilisation in Ukraine] (Kyiv, 1991)

Engel, B. A., *Between the Fields and the City: Women, Work and Family in Russia, 1861–1914* (Cambridge, 1994)

Eriksonas, L., *National Heroes and National Identities: Scotland, Norway, and Lithuania* (Brussels and New York, 2004)

Gerasimov, I. V., Glebov, S. V., Kaplunovskii, A. P., Mogilner, M. B. Semenov, A. M. (eds), *Novaia imperskaia istoriia postsovetskogo prostranstva: sbornik statei* [The New Imperial History of the Post-Soviet Space: A Collection of Essays] (Kazan, 2004)

Grushevskii, M., *Ocherk istorii ukrainskago naroda* [Outline of the history of the Ukrainian people] (1904; 2nd edn, repr. Kiev, 1991)

Gumilev, L. N., *Etnosfera: istoriia liudei i istoriia prirody* [Ethnosphere: A History of People and a History of Nature] (Moskva, 1993)

Gumilev, L. N., *Drevniaia Rus i Velikaia step* [Ancient Rus and the Great Steppe] (Moskva, 1993)

Gumilev, L. N., *Ritmy Evrazii* [Eurasia's Rhythms] (Moskva, 1993)

Hackmann, J., 'Ethnos oder Region? Probleme der baltischen Historiographie im 20. Jahrhundert', *Zeitschrift für Ostmitteleuropa-Forschung*, 50 (2001), 531–6

Hackmann, J., *Voluntary Associations and Region Building: A Post-national Perspective on Baltic History*, Center for European Studies, Working Paper Series, 105 (Harvard, MA, 2002)

Hagen, M. von, 'Writing the History of Russia as Empire: The Perspective of Federalism', in Evtuhov, C., Gasparov, B., Ospovat, A., Hagen, M. v. (eds), *Kazan, Moscow, St. Petersburg: Multiple Faces of the Russian Empire* (Moscow, 1997)

Halperin, C. J., 'Russia and the Steppe: George Vernadsky and Eurasianism', in *Forschungen zur Osteuropäischen Geschichte*, 36 (1985), 55–94

Hehn, J. von, 'Lettische Geschichtsschreibung: Zu A. Švabes "Geschichte Lettlands 1800–1914"', *Jahrbücher für Geschichte Osteuropas*, 8 (1960), 365–77

Hellmann, M., *Grundzüge der Geschichte Litauens*, 4th edn (Darmstadt, 1990)

Herzberg, J., Schmidt, C. (eds), *Vom Wir zum Ich: Individuum und Autobiographik im Zarenreich* (Köln, 2007)

Hildermeier, M., *Geschichte der Sowjetunion 1917–1991* (München, 1998)

Hofmann, A., Wendland, A. V. (eds), *Stadt und Öffentlichkeit in Ostmitteleuropa: Beiträge zur Entstehung moderner Urbanität zwischen Berlin, Charkiv, Tallinn und Triest* (Stuttgart, 2002)

Hroch, M., *Social Preconditions of National Revival in Europe: A Comparative Analysis of the Social Composition of Patriotic Groups among the Smaller European Nations* (Cambridge, 1985)

Hrushevskyi, M., *Istoriia Ukraiiny-Rusy* [History of Ukraine-Rus], t. I–XI (Kyïv, 1913–36; repr. Kyïv, 1991–8)

Hrytsak, I., *Narys istoriii Ukraiiny: formuvannia modernoii ukraiinskoii naciii XIX–XX stolit-tja* [Outline of the History of Ukraine: The Formation of the Modern Ukrainian Nation in the 19th and 20th Centuries] (Kyïv, 1996)

Iakovenko, N., *Narys istoriii Ukraiiny* [Outline of the History of Ukraine] (Kyïv, 1997)

Iakovenko, N., 'Ukraiina mizh Skhodom i Zakhodom: proektsiia odniieii ideii' [Ukraine between East and West: Projections of One Idea], in Iakovenko, N., *Paralelnyi svit. Doslidzhennia z istoriii uiavlen ta idej v Ukraiini XVI–XVII st.* (Kyïv, 2002), pp. 333–65

Ivanišević, A., Kappeler, A., Lukan, W., Suppan, A. (eds), *Klio ohne Fesseln? Historiographie im östlichen Europa nach dem Zusammenbruch des Kommunismus* (Wien et al., 2002 [=Österreichische Osthefte, 44 (2002), H. 1–2])

Jaeger, F., Rüsen, J., *Geschichte des Historismus: eine Einführung* (München, 1992)

Kahk, J., *Peasant and Lord in the Process of Transition from Feudalism to Capitalism in the Baltics: An Attempt of Interdisciplinary History* (Tallinn, 1982)

Kappeler, A., *Russland als Vielvölkerreich: Entstehung–Geschichte–Zerfall* (München, 1992)

Kappeler, A., *Kleine Geschichte der Ukraine* (München, 1994)

Kappeler, A., *Der schwierige Weg zur Nation: Beiträge zur neueren Geschichte der Ukraine* (Wien, Köln, Weimar, 2003)

Kliuchevskii, V. O., 'Kurs russkoi istorii' [A Course of Russian History], *Sochineniia v deviati tomach*, t. 1–5 (Moskva, 1987–9)

Kołakowski, L., *Der revolutionäre Geist*, 2nd edn (Stuttgart, 1977)

Kostomarov, N. I., *Russkaia istoriia v zhizneopisaniiakh ee glavnejshikh dejatelej* [Russian History in Biographies of Her Most Important Representatives'] (Sankt-Peterburg, 1873–1913)

Kostomarov, N. I., *Istoricheskie proizvedeniia: avtobiografiia* [Historical Works: Auto-biography] (Kiev, 1989)

Kostomarov, M. I., *Istorija Ukraiiny v zhyttepysakh vyznachnykh iiii diiachiv* [The History of Ukraine in Biographies of Her Most Important Representatives] (L'viv, 1876; 2nd edn, 1913)

Krapauskas, V., *Nationalism and Historiography: The Case of Nineteenth-Century Lithuanian Historicism* (New York, 2000)

Kruus, H., *Grundriss der Geschichte des estnischen Volkes* (Tartu, 1932)

Kuparinen, E. (ed.), *Am Rande der Ostsee: Aufsätze vom IV. Symposium deutscher und finnischer Historiker in Turku, 4.–7. September 1996* (Turku, 1998)

Kuzio, T., 'Historiography and National Identity among the Eastern Slavs: Towards a New Framework', *National Identities*, 3, 2 (2001), pp. 109–32

Lotman, J. A., *Russlands Adel: Eine Kulturgeschichte* (Köln, 1997)

Löwe, H.-D., *Antisemitismus und reaktionäre Utopie: russischer Konservatismus im Kampf gegen den Wandel von Staat und Gesellschaft 1890–1917* (Hamburg, 1978)

Luks, L., 'Die Ideologie der Eurasier im zeitgeschichtlichen Zusammenhang', *Jahrbücher für Geschichte Osteuropas*, 34 (1986), 374–95

Lypynskyi, V., 'Uchast shliakhty u velykomu ukraiinskomu povstanni pid provodom hetmana Bohdana Khmelnytskoho' [The Participation of the Gentry in the Great Ukrainian Rising under Hetman Bohdan Khmelnytskyi], *Tvory*, t. 2 (Philadelphia, 1980)

Lysiak-Rudnytsky, I., *Essays in Modern Ukrainian History* (Edmonton, 1986)

Lypynskyi, V., 'Ukraiina na perelomi 1657–1659' [Ukraine's Upheaval 1657–1659] in *Tvory*, t. 3 (Philadelphia, 1991)

Lysiak-Rudnytskyi, I., 'Mykhajlo Drahomanov' and 'Drahomanov iak politychnyi teoretyk' [Drahomanov as Political Theorist], *Istorychni ese*, t. 1 (Kyïv, 1994)

Lysiak-Rudnytskyi, I., 'Franciszek Duchiński i ioho vplyv na ukraiinsku politychnu dumku' [Franciszek Duchiński and his Influence on Ukrainian Political Thought], in *Istorychni ese*, t. 1 (Kyïv, 1994), pp. 265–80

Lysiak-Rudnytskyi, I., 'Viacheslav Lypynskyi' and 'Politychni ideii Viacheslava Lypynskoho z perspektyvy nashoho chasu' [The Political Ideas of Viacheslav Lypynskyi from Modern Perspective], *Istoryčni ese*, t. 2 (Kyïv, 1994), pp. 125–42; pp. 153–66

Magocsi, P.R., *A History of Ukraine* (Toronto, 1996)

Meinecke, F., *Weltbürgertum und Nationalstaat*, 6th edn (München and Berlin, 1922 [1907])

Mick, C., 'Die Ukrainermacher und ihre Konkurrenten', *Comparativ*, 2 (2005), 60–76

Miller, A., *'Ukrainskii vopros' v politike vlastej i russkom obshchestvennom mnenii (vtoraja polovina XIX v.)* [The 'Ukrainian Question' in the Policy of the Authorities and in Russian Public Opinion (Second Half of the 19th Century)] (Sankt-Peterburg, 2000)

Motyl, A., *The Turn to the Right: The Ideological Origins and the Development of Ukrainian Nationalism, 1919–1929* (Boulder, CO, 1980)

Neumann, D., *Studentinnen aus dem Russischen Reich in der Schweiz 1867–1914* (Zürich, 1987)

Pavlychko, S., *Feminizm* [Feminism] (Kyii, 2002)

Palli, H., 'Estonian Households in the 17th and 18th Centuries', in Wall, R. (ed.), *Family Forms in Historic Europe* (Cambridge, 1983), pp. 207–16

Pistohlkors, G. von, *Vom Geist der Autonomie: Aufsätze zur baltischen Geschichte* (Köln, 1995)

Plakans, A., 'Looking Backward: The Eighteenth and Nineteenth Centuries in Inter-war Latvian Historiography', *Journal of Baltic Studies*, 30, 4 (1999), 293–306

Rauch, G. von (ed.), *Geschichte der deutschbaltischen Geschichtsschreibung* (Köln, 1986)

Raun, T. U., 'The Image of the Baltic German Elites in Twentieth-Century Estonian Historiography: The 1930s vs. the 1970s', *Journal of Baltic Studies*, 30, 4 (1999), 338–51

Šapoka, A., *Lietuvos istorija* [A History of Lithuania] (Kaunas, 1936)
Saunders, D., *The Ukrainian Impact on Russian Culture, 1750–1850* (Edmonton, 1985)
Semyonov, A., *Ab imperio. Studies of New Imperial History and Nationalism in Post Soviet Space*, 2 (2003)
Sinjawskij, A., *Ivan der Dumme: Vom russischen Volksglauben* (Frankfurt/M, 1990)
Subtelny, O., *The Mazepists: Ukrainian Separatism in the 18th Century* (New York, 1981)
Subtelny, O., *Ukraine: A History* (Toronto, 1988)
Subtelnyi, O., *Ukraiina: istoriia* [Ukraine: A History] (Kyiiv, 1991)
Švābe, A., *Latvijas vēsture 1800–1914* [A History of Latvia, 1800–1914] (Uppsala, 1958)
Szűcs, J., *Die drei historischen Regionen Europas* (Frankfurt/M., 1990 [1983])
Tatishchev, V., *Istoriia rossiiskaia* [Russian [Imperial] History], vols 1–7 (1768; reprinted Moskva, 1962–3)
Thaden, E. C. (ed.), *Russification in the Baltic Provinces and Finland 1855–1919* (Princeton, NJ, 1981)
Theweleit, K., *Männerphantasien*, Bd. 1, *Frauen, Fluten, Körper, Geschichte*, 3rd edn (München and Zürich, 2000)
Trotzkij, L., *Geschichte der russischen Revolution*, 3rd edn (Frankfurt/M, 1983)
Velychenko, S., *National History as Cultural Process: A Survey of the Interpretations of Ukraine's Past in Polish, Russian, and Ukrainian Historical Writing from the Earliest Times to 1914* (Edmonton, 1992)
Vernadsky, G., *A History of Russia* (New Haven, CT, 1929)
Vulpius, R., *Nationalisierung der Religion: Russifizierungspolitik und ukrainische Nationsbildung 1860–1920* (Wiesbaden, 2005)
Wendland, A. V., *Die Russophilen in Galizien: Ukrainische Konservative zwischen Österreich und Russland, 1848–1915* (Wien, 2002)
Wendland, A. V., 'Volksgeschichte im Baltikum? Historiographien zwischen nationaler Mobilisierung und wissenschaftlicher Innovation in Estland, Lettland und Litauen (1919–1939)', in Hettling, M. (ed.), *Volksgeschichten im Europa der Zwischenkriegszeit* (Göttingen, 2003), pp. 205–38
Wendland, A. V., 'Region ohne Nationalität, Kapitale ohne Volk: Das Wilna-Gebiet als Gegenstand polnischer und litauischer nationaler Integrationsprojekte (1900–1940)', *Comparativ*, 2 (2005), 77–100

16 Mirrors for the Nation: Imagining the National Past among the Poles and Czechs in the Nineteenth and Twentieth Centuries

Capaldi, N., Livingston, D. (eds), *Liberty in Hume's History of England* (Dordrecht, 1990)
Cesarz, E., *Chłopi w polskiej myśli historycznej doby porozbiorowej 1795–1864* (Rzeszów, 1999)
Czapliński, W., *Zarys dziejów Polski do roku 1864* (Cracow, 1985)
Goll, J., *Posledních padesát let české práce dějepisné* (Prague, 1926)
Górka, O., *'Ogniem i Mieczem' a rzeczywistość historyczna*, 2nd edn (Warsaw, 1986; 1st edn, 1934)
Górny, M., *Między Marksem a Palackým: historiografia w komunistycznej Czechosłowacji* (Warsaw, 2001)
Gross, J. T., *Neighbors: The Destruction of the Jewish Community in Jedwabne* (Princeton, NJ, 2001)
Haubelt, J., 'O výkladu dějin českého a slovenského dějepisectví Františka Kutnara', *Československý Časopis Historický*, 27, 6 (1979), 907–15
Havelka, M. (ed.), *Spor o smysl českých dějin 1895–1938* (Prague, 1995)

Hoszowska, M., *Siła tradycji, presja życia: kobiety w dawnych podręcznikach dziejów Polski (1795–1918)* (Rzeszów, 2005)

Janion, M., *Niesamowita słowiańszczyzna: fantazmaty literatury* (Cracow, 2006)

Janion, M., 'Opowiadać o ludzkim cierpieniu: z Marią Janion rozmawia Andrzej Franaszek', *Tygodnik Powszechny*, no. 5, 11 February 2007

Janowski, M., 'Three Historians', *CEU History Department Yearbook* (2001–2), 199–232

Kizwalter, T., *O nowoczesności narodu: przypadek polski* (Warsaw, 1999)

Konopczyński, W., *Dzieje Polski nowożytnej*, vols 1 and 2 (Warsaw, 1936)

Kořalka, J., 'Pět tendencí moderního národního vývoje v Čechách', in idem, *Češi v Habsburské Říši a v Evropě* (Prague, 1996)

Kořalka, J., *František Palacký (1798–1876): životopis* (Prague, 1998)

Kostrzewa, R. (ed.), *Between East and West: Writings from Kultura* (New York, 1990)

Kraft, C., Steffen, K. (eds), *Europas Platz in Polen: Polnische Europa-Konzeptionen vom Mittelalter bis zum EU-Beitritt* (Osnabrück, 2007)

Kula, W., *An Economic Theory of the Feudal System: Towards a Model of the Polish Economy, 1500–1800* (London, 1976)

Kutnar, F., *Přehledné dějiny českého a slovenského dějepisectví*, 2 vols (Prague, 1973, 1977)

Lelewel, J., *Dzieła*, vol. 7 (Warsaw, 1961 [1829])

Lelewel, J., *Dzieła*, vol. 2, *Pisma metodologiczne* (Warsaw, 1964)

Litwin, H., *Narody Pierwszej Rzeczypospolitej*, in Sucheni-Grabowska, A., Dybkowska, A. (eds), *Tradycje polityczne dawnej Polski* (Warsaw, no date), pp. 168–218

Maclean, I., Montefiore, A., Winch, P. (eds), *The Political Responsibility of Intellectuals* (Cambridge, 1990)

Macura, V., *Znamení zrodu: české obrození jako kulturní typ* (Praha, 1983)

Malíř, J., Vlček, R. (eds), *Morava a české národní vědomí od středověku po dnešek* (Brno, 2001)

Małowist, M., *Wschód a zachód Europy w XIII–XVI wieku*, 2nd edn (Warsaw, 2006)

Naruszewicz, A., *Memoriał względem pisania historii narodowej* (1775), in Serejski, M.H. (ed.), *Historycy o historii*, vol. 1 (Warsaw, 1963), pp. 34–5

Palacký, F., *Dějiny národu českého v Čechách a v Moravě* (Prague, 1998 [facsimile of edition published Prague, 1907])

Polonsky, A. (ed.), *My Brother's Keeper? Recent Polish Debates on the Holocaust* (London, 1990)

Rádl, E., *Válka Čechů s Němci* (Prague, 1993; 1st edn, 1928)

Romek, Z., *Olgierd Górka: historyk w służbie myśli propaństwowej 1908–1955* (Warsaw, 1997)

Serejski, M. H., *Naród a państwo w polskiej myśli historycznej* (Warsaw, 1975)

Sulima Kamiński, A., *Historia Rzeczypospolitej wielu narodów, 1505–1795* (Lublin, 2000)

Tazbir, J., 'Cienie zapomnianych przodków', *Tygodnik Powszechny*, no. 3, 21 January 2007

Tigrid, P., *Kapesní průvodce inteligentní ženy po vlastním osudu* (Prague, 1990)

Tomek, V. V., 'O sinchronické methodě při dějepise rakouském', *Časopis Českeho Musea* (1854)

Vlnas, V., *Jan Nepomucký česká legenda* (Prague, 1993)

Walicki, A., *Poland between East and West: The Controversies over Self-Definition and Modernization in Partitioned Poland* (Cambridge, MA, 1994)

Wandycz, P. S., *The Lands of Partitioned Poland, 1795–1918* (Seattle and London, 1974)

Wierzbicki, A., *Wschód-Zachód w koncepcjach dziejów Polski: z dziejów polskiej myśli historycznej w dobie porozbiorowej* (Warsaw, 1984)

Wierzbicki, A., *Historiografia polska doby romantyzmu* (Wrocław, 1999)

17 National Historiographies in the Balkans, 1830–1989

Alter, P., *Nationalism* (London, 1994)

Anderson, B., *Imagined Communities: Reflections on the Origin and Spread of Nationalism*, rev. edn (London, 2006)

Antohi, S., 'Romania and the Balkans: From Geocultural Bovarism to Ethnic Ontology', *Tr@nsit Online*, 21 (2002) (accessed 15 October 2007)

Armbruster, A., *Românitatea românilor: istoria unei idei* (București, 1972)

Ahiska, M., 'Occidentalism: The Historical Phantasy of the Modern', *South Atlantic Quarterly*, 102, 2–3 (2003), 364

Bakić-Hayden, M., Hayden, R. M., 'Orientalist Variations on the Theme "Balkans": Symbolic Geography in Recent Yugoslav Cultural Politics', *Slavic Review*, 51, 1 (1992), 1–15

Bălcescu, N., The Course of Revolution in the History of the Romanians', in Ersoy, A., Górny, M., Kechriotis, V., *Discourses of Collective Identity in Central and Southeast Europe (1770–1945): Texts and Commentaries*, vol. 3 (Budapest, in press)

Banac, I., *The National Question in Yugoslavia: Origins, History, Politics* (Ithaca, NY, 1984)

Banac, I., 'Yugoslavia', *American Historical Review*, 97, 4 (1992), 1085

Barth, F. (ed.), *Ethnic Groups and Boundaries: The Social Organization of Culture Difference* (Oslo and London, 1969)

Baycroft, T., Hewitson, M. (eds), *What Is a Nation? Europe 1789–1914* (Oxford, 2006)

Benson, T. O. (ed.), *Central European Avant-Gardes: Exchange and Transformation, 1910–1930* (Cambridge, MA, 2002)

Berger, S., Donovan, M., Passmore, K. (eds), *Writing National Histories: Western Europe since 1800* (London, 1999)

Biondich, M., '"We Were Defending the State": Nationalism, Myth, and Memory in Twentieth-Century Croatia', in Lampe, J. R., Mazower, M. (eds), *Ideologies and National Identities: The Case of Twentieth-Century Southeastern Europe* (Budapest, 2004), pp. 54–81

Biondich, M., 'Controversies Surrounding the Catholic Church in Wartime Croatia, 1941–45', *Totalitarian Movements and Political Religions*, 7, 4 (2006), 429–57

Bjelić, D. I., Savić, O. (eds), *Balkan as Metaphor, between Globalization and Fragmentation* (Cambridge, MA, 2002)

Black, J. L., *Nicholas Karamzin and Russian Society in the Nineteenth Century: A Study in Russian Political and Historical Thought* (Toronto, 1975)

Boia, L. (ed.), *Miturile comunismului românesc* (București, 1998)

Todorova, M., 'Bulgaria', *American Historical Review*, 97, 4 (1992), 1117

Boia, L., *History and Myth in Romanian Consciousness* (Budapest, 2001)

Brătianu, I. I. *1821–1891: A Biographical Sketch* (București, 1893)

Brătianu, Gh. I., *La Mer Noire: des origines à la conquête ottomane* (Monachi, 1969)

Bucur, M., 'Between the Mother of the Wounded and the Virgin of Jiu: Romanian Women and the Gender of Heroism during the Great War', *Journal of Women's History*, 12, 2 (2000), 31

Bucur, M., Miroiu, M. (eds), *Patriarhat și emancipare în istoria gândirii politice românești* (Iași, 2002)

Chirot, D. (ed.), *The Origins of Backwardness in Eastern Europe: Economics and Politics from the Middle Ages until the Early Twentieth Century* (Berkeley, CA, 1991)

Ciobanu, V. *Poporanismul: geneză, evoluție, ideologie* (București, 1946)

Ciupală, A. (ed.), *Despre femei și istoria lor în Romania* (București, 2004)

Crampton, R. J., *A History of Bulgaria, 1878–1918* (New York, 1983)

Cuvalo, A., *The Croatian National Movement, 1966–1972* (Boulder, CO, 1990)

Daskalov, R., 'Ideas about, and Reactions to Modernization in the Balkans', *East European Quarterly*, 31, 2 (1997), 141–80

Daskalov, R., *The Making of a Nation in the Balkans: Historiography of the Bulgarian Revival* (Budapest, 2004)

Deletant, D., Hanak, H. (eds), *Historians as Nation-Builders: Central and South-East Europe* (London, 1988)

Dénes, I. Z. (ed.), *Liberty and the Search for Identity: Liberal Nationalisms and the Legacy of Empires* (Budapest, 2006)

Despalatović, E. M., *Ljudevit Gaj and the Illyrian Movement* (New York, 1975)

Dimitrov, S., *La Vie et l'œuvre de Hristo Botev* (Grenoble, 1941)

Duțu, A., *Romanian Humanists and European Culture: A Contribution to Comparative Cultural History* (Bucharest, 1977)

Edmunds, J., 'Redefining Britannia: The Role of "Marginal" Generations in Reshaping British National Consciousness', in Brocklehurst, H., Philips, R. (eds), *History, Nationhood and the Question of Britannia* (Basingstoke, 2004), pp. 73–84

Eidelberg, P. G., *The Great Rumanian Peasant Revolt of 1907: Origins of a Modern Jacquerie* (Leiden, 1974)

Falina, M., 'Between "Clerical Fascism" and Political Orthodoxy: Orthodox Christianity and Nationalism in Interwar Serbia', *Totalitarian Movements and Political Religions*, 8, 2 (2007), 247–58

Fătu, M., Spălățelu, I., *Garda de Fier: Organizație teroristă de tip fascist* (București, 1971)

Feldman, M., Turda, M. (eds), *'Clerical Fascism' in Interwar Europe*, special issue of *Totalitarian Movements and Political Religions*, 8, 2 (2007)

Fischer-Galati, S. et al. (eds), *Romania between East and West* (Boulder, CO, 1982)

Fleming, K. E., 'Orientalism, the Balkans, and Balkan Historiography', *American Historical Review*, 105, 4 (2000), 1218–33

Genchev, N., *The Bulgarian National Revival Period* (Sofia, 1977)

Glenny, M., *The Balkans, 1804–1999: Nationalism, War and the Great Powers* (New York, 1999)

Goldsworthy, V., *Inventing Ruritania: The Imperialism of the Imagination* (New Haven, CT, 1998)

Graubard, S. R. (ed.), *Eastern Europe ... Central Europe ... Europe* (Boulder, CO, 1991)

Haan, F. de, Daskalova, K., Loufti, A. (eds), *A Biographical Dictionary of Women's Movements and Feminisms: Central, Eastern, and South Eastern Europe, 19th and 20th Centuries* (Budapest, 2006)

Hașdeu, B. B., *Istoria critică a românilor* (București, 1984)

Hiemstra, P. A., *Alexandru D. Xenopol and the Development of Romanian Historiography* (New York, 1987)

Hitchins, K., 'Rumania', *American Historical Review*, 97, 4 (1992), 1064–83

Hitchins, K., *Rumania, 1866–1947* (Oxford, 1994)

Hitchins, K., *Mit și realitate în istoriografia românească* (București, 1997)

Hranova, A., 'Historical Myths: The Bulgarian Case of Pride and Prejudice', in Kolstø, P., *Myths and Boundaries in South-Eastern Europe* (London, 2005), pp. 297–323

Iggers, G., *The German Conception of History: The National Tradition of Historical Thought from Herder to the Present*, rev. edn (Middleton, CT, 1969)

Ioanid, R., *The Sword of the Archangel: Fascist Ideology in Romania* (Boulder, CO, 1990)

Ionescu, G., Gellner, E. (eds), *Populism: Its Meaning and National Characteristics* (London, 1969)

Iorga, N., *Desvoltarea ideii unității politice a Românilor* (București, 1915)

Iorga, N., *Histoire des Roumains des Balcans* (Bucarest, 1919)

Iorga, N., *Byzance après Byzance* (Bucarest, 1935)

Jelavich, C., Jelavich, B., *The Establishment of the Balkan National States, 1804–1920* (Seattle and London, 1977)

Jelavich, B., 'Mihail Kogălniceanu: Historian as Foreign Minister, 1876–8', in Deletant, D., Hanak, H. (eds), *Historians as Nation-Builders: Central and South-East Europe* (London: Macmillan, 1988), pp. 87–105

Jelavich, C., *South Slav Nationalisms: Textbooks and Yugoslav Union before 1914* (Columbus, OH, 1990)

Jowitt, K., *Revolutionary Breakthroughs and National Development: The Case of Romania, 1944–1965* (Berkeley, CA, 1971)

Jowith, K. (ed.), *Social Change in Romania: A Debate on Development in a European Nation* (Berkeley, CA, 1978)

Kellogg, F., *A History of Romanian Historical Writing* (Bakersfield, CA, 1990)

Kimball, S. B., *The Austro-Slav Revival: A Study of Nineteenth Century Literary Foundations* (Philadelphia, 1973)

Kitch, M., 'Constantin Stere and Romanian Populism', *Slavonic and East European Review*, 53, 131 (1975), 248–71

Livezeanu, I., *Cultural Politics in Greater Romania: Regionalism, Nation Building and Ethnic Struggle, 1918–1930* (Ithaca, NY, 1995)

Lorenz, C., 'Towards a Theoretical Framework for Comparing Historiographies: Some Preliminary Considerations', in Seixas, P. (ed.), *Theorizing Historical Consciousness* (Toronto, 2004), pp. 25–48

Mach, R. von, *The Bulgarian Exarchate: Its History and the Extent of Its Authority in Turkey* (London, 1907)

MacKenzie, D., *Ilija Garašanin: Balkan Bismarck* (Boulder, CO, 1985)

Markovich, S. G. et al. (eds), *Problems of Identity in the Balkans* (Belgrade, 2006)

Mazower, M., *The Balkans: From the End of Byzantium to the Present Day* (London, 2000)

McClellan, W. D., *Svetozar Markovic and the Origin of Balkan Socialism* (Princeton, NJ, 1964)

Michael, H., *Ours Once More: Folklore, Ideology and the Making of Modern Greece* (Austin, TX, 1982)

Mihăilescu, Ş., *Din istoria feminismului românesc: antologie de texte (1838–1929)* (Iaşi, 2002)

Miller, T., 'Incomplete Modernities: Historicizing Yugoslav Avant-Gardes', *Modernism/Modernity*, 12, 4 (2005), 713–22

Mishkova, D., 'The Uses of Tradition and National Identity in the Balkans', in Todorova, *Balkan Identities*, pp. 269–93

Miskolczy, A., 'Nicolae Iorga's Conception of Transylvanian Romanian History in 1915', in Péter, L. (ed.), *Historians and the History of Transylvania* (Boulder, CO, 1992), pp. 129–65

Mosse, G., *The Image of Man: The Creation of Modern Masculinity* (New York, 1996)

Mügge, M. A., *Serbian Folk Songs: Fairy Tales and Proverbs* (London, 1916)

Murgescu, M-L., *Între 'bunul creştin' şi 'bravul român': rolul şcolii primare în construirea identitaţii naţionale româneşti (1831–1878)* (Bucureşti, 2004)

Nagy-Talavera, N. M., *Nicolae Iorga: A Biography* (Iaşi, 1998)

Norton, C. (ed.), *Nationalism, Historiography and the (Re)Construction of the Past* (Washington, 2007)

Oldson, W., *The Historical and Nationalistic Thought of Nicolae Iorga* (Boulder, CO, 1973)

Ornea, Z., *Poporanismul* (Bucureşti, 1972)

Panu, G., 'Studiul istoriei la români', in Lovinescu, E. (ed.), *Antologia ideologiei junimiste* (Bucureşti, 1943), pp. 283–398

Pârâianu, R., 'The History Textbooks Controversy in Romania: Five Years On', in *Magyar Lettre International*, 58 (2005); http://www.eurozine.com/articles/2005-11-11-paraianu-en.html (accessed 10 January 2007)

Pascu, Ş., *Formarea naţiunii române* (Bucureşti, 1967)

Pavlowitch, S. K., *A History of the Balkans, 1804–1945* (London, 1999)

Péter, L. (ed.), *Historians and the History of Transylvania* (Boulder, CO, 1992)

Pinto, V., 'The Civic and Aesthetic Ideals of the Bulgarian *Narodnik* Writers', *Slavonic and East European Review*, 32, 74 (1954), 344–66

Pippidi, A., 'Changes of Emphasis: Greek Christendom, Westernization, South-Eastern Europe, and Neo-Mitteleuropa', *Balkanologie*, 3, 2 (1999), 93–106

Popov, S., *Anton Strashimirov* (Sofia, 1987)

Pundeff, M., 'Bulgarian Historiography, 1942–1958', *American Historical Review*, 66, 3 (1961), 682–93

Ramet, S. (ed.), *The Independent State of Croatia (NDH), 1941–45*, special issue of *Totalitarian Movements and Political Religions*, 7, 4 (2006)

Rihtman-Auguštin, D., Capo Žmegač, J., *Ethnology, Myth and Politics: Anthropologizing Croatian Ethnology* (Aldershot, 2004)

Riis, C., *Religion, Politics, and Historiography in Bulgaria* (Boulder, CO, 2002)

Roller, M. (ed.), *Istoria R.P.R.: manual pentru învăţămîntul mediu* (Bucureşti, 1952)

Rothschild, J., *East Central Europe between the Two World Wars* (Seattle, 1974)

Roudometof, V., 'The Social Origins of Balkan Politics: Nationalism, Underdevelopment, and the Nation-State in Greece, Serbia and Bulgaria, 1880–1920', *Mediterranean Quarterly*, 11, 3 (2000), 144–63

Schafir, M., '"Romania's Marx" and the National Question: Constantin Dobrogeanu-Gherea', *History of Political Thought*, 5, 2 (1984), 295–314

Schmidt, J., *Populismus oder Marxismus: zur Ideengeschichte der radikalen Intelligenz Rumäniens, 1875–1915* (Tübingen, 1992)

Sorin, M., *National Identity of Romanians in Transylvania* (Budapest, 2001)

Todorova, M., 'Self-Image and Ethnic Stereotypes in Bulgaria', *Modern Greek Studies Yearbook*, 8 (1992), 139–63

Todorova, M., *Imagining the Balkans* (Oxford, 1997)

Todorova, M. (ed.), *Balkan Identities: Nation and Memory* (London, 2003)

Todorova, M., 'The Trap of Backwardness: Modernity, Temporality, and the Study of Eastern European Nationalism', *Slavic Review*, 61, 1 (2005), 140–64

Trencsényi, B., Kopeček, M. (eds), *Discourses of Collective Identity and Central and Southeast Europe (1770–1945): Texts and Commentaries*, vol. 1 (Budapest, 2006)

Turda, M., 'Nation States and Irredentism in the Balkans, 1890–1920', in Eriksonas, L., Müller, L. (eds), *Statehood beyond Ethnicity: Trans-national Perspectives onto Smaller States in Europe, c. 1600–2000* (Brussels, 2005), pp. 275–301

Turda, M., Weindling, P. (eds), *'Blood and Homeland': Eugenics and Racial Nationalism in Central and Southeast Europe, 1900–1940* (Budapest, 2007)

Turda, M., Mishkova, D. (eds), *Discourses of Collective Identity in Central and Southeast Europe (1770–1945)*, vol. 4 (Budapest, in press)

Turda, M., 'The Nation as Object: Race, Blood and Biopolitics in Interwar Romania', *Slavic Review*, 66, 3 (Fall 2007), 413–41

Valota, B., 'Giuseppe Mazzini's "Geopolitics of Liberty" and Italian Foreign Policy toward "Slavic Europe"', *East European Quarterly*, 37, 2 (2003), 151–6

Vârcolici, T., *Alecu Russo* (Bucureşti, 1964)

Verdery, K., *National Ideology under Socialism: Identity and Cultural Politics in Ceauşescu's Romania* (Berkeley, CA, 1991)

Viroli, M., *For Love of Country: An Essay on Patriotism and Nationalism* (Oxford, 1995)
Vucinich, W. S., 'Postwar Yugoslav Historiography', *Journal of Modern History*, 23, 1 (1951), 41–57
Wachtel, A. B., *Making a Nation, Breaking a Nation: Literature and Cultural Politics in Yugoslavia* (Stanford, CA, 1998)
Werner, B., *Nicolae Bălcescu (1819–1852): ein rumänischer revolutionärer Demokrat im Kampf für soziale und nationale Befreiung* (Berlin, 1970)
Wingfield, N. M., Bucur, M. (eds), *Gender and War in Twentieth-Century Eastern Europe* (Bloomington, IN, 2006)
White, H., *Metahistory: The Historical Imagination in Nineteenth-Century Europe* (Baltimore, MD and London, 1974)
Wolff, L., *Inventing Eastern Europe: The Map of Civilization on the Mind of the Enlightenment* (Stanford, CA, 1996)
Yuval-Davis, N., Anthias, F. (eds), *Woman–Nation–State* (New York, 1989)
Zub, A., *Mihail Kogălniceanu istoric* (Iaşi, 1974)
Zub, A., *Istorie şi istorici în România interbelică* (Iaşi, 1989)

18   History Writing among the Greeks and Turks: Imagining the Self and the Other

Akçura, Y., *Türkçülüğün Tarihi* [The History of Turkishness] (Istanbul, 1998)
Anderson, B., *Imagined Communities* (London and New York, 1990)
Babinger, F., *Geschichtsschreiber der Osmanen und Ihre Werke* (Leipzig, 1927)
Cevdet Pasha, A., *Tarih-i Cevdet [History of Cevdet]*, 12 vols (Istanbul, 1853–91)
Daskalakis, A. B., *To Politeuma tou Riga Belestinli* [The Polity of Rigas Velestinlis] (Athens, 1976)
Delatant, D., Hanak, H. (eds), *Historians as Nation Builders* (London, 1988).
Divitçioğlu, S., *Asya Üretim Tarzı ve Osmanlı Toplumu* [Asian Mode of Production and Ottoman Society] (Istanbul, 2003; 1st edn, 1967)
Fallmerayer, J. P., *Geschichte der Halbinsel Morea wahrend des Mittelalters*, vol. 1 (Stuttgart, 1830)
Gökalp, Z., *Turkish Nationalism and Western Civilization: Selected Essays of Z. Gökalp* (London, 1959)
Inan, A., *Türkiye Halkının Antropolojik Karakterleri ve Türkiye Tarihi: Türk Irkının Vatanı Anadolu* [The Anthropological Characteristics of the Turkish People and the History of Turkey: Anatolia, the Fatherland of the Turkish Race] (Ankara, 1947)
Jacob Landau, M., *Pan-Turkism in Turkey: A Study of Irredentism* (London, 1981)
Kafesoğlu, İ., *Türk İslam Sentezi* [Turkish-Islamic Synthesis] (Istanbul, 1999)
Karolidis, P., *Sygkhronos Istoria ton Ellinon kai Lipon Laon tis Anatolis apo to 1821 mehri to 1921* [Modern History of Greeks and Other Nations of Anatolia from 1821 to 1921], vols 1–7 (Athens, 1922–6)
Keyder, Ç., *State and Class in Turkey: A Study in Capitalist Development* (London, 1987)
Kordatos, Y., *Istoria tis Neoteris Elladas*, vols 1–4 (Athens, 1957–8)
Küçükömer, İ., *Düzenin Yabancılaşması* [The Alienation of the Social Order] (Istanbul, 1989; 1st edn, 1969)
Metallinos, G., *Tourkokratia* [Turkish Rule] (Athens, 1988)
Millas, H., 'Milli Türk Kimliği ve Öteki (Yunan)' ('The National Turkish Identity and the Other/the Greek'), in *Modern Türkiye'de Siyasi Düşünce*, vol. 4, *Milliyetçilik* (İstanbul, 2002)
Özal, T., *La Turquie en Europe* (Paris, 1988)

Pamuk, Ş., *Osmanlı-Türk İktisadi Tarihi, 1500–1914* [Economic History of Ottoman State-Turkey, 1500–1914] (Gerçek, 1988)

Paparrigopoulos, K., *Istoria tou Ellinikou Ethnous* [The History of the Hellenic Nation], vols 1–5 (Athens, 1865–74)

Sonyel, S., *Minorities and the Destruction of the Ottoman Empire* (Ankara, 1993).

Svoronos, N., *Histoire de la Grèce moderne* (Paris, 1972)

Toprak, Z., *Türkiye'de Milli İktisat* [National Economy in Turkey] (Istanbul, 1982)

Trikoupis, S. (1788–1873), *I Istoria tis Ellinikis Epanastaseos* [The History of the Greek Revolution], vols 1–4 (London, 1853–1957)

Valoudis, G., 'J. Ph. Fallmerayer und die Entstehung des neugriechischen Historismus', *Südostforschungen*, 29 (1970)

Zambelios, S., *Asmata dimotika tis Ellados* [Folk Songs of Greece] (Athens, 1852)

19   Narratives of Jewish Historiography in Europe

Abrahams, B. L., 'The Condition of the Jews of England at the Time of Their Expulsion in 1290', *Transactions*, 2 (1894–5, 1896), pp. 77–8

Arendt, H., *Rahel Varnhagen: The Life of a Jewess* (London, 1957)

Baron, S. W., 'Graetzens Geschichtsschreibung: eine methodologische Untersuchung', *Monatsschrift für Geschichte und Wissenschaft des Judentums*, 62 (1918), 5–15

Baron, S. W., 'Ghetto and Emancipation: Shall We Revise the Traditional View?', *Menorah Journal*, 14 (1928), 515–26

Baron, S. W., *History and Jewish Historians* (Philadelphia, 1946)

Baron, S. W., *A Social and Religious History of the Jews*, 18 vols, 2nd edn (New York, 1952–83)

Blänkner, R., Göhler, G., Waszek, N. (eds), *Eduard Gans (1797–1839): politischer Professor zwischen Restauration und Vormärz* (Leipzig, 2001)

Brann, M. (ed.), *Heinrich Graetz: Abhandlungen zu seinem 100. Geburtstag* (Vienna and Berlin, 1917)

Brenner, M., Myers, D. N. (eds), *Jüdische Geschichtsschreibung heute: Themen, Positionen, Kontroversen* (Munich, 2002)

Brenner, M., Kauders, A., Reuveni, G., Römer, N. (eds), *Jüdische Geschichte lesen: Texte der jüdischen Geschichtsschreibung im 19. und 20. Jahrhundert* (Munich, 2003)

Brenner, M., *Propheten des Vergangenen: Jüdische Geschichtsschreibung im 19. und 20. Jahrhundert* (München, 2006)

Brenner, M., Reuveni, G. (eds), *Emancipation through Muscles: Jews in European Sport* (Lincoln, NB, 2006)

Brisch, C., *Geschichte der Juden in Cöln und Umgebung aus ältester Zeit bis auf die Gegenwart: nach handschriftlichen und gedruckten Quellen bearbeitet*, 2 vols (Mühlheim an der Rhein, 1879/82)

Caro, J., *Geschichte der Juden in Lemberg von den ältesten Zeiten bis zur Theilung Polens im Jahre 1792 aus Chroniken und archivalischen Quellen* (Cracow, 1894)

Dubnow, S., *Die Jüdische Geschichte. Ein geschichtsphilosophischer Versuch* (1893: Berlin, 1898)

Dubnow, S., *Weltgeschichte des jüdischen Volkes: von seinen Uranfängen bis zur Gegenwart*, 10 vols (Berlin, 1925–9)

Dubnow, S., *Mein Leben*, translated from the Russian (Berlin, 1937)

Dubnow, S., *Buch des Lebens: Erinnerungen und Gedanken. Materialien zur Geschichte meiner Zeit*, 3 vols. ed. V. Dohrn, trans. Vera Bischitzky and Barbara Conrad (Göttingen, 2005)

Elbogen, I., Sterling, E., *Die Geschichte der Juden in Deutschland* (Hamburg, 1993)

Feiner, S., *Haskalah and History: The Emergence of a Modern Jewish Historical Consciousness* (Oxford, 2002)

Geiger, L., *Geschichte der Juden in Berlin: Festschrift zur zweiten Säkular-Feier* (Berlin, 1871)

Glaser, A., *Geschichte der Juden in Straßburg von der Zeit Karls des Großen bis auf die Gegenwart* (Strasbourg, 1894)

Glatzer, N.N. (ed.), *Leopold Zunz: Jude – Deutscher – Europäer. Ein jüdisches Gelehrten-schicksal des 19. Jahrhunderts in Briefen an Freunde* (Tübingen, 1964)

Graetz, H., *Die Konstruktion der jüdischen Geschichte: eine Skizze* (1846; Berlin, 1936 [with footnotes and a postface by Ludwig Feuchtwanger])

Graetz, H., *Geschichte der Juden von den ältesten Zeiten bis auf die Gegenwart*, 11 vols (Berlin, Leipzig and Magdeburg, 1853–76), vol. 1, final rev. edn (Leipzig, 1908; [reprint Berlin, 1998])

Graetz, H., *Volkstümlich Geschichte der Juden von den ältesten Zeiten bis zur Gegenwart*, 3 vols (Leipzig, 1888)

Graetz, H., *Tagebuch und Briefe*, ed. Reuwen Michael (Tübingen, 1977)

Graetz, M. (ed.), *Schöpferische Momente des europäischen Judentums in der frühen Neuzeit* (Heidelberg, 2000)

Grözinger, E., *Glückel von Hameln: Kauffrau, Mutter und erste jüdisch-deutsche Autorin* (Teetz, 2004)

Haber, P., Petry, E., Wildmann, D., *Jüdische Identität und Nation: Fallbeispiele aus Mitteleuropa* (Cologne, 2006)

Herzig, A. (ed.), *Schlesische Lebensbilder*, vol. 8 (Neustadt an der Aisch, 2004)

Hoffmann, C. (ed.), *Preserving the Legacy of German Jewry: A History of the Leo Baeck Institute 1955–2005* (Tübingen, 2005)

Jaeger, F., Rüsen, J. *Geschichte des Historismus: eine Einführung* (Munich, 1992)

Jolowicz, H., *Geschichte der Juden in Königsberg in Preussen: ein Beitrag zur Sittengeschichte der preussischen Staaten* (Posen, 1867)

Jost, I.M., *Geschichte der Israeliten seit der Zeit der Maccabäer bis auf unsre Tage, nach den Quellen bearbeitet von I. M. Jost, Lehrer und Erzieher in Berlin*, 9 vols (Berlin, 1820–28), vol. 1

Kaplan, M., *The Making of the Jewish Middle Class. Women, Family, and Identity in Imperial Germany* (New York and Oxford, 1991)

Katz, J. *Messianismus und Zionismus: zur jüdischen Sozialgeschichte* (Frankfurt/M, 1993)

Kayserling, M., *Die jüdischen Frauen in der Geschichte, Literatur und Kunst* (Leipzig, 1879)

Lagumina, B., Lagumina, G. (eds), *Codice diplomatico dei giudei di Sicilia*, 3 vols (Palermo, 1884–95)

Liberles, R., *Salo Wittmayer Baron: Architect of Jewish History* (New York, 1995)

Mahler, R., *A History of Modern Jewry (1780–1815)* (London, 1971)

Malvezin, T., *Histoire des juifs à Bordeaux* (Bordeaux, 1875)

Meisl, J., *Heinrich Graetz: eine Würdigung des Historikers und Juden zu seinem 100. Geburtstag* (Berlin, 1917)

Meyer, M. A., 'The Emergence of Jewish Historiography: Motives and Motifs', *History and Theory*, 27 (1988), 160–75

Miron, G., 'History, Remembrance, and a "Useful Past" in the Public Thought of Hungarian Jewry (1938–1939)', *Yad Vashem Studies*, 32 (2004), 131–70

Myers, D. N., 'Was there a Jerusalem School? An Inquiry into the First Generation of Historical Researchers at the Hebrew University', *Studies in Contemporary Jewry*, 10 (1994), 66–92

Myers, D. N., *Re-inventing the Jewish Past: European Jewish Intellectuals and the Zionist Return to History* (New York, 1995)

Myers, D. N., Ruderman, D. B. (eds), *The Jewish Past Revisited: Reflections on Modern Jewish Historians* (New Haven, CT and London, 1998)

Nattermann, R., *Deutsch-jüdische Geschichtsschreibung nach der Shoah: die Gründungs- und Frühgeschichte des Leo Baeck Institute* (Essen, 2004)

Nusbaum, H., *Szkice historyczne z zycia Zydow w Warszawie* (Warsaw, 1881)

Perles, J., *Geschichte der Juden in Posen* (Breslau, 1865)

Philippson, M., *Neueste Geschichte des jüdischen Volkes*, 3 vols (Berlin, 1907–11)

Reuwen, M., 'I. M. Jost und sein Werk', *Boulettin des Leo Baeck Instituts*, 3 (1960), 239–58

Richarz, M. (ed.), *Die Hamburger Kauffrau Glikl: jüdische Existenz in der Frühen Neuzeit* (Hamburg, 2001)

Roth, C., *History of Jews in Venice* (Philadelphia, 1930)

Roth, C., *The Jewish Contribution to Civilisation* (London, 1938)

Roth, C., *A History of the Jews in England* (Oxford, 1941)

Roth, C., *The History of the Jews of Italy* (Philadelphia, 1946)

Salvador, J., *Histoire des institutions de Moïse et du peuple hébreu*, 3 vols (Paris, 1828), vol. 1

Sassenberg, M., *Selma Stern (1890–1981): das Eigene in der Geschichte. Selbstentwürfe und Geschichtsentwürfe einer Historikerin* (Tübingen, 2004)

Schäfer, B. (ed.), *Historikerstreit in Israel* (Frankfurt/M, 2000)

Scheid, E., *Histoire des juifs d'Alsace* (Paris, 1887)

Schieder, W., Sellin, V. (eds), *Sozialgeschichte in Deutschland: Entwicklungen und Perspektiven im internationalen Zusammenhang*, vol. 4, *Soziale Gruppen in der Geschichte* (Göttingen, 1987)

Schmidt, I., 'Martin Philippson: biographische Studien zur deutsch-jüdischen Geschichte des 19. und frühen 20. Jahrhunderts', MA thesis, Technical University of Berlin, 1988

Smith, G., Schäfer, P. (eds), *Gershom Scholem: zwischen den Disziplinen* (Frankfurt/M, 1995)

Scholtz, G., *Historismus als spekulative Geschichtsphilosophie: Christlieb Julius Braniß (1792–1873)* (Frankfurt/M, 1973)

Schorsch, I., *From Text to Context: The Turn to History in Modern Judaism* (Hanover, NH and London 1994)

Schulin, E., *Arbeit an der Geschichte: Etappen der Historisierung auf dem Weg zur Moderne* (Frankfurt/M and New York, 1997)

Schwarzschild, E., *Die Gründung der israelitischen Religionsgesellschaft zu Frankfurt am Main und ihre Weiterentwicklung bis zum Jahre 1876* (Frankfurt/M, 1896)

Servi, F., *La Donna israelita nella società* (Casale, 1896)

Simon-Nahum, P., 'Jüdische Historiographie im Frankreich des 19. Jahrhunderts', in Wyrwa, *Judentum und Historismus*, pp. 91–116

Stourzh, G. (ed.), *Annäherungen an eine europäische Geschichtsschreibung* (Vienna, 2002)

Torre, L.D., *Nuovi studi sulla donna israelita* (Padova, 1864)

Volkov, S., 'Die Erfindung einer Tradition: zur Entstehung des modernen Judentums in Deutschland', *Historische Zeitschrift*, 253 (1991), 603–28

Volkov, S., Stern, F. (eds), *Sozialgeschichte der Juden in Deutschland: Festschrift zum 75. Geburtstag von Jacob Toury*, Tel Aviver Jahrbuch für deutsche Geschichte, 20 (Gerlingen, 1991)

Weyden, E., *Geschichte der Juden in Köln am Rhein von der Römerzeit bis auf die Gegenwart: nebst Noten und Urkunden* (Cologne, 1867)

Wyrwa, U. (ed.), *Judentum und Historismus: zur Entstehung der jüdischen Geschichtswissenschaft in Europa* (Frankfurt am Main and New York, 2003), pp. 9–36

Wyrwa, U., 'Jewish Historiography in Europe: Transnational Biographies, Cultural Transfer and European Intellectual Exchange' (forthcoming)

Wyrwa, U., 'Das Bild von Europa in der jüdischen Geschichtsschreibung des 19. und frühen 20. Jahrhunderts', in Kerstin Armborst/Wolf-Friedrich Schäufele (Hg.) *Der Wert*

'Europa' und die Geschichte. Auf dem Weg zu einem europäischen Geschichtsbewusstein, Mainz 2007 (Veröffentlichungen des Instituts für Europäische Geschichte Mainz, Beiheft online 2), ss. 74–93. URL: <http://www.ieg-mainz.de/vieg-online-beihefte/02-2007.html>

Yerushalmi, Y. H., *Zakhor: Jewish History and Jewish Memory* (New York, 1989); A. Funkenstein, *Perceptions of Jewish History* (Berkeley, 1992)

Zimmermann, M. 'Volk und Land: Volksgeschichte im deutschen Zionismus', in Hettling, M. (ed.), *Volksgeschichten im Europa der Zwischenkriegszeit* (Göttingen, 2003), pp. 96–119

20   Conclusion: Picking up the Threads

Alter, P., *Out of the Third Reich: Refugee Historians in Post-War Britain* (London, 1998)

Bahlke, J., Strohmeyer, A. (eds), *Konfessionalisierung in Ostmitteleuropa. Wirkungen des religiösen Wandels im 16. Und 17. Jahrhundert in Staat, Gesellschaft und Kultur* (Stuttgart, 1999)

Berger, S., Donovan, M., Passmore, K. (eds), *Writing National Histories. Western Europe since 1800* (London, 1999)

Berger, S., Lambert, P., Schumann, P. (eds), *Historikerdialoge. Geschichte, Mythos und Gedächtnis im deutsch-britischen kulturellen Austausch 1750–2000* (Göttingen, 2003)

Berger, S., Miller, A., 'Nation-Building and Regional Integration, c. 1800–1914: The Role of Empires', *European Review of History* 15, 3 forthcoming 2008)

Berger, S., Eriksonas, L., Mycock, A. (eds), *Narrating the Nation. The Writing of National Histories in Different Genres* (Oxford, 2008)

Blaschke, O., 'Das 19. Jahrhundert: ein zweites konfessionelles Zeitalter?', *Geschichte und Gesellschaft*, 26 (2000), 38–75

Blom, I., Hagemann, K., Hall, C. (eds), *Gendered Nations. Nationalisms and Gender Order in the Long Nineteenth Century* (Oxford, 2000)

Boldt, A., *Leopold von Ranke and Ireland* (Lampeter, 2007)

Cannadine, D., *G. M. Trevelyan: a Life in History* (London, 1992)

Canning, K., *Gender History in Practice: Historical Perspectives on Bodies, Class, and Citizenship* (Ithaca, NY, 2006)

Dirlik, A., 'Performing the World: Reality and Representation in the Making of World History(ies)', *Bulletin of the German Historical Institute, Washington D.C*, 37 (2005) 9–27

Duchhardt, H. (ed.), *Nationale Geschichtskulturen – Bilanz, Ausstrahlung, Europabezogenheit* (Mainz, 2006)

Dworkin, D., *Class Struggles* (Harlow, 2007)

Epple, A., *Empfindsame Geschichtsschreibung: Eine Geschlechtergeschichte der Historiographie zwischen Aufklärung und Historismus* (Cologne, 2003)

Erdmann, K. D., *Toward a Global Community of Historians. The International Historical Congresses and the International Committee of Historical Sciences 1898–2000* (Oxford, 2005)

Eriksonas, L., *National Heroes and National Identities: Scotland, Norway and Lithuania* (Brussels, 2004)

Frevert, U., *A Nation in Barracks: Modern Germany, Military Conscription and Civil Society* (Oxford, 2004)

Frevert, U., 'Europeanising German History', *Bulletin of the German Historical Institute Washington*, 36 (2005), 9–24

Hagemann, K., *'Männlicher Muth und teutsche Ehre': Nation, Krieg und Geschlecht in der Zeit der antinapoleonischen Kriege Preussens* (Paderborn, 2002)

Haupt, H-G., Langewiesche, D. (eds), *Nation und Religion in der deutschen Geschichte* (Frankfurt/M, 2001)

Hettling, M. (ed.), *Volksgeschichten im Europa der Zwischenkriegszeit* (Göttingen, 2003)

Hürter, J., Woller, H. (eds), *Hans Rothfels und die deutsche Zeitgeschichte* (Munich, 2005)

Jarausch, K., Geyer, M., *Shattered Past. Reconstructing German Histories* (Princeton, NJ, 2003)

Kedourie, E., *Nationalism* (Oxford, 1993)

Keßler, M., *Exilerfahrung in Wissenschaft und Politik. Remigrierte Historiker in der frühen DDR* (Cologne, 2001)

Linden, M. van der, Voss, L. H. van (eds), *Class and other Identities. Entries to West European Labour Historiography* (Amsterdam, 2001)

Lorenz, C., 'Scientific/Critical History', in Tucker, A. (ed.), *The Blackwell Companion to Historiography and Philosophies of History* (Cambridge, 2008)

Maner, H-C., Schulze Wessel, M. (eds), *Kirche und Staat, Religion und Gesellschaft in Ostmitteleuropa in der Zwischenkriegszeit* (Stuttgart, 2002)

Marchal, G. P., Mattioli, A. (eds), *Erfundene Schweiz. Konstruktionen nationaler Identität* (Zurich, 1992)

Marchal, G. P., *Schweizer Gebrauchsgeschichte. Geschichtsbilder, Mythenbildung und nationale Identität* (Basel, 2006)

Oberkrome, W., *Volksgeschichte. Methodische Innovation und völkische Ideologisierung in der deutschen Geschichtswissenschaft 1918–1945* (Göttingen, 1993)

O'Dowd, M., Porciani, I. (eds), *Women Historians*, special issue of *Storia della Storiografia*, 46 (2004)

Osterhammel, J., Petersson, N., *Die Geschichte der Globalisierung* (Munich, 2003)

Pekora, V. P. (ed.), *Nations and Identities* (Oxford, 2001)

Porciani, I., 'Les historiennes et le Risorgimento', *Mélanges de l'école française de Rome – Italie et Méditerranée* 112 (2000), 317–57

Porciani, I., Tollebeek, J. (eds), *Writing the Nation*, vol. 2: *Institutions, Networks and Communities of National Historiography – Comparative Approaches* (Basingstoke, 2008)

Robbins, K., *History, Religion and Identity in Modern Britain* (London, 1993)

Sachsenmaier, D., 'Recent Trends in European History: the world Beyond', *Journal of Modern Europe History* (forthcoming 2008)

Schmale, W., 'Europäische Geschichte als historische Disziplin. "Überlegungen zu einer Europäistik"', *Zeitschrift für Geschichtswissenschaft*, 46 (1998), 389–405

Schöttler, P. (ed.), *Geschichtsschreibung als Legitimationswissenschaft 1918–1945* (Frankfurt/M, 1997)

Scott, J., *Gender and the Politics of History* (New York, 1988)

Smith, B., *The Gender of History: Men, Women and Historical Practice* (Cambridge, MA, 1998)

Stapleton, J., *Sir Arthur Bryan and National History in Twentieth-Century Britain* (Lanham, MD, 2005)

Stuchtey, B., Wende, P. (eds), *British and German Historiography 1750–1950. Traditions, Perceptions and Transfers* (Oxford, 2000)

Sundhausen, H., 'Jugoslawien und seine Nachfolgestaaten', in Flacke, M., *Mythen der Nationen: 1945: Arena der Erinnerungen*, vol. 1 (Berlin, 2004), pp. 373–426

Troebst, S. (ed.), 'Geschichtsregionen: Concept and Critique', special issue of the *European Review of History*, 10, 2 (2003)

White, H., *Metahistory: The Historical Imagination in Nineteenth Century Europe* (Baltimore, MD, 1974)

Index